Essentials of
Managerial
Finance

Second Edition

Essentials of
Managerial
Finance

Second Edition

J. Fred Weston
University of California, Los Angeles

Eugene F. Brigham
The University of Wisconsin

Holt, Rinehart and Winston, Inc.
New York   Chicago   San Francisco   Atlanta
Dallas   Montreal   Toronto   London   Sydney

Preface

$\mathcal{E}$ssentials of Managerial Finance is designed for use in introductory finance courses. Our principal goal is to show precisely what managerial finance is, how it relates to other functions of the business firm, and how financial decisions can further the basic enterprise goal of stockholder wealth maximization. A secondary goal, implicit in the first edition but explicit in this revised edition, is to show how financial decisions affect society at large and, especially, how optimal financial decisions are necessary if the economy is to function efficiently.

The emphasis in *Essentials* is on decisions, both decisions relating to the internal management of the firm and those relating to the acquisition of new assets and funds. Stress is given to how and why financial decisions affect the value of the firm rather than to rules or procedures.

Essentials of Managerial Finance is, in a sense, an abbreviated version of our larger book, *Managerial Finance*. While *Managerial Finance* explores in depth controversial and difficult conceptual problems, *Essentials* presents the fundamental materials of a business finance course with a minimum amount of the theoretical proofs of decision models. A contrast between two types of mathematics books will provide a useful analogy. One math book might develop theorems and proofs of the theorems, while another might present the theorems and illustrate their use without formal development of the proofs. *Managerial Finance* is comparable to the mathematics book that presents all proofs; *Essentials* is comparable to the book that utilizes theorems in practical applications.

RELATIONSHIP TO MANAGERIAL FINANCE

This contrast may be illustrated with specific comparisons between the two texts. In the "Capital Budgeting" chapter of *Managerial Finance,* we analyze the theoretical differences between the internal rate of return and the net present value methods of evaluating alternatives. In the same chapter in *Essentials,* on the other hand, we explain and

illustrate each of the alternative methods, then state our conclusion that on theoretical grounds the net present value method is
generally preferable. We refer interested readers to *Managerial Finance*
for the proof of our proposition.

Another difference between the two books is illustrated by certain
aspects of cost of capital—specifically, the cost of retained earnings
versus the cost of new external equity funds. *Managerial Finance* explores in depth the difficult theoretical issues. In *Essentials* we present
our conclusions on how the costs of retained earnings and the
cost of new equity should be calculated for practical cost of capital
applications.

Still another example of the difference in treatment of materials in the
two books can be observed in the discussion of risk and uncertainty.
In *Managerial Finance* we examine such topics as the use of certainty equivalents versus risk-adjusted discount rates. In *Essentials* we
base our discussions on risk-adjusted rates only, since this is the
procedure commonly used in practice.

In this revision, as in the first edition, we first "tried out" new concepts and ideas in *Managerial Finance,* then modified them for improved
clarity wherever experience in using *Managerial Finance* suggested that
changes were in order. The section on capital budgeting under uncertainty, as well as that on the cost of capital, reflects this practice of
pretesting difficult material.

CHANGES IN THE SECOND EDITION   The second edition of *Essentials* differs from the first in several key
respects. Some of the more significant alterations are itemized below.

1. Updating.   Finance is a highly dynamic area, and many changes
have occurred since the first edition came out in 1968. The federal tax
laws have been thoroughly overhauled; a Uniform Commercial Code
has been passed by all of the states; important theoretical advances
have been made; and, perhaps most important, a dramatic shift has
occurred in the level and structure of interest rates, stock prices, and
money and capital markets in general. All of these changes have been
reflected in this edition.

2. Uncertainty.   A major feature of this second edition is the addition
of a new chapter on uncertainty and risk analysis. Since this is a
difficult subject we pondered whether the formal treatment of risk
should be presented in *Essentials.* We concluded that the material could
be written in a manner to make it comprehensible at an introductory
level and that the importance of the subject necessitated its inclusion.
Nevertheless, the chapter is integrated into the book in a manner which

permits the instructor to omit it in the first course or not, according to his wishes, without problems of continuity.

3. Reorganization of the book.   Large sections of the book were reorganized to provide a more logical development and, accordingly, to make it easier for the reader to view finance as a united whole, as well as to retain the central focus of value maximization. Examples of this reorganization include both the placement of dividend policy within the capital structure/cost of capital section and a complete reorganization of the financial analysis, planning, and control sections.

4. Modifications in cost of capital presentation.   Students generally have more difficulty understanding the cost of capital concept than any other aspect of finance. We have made a major effort to clarify this concept, as well as its relationship to the capital budgeting process.

5. Summary chapter.   The last chapter in the first edition has been replaced with a new chapter summarizing the book and integrating the various chapters into a cohesive whole. We believe that this new chapter enables students to conclude the basic course with a clear over-all understanding of finance.

6. End-of-chapter questions and problems.   The problems have been thoroughly revised (a) to remove ambiguities that existed in the first edition problems and (b) to better illustrate the major points raised in the text chapters.

7. Other modifications.   The entire book was carefully examined, both by ourselves and by others, to locate passages that readers may find difficult. Considerable effort was devoted to rewriting these sections to improve their clarity.

ANCILLARY MATERIALS

Several additional items have been prepared to supplement *Essentials*. The first is a study guide, which highlights the key points in the text and presents a comprehensive set of problems similar to those at the end of each chapter. Each problem is solved in detail; thus, a student who has difficulty working the end-of-chapter problems can be aided by reviewing the study guide.

Many collections of readings, and many casebooks, are available to be used with *Essentials*. A new readings book, *Readings in Managerial Finance,* and a casebook, *Cases in Managerial Finance,* both designed especially to supplement *Essentials,* are available from Holt, Rinehart and Winston.

We are grateful not only to users of previous editions who have given us the benefit of their reactions and suggestions but also to our own students on whom we tested our ideas. We are particularly indebted to

Professors Michael Adler, Edward Altman, John Andrews, Robert Aubey, William Beranek, Stephen Hawk, Barry Gertz, Charles W. Haley, Robert S. Himes, Craig Johnson, Donald Kaplan, Stewart Myers, Richardson Pettit, Gerald Pogue, William Sharpe, and Keith Smith for their careful reviews and criticisms of this and previous editions. We would also like to express our appreciation to Messrs. George Engler, Harry Magee, Timothy Nantell, Patrick Smith, William Weyers, and Saul Yaari for aiding us in preparing the manuscript and in developing and checking the questions and problems.

The University of California and the University of Wisconsin, and our colleagues on these campuses, provided us with intellectual support in bringing this book to completion. To Ing. Leon Avalos Vez we express thanks for the continued opportunity of testing ideas in a different institutional setting through the programs of the Instituto de Administracion Cientifica de las Empresas in Mexico. Finally, we are indebted to the Holt, Rinehart and Winston staff, especially Seibert G. Adams, Jr., Jere Calmes, Louise Waller, and Sara Boyajian for assistance above and beyond the call of duty.

The field of finance will continue to experience significant changes and developments. It is stimulating to participate in these exciting developments, and we sincerely hope that *Essentials* will contribute to a better understanding of the theory and practice of finance.

J. Fred Weston
Eugene F. Brigham

Los Angeles, California
Madison, Wisconsin
January 1971

Contents

PART IV
Valuation and
financial
structure

PART VII
*Valuation in
mergers and
corporate
readjustments*

Part I

Introduction

Chapter 1

The Scope and Nature of Managerial Finance

WHAT is Managerial Finance? What is the finance function in the firm, and what specific tasks are assigned to the financial manager? What tools and techniques are available to him, and how does one go about measuring his performance? On a broader scale, what is the role of finance in the economy, and how can managerial finance be used to further our national goals? Providing at least tentative answers to these questions is the principal purpose of this book.

THE CHANGING ROLE OF FINANCE

Like so many things in the contemporary world, the subject matter of finance has undergone some significant changes in recent years. Prior to 1950, the primary function of finance was *obtaining* funds. Later on, more attention was given to the *use* of funds, and one of the important developments of the early 1950s was a systematic analysis of the internal management of the firm with a focus on flows of funds within the corporate structure.[1]

As procedures for using financial control in the internal management process have developed, the finance function has become an increasingly important part of the firm's general management. In the past, the financial officer was simply told how much money the firm needed and then given the responsibility for obtaining these funds. Under the new system, the financial manager is confronted with fundamental questions about the operations of the business enterprise. These questions—the new domain of finance—have been stated as follows:

1. How large should an enterprise be, and how fast should it grow?

2. In what form should it hold its assets?

3. What should be the composition of its liabilities?[2]

[1] Bion Howard and Miller Upton, *Introduction to Business Finance* (New York: McGraw-Hill, Inc., 1953).

[2] Ezra Solomon, *The Theory of Financial Management* (New York: Columbia University Press, 1963), pp. 8–9.

As it stands today, the principal focus of finance is on decisions and actions which affect the value of the firm. Reflecting this focus, the central theme of *Essentials of Managerial Finance* is the valuation of the business enterprise. The firm's value today depends upon the expected stream of earnings that it will generate in the future, as well as the riskiness of these projected future earnings. To illustrate, two firms may each be expected to earn $100,000 a year in the indefinite future. The earnings of one firm are relatively certain—for example, its business may consist of owning United States Treasury bonds and its income may be the interest received on these bonds—while the earnings of the other firm are somewhat uncertain because it is engaged in a risky enterprise—for instance, drilling offshore oil wells. The first firm, because of its lower risk, probably has a higher capital value. For example, it might have a total market value of $1.5 million, while the high-risk company might have a market value of $1 million.

Financial decisions affect both the size of the earnings stream, or profitability, and the riskiness of the firm. These relationships are diagrammed in Figure 1–1. Policy decisions affect risk and profitability, and these two factors jointly determine the value of the firm.

FIGURE 1–1
Valuation as the central focus of the finance function

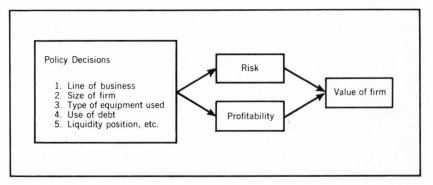

The primary policy decision is that of choosing the industry in which to operate—the product-market mix of the firm. When this choice has been made, both profitability and risk are determined by decisions relating to the size of the firm, the types of equipment that are used, the extent to which debt is employed, the firm's liquidity position, and so on.

These decisions generally affect both risk and profitability. An increase in the cash position, for instance, reduces risk, but since cash is not an earning asset, converting other assets to cash also reduces profitability. Similarly, the use of additional debt raises the rate of return, or the profitability, on the stockholders' net worth; at the same time, more debt means more risk. Financial analysis seeks to strike the particular balance between risk and profitability that will maximize the wealth of the firm's stockholders.

The nature and content of a field of study are likely to be responsive to the pressing problems of the day. To understand the evolution in finance, it is necessary to review some of the important new developments that have taken place both in the economies of the Free World and in the internal operations of business firms. Among the developments that have had an impact on the finance function are the following:

1. The rise of large-scale business units has made tasks formerly dealt with by the company president too numerous for any one person to handle.

2. Firms have increased both their product and geographic diversification.

3. The growth of spending on research and development has accelerated the tempo of change in the economy.

4. There has been an increased emphasis on growth in the economy and its major segments.

5. Accelerated progress in transportation and communication has brought the countries of the world closer together.

6. Profit margins have narrowed, reflecting heightened competition.

7. Continued inflation has produced a myriad of new problems, including tight money and high interest rates.

8. An increased awareness of social ills—such as air and water pollution, urban blight, and high levels of unemployment among minorities— has strengthened pressures to correct these problems.

These changes have had an important impact on the financial manager. Large-scale operations require decentralization and divisional responsibility for profit. Methods must be developed for segregating the contributions of smaller groups of activities and evaluating these contributions. The emphasis on growth and diversification requires the ability both to finance expansion and to adapt to changes in products and markets. Increased competition, narrowing profit margins, and higher interest rates heighten the need for techniques to make operations more efficient. International operations are more important than in earlier years, and many large firms do a substantial part of their business overseas.

Indeed, what has been referred to as a management revolution has occurred. Whether these changes deserve the term "revolution," or whether they simply reflect continuing changes that might be referred to as an "evolution," they have certainly broadened the responsibilities of financial management and led to the development of powerful new techniques and new ways of managing. One such change is the development of information-processing systems using the computer to acquire, store, retrieve, and analyze all kinds of business information. Computers are used to monitor the behavior of cash, receivables, inventories, and physical facilities. Another example is the accelerated development of management science methodology—linear programming, game theory, simulation, and so on. All are essentially mathematical techniques dealing with complex relations among business data.

Related to the development of management science is the significant progress which has been made in management planning and control techniques. These involve the following:

1. Establishing over-all profit goals

2. Establishing departmental and divisional goals which, taken together, achieve the over-all profit goal

3. Measuring progress and results against standards

4. Taking action through adjustments to keep the company moving toward its goal.

The direction in which business is moving, and the increasing importance of finance, is well illustrated by the following quotation:[3]

A realignment of management responsibilities at General Motors Corp. raises an intriguing question: Who will run the world's biggest manufacturer during the Seventies? . . . The increasing emphasis on cost controls raises the prospect that a financial man could [assume] the post of Chairman.

Similar events are taking place throughout the business world, and as the emphasis continues to shift toward not only the acquisition but also the effective use of funds, financial managers will play larger and larger roles in business firms.

ORGANIZATION OF THE BOOK The organization of this book reflects three elements: (1) theory, (2) financial decision models, and (3) descriptive and institutional material to provide content for both the theory and the decision models.

Ideally, the theory should first be set out in its totality, thereby providing the framework for a systematic approach to decision models. However, both theory and decision models must be built upon at least

[3] "General Motors Gears for the Seventies," *Fortune* (April 1970), p. 31.

some descriptive and institutional material. Because of this practical constraint, the organization of the book represents something of a compromise, blending together theories, decision tools, and descriptive materials as required for the subject at hand. This blend is reflected in our structuring the book into the following broad areas:

1. The tax environment

2. Financial analysis, planning, and control

3. Long-term investment decisions

4. Valuation and financial structure

5. Working capital management

6. Long-term financing

7. Valuation in mergers and corporate readjustment

8. An integrated view of financial management.

ORIENTATION OF MANAGERIAL FINANCE

Scope of Financial Management

Traditionally, the literature of business finance has emphasized either management of working capital or acquisition of funds. The acquisition of funds, or episodic financing, typically commits the firm for long periods and involves sizeable amounts of money. Errors here can be exceedingly costly. However, as the interval between episodes is long, the acquisition of funds takes only a small fraction of the financial manager's time.

Much of his energy is devoted to management of working capital. For this reason some persons have suggested that finance books should concentrate on this aspect of his duties. But a new and at least equally important emphasis is required: [the place of the financial manager in the general management framework and his greater role in the vital activities of planning and control.] However, the increased importance of new areas does not decrease the importance of traditional decision-making areas. This book, therefore, attempts to give full emphasis to the three major approaches to the financial manager's functions: (1) financial planning and control, (2) management of working capital, and (3) individual financing episodes.

The Insider versus the Outsider View

Should the study of finance take the insider's or the outsider's point of view? Phrased in another way, should a finance book emphasize the administrative, or the managerial, point of view, or should it be aimed at the person who is interested in business finance as a customer, a stockholder, or a voter? These two points of view are not incompatible. Although this book emphasizes the professional manager's job, neither point of view can be effectively developed without consideration of the other.

The financial manager, whose preoccupation is with the internal administration of the firm, must still take into account the reaction of outsiders to his operations. The claims and pressures of outsiders must be adjusted to the responsibilities and problems of internal financial administration. Hence, it seems essential to base financial decisions on a consideration of both points of view. Nevertheless, the internal point of view deserves primary emphasis because the financial manager is responsible for the financial affairs of his enterprise.

Small-Firm versus Large-Firm Financing
Similarly, the issue of the large firm versus the small firm as the appropriate focus of attention in finance courses is a false one. Principles of business finance are just as applicable to the small firm as to the large. The basic ideas are fundamentally the same, even though there are different factual environments in their application.

The distinction between corporate finance and other forms of business financing is also an artificial division. As the materials in Chapter 2 on the tax environment indicate, the boundaries between corporate and noncorporate forms are becoming increasingly blurred, particularly for small firms.

This book seeks to focus on generalizations that are applicable across a broad range of financing activities. It emphasizes effective use of principles, adaptation to the firm's external environment, and the role of the financial manager as a part of the general management process. A further foundation for this latter aspect is developed below.

PLACE OF FINANCE IN THE ORGANIZATION
The financial manager of the firm often carries the title of treasurer. Sometimes he is called vice-president—finance, controller, treasurer-controller, or secretary-treasurer. Whatever his title, the financial manager is usually close to the top of the organizational structure of the firm. Typically, he is a member of the first level of the corporate staff in a large organization.

Characteristically, financial planning is conducted by top-level management. Consequently, the chief financial manager is often a vice-president; or sometimes the president himself will carry the responsibilities of the financial manager. In large firms, major financial decisions are often made by a finance committee. For example, finance committees are used in General Motors, United States Steel, and American Telephone and Telegraph. In smaller firms the owner-manager himself typically conducts the financial operations, although he may delegate many other management functions.

One reason for the high place occupied by the financial manager in the organizational structure is the importance of planning, analysis, and control operations for which he is responsible. Often a "financial control" staff reports directly to the president or operates as an analytical staff for vice-presidents in charge of production, marketing, engineering, and other operations.

Another reason why financial authority is rarely decentralized or delegated to subordinates is that many financial decisions are crucial to the survival of the firm. Decisions which have major financial implications, such as taking on a new product or discarding an old one, adding a plant or changing locations, floating a bond or a stock issue or entering into sale and leaseback arrangements, are all major episodes in the life of a corporation.

Moreover, significant economies can be achieved through centralizing financial operations. A large corporation requiring $50 million can float a bond issue at a much lower interest cost per dollar than the rate at which a small firm can borrow $1,000. A small firm borrowing $1,000 will probably pay from 8 to 10 percent up to 14 to 18 percent. The large corporation is likely to be able to borrow at a rate ranging from 7 to 9 percent. It would be misleading, however, to imply that the advantages of centralization lie only in interest savings. The terms of the financial contract are also likely to be improved—a matter that may be of greater importance to the borrower than the interest rate. Contract terms refer to the extent to which borrowers can buy additional fixed assets, declare dividends, incur debt, and so forth.

Although the responsibility for carrying out major financial decisions is likely to be centered in the hands of a high-level official, a large number of day-to-day operations are conducted by the treasurer's office. These tasks are likely to be carried out by subordinates in lower level jobs. They include handling cash receipts and disbursements, borrowing from commercial banks on a regular and continuing basis, and formulating cash budgets.

MANAGERIAL FINANCE AND RELATED DISCIPLINES

Paradoxically, although some aspects of the finance function are conducted at the highest levels of the organization, a person aspiring to become a financial manager in a large company is likely to start as a trainee in a job with heavy accounting duties. Therefore, questions about the relation of finance to accounting and other studies naturally arise.

Accounting and Finance

Some persons find it difficult to distinguish between accounting and finance. They observe that in both subjects the same terminology and financial records are often used. Hence, it appears to them that accounting and finance are the same thing. But accounting is primarily data gathering; finance is data analysis for use in decision making. Although accounting has become increasingly useful in recent years in providing the information necessary for good management decisions, financial executives are responsible for analysis, planning, and control.

Quantitative Methods and the Behavioral Sciences Financial management deals with data and with people. The responsibilities for data analysis provide opportunities for application of the new and powerful tools of linear programming, game theory, and simulation referred to previously. Many of the concepts set out in this book may be used most effectively in business operations in conjunction with these new techniques. As the financial area can make much use of these skills, the student of finance is well advised to acquire them.

Operation of a business involves the interaction of physical assets, data, and people. The behavioral sciences are therefore also an essential part of the financial manager's training. Business involves authority relations between individuals and groups—political science. It also draws on sociology, which is the study of the behavior of people in groups. Of great importance, of course, is psychology, which deals with the personality and emotional make-up of both managers and managed.

Familiarity with these diverse areas of knowledge is required for making sound financial decisions. But perhaps of most direct significance for financial policies is the *economic* environment, whose nature and impact need to be sketched at least briefly at this point.

Economics and Finance Economics is defined as a study either of the efficient use of scarce resources or of the best means to fulfill socially defined ends or goals. The kinds of decisions made by firms in marketing, production, finance, and personnel are properly the subject matter of economics, and business finance is therefore an aspect of the economic theory of the firm. The characteristics of the economic environment are of vital significance for financial policies in ways briefly indicated below.

Separation of Savings and Investment The United States is a money economy, with savings and investment being performed by different persons. People save through institutions such as savings banks, commercial banks, savings and loan associations, life insurance companies, and pension funds—the "financial intermediaries." Businesses obtain funds from the intermediaries to make investments in land, buildings, equipment, and inventories. Financial intermediaries today own approximately two-thirds of the securities of all firms, contrasted with less than one quarter of the securities at the turn of the century.

Financing today is much more impersonal than it was earlier. Previously, wealth and income were not so equally distributed as they are now. People invested their funds directly in their own businesses or in local enterprises about which they had direct knowledge. Either they knew the persons running the firms or they were familiar with the operations. However, today most people save through financial intermediaries, which in turn buy the securities of the firms. Finance, therefore, is fundamentally a process for allocating economic resources among different users.

Prices and profits allocate resources in the United States. Allocation is made, not by administrative boards, but by relative prices and by income shares. Profit maximization, subject to risk-limiting strategies, is the framework for studying the operations of the firm. Most economics texts treat profit maximization, its variations, and its substitute goals in a formal way, with demand and supply curves to describe how the price system performs its functions. This book illustrates the concepts of profit maximization and other business strategies in terms of specific kinds of financial decisions. *Price and Profit System*

Fluctuations in the general level of business are a major cause of changes in the level of an individual firm's sales. Such changes result in changes in the firm's financing requirements. Differences in the degree of fluctuations influence the extent to which a financial manager may take on the risk of fixed-interest or fixed-rental obligations. Economic fluctuations result in many diverse forms of financing contracts. *Fluctuations and Economic Instability*

The economy of the United States has grown and will probably continue to grow at the rate of about 3 to 5 percent a year. To maintain its place in the economy, an industry must grow at least at this same rate. To hold its share of its industry market, a firm must also grow. Sales growth implies a continued growth in the firm's plant and equipment, inventories, receivables, and other assets. One of the financial manager's jobs is to obtain the funds to finance the expansion of the firm's ownership of these means of production and sale. *Growth*

In addition to the fluctuations in business and in the growth of the economy as a whole, there are fluctuations in price levels. Financial planning is necessary if a firm is to benefit from price level changes. The financial structure of the firm should reflect expectations about future price level changes. *Price Movements*

Fluctuations in interest rates and stock prices represent fluctuations in the cost of funds and the relative attractiveness of different forms and sources of financing. Interest rate levels are also an index of the availability of loanable funds. These factors are used by the financial *Interest Rates and Stock Market Prices* manager in analyzing the alternative forms of financing and in timing entry into the money markets.

Competition and Technological Change   Competition among firms, existing products, and newly created products pervades the economy. Technological changes present opportunities as well as threats. Adequate finances are required for the firm to make the adjustments necessary for survival and growth in the ever-changing economy, and it is the financial manager who must bear the responsibility for having the necessary funds on hand when they are needed.

Understanding the nature of the external environment, noting its impact on the firm, and recognizing the role of the firm in the operation of the economy—all are crucial and vital aspects of the decision process. The aim of the present book is to provide a meaningful body of concepts to guide the use of a broad variety of tools for financial decisions that advance the progress of the firm and the society of which it is a part.[4]

CRUCIAL ROLE OF FINANCING DECISIONS   The role of finance in the conduct of the firm has been expressed most aptly in the following statement: "A firm's success and even survival, its ability and willingness to maintain production and to invest in fixed or working capital are to a very considerable extent determined by its financial policies, both past and present."[5] This statement can be amply documented by examples of the lives of many firms. Let us consider a few.

General Motors was established in 1908 by W. C. Durant as a consolidation of a few companies in the automobile industry. When the working capital crisis of 1920–1921 developed, General Motors received financing aid from the Morgans and the du Ponts, and Durant lost his control of the company.

In contrast is the experience of Henry Ford. The Ford Motor Company needed some $75 million to meet its working capital needs. A group of Wall Street bankers formed a committee and offered to help Ford out of his difficulty in return for a portion of the control of the Ford Motor Company. Ford declined the proposal.

But Ford had to raise $75 million. How did he do it? First, he

---

[4] Cf. "It is important to recognize the fact that business also operates in a world of ideas. What business can or cannot do, as well as the way in which it must operate, is determined in part by the predominating concepts or theories in the society within which it exists. These may be religious, social, economic, or political and may be expressed in such forms as ethical standards, social values, and the objectives and methods of government."—Larson, *Guide to Business History* (Cambridge, Mass.: Harvard University Press, 1948), p. 5.

[5] Irwin Friend, "What Business Can Do to Prevent Recessions," in *Problems in Antirecession Policy* (New York: Committee for Economic Development, 1954), p. 6.

shipped his auto inventories to his dealers, with a telegram requesting cash. This forced them to borrow individually. He raised $25 million in this manner. Second, he allowed accounts and bills payable for raw materials to accumulate. Third, he reduced overhead in the factory and in the office. Fourth, by vigorous collection methods he collected some outstanding accounts receivable, foreign accounts, and by-product accounts. Fifth, he sold some $8 million of liberty bonds on hand. By all these methods he was able to meet his working capital needs and maintain complete control over his company.

A more recent illustration involves a consumer finance company. In 1966 the company sold $10 million of promissory notes to an insurance company. Later the firm needed additional funds, but it was unable to arrange with the holder of the original notes for an additional loan. The loan agreement had been so drawn that it was virtually necessary to call the entire issue and place a new one with another institutional investor. Because calling the original issue involved a substantial penalty, the company made it a point to see that the new loan agreement provided that additional funds could be secured from either the same lender or other lenders without the consent of the present holders and without paying penalties if any of the existing notes were to be retired. This illustration points up some of the pitfalls of the absence of planning in setting up loan agreements.

These examples illustrate a more general principle. It has been said with great truth that financing is the critical management function in that it provides the means of remedying weak management in other areas. If production or marketing efforts, for example, have deteriorated, adequate financial means may be used to rehabilitate and restore the weak departments to renewed effectiveness. On the other hand, money alone is no substitute for strength in the other operating areas of the firm. Finance is thus an interdependent part of the total fabric of the firm.

The financial manager plays a key role in the firm. He has a central **SUMMARY** responsibility in analysis, planning, and control, factors that guide the firm's resources into the most profitable lines and hold a tight rein on costs.

The importance of the financial manager is evidenced by his occupying a top-level position in the organization structure of the firm. Financial decisions are crucial for the well-being of a firm because they determine the ability of the company to obtain plant and equipment when needed, to carry the required amount of inventories and receivables, to avoid burdensome fixed charges when sales and profits fall, and to avoid losing control of the company.

These new dimensions in the nature and scope of the responsibilities of the financial manager have determined the central theme of this book, which is indicated by the following set of relations:

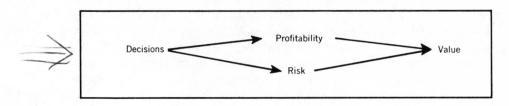

QUESTIONS **1–1** Are financial decisions likely to be more crucial for a failing business or for a successful, growing business? Would you, as chief executive officer, be more concerned about your financial manager in the failing firm or in the thriving firm?

1–2 What are the most important activities of the financial manager in terms of the importance of these activities to the firm's future and the amount of the financial manager's time they take up? Are these relationships likely to be the same for (a) large versus small firms, (b) stable versus growing firms, and (c) strong versus weak firms?

1–3 Would you expect the financial manager's role to be more important in a highly diversified, merger-minded conglomerate corporation or in a single-product firm that is concentrating on internal growth?

Chapter 2

The Tax
Environment[1]

*T*HE federal government is often called the most important stockholder in the American economy. This is not literally true, as the government does not "own" corporate shares in the strict sense of the word; it is, however, by far the largest recipient of business profits. Income of unincorporated businesses is subject to tax rates ranging up to 70 percent, and income of corporations is taxed at a 48 percent rate. State and sometimes city or county taxes must be added to these federal taxes, and dividends received by stockholders are subject to personal income taxes at the stockholders' individual tax rates.

With such a large percentage of business income going to the government, it is not surprising that taxes play an important role in financial decisions. To lease or to buy, to use common stock or debt, to make or not to make a particular investment, to merge or not to merge—all these decisions are influenced by tax factors. This chapter summarizes some basic elements of the tax structure relating to financial decisions.

The federal government uses both monetary policy and fiscal policy **FISCAL POLICY** to influence the level of economic activity. *Monetary policy*, which will be considered in a later chapter, deals with actions to influence the availability and cost of credit. *Fiscal policy* deals with altering the level and composition of government receipts and expenditures to influence the level of economic activity. Taxes constitute the primary receipt, hence they are an important element of fiscal policy.

Two principal methods have been employed to change tax receipts: (1) changing tax rates and (2) changing methods permitted for calculating tax-deductible depreciation (accelerating depreciation). Both of these points are discussed briefly in this section.

[1] This chapter has benefited from the assistance of Mr. R. Wendell Buttrey, tax attorney and lecturer on taxation at the University of California, Los Angeles, and Mr. J. Bruce Sefert, lecturer on taxation at the University of Wisconsin.

Changing Tax During periods of rapid and unsustainable economic expansion, and
Rates especially when such expansion has inflationary consequences, the federal government may attempt to dampen the level of economic activity
by increasing income tax rates. When tax rates are raised, both personal
disposable incomes and corporate profits after taxes are reduced. The
reduction in personal disposable income reduces individuals' purchasing power and thereby decreases their demand for goods and services.
The reduction in corporate after-tax profits reduces the profitability
of new investments and, at the same time, reduces corporate funds
available for investment. However, if the economy is depressed and
requires some form of stimulation, tax rates can be reduced, providing
both consumers and businesses with greater purchasing power and
increasing businesses' incentive to make investments in plant and
equipment.

During the period 1966–1969 the economy was operating at a very
high level, and prices were increasing at a rate of 3 to 6 percent
per year. Military expenditures associated with the Vietnam war were
stimulating the economy, and a government deficit was adding to the
inflationary pressure. The President, in January 1967, asked Congress
to increase taxes by 10 percent. After an 18-month delay, Congress,
in June 1968, did pass a 10 percent tax surcharge effective for the
period January 1, 1968, through December 31, 1969, for corporations,
and April 1, 1968, through December 31, 1969, for individuals.[2] Another comprehensive set of tax changes, including some adjustments
in basic tax rates, was passed in 1969. Some of the provisions of
the 1969 Act are discussed later in this chapter.

Tax rates have, in the past, been changed infrequently. Such changes
must be made by the Congress, and congressional action on a decision
with such a pervasive influence is not easy to obtain. Although economists and politicians have debated the idea of authorizing the President to change tax rates within certain prescribed limits, it appears
unlikely that Congress will be willing to give up this power. We expect,
therefore, that in the foreseeable future tax rates will be changed
infrequently.

Accelerated Depreciation charges are deductible when computing federal income
Depreciation taxes. Therefore, the larger the depreciation charge, the lower the actual
tax liability. The tax laws specify the allowed methods for calculating
depreciation for purposes of computing federal income taxes. If the
tax laws are changed to permit more rapid or *accelerated* depreciation,

---

[2] The tax increase took the form of a surcharge. That is, taxes were computed under the
rates given in the following pages of this book, then a surcharge equal to 10 percent of
this amount was added to the calculated tax. This surtax was reduced to 5 percent and
extended from January 1, 1970, to June 30, 1970, after which date it expired.

this will reduce tax payments and have a stimulating effect on business investments.[3]

A number of different depreciation methods are authorized for tax purposes: (1) straight line, (2) units of production, (3) sum-of-years-digits, and (4) double declining balance. These methods are explained briefly in the appendix to this chapter. The last two methods listed are generally referred to as *accelerated depreciation methods;* ordinarily, they are more favorable from a tax standpoint than is straight-line depreciation.

The fiscal policy implications of depreciation methods stem from two factors: (1) using accelerated depreciation reduces taxes in the early years of an asset's life, thus increasing corporate cash flows and making more funds available for investment, and (2) faster cash flows increase the profitability, or rate of return, on an investment. This second point is made clear in Chapter 8, where capital budgeting is discussed.

Depreciation methods, like tax rates, are determined by the Congress and are altered on occasion to influence the level of investment and thereby stimulate or retard the economy. The most sweeping changes in permitted depreciation methods were made in 1954, when the accelerated depreciation methods listed above were first permitted, and in 1962, when the depreciable lives of assets for tax purposes were reduced.

CORPORATE INCOME TAXES

Rate Structure

The first $25,000 of corporate taxable income is taxed at a 22 percent rate; all income over $25,000 is taxed at a 48 percent rate.[4] If a firm's taxable income was $100,000, for example, the tax would be computed as follows:

$$22\% \times 25,000 = \$\ 5,500$$
$$48\% \times 75,000 = \underline{36,000}$$
$$\$41,500$$

Table 2–1 shows that the average corporate income tax is moderately progressive up to $1 million, when it becomes virtually 48 percent.

This relatively simple tax structure has wide implications for business planning. Because the tax rate more than doubles when corporate income rises above $25,000, it clearly would pay to break moderately sized companies into two or more separate corporations in order to

---

[3] Federal tax statutes also consider the time over which assets must be depreciated. A reduction in the period over which an asset must be depreciated will have the same stimulating effect on the economy as would a change in permitted depreciation *methods* that increased depreciation expenses for tax purposes.

[4] Technically, there is a "normal" corporate tax of 22 percent plus a surtax of 26 percent on all income over $25,000.

hold the income of each unit under $25,000, and thus keep the tax rate at 22 percent. This was, in fact, done for many years by a number of firms, with some groups (retail chains, small loan companies) having literally thousands of separate corporations. However, the Tax Reform Act of 1969 limits the advantages of multiple corporations from 1970 through 1974 and abolishes all tax advantages in 1975. After 1974, if a group of firms having common ownership file separate returns for each company, then only one firm will be taxed at the initial 22 percent rate on the first $25,000 of income.

TABLE 2–1
Marginal and average corporate tax rates, 1968
In percentages

Corporate income (in dollars)	Marginal tax rate*	Average tax rate†
0–25,000	22	22.00
25,001–26,000	48	23.00
26,001–32,000	48	27.69
32,001–38,000	48	30.89
38,001–44,000	48	33.23
44,001–50,000	48	35.00
50,001–60,000	48	37.17
60,001–70,000	48	38.71
70,001–80,000	48	39.88
80,001–90,000	48	40.78
90,001–100,000	48	41.50
100,001–150,000	48	43.67
150,001–200,000	48	44.75
200,001–500,000	48	46.70
500,001–1,000,000	48	47.35
1,000,001–5,000,000	48	47.87
5,000,001–10,000,000	48	47.94
10,000,001–100,000,000	48	47.99
100,000,001–500,000,000	48	48.00

* The *marginal tax rate* is the tax on each additional dollar of taxable income received. The tax on each of the first $25,000 is 22 cents; on each dollar over $25,000, the marginal tax rate jumps to 48 cents. The total taxes paid, when divided by the taxable income, gives the average tax rate.
† Applied to the upper limit of each class interval.

Corporate Capital Gains and Losses[5]   Corporate taxable income consists of two components: (1) profits from the sale of capital assets and (2) all other income, defined as *ordinary income*.

[5] Corporate capital gains and losses (as well as most other tax matters) are subject to many technical provisions. This section and the others dealing with tax matters include only the most general provisions. For special cases the student is referred to *Federal Tax Course* (Englewood Cliffs, N.J.: Prentice-Hall, Inc., 1971), *passim*.

Capital assets are defined as assets, such as security investments, not bought and sold in the ordinary course of a firm's business. Gains and losses on the sale of capital assets are defined as capital gains, and under certain circumstances they receive special tax treatment. Real and depreciable property used in the business is not defined as a capital asset (Section 1221 of the Internal Revenue Code). However, Section 1231 of the code specifies that such property will be treated as a capital asset in the event of a net gain. In the event of a net loss, the full amount may be deducted from ordinary income without any of the limitations described for capital loss treatments.[6]

The sale of a capital asset held for six months or less gives rise to a *short-term* capital gain or loss; its disposal, when held for more than six months, produces a *long-term* gain or loss. Short-term capital gains less short-term capital losses equal *net short-term gains*. Net short-term gains are added to the firm's ordinary income and taxed at regular corporate income tax rates. For net long-term capital gains (long-term gains less long-term losses), the tax is limited to 30 percent. For example, if a corporation holds the common stock of another corporation as an investment for more than six months and then sells it at a profit, the gain is subject to a maximum tax of 30 percent. Of course, if income is below $25,000, regular tax rates of 22 percent will apply.[7]

If an asset, for example a machine tool, is subject to depreciation, *Depreciable Assets* its cost is defined as the original purchase price less accumulated depreciation. To illustrate, suppose a machine cost $10,000 and $5,000 of depreciation has been taken on it. Its book value, by definition, is $5,000 ($10,000 — $5,000).

If the company sells the machine for more than its book value, it may incur *either* a capital gain *or* ordinary income for tax purposes. If the gain is a recapture of depreciation, indicating that the firm had been depreciating the asset too rapidly (and charging off this depreciation as an expense to reduce ordinary income), the gain is ordinary income and is taxed accordingly. For example, if it sells the machine for $7,000, it incurs a $2,000 gain ($7,000 — $5,000). *This gain is not classified as a capital gain, however; it constitutes the recapture of depreciation and is taxed as ordinary income.*

---

[6] This special treatment of depreciable properties should be kept in mind in connection with the material in Chapter Eight on Capital Budgeting. The difference between the book value of an asset and its salvage value or abandonment value, if lower than book value, can be deducted from ordinary income, and thus the full amount of this difference represents a deductible expense.

[7] Prior to 1970 the corporate capital gains tax was 25 percent, the same as that imposed on individuals.

✗   The sale of a depreciable asset is subject to the capital gains tax when the gain exceeds the amount of depreciation taken. To continue with the preceding example, if our machine had been sold for $12,000, then a total profit of $7,000 ($12,000 — $5,000) would have been incurred. Of this amount, $5,000 would represent the recapture of depreciation (since this amount of depreciation had been charged off) and would be taxed as ordinary income; the remaining $2,000 would be classified as a capital gain for tax purposes and would be taxed at a rate of 30 percent.

Finally, if the firm sells the machine for $3,000, it incurs a $2,000 loss ($5,000 minus $3,000 received). This net loss can be deducted in full from ordinary income without any limitations.

Deductibility of Capital Losses   A net capital loss is not deductible from ordinary income. For example, if in 1970 a corporation had an ordinary income of $100,000 and a net capital loss of $25,000, it still paid a tax on the ordinary income at the normal rate of 22 percent on the $25,000 and 48 percent on the $75,000, a total tax of $41,500. The net capital loss may, however, be carried back for three years and then forward for five years and used to offset capital gains during that period. For example, if this corporation has a net capital gain of $75,000 in 1971, its *taxable net capital gain* in that year is $75,000 less the carry-over of $25,000, or $50,000. The tax on the net gain is 30 percent, or $15,000, which is added to the tax on its ordinary income.

Dividend Income   Another important rule is that 85 percent of dividends received by one corporation from another is exempt from taxation.[8] For example, if corporation H owns stock in corporation S and receives $100,000 in dividends from corporation S, it must pay taxes on only $15,000 of the $100,000. Assuming H is in the 48 percent tax bracket, the tax is $7,200, or 7.2 percent of the dividends received. The reason for this reduced tax is that to subject intercorporate dividends to the full corporate tax rate would, eventually, lead to triple taxation. First, firm S would pay its regular taxes. Then firm H would pay a second tax. Finally, H's own stockholders would be subject to taxes on their dividends. The 85 percent dividend exclusion thus reduces the multiple taxation of corporate income.

[8] If the corporation receiving the dividends owns 80 percent or more of the stock of a dividend-paying firm, it may file a consolidated tax return. In this case, there have been no dividends as far as the Internal Revenue Service (IRS) is concerned, so there is obviously no tax on dividends received. On the internal books of the related corporations there may be an accounting entry entitled "dividends" used to transfer funds from the subsidiary to the parent, but this is of no concern to the IRS.

Interest payments made by a corporation are a deductible expense *Deductibility of*
to the firm, but dividends paid on its own stock are not deductible. *Interest and*
Thus, if a firm raises $100,000 and contracts to pay the suppliers *Dividends*
of this money 7 percent, or $7,000 per year, the $7,000 is deductible
if the $100,000 is debt. It is not deductible if the $100,000 is raised
as stock and the $7,000 is paid as dividends.[9] This differential treat-
ment of dividends and interest payments has an important effect on
the manner in which firms raise capital, as we shall see in Chapter
12.

Before 1952, corporations paid their tax obligations in quarterly install- *Payment of Tax in*
ments in the year *following* the year in which the income was earned. *Installments*
For example, if a corporation earned $100,000 in 1949 and the tax
payable on this income was $50,000, the corporation paid $12,500
in each of four quarterly installments on March 15, June 15, September 15, and December 15, 1950. Now, however, firms must *esti-*
mate their taxable income for the current year and pay one-fourth of
the estimated tax on April 15, July 15, and October 15 of the current
year, and on January 15 of the following year.

Any ordinary corporate operating loss can be carried back three years *Net Operating*
and forward five years. The law states that the loss must first be *Carry-Back and*
carried back to the earliest year, the remainder applied to the second *Carry-Forward*
earliest year, and so on. For example, an operating loss in 1971 may
be used to reduce taxable income in 1968, 1969, 1970, 1972, 1973,
1974, 1975, and 1976; it *must* follow that sequence.

   The purpose of permitting this loss averaging is to avoid penalizing
corporations whose incomes fluctuate widely. To illustrate, suppose
the Ritz Hotel made $100,000 before taxes in all years except 1971,
when it suffered a $600,000 operating loss. The Ritz would use the
carry-back feature to recompute its taxes for 1968, use $100,000 of
the operating losses to reduce the 1968 profit to zero, and recover
the amount of taxes paid in that year. Since $500,000 of unrecovered
losses would still be available, Ritz would do the same thing for 1969
and 1970. Then, in 1972, 1973, and 1974, it would apply the *carry-*
forward loss to reduce its profits to zero in each of these years.

   The right to carry losses forward and backward has made some
corporations attractive buys. For example, Atlas Corporation and
Howard Hughes bought RKO Pictures because of a $30 million tax-loss
credit. A corporation may acquire another firm that has had a tax loss,

---

[9] There are limits on the deductibility of interest payments on some forms of securities
issued in connection with mergers. See Chapter 22.

operate it as a subsidiary, and then present consolidated returns for tax purposes. In the RKO Pictures case, the $30 million loss would be worth $15 million to Atlas, assuming Atlas pays state and federal income taxes at a 50 percent rate. Newspapers frequently contain advertisements such as "Tax-Loss Corporation for Sale," "Attractive Tax Loss Available." The corporation may be a doubly attractive buy if the purchaser is able to operate the business effectively and turn it into a profitable corporation at the same time that he benefits from the tax-loss carry-forward.

The tax law places certain restrictions on this privilege: (1) If more than 50 percent of the stock changes hands within two years after the purchase and (2) if any aspect of the old business is essentially abandoned, no loss carry-over is provided. The objective of the limitation is to prevent a firm from merging for the sole purpose of taking advantage of the tax law. If it merges for this purpose and files consolidated returns, the loss privilege may be disallowed. Moreover, deductions are denied where an acquisition appears to have been motivated largely by the prospects of such deductions.[10]

Improper Accumulation A special surtax on improperly accumulated income is provided for by Section 531 of the Internal Revenue Code, which states that earnings accumulated by a corporation are subject to penalty rates *if the purpose of the accumulation is to enable the stockholders to avoid the personal income tax*. Of income not paid out in dividends, a cumulative total of $100,000 (the balance sheet item "retained earnings") is prima facie retainable for the reasonable needs of the business. This is a benefit for small corporations. But there is a penalty rate on all amounts over $100,000 shown to be unnecessary to meet the reasonable needs of the business. The penalty rate is 27.5 percent on the first $100,000 of improperly accumulated taxable income for the current year and 38.5 percent on all amounts over $100,000.

Retained earnings are used to pay off debt, to finance growth, and to provide the corporation with a cushion against possible cash drains caused by losses. How much a firm should properly accumulate for uncertain contingencies is a matter of judgment. Fear of the penalty taxes that may be imposed under Section 531 may cause a firm to pay out a higher rate of dividends than it otherwise would.[11]

Sometimes Section 531 may stimulate mergers. A clear illustration is provided by the purchase of the Toni Company (home permanents)

[10] Sylvan Tobolowsky, "Tax Consequences of Corporate Organization and Distributions," *Journal of Taxation*, XII (January 1960), pp. 8–15.

[11] See materials in James K. Hall, *The Taxation of Corporate Surplus Accumulations* (Washington, D.C.: U.S. Government Printing Office, 1952), especially Appendix 3.

by the Gillette Safety Razor Company.[12] The sale was made early in 1948, when Toni's sales volume had begun to level off. Since earnings retention might have been difficult to justify, the owners of Toni, the Harris brothers, were faced with the alternatives of paying penalty rates for improper accumulation of earnings or of paying out the income as dividends. Toni's income after corporate taxes was $4 million a year; with the Harris brothers' average personal income tax of 75 percent, only $1 million a year would have been left after they paid personal taxes on dividends. By selling Toni for $13 million, they realized a $12 million capital gain (their book value was $1 million). After paying the 25 percent capital gains tax on the $12 million, or $3 million, the Harrises realized $10 million after taxes ($13 million sale price less $3 million tax). Thus, Gillette paid the equivalent of $3\frac{1}{4}$ years' after-corporate-tax earnings for Toni, while the Harris brothers received 10 years' after-personal-income-tax net income for it. The tax factor made the transaction advantageous to both parties.

The broad aspects of the federal corporate income tax have now been covered. For many business decisions, the federal income tax on individuals is equally important, so the main outlines of this part of the tax system must be discussed. In the next section, the individual tax structure is examined and compared with the corporate tax structure, thus providing a basis for making an intelligent choice as to which form of organization a firm should elect for tax purposes.

Election of Legal Form for Tax Purposes

Of some five million firms in the United States, over four million are organized as individual proprietorships or as partnerships. The income of businesses organized as individual proprietorships or partnerships is taxed as personal income to the owners or the partners. The net income of a proprietorship or a partnership is reported to provide a basis for determining the individual's income tax liability. Thus, as a business tax, the individual income tax may be as important as the corporate income tax.

PERSONAL INCOME TAX

The tax rates applicable to the single individual are set forth in Table 2–2, and rates applicable to married couples filing joint returns are shown in Table 2–3. Since joint returns are permitted whether or not one spouse earns the entire income, this privilege has the effect of lowering applicable tax rates.

Individual Income Tax Structure

[12] See J. K. Butters, J. Lintner, and W. L. Cary, *Effects of Taxation, Corporate Mergers* (Boston: Harvard Business School, 1951), pp. 96–111. The lucid presentation by these authors has been drawn on for the general background, but the data have been approximated to make the illustration simple. The principle involved is not affected by the modifications of the facts.

TABLE 2–2
Marginal and average tax rates for single individuals and married couples filing separate returns

Taxable income	Tax calculation			Average tax rate	
	Base amount	+ Marginal tax rate	= Tax*	Individual	Corporate
$0–$500	$0	14%	$70	14.0%	22.0%
500–1,000	70	15	145	14.5	22.0
1,000–1,500	145	16	225	15.0	22.0
1,500–2,000	225	17	310	15.5	22.0
2,000–4,000	310	19	690	17.3	22.0
4,000–6,000	690	21	1,110	18.5	22.0
6,000–8,000	1,110	24	1,590	18.6	22.0
8,000–10,000	1,590	25	2,090	20.9	22.0
10,000–12,000	2,090	27	2,630	21.9	22.0
12,000–14,000	2,630	29	3,210	22.9	22.0
14,000–16,000	3,210	31	3,830	23.9	22.0
16,000–18,000	3,830	34	4,510	25.1	22.0
18,000–20,000	4,510	36	5,230	26.1	22.0
20,000–22,000	5,230	38	5,990	27.2	22.0
22,000–26,000	5,990	40	7,590	29.2	23.0
26,000–32,000	7,590	45	10,290	32.1	27.7
32,000–38,000	10,290	50†	13,290	34.9	30.9
38,000–44,000	13,290	55	16,590	37.7	33.2
44,000–50,000	16,590	60	20,190	40.3	35.0
50,000–60,000	20,190	62	26,390	43.9	37.2
60,000–70,000	26,390	64	32,790	46.8	38.7
70,000–80,000	32,790	66	39,390	49.2	39.9
80,000–90,000	39,390	68	46,190	51.3	40.8
90,000–100,000	46,190	69	53,090	53.1	41.5
100,000–150,000	53,090	70	83,090	55.4	43.7
150,000–200,000	83,090	70	123,090	61.5	44.8
200,000–500,000	123,090	70	333,090	66.6	46.7
500,000–1,000,000	333,090	70	683,090	68.3	47.4
1,000,000–5,000,000	683,090	70	3,483,090	69.7	47.9
5,000,000–100,000,000	3,483,090	70	69,983,090	70.0	48.0

* Based on upper limit of each class interval.
† Maximum rate on earned income after 1971. See Footnote 13.

For some decisions, the taxpayer will compare the marginal tax rates. If a taxpayer has income from other sources and is deciding on whether to set up a new venture as a proprietorship or a corporation, he will be concerned with the tax rate applicable to the additional income. In comparing the relative advantages of the corporate versus noncorporate form of business organization, he is likely to compare the personal individual income tax rates to which his income will be subject with the marginal corporate income tax rates.

Taxable income	Tax calculation			Average tax rate	
	Base amount +	Marginal tax rate =	Tax*	Individual	Corporate
$0–$1,000	$0	14%	$140	14.0%	22.0%
1,000–2,000	140	15	290	14.5	22.0
2,000–3,000	290	16	450	15.0	22.0
3,000–4,000	450	17	620	15.5	22.0
4,000–8,000	620	19	1,380	17.4	22.0
8,000–12,000	1,380	22	2,260	18.8	22.0
12,000–16,000	2,260	25	3,260	20.4	22.0
16,000–20,000	3,260	28	4,380	21.9	22.0
20,000–24,000	4,380	32	5,660	23.6	22.0
24,000–28,000	5,660	36	7,100	25.4	24.8
28,000–32,000	7,100	39	8,660	27.1	27.7
32,000–36,000	8,660	42	10,340	28.7	29.9
36,000–40,000	10,340	45	12,140	30.4	31.8
40,000–44,000	12,140	48	14,060	32.0	33.2
44,000–52,000	14,060	50†	18,060	34.7	35.5
52,000–64,000	18,060	53	24,420	38.2	37.8
64,000–76,000	24,420	55	31,020	40.8	39.4
76,000–88,000	31,020	58	37,980	43.2	40.6
88,000–100,000	37,980	60	45,180	45.2	41.5
100,000–120,000	45,180	62	57,580	48.0	42.6
120,000–140,000	57,580	64	70,380	50.3	43.4
140,000–160,000	70,380	66	83,580	52.2	43.9
160,000–180,000	83,580	68	97,180	54.0	44.4
180,000–200,000	97,180	69	110,980	55.5	44.8
200,000–300,000	110,980	70	189,980	60.3	45.8
300,000–400,000	180,980	70	250,980	62.7	46.4
400,000–1,000,000	250,980	70	670,980	67.1	47.4
1,000,000–10,000,000	670,980	70	6,970,980	69.7	47.9
10,000,000–100,000,000	6,970,980	70	69,920,980	70.0	48.0

* Based on upper limit of each class interval.
† Maximum rate on earned income after 1971. See Footnote 13.

TABLE 2–3
Marginal and average tax rates for married couples filing joint returns

When the taxpayer's income will be derived mainly from the enterprise he contemplates forming, he is more likely to compare the average rates of taxation. The relation between the average tax rates of the corporate income tax and the individual income tax is shown in Figure 2–1. For single returns, the individual rate rises above the corporate rate at about $12,000. For joint returns, the individual tax is lower than the corporate rate up to $20,000, then approximately equal to $54,000, at which point the amount of taxes on personal income is $19,320 and that on corporate income is $19,420. From this point on, the individual tax rate rises to 70 percent, while the corporate rate rises more slowly toward 48 percent.[13]

Thus, for a firm with a net income of $1 million, there is no question but that the corporate form of business should be used. The tax advantage helps to explain why our largest businesses utilize the corporate form of organization. At incomes in the region of the $54,000 dividing line, whether the corporate or the noncorporate form will be most advantageous depends upon the facts of the case. If a firm finds it necessary to pay out a substantial part of its earnings in dividends, the noncorporate form is likely to be advantageous because the "double taxation" is avoided. However, the corporate form is satisfactory if most of the earnings are to be retained.

FIGURE 2–1
Comparison between average rates of personal income tax and corporation income tax (1970 tax rates)

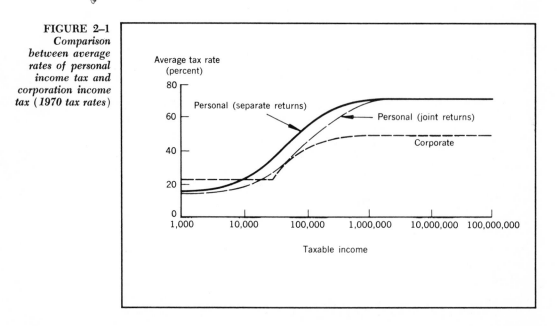

Capital Gains and Losses As with corporations, the distinction between short-term and long-term gains and losses is the six-month holding period. Net short-term gains are taxed at regular rates; the tax on long-term gains may be computed in either of two ways. First, the taxpayer may pay a flat rate of 25 percent on net long-term gains. Alternatively, he may pay the ordi-

---

[13] The personal income tax rate for both single and joint returns is limited to 60 percent in 1971 and 50 percent thereafter, if the income is in the form of salary or income from personal services. The income from a business organized as a partnership or a proprietorship is taxed at rates up to 70 percent unless the income of the business is primarily attributed to the personal services of the owner (as in the case of a partnership of doctors).

nary tax rate on *one-half* the amount of the net long-term gains.[14] The taxpayer should compute his tax under each of these methods and then select the one that results in the lower tax bill. For example, a married couple with an income of $32,000 from noncapital sources and a $10,000 long-term capital gain would compute their tax in two ways: (1) apply the normal tax rates on $32,000 plus 1/2 of $10,000, or $37,000, or (2) apply the normal tax on $32,000, plus 25 percent on $10,000. The first method would produce a tax of $10,790; the second, a tax of $11,160. The taxpayer would naturally elect the first method in this case. In general, for joint returns the 25 percent option is beneficial only if the taxable income exceeds $44,000, the point at which the marginal tax rate reaches 50 percent. Note that individual and corporate treatments differ in two ways: (1) corporations do not have the option of having only half of their capital gains taxed at normal rates, and (2) the corporate capital gains tax rate is 30 percent versus 25 percent for individuals.

Personal capital losses, short term or long term, can be carried forward without a time limit and deducted against either short-term or long-term capital gains. In addition, if the capital losses carried forward are not exhausted in the current year, 50 percent of long-term capital losses, up to a limit of $1,000 per year, may be charged off as a deduction against ordinary income. In other words, if an individual has $2,000 of long-term capital losses he may deduct 50 percent of this amount, or $1,000, from his ordinary income. If the net long-term capital loss is in excess of $2,000, any amount above $2,000 may be carried forward until it is exhausted. Short-term capital losses are not cut in half, that is, short-term losses can be deducted from ordinary income up to the $1,000 limit. Capital losses may not be carried back by individuals.

Moreover, Section 1244 of the Revenue Act of 1958 provides that individuals who invest in the stock of small corporations and suffer a loss on that stock may, for tax purposes, treat such a loss up to $25,000 a year ($50,000 on a joint return) as an ordinary loss rather than as a capital loss. A corporation is defined for this purpose as a small corporation, and the loss on its stock can be treated as an ordinary loss, if its common stock does not exceed $500,000 and if its total net worth—common stock plus retained earnings—does not exceed $1 million. This provision also encourages the formation of, and investment in, small corporations.

---

[14] The 25 percent option is not available on capital gains in excess of $50,000; thus on a $100,000 capital gain, $50,000 would be taxed at 25 percent, while one-half of the remainder would be taxed as ordinary income.

Dividend Income The first $100 of dividend income received by an individual stock-holder is excluded from taxable income. If stock is owned jointly by a husband and a wife, the exclusion is $200. However, if only one spouse owns stock, the total exclusion is generally only $100.

To illustrate, if a family's gross income consists of $12,000 of salary plus $500 of dividends on stock owned by the husband, the gross taxable income (before deductions) is $12,400. However, if the stock is jointly owned, the taxable gross income would be $12,300, because $200 of the dividend income would be excluded.

Personal Deductions In 1971 a $650 deduction is allowed for the taxpayer and each of his dependents; the deduction rises to $700 in 1972, then goes to $750 in 1973 and thereafter. The deduction is doubled for any tax-payer who is over sixty-five years. A family of four—husband, wife, and two dependent children, none over sixty-five—would thus have personal deductions of four times $650, or $2,600, in 1971.

Other Deductions Certain other items are also deductible from income before computing taxes—medical expenses (subject to limitations), interest payments, state and local taxes, and contributions, among others. A taxpayer has the choice of either itemizing these deductions or taking the standard deduction, which was computed as the lower of $1,000 or 10 percent of gross taxable income in 1970 and earlier. The 1969 Tax Reform Act changed these percentages and ceilings as follows: 1971, 13 percent and $1,500; 1972, 14 percent and $2,000; 1973 and thereafter, 15 percent and $2,000.

Illustration. In 1971 a family of four filing a joint return has an income consisting of $11,000 salary and $500 dividends on stock owned jointly by the husband and the wife. They take the standard deduction. Their gross income is $11,500, but $200 dividends are excluded, leaving a gross taxable income of $11,300. Personal deductions are $2,600 and the standard deduction is $1,000, the lesser of $1,000 or 10 percent of $11,300; their taxable income is therefore $7,700. From Table 2–3 we find that the tax is $1,323, calculated as $620 plus 19 percent of $3,700.

Partnership or Proprietorship, or Corporation? Subchapter S of the Internal Revenue Code provides that some incorporated businesses may elect to be taxed as proprietorships or partnerships. The main regulations governing permission to make this election include:

1. The firm must be a domestic corporation and must not be affiliated with a group eligible to file consolidated tax returns. (Ordinarily 80 percent ownership of a subsidiary is required for filing consolidated returns.)

2. The firm may not have more than ten stockholders, all of whom must be individuals.

3. The firm may not derive over 20 percent of its gross receipts from royalties, rents, dividends, interest, annuities, and gains on sales of securities.

Although the foregoing tax factors make it difficult to generalize on whether the corporate or the noncorporate form is more advantageous from a tax standpoint, the essential variables for making an analysis are provided. In general, the advantage now seems to be on the side of the corporation, particularly since a firm may obtain the many benefits of its corporate status and yet elect to be taxed as a proprietorship or a partnership.

SUMMARY

This chapter provides some basic background on the tax environment within which business firms operate.

Corporate Taxes

The *corporate tax rate* structure is simple: The tax rate is 22 percent on income up to $25,000 and 48 percent on all income over $25,000. Estimated taxes are paid in quarterly installments during the year in which the income is earned; when the returns are filed, the actual tax liability will result either in additional payments or in a refund due. *Operating losses* may be carried back for three years and forward for five years. *Capital losses* may not be treated as a deduction from operating income, but they may be used to offset capital gains. Corporate capital losses may be carried back for three years and forward for five years. Net long-term capital gains are taxed at a 30-percent rate (as compared with 25 percent for individuals).

Eighty-five percent of the *dividends received* by a corporation owning stock in another firm is excluded from the receiving firm's taxable income, and the receiving firm must pay full taxes on the remaining 15 percent of the dividends. *Dividends paid* are not treated as a tax-deductible expense. Regardless of the size of its earnings, a corporation does not have to pay dividends if it needs funds for expansion. If, however, the funds are not used for a legitimate purpose and if earnings are retained merely to enable stockholders to avoid paying personal income taxes on dividends received, the firm will be subject to an *improper accumulations tax. Interest received* is taxable as ordinary income; *interest paid* is a deductible expense.

Personal Income Tax   Unincorporated business income is taxed at the personal tax rates of the owners. Personal income tax rates for both individuals and married persons filing jointly are *progressive*—the higher one's income, the higher his tax rate. Personal income tax rates start at 14 percent of taxable income and rise to 70 percent of taxable income over $200,000. Corporate income tax rates range from 22 to 48 percent. Thus at lower incomes the personal income tax rate is lower if a business is organized as a proprietorship or a partnership; at higher incomes the corporate tax rate is lower. This fact has a significant bearing on whether a business chooses to be taxed as a corporation or as a proprietorship or a partnership.

Short-term *capital gains* are taxed at ordinary rates; long-term gains, at 25 percent or one-half the normal tax rate, whichever is lower, for individuals (but at 30 percent for corporations). Capital losses can be used to offset capital gains. One-half of an individual's net capital losses in any year can be deducted from ordinary income up to a limit of $1,000 a year. Capital losses in excess of $2,000 can be carried forward indefinitely until used up.

The foregoing material on the United States tax system is not designed to make a tax expert of the reader. It merely provides a few essentials for recognizing the tax aspects of business financial problems and for developing an awareness of the kinds of situations that should be taken to tax specialists for further guidance. These basics will, however, be referred to frequently in the remainder of the text, for income taxes are often an important factor in the making of business financial decisions.

QUESTIONS   **2–1**   Compare the marginal and the average tax rates of corporations with taxable incomes of $5,000, $50,000, $500,000, $5,000,000, and $50,000,000. Can you make such a comparison for sole proprietorships or for partnerships?

2–2   Which is the more relevant tax rate, the marginal or the average, in determining the form of organization for a new firm? Have recent changes in the tax laws made the form of organization more or less important than formerly?

2–3   For tax purposes, how does the treatment of interest expense compare with the treatment of common stock dividends from each of the following standpoints: a firm paying the interest or the dividends, an individual recipient, a corporate recipient?

2–4   Compare the treatment of capital gains and losses with ordinary gains and losses in income tax returns.

2–5   What is the present corporate carry-back and carry-forward tax provision for ordinary income? What is the purpose of this provision?

2–6   What is the purpose of the Internal Revenue Code provision dealing with improper accumulation of corporate surplus revenue?

2–7   Why is personal income tax information important for a study of business finance?

2–8 How do the tax rates for capital gains and losses affect an individual's investment policies and opportunities for financing a small business?

2–1 A corporation has a net income of $68,700 before interest charges. **PROBLEMS** Assuming interest charges amount to $6,500:

a) How much income tax must the corporation pay?
b) What is the marginal tax rate?

2–2 George G. Golden is a married man with one child. His gross income for 1971 is $15,000, which includes $1,400 of corporate dividends received by his wife. He files a joint return and takes the standard deduction. What is his personal income tax liability for 1971?

2–3 The taxable income (losses are shown in parentheses) of the Houston Corporation, formed in 1967, is shown below:

1967	$(300,000)
1968	150,000
1969	200,000
1970	300,000
1971	(150,000)

Ignoring the surtax that was in effect from January 1, 1968, to June 30, 1970, what is the corporate tax liability for each year?

2–4 The Benson Corporation income statement for 1971 is shown here:

Gross taxable income	$200,000
Tax payable (prepaid)	89,500
Net income after taxes	$110,500

ABC Manufacturing Corporation had a $60,000 loss in 1971. Benson feels that managerial talent can turn ABC into a profitable operation. If the two companies merged prior to January 1, 1972, what would be the merged corporation's income for 1971 after any refund of prepaid taxes? What is the difference in tax liability for Benson before and after the merger?

2–5 In 1971 White Manufacturing earned $300,000 before taxes on sales of $6 million. In 1969 it acquired working control of Dynamic Products, Inc., for $200,000, and it disposed of the stock in 1971 for $400,000. (White controlled less than 80 percent of Dynamic.) In addition, dividends paid by Dynamic to White during 1971 amounted to $20,000.

a) What is White's tax for 1971?
b) What would White's tax have been if Dynamics had declared a further dividend of $50,000 in 1971 and if White had sold the stock, purchased in 1969, for $300,000?

2–6 Edward Winters and Charles Bolen are planning to start a new business, W & B Manufacturing, and they are now trying to decide whether to incorporate for tax purposes or run the business as a partnership. They will each own 50 percent of the business and all profits will be paid out as dividends. Winters is married and has two children; Bolen is single. Winters has an income (dividends on stocks owned in his own name) of $15,000 per year exclusive of his interest in W & B Manufacturing. Bolen has no outside income, but he has enough savings to support himself until the business starts providing him with an income. Both men take the standard deduction. Assuming the company has the following income, what would their total personal and corporate taxes be under:

a) a partnership or
b) a corporation?

Year	Income before tax (thousands)
1973	$(30)*
1974	25
1975	95
1976	180
1977	280

* Personal business losses can be carried forward for five years.

Appendix
TO CHAPTER 2

DEPRECIATION METHODS

The four principal methods of depreciation—straight line, sum-of-years-digits, double declining balance, and units of production—and their effects on a firm's taxes can be illustrated. We will begin by assuming that a machine is purchased for $1,100 and has an estimated useful life of 10 years or 10,000 hours. It will have a scrap value of $100 after 10 years of use or after it has been used for 10,000 hours, whichever comes first. Table A2–1 illustrates each of the four depreciation methods and compares the depreciation charges of each method over the 10-year period.

Straight Line   With the straight-line methods, a uniform annual depreciation charge of $100 per year is provided. This figure is arrived at by simply dividing the functional life into the total cost of the machine minus the estimated salvage value:

$$\frac{(\$1,100 \text{ cost} - \$100 \text{ salvage value})}{10 \text{ years}} = \$100 \text{ per year depreciation charge.}$$

If the estimated salvage value is not in excess of 10 percent of the original cost, it can be ignored, but we are leaving it in for illustrative purposes.

Double Declining Balance   The double declining balance (DDB) method of accelerated depreciation requires the application of a constant rate of depreciation each year to the undepreciated value of the asset at the close of the previous year. In this case, since the annual straight-line rate is 10 percent per year ($1,000 ÷ $100), the double declining rate would be 20 percent (2 × 10 percent). This percentage is applied to the full purchase price of the machine, not the cost less salvage value. Therefore, depreciation under the DDB method is $220 during the first year (20 percent × $1,100).

Depreciation amounts to $176 in year 2 and is calculated by applying the 20 percent rate to the undepreciated value of the asset,

$$20\% \times (\$1{,}100 - \$220) = \$176,$$

and so on as the undepreciated balance declines. Notice that under DDB the asset is not fully depreciated at the end of the tenth year. In our example the remaining depreciation would be taken in the tenth year.[1]

TABLE A2–1
Comparison of depreciation methods for a 10-year, $1,100 asset with a $100 salvage value

		Depreciation methods		
Year	Straight line	Double declining balance	Sum-of-years-digits	Units of production*
1	$ 100	$220	$ 182	$ 200
2	100	176	164	180
3	100	141	145	150
4	100	113	127	130
5	100	90	109	100
6	100	72	91	80
7	100	56	73	60
8	100	46	55	50
9	100	37	36	30
10	100	30	18	20
Total	$1,000	$981	$1,000	$1,000

* The assumption is that the machine is used the following number of hours: first year, 2000; second year, 1800; third year, 1500; fourth year, 1300; fifth year, 1000; sixth year, 800; seventh year, 600; eighth year, 500; ninth year, 300; tenth year, 200.

Sum-of-Years-Digits Under the sum-of-years-digits method, the yearly depreciation allowance is determined as follows:

1. Calculate the sum of the years' digits; in our example there are a total of 55 digits: $1 + 2 + 3 + 4 + 5 + 6 + 7 + 8 + 9 + 10 = 55$. This figure can also be arrived at by means of the sum of an algebraic progression equation where N is the life of the asset:

$$\text{Sum} = N\left(\frac{N+1}{2}\right)$$

$$= 10\left(\frac{10+1}{2}\right) = 55.$$

[1] Actually, the company would switch from DDB to straight line whenever straight line depreciation on the remaining book value of the asset exceeds the DDB amount. Thus, in year 9 the book value is $86, so straight line depreciation would be $43 versus $37 if the change were not made.

2. Divide the number of remaining years by the sum-of-years-digits and multiply this fraction by the depreciable value of the asset:

$$\text{Year 1} \quad \frac{10}{55} (\$1{,}000) = \$182 \text{ depreciation}$$

$$\text{Year 2} \quad \frac{9}{55} (\$1{,}000) = \$164 \text{ depreciation}$$

.
.
.

$$\text{Year 10} \quad \frac{1}{55} (\$1{,}000) = \$18 \text{ depreciation.}$$

Units of Production

Under the units of production method, the expected useful life of 10,000 hours is divided into the depreciable cost (purchase price minus salvage value) to arrive at an hourly depreciation rate of $.10. Since, in our example, the machine is run for 2,000 hours in the first year, the depreciation in that year is $200; in the second year, $180; and so on. With this method, depreciation charges cannot be estimated precisely ahead of time; the firm must wait until the end of the year to see what usage and, hence, depreciation turn out to be.

Effect of Depreciation on Taxes Paid

The effect of the accelerated methods upon a firm's income tax payment is easily demonstrated. In the first year, should the firm choose to use the straight-line method, only $100 may be deducted from its earnings to arrive at earnings before taxes (the amount of earnings to which the tax rate applies). However, using either of the other three methods, the firm would have a much greater deduction and, therefore, a lower tax liability.

Changing the Depreciable Life of an Asset

Depreciation charges may actually be accelerated without resorting to changing the depreciation method simply by shortening the estimated life of an asset. The federal government establishes certain guidelines that set legal limits on the minimum life of classes of assets; by lowering these limits, the government can accomplish ends similar to permitting accelerated methods. Halving the minimum depreciable life of an asset, for example, would effectively double the annual rate of depreciation.

Part II

Financial Analysis, Planning, and Control

Chapter 3

Ratio Analysis

*P*LANNING is the key to the financial manager's success. Financial plans may take many forms, but a good plan must be related to the firm's existing strengths and weaknesses. Its strengths must be understood if they are to be used to proper advantage, and its weaknesses must be recognized if corrective action is to be taken. For example, are inventories adequate to support the projected level of sales? Does the firm have too heavy an investment in accounts receivable, and does this condition reflect a lax collection policy? The financial manager can plan his future financial requirements in accordance with the forecasting and budgeting procedures developed in succeeding chapters, but his plan must begin with the type of financial analysis developed below.

BASIC TYPES OF FINANCIAL RATIOS

Each type of analysis has a purpose or use that determines the different types of relationships emphasized in the analysis. The analyst may, for example, be a banker considering whether or not to grant a short-term loan to a firm. He is primarily interested in the firm's liquid position and stresses ratios that measure liquidity. In contrast, long-term creditors place far more emphasis on earning power and on operating efficiency than on liquidity. They know that unprofitable operations will erode asset values and that a strong current position is no guarantee that funds will be available to repay a 20-year bond issue. Equity investors are similarly interested in long-term profitability and efficiency. Management is, of course, concerned with all these aspects of financial analysis—it seeks to repay its debts to creditors and to earn profits for stockholders.

It is useful to classify ratios into four fundamental types:

1. *Liquidity ratios* measure the firm's ability to meet its maturing short-term obligations.

✗2. *Leverage ratios* measure the extent to which the firm has been financed by debt.

✗3. *Activity ratios* measure how effectively the firm is using its resources.

✗4. *Profitability ratios* measure management's over-all effectiveness as shown by the returns generated on sales and investment.

Specific examples of each ratio are given in the following sections with an actual case history used to illustrate their calculation and use. The company's name and the actual figures are disguised, of course, but the case is a good one to illustrate the process of financial analysis.

Walker-Wilson Manufacturing Company   The Walker-Wilson Manufacturing Company produces specialized machinery used in the automobile repair business. Formed in 1946, when Charles Walker and Ben Wilson set up a small plant to produce certain tools they had developed while in the Army, Walker-Wilson grew steadily and earned the reputation of being one of the best small firms in its line of business. In December 1968, both Walker and Wilson were killed in a crash of their private plane. For the next two years the firm was managed by Walker-Wilson's accountant. In 1970 the widows, who are the principal stockholders in Walker-Wilson, acting on the advice of the firm's bankers and attorneys, engaged David Thompson as president and general manager.

Thompson is experienced in this line of business, especially in production and sales; he does not, however, have a detailed knowledge of his new company. He has therefore decided to conduct a careful appraisal of the firm's position and, on the basis of this position, to draw up a plan for future operations. The most recent balance sheet and income statement—the starting points for any financial analysis—are presented in Tables 3–1 and 3–2.[1]

Liquidity Ratios   Generally, the first concern of the financial analyst is liquidity: Is the firm able to meet its maturing obligations? Walker-Wilson has debts totaling $300,000 that must be paid within the coming year. Can these obligations be satisfied? Although a full liquidity analysis requires the use of cash budgets (described in Chapter 6), ratio analysis,

---

[1] There is no "standard form" for the balance sheet, income statement, or other financial statements. Moreover, certain words can be given more than one meaning, and a single concept can be called by several different titles. For example, "net income after taxes" is also called "net income," "net profit," "income," and "profit." Depreciation can refer to the accumulated reserve for depreciation or to the annual charge against operating income. The balance sheet is also called the "statement of condition," and the income statement is called the "profit and loss statement." These and other ambiguities can cause confusion; if one is careful to determine the context within which the word is used, this confusion can be minimized.

TABLE 3–1
Walker-Wilson Company
Illustrative balance sheet
December 31, 1970

Assets		Claims on assets	
Cash	$ 50,000	Accounts payable	$ 60,000
Marketable securities	150,000	Notes payable, 8%	100,000
Receivables, net	200,000	Accruals	10,000
Inventories	300,000	Provision for federal income	
⁻Total current assets	$ 700,000	taxes	130,000
Gross plant and equip-		⁻Total current liabilities	$ 300,000
ment	$1,800,000	First mortgage bonds, 5%*	500,000
Less reserve for		Debentures, 6%	200,000
depreciation	500,000		1,000,000
Net plant and equipment	$1,300,000	Common stock	600,000
		Retained earnings	400,000
		Total net worth	$1,000,000
Total assets	$2,000,000	Total claims on assets	$2,000,000

* The annual sinking fund requirement is $20,000.

by relating the amount of cash and other current assets to the current obligations, provides some quick and easy-to-use measures of liquidity.

The current ratio is computed by dividing current liabilities into current ① *Current Ratio* assets. Current assets normally include cash, marketable securities, accounts receivable, and inventories; current liabilities consist of accounts payable, short-term notes payable, current maturities of long-term debt, accrued income taxes, and other accrued expenses (principally wages). The current ratio is the generally accepted measure of short-term solvency, since it indicates the extent to which the claims of short-term creditors are covered by assets that are expected to be converted to cash in a period roughly corresponding to the maturity of the claims.

The calculation of the current ratio for Walker-Wilson is shown below:

$$\text{Current ratio} = \frac{\text{current assets}}{\text{current liabilities}} = \frac{\$700,000}{\$300,000} = 2.3 \text{ times.}$$

$$\text{Industry average} = 2.5 \text{ times.}$$

The current ratio is slightly below the average for the industry, 2.5, but not low enough to cause concern. It appears that Walker-Wilson is about in line with most other firms in this particular line of business. Since current assets are near-maturing, it is highly prob-

TABLE 3–2
Walker-Wilson Company
Illustrative income statement
for the year ended December 31, 1970

Net sales		$3,000,000
Cost of goods sold		2,580,000
Gross profit		$ 420,000
Less: Operating expenses		
Selling	$22,000	
General and administrative	40,000	
Rent on office	28,000	90,000
Gross operating income		$ 330,000
Depreciation		100,000
Net operating income		$ 230,000
Add: Other income		
Royalties		15,000
Gross income		$ 245,000
Less: Other expenses		
Interest on notes payable	$ 8,000	
Interest on first mortgage	25,000	
Interest on debentures	12,000	45,000
Net before income tax		$ 200,000
Federal income tax (at 40 percent*)		80,000
Net income after income tax available to common stockholders		$ 120,000
Less: Common stock dividends		100,000
Increase in retained earnings		$ 20,000

* For most of the illustrations in the text a 50 percent corporate tax rate is used.

able that they could be liquidated at close to book value. With a current ratio of 2.3, Walker-Wilson could liquidate current assets at only 42.9 percent of book value and still pay off current creditors in full.

Although industry average figures are discussed later in the chapter, it should be stated at this point that the industry average is not a magic number which all firms should strive to maintain. In fact, some very good firms will be above it and other good firms will have ratios below the industry average. However, if a firm's ratios are very far removed from the average for its industry, the analyst must be concerned about why this variance occurs; that is, a deviation from the industry average should signal the analyst to check further.

2. Quick Ratio or Acid Test   The quick ratio is calculated by deducting inventories from current assets and dividing the remainder by current liabilities. Inventories are typically the least liquid of a firm's current assets and the assets on which losses are most likely to occur in the event of liquidation.

Therefore, this measure of ability to pay off short-term obligations without relying on the sale of inventories is important.

$$\text{Quick, or acid test ratio} = \frac{\text{(current assets} - \text{inventory)}}{\text{current liabilities}} = \frac{\$400,000}{\$300,000}$$

$$= 1.3 \text{ times.}$$

$$\text{Industry average} = 1.0 \text{ times.}$$

The industry average quick ratio is 1, so Walker-Wilson's 1.3 ratio compares favorably with other firms in the industry. Thompson knows that if the marketable securities can be sold at par and if he can collect the accounts receivable, he can pay off his current liabilities without selling any inventory.

Leverage Ratios

Leverage ratios, which measure the contributions of owners as compared with the financing provided by the firm's creditors, have a number of implications. First, creditors look to the equity, or owner-supplied funds, to provide a margin of safety. If owners have provided only a small proportion of total financing, the risks of the enterprise are borne mainly by the creditors. Second, by raising funds through debt, the owners gain the benefits of maintaining control of the firm with a limited investment. Third, if the firm earns more on the borrowed funds than it pays in interest, the return to the owners is magnified. For example, if assets earn 10 percent and debt costs but 8 percent, there is a 2 percent differential, which accrues to the stockholders. Leverage cuts both ways, however; if the return on assets falls to 7 percent, the differential between that figure and the cost of debt must be made up from equity's share of total profits. In the first instance, where assets earn more than the cost of debt, leverage is favorable; in the second it is unfavorable.

Firms with low leverage ratios have less risk of loss when the economy is in a recession, but they also have lower expected returns when the economy booms. In other words, firms with high leverage ratios run the risk of large losses but also have a chance of gaining high profits. The prospects of high returns are desirable, but investors are averse to risk. Decisions about the use of leverage, then, must balance higher expected returns against increased risk.

In practice, leverage is approached in two ways. One approach involves examining balance sheet ratios and determining the extent to which borrowed funds have been used to finance the firm. The other approach measures the risks of debt by income statement ratios designed to determine the number of times fixed charges are covered by operating profits. These sets of ratios are complementary, and most analysts examine both types of leverage ratios.

(3.) Debt to Total Assets This ratio, generally called the debt ratio, measures the percentage of total funds that have been provided by creditors. Debt includes current liabilities and all bonds. Creditors prefer moderate debt ratios, since the lower the ratio, the greater the cushion against creditors' losses in the event of liquidation. In contrast to the creditors' preference for a low debt ratio, the owners may seek high leverage either (1) to magnify earnings or (2) because raising new equity means giving up some degree of control. If the debt ratio is too high, there is a danger of encouraging irresponsibility on the part of the owners. The stake of the owners can become so small that speculative activity, if it is successful, will yield a substantial percentage return to the owners. However, if the venture is unsuccessful, only a moderate loss is incurred by the owners because their investment is small.

$$\text{Debt ratio} = \frac{\text{total debt}}{\text{total assets}} = \frac{\$1,000,000}{\$2,000,000} = 50\%.$$

$$\text{Industry average} = 33\%.$$

Walker-Wilson's debt ratio is 50 percent; this means that creditors have supplied half the firm's total financing. Since the average debt ratio for this industry—and for manufacturing generally—is about 33 percent, Walker-Wilson would find it difficult to borrow additional funds without first raising more equity capital. Creditors would be reluctant to lend the firm more money, and Thompson would probably be subjecting the stockholders to undue dangers if he sought to increase the debt ratio still more by borrowing.

(4.) Times Interest Earned The times-interest-earned ratio is determined by dividing earnings before interest and taxes (gross income in Table 3–2) by the interest charges. The times-interest-earned ratio measures the extent to which earnings can decline without resultant financial embarrassment to the firm because of inability to meet annual interest costs. Failure to meet this obligation can bring legal action by the creditors, possibly resulting in bankruptcy. Note that the before-tax profit figure is used in the numerator. Because income taxes are computed after deducting interest expense, the ability to pay current interest is not affected by income taxes.

$$\text{Times-interest-earned} = \frac{\text{profit before taxes} + \text{interest charges}}{\text{interest charges}}$$

$$= \frac{\$200,000 + \$45,000}{\$45,000} = \frac{\$245,000}{\$45,000} = 5.4 \text{ times.}$$

$$\text{Industry average} = 8.0 \text{ times.}$$

Walker-Wilson's interest charges consist of three payments totaling $45,000 (see Table 3–2). The firm's gross income available to service these charges is $245,000, so the interest is covered only 5.4 times. Since the industry average is 8 times, the company is covering its interest charges by a minimum margin of safety and deserves only a fair rating. This ratio reinforces the conclusion based on the debt ratio that the company is likely to face some difficulties in raising additional funds from debt sources.

The number of times fixed charges are covered is determined by divid-⑤ *Fixed Charge* ing profit before fixed charges by the total fixed charges—interest, lease *Coverage* payments, sinking fund requirements, and the tax related to sinking fund payments.[2] This more inclusive ratio provides an important supplement to the times interest earned figure, as it recognizes that financial problems may arise from the nonpayment of lease obligations or sinking fund charges as well as from the failure to meet interest payments.

$$\text{Fixed charge coverage} = \frac{\text{income available for meeting fixed charges}}{\text{fixed charges}}$$

$$= \frac{\text{gross income} + \text{rent on office}}{\text{interest} + \text{rent} + \text{before-tax sinking fund}}$$

$$= \frac{\$245,000 + \$28,000}{\$45,000 + \$28,000 + \$33,333}$$

$$= \frac{\$273,000}{\$106,333} = 2.6 \text{ times.}$$

Industry average = 4.0 times.

Walker-Wilson's fixed charges are covered 2.6 times, as opposed to an industry average of 4 times. Again, this indicates that the firm

[2] A sinking fund, discussed in detail in Chapter 19, is a required annual payment designed to pay off a bond issue. Sinking fund payments are not deductible for income tax purposes, so they must be paid with after-tax profits. This means, in effect, that the firm must earn sufficient profits before taxes to enable it to pay its tax bill and still have enough left to meet the sinking fund requirement. For this reason the tax requirement must be included in the denominator of the fixed charge coverage ratio.

Since it is in the 40 percent tax bracket, Walker-Wilson must have a before-tax income of $33,333 to enable it to pay the tax and still have $20,000 left after taxes. The general equation for finding the necessary before-tax income is:

$$\text{before-tax income required for sinking fund payment} = \frac{\text{sinking fund payment}}{1.0 - \text{tax rate}}$$

$$= \frac{\$20,000}{1.0 - 0.4} = \frac{\$20,000}{0.6}$$

$$= \$33,333.$$

is somewhat weaker than creditors would prefer it to be and further points up the difficulties Thompson would likely encounter if he should attempt additional borrowing.

Activity Ratios   Activity ratios measure how effectively the firm employs the resources at its command. These ratios all involve comparisons between the level of sales and the investment in various asset accounts. The activity ratios presume that a "proper" balance exists between sales and the various asset accounts—inventories, accounts receivable, fixed assets, and others. As we shall see in the following chapters, this is indeed a good assumption.

6. *Inventory Turnover*   The inventory turnover is defined as sales divided by inventories.

$$\text{Inventory turnover} = \frac{\text{sales}}{\text{inventory}} = \frac{\$3,000,000}{\$300,000} = 10 \text{ times.}$$

$$\text{Industry average} = 9 \text{ times.}$$

Walker-Wilson's turnover of 10 compares favorably with an industry average of 9 times. This suggests that the company does not hold excessive stocks of inventory; excess stocks are, of course, unproductive and represent an investment with a low or zero rate of return. This high inventory turnover also reinforces Thompson's faith in the current ratio. If the turnover had been low—perhaps 3 or 4 times—he would have wondered whether the firm was holding damaged or obsolete materials not actually worth their stated value.

Two problems arise in calculating and analyzing the inventory turnover ratio. First, sales are at market prices; if inventories are carried at cost, as they generally are, it would be more appropriate to use cost of goods sold in place of sales in the numerator of the formula. Established compilers of financial ratio statistics such as Dun & Bradstreet, however, use the ratio of sales to inventories carried at cost. To develop a figure that can be compared with those developed by Dun & Bradstreet, it is therefore necessary to measure inventory turnover with sales in the numerator, as we do here.

The second problem lies in the fact that sales occur over the entire year, whereas the inventory figure is for one point in time. This makes it better to use an average inventory, computed by adding beginning and ending inventories and dividing by 2. If it is determined that the firm's business is highly seasonal, or if there has been a strong upward or downward sales trend during the year, it becomes essential to make this relatively simple adjustment. Neither of these conditions holds for Walker-Wilson; to maintain comparability with industry averages, therefore, Thompson did not use the average inventory figure.

The average collection period, which is a measure of the accounts ⑦ *Average* receivable turnover, is computed as follows: First, the annual credit *Collection Period* sales are divided by 360 to get the average daily sales.[3] Second, daily sales are divided into accounts receivable to find the number of days' sales tied up in receivables. This is defined as the average collection period, for it represents the average length of time that the firm must wait after making a sale before receiving cash.

$$\text{Sales per day} = \frac{\$3,000,000}{360} = \$8,333$$

$$\text{Average collection period} = \frac{\text{receivables}}{\text{sales per day}} = \frac{\$200,000}{\$8,333} = 24 \text{ days.}$$

$$\text{Industry average} = 20 \text{ days.}$$

The calculations for Walker-Wilson show an average collection period of 24 days, slightly above the 20-day industry average. This ratio can also be evaluated by the terms on which the firm sells its goods. For example, Walker-Wilson's sales terms call for payment within 20 days, so the 24-day collection period indicates that customers, on the average, are not paying their bills on time. If the trend in the collection period over the past few years has been rising while the credit policy has not changed, this is even stronger evidence that steps should be taken to expedite the collection of accounts receivable.

One nonratio financial tool should be mentioned in connection with accounts receivable analysis—the aging schedule, which breaks down accounts receivable according to how long they have been outstanding. This schedule for Walker-Wilson is given below:

Age of account (days)	Percent of total value of accounts receivable
0–20	50
21–30	20
31–45	15
46–60	3
over 60	12
Total	100

The 24-day collection period looked bad by comparison with the 20-day terms, and the aging schedule shows that the firm is having especially serious collection problems with some of its accounts. Fifty percent are overdue, many for over a month. Others pay quite

---

[3] For convenience, the financial community generally uses 360 rather than 365 as the number of days in the year for purposes such as the present one.

promptly, bringing the average down to only 24 days, but the aging schedule shows this average to be somewhat misleading.

(8.) *Fixed Assets Turnover* The ratio of sales to fixed assets measures the turnover of capital assets.

$$\text{Fixed asset turnover} = \frac{\text{sales}}{\text{fixed assets}} = \frac{\$3,000,000}{\$1,300,000} = 2.3 \text{ times.}$$

Industry average = 5.0 times.

Walker-Wilson's turnover of 2.3 times compares poorly with the industry average of 5 times, indicating that the firm is not using its fixed assets to as high a percentage of capacity as are the other firms in the industry. Thompson should bear this fact in mind when his production officers request funds for new capital investments.

(9.) *Total Assets Turnover* The final activity ratio measures the turnover of all the firm's assets— it is calculated by dividing sales by total assets.

$$\text{Total assets turnover} = \frac{\text{sales}}{\text{total assets}} = \frac{\$3,000,000}{\$2,000,000} = 1.5 \text{ times.}$$

Industry average = 2.0 times.

Walker-Wilson's turnover of total assets is well below the industry average. The company is simply not generating a sufficient volume of business for the size of the asset investment. Sales should be increased or some assets should be disposed of or both steps should be taken.

Profitability Ratios Profitability is the net result of a large number of policies and decisions. The ratios examined thus far reveal some interesting things about the way the firm is operating, but the profitability ratios give final answers as to how effectively the firm is being managed.

(10.) *Profit Margin on Sales* This ratio, computed by dividing net income after taxes by sales, gives the profit per dollar of sales.

$$\text{Profit margin} = \frac{\text{net profit after taxes}}{\text{sales}} = \frac{\$120,000}{\$3,000,000} = 4\%.$$

Industry average = 5%.

Walker-Wilson's profit margin is somewhat below the industry average of 5 percent, indicating that the firm's sales prices are relatively low or that its costs are relatively high, or both. With a 4 percent after-tax margin on sales and a 40 percent corporate tax rate, unit sales prices can decline by 6⅔ percent (= .04/.6) or costs rise by 6⅔ percent before the firm suffers an over-all loss. In general, profit margins indicate the magnitude of the margin of protection against losses resulting from falling prices or rising costs.

The ratio of net profit to total assets measures the return on total investment in the firm.[4]   ⑪ *Return on Total Assets*

$$\text{Return on total assets} = \frac{\text{net profit after taxes}}{\text{total assets}} = \frac{\$120,000}{\$2,000,000} = 6\%.$$

$$\text{Industry average} = 10\%.$$

Walker-Wilson's 6 percent return is well below the 10 percent average for the industry. This low rate results from the low profit margin on sales and from the low turnover of total assets.

The ratio of net profit after taxes to net worth measures the rate of return on the stockholders' investment.   ⑫ *Return on Net Worth*

$$\text{Return on net worth} = \frac{\text{net profit after taxes}}{\text{net worth}} = \frac{\$120,000}{\$1,000,000} = 12\%.$$

$$\text{Industry average} = 15\%.$$

Walker-Wilson's 12 percent return is below the 15 percent industry average.

The individual ratios, which are summarized in Table 3–3, give Thompson a reasonably good idea of Walker-Wilson's main strengths and weaknesses. First, the company's liquidity position is reasonably good—its current and quick ratios appear to be satisfactory by comparison with the industry averages. Second, the leverage ratios suggest that the company is rather heavily indebted. With a debt ratio substantially higher than the industry average and with coverage ratios well below the industry averages, it is doubtful that Walker-Wilson could do much additional debt financing except on relatively unfavorable terms. Even if Thompson could borrow more, to do so would be sub-

Summary of the Ratios

$$\frac{S}{Inv.} \times \frac{Prof}{S} = \frac{Return}{on\ Invest}$$

---

[4] In calculating the return on total assets, it is sometimes desirable to add interest to net profits after taxes to form the numerator of the ratio. The theory here is that assets are "supplied" by both stockholders and creditors, and the ratio should measure the productivity of assets in providing returns to both classes of investors. We have not done so at this point for two reasons: (1) For manufacturing companies this addition is generally inconsequential. (2) The published averages we use for comparative purposes exclude interest. Later in the book, however, when we deal with public utilities, we do add back interest. This addition has a material bearing on the value of the ratio for utilities, and the revised ratio is the one normally used for them.

TABLE 3-3 Summary of financial ratio analysis

Ratio	Formula for calculation	Calculation	Industry average	Evaluation
I. Liquidity				
1. Current	$\dfrac{\text{Current assets}}{\text{Current liability}}$	$\dfrac{\$\,700,000}{\$\,300,000} = 2.3 \text{ times}$	2.5 times	Satisfactory
2. Quick, or acid test	$\dfrac{(\text{Current assets} - \text{inventory})}{\text{Current liabilities}}$	$\dfrac{\$\,400,000}{\$\,300,000} = 1.3 \text{ times}$	1.0 times	Good
II. Leverage				
3. Debt to total assets	$\dfrac{\text{Total debt}}{\text{Total assets}}$	$\dfrac{\$1,000,000}{\$2,000,000} = 50\%$	33%	Poor
4. Times interest earned	$\dfrac{\text{Profit before taxes plus interest charges}}{\text{Interest charges}}$	$\dfrac{\$\,245,000}{\$\,45,000} = 5.4 \text{ times}$	8.0 times	Fair
5. Fixed charge coverage	$\dfrac{\text{Income available for meeting fixed charges}}{\text{Fixed charges}}$	$\dfrac{\$\,273,000}{\$\,106,333} = 2.6 \text{ times}$	4.0 times	Poor
III. Activity				
6. Inventory turnover	$\dfrac{\text{Sales}}{\text{Inventory}}$	$\dfrac{\$3,000,000}{\$\,300,000} = 10 \text{ times}$	9 times	Satisfactory
7. Average collection period	$\dfrac{\text{Receivables}}{\text{Sales per day}}$	$\dfrac{\$\,200,000}{\$\,8,333} = 24 \text{ days}$	20 days	Satisfactory
8. Fixed assets turnover	$\dfrac{\text{Sales}}{\text{Fixed assets}}$	$\dfrac{\$3,000,000}{\$1,300,000} = 2.3 \text{ times}$	5.0 times	Poor
9. Total assets turnover	$\dfrac{\text{Sales}}{\text{Total assets}}$	$\dfrac{\$3,000,000}{\$2,000,000} = 1.5 \text{ times}$	2 times	Poor
IV. Profitability				
10. Profit margin on sales	$\dfrac{\text{Net profit after taxes}}{\text{Sales}}$	$\dfrac{\$\,120,000}{\$3,000,000} = 4\%$	5%	Poor
11. Return on total assets	$\dfrac{\text{Net profit after taxes}}{\text{Total assets}}$	$\dfrac{\$\,120,000}{\$2,000,000} = 6.0\%$	10%	Poor
12. Return on net worth	$\dfrac{\text{Net profit after taxes}}{\text{Net worth}}$	$\dfrac{\$\,120,000}{\$1,000,000} = 12.0\%$	15%	Poor

jecting the company to the danger of default and bankruptcy in the event of a business downturn.

Turning to the activity ratios, the inventory turnover and average collection period both indicate that the company's current assets are pretty well in balance, but the low fixed asset turnover suggests that there has been too heavy an investment in fixed assets. This low fixed asset turnover means, in effect, that the company probably could have operated with a smaller investment in fixed assets. Had the excessive fixed asset investment not been made, the company could have avoided some of its debt financing and would now have lower interest payments. This, in turn, would have led to improved leverage and coverage ratios.

The profit margin on sales is low, indicating that costs are too high or that prices are too low or both. In this particular case, the sales prices are in line with other firms; high costs are, in fact, the cause of the low margin. Further, the high costs can be traced (1) to high depreciation charges and (2) to high interest expenses. These costs are, in turn, both attributable to the excessive investment in fixed assets.

Returns on both the total investment and net worth are also below the industry average. These relatively poor results are directly attributable to the low profit margin on sales, which lowers the numerator of the ratios, and to the excessive investment, which raises the denominator.

While the preceding ratio analysis gives a reasonably good picture [*Trend Analysis*] of Walker-Wilson's operation, it is incomplete in one important respect—it ignores the time dimension. The ratios are snapshots of the picture at one point in time, but there may be trends in motion that are in the process of rapidly eroding a relatively good present position. Conversely, an analysis of the ratios over the past few years may suggest that a relatively weak position is being improved at a rapid rate.

The method of trend analysis is illustrated in Figure 3–1, which shows a graph of Walker-Wilson's sales, current ratio, debt ratio, fixed asset turnover, and return on net worth. These figures are compared with industry averages. Industry sales have been rising steadily over the entire period, and the industry average ratios have been relatively stable throughout. Thus, any trends in the company's ratios are due to its own internal conditions, not to environmental influences affecting all firms. Second, Walker-Wilson's deterioration since the death of the two principal officers is also apparent. Prior to 1968, Walker-Wilson was growing more rapidly than the average firm in the industry; during the next two years, however, sales actually declined.

FIGURE 3–1
Illustration of trend
analysis

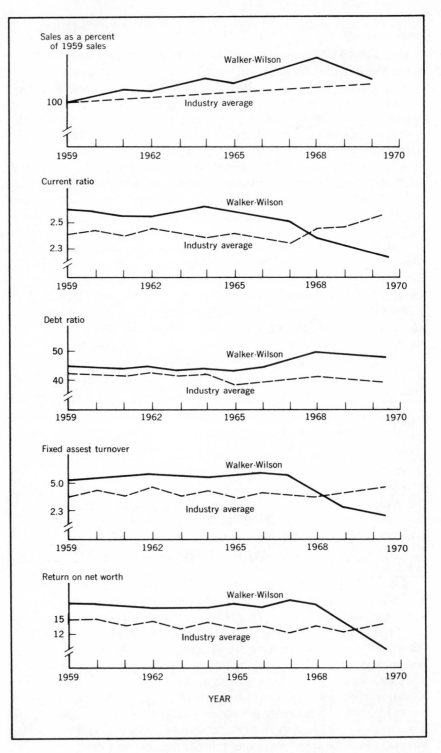

Walker-Wilson's liquidity position as measured by its current ratio has also gone downhill in the past two years. Although the ratio is only slightly below the industry average at the present time, the trend suggests that a real liquidity crisis may develop during the next year or two unless corrective action is taken immediately.

The debt ratio trend line shows that Walker-Wilson followed industry practices closely until 1968, when the ratio jumped a full 10 percentage points above the industry average. Similarly, the fixed asset turnover declined during 1968, even though sales were still rising. The records reveal that the company borrowed heavily during 1968 to finance a major expansion of plant and equipment. Walker and Wilson had intended to use this additional capacity to generate a still higher volume of sales and to retire the debt out of expected high profits. However, their untimely death led to a decrease in sales rather than an increase, and the expected high profits that were to be used to retire the debt did not materialize. The analysis suggests that the bankers were correct when they advised Mrs. Walker and Mrs. Wilson of the firm's need for a change in management.

The du Pont system of financial analysis has achieved wide recognition in American industry, and properly so. It brings together the activity ratios and profit margin on sales and shows how these ratios interact to determine the profitability of assets. The nature of the system, modified somewhat, is set forth in Figure 3–2.

DU PONT SYSTEM OF FINANCIAL ANALYSIS

The right side of the figure develops the turnover ratio. This section shows how current assets (marketable securities, inventories, accounts receivable, and cash) added to fixed assets gives total investment. Total investment divided into sales gives the turnover of investment. The left side of the figure develops the profit margin on sales. The individual expense items plus income taxes are subtracted from sales to produce net profits after taxes. Net profits divided by sales gives the profit margin on sales. When the asset turnover ratio is multiplied by the profit margin on sales, the product is the return on total investment in the firm. This can be seen from the following formula.

$$\frac{sales}{investment} \times \frac{profit}{sales} = \frac{profit}{investment}.$$

Walker-Wilson's turnover was seen to be 1.5 times, as compared to an industry average of 2 times; its margin on sales was 4 percent, as compared to 5 percent for the industry. Multiplied together, turnover and profit margin produced a return on assets equal to 6 percent, a rate well below the 10 percent industry average. If Thompson is

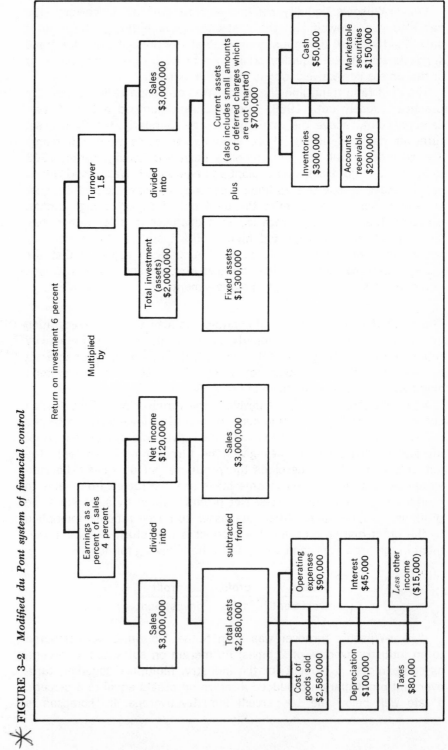

FIGURE 3–2 *Modified du Pont system of financial control*

to bring Walker-Wilson back to the level of the rest of the industry, he should strive to boost both his profit margin and his total asset turnover. Tracing back through the du Pont system should help him in this task.

Although Walker-Wilson's return on total investment is below the 10 percent industry average, the firm's 12 percent return on net worth is only slightly below the 15 percent industry average. How can the return on net worth end up so close to the industry average when the return on total assets is so far below the average? The answer is that Walker-Wilson uses more debt than the industry average.

Extending the du Pont System to Include Leverage

Only one-half of Walker-Wilson's assets are financed with net worth; the other half is financed with debt. This means that the entire 6 percent return on assets (which is computed after interest charges on debt) goes to the common stockholders, so their return is boosted substantially. The precise formula for measuring the effect of financial leverage on stockholder returns is shown below:

$$\text{percentage return on net worth} = \frac{\text{percentage return on assets}}{\text{percent of assets financed by net worth}}$$

$$= \frac{\text{percentage return on assets}}{1.0 - \text{debt ratio}}.$$

Calculation for Walker-Wilson:

$$\text{return on net worth} = \frac{6\%}{1.0 - 0.50} = \frac{6\%}{0.5} = 12\%.$$

Calculation for the industry average:

$$\text{return on net worth} = \frac{10\%}{1.0 - 0.33} = \frac{10\%}{0.67} = 15\%.$$

This formula is useful for showing how financial leverage can be used to increase the rate of return on net worth.[5] But increasing returns on net worth by using more and more leverage causes the leverage ratios to rise higher and higher above the industry norms. Creditors resist this tendency, so there are limitations to the practice. Moreover, greater leverage increases the risk of bankruptcy and thus endangers the firm's stockholders. Since Mrs. Walker and Mrs. Wilson, the widows of the firm's founders, are entirely dependent on income

---

[5] There are limitations on this statement—specifically, the return on net worth increases with leverage only if the return on assets exceeds the rate of interest on debt, after giving account to the tax deductibility of interest payments. This whole concept is explored in detail in Chapter 10, which is devoted entirely to financial leverage.

from the firm for their support, they would be in a particularly bad position should the firm go into default. Consequently, Thompson would be ill-advised to attempt to use leverage to boost the return on net worth much further.

RATES OF RETURN IN DIFFERENT INDUSTRIES

Would it be better to have a 5 percent margin on sales and an assets turnover of 2 times, or a 2 percent sales margin and a turnover of 5 times? It makes no difference—in either case the firm has a 10 percent return on investment. Actually, most firms are not free to make the kind of choice posed in the above question. Depending on the nature of its industry, the firm *must* operate with more or fewer assets, and it will experience a turnover that depends on the characteristics of its particular line of business. In the case of a dealer in fresh fruits and vegetables, fish, or other perishable items, the turnover should be high—every day or two would be most desirable. In contrast, some lines of business require very heavy fixed investment or long production periods. A hydroelectric utility company, with its heavy investment in dams and transmission lines, requires heavy fixed investment; a shipbuilder or an aircraft producer needs a long production period. Such companies necessarily have a low asset turnover rate but a correspondingly higher profit margin on sales.

If a grocery chain has a high turnover, and a chemical producer, with its heavy investment in fixed assets, a low turnover, would you expect to find differences in their profit margins on sales? In general, you would—the chemical producer should have a considerably higher profit margin to offset its lower turnover. Otherwise, the grocery business would be much more profitable than the chemical, investment would flow into the grocery industry, and profits in this industry would be eroded to the point where the rate of return was about equal to that in the chemical industry.

We know, however, that leverage must be taken into account when considering the rate of return on net worth. If the firms in one industry have a somewhat lower return on total assets but use slightly more financial leverage than do those in another industry, both sets of firms may end up with approximately the same rate of return on net worth.[6]

Analysis

These points, which are all necessary to a complete understanding of ratio analysis, are illustrated in Table 3–4. Here we see how turnover and profit margins interact with each other to produce varying returns on assets and also how financial leverage affects the returns on net worth. Hercules, Inc., Safeway Stores, and the average of all manufac-

[6] The factors that make it possible for firms to use more leverage are taken up in Chapters 10, 11, and 12. It may be stated now, however, that the primary factor favoring leverage is sales stability.

turing firms are compared. Hercules, with its very heavy fixed asset investment, is seen to have a relatively low turnover, while Safeway, a typical chain food store, has a very high sales-to-assets ratio. However, Hercules ends up with about the same rate of return on assets because its high profit margin on sales compensates for its low turnover. Both Safeway and Hercules use financial leverage to increase their return on net worth.

	Sales to total assets	Profit to sales	Profit to total assets	Debt to total assets	Profit to net worth*
All manufacturing firms	1.60X	5.6%	8.9%	41%	15.1%
Hercules, Inc. (chemical producer)	1.15	8.5	9.8	32	14.4
Safeway Stores (food retailer)	5.23	1.8	9.4	40	15.7

TABLE 3–4
Turnover, profit margins, and returns on net worth, 1968

* The figures in this column may be found as:

$$\text{Profit to net worth} = \frac{\text{profit to total assets}}{1 - \text{debt to total assets}}.$$

Sources: Moody's Investors Service; FTC-SEC Bulletins.

In the analysis of the Walker-Wilson Company, industry average ratios were frequently used. Where may one obtain such averages? Some important sources are listed below.

SOURCES OF COMPARATIVE RATIOS

Probably the most widely known and used of the industry average ratios are those compiled by Dun & Bradstreet, Inc. "Dun & Brad" provides fourteen ratios calculated for a large number of industries. Sample ratios and explanations are shown in Table 3–5. The complete data give the fourteen ratios, with the interquartile ranges[7] for 125 lines of business activity based on their financial statements. The 125 types of business activity consist of 71 manufacturing and construction categories, 30 types of wholesalers, and 24 types of retailers.

Dun & Bradstreet

[7] The median and quartile ratios can be illustrated by an example. The median ratio of current assets to current debt of manufacturers of airplane parts and accessories, as shown in Table 3–5, is 1.78. To obtain this figure, the ratios of current assets to current debt for each of the 55 concerns were arranged in a graduated series, with the largest ratio at the top and the smallest at the bottom. The median ratio of 1.78 was the ratio halfway between the top and the bottom. The ratio of 2.26, representing the upper quartile, was one quarter of the way down the series from the top (or halfway between the top and the median). The ratio of 1.36, representing the lower quartile, was one quarter of the way up from the bottom (or halfway between the median and the bottom).

TABLE 3-5 Dun & Bradstreet ratios for selected industries, 1967

Line of business (and number of concerns reporting)	Current assets to current debt (times)	Net profits on net sales (percent)	Net profits on tangible net worth (percent)	Net profits on net working capital (percent)	Net sales to tangible net worth (times)	Net sales to net working capital (times)	Collection period (day)	Net sales to inventory (times)	Fixed assets to tangible net worth (percent)	Current debt to tangible net worth (percent)	Total debt to tangible net worth (percent)	Inventory to net working capital (percent)	Current debt to inventory (percent)	Funded debts to net working capital (percent)
2871-72-79* Agricultural Chemicals (41)	3.71	4.46	11.13	25.05	4.69	13.45	28	13.1	26.5	18.6	72.1	46.6	86.4	23.9
	1.88	2.17	6.90	10.43	3.08	5.98	56	6.9	53.2	56.8	115.9	74.4	150.4	51.1
	1.34	0.79	1.45	3.95	1.67	3.91	107	4.3	68.5	110.4	244.5	153.8	258.4	185.9
3722-23-29 Airplane Parts & Accessories (53)	2.26	7.01	22.67	44.41	4.82	9.37	29	8.4	34.1	35.5	60.0	75.1	82.3	16.9
	1.78	4.44	16.67	26.26	3.23	5.22	39	5.9	55.1	61.8	93.5	103.7	98.1	44.3
	1.36	2.92	8.10	14.98	2.35	4.35	55	4.2	77.0	88.7	127.1	176.9	159.8	74.7
2051-52 Bakery Products (92)	2.39	4.46	16.54	67.52	5.59	28.67	13	38.5	60.2	21.4	39.2	39.2	150.1	41.5
	1.84	2.37	10.21	34.41	4.15	16.40	18	30.4	78.8	30.2	57.3	61.7	223.8	95.8
	1.39	0.94	3.79	12.75	2.98	10.32	24	22.5	103.9	48.5	103.6	99.5	315.2	214.8
3312-13-15-16-17 Blast Furnaces, Steel Works & Rolling Mills (63)	3.65	6.08	11.85	26.47	2.53	5.10	29	6.6	45.4	14.4	20.2	69.3	49.3	32.2
	2.58	4.07	8.01	19.18	1.90	4.21	35	4.9	61.4	23.4	50.8	92.4	67.1	67.5
	2.02	3.00	5.38	11.44	1.41	3.19	43	4.2	89.8	35.3	81.1	110.5	97.5	105.4
2331 Blouses & Waists, Women's & Misses' (71)	2.64	2.01	17.21	22.70	13.18	15.24	27	20.6	3.5	51.3	75.9	56.0	104.7	5.7
	1.73	0.69	7.86	9.28	8.58	9.80	36	13.0	7.2	130.7	175.3	86.0	152.0	23.6
	1.41	0.19	1.33	1.47	6.32	8.00	50	8.8	14.8	217.2	359.5	123.4	254.1	53.4
2731-32 Books; Publishers Publishing & Printing (43)	3.52	8.14	17.52	25.20	3.18	5.02	41	10.6	9.4	30.2	51.8	52.0	49.7	6.1
	2.63	5.20	10.44	16.13	2.32	2.86	58	4.1	28.8	45.7	77.2	71.4	85.4	28.1
	2.01	2.65	5.63	8.19	1.69	1.95	78	2.5	55.9	73.3	113.8	88.2	164.2	86.5
2211 Broad Woven Fabrics, Cotton (38)	4.32	5.67	10.90	22.49	2.11	5.35	26	6.8	45.1	12.1	22.0	57.5	49.5	9.7
	3.00	3.96	7.34	15.84	1.82	4.03	53	5.7	54.9	24.3	34.5	78.8	60.2	40.2
	2.24	2.58	4.09	7.50	1.43	3.10	58	3.9	65.6	32.4	59.7	105.5	81.4	65.8
2031-32-33-34-35-36-37 Canned & Pres. Fruits, Vegetables & Sea Foods (75)	2.40	6.16	17.28	43.40	4.91	13.41	15	7.6	39.3	30.7	51.7	82.9	59.9	24.6
	1.63	2.80	11.25	20.02	3.13	7.45	24	5.1	51.9	63.5	121.7	148.5	86.3	55.2
	1.25	1.75	6.23	11.21	2.06	4.31	40	3.3	75.4	118.6	152.5	255.3	119.6	123.0

* Standard Industrial Classification (SIC) Categories.
Source: Key Business Ratios in 125 Lines, 1967 (New York: Dun & Bradstreet, Inc.). Reprinted by permission of Dun & Bradstreet.

Another group of useful ratios can be found in the annual *Statement Studies* compiled and published by the Robert Morris Associates (RMA), which is the national association of bank loan officers. These are representative averages based on financial statements received by banks in connection with loans made. Eleven ratios are computed for 156 lines of business. The firms represented in the sample tend to be the larger and financially stronger firms; the averages contained in the RMA studies, therefore, provide a relatively high-quality basis for comparison. However, for most industries the RMA studies now compute ratios for groups of firms based on total asset size to show how financial ratios vary with firm size.

Robert Morris Associates

The Federal Trade Commission (FTC) and the Securities and Exchange Commission (SEC) jointly publish quarterly data on manufacturing companies. Both balance sheet and income statement data are developed from a systematic sample of corporations. The reports are published within perhaps six months after the financial data have been made available by the companies. They include an analysis by industry groups and by asset size, as well as financial statements in ratio form (or common-size analysis). The FTC-SEC reports are a rich source of information and are frequently used for comparative purposes.

Quarterly Financial Report for Manufacturing Corporations

Credit departments of individual firms compile financial ratios and averages (1) on their customers in order to judge their ability to meet obligations and (2) on their suppliers in order to evaluate their financial ability to fulfill contracts. The First National Bank of Chicago, for instance, compiles semiannual reports on the financial data for finance companies. The National Cash Register Company gathers data for a large number of business lines.

Individual Firms

Financial ratios for many industries are compiled by trade associations and constitute an important source to be checked by a financial manager seeking comparative data. In addition, accounting firms specializing in certain lines (for example, textiles or canning) will compile averages of financial ratios for the confidential use of their clients. These averages are usually the best obtainable. In addition to balance sheet data, they provide detailed information on operating expenses, which makes possible an informed analysis of the efficiency of the firms.

Trade Associations and Public Accountants

In this chapter we have discussed a rather long list of ratios and have learned what each ratio is designed to measure. Sometimes it will be unnecessary to go beyond a few calculations to determine that a firm is in very good or very bad condition, but often the analysis is equivalent to a detective-story investigation—what one ratio will not indicate, another may. Also, a relation vaguely suggested by one

USE OF FINANCIAL RATIOS IN CREDIT ANALYSIS

ratio may be corroborated by another. For these reasons, it is often useful to calculate a number of different ratios.

In numerous situations, however, a few ratios will tell the story. For example, a credit manager who has a large number of invoices flowing across his desk each day may limit himself to three ratios as evidence of whether the prospective buyer of his goods will pay promptly: (1) He may use either the current or the quick ratio to determine how burdened the prospective buyer is with current liabilities. (2) He may use the debt-to-total assets ratio to determine how much of the prospective buyer's own funds are invested in the business. If the funds of the prospective buyer are low, he is probably short of working capital and is likely to fall behind in his payments. (3) He may use any one of the profitability ratios to see whether or not the firm has favorable prospects. If the profit margin is high enough, it may justify the risk of dealing with a slow-paying customer. Profitable companies are likely to grow and, thus, to become better customers in the future. However, if the profit margin is low relative to other firms in the industry, if the current ratio is low, and if the debt ratio is high, a credit manager probably will not approve a sale involving an extension of credit.[8]

Of necessity, the credit manager is more than a calculator and a reader of financial ratios. Qualitative factors may override quantitative analysis. Oil companies, for instance, in selling to truckers often find that the financial ratios are adverse and that if they based their decisions solely on financial ratios, they would not make sales. Or, to take another example, profits may have been low for a period, but if the customer understands why profits have been low and can remove the cause of the difficulty, a credit man may be willing to approve a sale to him. The credit man's decision is also influenced by his own firm's profit margin. If the selling firm is making a large profit on sales, then it is in a better position to take credit risks than if its margin is low. Ultimately, the credit manager must judge a customer with regard to his character and management ability, and intelligent credit decisions must be based on careful consideration of conditions in the selling as well as in the buying firm.

---

[8] Statistical techniques have been developed to improve the use of ratios in credit analysis. One such development is the discriminant analysis model reported by Edward I. Altman ("Financial Ratios, Discriminant Analysis, and the Prediction of Corporate Bankruptcy," *Journal of Finance*, XXIII, September 1968). In this model, Altman combines a number of liquidity, leverage, activity, and profitability ratios to form an index of a firm's probability of going bankrupt. His model predicted bankruptcy quite well one or two years in the future. We can anticipate further work along these lines, and an increasing use of statistical techniques in credit and other types of financial analysis.

We have emphasized the use of financial analysis internally—by the financial manager to seek ways of improving his firm's performance—and in extending credit. However, this type of analysis is also useful in security analysis, or the analysis of the investment merits of stocks and bonds. When the emphasis is on security analysis, the principal focus is on judging the long-run profit potential of the firm. Profitability is dependent in large part on the efficiency with which the firm is run; since financial analysis provides insights into this factor, it is useful to the security analyst.

USE OF FINANCIAL RATIOS IN SECURITY ANALYSIS

Financial ratio analysis enables the financial manager to gauge the progress of his firm and to judge how it appears to others, especially stockholders and creditors. The number and the kinds of ratios he uses depend upon the nature of the industry and the size and age of the firm. The ratios discussed in this chapter are summarized with norms for large manufacturing firms, where such ratios are available, in Table 3–6. For most types of analyses the financial manager need not utilize all the ratios we have indicated. Usually, only a selected few are necessary. However, the financial manager will also find it useful to make trend comparisons or comparisons with other firms, or both.

REFERENCE GUIDES FOR RATIO ANALYSIS

I. Liquidity		
1. Current ratio	2/1	
2. Quick ratio	1/1	
II. Leverage		
3. Debt to total assets	40 percent	
4. Times interest earned	8 times	
5. Fixed charge coverage	4 times	
III. Activity		
6. Inventory turnover	9 times	
7. Average collection period	varies with credit terms	
8. Fixed assets turnover	varies	
9. Total asset turnover	varies	
IV. Profitability		
10. Gross profit on sales	4–6 percent	
11. Return on total assets	10–12 percent	
12. Return on net worth	13–15 percent	

TABLE 3–6 *Summary of financial ratios and reference guides for large manufacturing firms*

It is also important to realize that for many types of decisions, financial ratios are only a beginning. They give the financial manager just a fraction of the information he needs for making a decision. Ultimately, the financial manager's success rests on his judgment of men and on his ability to anticipate future events.

SUMMARY Ratio analysis, which relates balance sheet and income statement items to one another, permits the charting of the history of a firm and the evaluation of its present position. This type of analysis also allows the financial manager to anticipate reactions of investors and creditors and, thus, gives him a good insight into how his attempts to acquire funds are likely to be received.

Basic Types of Ratios Ratios are classified into four basic types: (1) liquidity, (2) leverage, (3) activity, and (4) profitability. Data from the Walker-Wilson Manufacturing Company are used to compute each type of ratio and to show how a financial analysis is made in practice. An almost unlimited number of ratios may be calculated, but in practice a limited number of each type are sufficient. What are probably the twelve most common ratios are discussed in this chapter.

Use of Ratios A ratio is not a meaningful number in and of itself—it must be compared with something before it becomes useful. The two basic kinds of comparative analysis are: (1) trend analysis, which involves computing the ratios of a particular firm for several years and comparing the ratios over time to see if the firm is improving or deteriorating; and (2) comparisons with other firms in the same industry. These two types of comparisons are often combined in the kind of graphic analysis illustrated in Figure 3–1.

Du Pont System The du Pont system shows how the return on investment is dependent upon turnover and the profit margin. The system is generally expressed in the form of the following relationship:

$$\frac{\text{sales}}{\text{investment}} \times \frac{\text{profit}}{\text{sales}} = \frac{\text{profit}}{\text{investment}}.$$

The first term, investment turnover, times the profit margin equals the rate of return on investment. The kinds of actions discussed in this chapter can be used to effect needed changes in turnover and the profit margin and thus to improve the return on investment.

The du Pont system can be extended to encompass financial leverage and to examine the manner in which turnover, sales margins, and leverage all combine to determine the rate of return on net worth. The following equation is used to show this relationship:

$$\text{Percent return on net worth} = \frac{\text{percent return on assets}}{1.0 - \text{debt ratio}}.$$

The formula is useful for examining the way financial leverage can be used to increase the rate of return on net worth.

The extended du Pont system shows why firms in different industries— *Rates of Return* even though they have widely different turnovers, profit margins, and *in Different* debt ratios—may end up with very similar rates of return on net worth. *Industries* In general, firms dealing with relatively perishable commodities would be expected to have high turnovers but low profit margins, and firms whose production processes require heavy investments in fixed assets would be expected to have low turnover ratios but high profit margins.

3–1 "A uniform system of accounts, including identical forms for balance **QUESTIONS** sheets and income statements, would be a most reasonable requirement for the SEC to impose on all publicly owned firms." Discuss.

3–2 There are four groups of financial ratios: liquidity, leverage, activity, and profitability. Financial analysis is conducted by four types of analysts: management, equity investors, long-term creditors, and short-term creditors.
a) Explain the nature of each type of ratio.
b) Explain the emphasis of each type of analyst.
c) Could the same basic approach to financial analysis be taken by each group of analysts?

3–3 How can a composite of industry averages be used as a norm for comparison with the financial ratios of an individual firm?

3–4 Why can norms with relatively well-defined limits be stated in advance for some financial ratios but not for others?

3–5 Why should financial ratio calculations be supplemented by trend analysis?

3–6 Why would the inventory turnover figure be more important to a grocery store than to a shoe repair store?

3–7 Can a firm have a high current ratio and still be unable to pay its bills?

3–8 Can the concept of financial ratio analysis be extended to the field of security analysis? Discuss.

3–9 "The higher the rate of return on investment, the better the firm's management." Is this statement true for all firms? Explain. If you disagree with the statement, give examples of businesses in which it might not be true.

3–10 What factors would you attempt to change if you wanted to increase a firm's rate of return (a) on assets or (b) on net worth?

3–11 Profit margins and turnover rates vary from industry to industry. What industry characteristics account for these variations? Give some contrasting examples to illustrate your answer.

3–12 Which relation would you, as a financial manager, prefer: a profit margin of 10 percent with a capital turnover of 2, or a profit margin of 25 percent and a capital turnover of 1? Can you think of any firm with a relationship similar to the latter?

3–1 The following data were taken from the financial statements of the Baxter **PROBLEMS** Corporation for the calendar year 1971. The norms given below are industry averages for the metal stamping industry.
a) Fill in the ratios for Baxter.
b) Indicate by comparison with the industry norms the errors in management policies reflected in these financial statements.

Baxter Corporation
Balance sheet
December 31, 1971

Cash	$ 44,000	Accounts payable	$ 33,000
Receivables	55,000	Notes payable (5%)	44,000
Inventory	165,000	Other current liabilities	22,000
Total current assets	$264,000	Total current liabilities	$ 99,000
Net fixed assets	121,000	Long-term debt (6%)	44,000
		Net worth	242,000
Total assets	$385,000	Total claims on assets	$385,000

Baxter Corporation
Income statement
(*for year ending December 31, 1971*)

Sales		$550,000
Cost of goods sold		
Materials	$209,000	
Labor	132,000	
Heat, light, and power	19,800	
Indirect labor	33,000	
Depreciation	12,100	405,900
Gross profit		$144,100
Selling expenses	55,000	
General and administrative expenses	63,360	118,360
Operating profit		25,740
Less: interest expense		2,640
Net profit before taxes		23,100
Less: federal income taxes		11,550
Net profit		$ 11,550

Ratios

Ratio	Baxter	Norm
current assets / current liabilities	$\frac{264}{99}$	2.5 times
sales / inventories	$\frac{550}{165}$	9.9 times
average collection period	$\frac{55(360)}{550} = 36$	33 days
sales / total assets	$\frac{550}{385}$	1.3 times
net profit / sales	$\frac{11,550}{550,500}$	3.3%
net profit / total assets	$\frac{11,550}{385,500}$	3.8%
net profit / net worth	$\frac{11,550}{242,500}$	10.7%

3–2 For one set of the pairs of companies listed below, chart the following financial ratios over the past seven years. (This problem requires library research. Data may be obtained from company reports or from an investment manual such as Moody's Industrials or Standard & Poor's Industrials.)

Ratios: Current ratio
Total debt to net worth
Sales to total assets
Average collection period
Sales to inventory (inventory turnover)
Profit after fixed charges and taxes to sales
Profit after fixed charges and taxes to net worth
Operating expenses to sales

Companies: General Motors and Chrysler
Boeing and Lockheed
Sperry Rand and International Business Machines
Standard Oil of New Jersey and Standard Oil of California
General Electric and Westinghouse

a) Compare the trends in the return on net worth for each of the two companies in the pair you are analyzing.
b) Indicate the reasons for any difference in trends in the rate of return on net worth suggested by your time-trend analysis.

3–3 Fill in the following outline of the du Pont pattern of analysis for one set of the pairs of companies listed below. (This problem requires library research. Data may be obtained from company annual reports or from an investment manual such as Moody's Industrials or Standard & Poor's Industrials. The data collected for Problem 3–2 is applicable to this problem.)

General Motors and Chrysler
Boeing and Lockheed
Sperry Rand and International Business Machines
Standard Oil of New Jersey and Standard Oil of California
General Electric and Westinghouse

Sales to operating investment _____%	Cash to sales (percentage)	_____
	Average collection period (days)	_____
	Inventory turnover (times)	_____
Return on investment _____%	Net fixed asset turnover (times)	_____
	Total operating assets	$_____
	Operating expenses to sales (percentage)	_____
Profit to sales _____%	Net income before fixed charges and taxes to total assets (percentage)	_____
	Net income after fixed charges and taxes	$_____

a) Using data for the most recent year available, compare the return on investment for the two companies.

b) Indicate reasons for the observed differences in rates of return suggested by the du Pont analysis.

3–4* Roger Elliot, Vice President and Loan Officer of the Hartford Bank, was recently alerted to the deteriorating financial position of one of his clients, Arden Products, Inc., by his bank's newly installed computer loan-analysis program. The bank requires quarterly financial statements—balance sheets and income statements—from each of its major loan customers. This information is punched on cards and fed into the computer, which then calculates the key ratios for each customer, charts trends in these ratios, and compares the statistics on each company with the average ratios and trends of other firms in the same industry. If any ratio of any company is significantly poorer than the industry average, the computer output makes note of this fact. Also, if the terms of a loan require that certain ratios be maintained at certain minimum levels, and these minimums are not being met by a company, then the computer output notes the deficiency.

When an analysis was run on Arden Products three months earlier, Elliot saw that certain of Arden's ratios were showing downward trends and were dipping below the averages for the dairy products industry. Elliot sent a copy of the computer output, together with a note voicing his concern, to Eric Swenson, President of Arden Products. Although Swenson acknowledged receipt of the material, he apparently took no action to correct the situation.

While problems appeared to be developing in the financial analysis three months ago, no ratio was below the level specified in the loan agreement between the bank and Arden Products. The latest analysis, however, showed that the current ratio was below the 2.0 times specified in the loan agreement. Legally, according to the loan agreement, the Hartford Bank could call upon Arden Products for immediate payment of the entire bank loan, and, if payment was not forthcoming within 10 days, the bank could force Arden Products into bankruptcy. Elliot had no intention of actually enforcing the contract to the full extent that he legally could, but he did intend to use the loan agreement provision to prompt Arden Products to take some decisive actions to improve its financial picture.

Arden Products is in the dairy products business, operating in northern Connecticut and serving the Hartford area. Seasonal working capital needs have been financed primarily by loans from the Hartford Bank, and the current line of credit permits Arden to borrow up to $120,000. In accordance with standard banking practices, however, the loan agreement requires that the bank loan be repaid in full by February 1971.

A limitation on dairy products prices, coupled with a new labor contract which increased wages substantially, caused a decline in Arden Products' profit margin and net income during the last half of 1969 as well as during most of 1970. Sales increased during both of these years, however, due to Arden Products' aggressive marketing program.

When he received Elliot's latest computer analysis and Elliot's blunt statement that the bank would insist on immediate repayment of the entire loan unless Arden Products presented a program showing how the poor current financial picture could be improved, Swenson began trying to determine what could be done. He rapidly concluded that the present level of sales could not be continued

* This case is taken from Eugene F. Brigham, Timothy J. Nantell, Robert T. Aubey, and Stephen L. Hawk, *Cases in Managerial Finance,* (New York: Holt, Rinehart and Winston, Inc., 1970), Case No. 2.

without an *increase* in the bank loan from $120,000 to $170,000, since payments of $50,000 for construction of a plant addition would have to be made in January 1971. Even though Arden Products has been a good customer of the Hartford Bank for over 50 years, Swenson was concerned whether the bank would continue to supply the present line of credit, let alone increase the loan outstanding. Swenson was especially troubled in view of the fact that the Federal Reserve recently tightened bank credit considerably, forcing the Hartford Bank to ration credit even to its best customers.

Questions

1. Calculate the key financial ratios for Arden Products and plot trends in Arden Products' ratios against the industry averages.

2. What strengths and weaknesses are revealed by the ratio analysis?

3. What sources of *internal* funds would be available for the retirement of the loan? If the bank were to grant the additional credit Arden Products needs and to extend the increased loan from a due date of February 1, 1971, to June 30, 1971, would the company be able to retire the loan on June 30, 1971?

4. On the basis of your financial analysis, do you believe that the bank should grant the additional loan and extend the entire line of credit to June 30, 1971?

5. If the credit extension is not made, what alternatives are open to Arden Products?

Arden Products, Inc.
Balance sheet
December 31

	1962	1968	1969	1970
Cash	$ 17,000	$ 25,500	$ 11,900	$ 8,500
Accounts receivable	68,000	102,000	115,600	161,500
Inventory	85,000	127,500	212,500	344,250
Total current assets	$170,000	$255,000	$340,000	$514,250
Land and building	25,500	20,400	54,400	51,000
Machinery	34,000	62,900	49,300	42,500
Other assets	20,400	11,900	3,400	2,550
Total assets	$249,900	$350,200	$447,100	$610,300
Notes payable, bank	—	—	42,500	119,000
Accounts and notes payable	37,400	40,800	64,600	127,500
Accruals	17,000	20,400	23,800	32,300
Total current liabilities	$ 54,400	$ 61,200	$130,900	$278,800
Mortgage	25,500	18,700	17,000	15,300
Common stock	85,000	85,000	85,000	85,000
Capital surplus	68,000	68,000	68,000	68,000
Earned surplus	17,000	117,300	146,200	163,200
Total liability and equity	$249,900	$350,200	$447,100	$610,300

Arden Products, Inc.
Income statement

	1968	1969	1970
Net sales	$1,105,000	$1,147,500	$1,190,000
Cost of goods sold	884,000	918,000	952,000
Gross operating profit	$ 221,000	$ 229,500	$ 238,000
General administration and selling	85,000	93,500	102,000
Depreciation	34,000	42,500	51,000
Miscellaneous	17,000	35,700	51,000
Net income before taxes	$ 85,000	$ 57,800	$ 34,000
Taxes (50%)	42,500	28,900	17,000
Net income	$ 42,500	$ 28,900	$ 17,000

	Dairy products industry ratios, 1970[a]
Quick ratio	1.0
Current ratio	2.7
Inventory turnover[b]	7 times
Average collection period	32 days
Fixed asset turnover[b]	13.0 times
Total asset turnover[b]	2.6 times
Return on total assets	9%
Return on net worth	15%
Debt ratio	50%
Profit margin on sales	3.5%

[a] Industry average ratios have been constant for the past three years.
[b] Based on year-end balance sheet figures.

Chapter 4

Profit Planning

*T*HE preceding chapter described how ratios are used in financial analysis and showed how the basic ratios are related to one another. A major area of financial management involves a continuous review of these ratios to insure that no aspects of the firm's existing operations are getting out of control—this key element of the system of financial controls designed to maximize operating efficiency is discussed in Chapter 5. Still other tools are available to aid the financial manager in the planning and control process. Two of these—break-even analysis, which is especially useful when considering plant expansion and new product decisions, and sources and uses of funds statements, which are an important aid in seeing how the firm has obtained funds and how these funds have been used—are discussed in this chapter.

Break-even analysis is basically an analytical technique for studying **BREAK-EVEN** the relations among fixed costs, variable costs, and profits. If a firm's **ANALYSIS** costs were all variable, the problem of break-even volume would never arise, but by having some variable and some fixed costs, the firm must suffer losses up to a given volume.

Break-even analysis is a formal profit planning approach based on established relations between costs and revenues. It is a device for determining the point at which sales will just cover total costs. If the firm is to avoid losses, its sales must cover all costs—those that vary directly with production and those that do not change as production levels change. Costs that fall into each of these categories are outlined as shown on page 70.

The nature of break-even analysis is depicted in Figure 4–1, the basic break-even chart. The chart is on a unit basis, with volume produced shown on the horizontal axis and costs and income measured on the vertical axis. Fixed costs of $40,000 are represented by a hori-

Fixed costs*	Direct or variable costs
Depreciation on plant and equipment	Factory labor
Rentals	Materials
Interest charges on debt	Sales commissions
Salaries of research staff	
Salaries of executive staff	
General office expenses	

* Some of these costs—for example, salaries and office expenses—
could be varied to some degree; however, firms are reluctant to reduce
these expenditures in response to temporary fluctuations in sales.

zontal line; they are the same (fixed) regardless of the number of units
produced. Variable costs are assumed to be $1.20 a unit. Total costs
rise by $1.20, the amount of the variable costs, for each additional
unit produced. Production is assumed to be sold at $2 a unit, so
the total income is pictured as a straight line, which must also increase

FIGURE 4–1
Break-even chart

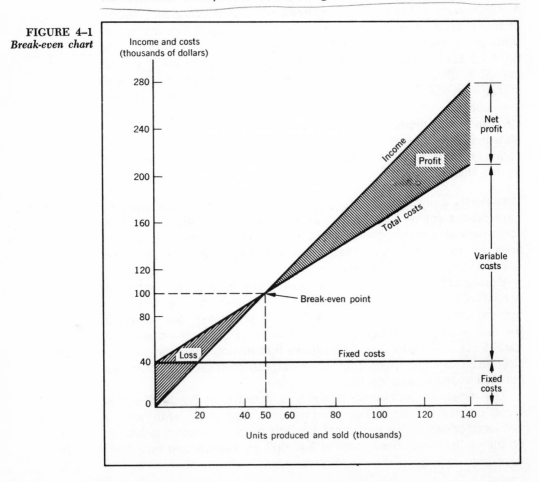

with production. The slope (or the rate of ascent) of the total-income line is steeper than that of the total-cost line. This must be true, because the firm is gaining $2 of revenue for every $1.20 paid out for labor and materials, the variable costs.

Up to the break-even point, found at the intersection of the total income and total-cost lines, the firm suffers losses. After that point, the firm begins to make profits. Figure 4–1 indicates a break-even point at a sales and costs level of $100,000 and a production level of 50,000 units. More exact calculations of the break-even point can be carried out algebraically or by trial and error. In section A of Table 4–1 profit-and-loss relations are shown for various levels of sales; in section B the algebraic calculations are carried out.

$$(2.00)(x) = (1.20)(x) + 40,000$$
$$.8x = 40,000$$
$$x = \frac{40,000}{.8} = 50,000$$

TABLE 4–1
Relations among units produced, total variable costs, fixed costs, total costs, and total income

A. Trial-and-error calculations

Units sold	Total variable costs	Fixed costs	Total costs	Sales	Net profit (loss)
20,000	$ 24,000	$40,000	$ 64,000	$ 40,000	$(24,000)
40,000	48,000	40,000	88,000	80,000	(8,000)
50,000	60,000	40,000	100,000	100,000	—
60,000	72,000	40,000	112,000	120,000	8,000
80,000	96,000	40,000	136,000	160,000	24,000
100,000	120,000	40,000	160,000	200,000	40,000
120,000	144,000	40,000	184,000	240,000	56,000
140,000	168,000	40,000	208,000	280,000	72,000

B. Algebraic solution to break-even point

1. The break-even quantity is defined as that volume of output at which revenue is just equal to total costs (fixed costs plus variable costs).

2. Let:

P = sales price per unit
Q = quantity produced and sold
F = fixed costs
V = variable costs per unit

3. Then:

$$P \cdot Q = F + V \cdot Q$$
$$P \cdot Q - V \cdot Q = F$$
$$Q(P - V) = F$$

$$Q = \frac{F}{P - V} \text{ at break-even } Q$$

4. Illustration:

$$Q = \frac{\$40,000}{\$2.00 - \$1.20}$$

$$= 50,000 \text{ units}$$

Nonlinear Break- In break-even analysis, linear (straight line) relationships are generally
Even Analysis assumed. It complicates matters slightly, but it is easy enough to
use nonlinear relationships. For example, it is reasonable to think that
increased sales can be obtained if sales prices are reduced. Similarly,
empirical studies suggest that the average variable cost per unit falls
over some range of output, then begins to rise. These assumptions
are illustrated in Figure 4–2. Here we see a loss region when sales
are low, a profit region (and a maximum profit), and another loss region
at very high output levels.

FIGURE 4–2
Nonlinear break-
even chart

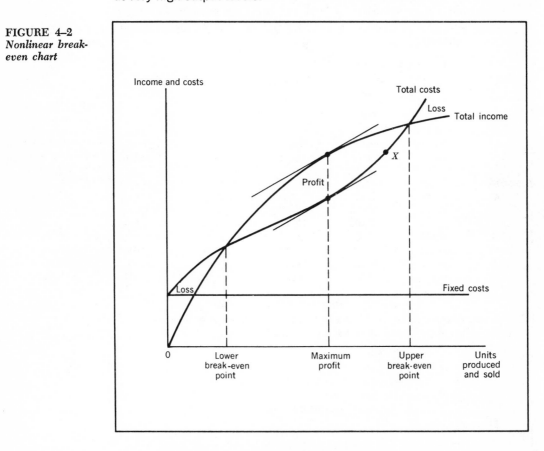

Note: The angle of a line from the origin to a point on the total-income line measures
price—that is, total income/units sold = price—and a line from the origin to the
total-cost curve measures cost per unit. It can be seen that the angle of the line to
the revenue curve declines as we move toward higher sales, which means the price
is falling. Unit costs (Total Cost/Units Produced) declines to point X, the tangency
point of a line from the origin to the total-cost curve, then begins to rise.
  The slopes of the total-cost and total-income lines measure marginal cost (MC)
and marginal revenue (MR) respectively. At the point where the slopes of the two
total curves are equal, $MR = MC$, and profits are at a maximum.

Although nonlinear break-even analysis is intellectually appealing, linear analysis is probably more appropriate for the uses to which it is put. Break-even charts allow focus to be placed on the key elements: sales, fixed costs, and variable costs. Even though linear break-even charts are drawn extending from *zero* output to very high output levels, no one who uses them would ordinarily be interested in or even consider the high and low extremes. In other words, users of break-even charts are really interested only in a "relevant range," and within this range linear functions are probably reasonably accurate.

Break-even analysis can be used in three separate but related ways: *An Example of Break-even Analysis*

1. It can be used in new product decisions: How large must the sales volume on a new product be if the firm is to break even on the project? This topic is illustrated in this section.

2. Break-even analysis can be used to analyze a modernization or automation program. Here, the firm operates in a more mechanized, automated manner and substitutes fixed costs for variable costs. This topic is covered later in the section on "Operating Leverage."

3. Break-even analysis can be used to study the effects of a general expansion in the level of operations. This topic is covered below in the section entitled "Break-even Point Based on Totals."

The textbook publishing business provides a good example of the effective use of break-even analysis for new product decisions. To illustrate, consider the following hypothetical example of the analysis for a college textbook. The costs and revenues are graphed in Figure 4–3.

Fixed costs

Copy editing	$ 3,000
Art work	1,000
Type setting	36,000
Total fixed costs	$40,000

Variable costs per copy

Printing and binding	$ 1.10
Bookstore commissions	2.00
Salesman's commissions	.25
Author's royalties	1.00
General and administrative costs	.50
Total variable costs per copy	$ 4.85
Sales price per copy	$10.00

The fixed costs can be estimated quite accurately; the variable costs, which are set by contracts, can also be precisely estimated (and they are linear). The sales price is variable, but competition keeps prices within a sufficiently narrow range to make a linear total-revenue curve reasonable. Applying the formula, we find the break-even sales volume to be 7,767 copies.

FIGURE 4–3
Break-even chart
for a hypothetical
textbook

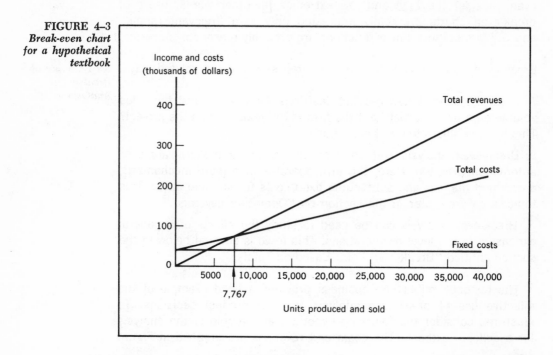

Publishers know the size of the total market for a given book, "the competition," and so forth. With this data as a base, they can estimate the possibilities that a given book will reach or exceed the break-even point. If the estimate is that it will not, the publisher may consider cutting production costs by doing less art work and editing, using a lower grade of paper, negotiating with the author on royalty rates, and so on. In this particular business—and especially for new product decisions in many others—linear break-even analysis has proved itself to be a useful tool.

Break-even Point Calculating break-even points on the basis of dollar sales instead of
Based on Totals on units of output is frequently useful. The main advantage of this method, which is illustrated in Table 4–2, is that it enables one to determine a general break-even point for a firm that sells several re-

lated products at varying prices. Furthermore, the procedure requires a minimum of data. Only three values are needed: sales, fixed costs, and variable costs. Sales and total-cost data are readily available from annual reports of corporations and from investment manuals. Total costs must then be segregated into fixed and variable components. The major fixed charges (rent, interest, depreciation, and general and administrative expenses) may be taken from the income statement. Finally, variable costs are calculated by deducting fixed costs from total costs.

$$\text{Break-even point (sales volume)} = \frac{\text{total fixed costs}}{1 - \dfrac{\text{total variable costs}}{\text{total sales volume}}}.$$

Procedure

Take any quantity and use the related data to determine the break-even point. For example, assume that 20,000 units are produced and use the data in Table 4–1:

$$\text{Break-even point} = \frac{\$40,000}{1 - \dfrac{\$24,000}{\$40,000}} = \frac{\$40,000}{0.4} = \$100,000.$$

Rationale

1. At the break-even point, sales (S) are equal to fixed cost (FC) plus variable cost (VC):

$$S = FC + VC. \tag{4-1}$$

2. Because both the sales price and the variable cost per unit are assumed to be constant in break-even analysis, the ratio VC/S is also constant and may be found from the annual income statement.

3. Since variable cost is a constant percentage of sales, equation (4–1) can be rewritten as:

$$S = FC + \frac{VC}{S}(S)$$

$$S\left(1 - \frac{VC}{S}\right) = FC$$

$$S = \frac{FC}{1 - \dfrac{VC}{S}} \text{ at break-even } S.$$

TABLE 4–2
Calculation of break-even point based on totals

Operating leverage reflects the extent to which fixed costs are used in operations, and break-even analysis can be used to analyze the degree of operating leverage employed.

Operating Leverage

The significance of the degree of operating leverage is clearly illustrated by Figure 4–4. Three firms, A, B, and C, with differing degrees of leverage, are contrasted. Firm A is considered to have a

Analysis

FIGURE 4-4 *Operating leverage*

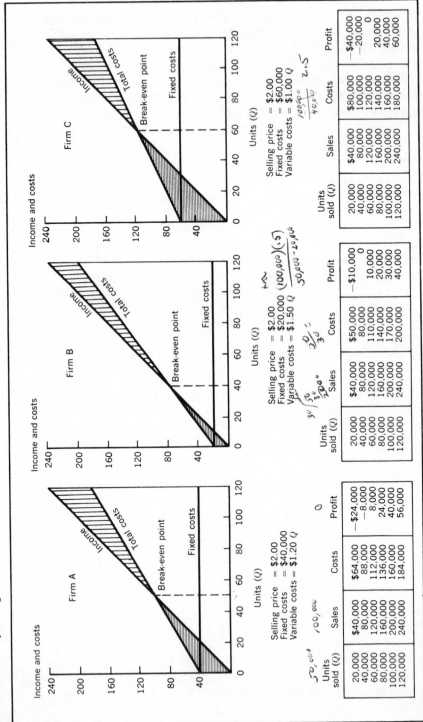

normal amount of fixed costs in its operations. It uses automated equipment (with which one operator can turn out a few or many units at the same labor cost) to about the same extent as the average firm in the industry. Firm B has lower fixed costs, but note the steeper rate of increase in variable costs of this firm over firm A. Firm B, however, breaks even at a lower level of operations than does firm A. At a production level of 40,000 units, firm A is losing $8,000 but firm B breaks even.

On the other hand, firm C has the highest fixed costs. It is highly automated, using expensive, high-speed machines that require very little labor per unit produced. With such an operation, its variable costs rise slowly. Because of the high overhead resulting from charges associated with the expensive machinery, firm C's break-even point is higher than that for either firm A or B. Once firm C reaches its break-even point, however, its profits rise faster than do those of the other firms. Operating leverage can be defined more precisely in terms of the way a given change in volume affects profits. For this purpose we use the following definition: *The degree of operating leverage is defined as the percentage change in operating income that results from a percentage change in units sold.* Algebraically:

$$\text{Degree of operating leverage} = \frac{\text{percentage change in operating income}}{\text{percentage change in sales}}.$$

For Firm A in Figure 4–4 the degree of operating leverage at 100,000 units of output is:

$$\text{Degree of } OL_A = \frac{\dfrac{\Delta \text{ profit}}{\text{profit}}}{\dfrac{\Delta Q}{Q}}$$

$$= \frac{\dfrac{\$56,000 - \$40,000}{\$40,000}}{\dfrac{120,000 - 100,000}{100,000}} = \frac{\dfrac{\$16,000}{\$40,000}}{\dfrac{20,000}{100,000}}$$

$$= \frac{40\%}{20\%} = \boxed{2.0}.$$

Here, Δ profit is the increase in profit, Q is the quantity of output in units, and ΔQ is the increase in output.

A formula has been developed to aid in calculating the degree of operating leverage at any level of output Q:[1]

$$\text{Degree of operating leverage at point } Q = \frac{Q(P - V)}{Q(P - V) - F}. \qquad (4\text{-}2)$$

Here, P is the price per unit, V is the variable cost per unit, and F is fixed costs. Using Equation 4–2, we find Firm A's degree of operating leverage at 100,000 units of output to be:

$$OL_A \text{ at 100,000 units} = \frac{100,000(\$2.00 - \$1.20)}{100,000(\$2.00 - \$1.20) - \$40,000}$$

$$= \frac{\$80,000}{\$40,000} = \boxed{2.0}.$$

The two methods must, of course, give consistent answers.

Equation 4–2 can also be applied to Firms B and C. When this is done, we find Firm B's degree of operating leverage at 100,000 units to be 1.5 and that of Firm C to be 2.5. Thus, for a 100 percent increase in volume Firm C, the company with the most operating leverage, will experience a profit increase of 250 percent; while for the same 100 percent volume gain Firm B, the one with the least leverage, will have only a 150 percent profit gain.

In summary, the calculation of the degree of operating leverage shows algebraically the same pattern that Figure 4–4 showed graphically—that the profits of Firm C, the company with the most operating leverage, are most sensitive to changes in sales volume, while those of Firm B, which has only a small amount of operating leverage, are

---

[1] Equation 4-2 is developed as follows:
The change in output is defined as ΔQ. Fixed costs are constant, so the change in profit is $\Delta Q(P - V)$, where P = price per unit and V = variable cost per unit.

The initial profit is $Q(P - V) - F$, so the percentage change in profit is:

$$\frac{\Delta Q(P - V)}{Q(P - V) - F}.$$

The percentage change in output is $\Delta Q/Q$, so the ratio of the change in profits to the change in output is:

$$\frac{\dfrac{\Delta Q(P - V)}{Q(P - V) - F}}{\dfrac{\Delta Q}{Q}} = \frac{\Delta Q(P - V)}{Q(P - V) - F} \cdot \frac{Q}{\Delta Q} = \frac{Q(P - V)}{Q(P - V) - F}.$$

relatively insensitive to volume changes. Firm A, with an intermediate
degree of leverage, lies between the two extremes.[2]

Some of the firm's fixed costs are noncash outlays, and for a period *Cash Break-*
some of its revenues may be in receivables. The cash break-even *even Analysis*
chart for Firm A, constructed on the assumption that $30,000 of the
fixed costs from the previous illustration are depreciation charges
and, therefore, a noncash outlay, is shown in Figure 4–5.[3] Because

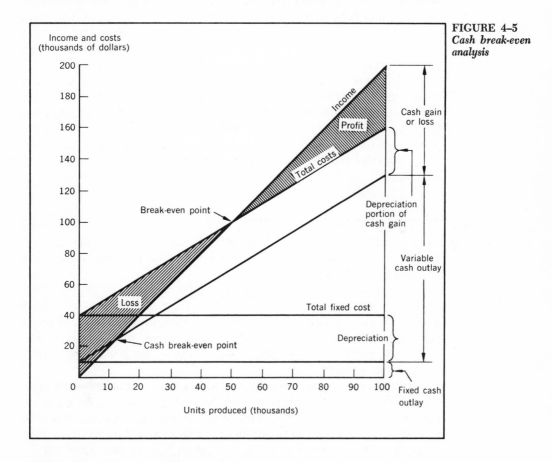

FIGURE 4–5
Cash break-even
analysis

---

[2] The degree of operating leverage is a form of the *elasticity concept* and, thus, is akin to
the familiar price elasticity developed in economics. Since operating leverage is an elasticity,
it varies depending upon the particular part of the break-even graph that is being considered.
For example, in terms of our illustrative firms the degree of operating leverage is greatest
close to the break-even point, where a very small change in volume can produce a very
large percentage increase in profits simply because the base profits are close to zero near
the break-even point.

[3] The nature of depreciation as a noncash outlay is explained in Footnote 5 of this chapter.

fixed-cash outlays are only $10,000, the cash break-even point is at 12,500 units rather than 50,000 units, which is the profit break-even point.

Cash break-even analysis does not fully represent cash flows—for this a cash budget is required. But cash break-even analysis is useful because it provides a picture of the flow of funds from operations. A firm could incur a level of fixed costs that would result in losses during periods of poor business but in large profits during upswings. If cash outlays are small, even during periods of losses, the firm might still be operating above the cash break-even point. Thus the risks of insolvency, in the sense of inability to meet cash obligations, would be small. This allows a firm to reach out for higher profits through automation and operating leverage.

Action taken by the federal government in the early 1960s made it possible for firms to claim larger depreciation allowances for tax purposes. This had the effect, in terms of Figure 4–5, of reducing the fixed cash outlay (but not the total fixed cost). With the cash break-even point reduced, U.S. firms were induced to employ additional operating leverage and, by doing so, to increase the efficiency of the U.S. economy.

Limitations of Break-Even Analysis Break-even analysis is useful in studying the relations among volume, prices, and cost structure; it is thus helpful in pricing, cost control, and other financial decisions. It has limitations, however, as a guide to managerial actions.

Linear break-even analysis is especially weak in what it implies about the sales possibilities for the firm. Any given break-even chart is based on a constant selling price. Therefore, in order to study profit possibilities under different prices, a whole series of charts is necessary, one chart for each price. Alternatively, nonlinear break-even analysis can be used.

With regard to costs, break-even analysis is also deficient—the relations indicated by the chart do not hold at all outputs. As sales increase, existing plant and equipment are worked to capacity, and both this situation and the use of additional workers and overtime pay cause variable costs to rise sharply. Additional equipment and plant are required, thus increasing fixed costs. Finally, over a period the products sold by the firm change in quality and quantity. Such changes in product mix influence the level and slope of the cost function. Linear break-even analysis is useful as a first step in developing the basic data required for pricing and making financial decisions. However, more detailed analysis, perhaps including nonlinear analysis, is required before final judgments can be made.

The sources and uses of funds statement is one of the most useful **SOURCES AND** tools in the financial manager's analytical kit. The basic purpose of **USES OF** the funds statement is to indicate, on an historical basis, where cash **FUNDS** came from and how it was used. **STATEMENT**

When a firm requests a loan, one of the first questions posed by the loan officer is, What has the firm done with the money it had? This question is answered by the sources and uses statement. The information it provides may indicate that the firm is making progress or that problems are arising.

To construct the sources and uses statement, one first tabulates the *Rough-and-Ready* changes in balance sheet items from one year to the next. Each change *Sources and Uses* in the balance sheet may be classified as either a source of funds *Analysis* or a use of funds, according to the following pattern:

Source of funds: (1) decrease in asset item or (2) increase in liability item.

Use of funds: (1) increase in asset item or (2) decrease in liability item.

An illustration of the financial manager's rough-and-ready analysis of sources and uses of funds is embodied in Tables 4–3 and 4–4 for Dallas Fertilizer and Chemical Company.

Dallas obtained funds by drawing down cash balances, by selling marketable securities, by increasing other current liabilities, by incurring long-term debt, and by retaining earnings. Total funds from these sources were $39 million. An additional $10 million accrued from an increase in the reserve for depreciation. Depreciation expense itself does not produce cash, but it is a noncash outlay. Since it was deducted from revenues to arrive at the retained earnings figure, it must be added back as a source of funds in cash flow analysis.[4]

---

[4] Treating depreciation as a source of funds is sufficiently worrisome to students to warrant elaboration. Consider Dallas's condensed 1970 income statement. Assume that sales are for cash and that all costs (except depreciation) and taxes are paid during the period.

Sales	$300,000,000
Costs excluding depreciation	270,000,000
Depreciation	10,000,000
Profit before taxes	20,000,000
Taxes	8,000,000
Profit after taxes	$ 12,000,000

Disregarding any possible changes in balance sheet accounts, how much cash was available from operations to finance new investment, to repay debt, and so on? The answer is $22 million, the sum of profits after taxes plus depreciation. In the actual case, of course, other events transpired and produced a different figure for total sources of funds. This example does show, however, the rationale behind the statement that depreciation is a source of funds.

TABLE 4–3
Dallas Fertilizer and Chemical Company
Comparative balance sheets and sources and uses of funds
In millions of dollars

	12/31/69	12/31/70	Sources	Uses
Cash	$ 10	$ 5	$ 5	
Marketable securities	25	15	10	
Net receivables	15	20		$ 5
Inventories	25	30		5
Gross fixed assets	150	180		30
Less: Allowance for depreciation*	(40)	(50)	10	
Net fixed assets	110	130		
Total assets	$185	$200		
Accounts payable	$ 10	$ 6		4
Notes payable	15	10		5
Other current liabilities	10	14	4	
Long-term debt	60	70	10	
Preferred stock	10	10	—	—
Common stock	50	50	—	—
Retained earnings	30	40	10	
Total claims on assets	$185	$200	$49	$49

*The allowance for depreciation is actually a liability account, even though it appears on the left side of the balance sheet. Note that it is deducted, not added, when totaling the column.

TABLE 4–4
Dallas Fertilizer and Chemical Company
Statement of sources and uses of funds, 1970
In millions of dollars

	Amount	Percent
X Uses		
Gross fixed assets expansion	$30	61.2
Inventory investment	5	10.2
Increase in receivables	5	10.2
Reduction in notes payable	5	10.2
Reduction in accounts payable	4	8.2
Total use of funds	$49	100.0
X Sources		
Increase in long-term debt	$10	20.4
Increase in retained earnings	10	20.4
Noncash depreciation outlay	10	20.4
Sale of marketable securities	10	20.4
Reduction in cash holdings	5	10.2
Increase in other liabilities	4	8.2
Total source of funds	$49	100.0

The total sources of funds, then, is $49 million. This amount was used to finance an increase in accounts receivable, to purchase inventories and fixed assets, and to reduce notes payable. Dallas Chemical had a net income of $12 million in 1970 and paid out $2 million in dividends, so that the retained earnings of $10 million completely reconciles the surplus account.

What does this rough-and-ready statement of sources and uses of funds tell the financial manager? It tells him that plant size was expanded and that fixed assets amounting to $30 million were acquired. Inventories and net receivables also increased as sales increased. The firm needed funds to meet working capital and fixed assets demands.

Previously, Dallas had been financing its growth through bank credit (notes payable). In the present period of growth, management decided to obtain some financing from permanent sources (long-term debt). It obtained enough long-term debt not only to finance some of the asset growth but also to pay back some of its bank credit and reduce accounts payable. In addition to the long-term debt, funds were acquired from retained earnings and from depreciation charges. Moreover, the firm had been accumulating marketable securities in anticipation of this expansion program, and these were sold to pay for new buildings and equipment. Finally, cash had been accumulated in excess of the firm's needs and was also worked down.

This example illustrates how the financial manager's rough-and-ready approach to sources and uses can give him a fairly complete picture of recent operations. Such an approach is not bogged down in details. Because refined adjustments usually amount to less than 4 or 5 percent of the total amounts involved, the financial manager can omit them and still obtain a good perspective on the flow of funds in his company.

A *pro forma*, or projected, sources and uses of funds statement can also be constructed to show how a firm plans to acquire and employ funds during some future period. In the next chapter we discuss financial forecasting, which involves the determination of future sales, the level of assets necessary to generate these sales (the left side of the projected balance sheet), and the manner in which these assets will be financed (the right side of the projected balance sheet). Given the projected balance sheet and supplementary projected data on earnings, dividends, and depreciation, the financial manager can construct a *pro forma* sources and uses of funds statement to summarize his firm's projected operations over the planning horizon. Such a statement is obviously of much interest to lenders as well as to the firm's own management.

Pro Forma Sources and Uses of Funds

SUMMARY   This chapter analyzes two important financial tools, *break-even analysis* and *sources and uses of funds statements,* and a key concept, that of *operating leverage.*

Break-Even Analysis   Break-even analysis is a method of relating fixed costs, variable costs, and total revenues to show the level of sales that must be attained if the firm is to operate at a profit. The analysis can be based on the number of units produced or on total dollar sales. It can also be used for the entire company or for a particular product or division. Further, with minor modifications, break-even analysis can be put on a cash basis instead of on a profit basis. Ordinarily, break-even analysis is conducted on a linear, or straight-line basis. However, this is not necessary—nonlinear break-even analysis is feasible and at times desirable.

$$\text{Units}$$
$$P(Q) = FC + VC(Q)$$

$$\text{Sales}$$
$$S = \frac{FC}{1 - \frac{VC}{P}}$$

Operating Leverage   Operating leverage is defined as the extent to which fixed costs are used in operations. The *degree of operating leverage,* defined as the percentage change in operating income that results from a specific percentage change in units sold, provides a precise measure of how much operating leverage a particular firm is employing. Break-even analysis gives a graphical view of the effects of changes in sales on profits; the degree of operating leverage presents the same picture in algebraic terms.

$$OL = \frac{\% \Delta \text{ Net Income}}{\% \Delta \text{ Sales}}$$

Sources and Uses of Funds Statement   The sources and uses of funds statement indicates where cash came from and how it was used. When a firm wishes to borrow funds one of the first questions posed by the loan officer is, "What has the firm done with the money it had?" This question is answered by the sources and uses statement. The information it provides may indicate that the firm is making progress or that problems are arising. Sources and uses data may also be analyzed on a *pro forma,* or projected, basis to show how a firm plans to acquire and employ funds during some future period.

Break-even analysis, operating leverage, and sources and uses statements are all fundamental concepts for the financial manager, and they will be encountered time and time again throughout the remainder of this book.

QUESTIONS   **4–1** Why is it particularly important for a rapidly growing young firm to concern itself with systems of control?

4–2 Are lower total costs *always* beneficial to a company? Why?

4–3 What benefits can be derived from break-even analysis?

4–4 What is operating leverage? Explain how profits or losses can be magnified in a firm with a great deal of operating leverage as opposed to a firm without this characteristic.

4–5 What portion of the selling price of a product goes toward covering fixed costs? Relate your answer to marginal analysis.

4–6 What data are necessary to construct a break-even chart?

4–7 What is the general effect of each of the following changes on a firm's break-even point?

a) An increase in selling price with no change in units sold.
b) A change from the leasing of a machine for $5,000 a year to the purchase of the machine for $100,000. The useful life of this machine will be 20 years, with no salvage value. Assume straight-line depreciation.
c) A reduction in variable labor costs.

4–8 What are the most important determinants of fixed asset and inventory requirements for a manufacturing firm?

4–9 Why do turnover ratios differ for firms in the same industry?

4–10 What effects would a price level increase have upon the level of investment in inventories and fixed assets, and what would be the net effect on the level of cash?

4–11 What are the similarities and differences between a sources and uses analysis and a cash budget?

4–12 Are increases in a surplus account and in depreciation considered to be sources of funds?

4–1 For Monroe Industries the following relations exist: each unit of output **PROBLEMS** is sold for $66; for output up to 20,000 units the fixed costs are $195,000; variable costs are $27 a unit.

a) What is the firm's gain or loss at sales of 4,000 units? of 6,000 units?
b) What is the break-even point? Illustrate by means of a chart.
c) What is Monroe's degree of operating leverage at sales of 4,000 and 6,000 units?
d) What happens to the break-even point if the selling price rises to $78? What is the significance of the change to financial management? Illustrate by means of a chart.
e) What occurs to the break-even point if the selling price rises to $78 but variable costs rise to $39 a unit? Illustrate by means of a chart.

4–2 The consolidated balance sheets for the Pelex Corporation at the beginning and end of 1970 are shown below.

Pelex Corporation
Balance sheet
Beginning and end 1970
In millions of dollars

	(Jan. 2)	(Dec. 31)	**Sources**	**Use**
Cash	$ 15	$ 7	————	————
Marketable securities	11	0	————	————
Net receivables	22	30	————	————
Inventories	53	75	————	————
Total current assets	$101	$112	————	————
Gross fixed assets	75	150	————	————
Less: Reserves for depreciation	(26)	(41)	————	————
Net fixed assets	49	109	————	————
Total assets	$150	$221	————	————

	(Jan. 2)	(Dec. 31)	Sources	Uses
Accounts payable	$ 15	$ 18	————	————
Notes payable	15	3	————	————
Other current liabilities	7	15	————	————
Long-term debt	8	26	————	————
Common stock	38	64	————	————
Retained earnings	67	95	————	————
Total claims on assets	$150	$221	————	————

The company bought $75 million worth of fixed assets. The charge for current depreciation was $15 million. Earnings after taxes were $38 million, and the company paid out $10 million in dividends.

a) Fill in the amount of source or use in the appropriate column.

b) Prepare a percentage statement of sources and uses of funds.

c) Briefly summarize your findings.

4-3 Indicate the effects of the transactions listed below on each of the following: total current assets, working capital, current ratio, and net profit. Use + to indicate an increase, — to indicate a decrease, and 0 to indicate no effect. State necessary assumptions and assume an initial current ratio of more than 1 to 1.

	Total current assets	Net working capital*	Current ratio	Effect on net profit
1. Cash is acquired through issuance of additional common stock.	+	0	0	0
2. Merchandise is sold for cash.	+	+	+	+
3. Federal income tax due for the previous year is paid.	—	0	0	0
4. A fixed asset is sold for less than book value.	—			
5. A fixed asset is sold for more than book value.				
6. Merchandise is sold on credit.				
7. Payment is made to trade creditors for previous purchases.				
8. A cash dividend is declared and paid.				
9. Cash is obtained through bank loans.				
10. Short-term notes receivable are sold at a discount.				
11. Previously issued stock rights are exercised by company stockholders.				
12. A profitable firm increases its fixed asset depreciation allowance account.				

	Total current assets	Net working capital*	Current ratio	Effect on net profit
13. Marketable securities are sold below cost.	____	____	____	____
14. Uncollectible accounts are written off against the allowance account.	____	____	____	____
15. Advances are made to employees.	____	____	____	____
16. Current operating expenses are paid.	____	____	____	____
17. Short-term promissory notes are issued to trade creditors for prior purchases.	____	____	____	____
18. Ten-year notes are issued to pay off accounts payable.	____	____	____	____
19. A wholly depreciated asset is retired.	____	____	____	____
20. A *cash* sinking fund for the retirement of bonds is created; a reserve for bond sinking fund is also created.	____	____	____	____
21. Bonds are retired by the use of the cash sinking fund.	____	____	____	____
22. Accounts receivable are collected.	____	____	____	____
23. A stock dividend is declared and paid.	____	____	____	____
24. Equipment is purchased with short-term notes.	____	____	____	____
25. The allowance for doubtful accounts is increased.	____	____	____	____
26. Merchandise is purchased on credit.	____	____	____	____
27. Controlling interest in another firm is acquired by the issuance of additional common stock.	____	____	____	____
28. Earnings are added to the reserve for bond sinking fund.	____	____	____	____
29. An unconsolidated subsidiary pays the firm a cash dividend from current earnings.	____	____	____	____
30. The estimated taxes payable are increased.	____	____	____	____

* Net working capital is defined as current assets minus current liabilities.

Chapter 5

Financial Forecasting

*T*HE planning process is an integral part of the financial manager's job. As will be seen in subsequent chapters, long-term debt and equity funds are raised infrequently and in large amounts. Further, the cost per dollar raised by selling such securities decreases as the size of the issue increases, and this increases the tendency to raise outside capital at infrequent intervals. Because of these considerations, it is important that the firm have a working estimate of its total needs for funds for the next few years. It is therefore useful to examine methods of forecasting the firm's over-all needs for funds, and this is the subject of the present chapter.

THE CASH FLOW CYCLE We must recognize that firms need assets in order to make sales, and if sales are to be increased, assets must also be expanded. Growing firms require new investments—immediate investment in current assets and, as full capacity is reached, investment in fixed assets as well. New investments must be financed. New financing carries with it commitments and obligations to service the capital obtained.[1] A growing, profitable firm is likely to require more cash for investments in receivables, inventories, and fixed assets. Therefore, a growing, profitable firm can have a cash flow problem. The nature of this problem, as well as the cause and effect relationship between assets and sales, is illustrated in the following discussion, where the consequences of a series of transactions are traced.

Effects on the Balance Sheet 1. Two partners invest a total of $50,000 to create the Glamour Galore Dress Company. The plant is rented, but equipment and other fixed assets cost $30,000. The resulting financial situation is shown by Balance Sheet 1.

[1] By "servicing" capital we refer to interest and repayment of principal on debt as well as dividends and retained earnings (the cost of equity capital) on common stocks.

Assets		Liabilities		*Balance sheet 1*
Current Assets				
Cash	$20,000			
Fixed Assets		Capital stock	$50,000	
Plant and equipment	30,000	Total liabilities		
Total assets	$50,000	and net worth	$50,000	

2. Glamour Galore receives an order to manufacture 10,000 dresses. The receipt of an order in itself has no effect on the balance sheet. However, in preparation for the manufacturing activity, the firm buys $20,000 worth of cotton cloth on terms of net 30 days. Without additional investment by the owners, total assets increase by $20,000, financed by the trade accounts payable to the supplier of the cotton cloth.

After the purchase, the firm spends $20,000 on labor for cutting the cloth to the required pattern. Of the $20,000 total cost, $10,000 is paid in cash and $10,000 is owed in the form of accrued wages. These two transactions are reflected in Balance Sheet 2.

Assets		Liabilities		*Balance sheet 2*
Current Assets		Accounts payable	$20,000	
Cash	$10,000	Accrued wages payable	10,000	
Inventories:				
Work in process:				
Materials	20,000	Total current liabilities	$30,000	
Labor	20,000			
Total current assets	$50,000	Capital stock	50,000	
Fixed Assets				
Plant and equipment	30,000	Total liabilities		
Total assets	$80,000	and net worth	$80,000	

Total assets increase to $80,000. Current assets are increased; net working capital, total current assets minus total current liabilities, remains constant. The current ratio declines to 1.67, and the debt ratio rises to 38 percent. The financial position of the firm is weakening. If it should seek to borrow at this point, Glamour Galore could not use the work-in-process inventories as collateral because a lender could find little use for partially manufactured dresses.

3. In order to complete the dresses, additional labor costs of $20,000 are incurred and paid in cash. It is assumed that the firm desires to maintain a minimum cash balance of $5,000. Since the initial cash balance is $10,000, Glamour Galore must borrow an additional $15,000 from its bank to meet the wage bill. The borrowing is reflected

in notes payable in Balance Sheet 3. Total assets rise to $95,000, with a finished goods inventory of $60,000. The current ratio drops to 1.4, and the debt ratio rises to 47 percent. These ratios represent a further weakening of the financial position.

Balance sheet 3

Assets		Liabilities	
Current Assets		Accounts payable	$20,000
Cash	$ 5,000	Notes payable	15,000
Inventory:		Accrued wages payable	10,000
Finished goods	60,000		
Total current assets	$65,000	Total current liabilities	$45,000
Fixed Assets		Capital stock	50,000
Plant and equipment	30,000		
		Total liabilities	
Total assets	$95,000	and net worth	$95,000

4. Glamour Galore ships the dresses on the basis of the original order, invoicing the purchaser for $100,000 within 30 days. Accrued wages and accounts payable have to be paid now, so Glamour Galore must borrow an additional $30,000 in order to maintain the $5,000 minimum cash balance.

Balance sheet 4

Assets		Liabilities	
Current Assets		Notes payable	$ 45,000
Cash	$ 5,000	Total current liabilities	$ 45,000
Accounts receivable	100,000		
Total	$105,000	Capital stock	$ 50,000
Fixed Assets		Retained earnings	40,000
Plant and equipment	30,000	Total net worth	$ 90,000
		Total liabilities	
Total Assets	$135,000	and net worth	$135,000

Note that in Balance Sheet 4, finished goods inventory is replaced by receivables, with the markup reflected as retained earnings. This causes the debt ratio to drop to 33 percent. Since the receivables are carried at selling price, the current assets increase to $105,000 and the current ratio rises to 2.3. Compared with the conditions reflected in Balance Sheet 3, most of the financial ratios show improvement. However, the absolute amount of debt is large.

Whether the firm's financial position is really improved depends upon the credit worthiness of the purchaser of the dresses. If the purchaser is a good credit risk, Glamour Galore may be able to borrow further on the basis of the accounts receivable.

5. The firm receives payment for the accounts receivable, pays off the bank loan, and is in the highly liquid position shown by Balance

Sheet 5. If a new order for 10,000 dresses is received, it will have no effect on the balance sheet, but a cycle similar to the one described in this section will begin.

Assets		Liabilities		
Assets		**Liabilities**		*Balance sheet 5*
Current Assets		Capital stock	$50,000	
Cash	$60,000	Earned surplus	40,000	
Fixed Assets				
Plant and equipment	$30,000			
		Total liabilities		
Total assets	$90,000	and net worth	$90,000	

The idea of the cash cycle can now be generalized. An order that requires the purchase of raw materials is placed with the firm. The purchase in turn generates an account payable. As labor is applied, work-in-process inventories build up. To the extent that wages are not fully paid at the time labor is used, accrued wages will appear on the liability side of the balance sheet. As goods are completed, they move into finished goods inventories. The cash needed to pay for the labor to complete the goods may make it necessary for the firm to borrow.

Cash flow cycle

Finished goods inventories are sold, usually on credit, which gives rise to accounts receivable. As the firm has not received cash, this point in the cycle represents the peak in financing requirements. If the firm did not borrow at the time finished goods inventories were at their maximum, it may do so as inventories are converted into receivables by credit sales. Income taxes, which were not considered in the example, can add to the problem. As accounts receivable become cash, short-term obligations can be paid off.

How the process just described results in the need for increased financing as the volume of sales rises can be illustrated by actual data for Amalgamated Motors Corporation (AMAG) during 1950–1970 (Table 5–1). During the first ten years of this period, sales rose by $800 million, which represents a 200 percent increase. Current assets increased by 220 percent, net plant and equipment by only 167 percent. The $800 million increase in sales gave rise to the need to finance a $330 million increase in current assets and a $125 million increase in net fixed assets. Thus current assets rose by about 40 percent of the increase in sales, and net fixed assets at somewhat over 15 percent of the increase in sales. Stated differently, for every $10 million increase in sales, AMAG had to finance an additional $4 million in current assets and $1.5 million in net fixed assets.

How Sales Require Financing

TABLE 5–1
Amalgamated Motors Corporation, 1950–1970
Dollars in millions

	1950	1960	1970	Percentage of increase 1950–1960	Percentage of increase 1960–1970
Sales	$400	$1,200	$1,800	200	50
Current assets	150	480	800	220	67
Net plant and equipment	75	200	300	167	50
Total	225	680	1,100	202	62
Current liabilities	60	175	310	192	77
Long-term debt	40	250	300	525	20
Shareholders' equity	140	300	525	114	75
Total	$240	$ 725	$1,135	202	57

Note: Totals do not balance because only the significant items were taken from the report.

During the first decade covered by the AMAG data, increased operating assets were financed about two-thirds by debt and one-third by shareholders' equity. Long-term debt increased by 525 percent.

The data for 1950–1960 may be compared with those for the subsequent ten years, thus testing to see if the generalizations made from the early years hold for the latter period. First, the rate of growth has slowed, so the percentage figures are smaller. However, there is strong confirmation of the generalizations made with respect to the decade between 1950 and 1960. During the later period, 1960 through 1970, sales increased by 50 percent and total assets by 62 percent. Note again the close correspondence between the percentage increase in sales and the percentage increase in financing requirements. When sales increased by 50 percent, net plant and equipment also increased by precisely 50 percent. Current assets increased by 67 percent.

An interesting contrast is provided by the methods of financing growth. In the earlier period, current liabilities increased by about the same percentage as sales increased. However, in that earlier period, long-term debt increased by over 500 percent, while net worth increased by somewhat over 100 percent. In the years 1960–1970 long-term debt increased by a much smaller percentage than did sales, and net worth increased by a much larger percentage.

These data, drawn from AMAG's actual experience, illustrate the close relationship between changes in the level of sales and changes in financing requirements.

The influence of sales on current asset levels was illustrated above. *Financing* Over the course of several cycles, the fluctuations in sales will be *Patterns* accompanied in most industries by a rising long-term trend. Figure 5–1 shows the consequences of such a pattern. Total permanent assets increase steadily in the form of current and fixed assets. Increases of this nature should be financed by long-term debt; by equity; by "spontaneous" increases in liabilities, such as accrued taxes and wages; and by accounts receivable, which naturally accompany increasing sales. However, temporary increases in assets can be covered by short-term liabilities. The distinction between temporary and permanent asset levels may be difficult to make in practice, but it is neither illusory nor unimportant. Short-term financing to finance long-term needs is dangerous. A profitable firm may become unable to meet its cash obligations if funds borrowed on a short-term basis have become tied up in permanent asset needs.

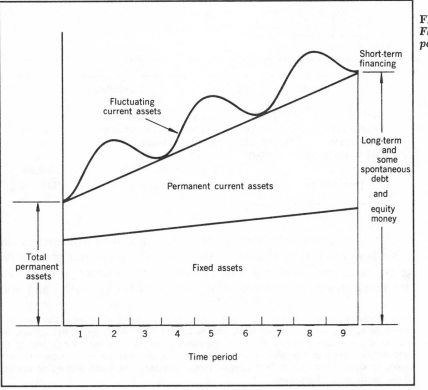

FIGURE 5–1
Fluctuating versus permanent assets

PERCENT-OF-SALES METHOD
It is apparent from the preceding discussion that the most important variable that influences a firm's financing requirements is its projected dollar volume of sales. A good sales forecast is an essential foundation for forecasting financial requirements. The principal methods of forecasting financial requirements are described in this and the following sections.

The simplest approach to forecasting financial requirements expresses the firm's needs in terms of the percentage of annual sales invested in each individual balance sheet item. As an example, consider the Moore Company, whose balance sheet as of December 31, 1970, is shown in Table 5–2. The company's sales are running at about $500,000 a year, which is its capacity limit; the profit margin after tax on sales is 4 percent. During 1970, the company earned $20,000 after taxes and paid out $10,000 in dividends, and it plans to continue paying out half of net profits as dividends. How much additional financing will be needed if sales expand to $800,000 during 1971? The calculating procedure, using the percent-of-sales method, is explained below.[2]

TABLE 5–2
The Moore Company
Balance sheet
December 31, 1970

Assets		Liabilities	
Cash	$ 10,000	Accounts payable	$ 50,000
Receivables	85,000	Accrued taxes and wages	25,000
Inventories	100,000	Mortgage bonds	70,000
Fixed assets (net)	150,000	Common stocks	100,000
		Retained earnings	100,000
Total assets	$345,000	Total liab. and net worth	$345,000

First, isolate those balance sheet items that can be expected to vary directly with sales. In the case of the Moore Company, this step applies to all the assets—a higher level of sales would necessitate more cash for transactions, more receivables, higher inventory levels, and addi-

---

[2] We recognize, of course, that as a practical matter, business firms plan their needs in terms of specific items of equipment, square feet of floor space, and other factors, and not as a percentage of sales. However, the outside analyst does not have access to this information, and the manager, even though he has the information on specific items, needs to check his forecasts in aggregate terms. The percent-of-sales method serves both these needs surprisingly well.

tional fixed plant capacity. On the liability side, accounts payable as well as accruals may be expected to increase with increases in sales. Retained earnings will go up as long as the company is profitable and does not pay out 100 percent of earnings, but the percentage increase is not constant. However, neither common stock nor mortgage bonds would increase spontaneously with an increase in sales.

Those items that can be expected to vary directly with sales are tabulated as a percentage of sales in Table 5–3. For every $100 increase in sales, assets must increase by $69; this $69 must be financed in some manner. Accounts payable will increase spontaneously with sales, as will accruals; these two items will supply $15 of new funds for each $100 increase in sales. Subtracting the 15 percent for spontaneously generated funds from the 69 percent funds requirement leaves 54 percent—thus, for each $100 increase in sales, the Moore Company must obtain $54 of financing either from retained earnings or from external sources.

TABLE 5–3
The Moore Company
Balance sheet items expressed as a percent of sales
December 31, 1970

Assets		Liabilities	
Cash	2.0%	Accounts payable	10.0%
Receivables	17.0	Accrued taxes and wages	5.0
Inventories	20.0	Mortgage bonds	na
Fixed assets (net)	30.0	Common stock	na
		Retained earnings	na
Total assets	69.0%	Total liab. and net worth	15.0%
na = not applicable			
Assets as a percent of sales			69.0%
Less: Spontaneous increase in liabilities			15.0
Percent of each additional dollar of sales that must be financed			54.0%

In the case at hand, sales are scheduled to increase from $500,000 to $800,000, or by $300,000. Applying the 54 percent to the expected increase in sales leads to the conclusion that $162,000 will be needed. Some of this need will be met by retained earnings. Total sales during 1971 will be $800,000; if the company earns 4 percent after taxes on this volume, profits will amount to $32,000. Assuming that the 50 percent dividend payout ratio is maintained, dividends will be $16,000 and $16,000 will be retained. Subtracting the retained earnings from the $162,000 that was needed leaves a figure of $146,000—this is the amount of funds that must be obtained through borrowing or by selling new common stock.

Notice what would have happened if the Moore Company's sales forecast for 1971 had been only $515,000—a not bad 3 percent gain. Applying the 54 percent net need for funds to the $15,000 sales increase gives an $8,100 funds requirement. Retained earnings ($10,300) would more than cover these requirements, so the firm would have no need of outside capital. The example shows not only that higher levels of sales bring about a need for funds, but also that while small percentage increases can be financed through retained earnings, larger increases cause the firm to go into the market for outside capital. In other words, a certain level of growth can be financed from internal sources, but higher levels of growth require external financing.

The percent-of-sales method of forecasting financial requirements is neither simple nor mechanical, although an explanation of the ideas requires simple illustrations. Experience in applying the technique in practice suggests the importance of understanding (1) the basic technology of the firm and (2) the logic of the relation between sales and assets for the particular firm in question. A substantial amount of experience and judgment is required to apply the technique in actual practice.

The percent-of-sales method is most appropriately used for forecasting relatively short-term changes in financing needs. It is less useful for longer term forecasting for reasons that are best described in connection with the analysis of the regression method of financial forecasting discussed in the next sections.

SCATTER DIA-GRAM, OR SIMPLE REGRESSION, METHOD   An alternative method used to forecast financial requirements is the scatter diagram, or simple regression, method. A scatter diagram is a graphic portrayal of joint relations. Proper use of the scatter diagram method requires practical but not necessarily statistical sophistication.

Table 5–4 and Figure 5–2 illustrate the use of the scatter diagram method and also demonstrate its superiority over the percent-of-sales method for long-range forecasting. As in all financial forecasting, the sales forecast is the starting point. The financial manager is given the sales forecast, or he may participate in formulating it. Suppose he has data through 1970 and is making a forecast of inventories for 1975, as indicated in Table 5–4. If he is using the simple regression method, he draws a line through the points for 1965 through 1970, as shown in Figure 5–2. The line that fits the scatter of points in this example is a straight line. It is called the line of best fit, or the regression line. Of course, all points seldom fall exactly on the regression line, and the line itself may be curved as well as linear.[3]

TABLE 5–4
*Relations between
inventory and sales*

Year	Sales	Inventory	Inventory as a percent of sales
1965	$ 50,000	$22,000	44
1966	100,000	24,000	24
1967	150,000	26,000	17
1968	200,000	28,000	14
1969	250,000	30,000	12
1970	300,000	32,000	11
.	.	.	.
.	.	.	.
.	.	.	.
1975 (estimated)	500,000	40,000	8

If the percent-of-sales method had been used, some difficulties would have arisen immediately. Table 5–4 gives percent of sales for 1965 through 1970. What relation could be used? the 44 percent for 1965? the 11 percent for 1970? or some average of the relations? If the relation for 1970 had been used, a forecast of $55,000 for inventories in 1975 would have been made, compared with $42,000 by the scatter diagram method. This forecast represents a large error.

The regression method is thus seen to be superior for forecasting financial requirements, particularly for longer term forecasts. When a firm is likely to have a base stock of inventory or fixed assets, the ratio of the item to sales declines as sales increase. In such cases the percent-of-sales method results in large errors.[4]

---

[3] In these illustrations, inventories are used as the item to be forecast. Much theory suggests that inventories increase as a square root of sales; see, for example, the inventory control model developed in Chapter 14. This characteristic would tend to turn the line of regression between inventories and sales slightly downward. Also, improvements in inventory-control techniques would curve the line of relation downward. However, the increased diversity of types, models, and styles tends to increase inventories. Applications by the authors' students of the regression method to hundreds of companies indicate that the linear straight line relations frequently represent the line of best fit or, at worst, involve only small error. If the line were in fact curved over, a curved line could be fitted to the data and used for forecasting purposes.

[4] The widespread use of the percentage method makes for lax control. It would be easy to improve on a $55,000 inventory level and still be inefficient because the correct target amount is closer to $40,000.

FIGURE 5–2
*Illustrative relation
between sales and
inventory*

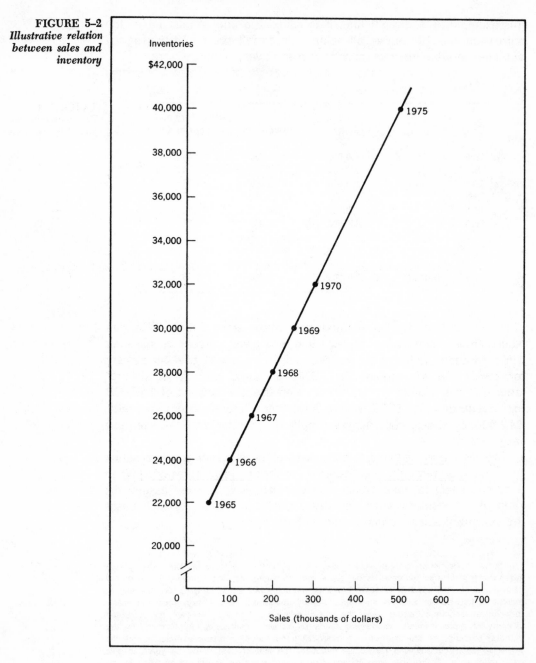

A more sophisticated approach to forecasting a firm's assets calls for the use of *multiple regression analysis*. In simple regression, sales are assumed to be a function of only one variable; in multiple regression, sales are recognized to depend upon a number of variables. For example, in simple regression we might state that sales are strictly a function of GNP. With multiple regression, we might say that sales are dependent upon both GNP and a set of additional variables. For example, the sale of ski equipment depends upon (1) the general level of prosperity as measured by GNP, personal disposable income, or other indicators of aggregate economic activity; (2) population increases; (3) number of lifts operating; (4) weather conditions; (5) advertising, and so forth.

    We shall not go into detail on the use of multiple regression analysis at this time. However, most computer installations have "canned" regression programs incorporated into their systems, making it extremely easy to use multiple regression techniques; multiple regression is widely used by at least the larger corporations.

MULTIPLE REGRESSION METHOD

Thus far we have considered four methods used in financial forecasting: (1) the percent-of-sales method, (2) the scatter diagram, or simple linear regression method, (3) curvilinear simple regression, and (4) multiple regression. This section summarizes and compares these four methods.

A COMPARISON OF FORECASTING METHODS

The percent-of-sales method of financial forecasting assumes that certain balance sheet items vary directly with sales; that is, that the ratio of a given balance sheet item to sales remains constant. The postulated relationship is shown in Figure 5–3. Notice that the percent-of-sales method implicitly assumes a linear relationship that passes through the origin. The slope of the line representing the relationship may vary, but the line always passes through the origin. Implicitly, the relationship is established by finding one point, or ratio, such as that designated as X in Figure 5–3, and then connecting this point with the origin. Then, for any projected level of sales, the level of the particular balance sheet item can be determined.

Percent-of-Sales Method

The scatter diagram method differs from the percent-of-sales method principally in that it does not assume that the line of relationship passes through the origin. In its simplest form, the scatter diagram method calls for calculating the ratio between sales and the relevant balance sheet item at two points in time, extending a line through these two points, and using the line to describe the relationship between sales and the balance sheet item. The accuracy of the regression is improved if more points are plotted, and the regression line can

Scatter Diagram, or Simple Linear Regression, Method

be fitted mathematically (by a technique known as the method of least squares) as well as drawn in by eye.

FIGURE 5–3
*Illustration of the
percent-of-sales
method*

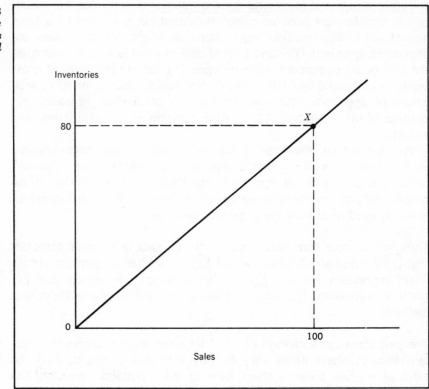

The scatter diagram method is illustrated in Figure 5–4, where the percent-of-sales relationship is also shown for comparison. The error induced by the use of the percent-of-sales method is represented by the gap between the two lines. At a sales level of 125, the percent-of-sales method would call for an inventory of 100 versus an inventory of only 90 using a scatter diagram forecast. *Notice that the error is very small if sales continue to run at approximately the current level, but the gap widens and the error increases as sales deviate in either direction from current levels, as they probably would if a long-run forecast was being made.*

Simple Curvilinear Regression   Linear scatter diagrams, or linear regressions, assume that the slope of the regression line is constant. This condition does frequently exist, but this is not a universal rule. Figure 5–5 illustrates the application of curvilinear simple regression to forecasting financial relationships.

We have drawn this hypothetical illustration to show a flattening curve, which implies a decreasing relationship between sales and inventory beyond point X, the current level of operations. In this case, the forecast of inventory requirements at a sales level of 125 would be too high if the linear regression method was used (but too low if sales declined from 100 to 50).

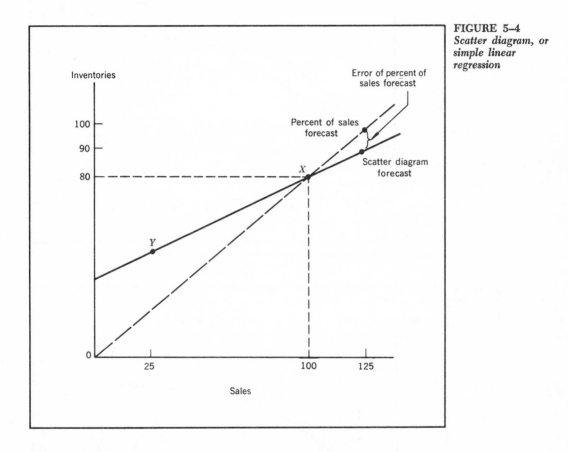

FIGURE 5–4
Scatter diagram, or simple linear regression

In our illustration to this point, we have been assuming that the observations fell exactly on the relationship line. This implies perfect correlation, something that, in fact, seldom occurs. In practice, the actual observations would be scattered about the regression line as shown in Figure 5–6. What causes the deviations from the regression line? One obvious answer, if linear regression is used, is that the actual line of relationship might be curvilinear. But if curvilinear regression is used and deviations occur, we must seek other explanations for the scatter around the regression line. The most obvious answer is that

Multiple Regression

FIGURE 5–5
Curvilinear simple regression

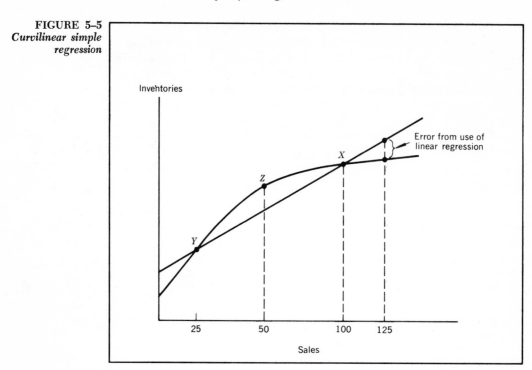

FIGURE 5–6
Multiple regression

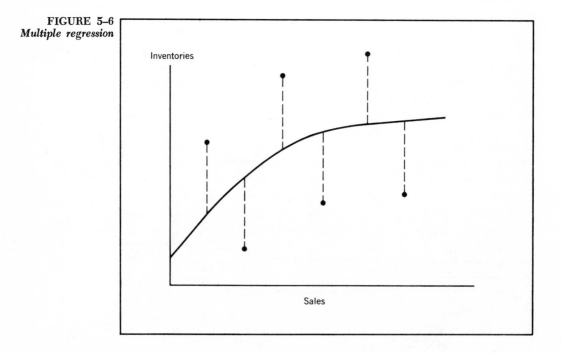

balance sheet items, such as inventories, are determined by factors other than just sales. For example, inventory levels are certainly influenced by work stoppages at the plants of suppliers. If a steel fabricator anticipates a strike in the steel industry, he will stock up on steel products in anticipation of the strike. Such hedge buying would cause actual inventories to be above the level forecast on the basis of sales projections. Then, assuming a strike does occur and continues for many months, inventories will be drawn down and may end up well below the predicted level. Multiple regression techniques, which introduce additional variables (such as work stoppages) into the analysis, are employed to further improve financial forecasting.

The need to employ more complicated forecasting techniques varies from situation to situation. For example, the percent-of-sales method may be perfectly adequate for making short-run forecasts where conditions are relatively stable, while curvilinear multiple regression may be deemed essential for longer-run forecasts in more dynamic industries. As in all other applications of financial analysis, the cost of using more refined techniques must be balanced against the benefits of increased accuracy.

✱ Which method is used depends on many things

SUMMARY

Firms need assets to make sales; and if sales are to be increased, assets must also be expanded. The first section of this chapter illustrates the relationship between sales and assets, and shows how even a growing, profitable firm can have a cash-flow problem.

The most important causal variable in determining financial requirements is a firm's projected dollar volume of sales; a good sales forecast is an essential foundation for forecasting financial requirements. The two principal methods used to make financial forecasts are (1) the percent-of-sales method and (2) the regression method. The first has the virtue of simplicity—the forecaster computes past relationships between asset and liability items and sales, assumes these same relationships will continue, and then applies the new sales forecast to get an estimate of the financial requirements.

However, since the percent-of-sales method assumes that the balance sheet/sales relationships will remain constant, it is only useful for relatively short-run forecasting. When longer forecasts are being made, the regression method is preferable because it allows for changing balance sheet/sales relationships. Further, linear regression can be expanded to curvilinear regression, and simple regression to multiple regression. These more complex methods are useful in certain circumstances, but their increased accuracy must be balanced against the increased costs of using them.

The tools and techniques discussed in this chapter are generally used in the following manner: As a first step, one of the long-range forecasting techniques is used to make a long-run forecast of the firm's financial requirements over a three-to-five-year period following the short-run planning period. This forecast is then used to make the strategic financing plans during the planning period. Long lead times are necessary when companies sell bonds or stocks; otherwise, financial managers might be forced to go into the market for funds during unfavorable periods.

In addition to this long-run, strategic forecasting, the financial manager must also make accurate short-run forecasts to be sure that bank funds will be available to meet seasonal and other short-run requirements. This topic is considered in the following chapter.

QUESTIONS 5–1 What is the first step in forecasting financial requirements? Why is this the first step?

5–2 If a firm's average collection period is 25 days and its daily credit sales are $1,000, what is the theoretical amount for accounts receivable on the balance sheet?

5–3 Describe the regression method for forecasting financial needs. What are the strengths and the weaknesses of this method?

5–4 What should be the approximate point of intersection between the sales/asset regression line and the vertical axis (Y-axis intercept) for the following: inventory, accounts receivable, fixed assets? State your answer in terms of positive, zero, or negative intercept. Can you think of any accounts that might have a negative intercept?

5–5 How does forecasting financial requirements in advance of needs assist the financial manager to perform his responsibilities more effectively?

5–6 Explain how a downturn in the business cycle could either cause a cash shortage for a firm or have the opposite effect and generate excess cash.

5–7 Why do many "young" firms find it difficult to obtain working capital loans from commercial banks? Do you suppose that a given firm would have an easier time getting a working capital loan than a loan to finance fixed assets?

5–8 Explain this statement: "Current assets to a considerable extent represent permanent assets."

5–9 What advantages might multiple regression technique have over simple regression in forecasting sales? What might be some drawbacks in the actual use of this technique?

PROBLEMS 5–1 The Pilgrim Supply Company is a wholesale steel distributor. It purchases steel in carload lots from more than twenty producing mills and sells to several thousand steel users. The items carried include sheets, plates, wire products, bolts, windows, pipe, and tubing.

The company owns two warehouses, each housing 10,000 square feet, and contemplates the erection of another warehouse of 15,000 square feet. The nature of the steel-supply business requires that the company maintain large inventories to take care of customer requirements in the event of mill strikes or other delays.

In examining patterns from 1965 through 1970 the company found a rather consistent relation between the following accounts as a percent of sales.

Current assets	50%
Net fixed assets	20%
Accounts payable	5%
Other current liabilities, including accruals and provision for income taxes but not bank loans	5%
Net profit after taxes	2%

The company's sales for 1971 were $9 million, and its balance sheet on December 31, 1971, was as follows:

Pilgrim Supply Company
Balance sheet
December 31, 1971

Current assets	$4,500,000	Accounts payable	$ 450,000
Fixed assets	1,800,000	Notes payable	900,000
		Other current liabilities	450,000
		Total current liabilities	1,800,000
		Mortgage loan	300,000
		Common stock	750,000
		Earned surplus	3,450,000
Total assets	$6,300,000	Total liabilities and net worth	$6,300,000

The company expects its sales to grow by $600,000 each year. If this growth is achieved, what will its financial requirements be at the end of the five-year period? Assume that accounts not tied directly to sales (for example, notes payable) remain constant. Assume also that the company pays no dividends.

a) Construct a *pro forma* balance sheet for the end of 1976, using "additional financing needed" as the balancing item.

b) What are the crucial assumptions made in your projection method?

5–2   The annual sales of the Random Company, a recently organized firm, are $6 million. Common stock and notes payable are constant. The percent of sales in each balance sheet item that varies directly with sales are expected to be as follows:

Cash	4
Receivables	12
Inventories	12
Net fixed assets	18
Accounts payable	10
Provision for income tax	4
Other current liabilities	5
Profit rate (after taxes) on sales	6

a) Complete the balance sheet below:

Random Company
Balance sheet
December 31, 1971

Cash	_____	Accounts payable	_____
Receivables		Notes payable	$480,000
Inventory	_____	Provision for income tax	_____
Total current assets	_____	Other current liabilities	_____
Fixed assets	_____	Total current liabilities	_____
		Common stock	780,000
		Retained earnings	_____
Government securities	0	Total liabilities and net worth	
Total assets			
	=========		=========

b) Now suppose that in one year sales increase by $1,200,000, to $7.2 million. What will be the new balance sheet (no dividends paid)? (Assume that any excess funds will be invested in government securities.)

c) For any given increase in sales in one year, what will be the additional external financing requirements, expressed as a percentage of sales?

Chapter 6

Financial Planning
and Control:
Budgeting

*I*N the preceding chapter we first examined the relationship between assets and sales, then considered several procedures which the financial manager can use in order to forecast his requirements. In addition to his long-range forecasts the financial manager is also concerned with short-term needs for funds. It is embarrassing for a corporate treasurer to "run out of money." Even though he may be able to negotiate a bank loan on short notice, his plight may cause the banker to question the soundness of the firm's management and, accordingly, to reduce the company's line of credit with the bank. Therefore, attention must be given to short-term budgeting, with special emphasis on cash forecasting, or *cash budgeting*, as it is commonly called.

The cash budget is, however, only one part of the firm's over-all budget system. The nature of the budget system, and especially the way it can be used for both planning and control purposes, is also discussed in this chapter.

A budget is simply a financial plan. A household budget itemizes the **BUDGETING** family's sources of income and describes how this income will be spent: so much for food, housing, transportation, entertainment, education, savings, and so on. Similarly, the federal budget indicates income sources and allocates funds to defense, welfare, agriculture, education, and the like. By the same token, a firm's budget is a plan detailing how funds will be spent on labor, raw materials, capital goods, and so on, as well as how the funds for these expenditures will be obtained. Just as the federal budget can be used as a device to insure that the Defense Department, Agriculture Department, and others limit their expenditures to specified amounts, the corporate budget can also be used as a device for formulating the firm's plans and for exercising control over the various departments.

Budgeting is, thus, a management tool used for both *planning* and *control.* Depending on the nature of the business, detailed plans may be formulated for the next few months, the next year, the next five years, or even longer. A heavy construction company that constantly has outstanding bids, which may or may not be accepted, cannot, and indeed need not, plan ahead as far as an electric utility company. The electric utility can base its projections on population growth, which is highly predictable for five- to ten-year periods; and it *must* plan asset acquisitions years ahead because of the long lead times involved in constructing dams, nuclear power plants, and the like.

THE NATURE OF THE BUDGETING PROCESS Fundamentally, the budgeting process is a method to improve operations; it is a continuous effort to get the job done in the best possible way. Historically, budgeting was treated as a device to limit expenditures. The more modern approach is to view the budgeting process as a tool for obtaining the most productive and profitable use of the company's resources. The budget requires a set of performance standards, or targets. Budgets are reviewed to compare plans and results, and this process has been called "controlling to plan." It is a continuous monitoring procedure, reviewing and evaluating performance with reference to the previously established standards.

Establishing standards requires a realistic understanding of the activities carried on by the firm. Arbitrary standards, set without a basic understanding of the minimum costs as determined by the nature of the firm's operations, can do more harm than good. Budgets imposed in an arbitrary fashion may represent impossible targets at the one extreme or standards that are too lax at the other. If standards are unrealistically high, frustrations and resentment will develop. If standards are unduly lax, costs will be out of control, profits will suffer, and morale will become flabby. However, a set of budgets based on a clear understanding and careful analysis of operations can play an important positive role for the firm.

Budgets, therefore, can provide valuable guides to both high-level executives and middle-management personnel. Well-formulated and effectively developed budgets make subordinates aware of the fact that top management has a realistic understanding of the nature of the operations in the business firm. Thus, the budget becomes an important communication link between top management and the divisional personnel whom they guide.

Budgets also represent planning and control devices that enable management to anticipate change and adapt to it. Business operations in today's economic environment are complex and subject to heavy competitive pressures. In such an environment many kinds of changes take place. The rate of growth of the economy as a whole fluctuates, and these fluctuations affect different industries in a number of different ways. If a firm plans ahead, the budget and control process can provide management with a better basis for understanding the firm's operations in relation to the general environment. This increased understanding leads to faster reactions to developing events, thus increasing the firm's ability to perform effectively.

The budgeting process, in summary, improves internal coordination. This element reflects the basic theme of this book: To show how financial decisions affect the profits and value of the firm and to show how these decisions may be improved. Decisions at every stage—for each product and at the research, engineering, production, marketing, personnel, and financial levels—all have an impact on the firm's profits. Planning and control is the essence of profit planning, and the budget system provides an integrated picture of the firm's operations as a whole. Therefore, the budget system enables the manager of each division to see the relation of his part of the enterprise to the totality of the firm. For example, a production decision to alter the level of work-in-process inventories, or a marketing decision to change the terms under which a particular product is sold, can be traced through the entire budget system to show its effects on the firm's over-all profitability. The budgeting system is a most important financial tool.

The over-all nature of the budget process is outlined in Figure 6–1. *The Budget* Budgeting is a part of the total planning activity in the firm, so we *System* must begin with a statement of corporate goals or objectives. The statement of goals (shown in the box at the top of the figure) determines the second part of the figure, the corporate long-range plan (shown in the second box). A segment of the corporate long-range plan includes a long-range sales forecast. This forecast requires a determination of the number and types of products that will be manufactured both at present and in the future years encompassed by the long-range plan. This is the product mix strategy.

Short-term forecasts and budgets are formulated within the framework of the long-range plan. One might, for example, begin with a sales forecast covering six months or one year. The short-term sales forecast provides a basis for (and is dependent on) the broad range of policies indicated in the center of Figure 6–1. First, there are manufacturing policies covering the choice of types of equipment, plant layout, and production-line arrangements. In addition, the kind of durability built into the products and their associated costs will be considered. Second, a broad set of marketing policies must be formulated. These relate to such items as (1) the development of the firm's own sales organization versus the use of outside sales organizations; (2) the number of salesmen and the method by which they will be compensated; (3) the forms, types and amounts spent on advertising; and other factors. (Third) are the research and general management policies. Research policies relate to relative emphasis on basic versus applied research and the product areas emphasized by both types of research. (Fourth) are financial policies, discussed in the following section.

FIGURE 6–1
Over-all view of the total budgeting process and relations

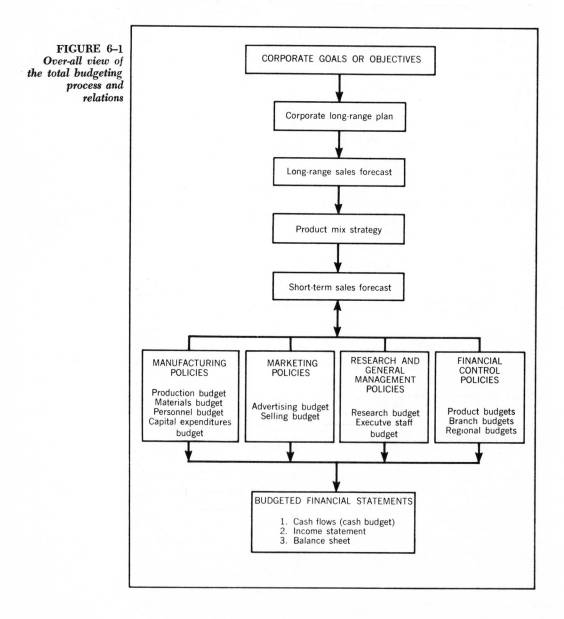

Financial control policies include the organization and content of various types of financial control budgets. These include a budget for individual products and for every significant activity of the firm. In addition, budgets will be formulated to control operations at individual branch offices. These budgets, in turn, are grouped and modified to control regional operations.

Financial Control Policies

In a similar manner, policies established at the manufacturing, marketing, research, and general management levels give rise to a series of budgets. For example, the production budget will reflect the use of materials, parts, labor, and facilities; each of the major elements in a production budget is likely to have its own individual budget program. There is likely to be a materials budget, a labor or personnel requirements budget, and a facilities or long-run capital expenditures budget. After the product is produced, the next step in the process will call for a marketing budget. Related to the over-all process are the general office and executive requirements, which will be reflected in the general and administrative budget system.

The results of projecting all these elements of cost are reflected in the budgeted, or projected, income statement. The anticipated sales give rise to the various types of investments needed to produce the products; these investments, plus the beginning balance sheet, provide the necessary data for developing the assets side of the balance sheet.

These assets must be financed; and a cash flow analysis—the cash budget—is required. The cash budget indicates the combined effects of the budgeted operations on the firm's cash flow. A positive net cash flow will indicate that the firm has ample financing. However, if an increase in the volume of operations leads to a negative cash flow, additional financing will be required. This leads directly to choices of financing, which is the subject of a considerable portion of the remainder of the book.

Since the structure of the income statement and balance sheet have already been covered in preceding chapters, the rest of this section will deal with the two remaining aspects of the budgeting process—the cash budget and the concept of variable, or flexible, budgets.

The cash budget, as indicated, determines not only the total amount of financing that will be required but its timing as well. The cash budget indicates the amount of funds that will be needed month by month, or even week by week, and is one of the financial manager's most important tools. Because a clear understanding of the nature of cash budgeting is important, the process is described by means of an example that makes the elements of the cash budget explicit.

CASH BUDGETING

Marvel Toy is a medium-sized toy manufacturer. Sales are highly seasonal, with the peak occurring in September when retailers stock up for the Christmas season. All sales are made on terms that allow a cash discount on payments made within 30 days; if the discount is not taken, the full amount must be paid in 60 days. But Marvel, like most other companies, finds that some of its customers delay payment up to 90 days. Experience shows that on 20 percent of the sales, payment is made within 30 days; on 70 percent of the sales, payment is made during the second month after the sale; and on 10 percent of the sales payment is made during the third month.

Production is geared to future sales. Purchased materials and parts amount to 70 percent of sales, and Marvel purchases materials and parts the month before the company expects to sell the finished product. Marvel's own purchase terms permit it to delay payment on its own purchases for one month. In other words, if August sales are forecast at $30,000, then purchases during July will amount to $21,000, and this amount will actually be paid in August.

Wages and salaries, rent, and other cash expenses are given in Table 6–1. The company also has a tax payment of $8,000 coming due in August. Its capital budgeting plans call for the purchase in July of a new machine tool costing $10,000, payment to be made in September. Assuming the company needs to keep a $5,000 cash balance at all times and it has $6,000 on July 1, what are Marvel's financial requirements for the period July–December?

The cash requirements are worked out in the cash budget shown as Table 6–1. The top half of the table provides a worksheet for calculating collections on sales and payments on purchases. The first line in the worksheet gives the sales forecast for the period May through December—May and June sales are necessary to determine collections for July and August. Next, cash collections are given. The first line of this section shows that 20 percent of the sales during any given month are collected that month. The second shows the collections on the prior month's sales—70 percent of sales in the preceding month. The third line gives collections from sales two months earlier—10 percent of sales in that month. The collections are summed to find the total cash receipts from sales during each month under consideration.

With the worksheet completed, the cash budget itself can be considered. Receipts from collections are given on the top line. Next, payments during each month are summarized. The difference between cash receipts and cash payments is the net cash gain or loss during the month; for July, there is a net cash loss of $4,200. The initial cash on hand at the beginning of the month is added to the net cash gain or loss during the month to yield the cumulative cash that will be on hand if no financing is done; at the end of July, Marvel Toy will have cumulative cash equal to $1,800. The desired cash balance,

TABLE 6-1 *Marvel Toy Company cash budget*

Worksheet

	May	June	July	Aug.	Sept.	Oct.	Nov.	Dec.	Jan.
Sales (net of cash discounts)	$10,000	$10,000	$20,000	$30,000	$40,000	$20,000	$20,000	$10,000	$10,000
Collections									
First month (20%)	$ 2,000	$ 2,000	$ 4,000	$ 6,000	$ 8,000	$ 4,000	$ 4,000	$ 2,000	$ 2,000
Second month (70%)		7,000	7,000	14,000	21,000	28,000	14,000	14,000	7,000
Third month (10%)			1,000	1,000	2,000	3,000	4,000	2,000	2,000
Total	$ 2,000	$ 9,000	$12,000	$ 21,000	$ 31,000	$35,000	$22,000	$18,000	$11,000
Purchases (70% of next month's sales)	$ 7,000	$14,000	$21,000	$ 28,000	$ 14,000	$14,000	$ 7,000	$ 7,000	
Payments (one month lag)		7,000	14,000	21,000	28,000	14,000	14,000	7,000	7,000

Cash budget

	May	June	July	Aug.	Sept.	Oct.	Nov.	Dec.	Jan.
Receipts									
Collections			$12,000	$ 21,000	$ 31,000	$35,000	$22,000	$18,000	$11,000
Payments									
Purchases			14,000	21,000	28,000	14,000	14,000	7,000	
Wages and salaries			1,500	2,000	2,500	1,500	1,500	1,000	
Rent			500	500	500	500	500	500	
Other expenses			200	300	400	200	200	100	
Taxes			—	8,000	—	—	—	—	
Payment on machine			—	—	10,000	—	—	—	
Total payments			$16,200	$ 31,800	$ 41,400	$16,200	$16,200	$ 8,600	
Net cash gain (loss) during month			$(4,200)	$(10,800)	$(10,400)	$18,800	$ 5,800	$ 9,400	
Initial cash at start of month			6,000	1,800	(9,000)	(19,400)	(600)	5,200	
Cumulative cash (if no financing)			$ 1,800	$ (9,000)	$(19,400)	$ (600)	$ 5,200	$14,600	
Desired level of cash			5,000	5,000	5,000	5,000	5,000	5,000	
Cash above minimum needs (or financing needs)—cumulative minus desired			$(3,200)	$(14,000)	$(24,400)	$(5,600)	$ 200	$ 9,600	

$5,000, is subtracted from the cumulative cash balance to determine the amount of financing that the firm needs if it is to maintain the desired level of cash. At the end of July we see that Marvel will need $3,200.

This same procedure is used in the following months. Sales will expand seasonally in August; with the increased sales will come increased payments for purchases, wages, and other items. Moreover, the $8,000 tax bill is due in August. Receipts from sales will go up too, but the firm will still be left with a $10,800 cash deficit during the month. The total financial requirements at the end of August will be $14,000—the $3,200 needed at the end of July plus the $10,800 cash deficit for August.

Sales peak in September, and the cash deficit during this month will amount to another $10,400. The total need for funds through September will increase to $24,400. Sales and, consequently, purchases and the payment for past purchases will fall markedly in October; the collections will be the highest of any month because they mainly reflect the high September sales. As a result, Marvel Toy will enjoy a healthy $18,800 cash surplus during October. This surplus can be used to pay off borrowings, so the need for financing will decline by $18,800 to $5,600.

Marvel will have another cash surplus in November, and this extra cash will permit the company to eliminate completely the need for financing. In fact, the company is expected to have $200 in extra cash by the month's end, and another cash surplus in December will swell the extra cash to $9,600. With such a large amount of unneeded funds, Marvel's treasurer will doubtless want to make investments in some type of interest-bearing securities or put the funds to use in some other way.

VARIABLE, OR FLEXIBLE, BUDGETS   Budgets are planned allocations of a firm's resources, based on forecasts for the future. Two important elements influence actual performance. One element is the impact of external influences—developments in the economy as a whole and competitive developments in the firm's own industry. The firm has essentially no control over these factors. The second element, which is controllable by the firm, is the level of efficiency at a given volume of sales. It is useful to separate the impact of these two elements, as this separation is necessary for evaluating individual performances.

The essence of the variable budget system is to introduce flexibility into budgets by recognizing that certain types of expenditures will vary at different levels of output. Thus, a firm might have an alternative level of outlay budgeted for different volumes of operation—high, low, medium. One of management's responsibilities is to determine which of these alternative budgets should be in effect for the planning period under consideration.

The scatter diagram method, described in the preceding chapter in connection with financial forecasting, may also be utilized to establish the basis for flexible budgeting. The use of the concept can be illustrated by a specific example. Suppose that a retail store has had the experience indicated by the historical data set forth in Table 6–2.

TABLE 6–2
Hubler Department Store
Relationship between sales and employees

Month	Sales (in millions of dollars)	Number of employees
January	4	42
February	5	51
March	6	60
April	7	75
May	10	102
June	8	83
July	5	55
August	9	92

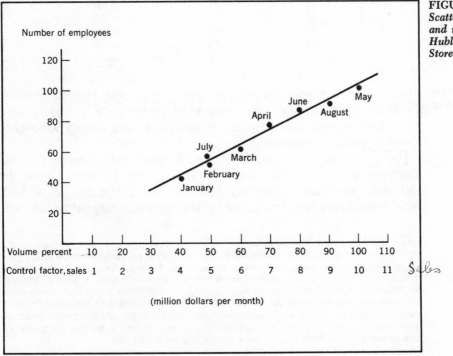

FIGURE 6–2
Scatter diagram and regression line: Hubler Department Store

It is apparent from the data that the number of employees the firm needs is dependent upon the dollar volume of sales that occurs during a month. This is seen more easily from a scatter diagram like that of Figure 6–2. The freehand regression line is sloped positively because the number of employees increases as the volume of sales increases. The independent variable, dollar volume of sales, is called the *control variable*. Variations in the control variable cause changes in total expenses. The volume of sales can be forecast, and the number of employees can be read from the regression chart. The relations can be expressed in tabular form (Table 6–3). Given the forecast of the volume of operations, standards are provided for the expected number of employees and the weekly payroll.[1]

TABLE 6–3
Hubler Department Store
Budget allowance

Volume (in percentages)	Employees	Weekly payroll estimate (average wage, $100)
60	62	$ 6,200
70	72	7,200
80	82	8,200
90	92	9,200
100	102	10,200
110	112	11,200

PROBLEMS OF BUDGETING Four major problems are encountered when using budget systems. First, budgetary programs can grow to be so complete and so detailed that they become cumbersome, meaningless, and unduly expensive. Overbudgeting is dangerous.

Second, budgetary goals may come to supersede enterprise goals. Budgets are a tool, not an end in themselves. Enterprise goals by definition supersede subsidiary plans of which budgets are a part. Also, budgets are based on future expectations that may not be realized.

[1] Note that regression analysis provides even more flexibility in budgeting than do the high, medium, and low levels mentioned earlier. Also, it is possible to include *confidence levels* when using the regression method. For example, Table 6–3 shows that when volume is at 80 percent, we expect to have 82 employees and a weekly payroll of $8,200. Although this relationship would probably not hold *exactly*, we might find that actual observations lie within 78 and 86 employees at this sales volume 95 percent of the time. Thus, 95 percent confidence levels would encompass the range 78–86. Similar ranges could be determined for other volumes; management might, as a matter of control policy, investigate whenever actual performances were outside this expected range.

There is no acceptable reason for neglecting to alter budgets as circumstances change. This reasoning is the core of the argument in favor of more flexible budgets.

Third, budgets can tend to hide inefficiencies by continuing initial expenditures in succeeding periods without proper evaluation. Budgets growing from precedent usually contain undesirable expenditures. They should not be used as umbrellas under which slovenly, inefficient management can hide. Consequently, the budgetary process must contain provision for reexamination of standards and other bases of planning by which policies are translated into numerical terms.

Finally, case study evidence suggests that the use of budgets as a pressure device defeats their basic objectives. Budgets, if used as instruments of tyranny, cause resentment and frustrations, which in turn lead to inefficiency. In order to counteract this effect, it has been recommended that top management increase the participation of subordinates during the preparatory stages of the budgets.

USE OF FINANCIAL PLANS AND BUDGETS

Forecasts, or long-range plans, are necessary in all the firm's operations. The personnel department must have a good idea of the scale of future operations if it is to plan its hiring and training activities properly. The production department must be sure that the productive capacity is available to meet the projected product demand, while the finance department must be sure that funds are on hand to meet the firm's financial requirements.

The tools and techniques discussed in this and the preceding chapters are actually used in several separate, but related, ways. First, the percent-of-sales method or, preferably, the regression method is used to make a long-range forecast of financial requirements over a projected three-to-five-year period. This forecast is then used to make the strategic financing plans during the planning period. The company might, for example, plan to meet its financial requirements with retained earnings and short-term bank debt during, say, 1971 and 1972, float a bond issue in 1973, use retained earnings in 1974, and finally sell an issue of common stock in 1975. Fairly long lead times are necessary when companies sell bonds or stocks; otherwise, they might be forced to go into the market during unfavorable periods.

In addition to this long-run strategic financial planning, the financial manager must also make accurate short-run forecasts to be sure that bank funds will be available to meet seasonal and other short-run requirements. He might, for example, have a meeting with his bank's loan officer to discuss his company's need for funds during the coming year. Prior to the meeting, he would have his accountants prepare a detailed cash budget showing the need for money during each of

Steps in trying to secure cash funds

the coming 12 months. The cash budget would show the maximum amount that would be needed during the year, how much would be needed during each month, and how cash surpluses would be generated at some point to enable the firm to repay the bank loan.

The financial manager would also have his firm's most recent, as well as its projected, balance sheets and income statements. He would have calculated the key financial ratios to show both its actual and its projected financial positions to the banker. If the firm's financial position is sound and if its cash budget appears reasonable, the bank will commit itself to make the required funds available. Even if the bank decides that the company's request is unreasonable and denies the loan request, the financial manager will have time to seek other sources of funds. While it might not be pleasant to have to look elsewhere for money, it is much better to know ahead of time that the loan request will be refused.

DIVISIONAL CONTROL IN A DECENTRALIZED FIRM   When we discussed the du Pont system of financial control in Chapter 3, its use was considered for the firm as a whole rather than for different divisions of a single firm. The du Pont system can, however, also be used to control the various parts of a multidivisional firm.

For organizational reasons large firms are generally set up on a decentralized basis. For example, a firm like General Electric establishes separate divisions for heavy appliances, light appliances, power transformers, steam generating equipment, nuclear generating equipment, and so on. Each of these divisions is defined as a *profit center*. Each profit center has its own investments—its fixed and current assets, together with a share of corporate overhead—and each is expected to earn an appropriate return on its investment.

The corporate headquarters, or central staff, typically controls the various divisions by a form of the du Pont system. When it is used for divisional control the procedure is frequently referred to as ROI (Return On Investment) control. If a particular division's ROI falls below a target figure then the centralized corporate staff assists the division's own financial staff to trace back through the du Pont system to determine the cause of the substandard ROI. Each division manager is judged by his division's ROI, and he is rewarded or penalized accordingly. Therefore, division managers are motivated to keep their ROI up to the target level. These individual actions, in turn, should maintain the total firm's ROI at an appropriate level.

In addition to its use in managerial control, ROI can be used to allocate funds to the various divisions. The firm as a whole has financial resources—retained earnings, cash flow from depreciation, and the ability to obtain additional debt and equity funds from capital markets. These funds can be allocated to different divisions on the basis of divisional ROI's; divisions with high ROI's receive more funds than those with low ROI's.[2]

A number of problems may arise if ROI control is used without proper safeguards. Since the divisional managers are rewarded on the basis of their ROI performance, if corporate morale at the upper echelons is to be maintained, it is absolutely essential that the divisional managers feel that their divisional ROI does indeed provide an accurate measure of relative performance. But ROI is dependent on a number of factors in addition to managerial competence. Some of these are listed below:

1. *Depreciation.* ROI is very sensitive to depreciation policy, and if one division is writing off assets at a relatively rapid rate, then its annual profits and, hence, its ROI will be reduced.

2. *Book value of assets.* If an older division is using assets that have been largely written off, then both its current depreciation charges and its investment base will be low, and its ROI high, relative to a new division.

3. *Transfer pricing.* In most corporations some divisions sell to other divisions. In General Motors, for example, the Fisher Body Division sells to the Chevrolet Division, and in such cases the price at which goods are transferred between divisions has a fundamental effect on divisional profits. If the transfer price of auto bodies is set relatively high, then Fisher Body will have a relatively high ROI and Chevrolet a relatively low ROI.

4. *Time periods.* Many projects have long gestation periods—expenditures must be made for research and development, plant construction, market development, and the like, and such expenditures will add to the investment base without a commensurate increase in sales for, possibly, several years. During this period a division's ROI could be seriously reduced, and, without proper constraints, its division manager could be improperly penalized. Especially when one recognizes the frequency of personnel transfers in large corporations one can see that the timing problem could, possibly, cause managers to refrain from making long-term investments that are in the best interests of the firm.

In summary, ROI control has been used with great success in American industry. However, this control system cannot be used in a mechanical sense by inexperienced personnel. Like most other tools, it is a good one if it is used properly, but it is a destructive one if it is misused.

---

[2] The point of this procedure is to increase the total firm's ROI. To maximize the over-all ROI, marginal ROI's between divisions should be equalized.

EXTERNAL USES OF FINANCIAL FORECASTS AND BUDGETS We have stressed the use of planning and budgeting for internal purposes—increasing the efficiency of a firm's operations. These same tools and techniques can, with relatively minor modifications, be used in both credit analysis and security analysis. For example, outside security analysts can make a forecast of a given firm's sales and, through the income statement and balance sheet relationships, make *pro forma* (or projected) balance sheets and income statements. Credit analysts can make similar projections to aid in estimating the likely need for funds by their customers and the likelihood that borrowers can make prompt repayment.

This type of analysis has actually been conducted on a large scale in recent years. Very complete financial data going back some 20 years on about 2,000 large, publicly owned corporations is now available on magnetic tapes (Standard and Poor's Compustat tapes). These tapes are being used by security analysts in highly sophisticated ways. From what we have seen, analyses conducted in such a manner offer large potential benefits. The same tapes, frequently supplemented with additional data, are being used by the major lending institutions— banks and insurance companies—to forecast their customers' needs for funds and, thus, to plan their own financial requirements.

SUMMARY A budget is a plan stated in terms of specific expenditures for specific purposes. It is used for both planning and control, with the over-all purpose being to improve internal operations, thereby reducing costs and raising profitability. A budgeting system starts with a set of performance standards, or targets. These targets constitute, in effect, the firm's financial plan. The budgeted figures are compared with actual results—this is the control phase of the budget system, and it is a critical step in well-operated companies.

Although the entire budget system is of vital importance to corporate management, one aspect of the system is especially important to the financial manager—the cash budget. The cash budget is, in fact, the principal tool for making short-run financial forecasts. Cash budgets, if used properly, are highly accurate and can pinpoint the funds that will be needed, when they will be needed, and when cash flows will be sufficient to retire any loans that might be necessary.

A good budget system will recognize that some factors lie outside the firm's control. Especially important here is the state of the economy and its effects on sales, and *flexible budgets* will be set up as targets for the different departments assuming different levels of sales. Also, a good system will insure that those responsible for carrying out a plan are involved in its preparation; this procedure will help guard against the establishment of unrealistic targets and unobtainable goals.

As a firm becomes larger it is necessary to decentralize operations to some extent, and decentralized operations require some type of centralized control over the various divisions. The principal tool used for such control is the Return On Investment (ROI) method. There are problems with ROI control, but if care is taken in its use, the method can be quite valuable to a decentralized firm.

6–1 What use might a confidence interval scheme have in variable budgeting? **QUESTIONS**

6–2 Why is a cash budget important even when there is plenty of cash in the bank?

6–3 How might individuals employ the techniques of financial planning and budgeting for their own use?

6–4 What is the difference between the long-range financial forecasting concept and the budgeting concept? How might they be used together?

6–5 Assume that a firm is making up its long-run financial budget. What period should this budget cover—one month, six months, one year, three years, five years, or what? Justify your answer.

6–6 Why would a detailed budget be more important to a large, multidivisional firm than to a small, single product firm?

6–1 The Henderson Company is planning to request a line of credit from its **PROBLEMS** bank. The following sales forecasts have been made:

May	$ 60,000
June	60,000
July	120,000
August	180,000
September	240,000
October	120,000
November	120,000
December	30,000
January 1970	60,000

Collection estimates were obtained from the credit and collection department as follows: cash sales, 5 percent; collected the month following the sale, 80 percent; collected the second month following the sale, 15 percent. Payments for labor and raw materials are typically made during the month following the month in which these costs are incurred. Total labor and raw materials costs are estimated for each month as follows (payments are made the following month):

May	$ 30,000
June	30,000
July	42,000
August	294,000
September	102,000
October	78,000
November	54,000
December	30,000

General and administrative salaries will amount to approximately $9,000 per month; lease payments under long-term lease contracts will be $3,000 per month; depreciation charges are $12,000 per month; miscellaneous expenses will be $900 per month; income tax payments of $21,000 will be due in both September and December; and a progress payment of $60,000 on a new research lab must be paid in October. Cash on hand on July 1 will amount to $45,000, and a minimum cash balance of $30,000 should be maintained throughout the cash budget period.

a) Prepare a monthly cash budget for the last six months of 1971.

b) Prepare an estimate of required financing for each month during the period, that is, the amount of money that the Henderson Company will need to borrow during each month.

c) Suppose receipts from sales came in uniformly during the month; that is, cash payments come in 1/30th each day, but both purchase invoices and wages are paid on the fifth of the month. Would this have an effect on the cash budget, that is, would the cash budget you have prepared be valid under these assumptions? If not, what could be done to make a valid estimation of financing requirements?

Part III

Long-term Investment Decisions

Chapter 7

The Interest Factor in Financial Decisions

THE investment in fixed assets should, logically, be taken up at this point. However, the long-term nature of fixed investments makes it necessary to consider first the theory of compound interest—the "math of finance." Compound interest is essential to an understanding of capital budgeting, the topic of the following chapter. However, interest rate theory is also an integral part of several other topics taken up later in the text. Financial structure decisions, lease versus purchase decisions, bond refunding operations, security valuation techniques, and the whole question of the cost of capital are some other subjects that cannot be understood without a knowledge of compound interest.

Many people are afraid of the subject of compound interest and simply avoid it. It is certainly true that many successful business-men—even some bankers—know essentially nothing of the subject. However, as technology advances, as more and more engineers become involved in general management, and as modern business administration programs turn out more and more highly qualified graduates, this "success in spite of himself" pattern will become more and more difficult to achieve. Furthermore, fear of compound interest relationships is quite unfounded—the subject matter is simply not that difficult. Practically all problems involving compound interest can be handled quite satisfactorily with only a few basic formulas.

A person deposits $1,000 in a savings and loan association that pays 4 percent interest compounded annually. How much will he have at the end of one year? To treat the matter systematically, let us define the following terms: **COMPOUND VALUE**

P = principal, or beginning amount

i = interest rate

I = dollar amount of interest earned during a period

V = ending amount, or the sum of $P + I$.

V may now be calculated as

$$V = P + I$$
$$= P + Pi$$
$$= P(1 + i). \tag{7-1}$$

This last equation shows that the ending amount is equal to the beginning amount times the factor $(1 + i)$. In the example, where $P = \$1,000$, V is determined as:

$$V = \$1,000(1.0 + .04) = \$1,000(1.04) = \$1,040.$$

If the person leaves the $1,000 on deposit for five years, to what amount will it have grown at the end of that period? Equation 7–1 can be used to construct Table 7–1, which indicates the answer. Note that V_2, the balance at the end of the second year, is found as:

$$V_2 = P_2(1 + i) = P_1(1 + i)(1 + i) = P_1(1 + i)^2.$$

TABLE 7-1
*Compound interest
calculations*

Year	Beginning amount (P)	$\times$ $(1 + i)$ =	ending amount (V)
1	$1,000	1.04 =	$1,040
2	1,040	1.04 =	1,082
3	1,082	1.04 =	1,125
4	1,125	1.04 =	1,170
5	1,170	1.04 =	1,217

Similarly, V_3, the balance after three years, is found as

$$V_3 = P_3(1 + i) = P_1(1 + i)^3.$$

In general, V_n, the compound amount at the end of any year n, is found as

$$V_n = P(1 + i)^n \tag{7-2}$$

This is the fundamental equation of compound interest, and it can readily be seen that Equation 7–1 is simply a special case of Equation 7–2 where $n = 1$.

While it is necessary to understand the derivation of Equation 7–2 in order to understand much of the material in the remainder of this chapter (as well as material to be covered in subsequent chapters), the concept can be applied quite readily in a mechanical sense. Tables have been constructed for values of $(1 + i)^n$ for wide ranges of i and n. Table 7–2 is illustrative, while Table A–1, in Appendix A, is a more complete table.

Letting *IF* (interest factor) = $(1 + i)^n$, Equation 7–2 may be written as $V = P(IF)$. It is necessary only to go to an appropriate interest table to find the proper interest factor. The correct interest factor for the above illustration is found in Table 7–2. Look down the year column to 5, then across this row to the appropriate number in the 4 percent column to find the interest factor—1.217. Then, using this interest factor, we find the compound value of the $1,000 after five years as

$$V = P(IF) = \$1,000(1.217) = \$1,217.$$

Notice that this is precisely the same figure that was obtained by the long method in Table 7–1.

Year	1%	2%	3%	4%	5%	6%	7%	8%	9%	10%
1	1.010	1.020	1.030	1.040	1.050	1.060	1.070	1.080	1.090	1.100
2	1.020	1.040	1.061	1.082	1.102	1.124	1.145	1.166	1.188	1.210
3	1.030	1.061	1.093	1.125	1.158	1.191	1.225	1.260	1.295	1.331
4	1.041	1.082	1.126	1.170	1.216	1.262	1.311	1.360	1.412	1.464
5	1.051	1.104	1.159	1.217	1.276	1.338	1.403	1.469	1.539	1.611
6	1.062	1.126	1.194	1.265	1.340	1.419	1.501	1.587	1.677	1.772
7	1.072	1.149	1.230	1.316	1.407	1.504	1.606	1.714	1.828	1.949
8	1.083	1.172	1.267	1.369	1.477	1.594	1.718	1.851	1.993	2.144
9	1.094	1.195	1.305	1.423	1.551	1.689	1.838	1.999	2.172	2.358
10	1.105	1.219	1.344	1.480	1.629	1.791	1.967	2.159	2.367	2.594
11	1.116	1.243	1.384	1.539	1.710	1.898	2.105	2.332	2.580	2.853
12	1.127	1.268	1.426	1.601	1.796	2.012	2.252	2.518	2.813	3.138
13	1.138	1.294	1.469	1.665	1.886	2.133	2.410	2.720	3.066	3.452
14	1.149	1.319	1.513	1.732	1.980	2.261	2.579	2.937	3.342	3.797
15	1.161	1.346	1.558	1.801	2.079	2.397	2.759	3.172	3.642	4.177

TABLE 7–2
Compound value of $1

Suppose you were offered the alternative of either $1,217 at the end of five years or *X* dollars today. There is no question but that the $1,217 will be paid in full (perhaps the payer is the United States government) and, having no current need for the money, you would deposit it in a savings association paying a 4 percent dividend. (Four percent is defined to be your "opportunity cost.") How small must *X* be to induce you to accept the promise of $1,217 five years hence?

PRESENT VALUE

Referring to Table 7–2, one finds that the initial amount of $1,000 growing at 4 percent a year yields $1,217 at the end of five years. Hence, you should be indifferent in your choice between $1,000 today and $1,217 at the end of five years. The $1,000 is defined as the *present value* of $1,217 due in five years when the applicable interest rate is 4 percent.

Finding present values (or discounting, as it is commonly called) is simply the reverse of compounding, and Equation 7–2 can quite readily be transformed into a present value formula. Dividing both sides by $(1 + i)^n$ and dropping the subscript n from V_n, we have

$$\text{Present value} = P = \frac{V}{(1 + i)^n} = V \left[\frac{1}{(1 + i)^n} \right]. \qquad (7\text{–}3)$$

Tables have been constructed for the term in brackets for various values of i and n; Table 7–3 is an example. A more complete table, Table A–2, is found in Appendix A. For the illustrative case being considered, look down the 4 percent column to the fifth row. The figure shown there, 0.822, is the interest factor used to determine the present value of $1,217 payable in five years, discounted at 4 percent.

$$P = V(IF)$$
$$= \$1,217(0.822)$$
$$= \$1,000.$$

TABLE 7–3
Present value of $1

Year	1%	2%	3%	4%	5%	6%	7%	8%	9%	10%	12%	14%	15%
1	.990	.980	.971	.962	.952	.943	.935	.926	.917	.909	.893	.877	.870
2	.980	.961	.943	.925	.907	.890	.873	.857	.842	.826	.797	.769	.756
3	.971	.942	.915	.889	.864	.840	.816	.794	.772	.751	.712	.675	.658
4	.961	.924	.889	.855	.823	.792	.763	.835	.708	.683	.636	.592	.572
5	.951	.906	.863	.822	.784	.747	.713	.681	.650	.621	.567	.519	.497
6	.942	.888	.838	.790	.746	.705	.666	.630	.596	.564	.507	.456	.432
7	.933	.871	.813	.760	.711	.665	.623	.583	.547	.513	.452	.400	.376
8	.923	.853	.789	.731	.677	.627	.582	.540	.502	.467	.404	.351	.327
9	.914	.837	.766	.703	.645	.592	.544	.500	.460	.424	.361	.308	.284
10	.905	.820	.744	.676	.614	.558	.508	.463	.422	.386	.322	.270	.247

COMPOUND VALUE OF AN ANNUITY   *An annuity is defined as a series of payments of a fixed amount for a specified number of years.* Each payment occurs at the end of the year.[1] For example, a promise to pay $1,000 a year for three years is a three-year annuity. If one were to receive such an annuity and were to deposit each annual payment in a savings account paying 4 percent interest, how much would he have at the end of three years? The answer is shown graphically in Figure 7–1. The first payment is made at the end of year 1, the second at the end of year 2, and so on. The last payment is not compounded at all; the next to the last is compounded for one year; the second from the last for two

---

[1] Had the payment been made at the beginning of the period, each receipt would simply have been shifted back one year. The annuity would have been called an *annuity due;* the one in the present discussion, where payments are made at the end of each period, is called a *regular annuity* or, sometimes, a *deferred annuity.*

years; and so on back to the first, which is compounded for $n - 1$ years. When the compound values of each of the payments are added, their total is the sum of the annuity. In the example, this total is $3,122.

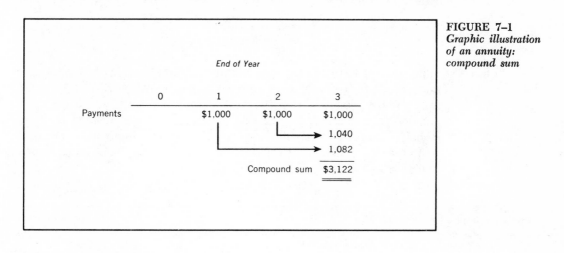

FIGURE 7–1
Graphic illustration of an annuity: compound sum

TABLE 7–4
Sum of an annuity of $1 for N years

Year	1%	2%	3%	4%	5%	6%	7%	8%
1	1.000	1.000	1.000	1.000	1.000	1.000	1.000	1.000
2	2.010	2.020	2.030	2.040	2.050	2.060	2.070	2.080
3	3.030	3.060	3.091	3.122	3.152	3.184	3.215	3.246
4	4.060	4.122	4.184	4.246	4.310	4.375	4.440	4.506
5	5.101	5.204	5.309	5.416	5.526	5.637	5.751	5.867
6	6.152	6.308	6.468	6.633	6.802	6.975	7.153	7.336
7	7.214	7.434	7.662	7.898	8.142	8.394	8.654	8.923
8	8.286	8.583	8.892	9.214	9.549	9.897	10.260	10.637
9	9.369	9.755	10.159	10.583	11.027	11.491	11.978	12.488
10	10.462	10.950	11.464	12.006	12.578	13.181	13.816	14.487

Expressed algebraically, with S_n defined as the compound sum, R as the periodic receipt, and n as the length of the annuity, the formula for S_n is

$$S_n = R(1 + i)^{n-1} + R(1 + i)^{n-2} + \cdots + R(1 + i)^1 + R(1 + i)^0$$
$$= R[(1 + i)^{n-1} + (1 + i)^{n-2} + \cdots + (1 + i)^1 + 1]$$
$$= R[IF].$$

The expression in brackets has been given values for various combinations of n and i. An illustrative set of these annuity interest factors is given in Table 7–4; a more complete set may be found in Table A–3 in Appendix A. To find the answer to the three-year $1,000 annuity problem, simply refer to Table 7–4, look down the 4 percent column to the row for the third year, and multiply the factor 3.122 by $1,000. The answer is the same as the one derived by the long method illustrated in Figure 7–1.

$$S_n = R \times IF$$
$$= \$1,000 \times 3.122 = \$3,122.$$

$(7\text{–}4)$

PRESENT VALUE OF AN ANNUITY Suppose you were offered the following alternatives: a three-year annuity of $1,000 a year or a lump-sum payment today. You have no need for the money during the next three years, so if you accept the annuity you would simply deposit the receipts in a savings account paying 4 percent interest. How large must the lump-sum payment be to make it equivalent to the annuity? The graphic illustration shown in Figure 7–2 will help explain the problem.

FIGURE 7–2
Graphic illustration of an annuity: present value

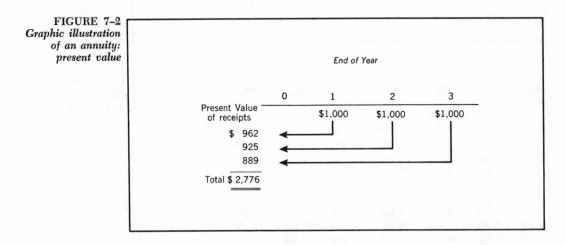

The present value of the first receipt is $R[1/(1 + i)]$; the second is $R[1/(1 + i)]^2$; and so on. Defining the present value of an annuity of n years as A_n, we may write the following equation:

$$A_n = R \left[\frac{1}{1 + i} \right]^1 + R \left[\frac{1}{1 + i} \right]^2 + \cdots + R \left[\frac{1}{1 + i} \right]^n$$
$$= R \left[\frac{1}{(1 + i)} + \frac{1}{(1 + i)^2} + \cdots + \frac{1}{(1 + i)^n} \right]$$
$$= R[IF].$$

$(7\text{–}5)$

Again, tables have been worked out for the interest factor, the term in the brackets. Table 7–5 is illustrative, and a more complete table is found in Table A–4 in Appendix A. From this table, the IF for a three-year, 4 percent annuity is found to be 2.775. Multiplying this factor by the $1,000 annual receipt gives $2,775, the present value of the annuity. This figure departs from the long-method answer shown in Figure 7–2 only by a rounding difference.

$$A_n = R \times IF$$
$$= \$1,000 \times 2.775 \qquad\qquad (7\text{–}6)$$
$$= \$2,775.$$

Notice that the *IF* for the present value of an annuity is always *less than* the number of years the annuity runs, whereas the *IF* for the sum of an annuity is *greater than* the number of years.

Year	1%	2%	3%	4%	5%	6%	7%	8%	9%	10%
1	0.990	0.980	0.971	0.962	0.952	0.943	0.935	0.926	0.917	0.909
2	1.970	1.942	1.913	1.886	1.859	1.833	1.808	1.783	1.759	1.736
3	2.941	2.884	2.829	2.775	2.723	2.673	2.624	2.577	2.531	2.487
4	3.902	3.808	3.717	3.630	3.546	3.465	3.387	3.312	3.240	3.170
5	4.853	4.713	4.580	4.452	4.329	4.212	4.100	3.993	3.890	3.791
6	5.795	5.601	5.417	5.242	5.076	4.917	4.766	4.623	4.486	4.355
7	6.728	6.472	6.230	6.002	5.786	5.582	5.389	5.206	5.033	4.868
8	7.652	7.325	7.020	6.733	6.463	6.210	6.971	5.747	5.535	5.335
9	8.566	8.162	7.786	7.435	7.108	6.802	6.515	6.247	5.985	5.759
10	9.471	8.983	8.530	8.111	7.722	7.360	7.024	6.710	6.418	6.145

TABLE 7–5
Present values of an annuity of $1

Thus far in the chapter all the equations are based upon Equation (7–2). The present value equation merely involves a transposition of Equation 7–2, and the annuity equations just take the sum of the basic compound interest equation for different values of *n*. We next examine some additional modifications of the equations.

Summary

Suppose we want to know the amount of money that must be deposited at 5 percent for each of the next five years, in order to have $10,000 available to pay off a debt at the end of the fifth year. Dividing both sides of equation 7–4 by *IF*, we obtain

ANNUAL PAYMENTS FOR ACCUMULATION OF A FUTURE SUM

$$R = \frac{S_n}{IF}.$$

Looking up the interest factor for five years at 5 percent in Table 7–4 and dividing this figure into $10,000, we find

$$R = \frac{\$10,000}{5.526} = \$1,810.$$

Thus, if $1,810 is deposited each year in an account paying 5 percent interest, at the end of five years the account will have accumulated $10,000.

ANNUAL RECEIPTS FROM AN ANNUITY   Suppose that on September 1, 1969, you receive an inheritance of $7,000. The money is to be used for your education and is to be spent during the academic years beginning September 1970, 1971, and 1972. If you place the money in a bank account paying 4 percent annual interest and make three equal withdrawals at each of the specified dates, how large can each withdrawal be to leave you with exactly a zero balance after the last one has been made?

The solution requires application of the present value of an annuity formula, Equation 7–6. Here, however, we know that the present value of the annuity is $7,000, and the problem is to find the three equal annual payments when the interest rate is 4 percent. This calls for dividing both sides of Equation 7–6 by IF to make Equation 7–7.

$$A_n = R \times IF \tag{7-6}$$

$$R = \frac{A_n}{IF}. \tag{7-7}$$

The interest factor (IF) is found in Table 7–5 to be 2.775, and substituting this value into Equation 7–7 we find the three equal annual withdrawals to be $2,523 a year:

$$R = \frac{\$7,000}{2.775} = \$2,523.$$

This particular type of calculation is used frequently in setting up insurance and pension plan benefit schedules, and it is also used to find the periodic payments necessary to retire a loan within a specified period. For example, if you wanted to retire a $7,000 bank loan, paying interest at 4 percent on the unpaid balance, in three equal annual installments, each payment would be $2,523. In this case, you would be the borrower, and the bank would be "buying" an annuity with a present value of $7,000.

DETERMINING INTEREST RATES   There are many instances where one knows the present values and cash flows associated with a payment stream, but one does not know the interest rate involved. For instance, suppose a bank offered to lend you $1,000 today if you would sign a note agreeing to pay the bank $1,217 at the end of five years. What rate of interest would you be paying on the loan? To answer the question requires the use of Equation 7–2:

$$V_n = P(1 + i)^n = P(IF). \tag{7-2}$$

Simply solve for *IF*, then look up this value of *IF* in Table 7–2 (or A–1) under the row for the fifth year:

$$IF = \frac{V_n}{P} = \frac{\$1,217}{\$1,000} = 1.217.$$

Looking across the row for the fifth year, we find the value 1.217 in the 4 percent column; therefore, the interest rate on the loan is 4 percent.

Precisely the same approach is taken to determine the interest rate implicit in an annuity. For example, suppose a bank will lend you $2,775 provided you sign a note in which you agree to pay the bank $1,000 at the end of each of the next three years. What interest rate is the bank charging you? To answer the question, solve Equation 7–6 for *IF*, then look up the *IF* in Table 7–5 (or A–4):

$$A_n = R \times IF \tag{7-6}$$

$$IF = \frac{A_n}{R} = \frac{\$2,775}{\$1,000} = 2.775.$$

Looking across the third year row, we find the factor 2.775 under the 4 percent column; therefore the bank is lending you money at 4 percent.

Recall that the definition of an annuity includes the words *fixed amount*—in other words, annuities deal with constant, or level, payments or receipts. Although many financial decisions do involve constant payments, many important decisions are concerned with uneven flows of cash. In particular, the kinds of fixed asset investments dealt with in the following chapter very frequently involve uneven flows. Consequently, it is necessary to expand the present analysis to deal with varying payment streams. Since most of the applications call for present values, not compound sums or other figures, this section is restricted to the present value (*PV*).

PRESENT VALUE OF AN UNEVEN SERIES OF RECEIPTS

To illustrate the calculating procedure, suppose someone offered to sell you a series of payments consisting of $300 after one year, $100 after two years, and $200 after three years. How much would you be willing to pay for the series, assuming the appropriate discount rate (interest rate) is 4 percent? To determine the purchase price, simply compute the present value of the series; the calculations are worked out in Table 7–6 on page 134. The receipts for each year are shown in the second column; the discount factors (from Table 7–3) are given in the third column; and the product of these two columns, the present value of each individual receipt, is given in the last column. When the individual present values in the last column are added, the sum is the present value of the investment, $558.90. Under the assumptions of the example, you should be willing to pay this amount for the investment.

Year	Receipt $\times$	Interest factor (IF) =	present value (PV)
1	$300	.962	$288.60
2	100	.925	92.50
3	200	.889	177.80
		PV of investment	$558.90

Had the series of payments been somewhat different—say $300 at the end of the first year, then nine annual payments of $100 each—we would probably want to use a different procedure for finding the investment's present value. We could, of course, set up a calculating table, such as Table 7–6, but the fact that most of the payments are part of an annuity permits us to use a short cut. The calculating procedure is shown in Table 7–7, and the logic of the table is diagrammed in Figure 7–3.

1. PV of $300 due in 1 year = $300(0.962)	$ 288.60
2. PV of nine-year annuity with $100 receipts	
a. PV at beginning of next year	
$100(7.435) = $743.50	
b. PV of $743.50 = $743.50(0.962)	715.25
3. PV of total series	$1,003.85

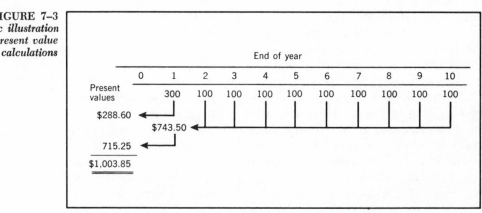

Section 1 of the table deals with the $300 received at the end of the first year; its present value is found to be $288.60. Section 2 deals with the nine $100 payments. In part (a), the value of a $100, 9-year, 4 percent annuity is found to be $743.50. However, the annuity does not start until *next* year—that is, the first receipt under the annuity comes in two years—so it is worth less than $743.50 today. Specifically, it is worth the present value of $743.50, discounted back one year at 4 percent, or $715.25; this calculation is shown in part (b) of section 2. When the present value of the initial payment is added to the present value of the annuity component, the sum is the present value of the entire investment, or $1,003.85.

In all the examples used thus far, it has been assumed that returns were received once a year, or annually. For example, in the first section of the chapter, dealing with compound values, it was assumed that funds were placed on deposit in a savings and loan association and grew by 4 percent a year. However, suppose the advertised rate had been 4 percent compounded *semiannually*. What would this have meant? Consider the following example.

SEMIANNUAL AND OTHER COMPOUNDING PERIODS

A person deposits $1,000 in a bank savings account and receives a return of 4 percent compounded semiannually. How much will he have at the end of one year? Semiannual compounding means that interest is actually paid each six months, a fact taken into account in the tabular calculations in Table 7–8. Here the annual interest rate is divided by 2, but twice as many compounding periods are used because interest is paid twice a year. Comparing the amount on hand at the end of the second six-month period, $1,040.40, with what would have been on hand under annual compounding, $1,040, shows that semiannual compounding is better from the standpoint of the saver. This result occurs, of course, because he earns interest on interest more frequently.

Period	Beginning amount (P)	$\times$ $(1 + i)$ =	ending amount (V)
1	$1,000.00	(1.02)	$1,020.00
2	1,020.00	(1.02)	1,040.40

TABLE 7–8
Compound interest calculations with semiannual compounding

General formulas can be developed for use when compounding periods are more frequent than once a year. To demonstrate this, equation

7–2 is modified as follows:

$$V_n = P(1 + i)^n.$$ (7-2)

$$V_n = P\left(1 + \frac{i}{m}\right)^{mn}.$$ (7-8)

Here m is the number of times per year compounding occurs. When banks compute daily interest, the value of m is set at 365 and Equation 7–8 is applied.

The tables can be used when compounding occurs more than once a year. Simply divide the nominal, or stated, interest rate by the number of times compounding occurs, and multiply the years by the number of compounding periods per year. For example, to find the amount to which $1,000 will grow after five years if semiannual compounding is applied to a stated 4 percent interest rate, divide 4 percent by 2 and multiply the five years by 2. Then look in Table 7–2 (or Appendix Table A–1) under the 2 percent column and the row for the tenth year. You find an interest factor of 1.219. Multiplying this by the initial $1,000 gives a value of $1,219, the amount to which $1,000 will grow in five years at 4 percent compounded semiannually. This compares with $1,217 for annual compounding.

The same procedure is applied in all the cases covered—compounding, discounting, single payments, and annuities. To illustrate semiannual compounding in finding the present value of an annuity, for example, consider the case described in the section on the present value of an annuity above—$1,000 a year for three years, discounted at 4 percent. With annual compounding (or discounting) the interest factor is 2.775, and the present value of the annuity is $2,775. For semiannual compounding look under the 2 percent column and year 6 row of Table 7–5, to find an interest factor of 5.601. This is now multiplied by half of $1,000, or the $500 received each six months, to get the present value of the annuity—$2,800. The payments come a little more rapidly—the first $500 is paid after only six months (similarly with other payments), so the annuity is a little more valuable if payments are received semiannually rather than annually.

By letting m approach infinity, Equation 7–8 can be modified to the special case of *continuous compounding*. Continuous compounding, while extremely useful in theoretical finance, has not been used frequently in practical applications. Further, its development is highly technical and requires the use of integral calculus. We have, therefore, elected not to treat it in this book.[2]

---

[2] For a discussion of continuous compounding, see *Managerial Finance*, third edition, Appendix to Chapter 6, pp. 161–168.

Throughout the chapter an assumed interest rate has been used in the examples. Before closing, however, it is necessary to give some idea of what the appropriate interest rate for a particular investment might be.

The starting point is, of course, the general level of interest rates in the economy as a whole. This level is set by the interaction of supply-and-demand forces, with demand for funds coming largely from businesses, individual borrowers, and, when it is running a deficit, the federal government. Funds are supplied by individual and corporate savers and, under the control of the Federal Reserve System, by the creation of money by banks. Depending on the relative levels of supply and demand, the basic pattern of interest rates is determined.

There is no one rate of interest in the economy—rather, there is, at any given time, an array of different rates. The lowest rates are found on the safest investments, the highest rates on the most risky ones. Usually, there is less risk on investments that mature in the near future than on longer term investments, so generally higher rates are associated with long-term investments. There are other factors that affect interest rate differentials (also called "yield" differentials), but a discussion of these factors is best deferred until later in the book.

A person faced with the kinds of decisions considered in this chapter must accept the existing set of interest rates found in the economy. If he has money to invest, he can invest in short-term United States government securities and incur no risk whatever. However, he will generally have to accept a relatively low yield on his investment. If he is willing to accept a little more risk, he can invest in high-grade corporate bonds and get a higher fixed rate of return. If he is willing to accept still more risk, he can move into common stocks to obtain variable (and hopefully higher) returns (dividends plus capital gains) on his investment. Other alternatives include bank and savings and loan deposits, long-term governments, mortgages, apartment houses, and so on.

Types of Investment dependent on risk

With only a limited amount of money to invest, one must pick and choose among investments, and the final selection will involve a choice between risk and returns. Suppose, for example, that you are indifferent between a five-year government bond yielding 4 percent a year, a five-year corporate bond yielding 5 percent, and a share of stock on which you can expect to receive a 6 percent return. Given this situation, you can take the government bond as a riskless security, and you attach a 1 percent risk premium to the corporate bond and a 2 percent risk premium to the share of stock. Risk premiums, then, are the added returns that risky investments must command over less risky

Risk Premiums

ones if there is to be a demand for risky assets. The concept of the risk premium is discussed in more detail in Chapter 9 and also in the chapters dealing with the cost of capital.

Opportunity Costs   Although there are many potential investments available in the economy at any given time, a particular individual actively considers only a limited number of them. After making adjustments for risk differentials, he ranks the various alternatives from the most attractive to the least. Then, presumably, our investor puts his available funds in the most attractive investment. If he is offered a new investment, he must compare it with the best of the existing alternatives. If he takes the new investment, he must give up the opportunity of investing in the best of his old alternatives. *The yield on the best of the alternatives is defined as the opportunity cost of investing in the new alternative.* The interest rates used in the preceding examples were all determined as opportunity costs available to the person in the example. This concept is also used in the following chapter, where we consider business decisions on investments in fixed assets, or the *capital budgeting decision.*

SUMMARY   A knowledge of compound interest and present value techniques is essential to an understanding of many important aspects of finance: capital budgeting, financial structure, security valuation, and many other topics. The basic principles of compound interest, together with the most important formulas used in practice, were described in this chapter.

Compound Value   Compound value (V_n), or compound amount, is defined as the sum to which a beginning amount of principal (P) will grow over n years when interest is earned at the rate of i percent a year. The equation for finding compound values is

$$V_n = P(1 + i)^n.$$

Tables giving the present value of $1 for a large number of different years and interest rates have been prepared. The present value of $1 is called the interest factor (IF); illustrative values are given in Table 7–2, and a more complete set of interest factors is given in Appendix Table A–1.

Present Value (PV)   The present value of a future payment (P) is the amount which, if we had it now and invested it at the specified interest rate (i), would equal the future payment (V) on the date the future payment is due. For example, if one is to receive $1,217 after five years and decides that 4 percent is the appropriate interest rate (it is called "discount" rate when computing present values), then he could find the present value of the $1,217 to be $1,000 by applying the following equation:

$$P = V \left[\frac{1}{(1 + i)^n} \right] = \$1,217[0.822] = \$1,000.$$

The term in brackets is called the present value interest factor (IF), and values for it have been worked out in Table 7–3 and Appendix Table A–2.

An annuity is defined as a series of payments of a fixed amount (R) *Compound Value* for a specified number of years. The compound value of an annuity *of an Annuity* is the total amount one would have at the end of the annuity period if each payment was invested at a certain interest rate and held to the end of the annuity period. For example, suppose we have a three-year $1,000 annuity invested at 4 percent. There are formulas for annuities, but tables are available for the relevant interest factors. The IF for the compound value of a three-year annuity at 4 percent is 3.122, and it can be used to find the present value of the illustrative annuity:

Compound value $= IF \times$ annual receipt $= 3.122 \times \$1,000 = \$3,122.$

Thus, $3,122 is the compound value of the annuity.

The present value of an annuity is the lump sum one would need *Present Value of* to have on hand today in order to be able to withdraw equal amounts *an Annuity* (R) each year and end up with a balance exactly equal to zero at the end of the annuity period. For example, if one wanted to withdraw $1,000 a year for three years, he could deposit $2,775 today in a bank account paying 4 percent interest, withdraw the $1,000 in each of the next three years, and end up with a zero balance. Thus, $2,775 is the present value of an annuity of $1,000 per year for three years when the appropriate discount rate is 4 percent. Again, tables are available for finding the present value of annuities. To use them, one simply looks up the interest factor (IF) for the appropriate number of years and interest rate, then multiplies the IF by the annual receipt.

PV of annuity $= IF \times$ annual receipt $= 2.775 \times \$1,000 = \$2,775.$

All interest factors (IF) given in the tables are for $1; for example, *Relation of Interest* 2.775 is the IF for finding the present value of a three-year annuity. *Factors to One* It must be multiplied by the annual receipt, $1,000 in the example, *Another* to find the actual value of the annuity. Students—and even financial managers—sometimes make careless mistakes when looking up interest factors, using the wrong table for the purpose. This can be avoided if one recognizes the following sets of relations.

Compound value, single payment. The *IF* for the compound value of a single payment, with the normal interest rates and holding periods generally found, is *always* greater than 1.0 but seldom larger than about 3.0.

Present value, single payment. The *IF* for the present value of a single payment is *always* smaller than 1.0; for example, 0.822 is the present value *IF* for 4 percent held for five years. The *compound* value *IF* is larger than 1.0; the *present* value *IF* is smaller than 1.0.

Compound value of an annuity. The *IF* for the compound value of an annuity is *always* larger than the number of years the annuity has to run. For example, the *IF* for a three-year annuity will be larger than 3.0, while the *IF* for a 10-year annuity will be larger than 10.0. Just how much larger depends on the interest rate—at low rates the interest factor is slightly larger than *n*; at high rates it is very much larger.

Present value of an annuity. The *IF* for the present value of an annuity is smaller than the number of years it has to run. For example, the *IF* for the present value of a three-year annuity is less than 3.0.

Other Uses of the Basic Equations The four basic interest formulas can be used in combination to find such things as the present value of an uneven series of receipts. The formulas can also be transformed to find (1) the annual payments necessary to accumulate a future sum, (2) the annual receipts from a specified annuity, (3) the periodic payments necessary to amortize a loan, and (4) the interest rate implicit in a loan contract.

$$(1)\ R = \frac{S_n}{IF} \qquad (4)\ IF = \frac{A_n}{R}$$
$$(2)\ R = \frac{A_n}{IF} \qquad (5)\ IF = \frac{S_n}{P}$$
$$(3)\ R = \frac{A_n}{IF}$$

Appropriate Interest Rate The appropriate interest rate to use is critical when working with compound interest problems. The true nature of the interest rates to be used when working with business problems can be understood only after the chapters dealing with the cost of capital have been examined; this chapter concluded with a brief discussion of some of the factors that determine the appropriate rate of interest for a particular problem—the risk of the investment and the investor's opportunity cost of money.

QUESTIONS **7–1** What types of financial decisions require explicit consideration of the interest factor?

7–2 Compound interest relations are important for decisions other than financial ones. Why are they important to marketing managers?

7–3 Would you rather have an account in a savings and loan association that pays 5 percent interest compounded semiannually or 5 percent interest compounded daily? Why?

7–4   For a given interest rate and a given number of years, is the interest factor for the sum of an annuity larger or smaller than the interest factor for the present value of the annuity?

7–5   Suppose you are examining two investments, A and B. Both have the same maturity, but A pays a 6 percent return and B yields 5 percent. Which investment is probably riskier? How do you know it is riskier?

7–1   At a growth rate of 9 percent, how long does it take a sum to double?   **PROBLEMS**

7–2   Which amount is worth more at 12 percent: $1,000 today or $2,000 after 6 years?

7–3   On December 31, George Goodman buys a building for $50,000 payable 10 percent down and the balance in twenty-five equal annual installments that are to include principal plus 8 percent compound interest on the declining balance. What are the equal installments?

7–4   a) What amount would be paid for a $1,000, 10-year bond that pays $25 interest semiannually ($50 a year) and is sold to yield 8 percent, compounded semiannually?
b) What would be paid if the bond is sold to yield 4 percent?
c) What would be paid if semiannual interest payments are $30 and the bond is sold to yield 12 percent?

7–5   The Apollo Company is establishing a sinking fund to retire a $500,000 mortgage that matures on December 31, 1980. The company plans to put a fixed amount into the fund each year for 10 years. The first payment will be made on December 31, 1971, the last on December 31, 1980. The company anticipates that the fund will earn 6 percent a year. What annual contributions must be made to accumulate the $500,000 as of December 31, 1980?

7–6   A bank agrees to lend you $1,000 today in return for your promise to pay the bank $1,311 four years from today. What rate of interest is the bank charging you?

7–7   You can buy a bond at a price of $6,930. If you buy the bond you will receive four annual payments of $2,000, the first payment to be made a year from today. What rate of return, or yield, does the bond offer?

7–8   You are considering two investment opportunities, A and B. A is expected to pay $200 a year for the first 10 years, $400 a year for the next 20 years, and nothing thereafter. B is expected to pay $800 a year for 11 years, and nothing thereafter. You find that alternative investments of similar risk yield 6 percent and 14 percent for A and B respectively.

a) Find the present value of each investment. Show calculations.
b) Which is the more risky investment? Why?
c) Assume that your rich uncle will give you your choice of investments without cost to you, and that (i) you must hold the investment for its entire life (cannot sell it) or (ii) you are free to sell it at its going market price. Which investment would you prefer under each of the two conditions?

Chapter 8

Capital Budgeting Techniques

CAPITAL budgeting involves the entire process of planning expenditures whose returns are expected to extend beyond one year. The choice of one year is arbitrary, of course, but it is a convenient cutoff period for distinguishing between types of expenditures. Obvious examples of capital outlays are expenditures for land, buildings, and equipment, and for permanent additions to working capital (especially inventories) associated with plant expansion. Also, an advertising or promotion campaign, or a program of research and development, is likely to have an impact beyond one year and, hence, come within the classification of a capital budgeting expenditure.[1]

Capital budgeting is not only important for the future well-being of the firm, but it is also a complex, conceptually difficult topic. As we shall see later in this chapter, the optimum capital budget—the level of investment that maximizes the present value of the firm—is simultaneously determined by the interaction of supply and demand forces under conditions of uncertainty. Supply forces refer to the supply of capital to the firm, or its *cost of capital schedule.* Demand forces relate to the investment opportunities open to the firm, as measured by the *stream of revenues* that will result from an investment decision. *Uncertainty* enters the decision because it is impossible to know exactly either the cost of capital or the stream of revenues that will be derived from a project.

To facilitate the exposition of the investment decision process, we

---

[1] Although this discussion is focused on capital budgeting related to expenditures on fixed assets, the theory and techniques are equally applicable to all kinds of asset investments by business. Therefore, while the authors follow traditional practices of relating capital budgeting to investment in fixed assets, it should be remembered that the techniques discussed are applicable to all types of management decisions. In concept, investments in cash, receivables, or inventory must be justified by earning a satisfactory return on these asset items.

have broken the topic down into its major components. In this chapter, we consider the capital budgeting process and the techniques generally employed by reasonably sophisticated business firms. Uncertainty is explicitly and formally considered in Chapter 9, and the cost of capital concept is developed and related to capital budgeting in Chapters 10 through 13.

A number of factors combine to make capital budgeting one of the most important areas of strategic decision-making with which financial management is involved. These points are discussed in this section.

SIGNIFICANCE OF CAPITAL BUDGETING

First and foremost, the fact that the results continue over an extended period means that the decision-maker loses some of his flexibility. He must make a commitment into the future. For example, the purchase of an asset with an economic life of ten years requires a long period of waiting before the final results of the action can be known. The decision-maker must commit funds for this period and, thus, become a hostage of future events.

Long-Term Effects

Asset expansion is fundamentally related to expected future sales. A decision to buy or to construct a fixed asset that is going to last five years involves an implicit five-year sales forecast. (Indeed, the economic life of an asset purchased represents an implicit forecast for the duration of the economic life of the asset.) Hence, failure to forecast accurately will result in overinvestment or underinvestment in fixed assets.

An erroneous forecast of asset needs can result in serious consequences for a firm. If the firm has invested too much in assets, it will be incurring unnecessarily heavy expenses. If it has not spent enough on fixed assets, two serious problems may arise. First, its equipment may not be sufficiently modern to enable it to produce competitively. Second, if it has inadequate capacity, it may lose a portion of its share of the market to rival firms. To regain lost customers typically requires heavy selling expenses or price reductions or both.

Another problem is to phase properly the availability of capital assets in order to have them come "on stream" at the correct time. For example, the executive vice-president of a decorative tile company recently gave the authors an illustration of the importance of capital budgeting. His firm tried to operate near capacity most of the time. For about four years there had been intermittent spurts in the demand for its product; when these spurts occurred, the firm had to turn away orders. After a sharp increase in demand, the firm would add capacity by renting an additional building, then purchasing and installing the appropriate equipment. It would take six to eight months to have the

Timing the Availability of Capital Assets

additional capacity ready. At this point the company would find that there was no demand for its increased output—other firms had already expanded their operations and had taken an increased share of the market, with the result that demand for this firm had leveled off. If the firm had properly forecast demand and had planned its increase in capacity six months or one year in advance, it would have been able to maintain its market—indeed, to obtain a larger share of the market.

Quality of Capital Assets Good capital budgeting will also improve the timing of asset acquisitions and the quality of assets purchased. This situation follows from the nature of capital goods and of their producers. Capital goods are not ordered by firms until they see that sales are going to press on capacity. Such occasions occur simultaneously for many firms. When the heavy orders come in, the producers of capital goods go from a situation of idle capacity to one where they cannot meet all the orders that have been placed. Consequently, large backlogs of orders accumulate. Since the production of capital goods involves a relatively long work-in-process period, a year or more of waiting may be involved before the additional capital goods are available. This factor has obvious implications for purchasing agents and plant managers.

Raising Funds Another reason for the importance of capital budgeting is that asset expansion typically involves substantial expenditures. When a firm is going to spend a considerable amount of money, it must make the proper plans—large amounts of funds are not available automatically. A firm contemplating a major capital expenditure program may need to arrange its financing several years in advance to be sure of having the funds required for the expansion.

Ability to Compete Finally, it has been said with a great deal of truth that many firms fail not because they have too much capital equipment but because they have too little. While the conservative approach of having a small amount of capital equipment may be appropriate at times, such an approach may also be fatal if a firm's competitors install modern, automated equipment that permits them to produce a better product and sell it at a lower price.

A SIMPLIFIED VIEW OF CAPITAL BUDGETING Capital budgeting is, in essence, an application of a classic proposition from the economic theory of the firm: namely, a firm should operate at the point where its marginal revenue is just equal to its marginal cost. When this rule is applied to the capital budgeting decision, marginal revenue is taken to be the percentage rate of return on investments, while marginal cost is the firm's cost of capital.

A simplified version of the concept is depicted in Figure 8–1(a). Here the horizontal axis measures the dollars of investment during a year, while the vertical axis shows both the percentage cost of capital and the rate of return on projects. The projects are denoted by the boxes—project A, for example, calls for an outlay of $3 million and promises a 17 percent rate of return; project B requires $1 million and yields about 16 percent; and so on. The last investment, project G, simply involves buying 4 percent government bonds, which may be purchased in unlimited quantities. In Figure 8–1(b) the concept is generalized to show smoothed investment opportunity schedules (IRR), and three alternative schedules are presented.[2]

The curve MCC designates the marginal cost of capital, or the cost of each additional dollar acquired for purposes of making capital expenditures. As it is drawn in 8–1(a), the marginal cost of capital is constant at 10 percent until the firm has raised $13 million, after which the cost of capital turns up. To maximize profits, the firm should accept projects A through D, obtaining and investing $11 million, and reject E, F, and G.

Notice that three alternative investment opportunity schedules are shown in 8–1(b). IRR_1 designates relatively many good investment opportunities, while IRR_3 designates relatively few good projects. The three different curves could be interpreted as applying either to three different firms or to one firm at three different times. As long as the IRR curve cuts the MCC curve to the left of Q_2—for example, at Q_1— the marginal cost of capital is constant. To the right of Q_2—for example, at Q_3—the cost of capital is rising. Therefore, if investment opportunities are such that the IRR cuts the MCC curve to the right of Q_2, the *actual* marginal cost of capital (a single point) is not constant; rather, it depends upon the IRR curve. In this chapter we generally *assume* that the IRR curve cuts the MCC curve to the left of Q_2, thus permitting us to assume that the cost of capital is constant. We might mention at this time that, while the assumption of a constant cost of capital certainly does not hold for all firms, and especially not for small, new, and rapidly growing ones, our investigations suggest that it generally is approximately correct for most large, mature corporations.

At the applied level, the capital budgeting process is considerably **APPLICATION** more complex than the preceding example would suggest. Projects do **OF THE** not just appear; a continuing stream of good investment opportunities **CONCEPT** results from hard thinking, careful planning, and, often, large outlays

---

[2] The investment opportunity schedules measure the rate of return on each project. The rate of return on a project is generally called the *internal rate of return* (IRR). This is why we label the investment opportunity schedules IRR. The process of calculating the IRR is explained later in this chapter.

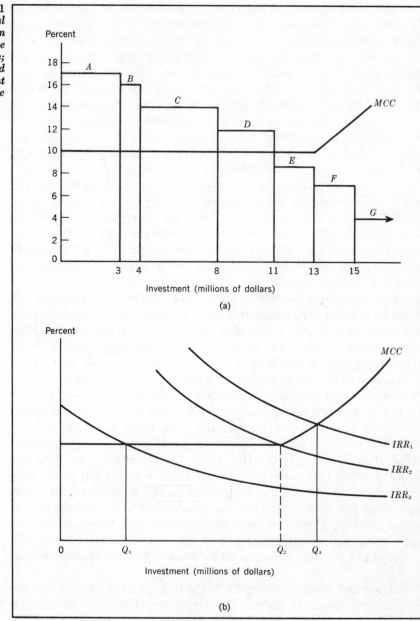

for research and development. In addition, some very difficult measurement problems are involved; the sales and costs associated with particular projects must be estimated, frequently for many years into the future, in the face of great uncertainty. Last, some difficult conceptual and empirical problems arise over the methods of calculating rates of return and the cost of capital.

Businessmen are required to take action, however, even in the face of the kinds of problems described; this requirement has led to the development of procedures that assist in making optimal investment decisions. One of these procedures, forecasting, was discussed in Chapter 6; uncertainty will be discussed in formal terms in the next chapter; and the important subject of the cost of capital is deferred to Chapter 12. The essentials of the other elements of capital budgeting are taken up in the remainder of this chapter.

Aside from the actual generation of ideas, the first step in the capital *Investment* budgeting process is to assemble a list of the proposed new invest- *Proposals* ments, together with the data necessary to appraise them. Although practices vary from firm to firm, proposals dealing with asset acquisitions are frequently grouped according to the following categories:

1. Replacements
2. Expansion: additional capacity in existing product lines
3. Expansion: new product lines
4. Other (for example, pollution control equipment)

These groupings are somewhat arbitrary, and it is frequently difficult to decide the appropriate category for a particular investment. In spite of such problems, the scheme is used quite widely and, as shall be seen, with good reason.

Ordinarily, replacement decisions are the simplest to make. Assets wear out and become obsolete, and they must be replaced if production is to continue. The firm has a very good idea of the cost savings to be obtained by replacing an old asset, and it knows the consequences of nonreplacement. All in all, the outcomes of most replacement decisions can be predicted with a high degree of confidence.

An example of the second investment classification is a proposal for adding more machines of the type already in use or the opening of another branch in a city-wide chain of food stores. Expansion investments are frequently incorporated in replacement decisions. To illustrate, an old, inefficient machine may be replaced by a larger and more efficient one.

A degree of uncertainty—sometimes extremely high—is clearly involved in expansion, but the firm at least has the advantage of examining past production and sales experience with similar machines or stores. When it considers an investment of the third kind, expansion into new product lines, little if any experience data are available on which to base decisions. To illustrate, when Union Carbide decided to develop the laser for commercial application, it had very little idea of either the development costs or the specific applications to which lasers could be put. Under such circumstances, any estimates must at best be treated as very crude approximations.

The "other" category is a catchall and includes intangibles; an example is a proposal to boost employee morale and productivity by installing a music system. Pollution control devices are another example of the "other" category. Major strategic decisions such as plans for overseas expansion or mergers might also be included here, but more frequently they are treated separately from the regular capital budget.

Administrative Details   The remaining aspects of capital budgeting involve administrative matters. Approvals are typically required at higher levels within the organization as we move away from replacement decisions and as the sums involved increase. One of the most important functions of the board of directors is to approve the major outlays in a capital budgeting program. Such decisions are crucial for the future well-being of the firm.

The planning horizon for capital budgeting programs varies with the nature of the industry. When sales can be forecast with a high degree of reliability for 10 to 20 years, the planning period is likely to be correspondingly long; electric utilities are an example of such an industry. Also, when the product-technology developments in the industry require an 8-to-10-year cycle to develop a new major product, as in certain segments of the aerospace industry, a correspondingly long planning period is necessary.

After a capital budget has been adopted, payments must be scheduled. Characteristically, the finance department is responsible for scheduling payments and for acquiring funds to meet payment schedule requirements. In addition, the finance department will be primarily responsible for cooperating with the members of operating divisions to compile systematic records on the uses of funds and the uses of equipment purchased in capital budgeting programs. Effective capital budgeting programs require such information as the basis for periodic review and evaluation of capital expenditure decisions—the feedback and control phase of capital budgeting.

The foregoing represents a brief overview of the administrative aspects of capital budgeting; the analytical problems involved are considered next.

In most firms there are more proposals for projects than the firm is able or willing to finance. Some proposals are good, others are poor, and methods must be developed for distinguishing between them. Essentially, the end product is a ranking of the proposals and a cutoff point for determining how far down the ranked list to go.

CHOOSING AMONG ALTERNATIVE PROPOSALS

In part, proposals are eliminated because they are *mutually exclusive*. Mutually exclusive proposals are alternative methods of doing the same job. If one piece of equipment is chosen to do the job, the others will not be required. Thus, if there is a need to improve the materials handling system in a chemical plant, the job may be done either by conveyer belts or by fork trucks. The selection of one method of doing the job makes it unnecessary to use the others. They are mutually exclusive items.

Independent items are pieces of capital equipment that are being considered for different kinds of projects or tasks that need to be accomplished. For example, in addition to the materials handling system, the chemical firm may need equipment to package the end items. The work would require a packaging machine, and the purchase of equipment for this purpose would be independent of the equipment purchased for materials handling.

To distinguish among the many items that compete for the allocation of the firm's capital funds, a ranking procedure must be developed. This procedure involves, first, calculating the estimated benefits from the use of equipment and, second, translating the estimated benefits into a measure of the advantage of the purchase of the equipment. Thus, an estimate of benefits is required, and a conversion of the benefits into a ranking measure must be developed.

Most discussions of measuring benefits are relatively brief, but it is important to emphasize that in the entire capital budgeting procedure, probably nothing is of greater importance than a reliable estimate of the cost savings or revenue increases that will be achieved from the prospective outlay of capital funds. However, these estimates are likely to be more closely related to the facts of particular situations than they are subject to generalizations.

IMPORTANCE OF GOOD DATA

The nature of the task of calculating savings from a proposed investment is indicated by a brief consideration of the items that may affect benefits: examples are changes in quality and quantity of direct labor, in amount and cost of scrap and rework time, and in maintenance expenses, down time, safety, flexibility, and so on. So many variables are involved that it is obviously impossible to make neat generalizations. However, this should not minimize the crucial importance of the required analysis of the benefits derived from capital expenditures. Each capital equipment expenditure must be examined in detail for possible additional costs and additional savings.

All the subsequent procedures for ranking projects are no better than the data input. Above all, the data formulation requires good judgment in expressing the amount of the benefits. This is not a routine clerical task to be performed on a mechanical basis. It requires continuous monitoring and evaluation of estimates by individuals competent to make such evaluations—engineers, accountants, economists, cost analysts, and other qualified persons.

After the estimates of costs and benefits have been made, they are utilized for ranking alternative investment proposals. How this grading is accomplished is the next topic.

RANKING INVESTMENT PROPOSALS   The point of capital budgeting—indeed, the point of all financial analysis—is to make decisions that will maximize the value of the firm's common stock. The capital budgeting process is designed to answer two questions: (1) Which of several mutually exclusive investments should be selected? (2) How many projects, in total, should be accepted, if the value of the stock is to be maximized?

Among the many methods for ranking investment proposals, three are discussed here. The first, payback, is included because it is so widely used; it is not, however, a conceptually sound method. The other two procedures are included because they are conceptually sound.[3] The name and a brief description of each are set forth below. *Future returns are, in all cases, defined as the net proceeds before depreciation but after taxes that result from a project. In other words, returns are synonymous with cash flows from investments.*

1. *Payback method:* number of years required to return the original investment.

2. *Net present value (NPV) method:* present value of future returns discounted at the appropriate cost of capital minus the cost of the investment.

3. *Internal rate of return (IRR) method:* interest rate which equates the present value of future returns to the investment outlay.

[3] There are also a number of "average rate of return" methods that are encountered in practice, and another conceptually sound discounted cash flow technique—the "profitability index" criterion. We have elected not to discuss the profitability index here in order to limit our coverage. See *Managerial Finance,* third edition, Chapter 7, for a discussion of these other methods.

The nature and characteristics of the three methods are illustrated and explained. To make the explanations more meaningful, the same data are used to illustrate each method.

Assume that two projects are being considered by a firm. Each requires an investment of $1,000. The firm's cost of capital is 10 percent.[4] The net cash flows from investments A and B are shown in Table 8–1.

Year	A	B	
1	$500	$100	*Net*
2	400	200	*Cash*
3	300	300	*Flows*
4	100	400	
5		500	
6		600	

TABLE 8–1
Net cash flows
Profit after taxes
plus depreciation

The *payback period* is the number of years it takes a firm to recover its original investment from net returns before depreciation but after taxes. The payback period is two and one-third years for project A and four years for project B. If the firm were employing a three-year payback period, project A would be accepted but project B would be rejected.

Although the payback period is very easy to calculate, it can lead to the wrong decisions. As the illustration demonstrates, it ignores income beyond the payback period. If the project is one maturing in later years, the use of the payback period can lead to the selection of less desirable investments. Projects with longer payback periods are characteristically those involved in long-range planning—developing a new product or tapping a new market. These are just the strategic decisions which determine a firm's fundamental position, but they also involve investments which do not yield their highest returns for a number of years. This means that the payback method may be biased against the very investments that are most important to a firm's long-run success.

In spite of its shortcomings, the payback method has been widely used by American industry. A survey made by the Machinery and Allied Products Institute indicated that 60 percent of the surveyed firms use the payback period. On equipment with a service life of 10 years or more, 28 percent of those using the method set a three-year payback, and 34 percent set a five-year payback. Only 16 percent use

[4] A discussion of how the cost of capital is calculated is presented in Chapter 12. At this point, cost of capital should be considered as the firm's opportunity cost of making a particular investment.

a payoff period of more than five years, even for such long-lived equipment. Thus, the relatively belated initiation of effective long-range planning by American firms is probably related to the widespread use of the payback period in analyzing alternative investments. Since its emphasis is on the very short run, the payback method simply does not require inquiry into the far-distant future.

Recognition of the longer period over which an investment is likely to yield savings points up another weakness in the use of the payback method for ranking investment proposals: its failure to take into account the interest factor. To illustrate, consider two assets, X and Y, each costing $300 and each having the following cash flows:

Year	X	Y
1	200	100
2	100	200
3	100	100

Each project has a two-year payback; hence, each would appear equally desirable. However, we know that a dollar today is worth more than a dollar next year, so project X, with its faster cash flow, is certainly more desirable.

The use of the payback period is sometimes defended on the ground that returns beyond three or four years are fraught with such great uncertainty that it is best to disregard them altogether in a planning decision. However, this is clearly an unsound procedure. Some of the investments with highest returns are those which may not come to fruition for eight or ten years. The new product cycle in industries involving advanced technologies may not have a payoff for eight or nine years. Furthermore, even though returns that occur after three or four or five years are most uncertain, it is important to make a judgment about the likelihood of their occurring. To ignore them is to assign a zero probability to these distant receipts. This can hardly produce the best results.

A final defense of the payback method is that a firm which is short of cash must necessarily give great emphasis to a quick return of its funds so that they may be put to use in other places or in meeting other needs. It can only be said that this does not relieve the payback method of its many shortcomings, and that there are better methods for handling the cash shortage situation.[5]

[5] We interpret a cash shortage to mean that the firm has a high opportunity cost for its funds and a high cost of capital. We would consider this high cost of capital in the internal rate of return method or the net present value method, thus taking account of the cash shortage.

As the flaws in the payback method were recognized, people began *Net Present Value* to search for methods of evaluating projects that would recognize *Method* that a dollar received immediately is preferable to a dollar received at some future date. This recognition led to the development of *discounted cash flow techniques* to take account of the time value of money. One such discounted cash flow technique is called the "net present value method," or sometimes simply the "present value method." *To implement this approach, simply find the present value of the expected net cash flow of an investment, discounted at the cost of capital, and subtract from it the initial cost outlay of the project.*[6] If the net present value is positive, the project should be accepted; if negative, it should be rejected. If the two projects are mutually exclusive, the one with the higher net present value should be chosen.

The equation for the net present value (*NPV*) is

$$NPV = \left[\frac{R_1}{(1 + k)^1} + \frac{R_2}{(1 + k)^2} + \cdots + \frac{R_N}{(1 + k)^N} \right] - C. \quad (8\text{--}1)$$

Here R_1, R_2, and so forth represent the net cash flows; k is the cost of capital; C is the cost of the project; and N is the project's expected life.

TABLE 8–2
Calculating the net present value (NPV) of projects with $1,000 cost

Year	**Project A**			**Project B**		
	Net cash flow	IF (10%)	PV of cash flow	Net cash flow	IF (10%)	PV of cash flow
1	$500	.91	$ 455	$100	.91	$ 91
2	400	.83	332	200	.83	166
3	300	.75	225	300	.75	225
4	100	.68	68	400	.68	272
5				500	.62	310
6				600	.56	336
	PV of inflows		$1,080			$1,400
	Less cost		−1,000			−1,000
	NPV		$ 80			$ 400

The net present values of projects A and B are calculated in Table 8–2. Project A has a *NPV* of $80, while B's *NPV* is $400. On this basis, both should be accepted if they are independent, but B should be the one chosen if they are mutually exclusive.

[6] If costs are spread over several years, this must be taken into account. Suppose, for example, that a firm bought land in 1965, erected a building in 1966, installed equipment in 1967, and started production in 1968. One could treat 1965 as the base year, comparing the present value of the costs as of 1965 to the present value of the benefit stream as of that same date.

Internal Rate of
Return Method

The internal rate of return (*IRR*) is defined as the *interest rate that equates the present value of the expected future receipts to the cost of the investment outlay*. The equation for calculating the internal rate of return is

$$C = \frac{R_1}{(1 + r)^1} + \frac{R_2}{(1 + r)^2} + \cdots + \frac{R_N}{(1 + r)^N}. \qquad (8\text{-}2)$$

Some value of *r* will cause the sum of the discounted receipts to equal the initial cost of the project, and that value of *r* is defined to be the internal rate of return.

Notice that the internal rate of return formula, Equation 8–2, is simply the *NPV* formula, Equation 8–1, solved for that particular value of *k* that causes the *NPV* to equal zero. In other words, the same basic equation is used for both methods, but (1) in the NPV method the discount rate (*k*) is specified and the *NPV* is found, while (2) in the *IRR* method the *NPV* is specified to equal zero and the value of *r* that forces the *NPV* to equal zero is found.

The internal rate of return may be found by trial and error. First, compute the present value of the cash flows from an investment, using an arbitrarily selected interest rate. Then compare the present value so obtained with the investment's cost. If the present value is higher than the cost figure, try a higher interest rate and go through the procedure again. Conversely, if the present value is lower than the cost, lower the interest rate and repeat the process. Continue until the present value of the flows from the investment are approximately equal to its cost. *The interest rate that brings about this equality is defined as the internal rate of return.*[7]

This calculation process is illustrated in Table 8–3 for projects A and B. First, the 4 percent interest factors are obtained from Appendix Table A–2. These factors are then multiplied by the cash flows for the corresponding years, and the present values of the annual cash flows are placed in the appropriate columns. For example, the IF (interest factor) 0.96 is multiplied by $500, and the product, $480, is placed in the first row of column A.

The present values of the yearly cash flows are then summed to get the investment's total present value. Subtracting the cost of the project from this figure gives the net present value. As the net present

---

[7] In order to reduce the number of trials required to find the internal rate of return, it is important to minimize the error at each iteration. One reasonable approach is to make as good a first approximation as possible, then to "straddle" the internal rate of return by making fairly large changes in the interest rate early in the iterative process. In practice, if many projects are to be evaluated or if many years are involved, one would not work out the calculations by hand but would use a computer. Computational techniques have been developed to enable the *IRR* to be found in three or four trials.

TABLE 8–3
Finding the internal rate of return

		Cash Flow	
	Year	A	B
Investment = $1,000	1	$500	$100
	2	400	200
	3	300	300
	4	100	400
	5		500
	6		600

	4 percent			**10 percent**			**15 percent**		
		Present value			Present value			Present value	
Year	IF	A	B	IF	A	B	IF	A	B
1	0.96	480	96	0.91	455	91	0.87	435	87
2	0.92	368	184	0.83	332	166	0.76	304	152
3	0.89	267	267	0.75	225	225	0.66	198	198
4	0.86	86	344	0.68	68	272	0.57	57	228
5	0.82		410	0.62		310	0.50		250
6	0.79		474	0.56		336	0.43		258
Present value		1,201	1,775		1,080	1,400		994	1,173
Net PV		201	775		80	400		(6)	173

	20 Percent			**24 Percent**			**32 Percent**		
		Present value			Present value			Present value	
Year	IF	A	B	IF	A	B	IF	A	B
1	0.83	415	83	0.81	405	81	0.76	380	76
2	0.69	276	138	0.65	260	130	0.57	228	114
3	0.58	174	174	0.52	156	156	0.43	129	129
4	0.48	48	192	0.42	42	168	0.33	33	132
5	0.40		200	0.34		170	0.25		125
6	0.33		198	0.28		168	0.19		114
Present value		913	985		863	873		770	690
Net PV		(87)	(15)		(137)	(127)		(230)	(310)

Note: Had the cash flows been constant, they would have been an annuity and the IRR could have been found from tables in the manner described on page 132 in Chapter 7.

values of both investments are positive at the 4 percent rate, increase the rate to 10 percent and try again. Once again the net present values are positive, so the rate is stepped up to 15 percent. *At this point the net present value of investment A is approximately zero, which indicates that its internal rate of return is approximately 15 percent. Continuing, B is found to have an internal rate of return of approximately 20 percent.*

What is so special about the particular interest rate that equates the cost of a project with the present value of its receipts? Suppose that a firm obtains all of its capital by borrowing from a bank and that the interest cost of this debt is 6 percent. If the internal rate of return on a particular project is calculated to be 6 percent, the same as the cost of capital, then the firm would be able to invest in the project, use the cash flow generated by the investment to pay off the principal and interest on the bank loan, and come out exactly even on the transaction. If the internal rate of return exceeded 6 percent, the project would be profitable, while if the internal rate of return was less than 6 percent, taking on the project would result in losses. It is this "break-even" characteristic that makes us interested in the internal rate of return.

TABLE 8–4
The prospective-projects schedule

Nature of proposal	Amounts of funds required	Cumulative total	IRR
1. Purchase of leased space	$2,000,000	$ 2,000,000	23%
2. Mechanization of accounting system	1,200,000	3,200,000	19
3. Modernization of office building	1,500,000	4,700,000	17
5. Addition of power facilities	900,000	5,600,000	16
5. Purchase of affiliate	3,600,000	9,200,000	13
6. Purchase of loading docks	300,000	9,500,000	12
7. Purchase of tank trucks	500,000	10,000,000	11
			10% cutoff
8. Installation of conveyor system	200,000	10,200,000	9
9. Construction of new plant	2,300,000	12,500,000	8
10. Purchase of executive aircraft	200,000	12,700,000	7

Assuming that the firm uses a cost of capital of 10 percent, the internal rate of return criterion states that, if the two projects are independent, both should be accepted—they both do better than "break even." If they are mutually exclusive, B ranks higher and should be accepted, while A should be rejected. A more complete illustration of how the internal rate of return would be used in practice is given in Table 8–4. Assuming a 10 percent cost of capital, the firm should accept projects 1 through 7, reject projects 8 through 10, and have a total capital budget of $10 million.

Under ordinary circumstances, both the net present value and the internal rate of return methods will give identical rankings to mutually exclusive projects. Therefore, using either of the methods will result in the same selection when choosing among competing projects. Further, the two methods ordinarily make identical (and "correct") statements about how far down the list of capital projects to go; that is, they give identical answers to the question of how large the total capital budget should be. However, under certain circumstances the two methods can give different answers.[8] When these differences arise, it is generally preferable to rely on the *NPV* method. Therefore, we shall concentrate on the *NPV* method for making capital budgeting decisions in the remainder of the text.

Which Discounted Cash Flow Technique Should Be Used?

Thus far the problem of measuring cash flows—the benefits used in the present value calculations above—has not been dealt with directly. This matter will now be discussed and a few simple examples given.

DETERMINING CASH FLOWS

One way of considering the cash flows attributable to a particular investment is to think of them in terms of comparative income statements. This is illustrated in the following example.

Simplified Model for Determining Cash Flows

The Widget Division of the Culver Company, a profitable, diversified manufacturing firm, purchased a machine five years ago at a cost of $7,500. The machine had an expected life of 15 years at time of purchase and a zero estimated salvage value at the end of the 15 years. It is being depreciated on a straight-line basis and has a book value of $5,000 at present. The division manager reports that he can buy a new machine for $10,000 (including installation) which, over its 10-year life, will expand sales from $10,000 to $11,000. Further, it will reduce labor and raw materials usage sufficiently to cut operating costs from $7,000 to $5,000. The old machine's current market value is $1,000. Taxes are at a 50 percent rate and are paid quarterly, and the firm's cost of capital is 10 percent. Should Culver buy the new machine?

The decision calls for three steps: (1) estimating the actual cash outlay attributable to the new investment, (2) determining the present

[8] See Eugene F. Brigham, "Differences between Discounted Cash Flow Capital Budgeting Techniques," *Readings in Managerial Finance* (New York: Holt, Rinehart and Winston, Inc., 1971), for a detailed discussion of differences between the two methods.

value of the incremental cash flows, and ③ seeing whether the *IRR* exceeds the cost of capital or the *NPV* is positive. These steps are explained further in the following discussion.

1. Estimated Cash Culver must make a $10,000 payment to the manufacturer of the
Outlay machine, but its next quarterly tax bill will be reduced by $2,000. The tax reduction occurs because the old machine, which is carried at $5,000, will be written down by $4,000 ($5,000 less $1,000 salvage value) immediately if the new one is purchased. To illustrate, suppose the Culver Company's taxable income in the quarter in which the new machine is purchased would be $100,000 without the purchase of the new machine and the consequent write-off of the old machine. With a 50 percent tax rate, Culver would have to write a check for $50,000 to pay its tax bill. However, if it buys the new machine and sells the old one, it takes an operating loss of $4,000—the $5,000 book value on the old machine less the salvage value. (The loss is an operating loss, not a capital loss, because it is in reality simply recognizing that depreciation charges, an operating cost, were too low during the old machine's five-year life.) With this $4,000 additional operating cost, taxable income is reduced from $100,000 to $96,000, and the tax bill from $50,000 to $48,000. This means, of course, that the firm's cash outflow for taxes is $2,000 less *because* it purchased the new machine. In addition, there is a cash inflow of $1,000 from the sale of the old machine. The result is that the purchase of the new machine involves a net cash outlay of $7,000; this is its cost for capital budgeting purposes.

Invoice price of new machine	$10,000
Less: Tax savings	−2,000
Salvage of old machine	−1,000
Net cash outflow (cost)	$ 7,000

2. Present Value The first column in Table 8–5 shows the Widget Division's estimated
of Benefits income statement as it would be without the new machine; the second column shows the statement as it will look if the new investment is made. (It is assumed that these figures are applicable for each of the next 10 years; if this is not the case, then cash flow estimates must be made for each year.) The difference between the new and the old cash flows, $1,750, is the incremental cash flow produced by the new machine; this is the benefit stream to be discounted at the cost of capital.

The interest factor for a 10-year, 10 percent annuity is found to be 6.145 from Appendix Table A–4. This factor, multiplied by the

$1,750 incremental cash flow, shows the investment to have a present value of $10,754.

$\underline{PV \text{ of inflows (benefits)}} = \$1,750 \times 6.145 = \$10,754.$

	Without new investment	With new investment
Sales	$10,000	$11,000
Operating costs	−7,000	−5,000
Depreciation (D)	−500	−1,000
Taxable income	$ 2,500	$ 5,000
Income taxes	−1,250	−2,500
Profit after taxes (P)	$ 1,250	$ 2,500
Cash flow $(P + D)$	$ 1,750	$ 3,500

Change in cash flow: $3,500 − $1,750 = $1,750

Note: The effects of the sale of the old machine on the income statement are not considered here. These effects are accounted for in the estimate of the cash outlay for the new machine.

TABLE 8–5
Comparative income statement framework for considering cash flows

Subtracting the $7,000 cost figure from the $10,754 gives the investment a net present value of $3,754. Since the net present value is positive, the new machine should be purchased.[9]

3. Net Present Value

$$PV \text{ of inflows (benefits)} = \$10,754$$
$$\text{Net cash outflow (cost)} = 7,000$$
$$\text{Net Present Value } (NPV) = \$ \,3,754$$

Table 8–6 shows a worksheet for making replacement decision calculations. The top section of the table sets forth the cash outflows at the time the investment is made. All these flows occur immediately, so no discounting is required, and the present value factor is 1.0. No tax adjustment is necessary on the invoice price of the new machine, but, as we saw above, the $4,000 loss on the old machine gives rise to a $2,000 tax reduction, which is deducted from the price of the new machine. Also, the $1,000 salvage value on the old machine is treated as a reduction in cash outflows necessary to acquire the new machine. Notice that since the $1,000 is a recovery of capital invest-

Worksheet for Replacement Decisions

[9] Alternatively, the internal rate of return on the project could have been computed and found to be 21 percent. Since this is substantially in excess of the 10 percent cost of capital, the internal rate of return method also indicates that the investment should be undertaken.

ment, it is not considered to be taxable income; hence, no tax adjustment is made for the salvage value.

In the lower section of the table we see that revenues increase by $3,000 a year—a sales increase of $1,000 plus a cost reduction of $2,000. However, this amount is taxable, so with a 50 percent tax, the after-tax benefits are reduced to $1,500. This $1,500 is received each year for 10 years, so it is an annuity. The present value of the annuity, discounted at the 10 percent cost of capital, is $9,217.

TABLE 8–6
Calculations for
replacement
decisions

	Amount before tax	Amount after tax**	Year event occurs	PV factor at 10%	PV
Outflows at time investment is made:					
Investment in new equipment	10,000	10,000	0	1.00	$10,000
Salvage value of old	(1,000)	(1,000)	0	1.00	(1,000)
Tax loss on sale	(4,000)	(2,000)	0	1.00	(2,000)
Total outflows (present value of costs)					$ 7,000
Inflows, or annual returns:					
Benefits*	3,000	1,500	1–10	6.145	9,217
Depreciation on new (annual)	1,000	500	1–10	6.145	3,073
Depreciation on old (annual)†	(500)	(250)	1–10	6.145	(1,536)
Salvage value on new‡	—	—	—	—	—
Total inflows (present value of benefits)					$10,754

PV of inflows less present value of outflows = $3,754

* $1,000 sales increase + $2,000 cost saving = $3,000 benefit.
† Had the replacement not been made, Culver would have had $500 depreciation a year on the old machine—$5,000 book value divided by 10 years. But since they made the replacement, this depreciation is no longer available. The $5,000 has been recovered as $1,000 salvage plus $4,000 deductible loss. The depreciation of $500 a year must, therefore, be substracted from inflows. It would be possible, of course, for Culver not to sell the old machine, not to take the immediate loss, and to continue getting the $500 yearly depreciation. If Culver chose to do this, however, the PV would be only $1,536 as against $3,000 ($2,000 + $1,000) for the sale and tax loss.
‡ The new machine has a zero estimated salvage value at the time it is purchased. However, the table is structured to show how salvage value would be handled in cases where it is applicable. Note also that where salvage value of the new machine is applicable, it is a *return of capital*, not income. Hence, the before-tax and after-tax amounts are the same.
** The values in the "amount after tax" column are equal to the "amount before tax" figure times $(1 - t)$, where t = tax rate. Here we are using $t = .5$, so $(1 - t) = (1 - .5) = .5$.

Cash inflows also come from the depreciation on the new machine—$1,000 before, or $500 after, taxes. Again, this is a 10-year annuity, and its present value is $3,073. Observe that the depreciation on the old machine is *subtracted* from the inflows section. The logic here is that, had the replacement *not* been made, the company would have had the benefit of the $500 depreciation each year for the next 10 years. With the replacement, however, all this depreciation is taken as an operating loss immediately and is shown as the tax loss on sale in the upper section of the table.[10]

Table 8–6 gives the same net present value, $3,754, as was derived under the comparative income statement approach. The annual inflows after taxes total $1,750 ($1,500 + $500 − $250), and the total outflows, or costs, are $7,000—these are the same figures as we obtained in the procedure based on Table 8–5, so the *NPV*'s must also be the same. In general, the tabular approach is more convenient for use in the management decisions illustrated in the end-of-chapter problems.

CAPITAL RATIONING

Ordinarily, firms operate as illustrated in Figure 8–1; that is, they take on investments to the point where the marginal returns from investment are just equal to their (constant) marginal cost of capital. For firms operating in this way the decision process is as described above—they make those investments having positive net present values, reject those whose net present values are negative, and choose between mutually exclusive investments on the basis of the higher net present value. However, a firm will occasionally set an absolute limit on the size of its capital budget in any one year that is less than the level of investment it would undertake on the basis of the criteria described above. The rationale behind such a decision is discussed in the following section.

Limiting the Firm's Expansion Rate

It is sometimes a fallacy to consider that what is true of the individual parts will be true of the whole. Although individual projects appear to promise a relatively attractive yield, when they are taken together difficulties might be involved in achieving all the favorable results simultaneously. One problem is that other firms in the same industry may be engaging in similar capital expenditure programs in an attempt to increase their capacity or, by cost and price reductions, to obtain a larger share of the product market. For a given growth rate in the industry, it is obviously impossible for every firm to obtain increases in sales that would fully utilize all the capital expenditure projects being undertaken.

Another problem is that while individual projects promise favorable yields, to undertake a large number of projects simultaneously might involve a very high rate of expansion by the individual firm. Such sub-

---

[10] An alternative way of handling depreciation in the table would simply be to show the *increase* in depreciation, that is, depreciation on the new minus that on the old machine. This procedure would yield identical results.

stantial additional personnel requirements and organizational problems may be involved that over-all rates of return will be diminished. Top management, at some point in the capital budgeting process, must therefore make a decision regarding the total volume of favorable projects that may be successfully undertaken without causing a significant reduction in the prospective returns from individual projects.

Reluctance to Obtain Outside Financing   The situation just described—that is, placing a ceiling on the total capital budget in order to keep the over-all rate of expansion within reasonable limits—is one reason for capital rationing. Another reason for limiting the capital budget, and one that perhaps better meets the strict definition of "capital rationing," is the reluctance of some managements to engage in external financing (borrowing, or selling stock).

One management, recalling the plight of firms with substantial amounts of debt in the 1930s, may simply refuse to use debt. Another management, which has no objection to selling debt, may not want to sell equity capital for fear of losing some measure of voting control. Still others may refuse to use any form of outside financing, considering safety and control to be more important than additional profits. These are all cases of capital rationing, and they result in limiting the rate of expansion to a slower pace than would be dictated by "purely rational profit-maximizing behavior."[11]

Project Selection under Capital Rationing   Under conditions of capital rationing, the net present value criterion may not give that ranking of projects which maximizes the value of the firm. For reasons too complex to warrant inclusion in this text, the authors recommend that investments be ranked by the internal rate of return whenever capital rationing causes a substantial number of otherwise acceptable projects to be rejected.[12] The firm should start at the top of its list of projects, taking investments of successively lower rank until the available funds have been exhausted. However,

---

[11] We should make two points here. First, we *do not* necessarily consider a decision to hold back on expansion irrational. If the owner of a firm has what *he* considers to be plenty of income and wealth, then it might be quite rational for him to "trim his sails," relax, and concentrate on enjoying what he has already earned rather than on earning still more. Such behavior would not, however, be appropriate for a publicly owned firm. More will be said on this subject in Chapter 9 in our discussion of utility theory.

The second point is that it is not correct to interpret as capital rationing a situation where the firm is willing to sell additional securities at the going market price but finds that it cannot because the market will simply not absorb more of its issues. Rather, such a situation indicates that the cost-of-capital curve is rising. If more acceptable investments are indicated than can be financed, then the cost of capital being used is too low and should be raised.

[12] See Eugene F. Brigham, "Differences between Discounted Cash Flow Capital Budgeting Techniques," in *Readings in Managerial Finance* (New York: Holt, Rinehart and Winston, Inc., 1971).

no investment with an internal rate of return below the cost of capital should be undertaken.

A firm might, for example, have the investment opportunities shown in Table 8–7 and only $6 million available for investment. In this situation, the firm would probably accept projects 1 through 4 and project 6, ending with a total capital budget of $5.9 million. Under no circumstances should it accept projects 8, 9, or 10, as they all have internal rates of return of less than 10 percent (and also net present values less than zero).

TABLE 8–7
The prospective-projects schedule

Nature of proposal	Project's cost	Cumu-lative total of costs	Internal rate of return	PV of benefits
1. Purchase of leased space	$2,000,000	$ 2,000,000	23%	$3,200,000
2. Mechanization of accounting system	1,200,000	3,200,000	19%	1,740,000
3. Modernization of office building	1,500,000	4,700,000	17%	2,070,000
4. Addition of power facilities	900,000	5,600,000	16%	1,125,000
5. Purchase of affiliate	3,600,000	9,200,000	13%	4,248,000
6. Purchase of loading docks	300,000	9,500,000	12%	342,000
7. Purchase of tank trucks	500,000	10,000,000	11%	540,000
			——10%—— cutoff	
8. Installation of conveyor system	200,000	10,200,000	9%	186,000
9. Construction of new plant	2,300,000	12,500,000	8%	2,093,000
10. Purchase of executive aircraft	200,000	12,700,000	7%	128,000

Before closing this section we should emphasize one point. Based on our experience, we doubt that many firms are subject to severe capital rationing. Accordingly, we believe that in the great majority of cases the net present value approach provides a completely satisfactory selection criterion for capital investment decisions.

SUMMARY

Capital budgeting, which involves commitments for large outlays whose benefits (or drawbacks) extend well into the future, is of the greatest significance to a firm. Decisions in these areas will, therefore, have a major impact on the future well-being of the firm. This chapter focused on how capital budgeting decisions can be made more effective in contributing to the health and growth of a firm. The discussion stressed the development of systematic procedures and rules for preparing a list of investment proposals, for evaluating them, and for selecting a cutoff point.

The chapter emphasized that one of the most crucial phases of the process of evaluating capital budget proposals is obtaining a dependable estimate of the benefits that will be obtained from undertaking the project. It cannot be overemphasized that the firm must allocate to competent and experienced personnel the making of these judgments.

Ranking Invest- Three commonly used procedures for ranking investment proposals
ment Proposals were discussed in the chapter:

Payback, defined as the number of years required to return the original investment. Although the payback method is used frequently, it has serious conceptual weaknesses, because it ignores the facts (a) that some receipts come in beyond the payback period and (b) that a dollar received today is more valuable than a dollar received in the future.

Net present value, defined as the present value of future returns discounted at the cost of capital minus the cost of the investment. The *NPV* method overcomes the conceptual flaws noted in the use of the payback method.

Internal rate of return, defined as the interest rate that equates the present value of future returns to the investment outlay. The internal rate of return method, like the *NPV* method, meets the objections to the payback approach.

Under ordinary circumstances the two discounted cash flow methods give identical answers to these questions: Which of two mutually exclusive projects should be selected? How large should the total capital budget be? However, under certain circumstances conflicts may arise. In general, the *NPV* method is preferred in the absence of capital rationing, but the *IRR* method may be the better choice if capital rationing is imposed.

Determining Cash The cash inflows from an investment consist of the incremental profit
Flows after taxes plus the incremental depreciation; the cash outflow is the cost of the investment less the sum of the salvage value received on an old machine plus any tax loss when the machine is sold.

Capital Rationing Although individual projects appear to promise a relatively attractive yield, if they are undertaken together difficulties might arise in achieving all the favorable projects simultaneously. Several factors must be considered in this connection: expansion plans of other firms in the industry, capital limitations, personnel problems if expansion rates are too high, and so on. Top management, at some point in the capital budgeting process, must make a decision regarding the total volume of favorable projects that can be successfully undertaken without causing a significant reduction in the returns from individual projects.

Ordinarily, however, this is not a problem for larger firms—they plan for expansion and are able to take advantage of good investment opportunities as they arise.

8–1 Why will a firm often continue to use obsolete equipment instead of installing new replacements? How does the use of this obsolete equipment affect the company and the economy?

8–2 Are there conditions under which a firm might be better off if it chooses a machine with a rapid payback rather than one with the largest rate of return?

8–3 Company X uses the payback method in evaluating investment proposals and is considering new equipment whose additional earnings will be $150 a year. The equipment costs $500 and its expected life is 10 years (straight-line depreciation). The company uses a three-year payback as its criterion. Should the equipment be purchased under the above assumptions?

8–4 What are the most critical problems that arise in calculating a rate of return for a prospective investment?

8–5 What other factors in addition to rate of return analysis should be considered in determining capital expenditures?

8–6 Would it be beneficial for a firm to review its past capital expenditures and capital budgeting procedures? Why?

8–7 Fiscal and monetary policies are tools used by the government to stimulate the economy. Explain, using the analytical devices developed in this chapter, how each of the following might be expected to stimulate the economy by encouraging investment.

a) A speed-up of tax-allowable depreciation (for example, the accelerated methods permitted in 1954 or the guideline depreciable life revisions of 1962).
b) An easing of interest rates.
c) Passage of the War on Poverty Program.

8–1 The Hercules Company is using a machine whose original cost was $60,000. The machine is five years old and has a current market (salvage) value of $8,000. The asset is being depreciated over a 15-year original life toward a zero estimated final salvage value. Depreciation is on a straight-line basis and the tax rate is 50 percent. .

Management is contemplating the purchase of a replacement which costs $40,000 and whose estimated salvage value is $4,000. The expected savings with the new machine are $12,000 a year. Depreciation is on a straight-line basis over a 10-year life, the cost of capital is 10 percent, and a 50 percent tax rate is applicable.

a) Should the firm replace the asset? Set up your solution as shown in Table 8–6.
b) How would your decision be affected if the expected savings from the investment in the new machine increase to $17,000 a year but the expected life of the new machine decreases to five years?
c) Disregarding the changes in b (that is, assuming again that expected savings are $12,000 a year and that the expected life is 10 years), how would your decision be affected if a second new machine is available that costs $80,000, has a $5,000 estimated salvage value, and is expected to provide $24,000 in annual savings over its 10-year life? (There are now three alternatives: (1) keep

old machine, (2) replace with $40,000 machine, or (3) replace with $80,000 machine.) Depreciation is still on a straight-line basis. For purposes of answering this question use both (1) the *NPV*, which you must calculate, and (2) the internal rate of return, which you may assume to be 35 percent for the $40,000 project and 21 percent for the $80,000 project.

d) Disregarding the changes in b and c (that is, under the original assumption that one $40,000 replacement machine is available), how would your decision be affected if a new generation of equipment is expected to be on the market in about two years that will provide increased annual savings and have the same cost, asset life, and salvage value?

e) What factors in addition to the quantitative factors listed above are likely to require consideration in a practical situation?

8–2   The Columbia Company is considering the purchase of a new machine tool to replace an obsolete one. The machine being used for the operation has both a tax book value and a salvage value of zero; it is in good working order and will last, physically, for at least an additional 10 years. The proposed machine will perform the operation so much more efficiently that Columbia Company engineers estimate that labor, material, and other direct costs of the operation will be reduced $6,000 a year if it is installed. The proposed machine costs $24,000 delivered and installed, and its economic life is estimated to be 10 years with zero salvage value. The company expects to earn 14 percent on its investment after taxes (14 percent is the firm's cost of capital). The tax rate is 50 percent, and the firm uses straight-line depreciation.

a) Should Columbia buy the new machine?

b) Assume that the tax book value of the old machine had been $8,000, that the annual depreciation charge would have been $800, and that it had no sale value. How do these assumptions affect your answer?

c) Change b to give effect also to the sale of the old machine for $4,000.

d) Change b to assume that the annual savings would be $8,000. (The change in c is not made; the machine is *not* sold for $4,000.)

e) Rework part a assuming the relevant cost of capital is now 5 percent. What is the significance of this? What can be said about parts b, c, and d under this assumption?

f) In general, how would each of the following factors affect the investment decision, and how should each be treated?

1) The expected life of the existing machine decreases.
2) Capital rationing is imposed upon the firm.
3) The cost of capital is not constant but is rising.
4) Improvements in the equipment to be purchased are expected to occur each year, and the result will be to increase the returns or expected savings from new machines over the saving expected with this year's model for every year in the foreseeable future.

8–3   Each of two mutually exclusive projects involves an investment of $3,000. Cash flows (after-tax profits plus depreciation) are $2,000 a year for two years for project S and $800 a year for six years for project L.

a) Compute the present value of each project if the firm's cost of capital is 0 percent, 6 percent, 10 percent, 20 percent.

b) Compute the internal rate of return for each project.

c) Graph the present values of the two projects, putting *PV* on the *Y* axis and the cost of capital on the *X* axis.

d) Which project is better?

Chapter 9

Capital Budgeting Under Uncertainty

*I*N order to focus on capital budgeting procedures and techniques as they are most commonly employed in industry, the "riskiness" of alternative projects was not treated explicitly in the preceding chapter. However, since investors and financial managers are risk averters, they should take into account whether one project is more risky than another when choosing between projects. Several approaches to risk analysis are discussed in this chapter.

We should point out at the outset that in the literature of finance, risk analysis is frequently treated in either of two distinctly different ways—either it is ignored, as we did for the most part in the preceding chapter, or it is treated in a highly formalistic, mathematical manner. The first approach, ignoring risk, is dangerous at best and downright misleading at worst. The second, the mathematical approach, is frequently not feasible in business situations because (1) vital statistical information is unavailable and (2) all the theoretical concepts have not yet been completely worked out. We are unwilling to ignore risk, but we are reluctant to take a formal, mathematical approach to the subject in an introductory textbook. Accordingly, we attempt to chart a middle course by presenting the essential elements of risk analysis in an intuitive manner.[1]

RISK IN FINANCIAL ANALYSIS

The riskiness of an asset is defined in terms of the likely variability of returns from the asset. For example, if one buys a $1 million short-term government bond expected to yield 5½ percent, then the return on the investment, 5½ percent, can be estimated quite precisely, and the investment is defined to be relatively risk free. However, if the $1 million is invested in the stock of a company just being orga-

---

[1] The reader is referred to *Managerial Finance*, third edition, Appendices to Chapter 8, for a more detailed discussion of risk analysis.

nized to prospect for uranium in Central Africa, then the probable return cannot be estimated precisely. The rate of return on the latter investment could range from minus 100 percent to some extremely large figure, and because of this high variability the project is defined as relatively risky.

Risk, then, is associated with income variability—the more variable the expected returns on an investment, the riskier the project. However, we can define risk more precisely, and it is useful to do so. This more precise definition requires a step-by-step development, which constitutes the remainder of this section.

Probability Any investment decision—or, for that matter, almost *any* kind of busi-
Distributions ness decision—implies a forecast of future events, with the forecast being either explicit or implicit. Ordinarily, the forecast of annual returns is a single figure, or point estimate, frequently called the "most likely outcome" or "best estimate." For example, one might forcast that the returns from a particular investment will be $500 per year for three years.

How good is this estimate—that is, how confident is the forecaster of his forecast figure? Is he very certain, very uncertain, or somewhere in between? This degree of uncertainty can be defined and measured in terms of the forecaster's "probability distribution"—the probability estimates associated with each possible outcome. In its simplest form, a probability distribution could consist of just a few potential outcomes. For example, in forecasting profits we could make an optimistic estimate, a pessimistic estimate, and a most likely estimate; or, alternatively, we could make a high, low, and "best guess" estimate. We might expect our high, or optimistic, estimate to be realized if the national economy booms; our pessimistic estimate to hold if the economy is depressed; and our best guess to occur if the economy runs at a normal level. These ranges are illustrated below:

State of the economy	Profits
Recession	$400
"Normal"	$500
Boom	$600

The tabulation above represents some improvement over our earlier "best guess" estimate of $500, as additional information has been provided. However, some critical information is still missing: How likely is it that we will have a boom, a recession, or normal economic conditions? If we have estimates of the probabilities of these events, we can develop a weighted average profit estimate and a measure of our degree of confidence in this estimate. This point is explored in the next subsection.

To illustrate how the probability distribution concept can be used to compare the riskiness of alternative investment projects, suppose we are considering two investment decisions, each calling for an outlay of $1,000 and each expected to produce a cash inflow of $500 per year for three years—the "best estimate" cash flow is $500 per year for each project. If the discount rate is 10 percent, we can use the methods developed in the preceding chapter to estimate each project's net present value:

$$NPV = \$500 \times 2.487 - \$1,000 = \$243.50.$$

The projects have the same expected returns; does this mean that they are equally desirable? To answer this question, we need to know whether the projects are also equally risky, since "desirability" depends upon both returns and risk.

Let us suppose that Project A calls for the replacement of a machine used in normal operations, and the benefits are labor and raw materials savings that will occur if the old machine is replaced by a more efficient one. Project B, on the other hand, calls for the purchase of an entirely new machine to produce a new product, the demand for which is highly uncertain. The replacement machine (Project A) will be used more—hence savings will be greater—if demand for the product is high, and product demand is high when the national economy is booming, low when the national economy is in a recession. We can also expect demand for the new product (Project B) to be greatest when the economy is booming.

We stated above that the *expected* annual return from each project is $500. Let us assume that these figures are developed in the following manner:

1. First, we estimate project returns under different states of the economy:

State of the economy	Annual dollar return	
	Project A	Project B
Recession	$400	$ 0
"Normal"	$500	$ 500
Boom	$600	$1,000

2. Next, we estimate the likelihood of different states of the economy. Our economic forecasts indicate that, given current trends in leading

economic indicators, the odds are two out of ten that a recession will occur, six out of ten that the economy will be normal, and two out of ten that there will be a boom.

③ Redefining the word "odds" as "probability," we find that the probability of a recession is 2/10 = .2, or 20 percent; the probability of "normal" times is 6/10 = .6, or 60 percent; and the probability of a boom is 2/10 = .2, or 20 percent. Notice that the probabilities add up to 1.0, or 100 percent: .2 + .6 + .2 = 1.0, or 100 percent.

④ Finally, in Table 9–1 we calculate weighted averages of the expected returns. When column 4 of the table is summed, we obtain a weighted average of the outcomes under various states of the economy; this weighted average is defined as the *expected value* of the cash flows from the project.

We can graph the results shown in Table 9–1 to obtain a picture of the variability of actual outcomes; this is shown as a bar chart in Figure 9–1. The height of each bar signifies the probability that a given outcome will occur. The range of probable outcomes for Project A is from $400 to $600, with an average or expected value of $500. The expected value for Project B is also $500, but the range of possible outcomes is from $0 to $1,000.

TABLE 9–1 *Calculation of expected values*	State of the economy (1)	Probability of this state occurring (2)	Outcome if this state occurs (3)	Column (2) times column (3) (4)
Project A:	Recession	.2	$400	$ 80
	"Normal	.6	$500	$300
	Boom	.2	$600	$120
		1.0	Expected value =	$500
Project B:	Recession	.2	$ 0	$ 0
	"Normal"	.6	$ 500	$300
	Boom	.2	$1,000	$200
		1.0	Expected value =	$500

Thus far we have assumed that only three states of the economy can exist: recession, "normal," and boom. Actually, of course, the state of the economy could range from deep depression, as in the early 1930s, to an inflationary boom, as in the late 1960s, and there are an unlimited number of possibilities in between. Suppose we had the time and patience to assign a probability to each possible state

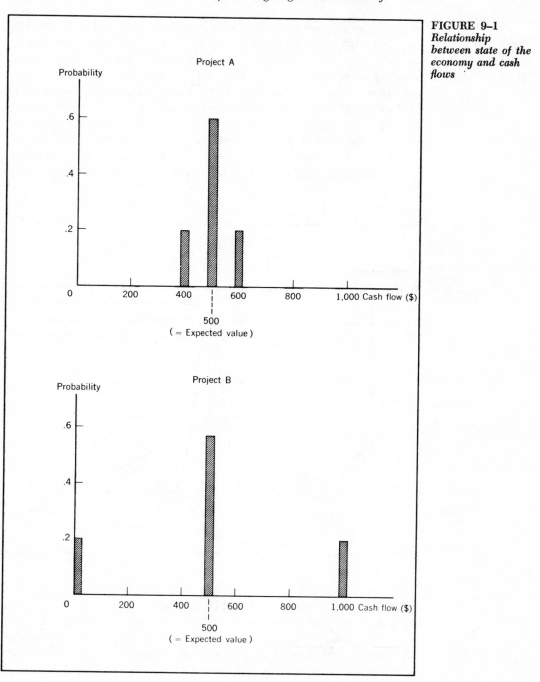

FIGURE 9-1
Relationship between state of the economy and cash flows

of the economy (with the sum of the probabilities still equaling 1.0), and to assign a monetary outcome to each project for each state of the economy. We would have a table similar to Table 9–1 except that it would have many more entries for "Probability" and "Outcome if this state occurs." This table could be used to calculate expected values as shown above, and the probabilities and outcomes could be graphed, as they are in Figure 9–2. In this graph we have modified the assumptions somewhat: We assume that there is 0 probability that Project A will yield less than $400 or more than $600, as well as that there is 0 probability that Project B will yield less that $0 or more than $1,000.

FIGURE 9–2
Probability distribution showing relationship between state of the economy and cash flows

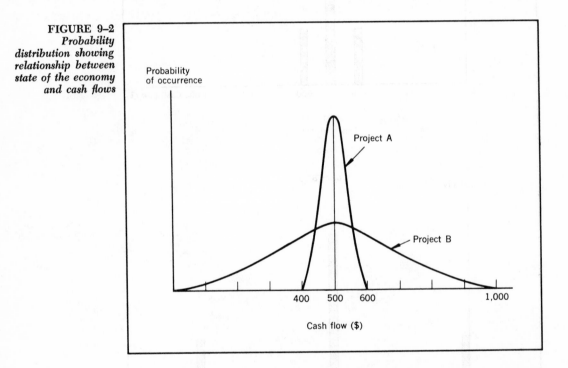

Figure 9–2 could be defined as a graph of the *probability distributions of returns* on Projects A and B. In general, the tighter the probability distribution (or, alternatively stated, the more peaked the distribution), the lower the risk on a project. The tighter the probability distribution, the more likely it is that the actual outcome will be close to the expected value. Since Project A has a relatively tight probability distribution, its *actual* cash flows are likely to be closer to the *expected* $500 than are those of Project B.

Risk is a difficult concept to grasp, and a great deal of controversy *Measuring Risk* has surrounded attempts to define and measure it. However, the most common definition of risk, and one that is satisfactory for our purposes, is stated in terms of the probability distributions presented in Figure 9–2: *The tighter the probability distribution of expected future returns, the smaller the risk of a given project.* According to this definition, as we have found, Project A is less risky than Project B.

To be most useful, our measure of risk should have some definite value—we need a *measure* of the tightness of the probability distribution of project returns. One such measure, and the one we shall use, is the *standard deviation*, the symbol for which is σ. The smaller the standard deviation, the tighter the probability distribution and, accordingly, the lower the riskiness of the project.[2] Project A's standard deviation is found to be $63.20, while that of Project B is $316.20. Other projects available to the firm could be evaluated for riskiness in similar fashion,

---

[2] Although it is not necessary to understand how the standard deviation is calculated to see how it is used in risk analysis, some students may be interested in the calculations. The standard deviation of a distribution is found as follows:

1. Calculate the expected value of the distribution.

2. Subtract the expected value from each possible outcome; square this difference; then multiply the squared deviation by the probability of occurrence of the particular outcome.

3. Obtain the sum of the squared deviation probabilities found in Step 2.

4. Find the square root of the sum found in Step 3.

In equation form, the standard deviation is found as follows:

$$1. \quad \bar{R} = \sum_{i=1}^{N} (R_i P_i) = \text{expected value}$$

R_i = return associated with the ith outcome
N = number of possible outcomes
P_i = probability of occurrence of the ith outcome

$$2. \quad \sigma = \sqrt{\sum_{i=1}^{N} (R_i - \bar{R})^2 P_i}.$$

Using these equations, we can find σ_A, the standard deviation of Project A, to be $63.20, and σ_B to be $316.20. Since B's standard deviation is larger, it is the riskier of the two projects.

If a probability distribution is normal (bell-shaped), the *actual outcome* will lie within ± 1 standard deviation of the *expected value* 68 percent of the time. Although some researchers have suggested that another dimension of the probability distribution, its skewness, may also affect risk, and we could expand our treatment of risk analysis to encompass this factor, we shall refrain from doing so.

thus providing the financial manager with information on both the risk
(σ) and the expected profitability (*NPV* or *IRR*) of capital projects.[3]

**RISKINESS OF
TIME**

We can also use Figure 9–2 to consider the riskiness of a stream
of receipts over time. Visualize, for example, investment A as being
the expected cash flow from a particular project during year 1 and
investment B as being the expected cash flow from the *same* project
in the tenth year. The expected return is the same for each of the
two years, but the subjectively estimated standard deviation is larger
for the more distant return. In this case, riskiness is *increasing over
time.*

FIGURE 9–3
*Risk as a function of
time*

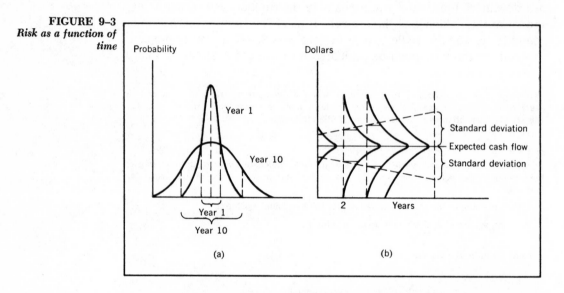

(a)   (b)

Figure 9–3 may help to clarify the concept of increasing riskiness
over time. Figure 9–3(a) simply shows the probability distribution
of expected cash flows in two years—years 1 and 10. The dashed

[3] We should note that problems can arise using the standard deviation as the measure
of risk. Specifically, if one project is larger than another—that is, has a larger cost and
larger expected cash flows—then it will normally have a larger standard deviation without
necessarily being more risky. For example, if a project had expected returns of $1 million
and a standard deviation of only $1,000, it would be less risky than a project with ex-
pected returns of $1,000 and $\sigma = \$500$. One way of eliminating this problem is to divide
the standard deviation by the mean expectation to obtain the *coefficient of variation.*
In general, the standard deviation is satisfactory when percentage *rates of return* are
considered, but the coefficient of variation is mandatory if *dollar* returns are considered. The reason for this distinction is that rates of return are already "standardized"
for size of investment, but some form of standardization is necessary when dollar returns
are considered.
    Also, effects of diversification, or portfolio effects, could influence the actual riskiness
of a given investment. This point is considered later in the chapter.

lines denote one standard deviation on each side of the expected value, so 68 percent of the time the actual outcomes can be expected to fall within the dashed lines for years 1 and 10, respectively. Figure 9–3(b) represents a three-dimensional plot of the expected cash flows over time, and their probability distributions. The probability distributions should be visualized as extending out from the page. The dashed lines show the standard deviations attached to the cash flows of each year, and the fact that these lines diverge from the expected cash flow line indicates that riskiness is increasing over time. If risk was thought of as being constant over time—that is, if the cash flow in a distant year could be estimated equally as well as the cash flow of a close year—then the standard deviation would be constant and the boundary lines would not diverge from the expected cash flow line.

PORTFOLIO RISK[4]

When considering the riskiness of a particular investment, it is frequently useful to [consider the relationship between the investment in question and other existing assets or potential investment opportunities.] To illustrate, a steel company may decide to diversify into residential construction materials. It knows that when the economy is booming, the demand for steel is high and the returns from the steel mill are large. Residential construction, on the other hand, tends to be countercyclical; when the economy as a whole is in a recession, the demand for construction materials is high.[5] Because of these divergent cyclical patterns, a diversified firm with investments in both steel and construction could expect to have a more stable pattern of revenues than would a firm engaged exclusively in either steel or residential construction. In other words, the deviations of the returns on the *portfolio of assets* may be less than the sum of the deviations of the returns from the individual assets.[6]

This point is illustrated in Figure 9–4: 9–4(a) shows the cyclical cash flow variations for the steel plant, 9–4(b) shows the cash flow fluctuations for the residential construction material division, and

---

[4] For an expanded discussion of portfolio risk, see Eugene F. Brigham, "Reduction of Risk Through Diversification: Portfolio Theory," *Readings in Managerial Finance.*

[5] The reason for the countercyclical behavior of the residential construction industry has to do with the availability of credit. When the economy is booming, interest rates are high. High interest rates seem to discourage potential home buyers more than they do other demanders of credit. As a result, the residential construction industry shows marked countercyclical tendencies.

[6] These conclusions obviously hold also for portfolios of financial assets—stocks and bonds. In fact, the basic concepts of portfolio theory were developed specifically for common stocks by Harry Markowitz and first presented in his article, "Portfolio Selection," *Journal of Finance*, VII, No. 1 (March 1952), pp. 77–91. The logical extension of portfolio theory to capital budgeting calls for considering firms as having "portfolios of tangible assets."

9–4(c) shows the cash flows for the combined company. When the cash flows from steel are large, those from residential construction are small, and vice versa. As a consequence, the combined cash flows are relatively stable.

FIGURE 9–4
*Relationship of
returns on two
hypothetical
investments*

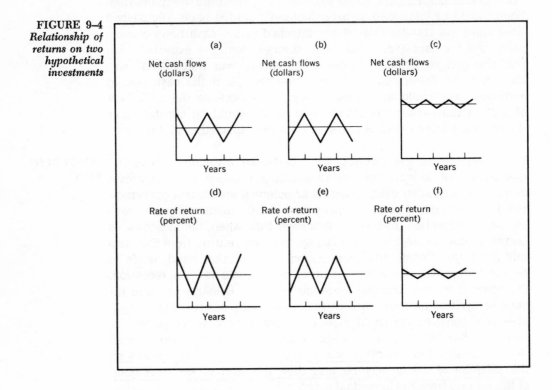

Assuming that the funds invested in the projects remain relatively constant over time, then annual rates of return on steel and on residential construction fluctuate in the same manner as do the net cash flows; the computed annual rate of return on the combined projects is more stable than is that on either plant considered separately. These relationships are shown in Figure 9–4(d), 9–5(e), and 9–5(f).

If we calculated the correlation between rates of return on the steel and construction divisions, we would find the correlation coefficient to be negative—whenever rates of return on the steel plant are high, those on the construction material plant are low. If any two projects have a high degree of *negative correlation*, then taking on the two investments reduces the firm's over-all risk, and this risk reduction is defined as a *portfolio effect.*

On the other hand, had there been a high *positive correlation* between the two projects—that is, if returns on A were high at the same time those on B were high—over-all risk could not have been reduced significantly by diversification. If the correlation between A and B had been $+1.0$, the risk reduction would have been zero, so no portfolio effects would have been obtained.

If the returns from the two projects were *completely uncorrelated, that is, if the correlation coefficient between them was zero, then diversification would benefit the firm to at least some extent.* The larger the number of uncorrelated, or independent, projects the firm takes on, the smaller will be the variation in its over-all rate of return.[7] Uncorrelated projects are not as useful for reducing risk as are negatively correlated ones, but they are better than positively correlated projects.

We can summarize the arguments on portfolio risk that have been presented thus far:

1. If *perfectly negatively correlated* projects are available in sufficient number, then diversification can completely eliminate risk. Perfect negative correlation is, however, almost never found in the real world.

2. If *uncorrelated* projects are available in sufficient number, then diversification can reduce risk significantly—to zero at the limit.

3. If all alternative projects are *perfectly positively correlated*, then diversification does not reduce risk at all.

In fact, most projects are positively correlated, but not perfectly correlated. The degree of intercorrelation among projects depends upon economic factors, and these factors are usually amenable to analysis. Returns on investments in projects closely related to the firm's basic products and markets will ordinarily be highly correlated with returns on the remainder of the firm's assets, and such investments will not generally reduce the firm's risk. However, investments in other product lines and in other geographic markets may have a low degree of correlation with other components of the firm and may, therefore, reduce overall risk. Accordingly if an asset's returns are not too closely related to the firm's other major assets (or, better yet, are negatively correlated with other investments), this asset is more valuable to a risk-averting firm than is a similar asset whose returns are positively correlated with the bulk of the assets. The recognition of this fact was one of the driving forces behind the trend toward conglomerate mergers during the 1950s and 1960s.

---

[7] The principle involved here is the so-called law of large numbers. As the number of independent projects is increased, then the standard deviation of the returns on the portfolio of projects will decrease with the square root of the number of projects taken on. This statement assumes, of course, that the means and standard deviations of the individual projects are approximately equal.

The effect of correlations among investments has been developed into a formal body of knowledge known as *portfolio theory*. These formal relationships are interesting, but we have elected not to incorporate them into this text because, given the state of the art and the availability of data on correlations, it is not generally possible to use these formal processes in capital budgeting decisions. Correlations among projects are, however, considered on an informal, subjective basis by most business executives.[8]

ALTERNATIVE METHODS OF TREATING RISK   Investors and managers are risk averters, so if two projects have different degrees of riskiness, this fact should be taken into account. The definition of risk should take account of the correlation between the returns on a particular project and the firm's other existing or potential assets (the "portfolio effect" of the project). For simplification, in this section we shall assume that all projects are perfectly correlated with one another, permitting us to disregard portfolio effects and to define a project's risk simply in terms of its variability.

Several different approaches may be taken to risk analysis. The most common—(1) the *informal treatment* method and (2) the *risk-adjusted discount rate* method—are examined in the following discussion.[9]

Informal Treatment   The most common method of dealing with risk is on a strictly informal basis. For example, the net present values, based on single-valued estimates of annual returns and the firm's average cost of capital, might be calculated. The decision-maker would recognize that some projects are "riskier" than others. If the net present values on two mutually exclusive projects are "reasonably" close to one another, the "less risky" one is chosen. The extent by which the net *PV* of the riskier project must exceed that of the less risky project before the riskier project will be selected is not specified—the decision rules are strictly internal to the decision-maker.

This approach may be formalized slightly by presenting the decision-maker with both the mean expectation and the standard deviation of the net *PV's*. These provide the decision-maker with an objective estimate of risk, but he still chooses among risky projects in an unspecified manner.

[8] A method has been developed to select a portfolio of risky assets such that the rate of return is maximized for a given degree of risk or, conversely, such that the risk is minimized for a given rate of return. Stated another way, if the maximum risk that a particular investor is willing to accept is equal to σ, then the technique selects the particular portfolio that provides the maximum possible return without exceeding this specified risk limit. The procedure is largely attributable to Markowitz, *op. cit.*

[9] A third procedure, the *certainty equivalent* method, is discussed in theoretical finance literature but rarely used in practice. See *Managerial Finance*, Chapter 8.

The process of choosing among risky assets can be formalized by **Risk-Adjusted** using higher discount rates for more risky projects. Suppose, for exam- **Discount Rate** ple, that a firm has determined its cost of capital (k) to be 10 percent. It could use this figure as the discount rate for computing the net present value of projects that are estimated to be of "average" risk. It could use progressively lower discount rates for less risky projects, and higher rates for riskier projects.

To illustrate, an integrated oil company might compute its over-all average cost of capital to be 10 percent and use this figure for evaluating "standard" investments—refinery additions, development wells for proven reserves, and so on. For evaluating service stations on toll roads, where competition is limited and demand is highly predictable, a discount rate of only 8 percent might be deemed appropriate. However, 20 percent might be used to evaluate investments in off-shore exploratory drilling operations.

When the risk-adjusted discount rate approach is employed—and it is by far the most widely used formal method of recognizing differing degrees of project riskiness—different discount rates are prescribed for the various divisions. In the oil company example, the refining division might be told by corporate headquarters to use 10 percent as its cost of capital; the service station division might be directed to use 8 percent; and the exploratory drilling division might be given a 20 percent discount rate.

These divisional figures would, of course, be averages, and the various divisions would differentiate among types of investments by the investments' individual riskiness. Within the refining division, for example, cost-reducing replacement decisions with rather precisely estimated savings might be evaluated with an 8 percent cost of capital, while projects calling for expansion into such new product lines as petrochemicals might call for a 15 percent discount rate.

These discount rate differentials, or *risk adjustments*, should reflect both the estimated standard deviation (or coefficient of variation) of expected returns and investors' attitudes toward risk.[10] For example, suppose a firm determines that its stockholders are willing to trade between risk and returns as shown in Figure 9–5. The curve is defined as a *market indifference curve*, or *risk/return trade-off function*. The average investor is indifferent to a riskless asset with a "sure" 5 percent rate of return, a "moderately" risky asset with a 7 percent expected return, and a "very" risky asset with a 15 percent expected return. As risk increases, higher and higher expected returns on investment are required to compensate investors for the additional risk.

---

[10] In addition, if favorable portfolio effects would result from the investment, this fact should be considered.

FIGURE 9–5
*Hypothetical
relationship between
risk and rate of
return*

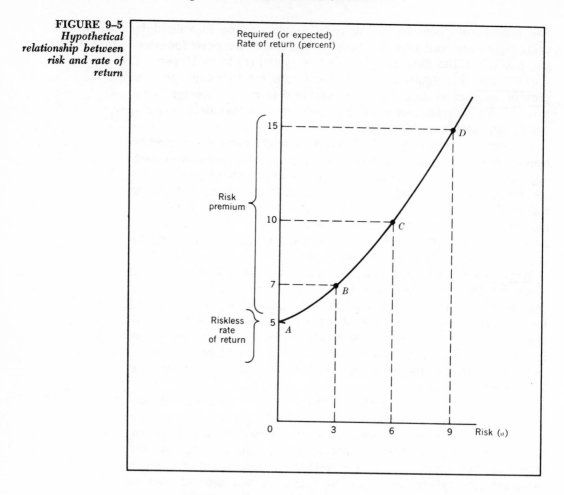

The difference between the expected rate of return on a particular risky asset and the rate of return on a riskless asset is defined as the *risk premium* on the risky asset. In the hypothetical situation depicted in Figure 9–5, the riskless rate is assumed to be 5 percent; a 2 percent risk premium is required for a standard deviation of 3 percent; and a 5 percent risk premium is attached to an investment with a standard deviation as high as 6 percent. The "average investor" is indifferent to risky investments B, C, and D, and the riskless asset A; the rate of return on the riskless asset is the *riskless rate of return,* or the *risk-free yield.*

If a particular firm's stock is located at point C on the risk indifference curve—that is, investors' expect the rate of return on the stock to be 10 percent, but the standard deviation of returns is 6 percent—then it should use a 10 percent discount rate for "average" projects, higher rates for more risky projects (15 percent at point D where $\sigma = 9$ percent), and lower rates for less risky projects (7 percent for point B where $\sigma = 3$ percent).[11]

We can illustrate the use of risk-adjusted discount rates with an example. The Walter Watch Company is considering two mutually exclusive types of watchbands. One band is specifically designed for Walter watches and cannot be used with those of other manufacturers, while the other is adaptable to a wide variety of watches, both Walter's and those of competitive watch companies. The expected investment outlay for design, engineering, production setup, and so on is $100,000 for each alternative. Expected cash inflows are $20,000 per year for eight years if the bands are usable only with Walter watches (Project A), and $22,000 per year for eight years if the bands can be used with a wide variety of watches (Project B). However, because of its "captive market," the standard deviation of expected annual returns from Project A is only $3,000, while that of Project B is $20,000. In view of this risk differential, Walter Watch's management decides that Project A should be evaluated with a 10 percent cost of capital, while the appropriate cost of capital for Project B is 14 percent. Which project should be selected?

USING RISK-ADJUSTED DISCOUNT RATES: AN ILLUSTRATION

We can calculate the risk-adjusted *NPV* for each project as follows:

$$NPV_A = \$20,000 \; (IF \text{ for eight year, 10\% annuity}) - \$100,000$$
$$= \$20,000 \; (5.335) - \$100,000$$
$$= \$6,700.$$

$$NPV_B = \$22,000 \; (IF \text{ for eight year, 14\% annuity}) - \$100,000$$
$$= \$22,000 \; (4.639) - \$100,000$$
$$= \$2,058.$$

Project B would have had the higher *NPV* if both projects had been evaluated at the same cost of capital, but when different discount rates are used to account for risk differentials, the analysis indicates that Walter Watch should choose the less risky alternative of manufacturing bands for its own watches.

One additional question should be raised in connection with risk analysis: Whose risk preferences, managements' or stockholders', are relevant in the capital budgeting decision? Put another way, if stockholders are able to diversify their own investment portfolios, why should individual firms be concerned with diversification?

MANAGEMENT VERSUS STOCK-HOLDERS

[11] For simplification, we assume at this point that the firm is financed with only equity capital. This assumption is relaxed when the cost of capital is considered in detail in Chapter 12.

If capital markets were perfect, if management personnel were concerned only with maximizing stockholders' wealth, if bankruptcy costs (both money costs and the intangible stigma attached to bankruptcy and reorganization) were minimal, if income taxes were zero, and if no frictions were involved in contracting and expanding business organizations, then perhaps diversificaton at the investor level would be sufficient. However, bankruptcy is extremely inefficient and costly; lenders (and to a lesser extent stockholders) are very much averse to the prospects of taking losses and of having to explain why they incurred losses; good managements would be hard to obtain and retain if they faced strong probabilities of losing their jobs through the failure of their firms; the tax laws make it preferable for losses to be sustained by a division of a profitable firm rather than by a separate firm; and so forth.

In consequence, we doubt that investors' diversification can completely replace corporate diversification. Accordingly, we believe that firms should be and are concerned about risk.[12] The question of how stockholder diversification and corporate diversification should be balanced, however, is still an open one, a subject for further research.

PUBLIC EXPENDITURE DECISIONS   Before concluding this chapter, we should point out that capital budgeting under uncertainty faces governmental agencies as well as individuals and firms. A series of hearings before Congress on methods and procedures of capital budgeting at the federal level revealed (1) that congressional leaders and the heads of the major governmental agencies agreed that governmental capital budgeting should be conducted under a method equivalent to our risk-adjusted discount rate procedure, but (2) the federal agencies are having a difficult time determining appropriate discount rates.[13] In other words, the federal

---

[12] An analogy with the theory of financial leverage is, perhaps, relevant here. As will be noted in Chapter 12, a theory has been put forth by two distinguished economists, Franco Modigliani and Merton Miller, that corporate leverage is irrelevant because individuals, by lending or borrowing on their own personal account, can alter the effects of corporate leverage. In other words, if a company has no debt (is unleveraged), an individual can create "home made" leverage by buying the company's stock on margin (borrowing to buy the stock). Modigliani and Miller's theoretical arguments are impeccable; on the grounds that their assumptions are incorrect—individuals are reluctant to borrow on personal account because they do not have limited liability (as do corporations), individuals pay higher interest rates than corporations, and so on—their theory has been criticized as not being relevant in the real world. The same kind of argument could be made against replacing corporate diversification by investor diversification.

[13] U.S. Congress, Subcommittee on Economy in Government of the Joint Economic Committee, *Economic Analysis of Public Investment Decisions: Interest Rate Policy and Discounting Analysis* (Washington, D.C.: U.S. Government Printing Office, 1968).

government is (or soon will be) following the same capital budgeting procedures as do the more sophisticated business firms, and the procedures described in this and the preceding chapter are applicable to both.

Two facts of life in finance are (1) that investors are averse to risk, **SUMMARY** and (2) that at least some risk is inherent in most business decisions. Given investor aversion to risk, and differing degrees of risk in different financial alternatives, it is necessary to consider risk in financial analysis.

Our first task is to define what we mean by risk; our second task is to measure it. The concept of *probability* is a fundamental element in both the definition and measurement of risk. A *probability distribution* shows the probability of occurrence of each possible outcome, assuming a given investment is undertaken. The mean, or weighted average of the distribution is defined as the *expected value* of the investment. The *standard deviation* of the distribution, which is a measure of the extent to which actual outcomes are likely to deviate from the expected value, is used as our measure of project risk. Thus, the greater the dispersion of the probability distribution of returns, the riskier the project, and actual project risk is measured by the standard deviation.

In appraising the riskiness of an individual capital investment, not only the variability of expected returns of the project itself but also the correlation between expected returns on this project and the remainder of the firm's assets must be taken into account. This relationship is called the *portfolio effect* of the particular project. Favorable portfolio effects are strongest when a project is negatively correlated with the firm's other assets; weakest when positive correlation exists. Portfolio effects lie at the heart of the firm's efforts to diversify into product lines not closely related to the firm's main line of business.

Risk differentials are frequently dealt with in a strictly informal manner. However, as firms become increasingly sophisticated, greater and greater efforts are being expended to deal with risk in a formal manner. When risk is treated explicitly, the typical procedure is by the *risk-adjusted discount rate method*—higher discount rates are used to evaluate riskier projects in the capital budgeting process. To use this method the firm must first estimate investors' *risk/return trade-off function,* then use this estimate to develop *risk premiums* for the riskier projects. A great deal of judgment is necessary when implementing these concepts, but more and more firms are deciding that even inexact attempts to account for risk are better than no attempts at all.

The concepts developed in this chapter are useful throughout the field of finance—indeed, in all aspects of business administration. In particular, it will be useful to keep the key ideas presented in this chapter—especially the definitions of risk, risk premiums, and risk-adjusted discount rates—in mind in the next three chapters, where capital structure, valuation, and the cost of capital are considered.

QUESTIONS   9–1   Define the following terms:
   a) Risk
   b) Uncertainty
   c) Objective probability
   d) Subjective probability
   e) Portfolio effects
   f) Risk-adjusted discount rate

9–2   The probability distribution of a less risky expected return is more peaked than that of a risky return. What shape would the probability distribution have for (1) completely certain returns and (2) completely uncertain returns?

9–3   In this chapter we have defined risk in terms of the variability of expected returns, where the expectations may be derived either subjectively or objectively. In constructing this measure of risk, we have implicitly given equal weight to variations on both sides of the expected return—higher returns or lower returns. Can you see any problems resulting from this treatment?

9–4   One frequently encounters the term "utility theory," which deals with the marginal utility of money, in economics courses. What is the relationship between utility theory and the type of risk analysis discussed in this chapter? (See pages 195-198.)

9–5   "On reflection, the use of the market indifference curve concept illustrated in Figure 9–5 as a basis for determining risk-adjusted discount rates is all right in theory, but it cannot be applied in practice. Market estimates of investors' reaction to risk cannot be measured precisely, so it is impossible to actually construct a set of risk-adjusted discount rates for different classes of investment." Comment on this statement.

9–6   Assume that residential construction and industries related to it are countercyclical to the general economy and are countercyclical to steel in particular. Does this negative correlation between steel and construction-related industries necessarily mean that a savings and loan association, whose profitability tends to vary with construction levels, would be less risky if it diversified by acquiring a steel distributor?

PROBLEMS   9–1   The Gertz Products Co., Inc., is considering replacing a 10-year-old machine that has a book value of $10,000 and a current salvage value of $35,000. It is looking at two mutually exclusive alternatives:

a) Replacement with a similar new machine with a $100,000 cost and net cash flows (after-tax profits plus depreciation) of $12,500 a year.
b) Replacement with a new type of machine, previously untried by either the company or its competitors, for sale by its inventor for $150,000. The expected net cash flows with the new type machine are $25,000 a year.

The first machine has an expected salvage value of $10,000 at the end of its 10-year life, and the new type machine has no expected salvage value at the end of its 10-year life. Net depreciation benefits for both machines are included in the calculations of net cash flows above. The firm's cost of capital is 10 percent.

a) Should the firm replace the existing machine, and if so, should replacement be with a similar new machine or with the new type of machine?

b) How would your results be affected if a risk-adjusted discount rate of 14 percent were used for the new type machine?

c) What factors and issues in addition to those treated above are likely to require consideration in a practical situation?

9–2 Ressner, Inc.'s marketing division is reviewing its annual advertising plans in conjunction with the firm's annual capital budget. Due to management's desire to retain a controlling equity position, each division has been given a budget limitation—$150,000 has been allocated to the marketing division. This department is considering two mutually exclusive investments for promotion of new business for the firm's plastic products. The first is the continuation of the firm's direct mail advertising program. Its costs are $.10 a mailing, enabling the firm to mail 1,500,000 pieces a year. Over many years, responses have averaged 1 percent of pieces mailed—ranging from 0.8 to 1.2 percent in 95 percent of the years for which experience is available. One-third of these responses are converted to sales that average $125 with a $50 pretax profit margin after all costs except advertising. There are no substantial lagged effects for direct mail returns, but there may be additional lagged benefits from the newspaper advertising described below.

The local sales representative of a five-city national newspaper chain has proposed the following contract to the director of marketing: A four-column, 4-inch ad (usual cost $224 a day) running 365 days in five major newspapers with an average circulation of 800,000 each (4,000,000 guaranteed minimum average circulation) for a total cost of $150,000. This represents an average daily cost of $412 versus a $1,120 normal daily rate for the five papers. The newspaper chain also agrees to provide 100 hours of free copywriting consulting time. Depending upon the effectiveness of the advertising copy, responses per day could be expected to range from 200 to only two. Profits per response should be the same as with direct mail advertising. The following subjective probabilities have been assigned to responses by the marketing director.

Daily responses	Probability
200	.4
50	.2
20	.2
2	.2

The applicable tax rate is 50 percent.

a) Calculate the expected return for each project. Which project should the division adopt?

b) What other factors not specified in the problem should be considered?

9–3 The Lakeshore Company is faced with two mutually exclusive investment projects. Each project costs $3,000 and has an expected life of three years.

Annual net cash flows from each project begin one year after the initial investment is made and have the following characteristics:

	Probability	Cash flow
Project A	.2	$2,400
	.6	3,000
	.2	3,600
Project B	.2	0
	.6	3,000
	.2	7,500

Lakeshore has decided to evaluate the riskier project at a 10 percent cost of
capital versus 8 percent for the less risky project.

a) What is the expected value of the annual net cash flows from each project?

b) What is the risk-adjusted *NPV* of each project?

Appendix A
TO CHAPTER 9

Although the examples we used in the text to illustrate uncertainty concepts are quite simple, real life decisions frequently require rather complex procedures. Two of these, *decision trees* and *computer simulation,* are described in Appendix A.

OTHER TECHNIQUES FOR DEALING WITH UNCERTAINTY

OTHER TECHNIQUES FOR DEALING WITH UNCERTAINTY

Most important decisions are not made once-and-for-all at one point in time. Rather, decisions are made in stages. For example, a petroleum firm considering the possibility of expanding into agricultural chemicals might take the following steps: (1) spend $100,000 for a survey of supply-demand conditions in the agricultural chemical industry; (2) if the survey results are favorable, spend $2 million on a pilot plant to investigate production methods; and (3) depending on the costs estimated from the pilot study and the demand potential from the market study, choose either to abandon the project, build a large plant, or build a small one. Thus, the final decision actually is made in stages, with subsequent decisions depending on the results of past decisions.

Decision Trees

The sequence of events can be mapped out to look like the branches of a tree, hence the name *decision tree.* As an example, consider Figure 9–6. The firm faces two choices—to build a large plant or a small one. Demand expectations for the plant's products are 50 percent for high demand, 30 percent for medium demand, and 20 percent for low demand. Depending upon demand, net cash flows (sales revenues minus operating costs, all discounted to the present) will range from $8.8 million to $1.4 million if a large plant is built, and from $2.6 million to $1.4 million if the decision is to build a small plant.

Since the demand probabilities are known, we can find the expected values of the cash flows, which are given in column 5 of the figure. Finally, we can deduct the investment outlays from the expected reve-

187

FIGURE 9-6 *Illustrative decision tree*

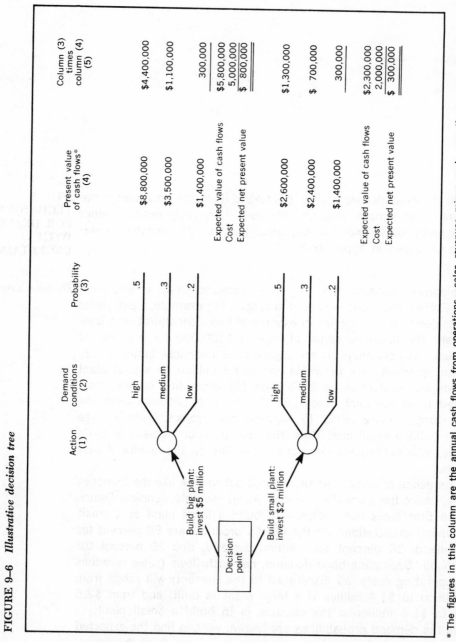

Action (1)	Demand conditions (2)	Probability (3)	Present value of cash flows* (4)	Column (3) times column (4) (5)
Build big plant: invest $5 million	high	.5	$8,800,000	$4,400,000
	medium	.3	$3,500,000	$1,100,000
	low	.2	$1,400,000	300,000
			Expected value of cash flows	$5,800,000
			Cost	5,000,000
			Expected net present value	$ 800,000
Build small plant: invest $2 million	high	.5	$2,600,000	$1,300,000
	medium	.3	$2,400,000	$ 700,000
	low	.2	$1,400,000	300,000
			Expected value of cash flows	$2,300,000
			Cost	2,000,000
			Expected net present value	$ 300,000

Decision point

* The figures in this column are the annual cash flows from operations—sales revenues minus cash operating costs—discounted at the firm's cost of capital.

nues to obtain the expected net present value of each decision. In the example the expected net present value is $800,000 for the large plant, $300,000 for the small one.

Since its net present value is higher, should the decision be to construct the large plant? Perhaps, but not necessarily. Notice that the range of outcomes is greater if the large plant is built—actual net present values (actual outcome minus investment cost) range from $3.8 million to *minus* $3.6 million, versus a range of only $600,000 to *minus* $600,000 for the small plant. Thus, risk is greater if the decision is to build the large plant. The decision-maker could take account of the risk differentials by using risk-adjusted discount rates to evaluate the two projects; thus, the values in columns 4 and 5 would be adjusted for risk.

The decision tree illustrated in Figure 9–6 is quite simple; in actual use the trees are frequently far more complex and involve a number of sequential decision points. As an example of a more complex tree, consider Figure 9–7. The boxes numbered ①, ②, and so on are *decision points*, instances when the firm must choose between alternatives, while the circles represent the possible actual outcomes, one of which will follow these decisions. At decision point ① the firm has three choices: To invest $3 million in a large plant, to invest $1.3 million in a small plant, or to spend $100,000 on market research. If the large plant is built, the firm follows the upper branch, and its position has been fixed—it can only hope that demand will be high. If it builds the small plant it follows the lower branch. If demand is low no further action is required, but if demand is high decision point ② is reached and the firm must either do nothing or else build a large plant at a cost of another $2.2 million. (Thus, if it obtains a large plant via expansion the cost is $500,000 greater than if it had built the large plant in the first place.)

If the decision at point ① is to pay $100,000 for more information, the firm moves to the center branch. The research modifies the firm's information about potential demand. Initially, the probabilities were 70 percent for high demand and 30 percent for low demand. The research survey will show either favorable (positive) or unfavorable (negative) demand prospects: If they are positive, the probabilities for high final demand will be 87 percent and 13 percent for low demand, while if the research yields negative results the odds on high final demand are only 35 percent versus 65 percent for low demand. These results will, of course, influence the firm's decision on building a large or a small plant.

If the firm builds a large plant and demand is high, then sales and profits will be large. However, if it builds a large plant and demand

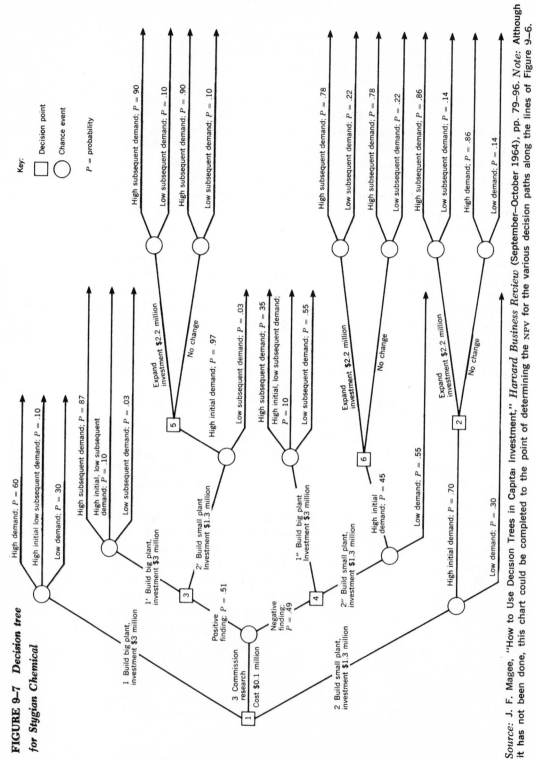

FIGURE 9-7 *Decision tree for Stygian Chemical*

Key:
□ Decision point
○ Chance event
P = probability

High demand; *P* = 60
High initial low subsequent demand; *P* = .10
Low demand; *P* = 30

1 Build big plant, investment $3 million

3 Commission research
Cost $0.1 million

Positive finding; *P* = .51

2 Build small plant, investment $1.3 million

High subsequent demand; *P* = 87
High initial, low subsequent demand; *P* = .10
Low subsequent demand; *P* = .03

1' Build big plant, investment $3 million

3

2' Build small plant investment $1.3 million

Negative finding; *P* = .49

4

1'' Build big plant investment $3 million

2'' Build small plant, investment $1.3 million

5

Expand investment $2.2 million

No change

High initial demand; *P* = .97

Low subsequent demand; *P* = .03

High subsequent demand; *P* = 35
High initial, low subsequent demand; *P* = .10
Low subsequent demand; *P* = .55

6

Expand investment; $2.2 million

No change

High initial demand; *P* = 45

Low demand; *P* = .55

High initial demand; *P* = .70

Low demand; *P* = .30

2

Expand investment $2.2 million

No change

High subsequent demand; *P* = 90
Low subsequent demand; *P* = .10
High subsequent demand; *P* = 90
Low subsequent demand; *P* = .10

High subsequent demand; *P* = .78
Low subsequent demand; *P* = .22
High subsequent demand; *P* = .78
Low subsequent demand; *P* = .22

High subsequent demand; *P* = .86
Low subsequent demand; *P* = .14

High demand; *P* = .86
Low demand; *P* = .14

Source: J. F. Magee, "How to Use Decision Trees in Capital Investment," *Harvard Business Review* (September–October 1964), pp. 79–96. *Note:* Although it has not been done, this chart could be completed to the point of determining the NPV for the various decision paths along the lines of Figure 9–6.

is weak, sales will be low and losses rather than profits will be incurred. On the other hand, if the firm builds a small plant and demand is high, sales and profits will be lower than they could have been had a large plant been built, but the chances of losses in the event of low demand will be eliminated. Thus, the decision to build the large plant is riskier than the one to build the small plant. The decision to commission the research is, in effect, an expenditure to reduce the degree of uncertainty in the decision on which plant to build; the research provides additional information on the probability of high versus low demand, thus lowering the level of uncertainty.

The decision tree in Figure 9–7 is incomplete in that no dollar outcomes (or utility values) are assigned to the various situations. If this step were taken, along the lines shown in the last two columns of Figure 9–6, then expected values could be obtained for each of the alternative actions. These expected values could then be used to aid the decision-maker in choosing among the alternatives.

Another technique designed to assist managers in making decisions **SIMULATION** under uncertainty is computer simulation. To illustrate the technique, let us consider a situation where a new oil refinery is to be built. The cost of the plant is not known for certain. It is expected to cost about $150 million, but if no problems are involved, the cost can be as low as $125 million, while an unfortunate series of events—strikes, increased material costs, technical problems, and the like—could result in costs running as high as $225 million.

Revenues from the new facility, which will operate for many years, will depend on population growth and income in the region, competition, developments in the auto industry, and so on. Operating costs will depend on petroleum discoveries, oil import quotas, labor cost trends, and the like. Since both sales revenues and operating costs are uncertain, annual profits are also uncertain.

Assuming that probability distributions can be assigned to each of the major cost and revenue determinants, then a computer program can be constructed to simulate what is likely to happen. In effect, the computer selects one value from each of the relevant distributions, combines it with other values selected from the other distributions, and produces an estimated profit and rate of return on investment. This particular profit and rate of return occur only for the particular combination of values selected during this particular trial. The computer goes on to select other sets of values and to compute other profits and rates of return, over and over, for perhaps several hundred trials. A count is kept of the number of times the various rates of return are computed, and when the computer runs are completed,

FIGURE 9–8
Simulated rate of return for Project X

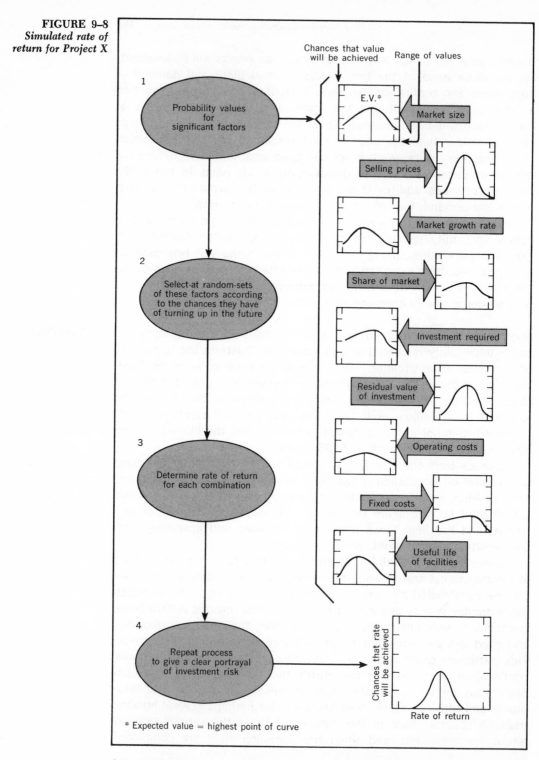

Source: Adapted from an article by David B. Hertz, "Risk Analysis in Capital Investment," *Harvard Business Review* (January–February 1964), pp. 95–106.

the frequency with which each rate of return occurred can be plotted as a frequency distribution.

The procedure is illustrated in Figures 9–8 and 9–9. Figure 9–8 shows how probability distributions for various factors that affect the rate of return are combined for Project X; a similar calculation is run for Project Y. Figure 9–9 shows that the expected rate of return on Investment X is 15 percent, while that of Investment Y is 20 percent. However, these are only the *average* rates of return generated by the computer—simulated rates ranged from −10 percent to +45 percent for Investment Y, and from 5 to 25 percent for Investment X. The standard deviation generated for X is only 4 percent—68 percent of the computer runs had rates of return between 11 and 19 percent—while that for Y is 12 percent. Clearly, then, Investment Y is riskier than Investment X. The computer simulation has provided us with both an estimate of the expected returns on the two projects and an estimate of their relative risks.

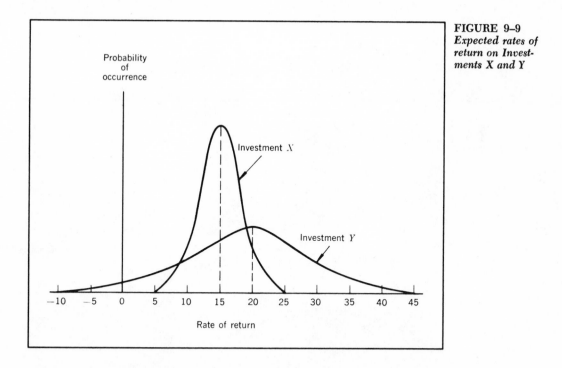

FIGURE 9–9
Expected rates of return on Investments X and Y

One final point should be made about the use of computer simulation in risk analysis. The technique involves obtaining probability distributions about a number of variables—investment outlays, unit sales, product prices, input prices, asset lives, and so on—and it involves a large amount of programming and machine time costs. Therefore, simulation is not generally feasible except for large and expensive projects such as major plant expansions or new product decisions. In these cases, however, when a firm is considering a major decision involving millions of dollars, computer simulation can provide valuable insights into the relative merits of alternative investment strategies.

In Chapter 9 we assumed that investors are averse to risk, that is, **UTILITY** they prefer less risk to more risk, other things being the same. Most **THEORY AND** people agree that this is "logical" and do not question the idea of **RISK AVERSION** risk aversion. However, one's understanding of the effect of risk on the value of assets is perhaps greater if he understands the theory that underlies the principle of risk aversion. The most widely held theory of risk aversion is presented here.

In theory we can identify three possible attitudes toward risk: a desire *Attitudes toward* for risk, an aversion to risk, and an indifference to risk. A *risk seeker* *Risk* is one who prefers risk; given a choice between more and less risky investments with identical expected money returns, the risk seeker would prefer the riskier investment. Faced with the same choice, the *risk averter* would select the less risky investment. The person who is *indifferent to risk* would not care which investment he received.

There undoubtedly are individuals who prefer risk and others who are indifferent to it, but both logic and observation suggest that business managers and stockholders are predominately risk averters. Why do you suppose risk aversion generally holds? Given two investments, each with the same expected dollar returns, why would most investors prefer the less risky one? Several theories have been advanced in answer to this question, but perhaps the most logically satisfying one involves *utility theory*.

At the heart of utility theory is the notion of *diminishing marginal utility for money*. If an individual with no money received $100, he could satisfy his most immediate needs. If he then received a second $100, he could utilize it, but the second $100 would not be quite as necessary to him as the first $100. Thus, the "utility" of the second, or *marginal*, $100 is less than that of the first $100. Therefore, we say that *the marginal utility of money is diminishing*.

Figure 9–10 graphs the relationship between income or wealth and its utility, where utility is measured in units called "utils." Curve A, the one of primary interest, is for someone with a diminishing utility for money. If this particular individual had $5,000, then he would have 10 utils of "happiness" or "satisfaction." If he received an additional $2,500, his utility would rise to 12 utils, an increase of two units. However, if he lost $2,500, his utility would fall to six utils, a loss of four units.

FIGURE 9–10
Relationship between money and its utility

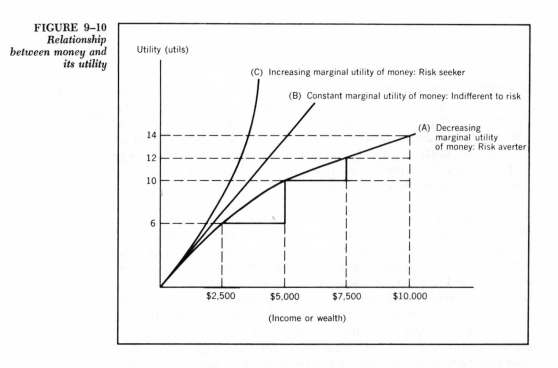

Utility (utils)

(C) Increasing marginal utility of money: Risk seeker

(B) Constant marginal utility of money: Indifferent to risk

(A) Decreasing marginal utility of money: Risk averter

14

12

10

6

$2,500 $5,000 $7,500 $10,000

(Income or wealth)

Most investors (as opposed to people who go to Las Vegas for the fun of it or because of psychological problems) appear to have a declining marginal utility for money, and this directly affects their attitudes toward risk. Risk means, in essence, the likelihood that a given return will turn out to be lower than the expected return. Someone who has a constant marginal utility for money will value each dollar of "extra" returns just as highly as each dollar of "lost" returns. On the other hand, someone with a diminishing marginal utility for money will get more "pain" from a dollar lost than "pleasure" from a dollar gained. Because of his utility of money function, the second individual will be very much opposed to risk, and he will require a very high return on any investment that is subject to much risk. In curve A of Figure

9–10 for example, a gain of $2,500 from a base of $5,000 would bring 2 utils of additional satisfaction, but a $2,500 loss would cause a 4 util satisfaction loss. Therefore, a person with this utility function and $5,000 would be unwilling to make a bet with a 50–50 chance of winning or losing $2,500. The risk-indifferent individual with curve B would be indifferent to the bet, and the risk-seeker would be eager to make it.

Diminishing marginal utility leads directly to risk aversion, and this risk aversion is reflected in the capitalization rate investors apply when determining the value of a firm. To make this clear, let us assume that government bonds are riskless securities and that such bonds currently offer a 5 percent rate of return.[14] Thus, if someone bought a $5,000 U.S. Treasury bond and held it for one year, he would end up with $5,250, a profit of $250. Suppose he had an alternative investment opportunity which called for the $5,000 to be used to back a wildcat oil drilling operation. If the drilling operation is successful, the investment will be worth $7,500 at the end of the year. If it is unsuccessful, the investor can liquidate his holdings and recover $2,500. There is a 60 percent chance that oil will be discovered, a 40 percent chance of a "dry hole." If he has only $5,000 to invest, should our investor choose the riskless government bond or the risky drilling operation?

Let us first calculate the expected monetary values of the two investments.

	Drilling operation			Government bond		
	Probability (1)	Outcome (2)	(1) × (2) (3)	Probability (1)	Outcome (2)	(1) × (2) (3)
Oil	.6	$7,500	$4,500	.6	$5,250	$3,150
No oil	.4	2,500	1,000	.4	$5,250	2,100
Expected value			$5,500			$5,250

The tabular calculation is not really necessary for the government bond, as the $5,250 outcome will occur regardless of what happens in the oil field; we include it simply for completeness. The drilling operation calculation, however, shows that the expected value of this venture, $5,500, is higher than that of the bond. Does this mean that our investor should put his money in the wildcat well? Not necessarily—it depends on his utility function. If his marginal utility for

[14] We shall abstract from any risk of price declines in bond prices caused by increases in the level of interest rates. Thus, the risk with which we are concerned at this point is *default risk,* the risk that principal and interest payments will not be made as scheduled.

money is sharply diminishing, then the potential loss of utility that would result from a dry hole, or "no oil," might not compensate for the potential gain in utility that would result with the development of a producing well. If the utility function shown in curve A of Figure 9–10 above is applicable, this is exactly the case. Four utils would be lost if "no oil" occurs, while only two would be gained if oil is found.

We can modify the expected monetary value calculation to reflect utility considerations. Reading from Figure 9–10 we see that our risk-averse investor would have approximately 12 utils if he invests in the wildcat venture and oil is found, 6 utils if he makes this investment and no oil is found, and 10.5 utils with certainty if he chooses the government bond. This information can be used to calculate the *expected utility values* for the oil investment. (No calculation is needed for the government bond, as we know its expected utility is 10.5.)

	Probability (1)	Monetary outcome (2)	Associated utility (3)	Column (1) × column (3) (4)
Oil	.6	$7,500	12.0	7.2
No oil	.4	2,500	6.0	2.4
			Expected utility	9.6 utils

Since the *expected utility* from the wildcat venture is only 9.6 utils versus 10.5 from the government bond, we see that the government bond is the preferred investment. Thus, even though the *expected monetary value* for the oil venture is higher, *expected utility* is higher for the bond; risk considerations therefore lead us to choose the safer government bond.

Part IV

Valuation and Financial Structure

Chapter 10

Financial Structure
and the
Use of Leverage

ONCE the financial manager has determined his firm's approximate financial requirements, his next task is to see to it that these funds are on hand.[1] Assuming that the company has a history of sound management and is not trying to expand too rapidly, there should be no problem in raising the necessary capital. However, capital comes in many forms—long- and short-term debt, secured and unsecured debt, preferred stock, common stock, retained earnings, and such hybrid instruments as convertibles and long-term leases. What are the characteristics of these different securities? Which particular form is the best one to use in a given situation? Or should a package consisting of some of each kind be tried? These are the questions to which we now turn. Our first task, and the one considered in this chapter, is to examine the firm's financial structure and the effects of using financial leverage.

To avoid ambiguity in the use of key concepts, the meanings of frequently used expressions are given here. *Financial structure* refers to the right-hand side of the balance sheet—the financing of the resources acquired by the firm. *Capital structure* is the permanent financing of the firm, represented by long-term debt, preferred stock, and net worth. *Net worth* is the *common stockholders' equity* and includes common stock, capital surplus, earned surplus (retained earnings), and net worth reserves.[2]

BASIC DEFINITIONS

---

[1] The financial manager cannot, of course, determine his financial requirements *precisely* until he knows the firm's cost of capital schedule. In the two preceding chapters we *assumed* that the cost of capital was given and examined the investment opportunities schedule. Now we shall assume the investment schedule to be given and examine the cost of capital schedule. In Chapter 13, these two schedules will be combined.

[2] Note that preferred stock is excluded from net worth here. Preferred stock is a hybrid security with some of the characteristics of common stock and some of the characteristics of bonds. When viewed from the point of view of the firm's creditors, preferred is very much like common. From the viewpoint of common stockholders, preferred shares are similar to debt. Consequently, preferred stock can be classified either as a part of net worth or not, depending on the purpose of the analysis. If we look at leverage from the creditor's point of view, preferred is included with equity. If we look at leverage from the position of the common stockholder, it is excluded from net worth. This seemingly ambiguous point is discussed in more detail in Chapter 19.

Our key concept for this chapter is *financial leverage, or the leverage factor,* defined as the ratio of total debt to total assets. For example, a firm having assets of $100 million and a total debt of $50 million would have a leverage factor of 50 percent. Some writers use only long-term debt in the numerator of the ratio, but this is not generally an accurate measure of financial leverage. While long-term debt might be more or less appropriate in an industry such as electric utilities, where little short-term debt is employed, it would be clearly inappropriate in other industries, such as aerospace, where firms rely on current debt as an important source of financing. Further, the smaller firms in most industries tend to make extensive use of short-term liabilities, particularly trade accounts payable. Therefore, to ignore current debt in measuring the risk incurred by using financial leverage would be to ignore the major (sometimes the only) form of debt employed.

Finally, we should distinguish at the outset between business risk and financial risk. By *business risk* we mean the inherent uncertainty, or variability of expected returns, on the firm's "portfolio" of assets. By *financial risk* we mean the additional riskiness to the common stock that is induced by the use of financial leverage.

THEORY OF FINANCIAL LEVERAGE Perhaps the best way to understand the proper use of financial leverage is to analyze its impact on profitability under varying conditions. Suppose there are three firms in a particular industry, and these firms are identical except for their financial policies. Firm A has used no debt and consequently has a leverage factor of zero; firm B, financed half by debt and half by equity, has a leverage factor of 50 percent; firm C has a leverage factor of 75 percent. Their balance sheets are shown in Table 10–1.

TABLE 10–1
Alternative financial structures

		Firm A	
		Total debt	$ 0
		Net worth	200
Total assets	$200	Total claims	$200
		Firm B	
		Total debt (6%)	$100
		Net worth	100
Total assets	$200	Total claims	$200
		Firm C	
		Total debt (6%)	$150
		Net worth	50
Total assets	$200	Total claims	200

How do these different financial patterns affect stockholder returns? As can be seen from Table 10–2, the answer depends upon the state of the industry's economy. When the economy is depressed, sales and profit margins are low; the firms earn only 2 percent on assets. When conditions become somewhat better, the return on assets is 5 percent. Under normal conditions, the return on assets rises to

		Economic conditions						TABLE 10–2 *Stockholder returns under various leverage and economic conditions*
	Very poor	Poor	(Indif- ference level)	Normal	Good	Very good
Rate of return on total assets before interest	2%	5%	6%	8%	11%	14%
Dollar returns on total assets before interest	$4	$10	$12	$16	$22	$28
Firm A: Leverage Factor 0%						
Earnings in dollars	$4	$10	$12	$16	$22	$28
Less: Interest expense	0	0	0	0	0	0
Gross income	4	10	12	16	22	28
Taxes (50%)*	2	5	6	8	11	14
Available to common stock	2	5	6	8	11	14
Percent return on common stock	1%	2.5%	3%	4%	5.5%	7%
Firm B: Leverage Factor 50%						
Earnings in dollars	$4	$10	$12	$16	$22	$28
Less: Interest expense	6	6	6	6	6	6
Gross income	(2)	4	6	10	16	22
Taxes (50%)*	(1)	2	3	5	8	11
Available to common stock	(1)	2	3	5	8	11
Percent return on common stock	−1%	2%	3%	5%	8%	11%
Firm C: Leverage Factor 75%						
Earnings in dollars	$4	$10	$12	$16	$22	$28
Less: Interest expense	9	9	9	9	9	9
Gross income	(5)	1	3	7	13	19
Taxes (50%)*	(2.5)	.5	1.5	3.5	6.5	9.5
Available to common stock	(2.5)	.5	1.5	3.5	6.5	9.5
Percent return on common stock	−5%	1%	3%	7%	13%	19%

* The tax calculation assumes that losses are carried back and result in tax credits.

8 percent, while in a moderate boom the figure goes to 11 percent. Finally, under extremely favorable circumstances, the companies have a 14 percent return on assets. These percentages, multiplied by the $200 of assets, give the earnings before interest and taxes for the three companies under the various states of the economy.

FIGURE 10–1
Relation between rates of return on assets and rates of return on net worth under different leverage conditions

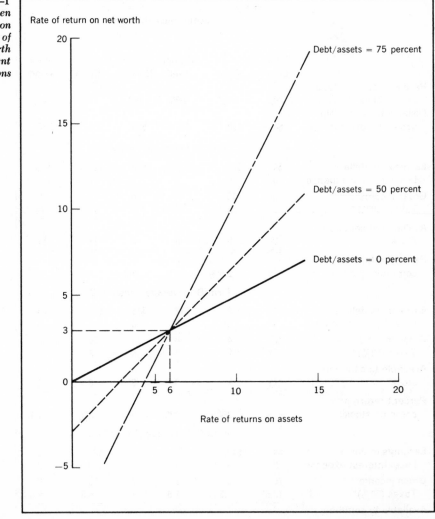

Table 10–2 demonstrates how the use of financial leverage magnifies the impact on the stockholders of changes in the rate of return on assets. When economic conditions go from normal to good, for example, returns on assets go from 8 to 11 percent, an increase of 37.5 percent.

Firm A uses no leverage, gets no magnification, and consequently experiences the same 37.5 percent jump in the rate of return to stockholders. Firm B, on the other hand, enjoys a 60 percent increase in stockholder returns as a result of the 37.5 percent rise in returns on assets. Firm C, which uses still more leverage, has an 85.7 percent increase. Just the reverse holds in economic downturns, of course; the 37.5 percent drop in returns on assets when the economy goes from normal to poor results in return-on-net-worth declines of 37.5 percent, 60 percent, and 85.7 percent for firms, A, B, and C, respectively.

Using the same illustrative numbers, Figure 10–1 gives a graphic presentation of the interaction between the rates of return on assets and net worth, given the three different leverage factors. The interesting point to note here is the intersection of the three lines at the point where assets are returning 6 percent, the interest cost of debt. At this point, the return on net worth is 3 percent. The assumed 50 percent tax rate reduces the 6 percent return on total assets to a return of 3 percent on net worth, regardless of the degree of leverage. When returns on assets are higher, leverage improves stockholder returns and is said to be *favorable*; when assets earn less than 6 percent, returns to stockholders are reduced and the leverage is defined as *unfavorable*. *In general, whenever the return on assets exceeds the cost of debt, leverage is favorable, and the higher the leverage factor the higher the rate of return on common equity.*

To show that the results of alternative financial decisions are useful in judging the relative merits and demerits of various plans, a specific example is given. This example illustrates how future earnings prospects affect financing decisions.

EFFECTS OF FINANCIAL LEVERAGE

TABLE 10–3
Universal Machine Company Balance sheet*
December 31, 1971

Cash	$ 200,000	Accounts payable	$1,200,000
Receivables (net)	1,100,000	Other current liabilities	800,000
Inventories	1,600,000	Total liabilities	$2,000,000
Plant (net)	2,500,000	Common stock ($10 par)	2,500,000
Equipment (net)	2,800,000	Surplus	3,700,000
Total assets	$8,200,000	Total claims on assets	$8,200,000

* Figures are rounded for convenience.

The Universal Machine Company, whose latest balance sheet is shown in Table 10–3, manufactures equipment used by steel producers. The major product is a lathe used to trim the rough edges off hot rolls of steel; the lathes sell for $10,000 each. As is typically the case for the producers of durable capital assets, the company's sales fluctuate widely, far more than does the over-all economy. For example, during 9 of the last 25 years, sales have been below the break-even point, so losses have been relatively frequent. In the past few years, however, machinery demand has been heavy and has actually been rising; if Universal is to continue sharing in this expansion, it will have to increase capacity. For this increase, $3 million is required. James Walter, the financial vice-president, learns that he can net $3 million by selling bonds with a 5 percent coupon. Alternatively, he can raise the money by selling 75,000 shares of common stock.

During the past five years, Universal's sales have fluctuated between $500,000 and $4,000,000; at the higher volume, the firm is operating at full capacity and has to turn down orders. With the additional plant expansion, sales capacity will increase to $6 million. Fixed costs, after the planned expansion, will be $500,000 a year, and variable costs (excluding interest on the debt) will be 40 percent of sales.

Although Walter's recommendation will be given much weight, the final decision for the method of financing rests with the company's board of directors. Procedurally, the financial vice-president will analyze the situation, evaluate all reasonable alternatives, come to a conclusion, and then present the alternatives with his recommendations to the board. For his own analysis, as well as for presentation to the board, Walter prepares the materials shown in Table 10–4.

In the top third of the table, earnings before interest and taxes (EBIT) are calculated for different levels of sales ranging from $0 to $6 million. The firm suffers an operating loss until sales are almost $1 million, but beyond that point it shows a rapid rise in gross profit.

The middle third of the table shows the financial results that will occur with bond financing at the various sales levels. First, the $150,000 annual interest charges are deducted from the earnings before interest and taxes calculated above. Next, taxes are taken out. Notice that if the sales level is so low that losses are incurred, the firm receives a tax credit. Finally, net profits after taxes are divided by the 250,000 shares outstanding to obtain earnings per share of common stock.[3]

In the bottom third of the table, the financial results that will occur with stock financing are calculated. No interest payments are involved, so the earnings-before-tax figure is the same as the one computed at the top of the table. Net profit after taxes is divided by 325,000 shares—the original 250,000 plus the new 75,000—to find earnings per share.

---

[3] The shares outstanding can be calculated by dividing the $2,500,000 common stock figure given on the balance sheet by the $10 par value.

TABLE 10-4 *Universal Machine Company, profit calculations at various sales levels*

Sales in units	0	50	100	200	400	600
Sales in dollars	$ 0	$ 500,000	$1,000,000	$2,000,000	$4,000,000	$6,000,000
Fixed costs	$ 500,000	$ 500,000	$ 500,000	$ 500,000	$ 500,000	$ 500,000
Variable costs (40% of sales)	-0-	200,000	400,000	800,000	1,600,000	2,400,000
Total costs (except interest)	$ 500,000	$ 700,000	$ 900,000	$1,300,000	$2,100,000	$2,900,000
Earnings before interest and taxes (EBIT)	$(500,000)	$(200,000)	$ 100,000	$ 700,000	$1,900,000	$3,100,000
Financing with bonds						
Less: Interest (5% × $3,000,000) (i)	$ 150,000	$ 150,000	$ 150,000	$ 150,000	$ 150,000	$ 150,000
Earnings before taxes	$(650,000)	$(350,000)	$ (50,000)	$ 550,000	$1,750,000	$2,950,000
Less: Income taxes (50%)*	(325,000)	(175,000)	$ (25,000)	275,000	875,000	1,475,000
Net profit after taxes	$(325,000)	$(175,000)	$ (25,000)	$ 275,000	$ 875,000	$1,475,000
Earnings per share on 250,000 shares of common (EPS)	$ -1.30	$ -0.70	$ -0.10	$1.10	$3.50	$5.90
Financing with stock						
Earnings before taxes†	$(500,000)	$(200,000)	$ 100,000	$ 700,000	$1,900,000	$3,100,000
Less: Income taxes (50%)*	$(250,000)	(100,000)	50,000	350,000	950,000	1,550,000
Net profit after taxes	$(250,000)	$(100,000)	$ 50,000	$ 350,000	$ 950,000	$1,550,000
Earnings per share on 325,000 shares of common (EPS)	$ -0.77	$ -0.31	$ +0.15	$1.08	$2.92	$4.77

* Assumes tax credit on losses.
† Earnings before tax is the same as earnings before interest and tax because interest is zero with stock financing.

Walter next plots the earnings for each share under the two methods of financing, as shown in Figure 10–2. If sales were depressed to zero, the debt financing line would cut the Y axis at —$1.30, below the —$0.78 intercept of the common stock financing line. The debt line has a steeper slope and rises faster, however, showing that earnings per share will go up faster with increases in sales if debt is used. The two lines cross at sales of about $2 million. Below that volume of sales the firm would be better off issuing common stock; above that level, debt financing would produce higher earnings per share.

FIGURE 10–2
*Earnings per share
for stock and debt
financing*

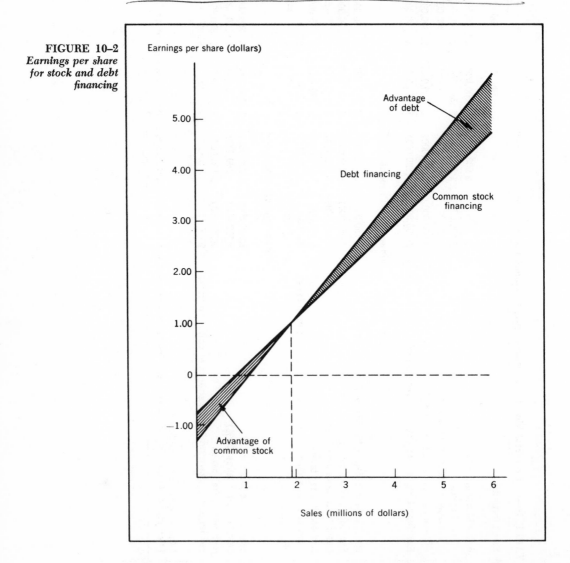

If Walter and his board of directors *knew for sure* that sales would never again fall below $2 million, bonds would be the preferred method of financing the asset increase. But they cannot know this for certain; in fact, they probably have good reason to expect future business cycles to drive sales down to, and even below, this critical level. They know that during the past five years sales have been as low as $500,000. If sales fall to this level again, the company would not be earning enough to cover its interest charges. Such a situation, if it continues for several years, could jeopardize the very existence of the firm. However, if sales continue to expand, there would be higher earnings per share from using bonds; no officer or director would want to forgo these substantial advantages.

Debt - good

Debt - bad

When industry standards for leverage are applied, we see that the firm's debt ratio, after financing, will be 45 percent as compared to a norm for manufacturing firms of only 37 percent (see Table 10–5). Since Universal Machine is a capital goods producer and is thus subject to wider fluctuations than the average manufacturer, it might be argued that a 45 percent debt ratio is too high for Universal Machine.

TABLE 10–5
Variation in financial leverage in industry groups, 1963–1964

Name of industry	Debt to total assets (in percentages)
Service	65
Public utilities	61
Wholesale trade	54
Agriculture	54
Retail trade	51
Mining	38
Manufacturing	37

Source: U.S. Treasury Department, Internal Revenue Service, *Statistics of Income, U.S. Business Tax Returns* (Washington, D.C.: U.S. Government Printing Office, 1967).

Walter's recommendation, and the decision of each director, will depend (1) upon each person's appraisal of the future and (2) upon his psychological attitude toward risks. The pessimists, or risk-averters, will prefer to employ common stock, while the optimists, or those less sensitive to risk, will favor bonds. This example, which is typical of many real-world situations, suggests that the major disagreements over the choice of forms of financing are likely to reflect uncertainty about the future levels of the firm's sales. Such uncertainty, in turn, reflects the characteristics of the firm's environment—general business conditions, industry trends, and quality and aggressiveness of management.[4]

RELATIONSHIP OF FINANCIAL LEVERAGE TO OPERATING LEVERAGE[5]   In Chapter 4 it was shown that a firm has some degree of control over its production processes; it can, within limits, use either a highly automated production process with high fixed costs but low variable costs or a less automated process with lower fixed costs but higher variable costs. If a firm uses a high degree of operating leverage, its break-even point was seen to be at a relatively high sales level, and changes in the level of sales were shown to have a magnified (or "leveraged") impact on profits. Notice that financial leverage has exactly the same kind of effect on profits: the higher the leverage factor, the higher the break-even sales volume and the greater the impact on profits from a given change in sales volume.

The *degree of operating leverage* was defined as the percentage change in operating profits associated with a given percentage change in sales volume, and Equation 4–2 was developed for calculating operating leverage:

$$\text{Degree of operating leverage at point } Q = \frac{Q(P - V)}{Q(P - V) - F}. \quad (4\text{-}2)$$

Here Q is units of output, P is the average sales price per unit of output, V is the variable cost per unit, and F is total fixed costs. Applying the formula to Universal Machine at an output level of 200 units (see Table 10–4 on page 207), we find its operating leverage to be 1.71, so a 100 percent increase in volume produces a 171 percent increase in operating profit:

$$\text{Degree of operating leverage} = \frac{200(\$10,000 - \$4,000)}{200(\$10,000 - \$4,000) - \$500,000}$$

$$= \frac{\$1,200,000}{\$700,000} = 1.71 \text{ or } 171\%.$$

Operating leverage affects *earnings before interest and taxes* (EBIT), while financial leverage affects *earnings after interest and taxes,* the

[4] Investors' appraisal of uncertainty is embodied in the capitalization rate applied to earnings to determine the value of the firm. Maximizing expected earnings will not be the best policy for stockholders if, by so doing, risk is increased to the point where the rising risk-adjusted discount rate more than off-sets the higher expected earnings. This point is discussed in more detail in the next three chapters.

It would, of course, be possible to appraise financial risk through the same types of probability analysis discussed in Chapter 9. This is not generally done in practical decision making, and we see no pedagogic advantages in formalizing leverage risk analysis. Therefore, we have elected not to take a formal subjective probability approach to leverage decisions in this book.

[5] This section can be omitted without losing the continuity of the chapter.

earnings available to common stockholders. In terms of Table 10–4 on page 207, operating leverage affects the top section of the table, financial leverage the lower sections. Thus, if Universal Machine had more operating leverage, its fixed costs would be higher than $500,000, its variable cost ratio would be lower than 40 percent of sales, and earnings before interest and taxes would vary with sales to a greater extent. Financial leverage takes over where operating leverage leaves off, further magnifying the effect on earnings per share of a change in the level of sales. For this reason, operating leverage is sometimes referred to as *first-stage leverage* and financial leverage as *second-stage leverage*.

The *degree of financial leverage* is defined as the percentage change in earnings available to common stockholders that is associated with a given percentage change in earnings before interest and taxes (*EBIT*). An equation has been developed to aid in calculating the degree of financial leverage for any given level of *EBIT* and interest charges (*I*):[6] **The Degree of Financial Leverage**

$$\text{Degree of financial leverage} = \frac{EBIT}{EBIT - I}. \qquad (10\text{--}1)$$

For Universal Machine at 200 units of output and an *EBIT* of $700,000, the degree of financial leverage with bond financing is

$$\text{Financial leverage: Bonds} = \frac{\$700,000}{\$700,000 - \$150,000} = 1.27.$$

[6] The equation is developed as follows:

1. Notice that $EBIT = Q(P - V) - F$.

2. Earnings per share $(EPS) = \dfrac{(EBIT - I)(1 - t)}{N}$ where *EBIT* is earnings before interest and taxes, *I* is interest paid, *t* is the corporate tax rate, and *N* is the number of shares outstanding.

3. *I* is a constant, so ΔEPS, the change in *EPS*, is

$$\Delta EPS = \frac{\Delta EBIT(1 - t)}{N}.$$

4. The percentage increase in *EPS* is the change in *EPS* over the original *EPS*, or

$$\frac{\dfrac{\Delta EBIT(1 - t)}{N}}{\dfrac{(EBIT - I)(1 - t)}{N}} = \frac{\Delta EBIT}{EBIT - I}.$$

5. The degree of financial leverage is the percentage change in *EPS* over the percentage change in *EBIT*, so

$$\text{Financial leverage} = \frac{\dfrac{\Delta EBIT}{EBIT - I}}{\dfrac{\Delta EBIT}{EBIT}} = \frac{EBIT}{EBIT - I}.$$

Therefore, a 100 percent increase in *EBIT* would result in a 127 percent increase in earnings per share. If stock financing is used, the degree of financial leverage is 1.0, so earnings per share would rise proportionately with *EBIT*: A 100 percent increase in *EBIT* would produce a 100 percent increase in *EPS*.

Combining Operating and Financial Leverage   Operating leverage causes a given change in sales volume to have a magnified effect on *EBIT*, and if financial leverage is superimposed on operating leverage, changes in *EBIT* will have a magnified effect on earnings per share. Therefore, if a firm uses a considerable amount of both operating leverage and financial leverage, even small changes in the level of sales will produce wide fluctuations in *EPS*.

Equation 4–1 for the degree of operating leverage can be combined with Equation 10–1 for financial leverage to show the total leveraging effect of a given change in sales on earnings per share:[7]

$$\text{Combined leverage effect} = \frac{Q(P - V)}{Q(P - V) - F - I}. \tag{10–2}$$

For Universal Machine at an output of 200 units (or \$2 million of sales), the combined leverage effect using debt financing is

$$\text{Combined leverage effect} = \frac{200(\$10,000 - \$4,000)}{200(\$10,000 - \$4,000) - \$500,000 - \$150,000}$$

$$= \frac{\$1,200,000}{\$1,200,000 - \$500,000 - \$150,000}$$

$$= 218 \text{ percent.}$$

Therefore, a 100 percent increase in sales from 200 units to 400 units will cause *EPS* to increase by 218 percent, or by a

---

[7] Equation 10–2 is developed as follows:

1. Recognize that $EBIT = Q(P - V) - F$ and rewrite Equation 10–1 as:

$$\frac{EBIT}{EBIT - I} = \frac{Q(P - V) - F}{Q(P - V) - F - I}. \tag{10–1a}$$

2. The total leverage effect is equal to the degree of operating leverage times the degree of financial leverage, or Equation 4–1 times Equation 10–1a:

$$\text{Combined leverage effect} = \text{Equation 4–1} \times \text{Equation 10–1a}$$

$$= \frac{Q(P - V)}{\cancel{Q(P - V) - F}} \cdot \frac{\cancel{Q(P - V) - F}}{Q(P - V) - F - I}$$

$$= \frac{Q(P - V)}{Q(P - V) - F - I}. \tag{10–2}$$

factor of 3.18:

$$EPS_{(400 \text{ units})} = EPS_{(200 \text{ units})} \times 3.18$$
$$= \$1.10 \times 3.18 = \$3.50.$$

These figures must, of course, agree with those worked out in Table 10–4.

The usefulness of the degree of leverage concept lies in the facts that (1) it enables us to specify the precise effect of a change in sales volume on earnings available to common stock and (2) it permits us to show the inter-relationship between operating and financial leverage. The concept can be used to show a businessman, for example, that a decision to automate and to finance new equipment with bonds will result in a situation wherein a 10 percent decline in sales will produce a 50 percent decline in earnings, while a different operating and financial leverage package will be such that a 10 percent sales decline will cause earnings to decline by only 20 percent. In our experience, having the alternatives stated in this manner gives the decision-maker a better idea of the ramifications of his actions.[8]

Usefulness

As might be expected, wide variations in the use of financial leverage may be observed among industries and among the individual firms in each industry. Illustrative of these differences is the range of ratios of debt to total assets, shown on page 209 in Table 10–5, for certain broad groups of industries. Service industries use the most leverage, reflecting (1) that services include certain financial institutions that typically have high liabilities and (2) that there are many smaller firms in the service industries, and small firms as a group are heavy users of debt. Public utility use of debt stems from a heavy fixed asset investment, coupled with extremely stable sales. Mining and manufacturing firms use relatively little debt because of their exposure to fluctuating sales.

VARIATIONS IN FINANCIAL STRUCTURE

Within the broad category "manufacturing," wide variations are observed for individual industries. Table 10–6 presents an array of total-debt-to-total-assets ratios for selected manufacturing industries. The lowest ratios are found among textile companies, in which competitive pressures continue to be great. Low debt ratios are also found among the durable goods industries. The highest debt ratios are found in consumer nondurable goods, where demand is relatively insensitive to fluctuations and general business activity.

[8] The concept is also useful for investors. If firms in an industry are classified as to their degrees of total leverage, an investor who is optimistic about prospects for the industry might favor those with high leverage, and vice-versa if he expects industry sales to decline.

Even within a given industry there are wide variations in the use
of financial leverage, as illustrated for the electric utility industry in
Table 10–7. These variations reflect a number of different considerations, including the volatility of business in the companies' operating
areas, the extent to which they use preferred stock, and their managements' willingness to assume risk. Montana Power, for example, sells
a large proportion of its electricity to copper producers, whose volume
of business, hence demand for power, is quite cyclical. This largely
explains its low debt ratio. Missouri Public Service, by contrast, has
a stable demand pattern, which permits its relatively high leverage
factor.

TABLE 10–6
*Total-debt-to-assets
ratios for selected
manufacturing
industries (1965)*

Manufacturing industries	Percent
Fabrics: Cotton, silk, wool, synthetic	27
Household furniture except upholstered	32
Automotive parts and accessories	35
Flour and other grain mill products	35
Iron and steel forgings	35
Iron and steel foundries	39
Drugs and medicines	40
Machine tools and metalworking equipment	40
Canned and dried fruits and vegetables	41
Industrial chemicals	42
Electronic components and accessories	42
Precision instruments	44
Books	45
Bread and other bakery products	46
Ready mixed concrete	47
Sporting and athletic goods	48
Meat packing	49
Dairy products	53
Veneer and plywood	55
Distilled liquor, wines, and liqueurs	59

Source: Annual Statement Studies (Philadelphia: Robert Morris
Association, 1966).

TABLE 10–7
*Debt-to-total-assets
ratio (Selected
electric utility
companies, 1966)*

Montana Power	46
Consolidated Edison of New York	55
Central Illinois Public Service	59
Detroit Edison	60
Tampa Electric	65
Missouri Public Service	66

Source: Moody's Public Utility Manual, 1967.

Thus far the discussion has touched on the factors that are generally considered when a firm formulates basic policies relating to its financial structure. The more important of these capital structure determinants are now listed and briefly discussed.

FACTORS INFLUENCING FINANCIAL STRUCTURE

1. Growth rate of future sales

2. Stability of future sales

3. Competitive structure of the industry

4. Asset structure of the firm

5. Control position and attitudes toward risk of owners and management

6. Lenders' attitudes toward the firm and industry

The future growth rate of sales is a measure of the extent to which the earnings per share of a firm are likely to be magnified by leverage. If sales and earnings grow at an 8-to-10 percent rate a year, for example, financing by debt with limited fixed charges should magnify the returns to owners of the stock.[9] This can be seen from Figure 10–2 on page 208.

Growth Rate of Sales

However, the common stock of a firm whose sales and earnings are growing at a favorable rate commands a high price; thus, it sometimes appears that equity financing is desirable. The firm must weigh the benefits of using leverage against the opportunity of broadening its equity base when it chooses between future financing alternatives. Such firms may be expected to have a moderate-to-high rate of debt financing.

Sales stability and debt ratios are directly related. With greater stability in sales and earnings, a firm can incur the fixed charges of debt with less risk than it can when its sales and earnings are subject to periodic declines; in the latter instance it will have difficulty in meeting its obligations. The stability of the utility industry, combined with relatively favorable growth prospects, has resulted in high leverage ratios in that industry.

Sales Stability

Debt servicing ability is dependent upon the profitability as well as the volume of sales. Hence, the stability of profit margins is as important as the stability of sales. The ease with which new firms may enter the industry and the ability of competing firms to expand capacity will influence profit margins. A growth industry promises higher profit margins, but such margins are likely to narrow if the industry is one in which the number of firms can be easily increased through addi-

Competitive Structure

---

[9] Such a growth rate is also often associated with a high profit rate.

tional entry.] For example, pleasure-boat manufacturing and neighborhood bowling alleys were highly profitable industries in the later 1950s, but it was relatively easy for new firms to enter these industries and go into competition with the older firms. As these industries matured during the early 1960s, the capacity of the old and the new firms grew at an increased rate. As a consequence, profit margins declined.

Other firms in other industries are better able to resist competitive pressures. For example, to duplicate the unique technical, service, and distribution facilities of the International Business Machines Corporation would be very difficult, a fact suggesting that profit margins for this firm are less subject to erosion.

Asset Structure   Asset structure influences the sources of financing in several ways. Firms with long-lived fixed assets, especially when demand for their output is relatively assured—for example, utilities—use long-term mortgage debt extensively. Firms whose assets are mostly receivables and inventory whose value is dependent on the continued profitability of the individual firm—for example, those in wholesale and retail trade—rely less on long-term debt financing and more on short term.

Management   The management attitudes that most directly influence the choice of
Attitudes   financing are those concerning (1) control of the enterprise and (2) risk. Large corporations whose stock is widely owned may choose additional sales of common stock because they will have little influence on the control of the company. Also, because management represents a stewardship for the owners, it is often less willing to take the risk of heavy fixed charges.[10]

In contrast, the owners of small firms may prefer to avoid issuing common stock in order to be assured of continued control. Because they generally have confidence in the prospects of their companies

[10] It would be inappropriate to delve too far into motivational theory in an introductory finance textbook, but it is interesting to note that the managers of many larger, publicly owned corporations have a relatively small ownership position and derive most of their income from salaries. Some writers assert that in such cases managements do not strive for profits, especially if this effort involves using leverage with its inherent risk. Presumably, these managers feel that the risks of leverage for them, the ones who actually decide to use debt or equity, outweigh the potential gains from successful leverage. If sales are low, there is a chance of failure and the loss of their jobs, whereas if sales and profits are high, it is the stockholders, not management, who receive the benefits. Another way of looking at the situation is to say that most stockholders are more diversified than most managers—if the firm fails, a stockholder only loses that percentage of his net worth invested in the firm, but the manager loses 100 percent of his job. While there is undoubtedly some merit to this argument, it should be pointed out that companies are increasingly using profit-based compensation schemes—bonus systems and stock-option plans—to motivate management to seek profitability, and low leverage companies are subject to take-over bids. (See Chapter 21.)

and because they can see the large potential gains to themselves resulting from leverage, managers of such firms are often willing to incur high debt ratios.

The converse can, of course, also hold—the owner-manager of a small firm may be *more* conservative than the manager of a large company. If the net worth of the small firm is, say, $1 million, and if it all belongs to the owner-manager, he may well decide that he is already pretty well off and elect not to risk using leverage in an effort to become still more wealthy.

Regardless of managements' analysis of the proper leverage factors *Lender Attitudes* for their firms, there is no question but that lenders' attitudes are frequently an important—sometimes the most important—determinant of financial structures. In the majority of cases, the corporation discusses its capital structure with lenders and gives much weight to their advice. But when management is so confident of the future that it seeks to use leverage beyond norms for the industry, lenders may be unwilling to accept such debt increases. They will emphasize that excessive debt reduces the credit standing of the borrower and the credit rating of the securities previously issued. The lenders' point of view has been expressed by a borrower, a financial vice-president, who stated, "Our policy is to determine how much debt we can carry and still maintain an AA bond rating, then use that amount less a small margin for safety."[11]

On the basis of the foregoing considerations, broad guidelines or refer- **GUIDELINES** ence levels for the financial structures of wide industrial segments **FOR** are presented in Table 10–8. *In examining these figures, keep in mind* **FINANCIAL** *all that has been said about the importance of carefully appraising the* **STRUCTURES** *individual situation and the dangers of relying on industry norms.* The guidelines do, however, have a rational basis, and it would be wise to evaluate critically the reasons behind any given company's decision to step outside the reference boundaries.

Chapter 3 described how financial data summarized by industry aver- **USE OF** ages can be used to evaluate the financial ratios for individual firms **FINANCIAL** in these industries. Such industry composites can also be used to **RATIO** provide a basis for formulating the financial plan of an individual **COMPOSITES IN** firm. Financial structures so developed conform to general industry **DETERMINING** practice. While simply conforming to the structure of other firms in **THE** a particular line of business is not necessarily desirable, such a stan- **FINANCIAL** **PLAN**

---

[11] Bond ratings, which are discussed in detail in Chapter 19, are basically indices of the risk that lenders incur when buying particular bonds. A rating of AAA is the best, denoting the lowest risk, and AA is just below it.

dard can be a useful starting point. This is especially true if the capital structure of a new enterprise is being planned; here the use of such guidelines can be helpful in suggesting what the financial requirements are likely to be.[12]

	Percentage of total assets					
	Current liabilities	Long-term debt	Preferred stock	Common equity or net worth	Current ratio	Times interest earned
Large, established firms						
Manufacturing	20–25%	15–20%	0–4%	55–65%	2X	8X
Utilities	5–10	45–50	10–15	30–35	1	4
Trade	30–35	16–18	0–2	50–55	2.5	7
Small, rapidly growing, profit- able firms						
Manufacturing	40–45%	0–5%	0–10%	40–60%	1X	9X
Trade	50–60	0–5	0–5	30–40	1.5	10

Developing a *pro forma* balance sheet,[13] based on the average of financial ratios of firms in a given line of business, is the first step. To use the method of financial ratio composites to construct the *pro forma* financial plan, it is necessary to know only two things: (1) the industry of the firm and (2) its size, measured by estimated annual sales. An illustration of the technique is given for an industrial machinery firm with estimated annual sales of $120,000. The Dun & Bradstreet median financial ratio composites for that industry for the most recent year are:

Sales to net worth	3 times
Current debt to net worth	40%
Total debt to net worth	60%
Current ratio	3 times
Net sales to inventory	4 times
Average collection period	42 days
Fixed assets to net worth	40%

[12] Provisions must also be made for organization expenses and various start-up costs, such as losses incurred. The losses incurred may result from relatively heavy fixed costs that will cause losses until sale volume grows to the point where initial fixed capacity is effectively utilized.

[13] A *pro forma* financial statement is one that is *projected.* It is an estimate of how a future statement will appear.

On the basis of this information, the following *pro forma* balance sheet can be constructed:

Cash	$ 4,000		Current debt	$16,000	
Accounts receivable	14,000		Long-term debt	8,000	
Inventory	30,000		Total debt	24,000	
Current assets		$48,000	Net worth	40,000	
Fixed assets		16,000			
			Total liabilities		
Total assets		$64,000	and net worth	$64,000	

Pro forma balance sheet

Here are the calculations:

1. Net worth = sales ÷ net worth turnover

$$\frac{\$120,000}{3} = \$40,000$$

2. Total debt = 60% of net worth

$$\$40,000 \times 60\% = \$24,000$$

3. Current debt = 40% of net worth

$$\$40,000 \times 40\% = \$16,000$$

4. Long-term debt = total debt — current debt

$$\$24,000 - \$16,000 = \$8,000$$

5. Total claims on assets = net worth + total debt

$$\$40,000 + \$24,000 = \$64,000$$

6. Current assets = current debt × current ratio

$$\$16,000 \times 3 = \$48,000$$

7. Inventory = sales ÷ inventory turnover

$$\frac{\$120,000}{4} = \$30,000$$

8. Accounts receivable = average collection period × sales per day

$$\frac{\$120,000}{360} \times \frac{42}{1} = \$14,000$$

9. Cash = current assets — (receivables + inventory)

$$\$48,000 - (\$14,000 + \$30,000) = \$4,000$$

10. Fixed assets = net worth × 40%

$$\$40,000 \times 40\% = \$16,000$$

11. Total assets = current assets + fixed assets

$$\$48,000 + \$16,000 = \$64,000.$$

Profitability and income statement relations can also be developed by reference to industry data, with the data being based on any of the wide variety of sources of financial ratio compilations described in Chapter 3. Alternatively, a financial manager may develop his own guidelines by constructing averages based on a selected number of firms most similar (in his judgment) to his own business—for example, firms of comparable age and size operating in his same geographic market area.

The use of financial ratio composites as a guideline to financial structures may be questioned on theoretical grounds. Because these composites are computed averages, some firms must be above the average and some below. But it is of interest to know on which side of the average an individual firm stands. Further, a strong practical consideration reinforces the value of such comparisons—bank lending officers and other credit and financial analysts place heavy reliance on such comparisons between individual firms and industry norms. Thus the financial structure of the firm will, in practice, be checked against industry data.

Of course, neither financial managers nor lenders need be held in a strait jacket by an industry average. *The average is primarily a standard for reference, and many factors may cause an individual firm to depart from the industry pattern.* For example, it has already been noted that age, size, growth rate, control position of owners, and management attitudes toward risk may all strongly influence the financial policies of a firm.

Financial structures suggested by industry practices actually represent only a starting point. Sound reasons may exist to cause an individual firm's financial structure to depart from the reference levels provided by industry data. But it is important that the financial manager understand the reasons for these differences and be able to explain them effectively to potential creditors. Sometimes the differences may represent elements of strength or the almost unavoidable growing pains of a rapidly developing company. However, departures from industry norms may also signal weaknesses requiring correction.

SUMMARY Financial leverage, which means using debt to boost rates of return on net worth over the returns available on assets, is the primary topic covered in this chapter. Whenever the return on assets exceeds the cost of debt, leverage is favorable and the return on equity is raised by using it. However, leverage is a two-edged sword, and if the returns on assets are less than the cost of debt, then leverage reduces the returns on equity. This reduction is greater the more leverage a firm employs. As a net result, leverage may be used to boost stockholder returns, but using it is done at the risk of increasing losses if the firm's economic fortunes decline.

Financial leverage is similar to operating leverage, a concept discussed in Chapter 4. As was true for operating leverage, financial leverage can be defined rigorously and measured in terms of the *degree of financial leverage*. In addition, the effects of financial and operating leverage may be combined, with the combined leverage factor showing the percentage changes in earnings per share that will result from a given percentage change in sales.

Financial structure, defined as the method of financing a firm's assets, represents another way of looking at the leverage question. In part, financial structures are determined by management. But firms are constrained by the amount of debt lenders are willing to advance, and this willingness is partially conditioned by the characteristics of the industry and by the financial structures of other firms in the industry. For this reason, the factors causing capital structures to differ among industries are analyzed.

In the following two chapters the concepts developed to this point in the book will be extended to the formal theory of the cost of capital and the theory of security valuation. The way investors appraise the relative desirability of increased returns versus higher risks is seen to be a most important consideration, one that, in general, invalidates the theory that firms should strive for maximum earnings per share regardless of the risks involved.

10–1 How will each of the following be changed by the occurrences listed **QUESTIONS** below: financial structure, capital structure, and net worth?

a) The firm has retained earnings of $100 for the year.

b) A preferred stock issue is refinanced with bonds.

c) Bonds are sold for cash.

d) The firm repurchases 10 percent of its outstanding common stock with excess cash.

e) An issue of convertible bonds is converted.

10–2 From an economic and social standpoint, is the use of financial leverage justifiable? Explain by listing some advantages and disadvantages.

10–3 Financial leverage and operating leverage are similar in one very important respect. What is this similarity and why is it important?

10–4 What are some reasons for variations of debt ratios among the firms in a given industry?

10–5   Why is the following statement true? "Other things being the same, firms with relatively stable sales are able to incur relatively high debt ratios."

10–6   Why do public utility companies usually pursue a different financial policy from that of trade firms?

10–7   The use of financial ratios and industry averages in the financial planning and analysis of a firm should be approached with caution. Why?

10–8   Some economists believe that the swings in the business cycles have not been as wide in recent years as they have been in the past. Assuming that they are correct in their analysis, what effect can this added stability have on the types of financing used by firms in the United States? Would your answer be true for all firms?

PROBLEMS   **10–1**   One useful test or guide for evaluating a firm's financial structure in relation to its industry is by comparison with financial ratio composites for its industry. A new firm or one contemplating entering a new industry may use such industry composites as a guide to what its financial position is likely to approximate after the initial settling-down period.

The following data represent the ratios for the furniture manufacturing industry for 1971:

Estimated annual sales	$1,200,000
Sales to net worth	4 times
Current debt to net worth	50%
Total debt to net worth	80%
Current ratio	2.2 times
Net sales to inventory	8 times
Average collection period	40 days
Fixed assets to net worth	70%

Ayres Furniture Designs
Pro forma
balance sheet
December 31, 1971

Cash	$_____	Current debt	$_____
Accounts receivable	_____	Long-term debt	_____
Inventory	_____	Total debt	_____
Current assets	_____	Net worth	_____
Fixed assets	_____	Total liabilities	
Total assets	$_____	and net worth	$_____

a) Complete the above *pro forma* balance sheet. (Round to nearest thousands.)
b) What does the use of the financial ratio composites accomplish?
c) What other factors will influence the financial structure of the firm?

10–2   In early 1971, the Gusher Company was planning to raise $300 million additional funds to finance growth. About the same time the Streamer Company was planning to raise $100 million for the same purpose. From data given below, which firm should sell 4.5 percent debentures and which should sell common stock? (In your answer, *do not* try to determine the effects of stock or bond financing on earnings per share. Rather, look at such things as debt ratios, interest costs, and so on, and make a subjective evaluation of the situation.)

Gusher and Streamer
Oil Companies
Balance sheets
In millions of dollars

	Gusher	Streamer
Current assets	$3,000	$ 650
Investments	400	100
Net fixed assets	4,600	1,750
Total assets	$8,000	$2,500
Current liabilities	$1,400	$ 300
Long-term debt	1,600	200
Total debt	$3,000	$ 500
Common stock outstanding		
Gusher (200 million shares), $10 par	$2,000	
Streamer (40 million shares), $25 par		$1,000
Surplus (earned and paid in)	3,000	1,000
Net worth	$5,000	$2,000
Total claims	$8,000	$2,500

Sales (in billions of dollars)		
1962	5.4	1.7
1963	5.6	1.7
1964	5.8	1.8
1965	6.4	1.9
1966	7.1	2.0

Net income (in millions of dollars)	Gusher	Streamer
1962	540	136
1963	560	136
1964	580	144
1965	640	152
1966	700	152

Gusher and Streamer Oil Companies
Income statements for
period ended June 30, 1970
In millions of dollars

	Gusher	Streamer
Sales	$7,100	$2,000
Total costs	6,128	1,820
Net income before taxes	$ 972	$ 180
Interest on debt (4.5% for Gusher, 4% for Streamer)	72	8
	$ 900	$ 172
Federal income taxes	200	20
Net income after taxes	$ 700	$ 152

	Gusher	Streamer
Sales to total assets	0.89	0.80
Earnings per share	$3.50	$3.80
Dividends per share	1.85	1.25
Price/earnings ratio*	20×	15×
Market price	$ 70	$ 57

*The price/earnings ratio is the market price per share divided by earnings per share. It represents the amount of money an investor is willing to pay for $1 of current earnings. The higher the riskiness of a stock, the lower its P/E ratio. The concept of price-earnings ratios is discussed at some length in Chapter 11.

10–3 The Beaumont Company plans to expand assets by 50 percent; to finance the expansion, it is choosing between a straight 6 percent debt issue and common stock. Its current balance sheet and income statement are shown below.

Beaumont Company
Balance sheet
December 31, 1971

		Debt, 5%	$ 40,000
		Common stock, $10 par	100,000
		Earned surplus (ℓ𝓈)	60,000
Total assets	$200,000	Total claims	$200,000

Beaumont Company
Income statement
for year ended
December 31, 1971

Sales	$600,000
Total costs (excluding interest)	538,000
Net income before taxes	$ 62,000
Debt interest	2,000
Income before taxes	$ 60,000
Taxes at 50%	30,000
Net income	$ 30,000

Earnings per share: $\dfrac{30,000}{10,000} = \$3$

Market price: $12 \times 3 = \$36$

If the Beaumont Company finances the $100,000 expansion with debt, the rate on the incremental debt will be 6 percent and the price/earnings ratio of the common stock will be 10 times.* If the expansion is financed by equity, the new stock can be sold at $33⅓, the rate on debt will be 5 percent, and the price/earnings ratio of all the outstanding common stock will remain at 12 times earnings.

a) Assuming that net income before interest on debt and before taxes is 10 percent of sales, calculate earnings per share at sales assumptions of $0, $50,000, $200,000, $280,000, $400,000, $600,000, $800,000 and $1,000,000, when financing is with common stock in contrast to debt. Assume no fixed costs.
b) Make a break-even chart for the earnings under *a*.
c) Using the price/earnings ratio indicated, calculate the market value per share of common stock for each sales level for both the debt and the equity methods of financing.
d) Make a break-even chart of market value per share for the company with data found in *c*.
e) If the firm follows the policy of seeking to maximize the market price of its stock, which form of financing should be employed?
f) What other factors should be taken into account in choosing between the two forms of financing?
g) Would it matter if the presently outstanding stock was all owned by Mr. Beaumont and that this represented his entire net worth? Would it matter if the final decision maker, the president, was compensated entirely by a fixed salary? that he had a substantial number of stock options?

* The price/earnings ratio is the market price per share divided by earnings per share. It represents the amount of money an investor is willing to pay for $1 of current earnings. The higher the riskiness of a stock, the lower its P/E ratio. The concept of price/earnings ratios is discussed at some length in Chapter 11.

Valuation and Rates of Return

*I*N the discussion of capital budgeting in Chapters 8 and 9, it was seen that the discount rate used in the calculations is of vital importance. Relatively small changes in the discount rate produce significant changes in computed net present values and sometimes cause a reversal in the decision to accept or to reject a particular project. In the discussion of capital budgeting, it was *assumed* that the cost of capital—the discount rate used in the present value process—was known, and this rate was used in the calculations. We did indicate in both Chapters 8 and 9, however, that the cost of capital was related (1) to the firm's riskiness and (2) to the amount of funds raised during a given period. Then, in Chapter 10, we showed how risk is magnified through the use of financial leverage. Now we devote specific attention to the problem of deriving the cost of capital for individual firms.

Since the cost of capital to the firm is integrally connected with investors' returns on capital, the basic principles underlying valuation theory are discussed in the present chapter. The following chapter, building on valuation theory, considers the costs of various types of capital and shows how they may be combined to produce the firm's over-all cost of capital.

DEFINITIONS OF VALUE

While it may be difficult to ascribe monetary returns to certain types of assets—works of art, for instance—the fundamental characteristic of business assets is that they give rise to income flows. Sometimes this flow is easy to determine and measure—the interest return on a bond is an example. At other times, the cash flows attributable to the asset must be estimated, as was done in Chapter 8 in the evaluation of projects. Regardless of the difficulties of measuring income flows, it is the prospective income from assets that gives them value.

Liquidating versus Going Concern Value

Several different definitions of "value" exist in the literature and are used in practice, with different ones being appropriate at different times. The first distinction that must be made is that between *liquidating value* and *going concern value*. Liquidating value is defined as the amount that could be realized if an asset or a group of assets (the entire assets of a firm, for example) are sold separately from the organization that has been using them. If the owner of a machine shop decides to retire, he might auction off his inventory and equipment, collect his accounts receivable, then sell his land and buildings to a grocery wholesaler for use as a warehouse. The sum of the proceeds from each category of assets that he receives would be the liquidating value of the assets. If his debts are subtracted from this amount, the difference would represent the liquidating value of his ownership in the business.

On the other hand, if the firm is sold as an operating business to a corporation or another individual, the purchaser would pay an amount equal to the going concern value of the company. If the going concern value exceeds the liquidating value, the difference represents the value of the organization as distinct from the value of the assets.[1]

Book Value versus Market Value

Another distinction must be made between *book value,* or the accounting value at which an asset is carried, and *market value,* the price at which the asset can be sold. If the asset in question is a firm, it actually has two market values—a liquidating value and a going concern value. Only the higher of the two is generally referred to as *the* market value.

Market Value versus Intrinsic Value

The distinction between *intrinsic value* and *market value* has been stated clearly and succinctly by Graham, Dodd, and Cottle:

A general definition of intrinsic value would be "that value which is justified by the facts, e.g., assets, earnings, dividends, definite prospects, including the factor of management." The primary objective in using the adjective "intrinsic" is to emphasize the distinction between *value* and *current market price,* but not to invest this "value" with an aura of permanence. In truth, the computed intrinsic value is likely to change at least from year to year, as the various factors governing that value are modified. But in most cases intrinsic value changes less rapidly and drastically than market price, and the investor usually has an opportunity to profit from any wide discrepancy between the current price and the intrinsic value as determined at the same time.[2]

Although Graham, Dodd, and Cottle develop this concept for security (that is, stocks and bonds) valuation, the idea is applicable to all business assets. What it involves, basically, is estimating the future net cash flows attributable to an asset; determining an appropriate capitalization, or discount rate; and then finding the present value of the cash flows. This, of course, is exactly what was done in Chapters

---

[1] Accountants have termed this difference "goodwill," but "organization value" would be a more appropriate description.

[2] B. Graham, D. L. Dodd, and S. Cottle, *Security Analysis* (New York, McGraw-Hill, Inc., 1961), p. 28.

7, 8, and 9, where the concept of intrinsic value was developed for application in finding the present value of investment opportunities.

The procedure for determining an asset's intrinsic value is known as the *capitalization-of-income method of valuation.* This is simply a fancy name for an old friend, the present value of a stream of earnings, discussed at length in Chapter 7. The following example illustrates the technique for valuing a bond. Following this, the method is illustrated with preferred and common stocks. From this point on, whenever the word "value" is used, we mean the intrinsic value found by capitalizing future cash flows. Further, for purposes of exposition, we shall assume that the current market prices of stocks or bonds are equal to their intrinsic values. This assumption is relaxed in future chapters, where we see that *differences* between management estimates of intrinsic values and market prices have a significant bearing on the type of security—stock or bond—used to raise funds at a given time.

CAPITALIZA-TION OF INCOME

Bond values are relatively easy to determine. As long as the bond is not expected to go into default, the expected cash flows are the annual interest payments plus the principal amount to be paid when the bond matures. Capitalization rates applied to bonds differ among bonds depending primarily upon differences in risk of default on interest or principal. A U.S. Treasury security, for example, would have less risk than one issued by the Westbrig Corporation; consequently, a lower discount (or capitalization) rate would be applied to its interest payments. The actual calculating procedures employed in bond valuation are illustrated by the following examples.

Bond Valuation

After the Napoleonic Wars (1814), England sold a huge bond issue which was used to pay off many smaller issues that had been floated in prior years to pay for the war. Since the purpose of the new issue was to consolidate past debts, the individual bonds were called Consols. Suppose the bonds had a par value of $1,000 (actually, they were stated in pounds) and paid $50 interest annually into perpetuity. What would the bonds be worth under current market conditions?

Example 1

First, note that the value (V) of any perpetuity[3] is computed as follows:[4]

$$V = \frac{\text{constant annual receipts}}{\text{capitalization rate}} = \frac{R}{i}. \tag{11-1}$$

[3] A perpetuity is a bond that never matures; it pays interest indefinitely.

[4] The proof of this equation is given in *Managerial Finance,* third edition. See note 2, p. 313.

We know that the Consol's annual interest payment is $50; therefore, the only other thing we need in order to find its value is the appropriate capitalization rate. This is commonly taken as the going interest rate, or yield, on bonds of similar risk. Suppose we find such bonds to be paying 4 percent under current market conditions. Then the Consol's value is determined as:

$$V = \frac{R}{i} = \frac{\$50}{0.04} = \$1,250.$$

If the going rate of interest rises to 5 percent, the value of the bond falls to $1,000 ($50/0.05 = 1,000). If interest rates continue rising, when the rate goes as high as 6 percent the value of the Consol will be only $833.33. Values of this perpetual bond at a range of interest rates are given in the following tabulation.

Current market interest rate	Current market value
0.02	$2,500.00
0.03	1,666.67
0.04	1,250.00
0.05	1,000.00
0.06	833.33
0.07	714.29
0.08	625.00

Example 2 Now suppose the British government issues bonds with the same risk of default as the Consols, but with a three-year maturity. The new bonds also pay $50 interest and have a $1,000 par value. What will be the value of these new bonds at the time of issue if the going rate of interest is 4 percent? The solution requires the calculations given in the following tabulation.[5]

Year	Receipt	4 percent discount factors	Present value
1	$50	0.962	$ 48.10
2	$50	0.925	46.25
3	$50 + $1,000	0.889	933.45
		Bond value	$1,027.80

[5] If the bond has a longer maturity, 20 years for example, we would certainly want to calculate its present value by finding the present value of a 20-year annuity and then adding to that the present value of the $1,000 principal amount received at maturity. Special bond tables have been devised to simplify the calculation procedure.

At the various rates of interest used in the preceding example, this three-year bond would have the following values.

Interest rate	Capital value
0.02	$1,086.15
0.03	1,056.45
0.04	1,027.80
0.05	1,000.00
0.06	973.65
0.07	947.20
0.08	922.85

Figure 11–1 shows how the values of the long-term bond (the Consol) and the short-term bond change in response to changes in the going market rate of interest. Note how much less sensitive the short-term bond is to changes in interest rates. At a going rate of interest equal to 5 percent, both the perpetuity and the short-term bond are valued at $1,000. When rates fall to 2 percent, the long-term bond rises to $2,500, while the short-term security goes to only $1,086. A similar situation occurs when rates rise above 5 percent. *This differential responsiveness to changes in interest rates always holds true—the longer the maturity of a security, the greater its price change in response to a given change in capitalization rates.* Thus, even if the risk of default on two bonds is exactly the same, the value of the one with the longer maturity is exposed to more risk from a rise in interest rates. This greater risk explains why short-term bonds usually have lower yields, or rates of return, than long-term bonds. It also explains why corporate treasurers are reluctant to hold their near-cash reserves in the form of long-term debt instruments—these near-cash reserves are held for precautionary purposes, and a treasurer would be unwilling to sacrifice safety for a little higher yield on a long-term bond.

Preferred Stock Valuation

Most preferred stocks entitle their owners to regular, fixed dividend payments similar to bond interest. Although some preferred issues are retired, most are perpetuities whose value is found as follows:

$$V = \frac{R}{i}.$$

In this case, R is simply the dividend on the preferred stock. For example, General Motors has a preferred stock outstanding that pays

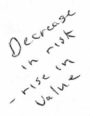

Decrease in risk → rise in value

a \$3.75 annual dividend. The appropriate capitalization rate at the time the stock was issued (1925) was 7.5 percent, so it sold at \$50 at the time of issue. Today, however, GM is a much stronger company, and its preferred stock is much less risky. So, in spite of a rise in interest rates and preferred yields generally, the net result is that the yield on GM's preferred issue has fallen to 6.8 percent, and the value of the stock has climbed to \$55 a share.

$$V = \frac{\$3.75}{.068} = \$55.$$

FIGURE 11–1
Values of long-term and short-term bonds at different interest rates

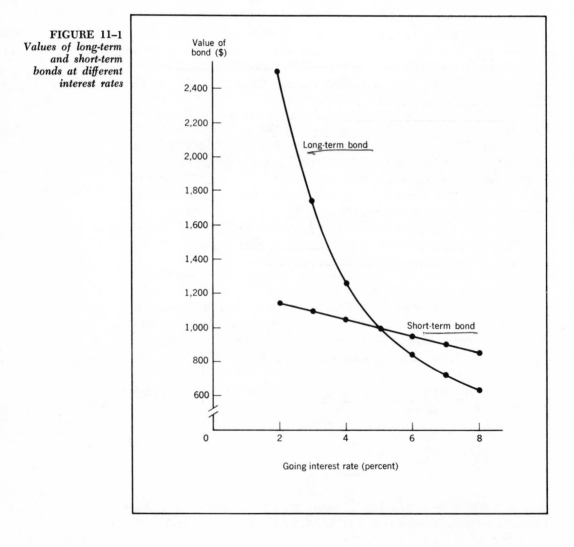

While the same principles apply to the valuation of common stocks *Common Stock* as to bonds or preferred stocks, two features make their analysis much *Valuation*[6] more difficult. First is the degree of certainty with which receipts can be forecast. For bonds and preferred stocks, this forecast presents very little difficulty, as the interest payments or preferred dividends are known with relative certainty. But in the case of common stocks, the forecasting of future earnings, dividends, and stock prices is exceedingly difficult, to say the least. The second complicating feature is that, unlike interest and preferred dividends, common stock earnings and dividends are generally expected to grow, not remain constant. Hence, standard annuity formulas cannot be applied, and more difficult conceptual schemes must be used.

The investment value of a share of common stock depends upon the dollar returns an investor will receive if he buys the stock. Now what are the returns? They are, of course, the dividends the investor receives while he holds the stock plus the price he receives when he sells it; the ending price is equal to the beginning price plus capital gains or minus capital losses.

To illustrate, suppose you are thinking of buying a share of American Rubber common stock. If you buy the stock, you plan to hold it for one year. The current market price is $40 a share. You note that American Rubber is earning $3.60 a share and paying $2 a year in dividends and that earnings, dividends, and the price of the company's stock have been rising at about 4 percent a year over the past 10 to 15 years.

Using this information and the investment evaluation techniques described in Chapters 7 and 8, you could calculate the expected rate of return, k, on American Rubber's stock as follows:

$$\text{Present price} = \frac{\text{dividend}}{(1+k)} + \frac{\text{price in 1 year}}{(1+k)}$$

$$= \frac{\text{dividend}}{(1+k)} + \frac{\text{present price} \times (1+\text{growth rate})}{(1+k)}$$

$$\$40 = \frac{\$2.00}{(1+k)} + \frac{\$40(1.04)}{(1+k)}$$

$$= \frac{\$2.00}{(1+k)} + \frac{\$41.60}{(1+k)} = \frac{\$43.60}{(1+k)}$$

$$1 + k = \frac{\$43.60}{\$40.00} = 1.090$$

$$k = 1.090 - 1.00 = 0.090, \text{ or } 9\%.$$

[6] The concepts involved in the theory of common stock valuation are, unfortunately, relatively difficult. Only the basic elements are covered in this text, but for a more detailed treatment see *Managerial Finance*, third edition, Chapter 10.

Let us examine the steps here and the assumptions involved. First, note that the first equation sets up the purchase of the share of stock as an investment (1) with a cost equal to the present price and (2) with returns equal to the dividend plus the ending price one year from now. The second equation shows that the ending price is equal to the present price plus the 4 percent expected price increase. The remainder of the equations simply substitute in the appropriate values and solve the basic equation for k, the rate of return on the stock, which turns out to be 9 percent.

The expected rate of return, k, can be split into two components, one from capital gains and one from dividends. This is done below:

$$\text{Dividend yield} = \frac{\text{dividend}}{\text{current price}} = \frac{\$2}{\$40} = 0.05, \text{ or } 5\%.$$

$$\text{Capital gains yield} = \frac{\text{price increase}}{\text{current price}} = \frac{\$1.60}{\$40.00} = 0.04, \text{ or } 4\%.$$

In this instance, the expected dividend yield turns out to be 5 percent, and the capital gains yield, 4 percent. The total expected return is equal to the dividend yield plus the capital gains yield:

$$\text{Total return} = \text{dividend yield} + \text{capital gains yield}$$

$$= \frac{\text{expected dividend}}{\text{current price}} + \frac{\text{expected increase in price}}{\text{current price}}.$$

Dividends are abbreviated to D, the current price to P, and the second term in the equation—the increase in price divided by the current price, or the growth rate—to g. The following fundamental equation is thus produced:

$$k = \text{rate of return} = \frac{D}{P} + g. \tag{11-2}$$

To repeat, the rate of return on a share of common stock is equal to its dividend yield plus the expected growth in the price of the stock, or the capital gains yield.[7]

Two critical assumptions are involved in the calculations: (1) that the dividend will be paid and (2) that the stock price will continue to grow at a 4 percent rate.[8] For a stable, solid company like American

---

[7] Strictly speaking, this equation holds only if the growth rate is expected to remain constant in the future.

[8] We are only using a one-year holding period. In the general case, where the holding period is of any length, the equation is still used, but another assumption must be added: namely, the dividend must grow at the same rate as the stock price. Again, for a stable company such as American Rubber this is a good assumption—dividends and stock prices *do* move more or less together.

Rubber the dividend assumption is probably a good one, but the growth assumption will almost surely not hold exactly. Depending on a great many factors—but most importantly the performance of the entire stock market—the ending price will probably turn out to be more or less than $41.60. And, depending on whether the final price is higher or lower than the one forecast, the rate of return will turn out to be more or less than anticipated. If, for example, the stock market soars and American Rubber goes up to $50 a share, the $10 capital gain plus the $2 dividend will provide a 30 percent rate of return. If, however, the market slumps badly and American Rubber falls to $30, the return will be *minus* 20 percent.

One other point should be observed in connection with these calculations for American Rubber. Notice that the company is expected to earn $3.60 a share and to pay out $2 in dividends. This means that $1.60 will be retained. Suppose the company reinvests these retained earnings in projects that yield 9 percent. Future earnings will increase by $0.14 ($1.60 × 0.09). Capitalized at 9 percent, the additional earnings add $1.60 to the value of the stock ($0.14/0.09). This $1.60 is exactly equal to the expected capital gain found above. The company *has* been retaining about 45 percent of its earnings, and it *has* been earning about 9 percent on new equity. The fact that earnings have been retained and reinvested in profitable projects explains why American Rubber has enjoyed a record of rising stock prices.

This exposition has been based on only a one-year holding period, but it can be expanded to any holding period with exactly the same results. The procedures are much more complicated, however, and go beyond the scope of this book.[9]

Price-earnings Ratios

Security analysts and investors have long used the price/earnings (P/E) ratio when comparing stocks. For example, American Rubber sells for $40 and earns $3.60 per share, so its P/E ratio is 11.1 times—investors are willing to pay $11.10 for every dollar of earnings.

P/E ratios vary considerably among companies; in 1970, while American Rubber was selling for 11.1 times earnings, Computer Corporation of America had a P/E ratio as high as 40, while Bolivian Metals had a ratio of only 5.2. These differences are, of course, caused by differences in *expectations* about the companies' futures. American Rubber's earnings have been growing at about 4 percent per year,

[9] While most authorities would agree with our beliefs that stock prices are determined by such fundamentals as earnings, dividends, and rates of return on retained earnings, some argue that securities, especially common stocks, are valued by an essentially irrational process which involves psychology, stockbroker recommendations, and several other factors. Such essentially random phenomena do have a profound influence on short-run price movements. Nevertheless, we argue that the long-run value of a stock is determined by investors capitalizing expected future returns.

while those of Computer Corporation have been climbing at about a 15 percent rate. Bolivian Metals, on the other hand, has experienced a *decline* in earnings, and investors are worried that the firm's Latin American properties will be expropriated.

We should also note that *there is not necessarily any relationship between a firm's P/E ratio and k, the rate at which investors capitalize the firm's expected dividend stream.* The differences noted in the P/E ratios of American Rubber, Computer Corporation, and Bolivian Metals could have resulted from different growth expectations, in which case the k values of the firms could all be *identical,* or from differences in investors' feelings about risk, in which case the k values would *not be identical.* In the present illustration, for example, our own studies suggest that Bolivian Metals has a low P/E ratio partly because its expected growth rate is low and partly because investors consider it to be a much riskier company than either of the other two.[10]

We next look at the factors that cause differentials in the expected rates of returns among securities; then we examine historical patterns of returns on stocks and bonds.

FACTORS LEADING TO VARIATIONS IN RETURNS AMONG SECURITIES

Risk and Rates of Return

The most important factor leading to differential expected rates of return among different securities is differences in risk. Here *risk* is defined as uncertainty about the return that will actually be realized. For example, if the asset in question is a 60-day Treasury bill, the expected return can be estimated quite accurately—there is little risk of not realizing in full the promised yield. If the security is a corporate bond, there is always some danger that the firm will default; thus, there is some uncertainty about the final return.

Uncertainty is greater yet when we move to common stocks. Dividends are not always predictable, and the capital gains component is quite uncertain. Within common stocks, different companies' stocks are more uncertain than others. Such well-established firms as AT & T, General Motors, and du Pont have long histories of earnings, dividends, and management performance. On the other hand, there is more uncertainty in the case of new companies and those developing new and essentially untried products—in these cases, risk is high relative to the AT & T's, GM's, and other blue chips.

Would you expect returns to be higher or lower on risky invest-

[10] Relationships between P/E ratios, growth rates, and capitalization rates (k) are discussed in some detail in Brigham and Pappas, "Duration of Growth, Changes in Growth Rates, and Corporate Share Prices," in *Readings in Managerial Finance.* There it is shown that a change in k can cause a change in the price of a firm's stock, and that this change in P results in a changed P/E ratio. But a changing P/E ratio can also be the result of changing growth expectations, so it is not generally correct to associate either relative P/E ratios among firms, or changing P/E ratios over time for a given firm, with investor capitalization rates. Such an association is valid *only* if growth is held constant.

ments? Although some individuals are gamblers by nature and seem to prefer more to less risk, investors as a group dislike risk, or are "risk averters." Given risk aversion, securities with higher risk must sell on the basis of higher expected yields. For example, a 9 percent expected return might be acceptable for American Rubber's stock, but a more stable and predictable electric utility common stock might sell on an 8 percent return basis. On the other hand, investors might be unwilling to buy stock in a wildcat oil drilling concern unless they can expect to make 50 percent. This is, of course, an informal application of the risk-adjusted discount rate concept discussed in Chapter 9.

For a given firm, its bonds are less risky to investors than its common stocks, so expected yields are higher on stocks than on bonds. Risks on preferred stocks lie between those on bonds and common stocks, so returns on these securities should fall in the middle.

One might also observe that different degrees of risk are incurred by individual firms within particular industries. If, for example, one firm has a strong research and development (R & D) program, excellent management training programs, and broad geographic and product diversification, while another has none of these features, the first will be regarded as less risky than the second and will sell on a lower yield basis. If small firms, because of less product or geographic diversification, lower R & D expenditures, more serious management succession problems, or any other reasons, are considered to be more risky than large firms, investors will require a higher rate of return on small firms' securities.

Marketability and Rates of Return

Investors also value flexibility, or maneuverability. If one becomes disenchanted with a particular investment, or if he needs funds for consumption or other investments, it is highly desirable for him to be able to liquidate his holdings. Other things the same, the higher the liquidity, or marketability, the lower an investment's required rate of return. Accordingly, one would expect to find listed stocks selling on a lower yield basis than over-the-counter stocks, and widely traded stocks selling at lower yields than stocks with no established market. Since investments in small firms are generally less liquid than those in large companies, we have another reason for expecting to find higher required yields among smaller companies.

Changes in Stock Price Levels

Equity yields differ among firms because of differences in inherent risks and marketability, but they also differ for an individual stock over time. If the demand for funds is relatively heavy and, at the same time, the supply is restricted, the law of supply and demand requires that the price of funds—the interest rate on debt or the required rate of return on equity—be higher than when supply and demand conditions are reversed. In the late 1940s, for example, many corporations were expanding and seeking equity funds to finance this expansion, while many investors were expecting a serious postwar depression and were not interested in purchasing stocks. The result was a very high required rate of return on equity issues and low common stock prices.

As it became clear that the booming economy was not headed for a depression, investors began shifting funds from the bond market to equity markets. Simultaneously, productive capacity began to catch up with demand, lowering corporate demands for funds. The net result was a pronounced decline in required rates of return and a much higher level of stock prices. These changes are illustrated in Figure 11–2.

FIGURE 11–2
Hypothetical supply and demand for equity securities

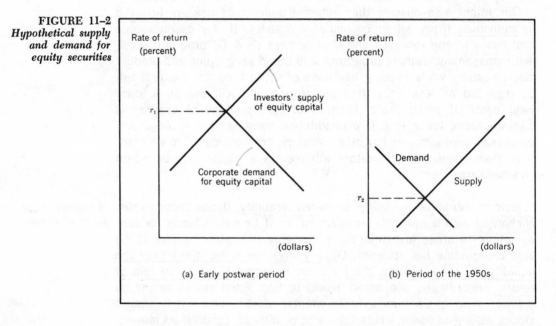

(a) Early postwar period   (b) Period of the 1950s

Stock prices change for either of two reasons—changes in required rates of return or changes in growth expectations. For example, the 1949–1968 increase in stock prices may have been caused by either declining required equity yields, higher growth expectations, or a combination of the two.

This idea can be illustrated by reference to American Rubber. Recall that when the stock is selling for $40, is paying a $2 dividend, and is expected to grow at about 4 percent during the next year, the expected rate of return is calculated to be 9 percent.

Now suppose supply and demand conditions in the capital markets

Example

change so that the equilibrium rate of return—the point where supply equals demand—on American Rubber's stock declines to 8 percent. Assuming that dividend and growth expectations remain constant, this decline in the capitalization rate causes the current price to jump from $40 to $50. The reasons are explained below. First, note that the current price is determined as

$$\text{Current price or value} = \frac{\text{dividend}}{1 + \text{capitalization rate}}$$

$$+ \frac{\text{current price} \times (1 + \text{growth rate})}{1 + \text{capitalization rate}}.$$

Substituting in the known quantities—the $2 dividend, the 8 percent capitalization rate, and the 4 percent growth rate—we find the current price of the stock as follows:

$$\text{Current price} = P = \frac{\$2.00}{1.08} + \frac{P(1.04)}{1.08}$$

$$= \frac{\$2.00 + 1.04P}{1.08}$$

$$1.08P = \$2.00 + 1.04P$$

$$1.08P - 1.04P = \$2.00$$

$$0.04P = \$2.00$$

$$P = \frac{\$2.00}{0.04} = \$50 \text{ a share.}$$

Therefore, if the average investor expects American Rubber to pay a $2 dividend and to experience a 4 percent stock price appreciation from the reinvestment of retained earnings, and if he is to receive an 8 percent return on his investment, then the initial investment—the current price—must be $50.[11]

A change in growth expectations could produce a similar change.

---

[11] For those interested in generalized formulas, one applicable to a perpetual growth situation is

$$P = \frac{D}{k - g},$$

where P = current price, D = current dividend, k = required rate of return, and g = the growth rate.

$$P = \frac{\$2.00}{0.08 - 0.04} = \frac{\$2.00}{0.04} = \$50 \text{ in the example.}$$

This equation is proved in *Managerial Finance*, third edition, pp. 334 and 404–409.

With the capitalization rate 9 percent and the growth rate 4 percent, the current price is $40. Now suppose the company announces a new development that leads investors to expect a higher rate of growth—say 5 percent a year. Substituting this new growth rate into the price equation and solving for the current price, we find a new price of $50 per share.

$$\text{Current price} = \frac{\$2.00}{1.09} + \frac{\text{current price } (1.05)}{1.09} = \$50.$$

For American Rubber, then, we see that a sharp stock price increase (or decrease) can arise from changes in market capitalization rates or growth expectations, or from a combination of the two. These ideas can be generalized for the stock market as a whole, and they can be used to explain changes in the level of stock prices.

Historical Rates Various financial researchers investigating returns on publicly-owned
of Return stocks over long periods have found them to average about 9 percent.
Equity Yields When measured from stock market lows, returns are relatively high; conversely, when the market is high in the base period, stockholder yields are relatively low. For example, had one bought a portfolio of stocks at the average price prevailing in the depressed year 1949 and held them until 1965, his return would have been about 15 percent. The same group of stocks, bought during the high market in 1961, would have yielded a little over 6 percent by 1965.

Some rough averages of estimated stock yields under different market conditions are shown in Table 11–1. To the extent (1) that the future approximates the past and (2) that investors base expected future returns on those realized in the past, the figures in the table should give some idea of stockholders' required rates of return under different market, risk, and liquidity conditions.[12]

Debt Yields Debt yields, or rates of return, also vary over time and with the characteristics of the individual loan. Many different statistics could be presented to support this assertion, but Table 11–2 illustrates it sufficiently. The year 1958 was a period of monetary ease, 1962 was "normal" in the sense that neither serious inflation nor deflation was present, and 1969 was a period of inflation and extremely tight money.

[12] We should note, however, that the Table 11–1 figures are based on a period when interest rates were lower than they are today. Because of the interrelationship between bond interest rates and stock prices, it may be necessary to raise the Table 11–1 figures by about 2 percentage points unless bond yields fall back to their earlier levels.

A glance down any of the columns will show how bank interest rates varied among periods.

Company Characteristics	Stock market condition		
	High	Normal	Low
Low risk, high marketability	6 ½	7	9 ½
Average risk and marketability	7–8	8–10	12–15
High risk, low marketability	9	12	20

TABLE 11–1
Estimated rates of return on common stocks

Variations across the rows of the table are somewhat more difficult to explain. In part, interest rates on loans decline as the size of the loan increases because of the fixed costs of making and servicing loans. In addition, part of the decline occurs because small firms borrow small amounts, and small firms are generally more risky than large ones. At any rate, it is clear that returns on debt, like those on stock, vary over time and with the characteristics of the borrower.

	Size of loan (in thousands of dollars)			
	1–10	10–100	100–200	200 and over
1958	5.5%	5.0%	4.6%	4.1%
1962	5.9	5.5	5.2	4.8
1969	9.4	9.2	9.0	8.7

Source: *Federal Reserve Bulletin.*

TABLE 11–2
Bank rates on business loans

The concepts of valuation and rates of return on debt and equity securities developed in this chapter are fundamentally related to the cost of capital concept. This is the subject of the following chapter.

In the discussion of the capital budgeting process in Chapter 8, the discount rate used in the calculations was seen to be of vital importance. At that time, we simply assumed that the cost of capital— the discount rate used in the present value process—was known, and we used this assumed rate in the calculations. In this chapter, however, we turned our attention to the theory of the cost of capital.

Since the cost of capital is integrally related to investors' returns on capital, the basic principles underlying valuation theory were discussed and a number of definitions of value were presented: (1) liq-

SUMMARY

uidating versus going concern value, (2) book versus market value, and (3) market versus "intrinsic" value. This last concept, intrinsic value, is fundamentally dependent upon discounted cash flow concepts and procedures; it involves estimating future cash flows and discounting them back to the present at an appropriate rate of interest. This rate of interest, defined as the "required rate of return," is a function of the investment's risk and the investor's opportunity costs.

Rates of return on bonds and preferred stocks are simple to understand and to calculate, but common stock returns are more difficult. First, common stock returns consist of (1) dividends and (2) capital gains, not a single type of payment as occurs with bonds and preferred stocks. This fact necessitates the development of a rate of return formula that considers both dividends and capital gains; the rate of return formula for common stock is, therefore, a two-part equation:

$$\text{Rate of return} = \text{dividend yield} + \text{capital gains yield.}$$

The second complicating feature of common stock is the degree of uncertainty involved. Bond and preferred stock payments are relatively predictable, but forecasting common stock dividends and, even more, capital gains, is a highly uncertain business.

Note also that risk is of two types: (1) a basic business risk having to do with the nature of the industry and the extent to which operating leverage is employed and (2) a financial risk dependent upon the extent to which financial leverage is employed. A firm that manufactures producers' durables—for example, railroad locomotives—is inherently more risky than an electric utility or chain of grocery stores. However, firms can and do alter their basic risks by using more or less financial leverage. As a result, a firm in a relatively stable industry may, because of excessive financial leverage, end up in a more risky position than one in an unstable industry.

As investors generally dislike risk, the required rate of return is higher on more risky securities. Bonds, as a class, are less risky than preferred stocks, and preferred stocks, in turn, are less risky than common stocks. As a result, the required rate of return is lowest for bonds, next for preferred stocks, and highest for common stocks. Within each of these security classes, there are variations among the issuing firms' risks and, hence, required rates of return vary among firms. Also, supply and demand conditions in the capital markets change over time, so a given firm's securities will have different required rates of return at different points in time.

QUESTIONS   **11–1**   Most inheritance tax laws state that for estate tax purposes, property shall be valued on the basis of "fair market value." Describe how an inheritance tax appraiser might use the valuation principles discussed in this chapter to establish the value (1) of shares of a stock listed on the New York Stock Exchange and (2) of shares representing 20 percent of a stock that is not publicly traded.

11–2 How does the level of interest rates influence stock and bond prices?

11–3 Using the theoretical concepts developed in this chapter and certain preceding ones, develop an argument to support the frequently encountered statement that a rising level of interest rates depresses the stock market. (It is true that higher interest rates tend to deflate the economy, hence corporate profits and stock prices, but this is not the desired answer to this question.)

11–4 Explain why bonds with longer maturities experience wider price movements from a given change in interest rates than do shorter maturity bonds. Preferably give your answer (1) in words (intuitively) and (2) mathematically.

11–5 Describe the factors that determine the market rate of return on a particular stock at a given point in time.

11–6 Table 11–1 gives some estimates of rates of return on common stocks. Using this or similar tables, would you expect ten "experts" to reach the same conclusion about expected market yields on a given firm's common stock? Why or why not?

11–1 a) The Spalding Company is earning $6 million a year after taxes. Its **PROBLEMS** common stock has a $10 par value; 3 million shares are authorized; and 2 million shares are outstanding. What are the company's earnings per share?
b) Common stocks of electronic companies in the same risk class as Spalding sell to yield 5 percent on earnings. What would be the expected price of Spalding's stock? Why? (Note: Earnings yield is the earnings/price ratio.)
c) At what price/earnings ratio does Spalding common sell?
d) If Spalding common sold on an 8 percent earnings yield basis, what would be its price? its price/earnings ratio?
e) Spalding pays a yearly dividend of $2 a share. If Spalding sells to yield 5 percent on earnings, what is the dividend yield basis on which it sells? (Note: Dividend yield is dividend/price.)

11–2 a) The bonds of the National Corporation are perpetuities bearing a 7 percent coupon and rated AAA. Bonds of this type yield 6 percent. What is the price of National's bonds? Their par value is $1,000.
b) Interest rate levels rise to the point where such bonds now yield 9 percent. What will be the price of the National bonds now?
c) Interest rate levels drop to 7 percent. At what price will the National bonds sell?
d) How would your answer to parts *a*, *b*, and *c* change if the bonds had a definite maturity date of 20 years?

11–3 Mike Dunn contemplates the purchase of a small electronic firm. Expected sales of the company are $4 million a year. For this line of business, firms earn 6 percent on sales after taxes.
  Dunn feels that his money should earn a 20 percent return on investment in an area as risky as electronics. What is the largest amount he would pay for the electronics firm?

11–4 Because of ill health and old age Robert McKenzie contemplates the sale of his hardware store. His corporation has the following balance sheet:

Assets		Liabilities and net worth	
Cash	$ 8,000	Notes payable—bank	$ 3,500
Receivables, net	3,000	Accounts payable	5,000
Inventories	19,000	Accruals	1,500
Fixtures and equipment less $10,000 reserve for depreciation	20,000	Common stock plus surplus	40,000
Total assets	$50,000	Total liabilities and net worth	$50,000

Annual before-tax earnings (after rent, interest, and salaries) for the preceding three years have averaged $12,000.

McKenzie has set a price of $60,000, which includes all the assets of the business except cash; the buyer assumes all debts. The assets include a five-year lease and the goodwill associated with the name of McKenzie Hardware. Assume both McKenzie and the potential purchaser are in the 50 percent tax bracket.

a) Is the price of $60,000 a reasonable one? Explain?
b) What other factors should be taken into account in arriving at a selling price?
c) What is the significance, if any, of the lease?

11–5 The Doyle Company is a small machine-tool manufacturer. It has been successful and has grown. Doyle is planning to sell an issue of common stock to the public for the first time. It faces the problem of setting an appropriate price on its common stock. The company feels that the proper procedure is to select firms similar to Doyle with publicly traded common stock and to make relevant comparisons.

The company finds several machine-tool manufacturers similar to it with respect to product mix, size, asset composition, and debt/equity proportions. Of these, Western and Olympic are most similar.

Relation	Western	Olympic	Doyle totals
Earnings per share, 1971	$ 3.00	$ 5.00	$ 800,000
Average, 1965–1971	2.00	4.00	600,000
Price per share, 1971	24.00	50.00	—
Dividends per share, 1971	1.50	2.50	400,000
Average, 1965–1971	1.20	2.50	300,000
Book value per share	20.00	50.00	6,000,000
Market-book ratio	120%	100%	—

a) How would these relations be used in guiding Doyle in arriving at a market value for its stock?
b) What price would you recommend if Doyle sells 200,000 shares?

*I*N the preceding chapter, the nature of the valuation process and the concept of expected rates of return were considered in some detail. In the discussion of the cost of capital, the subject of this chapter, extensive use will be made of these valuation concepts. First, the costs of the individual components of the capital structure—debt, preferred stock, and equity—are considered; because investors perceive different classes of securities to have different degrees of risk, there are variations in the costs of different types of securities. Second, the individual component costs are brought together to form a weighted cost of capital. Third, the conceptual ideas developed in the first two sections are illustrated with an example of the cost of capital calculation for an actual company. Finally, the interrelationship between the cost of capital and the investment opportunity schedule is developed, and the simultaneous determination of the marginal cost of capital and the marginal return on investment is discussed.

DEBT CAPITAL

If a firm borrows $100,000 for one year at 6 percent interest, its before-tax dollar cost is $6,000, and its before-tax percentage cost is 6 percent. *As a first approximation, the cost of debt is defined as the rate of return that must be earned on debt-financed investments in order to keep unchanged the earnings available to common shareholders.*[1] Hence, the cost of debt turns out to be the interest rate on debt, for if the firm borrows and invests the borrowed funds to earn a before-tax return just equal to the interest rate, then the earnings available to common stock remain unchanged. This is demonstrated below.

---

[1] Note that this definition is a *first approximation;* it will be modified to take account of the deductibility of interest payments for income tax purposes. Note also that here the cost of debt is considered in isolation. The impact of the debt on the cost of equity, as well as on future increments of debt (in a sense, the true marginal cost of debt), will be treated when the weighted cost of a combination of debt and equity is derived.

Example The ABC Company has sales of $1 million, operating costs of $900,000, and no debt, and it is taxed at the rate of 50 percent. Its income statement is shown in the Before column below. Then it borrows $100,000 at 6 percent and invests the funds in assets whose use causes sales to rise by $7,000 and operating costs to rise by $1,000. Hence, profits before interest rise by $6,000. The new situation is shown in the After column. Earnings after taxes are unchanged, as the investment just earns its cost of capital.

	Income statements	
	Before	After
Sales	$1,000,000	$1,007,000
Operating costs	900,000	901,000
Earnings before interest and taxes ($EBIT$)	$ 100,000	$ 106,000
Interest (I)	—	6,000
Earnings before taxes (EBT)	$ 100,000	$ 100,000
Taxes (T)	50,000	50,000
Earnings after taxes (EAT)	$ 50,000	$ 50,000

Note that the cost of debt is applicable to *new* debt, not to the interest on old, previously outstanding debt. In other words, we are interested in the cost of new debt, or the *marginal* cost of debt. The primary concern with the cost of capital is to use it in a decision-making process—the decision whether to obtain capital to make new investments; the fact that the firm borrowed at high or low rates in the past is irrelevant.[2]

PREFERRED STOCK Preferred stock, described in detail in Chapter 19, is a hybrid between debt and common stock. Like debt, preferred stock carries a fixed commitment on the part of the corporation to make periodic payments; in liquidation, the claims of the preferred stockholders take precedence over those of the common stockholders. Unlike debt, however, failure to make the preferred dividend payments does not result in bankruptcy. Preferred stock is thus somewhat more risky *to the firm* than common stock, but it is less risky than bonds. Just the reverse holds

[2] The fact that the firm borrowed at high or low rates in the past is, of course, important in terms of the effect of the interest charges on current profits, but this past decision is not relevant for *current* decisions. For current financial decisions, only current interest rates are relevant.

for investors. To the investor, preferred is less risky than common but more risky than debt.

The definition of the cost of preferred stock is similar to that of the cost of debt—it is that rate of return that must be earned on preferred stock-financed investments in order to keep unchanged the earnings available to common shareholders. This required rate of return turns out to be the preferred dividend per share (D_p) divided by the net price that the firm could realize from the sale of one share of a new issue of preferred stock (P_n).

$$\text{Cost of preferred stock} = \frac{D_p}{P_n}.$$

For example, if a firm sells an issue of $100 par value preferred stock with a $6 dividend and nets $95 a share after underwriting commissions, then its cost of preferred stock is 6.3 percent ($6/$95).

As they stand, the definitions of the cost of debt and preferred stock **TAX** capital are incompatible because, for tax purposes, interest payments **ADJUSTMENT** are deductible and preferred dividends are not. The following example is an illustration.

The ABC Company can borrow $100,000 at 6 percent, or it can sell *Example* 1,000 shares of $6 preferred stock to net $100 a share. Its before-investment situation is given in the Before column below. At what rate of return must it invest the proceeds from the new financing to keep the earnings available to common shareholders from changing?

		Invest in assets yielding		
		6%		12%
	Before	Debt	Preferred	Preferred
EBIT	$100,000	$106,000	$106,000	$112,000
I	—	6,000	—	—
EBT	100,000	100,000	106,000	112,000
T (50%)	50,000	50,000	53,000	56,000
Preferred dividends	—	—	6,000	6,000
Available for common dividends	$ 50,000	$ 50,000	$ 47,000	$ 50,000

As can be seen from the tabulations, if the funds are invested to yield 6 percent before taxes, earnings available to common stockholders are constant if debt is used, but they fall if the financing is with preferred stock. To maintain the $50,000 net earnings requires that funds generated from the sale of preferred stock be invested to yield 12 percent before taxes or 6 percent after taxes.

Cost-of-capital calculations may be made either on a before-tax or an after-tax basis. Ultimately, however, business decision-makers must consider after-tax effects. Therefore, just as in Chapter 10 in the discussion of the rates of return on investments, only the cost of capital *after* corporate taxes will be dealt with. The cost of preferred stock is already on an after-tax basis as defined, but a simple adjustment is needed to arrive at the after-tax cost of debt. It is recognized that interest payments are tax deductible—the higher the firm's interest payments, the lower its tax bill. In effect, the federal government pays part of a firm's interest charges. Therefore, the cost of debt capital is reduced as follows:

After-tax cost of debt = (before-tax cost) $\times$ (1.0 − tax rate).

Example   Before-tax cost of debt = 6 percent; tax rate = 48 percent.
After-tax cost = (0.06) (1 − 0.48) = (0.06)(0.52) = 3.12 percent.

Had the tax rate been 50 percent, as is usually assumed for ease of calculations, the after-tax cost of debt would have been one-half the interest rate. Also, we should note that for a firm with losses the tax rate is zero. Therefore, for a loss corporation the cost of debt is not reduced; that is, in the equation "tax rate" equals zero, so the after-tax cost of debt is equal to the before-tax cost (the interest rate).

COST OF EQUITY[3]   *The cost of equity capital is defined as the minimum rate of return that must be earned on equity-financed investments to keep unchanged the value of the existing common equity.* In other words, if 10 percent is a corporation's cost of equity capital, then the value of the equity used to finance an investment will exceed its cost if—and only if—the internal rate of return on the investment exceeds 10 percent. This is an opportunity cost concept. If investors can find investments of similar risk outside the firm that yield at least 10 percent—that is, if their opportunity cost of funds tied up in the business is 10 percent—then they do not want the firm to invest equity capital to yield less than 10 percent.

In general, there is a different cost of capital applicable to equity capital raised by retaining earnings than to that raised by selling new common stock. These points are covered below.

---

[3] "Equity" is defined here to *exclude* preferred stock. Equity, or net worth, is the sum of capital stock, capital surplus, and earned surplus (the accumulated retained earnings).

The cost of retained earnings, or the return that must be earned on **Retained Earnings[4]**
investments financed by retained earnings, is equal to the rate of return
that investors expect to receive on the stock. To illustrate, consider
Aubey Rents, a firm currently earning $2 a share, paying a $1 dividend, and selling at $20 a share. The company's earnings, dividends,
and stock price have all been growing at about 5 percent a year;
this growth rate is expected to continue indefinitely. Using this information and the procedures developed in Chapter 11, we compute the
expected rate of return on the stock as follows:

$$\text{Expected, or required, rate of return} = \frac{\text{dividend}}{\text{price}} + \text{expected growth}$$

$$k = \frac{\$1}{\$20} + 5\% = 10\%.$$

The expected growth rate in the price of the shares is 5 percent; on
the $20 initial price, this leads to a $1 increase in the value of the
stock. This price increase will be attained (barring changes in the
general level of stock prices) if the company retains $1 and invests
this amount to yield 10 percent. However, if the $1 of retained earn-
ings is invested to yield only 5 percent, then earnings will grow by
only $0.05 during the year, not by the expected $0.10 a share. The
new earnings will be $2.05, not the expected $2.10. This represents
a growth of only 2½ percent, not 5 percent. If investors believe that
the firm will earn only 5 percent on retained earnings in the future
and thus attain only a 2½ percent growth rate, they will reappraise
the value of the stock downward as follows:

$$\text{Current price} = \frac{\text{dividend}}{(1 + k)} + \frac{\text{current price} \times (1 + \text{expected growth})}{(1 + k)}$$

$$P = \frac{\$1.00}{1.10} + \frac{P \times (1.025)}{1.10}$$

$$P = \frac{\$1.00 + 1.025P}{1.10}$$

$$1.10P = \$1.00 + 1.025P$$

$$1.100P - 1.025P = \$1.00$$

$$0.075P = \$1.00$$

$$P = \$13.33.$$

[4] Our treatment of the cost of retained earnings abstracts from certain complications
caused by personal income taxes on dividend income and by brokerage costs incurred in
reinvesting dividend income. Similarly, we do not explicitly treat the cost of depreciation-
generated funds in the chapter. These topics are, however, discussed at length in *Managerial Finance*, third edition, Appendix to Chapter 11.

Note, however, that Aubey Rents suffered this price decline *because it invested equity funds—retained earnings—at less than its cost of capital.* Had it refrained from making this investment and paid all its earnings out in dividends, it would have cut its growth rate to zero. However, the price of the stock would not have fallen because investors would still have been getting the required 10 percent rate of return on their investments:

$$k = \frac{D}{P} + g = \frac{\$2}{\$20} + 0 = 10 \text{ percent.}$$

All the return would have been coming in the form of dividends, but the actual rate of return would have matched the required 10 percent.

New Common Stock   The cost of new common stock, or *external* equity capital, k_e, is higher than the cost of retained earnings, k, because of the flotation costs involved in selling new common stock. To demonstrate, let us continue with the example of Aubey Rents. The company has 10,000 shares of stock outstanding, no debt, and is expected to earn $20,000, or $2 a share during the coming year. Investors anticipate that the company will continue its policy of paying out 50 percent of earnings as dividends, so $1 is the dividend expectation for the coming year. The firm has also been growing at 5 percent a year, and this growth rate is expected to be maintained. Investors require a 10 percent rate of return on the stock, so it is selling for $20 a share.

Now suppose Aubey Rents sells 5,000 shares of stock to the public at $20 a share, incurs a selling cost of $2 a share, and thus nets $18 a share, or a total of $90,000. If this $90,000 is invested to yield 10 percent, will the earnings, dividend, and price expectations be met? First, we calculate the new earnings per share, giving effect to the stock sale and to the new investment.

$$\text{Incremental profits} = \$90,000 \times 0.10 = \$9,000$$
$$\text{Total profits} = \$20,000 + \$9,000 = \$29,000$$
$$\text{Incremental shares} = 5,000$$
$$\text{Total shares} = 10,000 + 5,000 = 15,000$$
$$\text{New earnings per share} = \frac{\$29,000}{15,000} = \$1.93.$$

The $1.93 is below the expected $2 a share. The sale of the new shares has diluted earnings, and the price of the stock will fall below $20 a share. Thus, the investment has not met the definition of the cost of capital—the return on the investment financed by new stock did not

earn the cost of capital because the incremental profits were not sufficient to keep the price of the stock from falling.

What rate of return must be earned on funds raised by selling stock
to make this action worthwhile, or, to put it another way, what is the
cost of new common stock? The answer is found by applying the following formula:

$$k_e = \frac{\text{required rate of return on common stock}}{1 - \text{percentage cost of floating new common stock}}.$$

In our example, the flotation cost on new equity issues (F) is 10 percent ($2/$20) and the required rate of return (k) is 10 percent, so
applying the formula we find the cost of new common stock (k_e) to be
11.1 percent:

$$k_e = \frac{k}{1.0 - F} = \frac{.10}{1.0 - 0.10} = \frac{.10}{0.9} = 11.1\%.$$

If Aubey earns 11.1 percent on investments financed by new common
stock issues, earnings per share will not fall below previous expectations, the price of the stock will not fall, and the investments will
have covered their cost of capital.

It is obvious by now that the basic rate of return required by investors
on a firm's common stock, k, is a most important quantity. This required rate of return is the cost of retained earnings, and, used with
the cost of floating common stock, it forms the basis for the cost
of capital obtained from new stock issues. How is this all-important
quantity estimated? *Finding the Basic Required Rate of Return on Common Stock*

Although one *can* use very involved, highly complicated procedures
for making this estimation, satisfactory estimates may, in general,
be obtained in either of two ways.

(1) Simply look at the average rate of return that investors have
obtained in the past, assume that in the future stocks will continue
to have about the same rates of return as in the past, and use these
historical averages as estimates of the current cost of equity capital.

For this, we recommend the figures given in Table 11–1 in the preceding chapter. To use the table for this purpose, one must first make
judgment decisions (a) about the risk/liquidity position of the stock
in question and (b) about the state of the stock market. Suppose,
for example, we decide that our particular company is of about average
risk and liquidity and that the stock market is about normal—the
market is not, in our judgment, either abnormally high or abnormally
low. In this case we would simply assign 9 percent as the basic cost
of equity capital. Later on, if the market dropped sharply, we might

re-evaluate the cost of equity upward to 10 or, perhaps, to 12 or even 15 percent.

Notice that some very fine judgments are required in this process. It would be nice to pretend that these judgments are unnecessary and to specify a precise way of determining the exact cost of equity capital. Unfortunately, this is not possible. Finance is in large part a matter of judgment, and one simply must face this fact.

(2.) An alternative procedure, the use of which is recommended in conjunction with the one described above, is to estimate the basic required rate of return as

$$\text{Rate of return} = \frac{\text{dividends}}{\text{price}} + \text{average growth rate}$$

$$k = \frac{D}{P} + g.$$

The rationale for this equation, which was discussed in Chapter 11, is that stockholder returns are derived from dividends and capital gains. The total of the dividend yield plus the average growth rate over the past 5 to 10 years gives an estimate of the total returns that stockholders probably expect in the future from a particular share of stock.

For normal companies—those that are growing at a rate approximately equal to that of the entire economy—the two procedures generally give similar results. If recent growth has been extremely high, so high that it is doubtful the rate can be maintained, then the first procedure is the better one.

WEIGHTED COST OF CAPITAL Suppose a particular firm's after-tax cost of debt is estimated to be 2½ percent (the interest rate on new debt issues is 5 percent), its cost of equity is estimated to be 10 percent, and the decision has been made to finance next year's projects by selling debt. The argument is frequently advanced that the cost of these projects is 2½ percent because debt will be used to finance them.

This position contains a basic fallacy. To finance a particular set of projects with debt implies that the firm is also using up some of its potential for obtaining new low-cost debt. As expansion takes place in subsequent years, at some point the firm will find it necessary to use additional equity financing or else the debt ratio will become too large.

To illustrate this point, suppose the firm has a 2½ percent cost of debt and a 10 percent cost of equity. In the first year it borrows heavily, using up its debt capacity in the process, to finance projects yielding 3 percent. In the second year it has projects available that yield 9 percent, three times the return on first-year projects, but it cannot accept them because they would have to be financed with 10 percent equity money. To avoid this problem, the firm should be viewed as an on-going concern and its cost of capital should be calculated as a weighted average of the various types of funds it uses: debt, preferred stock, and equity.

Before discussing the proper set of weights to be employed in com- *Calculating* puting the weighted average, it is useful to look briefly at the calculat- *Procedure* ing procedure. The method is demonstrated in the following example.

The right-hand-side of the Simple Company's balance sheet is shown *Example* in column 2 of Table 12–1, and the dollars are converted to percentages of the total in column 3. The firm wants to expand assets by 10 percent, or $10 million, during the coming year, and it wishes to keep its capital structure constant, with 30 percent debt, 5 percent preferred stock, and 65 percent equity. This means that the $10 million of new capital must be raised in the manner shown in column 4: $3 million debt, $500,000 preferred, and $6.5 million equity. Only if it finances in this manner can it maintain the existing capital structure proportions. Column 5 gives the after-tax component costs of the different types of capital: debt, preferred stock, and equity. Column 6 shows the product of columns 3 and 5. Summing column 5 gives the weighted average cost of the firm's capital—0.0775, or 7.75 percent.

An alternative method that gives identical results is to multiply the dollar figures in column 4 by the component costs in column 5 to get the figures in column 7, then add column 7 and divide the sum by the total amount of capital raised. Thus, the $775,000 total dollar cost divided by the $10 million of new capital is 7.75 percent. We use whichever method provides the easiest calculations for the specific application.

Although financial theorists and corporate financial managers disagree *Weighting System* over particular aspects of debt policy, there is general agreement that firms do seek optimum capital structures. "Optimum" is defined as the capital structure that minimizes the weighted cost of capital, and the concept is now illustrated. To avoid unnecessary confusion, it is assumed that firms have no preferred stock.

Figure 12–1 shows, for a hypothetical industry, how the cost of debt, the cost of equity, and the average cost of capital might vary as the debt ratio increases. (The average cost of capital figures are calculated in Table 12–2.) In the figure each dot represents one of the firms in the industry. For example, the dots labeled "1" represent firm 1, a company with no debt. Since it is financed entirely with 12 percent equity money, firm 1's average cost of capital is 12 percent. Firm 2 uses 10 percent debt and has a 3 percent cost of debt and

TABLE 12–1 *Simple Company*

Capital components (1)	Balance sheet figures (2)	Percent of totals (3)	New funds raised (4)	Component cost (after taxes) (5)	Column 3 times column 5 (6)	Column 4 times column 5 (7)
Debt	$ 30,000,000	30%	$ 3,000,000	3%	0.0090	$ 90,000
Preferred stock	5,000,000	5%	500,000	7%	0.0035	35,000
Net worth	65,000,000	65%	6,500,000	10%	0.0650	650,000
Total	$100,000,000	100%	$10,000,000		0.0775 or 7.75%	$775,000

a 12 percent cost of equity, and Firm 3 uses 20 percent debt and also has a 3 percent cost of debt and 12 percent cost of equity. Firm 4 has a 14 percent cost of equity and a 4 percent cost of debt. It uses 35 percent debt, and investors feel that, because of the added risk of financial leverage, at this high debt level they should obtain higher yields on the firm's securities. In this particular industry, the threshold debt ratio that begins to worry investors is 20 percent. Below 20 percent debt, investors are totally unconcerned about any risk induced by debt; above 20 percent, they are aware of the higher risk and require compensation in the form of higher rates of return.

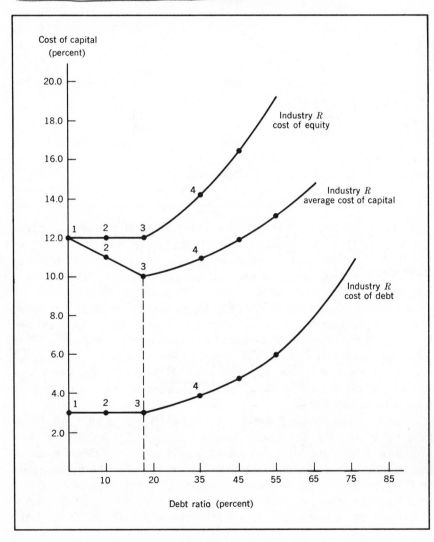

FIGURE 12–1
Hypothetical cost of capital schedules for an industry

TABLE 12–2
*Calculation of
average cost of
capital for
hypothetical firms
with different debt
ratios*

		Percent of total (1)	Component cost (2)	Col. (1) × Col. (2) ÷ 100* (3)
Firm 1				
	Debt	0	3.0	0
	Equity	100	12.0	12.0
		100%	average cost	12.0%
Firm 2				
	Debt	10	3.0	.3
	Equity	90	12.0	10.8
		100%	average cost	11.1%
Firm 3				
	Debt	20	3.0	.6
	Equity	80	12.0	9.6
		100%	average cost	10.2%
Firm 4				
	Debt	35	4.0	1.4
	Equity	65	14.0	9.1
		100%	average cost	10.5%

* We divide by 100 to put figures on a percentage basis.

In Table 12–2 the debt and the equity costs of the various firms are averaged on the basis of their respective weights of debt and equity capital. Firm 1 has a weighted average cost equal to 12 percent, firm 2 has a weighted average cost of 11.1 percent, firm 3 has a weighted cost of 10.2 percent, and firm 4 has a weighted cost of 10.5 percent. These weighted costs, together with those of the other firms in the industry, are also plotted in Figure 12–1. We can see that firm 3 has the lowest weighted cost of capital—*20 percent debt is the debt ratio that minimizes the average cost of capital, so the optimal capital structure requires that firms use 20 percent debt.* According to the theory, the other firms in the industry should move toward a 20 percent debt ratio.

Shown in Figure 12–2 are the cost-of-capital schedules for firms in a risky industry (*R*) and a stable industry (*S*). Industry *R*, the one on which Figure 12–1 was based, might consist of diesel locomotive manufacturers, and industry *S* of electric utilities. The highest line on the graph shows the relationship between the cost of equity and the debt ratio for firms in industry *R*. With no debt, their cost of equity is 12 percent. It remains at this level until debt reaches 20 percent, but beyond this point costs rise because of the increasing risk of greater amounts of debt. The second curve from the bottom shows the relationship between the cost of debt and the debt ratio for the R firms. This curve starts at 3 percent after taxes, is constant for a while, and then rises as a larger percentage of assets is financed with debt. The average cost of capital for R firms, the second line from the top, is 12 percent where all financing is with relatively expensive equity capital. After declining for a while as additional low-cost debt is averaged in with equity, the average cost of capital for R industry begins to rise when debt has reached 20 percent of total capital. Beyond this point, the fact that both debt and equity are becoming more expensive offsets the fact that debt costs less than common equity.

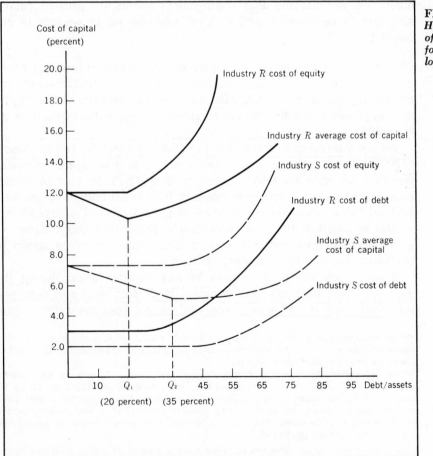

FIGURE 12–2
Hypothetical cost of capital schedules for high-risk and low-risk industries

While the same principles apply to firms in the less risky industry S, its cost functions are quite different from those of industry R. In the first place, S's over-all business risk is lower, giving rise to lower debt and equity costs at all debt levels. Further, its relative stability means that less risk is attached to any given percentage of debt; therefore, its costs of both debt and equity—and, consequently, its average cost of capital—turn up further to the right than do those for R firms. Its optimum debt ratio (Q_2) is at 35 percent as compared to only 20 percent for industry R firms.

Determining the actual optimum capital structure for a specific firm requires both analysis and judgment, and it is up to a firm's financial manager to decide on the best capital structure for his company. Once this decision has been reached, the weighting system for the average cost of capital calculation is also determined. Unless otherwise noted, we will assume that management deems its present capital structure to be optimal, and we shall use this set of weights in our calculations.[5]

INCREMENTAL COST VERSUS HISTORICAL COST

We could define the weighted average cost of capital in terms of either past or present values, and, depending on which definition we employed, we would either calculate the weighted average of the capital now employed in the firm or the weighted average of future increments of capital.

We are interested in estimating the cost of capital for two purposes: (1) capital is a resource and it has a cost, and if we are to minimize this cost we must be able to measure it; and (2) the cost of capital must be estimated if we are to use it in the capital budgeting process. Both of these uses require that we concentrate on *new* capital, not capital acquired in the past. Accordingly, throughout this chapter we are concerned only with the cost of funds that are to be raised in the future, not with funds already on hand.[6]

If we define the total amount of new capital raised during the year—retained earnings, new common stock sold, and new debt and preferred stock issued—as *incremental capital,* then our primary con-

---

[5] If the book value of a firm's capital differs from its market value, it is possible to define two alternative sets of capital weights. In strict accordance with theoretical concepts it is preferable to use market value weights.

However, neither the average cost of new capital raised during the year nor the marginal cost of each additional dollar raised during the year is generally influenced to any significant degree by the choice of weights used. The reason for this is that the market value of new debt and equity are approximately equal to the amount of book value they add to the firm's balance sheet. This point is discussed at greater length in *Managerial Finance,* third edition, pp. 352–353.

[6] We might note, however, that the historical average cost of all capital employed by the firm is used by public utility regulators as an estimate of the "fair rate of return" to allow regulated utilities.

cern is with the *cost of this incremental capital.* Henceforth, when we speak of either the average or the marginal cost of capital, we are referring to incremental capital, or capital raised during the current year.

The procedures discussed above are now applied to an actual company, the Continental Container Company, to illustrate the cost-of-capital calculation. Continental Container is a large firm, with assets of over $950 million and sales of over $1 billion. Sales and earnings are relatively stable, as food and beverage companies make up the bulk of the firm's customers. Dividends have been paid since 1923, even during the depression of the 1930s. Based on an indicated dividend rate of $2 and a current price of $50 per share, the dividend yield is 4 percent. Over the past ten years, earnings, dividends, and the price of the stock have grown at a rate of about 6 percent; all indications suggest that this same rate of growth will be maintained in the foreseeable future. Since internally generated funds provide sufficient equity, only the costs of internal equity, found in this case to be the 4 percent dividend yield plus the 6 percent growth rate, or a total of 10 percent, need be considered.

CALCULATING COST OF CAPITAL FOR AN ACTUAL COMPANY

The average interest rate on Continental Container's outstanding debt is 4.5 percent, but much of this debt was issued in earlier years when interest rates were much lower than they are now. Current market yields on both long- and short-term debt are about 7 percent, and approximately this cost will be associated with new debt issues. After a 48 percent income tax, the cost of debt is estimated to be 3.6 percent. The preferred stock is stated to be 3.75 percent preferred, but it was also issued when rates were low. Based on current market yields, the estimated cost of preferred stock is 7½ percent.

The right-hand side of Continental Container's balance sheet is given in Table 12–3. A large portion (24 percent) of the firm's funds are "free" in the sense that no interest is charged for them—accounts payable, accruals, and reserves are in this class. Some would argue that in the calculation of the over-all cost of capital, this "free" capital should be included. Under certain circumstances this procedure is valid; usually, however, only nonfree capital need be considered.[7] Of

---

[7] The primary justification for ignoring "free" capital is that, in the capital budgeting process, these spontaneously generated funds are netted out against the required investment outlay, then ignored in the cost-of-capital calculation. To illustrate, consider a retail firm thinking of opening a new store. According to customary practices, the firm should (1) estimate the required outlay, (2) estimate the net receipts (additions to profits) from the new store, (3) discount the estimated receipts at the cost of capital, and (4) accept the decision to open the new store only if the net present value of the expected revenue stream exceeds the investment outlay. The estimated accruals, trade payables, and other costless forms of credit are deducted from the investment before making the calculation.

the target, or chosen long-term capital structure, 22 percent is debt, 1 percent is preferred stock, and 77 percent is common equity.

TABLE 12–3
*Continental
Container Company
Right-hand side of
balance sheet
Millions of dollars*

			Nonfree funds only	
Payables and accruals	$120	12.5%		
Tax accruals	33	3.5		
Total "free" current liabilities	$153	16.0%		
Reserve for deferred taxes	$ 66	6.9%		
Other reserves (primarily pension fund)	11	1.1		
Total reserves	$ 77	8.0%		
Total "free" funds	$230	24.0%		
Interest-bearing debt	$160	16.7%	$160	22%
Preferred stock	7	0.8	7	1
Common equity	560	58.5	560	77
Nonfree funds	727	76.0%	$727	100%
Total financing	$957	100.0%		

If management believed that some other capital structure was optimal, then other weights would be used; for purposes of illustration it is assumed that the existing structure has been determined to be the optimum. Further, let us assume that Continental Container plans to raise $41.6 million during the current year. To maintain the target capital structure this $41.6 million must be raised as follows: $9.2 million as debt, $0.4 million as preferred stock, and $32.0 as equity. Also, note that all equity is obtained in the form of retained earnings. On the basis of these weights and the previously determined costs of debt, equity, and preferred stock, the calculations shown in Table 12–4 indicate that Continental Container's average cost of new capital is 8.6 percent. As long as Continental Container finances in the indicated manner, and uses only retained earnings for equity, its new funds should cost this amount.

MARGINAL COST OF CAPITAL In the preceding example of Continental Container, we assumed that the company would finance only with debt, preferred stock, and internally generated equity. On this basis we found the weighted average cost of new capital to be 8.6 percent. What would have occurred had the firm's need for funds been so great that it was forced to sell new common stock? The answer is that its marginal cost of new capital would have increased significantly. To show why this is so, we shall extend the Continental Container example.

First, suppose that during 1970 Continental Container had total earnings of $59 million available for common stockholders, paid $27 million in dividends, and retained $32 million. We know that to keep the capital structure in balance, the retained earnings should equal 77 percent of the net addition to capital, the other 23 percent being debt and preferred stock. Therefore, the total amount of new capital that can be obtained on the basis of the retained earnings is

$$\text{Retained earnings} = (0.77)(\text{new capital})$$

$$\text{New capital} = \frac{\text{retained earnings}}{0.77}$$

$$= \frac{\$32 \text{ million}}{0.77} = \$41.6 \text{ million.}$$

Next, we note that 1 percent of the new capital, or about $400,000, should be preferred stock and that 22 percent, or $9.2 million, should be debt. In other words, Continental Container can raise a total of $41.6 million—$32 million from retained earnings, $9.2 million in the form of debt, and $400,000 in the form of preferred stock—and still maintain its target capital structure in exact balance.

TABLE 12–4
Continental Container
Illustrative calculation of
average cost of capital
Dollars in millions

	Using dollar amounts of capital for weights (millions of dollars)		
	Amount of capital (1)	Component cost (2)	Amount of cost (Column 1 times column 2) (3)
Debt	$ 9.2	3.6%	$ .33
Preferred stock	.4	7.5	.03
Common equity	32.0	10.0	3.20
	$41.6		$3.56

$$\text{Average cost} = \frac{\$3.56}{\$41.6} = 8.56\%$$

	Using capital proportions for weights		
Debt	22.0%	3.6%	.0079
Preferred stock	1.0	7.5	.0007
Common equity	77.0	10.0	.0770
	100.0%		.0856 = 8.56%

If all financing up to $41.6 million is in the prescribed proportions, the cost of each dollar of new capital *up to $41.6 million* is still 8.6

percent, the previously computed average cost of capital. As soon as the total of the required funds exceeds $41.6 million, however, Continental Container must begin relying on more expensive new common stock. Therefore, beyond $41.6 million we must compute a new average cost of capital. Assuming Continental Container would incur a flotation cost on new equity issues equal to 10 percent, we could compute the cost of capital for funds over $41.6 million as shown in Table 12–5.

TABLE 12–5
Calculation of Continental Container's cost of capital using new common stock

1. Find the cost of new equity:

$$\text{Cost of new common stock} = \frac{\text{required rate of return}}{1 - \text{flotation costs}}$$

$$= \frac{.10}{0.9} = 11.1\%.$$

2. Find a new weighted cost of each dollar of new capital in excess of $41.6 million, using only new common stock for the equity component:

	Proportion $\times$	Component cost	$=$ product
Debt	22%	3.6	.0079
Preferred stock	1	7.5	.0008
Equity (new)	77	11.1	.0855
	100.0%		.0942 or 9.4%

According to Table 12–5, so long as Continental Container raises no more than $41.6 million, its average cost of new or incremental capital is 8.6 percent, but every dollar over $41.6 million has a cost of 9.4 percent.

The marginal cost of capital is defined as the cost of the last dollar of new capital raised during the year. Notice that the marginal cost of capital is itself an average of the cost of debt, preferred, and equity. Continental Container raises a new dollar as 22 cents debt, 1 cent preferred, and 77 cents equity, and the cost of this *composite dollar* is an average of the cost of debt, preferred, and equity. The cost of each (composite) dollar, up to $41.6 million, is constant at 8.6 percent, so this is the marginal cost of funds up to $41.6 million. Beyond $41.6 million the marginal cost of capital jumps to 9.4 percent because the firm must employ new common stock, which is more expensive than retained earnings.

The average cost of new capital—the figure the firm seeks to minimize—is found as an average of the marginal cost of capital before and after new outside equity is required, weighted according to the extent of new common stock financing. This calculation is made for Continental Container in Table 12–6, and the points are graphed in Figure 12–3(a). In the table, column 1 shows the amount of funds raised during the year, both in total and broken down into capital raised on the basis of internal equity only (retained earnings plus debt and preferred stock supported by retained earnings) and new common stock (external equity). Column 2 puts the column 1 figures into percentages, while column 3 gives the marginal costs of funds below and above $41.6 million (taken from Tables 12–4 and 12–5 respectively). Column 4 derives the average cost of the new funds raised, or the incremental capital obtained during the year.

	Dollar amount (1)	Percentage (weight) (2)	Marginal cost (3)	(2) × (3) product (4)
TABLE 12–6
1. Below $41.6 million raised during year:				
Marginal cost when no external equity is used:	all	100%	8.6%	8.60%
Marginal cost using external equity:	$ 0	0	9.4%	.00
	—	100%		
			Average cost =	8.60%
2. $50 million raised during year:				
Marginal cost when no external equity is used:	$ 41.6	83.2%	8.6%	7.16%
Marginal cost using external equity:	8.4	16.8	9.4	1.58
	$ 50.0	100.0%		
			Average cost =	8.74%
3. $250 million raised during year:				
Marginal cost when no external equity is used:	$ 41.6	16.6%	8.6%	1.43%
Marginal cost using external equity:	208.4	83.4	9.4	7.84
	$250.00	100.0%		
			Average cost =	9.27%

TABLE 12–6
Calculating Continental Container's average cost of capital for different amounts of funds

Up to $41.6 million—the total of retained earnings, incremental debt, and incremental preferred stock—the marginal cost of capital is constant at 8.6 percent. Immediately beyond $41.6 million, however, the marginal cost of capital jumps to 9.4 percent. The average cost of new capital is also constant and equal to 8.6 percent up to $41.6 million; beyond $41.6 million the average cost begins to rise.

FIGURE 12–3
Relation between the marginal cost of capital and the amount of funds raised

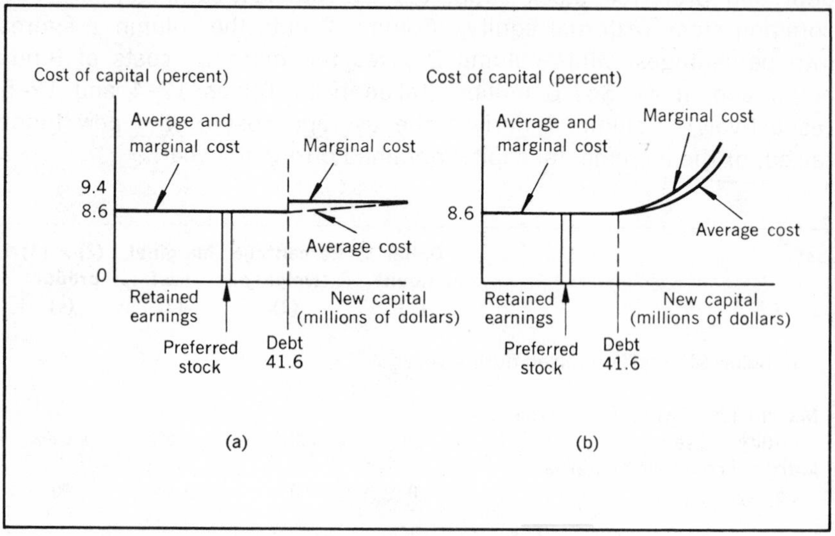

Figure 12–3(a) is, of course, highly idealized; in fact, the actual cost of capital curve looks much more like that shown in Figure 12–3(b). Here we see that the curve is flat until it reaches the vicinity of $41.6 million; then it turns up gradually and continues rising. It will go up gradually rather than suddenly because the firm will probably make small adjustments in its target debt ratio, in the actual types of securities it uses, and so on. And the curve will continue to rise because, as more and more of its securities are put on the market during a fairly short period, it will experience more and more difficulty in getting the market to absorb the new securities. These two topics—the wide assortment of securities available to the financial manager and the ability of the securities markets to absorb the firm's debt and equity instruments—are considered in the following chapters of the book. Note also that we cannot specify the exact cost of capital until we know how much capital will be raised. But the amount of capital that we raise depends on investment opportunities as determined in the capital budgeting decision. Capital budgeting and cost of capital operate jointly on one another, and both must be determined

simultaneously. This simultaneous determination is considered in Chapter 13, where dividend policy and internal financing decisions are discussed.

To this point we have considered the costs of various capital components and have seen how these component costs may be combined to form (1) the average cost of the increment of capital raised during the current year, and (2) the marginal cost of each dollar of capital raised during the current year. The following tabulation summarizes the use of each of these cost figures:

USING THE AVERAGE AND MARGINAL COSTS OF CAPITAL

The average cost of funds raised during the current year is of interest to the firm because this is the figure which the firm seeks to minimize by properly planning its capital structure. In general, the average cost of capital is constant until internal equity funds (and debt and preferred stock supported by this equity) have been exhausted, after which it begins to rise as larger and larger amounts of external equity capital are raised and averaged in with low cost retained earnings. (See Figure 12–3 on page 262.)

1. Average Cost of Incremental Capital

The marginal cost, also illustrated in Figure 12–3, gives the cost of each additional dollar raised during the current year. The marginal cost is of interest because it is the interest rate that should be used in the capital budgeting process—the firm should take on new capital projects only if their internal rates of return exceed the marginal cost of capital, or if net present values are positive when evaluated at the marginal cost of capital. The marginal cost of capital is constant and equal to average cost of capital until internal equity has been exhausted, at which point the marginal cost of capital jumps (or rises sharply).[8]

2. Marginal Cost

Before closing this chapter we should note that significant differences in capital costs exist between large and small firms, and these differences are especially pronounced in privately owned small firms.

LARGE FIRMS VERSUS SMALL FIRMS[9]

---

[8] Note, however, that if the cost of capital schedule is rising at the amount of funds called for in the capital budget, neither the NPV method nor the IRR method necessarily give "correct" answers to the questions: (1) how large should the capital budget be, and (2) which of two mutually exclusive projects should be selected? If the IRR method is used, the marginal cost of capital should be used as the cut-off point. If the NPV method is used, the marginal cost should also be used. A difficulty exists if the marginal cost of capital is not constant. This point was considered in Chapter 8, "Capital Budgeting Techniques."

Of course, if the firm does not use outside equity capital, the marginal and average costs are constant and equal to each other; fortunately, this situation generally holds for most firms.

[9] For an extended discussion of this subject, see Eugene F. Brigham and Keith V. Smith, "The Cost of Capital to Small Firms," in *Readings in Managerial Finance.*

The same concepts are involved, and the methods of calculating the average and marginal costs of capital are similar, but several points of difference arise:

1. It is especially difficult to obtain reasonable estimates of equity capital costs for small, privately owned firms.

2. Tax considerations are generally quite important for privately owned companies, as owner-managers may be in the top personal tax brackets. This factor can cause the effective after-tax cost of retained earnings to be considerably lower than the after-tax cost of new outside equity.[10]

3. Flotation costs for new security issues, especially new stock issues, are much higher for small than for large firms (see Chapter 17).

Points 2 and 3 above both cause the marginal cost curves for small firms to rise rapidly once retained earnings are exhausted.

These relationships have implications for the growth and development of large versus small firms, and, recognizing the plight of smaller companies, the federal government has set up programs to aid small businesses to obtain capital. (The principal agency, the Small Business Administration, is discussed in Chapter 20.)

SUMMARY In Chapter 11, the nature of the valuation process and the concept of expected rates of return were considered in some detail. The present chapter used these valuation concepts to develop an average cost of capital for the firm. First, the cost of the individual components of the capital structure—debt, preferred stock, and equity—were analyzed. Next, these individual component costs were brought together to form an average cost of capital. Finally, the conceptual ideas developed in the first two sections were illustrated with an example of the cost of capital for an actual company—Continental Container Company.

Cost of Individual Capital Components The cost of debt is defined to be the interest rate that must be paid on new increments of debt capital. Preferred stock's cost to the company is the effective yield and is found as the annual preferred dividend divided by the net price the company receives when it sells new preferred stock. In equation form, the cost of preferred stock is

$$\text{Cost of preferred stock} = \frac{\text{preferred dividend}}{\text{net price of preferred}}.$$

[10] This point is covered in *Managerial Finance*, third edition, pp. 365–366.

Since interest payments on debt are deductible for tax purposes but preferred dividends are not, it is necessary to make an adjustment to reconcile the cost of debt and that of preferred stock. Our procedure is to put both costs on an after-tax basis. The cost of preferred as calculated above is already on an after-tax basis; debt cost can be adjusted for taxes by multiplying the effective interest rate by a tax factor.

$$\text{After-tax cost of debt} = \text{interest rate} \times (1.0 - \text{tax rate}).$$

The cost of equity is defined as the minimum rate of return that must be earned on equity-financed investments to keep the value of the existing common equity unchanged. This required rate of return is the rate of return that investors expect to receive on the company's common stock—the dividend yield plus the capital gains yield. Generally, we assume that investors expect to receive about the same rates of return in the future that they have received in the past; therefore, we estimate the required rate of return on the basis of actual historical returns.

Equity capital comes from two sources, retained earnings and sale of new issues of common stock. The basic required rate of return is used for the cost of retained earnings. However, new stock has a higher cost because of the presence of flotation costs associated with the sale of stock. The cost of new common stock issues is computed as follows:

$$\text{Cost of new stock} = \frac{\text{required rate of return on common stock}}{1.0 - \text{percentage cost of floating new common stock}}.$$

New common stock is, therefore, more expensive than retained earnings.

The first step in calculating the average cost of capital is to determine *Average Cost of* the cost of the individual capital components as described above. The *Capital* next step is to establish the proper set of weights to be used in the averaging process. Unless we have reason to think otherwise, we generally assume that the present capital structure of the firm is at an optimum, where optimum is defined as the capital structure that will produce the minimum average cost of capital for raising a given amount of funds. The optimum capital structure varies from industry to industry, with more stable industries having optimum capital structures that call for the use of more debt than in the case of unstable industries.

Relation between Generally, the average and marginal cost of capital of a firm is con-
Cost of Capital stant until it has raised an amount of new capital equal to its retained
and Amount of earnings plus the amount of incremental debt and preferred stock
Funds Raised that can be supported by retained earnings. Beyond this point, the
firm must sell new common stock. Since new common stock has a
higher cost than retained earnings, the marginal cost of capital rises
when new common stock must be sold, and this higher marginal cost
raises the average cost.

The cost of capital rises gradually, not abruptly, once internal equity
has been exhausted: Firms make small adjustments in their target debt
ratios, begin to use an assortment of securities, retain more of their
earnings, and so on, as they reach the limit of internally generated
equity funds. These important topics—the wide assortment of securities available to the financial manager, changing debt ratios, and the
decision to retain earnings or pay them out in dividends—are covered
in the following chapters of the book.

QUESTIONS **12–1** Suppose the basic business risks to all firms in a given industry are
similar.

a) Would you expect all firms in each industry to have approximately the same
cost of capital?
b) How would the averages differ among industries?

12-2 Why are internally generated retained earnings less expensive than equity
raised by selling stock?

12–3 Prior to the 1930s the corporate income tax was not very important,
as rates were fairly low. Also prior to the 1930s preferred stock was much more
important than it has been since that period. Is there a relation between the
rise of corporate income taxes and the decline in importance of preferred stock?

12–4 Describe how each of the following would affect the cost of capital to
corporations in general.

a) The federal government solves the problem of business cycles (that is,
cyclical stability is increased).
b) The Federal Reserve Board takes action to lower interest rates.
c) The cost of floating new stock issues rises.

12–5 The formula $k = (D/P) + g$, where D = current dividend, P = the current price of a stock, and g = the past rate of growth in dividends, is sometimes used to estimate k, the cost of equity capital. Explain the reasoning behind the formula and this use of it.

PROBLEMS **12-1** On January 1, 1971, the total assets of RST Company were $100
million. By the end of the year total assets are expected to be $150 million. The
firm's capital structure, shown below, is considered to be optimal. Assume
there is no short-term debt.

Debt (6% coupon bonds)	$ 40,000,000
Preferred stock (7%)	10,000,000
Net worth	50,000,000
	$100,000,000

New bonds will have an 8 percent coupon rate and will be sold at par. Preferred will have a 9 percent rate and will also be sold at par. Common stock, currently selling at $50 a share, can be sold to net the company $45 a share. Stockholders' required rate of return is estimated to be 12 percent. Retained earnings are estimated to be $5 million. (Ignore depreciation.) The marginal corporate tax rate is 50 percent.

a) Assuming all asset expansion (gross expenditures for fixed assets plus related working capital) is included in the capital budget, what is the dollar amount of the capital budget? (Ignore depreciation.)
b) To maintain the present capital structure, how much of the capital budget must be financed by equity?
c) How much of the new equity funds needed must be generated internally? externally?
d) Calculate the cost of each of the equity components.
e) Compute the weighted average cost of equity.
f) Compute an average cost of capital for RST for funds raised *during* 1971.
g) According to the information given, would the average cost of capital have been higher or lower if the firm's rate of expansion had been lower? Why?

12–2 The Evans Manufacturing Company has the following capital structure as of December 31, 1971:

Debt (6½%)		$30,000,000
Preferred (7½%)		10,000,000
Common stock	10,000,000	
Retained earnings	30,000,000	
		40,000,000
Total capitalization		$80,000,000

Earnings per share have grown steadily from $1.54 in 1964 to $3.00 estimated for 1971. The investment community, expecting this growth to continue, applies a price/earnings ratio of 20 to yield a current market price of $60.00. Evans is paying a current annual dividend of $2, and it expects the dividend to grow at the same rate as earnings. The addition to retained earnings for 1971 is projected at $10 million; these funds will be available during the next budget year. Assume a 50 percent corporate tax rate.

Assuming that the capital structure relations set out above are maintained, new securities can be sold at the following costs:

Bonds: Up to and including $7.5 million of new bonds, 8% yield to investor on all new bonds.

From $7.51 to $15 million of new bonds, 8½% yield to investor on all new bonds.

Over $15 million of new bonds, 10% yield to investor on all new bonds.

Preferred: Up to and including $2.5 million of preferred stock, 8½% yield to investor on all new preferred stock.

From $2.51 to $5 million of preferred stock, 9% yield to investor on all new preferred stock.

Over $5 million of preferred stock, 10% yield to investor on all new preferred stock.

Common: Up to $10 million of new outside common stock, $60 per share less $4 per share flotation cost.

Over $10 million of new outside common stock, $60 per share less $8 per share flotation cost.

a) Compute the average and marginal costs of new capital for asset expansion levels of (1) $20 million, (2) $40 million, and (3) $60 million.

b) Graph the average and marginal costs of capital.

c) Discuss the breaking points in the marginal cost curves. What factors in the real world would tend to make the marginal cost curve smooth?

Chapter 13

*Dividend Policy
and Internal
Financing*

DIVIDEND policy determines the division of earnings between payments to stockholders and retained earnings. Retained earnings are one of the most significant sources of funds for financing corporate growth, but dividends constitute the cash flows that accrue to equity investors. Although both growth and dividends are desirable, these two goals are in conflict—a higher dividend rate means less retained earnings and, consequently, a slower rate of growth in earnings and stock prices. One of the financial manager's most important functions is to determine the allocation of profits after taxes between dividends and retained earnings, as this decision can have a critical influence on the value of the firm. The factors that influence the allocation of earnings to dividends or retained earnings are the subject of this chapter.

IMPORTANCE OF DIVIDEND POLICY

Table 13–1 sets forth the relationship between corporate internal sources of funds and total funds requirements since 1955. For the 14-year period between 1955 and 1968, the total of corporate funds raised was $952 billion. Internal sources financed about two-thirds of the total, with depreciation accounting for 42 percent and retained earnings for about 23 percent. If depreciation charges are deducted from gross total funds, net total funds in the amount of $617 billion is obtained. Retained earnings financed 65 percent of the net total increase in corporate funds—the firms' growth—during the 14-year period. And, as we shall see in a later chapter, most of the external funds raised by corporations is debt, so retained earnings make up an even more significant part of new equity acquired by firms.

Significance of Internal Financing

Comprehensive studies in capital formation and financing underscore the important role of internal financing. In commenting on the progress report of a National Bureau of Economic Research project on "Long-

TABLE 13-1   Corporate internal sources as percent of total funds, 1955–1968   In billions of dollars

Year (1)	Total funds from all sources (2)	Retained earnings (3)	Percentage of retained earnings to total funds (4)	Depreciation (5)	Percentage of depreciation to total sources (6)	Total internal sources (7)	Percentage of total internal sources to total sources* (8)
1955	$ 53.6	$ 13.9	25.9	$ 17.0	31.7	$ 30.9	57.6
1956	47.2	13.2	28.0	18.4	39.0	31.6	57.0
1957	42.0	11.8	28.1	20.3	48.3	32.1	76.4
1958	44.2	8.3	18.8	21.4	48.4	29.7	67.2
1959	57.9	12.6	21.8	22.9	39.6	25.5	61.4
1960	48.1	10.0	20.8	24.2	50.3	34.2	71.1
1961	56.6	10.2	18.0	25.4	44.8	35.6	62.8
1962	64.9	12.4	19.1	29.2	45.0	41.6	64.1
1963	67.1	13.6	20.3	30.8	45.9	44.4	66.2
1964	71.8	18.3	25.5	32.8	45.8	51.1	71.3
1965	93.1	23.1	24.8	35.2	37.8	58.3	62.2
1966	100.6	24.7	24.6	38.2	38.0	62.9	62.6
1967	94.2	21.2	22.5	41.2	43.7	62.4	66.2
1968	110.4	22.0	19.9	44.3	40.1	66.3	60.0
1955–60	293.0	69.8	23.8	124.2	42.4	194.0	66.2
1961–68	658.7	145.5	22.1	277.1	42.1	422.6	64.2
1955–68	$951.7	$215.3	22.6	$401.3	42.2	$616.6	64.8

Source: Economic Report of the President: (Washington, D.C.: U.S. Government Printing Office, 1970), p. 264.
*Note: Corporate inventory valuation adjustment has been ignored in computing total internal sources.

term Trends in Capital Formation and Financing," Eli Shapiro has called attention to the significance of internal financing:[1]

> Indeed, it may be stated categorically that one of the most important features of all three papers is the stress placed on internal financing over the first half of the twentieth century. The dominance of internal financing is hard to rationalize in the light of the disproportionate space devoted to the role of financial institutions in the so-called business or corporate finance textbooks published as recently as the late forties or early fifties.

Because of the great importance of internal financing, dividend policy, which determines the division of corporate earnings between outflows and retained earnings, must be recognized as one of the central decision areas for financial managers.

Studies of dividend patterns over extended periods beginning in 1870 indicate that, over all, corporations have paid in dividends about half of their earnings after taxes. However, this percentage has varied considerably from year to year. Table 13–2 shows that immediately following World War II dividend payout dropped to about 36 percent. This decrease was due to the rapid growth of firms and their need for funds to finance inventories and fixed assets at higher price levels. *Patterns in Dividend Payouts*

In the period 1950–1955, dividend payouts averaged about 41 percent of earnings. Writers in the mid-fifties observed that, of corporate earnings before taxes, one half was paid to the government. Of the remainder, 40 to 45 percent was distributed to the stockholders. Thus, if a corporation earned $20 million, the corporate income tax would take $10 million, corporate dividends would be about $4 million, and retained earnings would be about $6 million.

It is interesting to note the payout pattern during the 1960s (1960–1968). In the early part of the period, payouts were high, averaging about 50 percent. This was a period of relatively slack economic activity—investment opportunities were not particularly strong, and debt funds were available at low rates of interest. Without an especially pressing need for funds and with plenty of low-cost debt money available, dividend payouts were high. In the later years, however, investment demand was booming and debt funds were scarce and expensive. This caused firms to reduce dividend payouts and to rely more heavily on retained earnings.

The economic patterns described above indicate the great significance of retained earnings in financing the growth of firms. This poses the fundamental question: What determines the extent to which a firm will pay out dividends instead of retain earnings? This question may be answered by a consideration of the factors influencing dividend policy. **FACTORS INFLUENCING DIVIDEND POLICY**

[1] *Journal of Finance,* X (May 1955), p. 281.

TABLE 13–2
*Corporate profits
and dividends,
1929–1968*
*Dollar amounts in
billions*

Year	Corporate profits after tax	Dividends	Payout percentage
1929	$ 8.6	$ 5.8	6%
1930	2.9	5.5	190
1931	−0.9	4.1	0
1932	−2.7	2.5	0
1933	0.4	2.0	500
1934	1.6	2.6	163
1935	2.6	2.8	108
1936	4.9	4.5	92
1937	5.3	4.7	89
1938	2.9	3.2	110
1939	5.6	3.8	68
1940	7.2	4.0	56
1941	10.1	4.4	44
1942	10.1	4.3	43
1943	11.1	4.4	40
1944	11.2	4.6	41
1945	9.0	4.6	51
1946	15.5	5.6	36
1947	20.2	6.3	31
1948	22.7	7.0	31
1949	18.5	7.2	39
1950	24.9	8.8	35
1951	21.6	8.6	40
1952	19.6	8.6	44
1953	20.4	8.9	44
1954	20.6	9.3	45
1955	27.0	10.5	39
1956	27.2	11.3	42
1957	26.0	11.7	45
1958	22.3	11.6	52
1959	28.5	12.6	44
1960	26.7	13.4	50
1961	27.2	13.8	51
1962	31.2	15.2	49
1963	33.1	16.5	49
1964	38.4	17.8	46
1965	46.5	19.8	43
1966	49.9	20.8	42
1967	47.3	21.5	45
1968	49.8	23.1	46
1929–1939	31.2	41.5	133
1940–1945	58.7	26.3	45
1945–1950	110.8	39.5	36
1950–1955	134.1	54.7	41
1955–1960	157.7	71.1	45
1960–1965	203.1	96.5	48
1965–1968	244.3	109.8	45

Source: Economic Report of the President (Washington, D.C.: U.S. Government Printing Office, 1970), p. 260.

First, the major influences on dividend policy will be described. Second, this check list will be used to attempt to explain differences in dividend patterns observed among different industries and among firms in the same industry.

The state statutes and court decisions governing dividend policy are *Legal Rules* complicated, but their essential nature may be stated briefly. The legal rules provide that dividends be paid from earnings, either from the current year's earnings or from past years' earnings as reflected in earned surplus. State laws emphasize three rules: (1) the net profits rule, (2) the capital impairment rule, and (3) the insolvency rule.

The *net profits* rule provides that dividends may be paid from past and present earnings. The *capital impairment* rule protects shareholders and creditors by forbidding the payment of dividends from capital. Paying dividends from capital would be distributing the investment in the company rather than its earnings.[2] The *insolvency* rule provides that corporations may not pay dividends while insolvent. Insolvency is here defined in the bankruptcy sense that liabilities exceed assets.

Legal aspects are significant. They provide the framework within which dividend policies can be formulated. However, within these boundaries financial and economic factors have a major influence on policy.

Profits held as retained earnings (which show up in the right-hand *Liquidity Position* side of the balance sheet in the surplus or retained earnings account) may be invested in assets required for the conduct of the business. Thus, although a firm has had a record of earnings, it may not be able to pay cash dividends because of its liquidity position. Indeed, a growing firm, even a very profitable one, typically has a pressing need for funds. In such a situation the firm may elect not to pay cash dividends.

When a firm has sold debt to finance expansion or to substitute for *Need to Repay* other forms of financing, it is faced with two alternatives: It can refund *Debt* the debt at maturity by replacing it with another form of security, or it can make provision for paying off the debt. If the decision is to retire the debt, this will generally require the retention of earnings.

Debt contracts, particularly when long-term debt is involved, frequently *Restrictions in* restrict a firm's ability to pay cash dividends. Such restrictions, which *Debt Contracts* are designed to protect the position of the lender, usually state (1)

---

[2] It is possible, of course, to return stockholders' capital; however, when this is done, it must be clearly stated as such. A dividend paid out of capital is called a *liquidating* dividend.

that future dividends can be paid only out of earnings generated *after* the signing of the loan agreement (that is, future dividends cannot be paid out of past earned surplus) and ② that dividends cannot be paid when net working capital (current assets minus current liabilities) is below a specified amount. Similarly, preferred stock agreements generally state that no cash dividends can be paid on the common stock until all accrued preferred dividends have been paid. Such restrictions are discussed in Chapter 19.

Rate of Asset Expansion The more rapid the rate at which the firm is growing, the greater will be its needs for financing asset expansion. The greater the future need for funds, the more likely the firm is to retain earnings rather than pay them out.

Profit Rate The rate of return on assets determines the relative attractiveness of paying out earnings in the form of dividends to stockholders who will use them elsewhere, compared with the productivity of their use in the present enterprise.

Stability of Earnings If earnings are relatively stable, a firm is better able to predict what its future earnings will be. A stable firm is therefore more likely to pay out a higher percentage of its earnings than is a firm with fluctuating earnings. The unstable firm is not certain that in subsequent years the hoped-for earnings will be realized, so it is more likely to retain a high proportion of earnings in order to maintain dividends if earnings should fall off in the future.

Access to the Capital Markets A large, well-established firm with a record of profitability and some stability of earnings will have easy access to capital markets and other forms of external financing. The small, new, or venturesome firm, however, has a greater amount of risk for potential investors. Its ability to raise equity or debt funds from capital markets is restricted, and it must retain more earnings to finance its operations. A well-established firm is thus likely to have a higher dividend payout rate than is a new or small firm.

Control Another important variable is the effect of alternative sources of financing on the control situation in the firm. Some corporations, as a matter of policy, will expand only to the extent of their internal earnings. This policy is defended on the grounds that raising funds by selling additional common stock dilutes the control of the dominant group in the company. At the same time, selling debt increases the risks of fluctuating earnings to the present owners of the company. Reliance on internal financing in order to maintain control reduces the dividend payout.

The tax position of the owners of the corporation greatly influences the desire for dividends. For example, a corporation closely held by a few taxpayers in high income tax brackets is likely to pay out a relatively low dividend. The owners of the corporation are interested in taking their income in the form of capital gains rather than in ordinary dividends, which are subject to higher personal income tax rates. However, the stockholders in a large, widely held corporation may be interested in a high dividend payout. *Tax Position of Stockholders*

At times there is a conflict of interest in large corporations between stockholders in high income tax brackets and those in low income tax brackets. The former may prefer to see a low dividend payout and a high rate of earnings retention in the hope of an appreciation of the capital stock of the company. The lower income stockholder may prefer a relatively high dividend payout rate. The dividend policy of such a firm may be a compromise between a low and a high payout— an intermediate payout ratio. If, however, one group dominates and sets, let us say, a low payout policy, those stockholders who seek income are likely to sell their shares over time and shift into higher yielding stocks. Thus, to at least some extent, a firm's payout policy determines its stockholder types, as well as vice versa.

In order to prevent wealthy stockholders from using the corporation as an "incorporated pocketbook" by which they can avoid the high rates of personal income tax, tax regulations applicable to corporations provide for a special surtax on improperly accumulated income. However, Section 531 of the Revenue Act of 1954 placed the burden of proof on the Internal Revenue Service to justify penalty rates for accumulation of earnings. That is, earnings retention is justified unless the Internal Revenue Service can prove otherwise. *Tax on Improperly Accumulated Earnings*

The eleven factors outlined above influence corporations to different degrees, depending upon their particular situations. The effects of these factors result in different dividend patterns from industry to industry and from company to company. How these forces influence dividend policy is indicated in the following section.

A fundamental relation observed in dividend policy is the widespread tendency of corporations to pursue a relatively stable dividend policy. Profits of firms fluctuate considerably with changes in the level of business activity, but Figure 13–1 shows that dividends are more stable than earnings. **STABILITY OF DIVIDEND POLICY**

FIGURE 13–1
Corporate earnings
after taxes and
dividends (billions
of dollars)

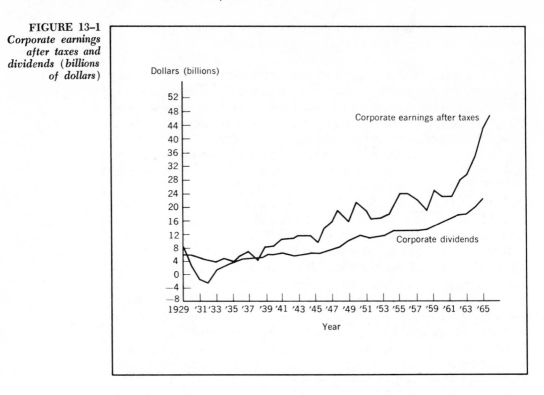

Most corporations seek to maintain a target dividend per share. However, dividends increase with a lag after earnings rise. Only after an increase in earnings appears clearly sustainable and relatively permanent are dividends increased. When dividends have been increased, strenuous efforts are made to maintain them at the new level. If earnings decline, until it is clear that an earnings recovery will not take place, dividends will be maintained.

Figure 13–2 illustrates these ideas by showing the earnings and dividend patterns for the Walter Watch Company over a 25-year period. Initially, earnings are $2 and dividends $1 per share, providing a 50 percent payout ratio. Earnings rise for four years, while dividends remain constant; thus, the payout falls during this period. During 1950 and 1951, earnings fall substantially; however, the dividend is maintained and the payout rises above the 50 percent target. During the period between 1951 and 1958, earnings experience a sustained rise. Dividends are held constant for a time, while management seeks to determine whether the earnings increase is permanent. In 1956, the earnings gain seems permanent, and dividends are raised in three steps to re-establish the 50 percent payout. During 1960 a strike causes earnings to fall below the regular dividend; assuming the earnings decline to be temporary, management maintains the dividend. Earnings fluctuate on a fairly high plateau from 1961 through 1967, during which time dividends remain constant. A new increase in earnings induces management to raise the dividend in 1968 to re-establish the 50 percent payout ratio. Most firms use a similar dividend policy, which explains why, in Figure 13–1, the amount of dividends rises only moderately in years when earnings increase sharply.

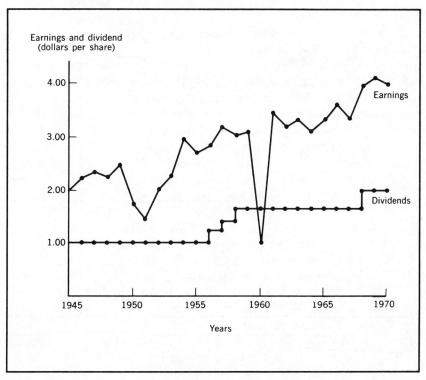

FIGURE 13–2
Dividend and earnings pattern, Walter Watch Company

Walter Watch kept its dividend at a steady dollar amount but allowed its payout ratio to fluctuate. An alternative policy that is followed by a few firms would have been to maintain a stable payout ratio and let the dollar dividends fluctuate.

Still a third alternative—and one favored by such firms as General Motors—is to set a relatively low "regular" dividend and then supplement it with year-end "extras" in years when earnings are high. As earnings of the firm increase, at first the customary quarterly dividend will not be altered. Year-end "extras," however, will be declared.

Only after it is clear that earnings have risen to a new plateau will the "regular" dividend be increased.

We may now evaluate this practice of following a stable dollar dividend policy. First, consider the stable dividend policy from the standpoint of the stockholders as owners of a company. Their acquiescence with the general practice must imply that stable dividend policies lead to higher stock prices on the average than do alternative dividend policies. Is this a fact? Does a stable dividend policy maximize security values for a corporation? There has been no truly conclusive empirical study of dividend policy, so any answer to the question must be regarded as tentative.

On a priori grounds, there is reason to believe that a stable dividend policy will lead to higher stock prices. First, a stable dividend policy could lead to higher stock prices because investors might be expected to value more highly dividends they are more sure of receiving. If dividends fluctuate, investors may consider them more risky than stable dividends. Accordingly, the same average amount of dividends received under a fluctuating dividend policy is likely to have a higher discount factor applied to it than is applied to dividends under a stable dividend policy. In the terms used in Chapter 12, this means that a firm with a stable dividend would have a lower required rate of return—or cost of capital—than one whose dividends fluctuated.

Second, many stockholders live on income received in the form of dividends. Such stockholders would be greatly inconvenienced by fluctuating dividends, and they would likely pay a premium for a stock with a relatively assured minimum dollar dividend.

A third advantage of a stable dividend from the standpoint of a corporation and its stockowners is the requirement of legal listing. Legal lists are lists of securities in which mutual savings banks, pension funds, insurance companies, and other fiduciary institutions are permitted to invest. One of the criteria for placing a stock on the legal list is that dividend payments not be reduced. Thus, legal listing encourages pursuance of a stable dividend policy.

On the other hand, if a firm's investment opportunities fluctuate from year to year, should it not retain more earnings during some years in order to take advantage of these opportunities when they appear, then increase dividends when good internal investment opportunities are scarce? This line of reasoning would lead to the recommendation of a fluctuating payout for companies whose investment opportunities are unstable. However, the logic of the argument is diminished by recognizing that it is possible to maintain a reasonably stable dividend by using outside financing, especially debt, to smooth out the differences between the funds needed for investment and the amount of money provided by retained earnings.

Before going on to consider dividend policy at a theoretical level, it is useful to summarize the three major types of dividend policies discussed in the preceding section: **ALTERNATIVE DIVIDEND POLICIES**

1. *Stable Dollar Amount per Share.* This is the policy followed by most firms, and it is this policy that is implied when one says "stable dividend policy."

2. *Constant Payout Ratio.* Some firms follow a policy of paying out a constant percentage of earnings. Since earnings will surely fluctuate, following this policy necessarily means that the dollar amount of dividends will fluctuate.

3. *Low Regular Dividend Plus Extras.* This policy is a compromise between the first two. It gives the firm flexibility, but it leaves investors somewhat uncertain as to what their dividend income will be.

The relative merits of these three policies can be evaluated better after a discussion of the residual theory of dividend policy, the topic covered in the next section.

In the preceding chapters on capital budgeting and the cost of capital, we indicated that, generally, the cost of capital schedule and the investment schedule must be combined before the cost of capital can be established. In other words, the optimum capital budget, the marginal cost of capital, and the marginal rate of return on investment are *simultaneously* determined. In this section we examine this simultaneous solution in the framework of what might be called *the residual theory of dividend policy.* The theory draws on materials developed earlier in the book—capital budgeting and the cost of capital—and serves to provide a bridge between these key concepts. **RESIDUAL THEORY OF DIVIDEND POLICY[3]**

The starting point in the theory is that investors prefer to have the firm retain and reinvest earnings rather than pay them out in dividends *if the return on reinvested earnings exceeds the rate of return the investor could, himself, obtain on other investments of comparable risk.* If the corporation can reinvest retained earnings at a 20 percent rate of return, while the best rate the stockholder can obtain if the earnings are passed on to him in the form of dividends is 10 percent, then the stockholder would prefer to have the firm retain the profits.

We have seen in Chapter 12 that the cost of equity capital obtained from retained earnings is an *opportunity cost* that reflects rates of return open to equity investors. If a firm's stockholders could buy other stocks of equal risk and obtain a 10 percent dividends-plus-capi-

---

[3] "Residual" implies "left over." The residual theory of dividend policy implies that dividends are paid after internal investment opportunities have been exhausted.

tal-gains yield, then 10 percent is the firm's cost of retained earnings. The cost of new outside equity raised by selling common stock is higher because of the costs of floating the issue.

Most firms have an optimum debt ratio that calls for at least some debt, so new financing is done partly with debt and partly with equity. Debt has a different, and generally lower, cost than equity, so the two forms of capital must be combined to find the *average cost of capital.* As long as the firm finances at the optimum point, using an optimum amount of debt and equity, and provided it uses only internally generated equity (retained earnings), its marginal cost of capital is equal to the average cost of capital.[4]

Internally generated equity is available for financing a certain amount of new investment; beyond this amount, the firm must turn to more expensive new common stock. At the point where new stock must be sold, the cost of equity and, consequently, the marginal cost of capital, rises.

These concepts, which were developed in Chapter 12, are illustrated in Figure 13–3. The firm has a marginal cost of capital of 10 percent so long as retained earnings are available; however, the cost of capital rises to 13 percent when new stock must be sold.[5]

FIGURE 13–3
The marginal cost of capital

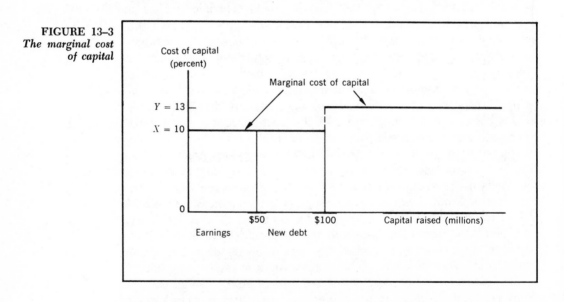

[4] It is demonstrated in elementary economics textbooks that the marginal cost curve cuts the average cost curve where the average is at a minimum—that is, the marginal and the average curves are *equal* where the average curve is at a *minimum.*

[5] Again, Figure 13–3 is unrealistic in the sense that the marginal cost of capital would rise steeply in the vicinity of $100 million, not have a discontinuity gap.

Our hypothetical firm has $50 million of retained earnings and a 50 percent optimum debt ratio. Therefore, it can make net investments (investments in addition to asset replacements financed from depreciation) up to $100 million—$50 million retained earnings plus $50 million new debt supported by the retained earnings. Therefore, its marginal cost of capital is constant at 10 percent for up to $100 million of capital. Beyond $100 million, the marginal cost of capital rises to 13 percent as the firm begins to use more expensive new common stock.

Next, suppose the firm's capital budgeting department draws up a list of investment opportunities, ranked in the order of their *IRR,* and plots them on a graph. The investment opportunity curves of three different years—one for a "good" year (IRR_1), one for a "normal" year (IRR_2), and one for a "bad" year (IRR_3)—are shown in Figure 13–4. IRR_1 shows that the firm can invest more money, and at higher rates of return, than it can when the investment opportunities are those given in IRR_2 and IRR_3.

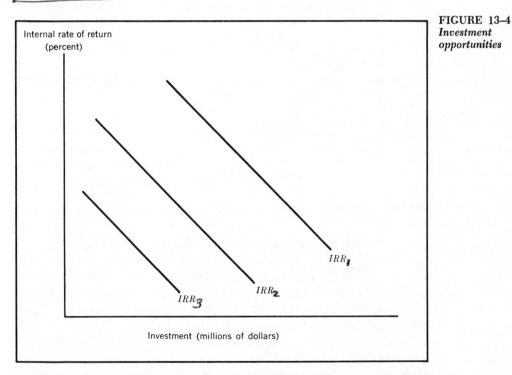

FIGURE 13–4
Investment opportunities

Now we combine the investment opportunities schedules with the cost of capital; this is done in Figure 13–5. The point where the investment opportunity curve cuts the cost of capital curve defines the proper level of new investment⟩ When investment opportunities are relatively poor, the optimum level of investment is $25 million; when opportunities are about normal, $75 million should be invested; and when opportunities are relatively good, the firm should make new investments in the amount of $125 million.

FIGURE 13–5
Interrelation among cost of capital, investment opportunities, and new investment

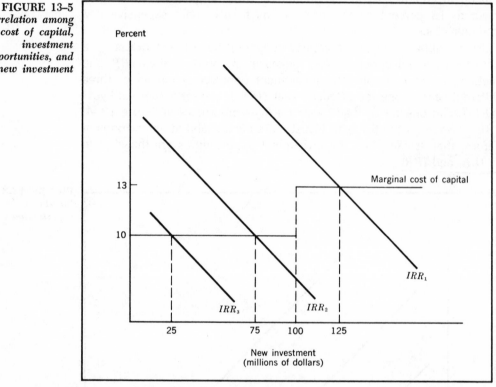

Consider the situation where IRR_1 is the appropriate schedule. The firm has $50 million in earnings and a 50 percent target debt ratio, so it can finance $100 million, $50 million earnings plus $50 million debt, from retained earnings plus new debt *if it retains all its earnings.* If it pays part of the earnings in dividends, then it will have to begin using expensive new common stock sooner, so the cost of capital curve will jump sooner. This suggests that under the conditions of IRR_1 the firm should retain all its earnings and actually sell some new common stock in order to take advantage of its investment opportunities. Its payout ratio is thus zero percent.

Under the conditions of IRR_2, however, the firm should invest only

$75 million. How should this investment be financed? First, notice that if it retains the full amount of its earnings, $50 million, it will need to sell only $25 million of new debt. But retaining $50 million and selling only $25 million of new debt will cause the company to move away from its target capital structure. To stay on target, the required $75 million must be financed half by equity—retained earnings—and half by debt, or $37.5 million of retained earnings and $37.5 million of debt. Now if the firm has $50 million in total earnings and decides to retain and reinvest $37.5 million, it must pay $12.5 million in dividends.[6] In this case, the payout ratio is 25 percent ($12.5 divided by $50).

Finally, under the "bad" conditions of IRR_3 the firm should invest only $25 million. Because it has $50 million in earnings, it could finance the entire $25 million out of retained earnings and still have $25 million available for dividends. Should this be done? Under the assumptions, this would not be a good decision because it would move the firm away from its target debt ratio. To stay in the 50–50 debt/equity position, the firm must retain $12.5 million and sell $12.5 million of debt. When the $12.5 million of retained earnings is subtracted from the $50 million of earnings, we are left with a residual of $37.5, the amount that should be paid out in dividends. In this case the payout ratio is 75 percent.

There seems to be a conflict between the theory and the statement **LONG-RUN** made in an earlier section that firms should and do maintain reason- **VIEWPOINT** ably stable cash dividends. How can this conflict be reconciled?

Actually, this reconciliation is quite simple if we recognize that the theory is not meant to be applied *exactly*. In other words, we would not recommend that a firm adjust its dividend each and every year— indeed, this is not necessary. Firms do have target debt ratios, but they also have a certain amount of flexibility—they can be moderately above or below the target debt position in any one year with no adverse consequences. This means that if an unusually large number of good investments are available in a particular year, the firm does not necessarily have to cut its dividend to take advantage of them—it can borrow somewhat more heavily than usual in that particular year without getting its debt ratio too far out of line. Obviously, however, this excessive reliance on debt could not continue for too many years without getting the debt ratio seriously out of line, necessitating either a sale

---

[6] Actually, it could buy back its common stock instead of paying dividends. Also, the firm might prefer to engage in merger activities rather than raise its payout ratio, using retained earnings to acquire other firms. This possibility is discussed in Chapter 21.

of new stock or a cut in dividends and an attendant increase in the level of retained earnings.

HIGH AND LOW DIVIDEND PAYOUT INDUSTRIES Some industries are experiencing rapid growth in the demand for their products, providing the firms in these industries with many good investment opportunities. Electronics, office equipment, and color television are examples of such industries in recent years. Other industries, however, have experienced much slower growth, or perhaps even declines. Examples of such slow-growth industries are cigarette manufacturing, textiles, and coal mining. Still other industries are growing at about the same rate as the general economy—oil, steel, and banking are representative.

The theory suggests that firms in rapidly growing industries should generally have *IRR* curves that are relatively far out to the right on graphs such as Figure 13–5; for example, Xerox, Fairchild Camera, and IBM might have investment opportunities similar to IRR_1. The tobacco companies, on the other hand, could be expected to have investment schedules similar to IRR_3, while IRR_2 might be appropriate for Standard Oil of New Jersey or U.S. Steel.

Each of these firms would, of course, experience shifts in investment opportunities from year to year, but the curves would *tend* to be in about the same part of the graph. In other words, firms like Xerox would *tend* to have more investment opportunities than money, so they would *tend* to have a zero (or very low) payout ratio. Reynolds Tobacco, on the other hand, would *tend* to have more money than good investments, so we would expect to find Reynolds paying out a relatively high percentage of earnings in dividends. These companies do, in fact, conform with our expectations.

CONFLICTING THEORIES ON DIVIDENDS Two basic schools of thought on dividend policy have been expressed in the theoretical literature of finance. One school, associated with Myron Gordon and John Lintner, among others, holds that the capital gains expected to result from earnings retention are more risky than are dividend expectations. Accordingly, this school suggests that the earnings of a firm with a low payout ratio will typically be capitalized at higher rates than are the earnings of a high payout firm.

The other school, associated with Merton Miller and Franco Modigliani, holds that investors are basically indifferent between returns coming in the form of dividends or as capital gains. Miller and Modigliani believe that any effect that a change in dividends has on the price of a firm's stock is related primarily to *information about expected future earnings conveyed by a change in dividends*. Recalling that corporate managements dislike cutting dividends, Miller and

Modigliani argue that increases in cash dividends raise expectations about the level of future earnings—dividend increases have favorable *information content.* In terms of Figure 13–2 above, Miller and Modigliani would say that the dividend increases in 1956, 1957, 1958, and 1968 had information content about future earnings—these dividend increases signaled to stockholders that management expected the recent earnings increases to be permanent.

Dividends are probably less uncertain than capital gains, but dividends are taxed at a higher rate than capital gains. How do these two forces balance out? Some argue that the uncertainty factor dominates, others feel that the differential tax rate is the stronger force and causes investors to favor corporate retention of earnings. Still others—and we put ourselves in this group—argue that it is difficult to generalize. Depending on the tax status and current income needs of its set of stockholders (both brokerage costs and capital gains taxes make it difficult for stockholders to shift companies), as well as the firm's internal investment opportunities, the optimum dividend policy will vary from firm to firm.[7]

DIVIDEND PAYMENTS

Dividends are normally paid quarterly. For example, Union Carbide paid dividends of $2.00 during 1969, 50 cents each quarter. In common financial language, we say that Union Carbide's *regular quarterly dividend* is 50 cents, or that its *regular annual dividend* is $2.00. Management, sometimes by an explicit statement in the annual report and sometimes by implication, conveys to stockholders an expectation that the regular dividend will be maintained if at all possible. Further, management conveys its belief that earnings will be sufficient to maintain the dividend.

Under other conditions, a firm's cash flows and investment needs may be too volatile for it to set a very high regular dividend; on the average, however, it needs a high dividend payout to dispose of funds not necessary for reinvestment. In such a case, the directors can set a relatively low regular dividend—low enough that it can be maintained even in low profit years or in years when a considerable amount of reinvestment is needed—and supplement it with an *extra dividend* in years when excess funds are available. As was pointed out earlier, General Motors, whose earnings fluctuate widely from year to year, has long followed the practice of supplementing its regular dividend with an *extra dividend* paid at the end of the year, when its profits and investment requirements are known.

---

[7] Some of these questions are considered in more detail—at both a theoretical and an empirical level—in *Managerial Finance,* third edition, Appendix A to Chapter 12.

PAYMENT The actual payment procedure is of some importance, and the follow-
PROCEDURE ing is an outline of the payment sequence.

1. The directors meet, say on November 15, and declare the regular dividend. The directors would, on this date, issue a statement similar to the following: "On November 15, 1970, the directors of the XYZ Company met and declared the regular quarterly dividend of $0.50 per share, plus an extra dividend of $0.75 per share, to holders of record on December 15, payment to be made on January 2, 1971."

2. On December 15, the *holder of record date*, the company closes its stock transfer books and makes up a list of the shareholders as of that date. If XYZ Company is notified of the sale and transfer of some stock before December 16, the new owner receives the dividend. If notification is received on or after December 16, the old stockholder gets the dividend.

3. Suppose Edward Johns buys 100 shares of stock from Robert Noble on December 13; will the company be notified of the transfer in time to list Noble as the new owner and, thus, pay the dividend to him? To avoid conflict, the stock brokerage business has set up a convention of declaring that the right to the dividend remains with the stock until four days prior to the holder of record date; on the fourth day before the record date, the right to the dividend no longer goes with the shares. The date when the right to the dividend leaves the stock is called the *ex-dividend date*.

In this case, the ex-dividend date is four days prior to December 15, or December 11. Therefore, if Johns is to receive the dividend, he must buy the stock by December 10. If he buys it on December 11 or later, Noble will receive the dividend.

The total dividend, regular plus extra, amounts to $1.25, so the ex-dividend date is important. Barring fluctuations in the stock market, we would normally expect the price of a stock to drop by approximately the amount of the dividend on the ex-dividend date.

4. The company actually mails the checks to the holders of record on January 2, the payment date.

STOCK One of the significant aspects of dividend policy in which the financial
DIVIDENDS manager plays an important role is that of *stock dividends* and *stock*
AND STOCK *splits*. A *stock dividend* is paid in additional shares of stock instead
SPLITS of cash, and simply involves the transfer of earned surplus to the capi-
tal stock account.[8]

---

[8] One point that should be made in connection with stock dividends is that the transfer from earned surplus to the capital stock account must be based on market value. In other

In a *stock split* there is no change in the total capital account or surplus. A larger number of shares of common stock is issued. In a two-for-one split, each stockholder would receive two shares for each one previously held. Book value per share would be cut in half. The par, or stated, value per share of common stock is similarly changed.

From a practical standpoint there is little difference between a stock dividend and a stock split. The New York Stock Exchange considers any distribution of stock totaling 24 percent or less of outstanding stock to be a stock dividend. Any distribution of stock of 25 percent or more is regarded as a stock split. Since the two are similar, the issues outlined below are discussed in connection with both stock dividends and stock splits.

The results of a careful empirical study of the effects of stock dividends are available and can be used as a basis for observations on the price effects of stock dividends.[9] The findings of the study are presented in Table 13–3. When stock dividends were associated with a cash dividend increase, the value of the company's stock six months after the ex-dividend date had risen by 8 percent. On the other hand, where stock dividends were not accompanied by cash dividend increases, stock values fell by 12 percent during the subsequent six-month period.

Price Effects

	Price at selected dates (in percentages)		
	Six months prior to ex-dividend date	At ex-dividend date	Six months after ex-dividend date
Cash dividend increase	100	109	108
No cash dividend increase	100	99	88

*TABLE 13–3
Price effects of
stock dividends*

These data seem to suggest that stock dividends are seen for what they are—simply additional pieces of paper—and that they do not represent true income. When they are accompanied by higher earnings

words, if a firm's shares are selling for $100 and it has 1 million shares outstanding, a 10 percent stock dividend requires the transfer of $10 million (100,000 × $100) from earned surplus to capital stock. Quite obviously, stock dividends are thus limited by the size of earned surplus. The rule was put into effect to prevent the declaration of stock dividends unless the firm has had earnings. This is another in a long series of rulings designed to prevent investors from being fooled by the practices of unscrupulous firms.

[9] C. A. Barker, "Evaluation of Stock Dividends," *Harvard Business Review*, XXXVI (July–August 1958), pp. 99–114.

and cash dividend increases, investors bid up the value of the stock. However, when stock dividends are not accompanied by increases in earnings and cash dividends, the dilution of earnings and dividends per share causes the price of the stock to drop. The fundamental determinant is underlying earnings and dividend trends.

Effects on Extent Table 13–4 shows the effect of stock dividends on common stock
of Ownership ownership. Large stock dividends resulted in the largest percentage increases in stock ownership. The use of stock dividends increased shareholders by 25 percent on the average. For companies and industries that did not offer stock splits or stock dividends, the increase in ownership was only 5 percent. Furthermore, the degree of increase in ownership increased with the size of the stock dividend.

TABLE 13–4
Effects of stock
dividends on stock
ownership

	Percentage increase in stockholders, 1950–1953
Stock dividend, 25% and over	30
Stock dividend, 5–25%	17
All stock dividends	25
No stock dividends or splits	5

Source: C. Austin Barker, "Evaluation of Stock Dividends," *Harvard Business Review,* XXXVI (July–August 1958), pp. 99–114.

This evidence suggests that stock dividends increase share ownership. Regardless of the effect on the total market value of the firm, the use of stock dividends and stock splits effectively increases stock ownership by lowering the price at which shares are traded to a more popular range.

SUMMARY Dividend policy determines the extent of internal financing by a firm. The financial manager decides whether to release corporate earnings from the control of the enterprise. Because dividend policy affects the financial structure, the flow of funds, corporate liquidity, stock prices, and investor satisfaction—to list a few ramifications—the manager exercises a high degree of judgment in establishing a dividend pattern.

In theory, once the firm's debt policy and cost of capital have been determined, dividend policy should automatically follow. Under our theoretical model, dividends are simply a residual after investment needs have been met; if this policy is followed, and if investors are indifferent between receiving their investment returns in the form of dividends or capital gains, stockholders are better off than under any other possible dividend policy. However, the financial manager simply does not have all the information assumed in the theory, and rule-of-thumb guidelines are needed.

As a guide to boards of directors responsible for dividend policy, the following check list summarizes the major economic and financial factors influencing dividend policy.

1. Rate of Growth and Profit Level.   Economic theory suggests that high growth rates are associated with higher profit opportunities and lower growth rates with smaller profit margins. The higher the growth rate and the larger the prospective margins, the lower the dividend payout is likely to be.

2. Stability of Earnings.   If earnings are relatively stable from the standpoint of both long-term growth and cyclical fluctuations, the dividend payout is likely to be higher.

3. Age and Size of Firm.   A well-established, large firm has better access to the capital markets than has a new and small firm. Hence, the dividend payout, other things being equal, will be higher for the larger and older firm.

4. Cash Position.   The stronger a firm's cash or liquidity position in relation to its prospective future need for funds, the higher the probable dividend payout.

5. Need to Repay Debt.   A firm that has incurred heavy indebtedness has implicitly committed itself to a relatively high rate of earnings retention unless it seeks to prepare the markets for a common stock or debt-refunding issue. This factor may be reinforced by provisions in the debt contract that prevent the payment of cash dividends unless certain conditions are met.

6. Control.   If maintenance of existing voting control is an important consideration, the dividend payout may be lower to permit financing from retained earnings. The procedure avoids issuance of additional securities, which would involve dilution of ownership or the increased risks of debt. However, if a struggle for control of the firm with opposition groups is in progress or is threatened, the dividend payout may be higher to appeal to stockholder goodwill.

7. Maintenance of a Target Dividend.   The objective of a stable dividend policy will make for low payouts when profits are temporarily high and high payouts when profits are temporarily depressed; and it will cause dividends to lag behind profit growth until the establishment of new earnings levels is strongly assured.

8. Tax Position of Stockholders. Corporations closely held by a few taxpayers in high income brackets are likely to have a lower dividend payout. Corporations widely held by small investors will tend to have higher dividend payouts.

9. Tax Position of the Corporation. Potential penalties for excessive accumulation of retained earnings may cause dividend payouts to be higher than economic and financial considerations alone would indicate.

Of the factors listed, some make for higher dividend payouts, some for lower. It is not possible to provide a formula that can be used to establish the proper dividend payout for a given situation. This is a task requiring the exercise of judgment. The considerations summarized above provide a check list for guiding dividend decisions.

Empirical studies indicate a wide diversity of dividend payout ratios not only among industries but also among firms in the same industry. Studies also show that dividends are more stable than earnings. Firms are reluctant to raise dividends in years of good earnings, and they resist dividend cuts as earnings decline. In view of investors' observed preference for stable dividends and of the probability that a cut in dividends is likely to be interpreted as forecasting a decline in earnings, stable dividends make good sense.

Stock Dividends and Splits Neither stock splits nor stock dividends alone exert a fundamental influence on prices. The fundamental determinant of the price of the company's stock is the company's earning power compared with the earning power of other companies. However, both stock splits and stock dividends can be used as an effective instrument of financial policy. They are useful devices for reducing the price at which stocks are traded, and studies indicate that stock dividends and stock splits tend to broaden the ownership of a firm's shares.

QUESTIONS **13–1** Discuss the advantages and disadvantages of each of the following dividend policies:

a) Constant payout ratio.
b) Constant dollar dividend per share.
c) Constant regular quarterly dividend plus a year-end extra when earnings are sufficiently high or corporate investment needs are sufficiently low.

13–2 How would each of the following changes probably affect aggregate payout ratios? Explain your answer.

a) An increase in the personal income tax rate.
b) A liberalization in depreciation policies for federal income tax purposes.
c) A rise in interest rates.
d) An increase in corporate profits.
e) A decline in investment opportunities.

13–3 Aggregate dividend payout ratios have been increasing since the end of World War II. Why?

13–4 Discuss the pros and cons of having the directors formally announce what a firm's dividend policy will be in the future.

13–5 What purpose do stock dividends and stock splits accomplish?

13–6 What is the difference between a stock dividend and a stock split? As a stockholder, would you prefer to see your company declare a 100 percent stock dividend or a two-for-one-split?

13–7 "The cost of retained earnings is less than the cost of new outside equity capital. Consequently, it is totally irrational for a firm to sell a new issue of stock and, during the same year, pay dividends." Discuss this statement.

13–1 Listed below are pertinent financial data for the common stocks of Pirro **PROBLEMS** Corporation, Dynamic Systems, and Eastern Fuel Gas. Pirro is a leading producer of copper, zinc, and lead, whose product demand is quite cyclical. Dynamic Systems is a computer manufacturer. Eastern Fuel Gas is an integrated gas system serving the northeastern United States.

Year	Earnings	Dividends	Price range	Payout	Price/ earnings* ratio	*Pirro Corporation*
1970	$4.59	$1.14	46–19	25%	10–4	
1969	2.25	0.73	21–12	32	9–5	
1968	0.99	0.69	21–11	70	18–10	
1967	0.87	0.66	27–18	76	25–17	
1966	2.01	0.58	24–15	29	11–7	
1965	1.73	0.54	27–19	31	14–9	
1964	0.95	0.46	25–13	48	20–10	
1963	1.11	0.79	29–12	71	22–9	
1962	2.19	0.75	37–26	34	12–8	
1961	2.78	0.64	28–16	23	7–4	
1970	$1.16	$0.06	46–32	5%	40–28	*Dynamic Systems*
1969	0.71	0.05	53–30	7	88–32	
1968	0.63	0.05	55–20	8	115–85	
1967	0.52	0.05	60–44	10	116–72	
1966	0.56	0.05	65–41	9	68–35	
1965	0.69	0.05	47–24	7	59–23	
1964	0.47	0.05	27–11	11	37–18	
1963	0.36	0.04	13–6	11	30–13	
1962	0.22	0.03	7–3	14	21–11	
1961	0.13	0.02	3–2	15	23–15	

Eastern Fuel Gas

1970	$2.17	$1.36	34–31	63%	16–14
1969	2.29	1.30	37–29	57	16–13
1968	2.15	1.23	31–23	57	14–11
1967	1.84	1.20	33–24	65	18–13
1966	1.86	1.20	24–22	64	13–12
1965	1.74	1.15	25–21	66	14–12
1964	1.78	1.10	24–17	62	13–10
1963	1.30	1.10	20–16	85	15–13
1962	1.58	1.03	22–19	65	14–12
1961	1.57	1.00	23–20	64	15–12

* Price/earnings ratios are the high and the low for the year according to *Standard & Poor's Reports.*

What differences are revealed by the data on the dividend policies of the three firms? What explanations can be given for these differences? What is the relationship of dividend policy to the market price of the stock?

13–2 In the following table, earnings and dividend data are shown for U.S. Telephone and Telegraph and Moon Oil Company, a closely held growing firm. Explain the difference in the percentage of dividends paid out by each.

U.S. Telephone and Telegraph

Year	Earnings	Dividend	Payout	Average price
1970	$3.24	$1.95	60%	70
1969	3.03	1.80	59	64
1968	2.90	1.80	62	59
1967	2.76	1.73	63	60
1966	2.77	1.65	60	47
1965	2.61	1.58	60	40
1964	2.34	1.50	64	33
1963	2.17	1.50	69	28
1962	2.20	1.50	68	30
1961	2.19	1.50	68	30

Moon Oil Company

Year	Earnings	Dividend	Payout	Average price
1970	$4.30	$0.95	22%	59
1969	3.85	0.90	23	46
1968	3.29	0.85	26	41
1967	3.09	0.81	26	43
1966	3.05	0.75	25	37
1965	2.64	0.73	28	44
1964	1.98	0.70	35	46
1963	2.93	0.67	23	50
1962	3.48	0.63	18	49
1961	2.95	0.58	20	44

13–3 Union spokesmen have presented arguments similar to the following: "Corporations such as General Foods retain about one half their profits—that is, they do not pay them out in dividends. Therefore, their profits are too high, because if they financed by selling common stock instead of by retained earnings, their prices or profits would not need to be so high." Evaluate the statement.

13–4 Select a pair of companies in problems 1 and 2 and calculate dividend payout based on cash flows. Would your previous explanation of dividend policies be affected by the cash flow payout patterns? The following financial data are appropriately scaled.

Pirro Corporation

Year	Net income*	Depreciation and depletion*
1970	$26.00	$8.78
1969	12.69	8.83
1968	5.53	8.98
1967	4.94	8.18
1966	9.38	7.56
1965	8.00	6.95
1964	3.98	6.27

U.S. Telephone and Telegraph

Year	Net income*	Depreciation and depletion*
1970	$1,658.6	$1,469.4
1969	1,479.5	1,332.1
1968	1,388.2	1,219.0
1967	1,284.6	1,099.9
1966	1,213.0	1,007.8
1965	1,113.2	930.0
1964	952.3	834.0

Dynamic Systems Corporation

Year	Net income*	Depreciation and depletion*
1970	$18.32	$5.24
1969	11.22	4.39
1968	9.96	3.41
1967	8.11	3.75
1966	8.81	2.87
1965	10.74	2.18
1964	7.21	1.58

Moon Oil Company

Year	Net income*	Depreciation and depletion*
1970	$68.51	$57.71
1969	61.22	62.19
1968	53.19	57.12
1967	49.79	65.60
1966	49.27	63.33
1965	42.84	52.81
1964	32.06	56.42

Eastern Fuel Gas

Year	Net income*	Depreciation and depletion*
1970	$11.05	$4.64
1969	11.66	4.65
1968	10.96	4.60
1967	9.35	4.20
1966	9.16	3.96
1965	8.56	3.95
1964	8.78	3.90

* After taxes, in millions of dollars.

Part V

Working Capital
Management

*W*ORKING *capital* refers to a firm's investment in short-term assets—cash, short-term securities, accounts receivable, and inventories. *Gross working capital* is defined as the firm's total current assets. *Net working capital* is defined as current assets minus current liabilities. If the term "working capital" is used without further qualification, it generally refers to gross working capital.

There are advantages and disadvantages to using the concept "working capital management." In the modern systems approach to business management everything is recognized to be related to everything else, and the operations of the firm are viewed as a total, integrated system. In this sense, it is artificial to study one segment of the firm, such as its current assets or its current liabilities. However, if one is really to understand the integrated whole, he must first understand the individual parts of the business firm. Therefore, it is useful to break down the total system and to analyze the component parts before taking an integrated view, as we do in Part VIII.

There are a number of aspects of working capital management that make it an important topic for study. Among them are the following.

IMPORTANCE OF WORKING CAPITAL MANAGEMENT

Surveys indicate that the largest portion of a financial manager's time is devoted to the day-by-day internal operations of the firm; this may be appropriately subsumed under the heading "working capital management." Since so much time is spent on working capital decisions, it is appropriate that the subject be covered carefully in managerial finance courses.

Time Devoted to Working Capital Management

Characteristically, current assets represent more than one-half the total assets of a business firm. Because they represent a large investment and because this investment tends to be relatively volatile, current assets are worthy of the financial manager's careful attention.

Investment in Current Assets

Relationship between Sales Growth and Current Assets The relationship between sales growth and the need to finance current assets is close and direct. For example, if the firm's average collection period is 40 days and if its credit sales are $1,000 a day, it will have an investment of $40,000 in accounts receivable. If sales rise to $2,000 a day, the investment in accounts receivable will rise to $80,000. Sales increases produce similar immediate needs for additional inventories and perhaps for working cash balances. All these needs must be financed, and since they arise so quickly, it is imperative that the financial manager keep himself aware of developments in the working capital segment of the firm. Of course, continued sales increases will require additional long-term assets, and these fixed asset additions must also be financed. However, fixed asset investments, while critically important to the firm in a strategic long-run sense, do not generally have the same urgency as do current asset investments.

Importance for Small Firms Working capital management is particularly important for small firms. A small firm may minimize its investments in fixed assets by renting or leasing plant and equipment. However, there is no way of avoiding an investment in cash, receivables, and inventories. Therefore, current assets are particularly significant for the financial manager of a small firm. Similarly, a small firm has relatively limited access to the long-term capital markets; therefore, it must necessarily rely heavily on trade credit and short-term bank loans, both of which affect net working capital by increasing current liabilities.

CONTROLLING INVESTMENT IN CASH AND MARKETABLE SECURITIES The starting point in controlling the investment in current assets is effective control of cash and cash equivalent. Cash equivalent includes marketable securities—for example, short-term government securities—characteristically held for liquidity purposes. These interest-bearing liquid assets can be converted to cash rapidly if the firm should need additional funds. "Cash" is primarily held as balances with commercial banks, largely in the form of demand deposits. Approximately 85 to 90 percent of all transactions in the United States are accomplished through the use of "cash" in the form of demand deposits.[1]

---

[1] A comment on the growing use of credit cards and the approach of the so-called checkless, cashless society is appropriate. As an increasing number of transactions are made with credit cards, individuals need smaller cash balances. If and when computerized transactions between accounts is feasible—A makes a purchase from B and instructs a computer to make a transfer from his balance to that of B—the need for working balances of both businesses and individuals will be greatly reduced. Trends in this direction have already caused huge increases in the income velocity of money (national income/money supply), and all indications are for a continuation if not acceleration of the trend.

Businesses or individuals have three primary motives for holding cash:
(1) the transactions motive, (2) the precautionary motive, and (3)
the speculative motive.

The transactions motive for holding cash is to enable the firm to conduct its ordinary business—making purchases and sales. In some lines of business, such as the utilities, where billings can be cycled throughout the month, cash inflows can be scheduled and synchronized closely with the need for the outflow of cash. Hence, we expect the cash-to-revenues ratio and cash-to-total-assets ratio for utility firms to be relatively low. In retail trade, by contrast, a large number of transactions may actually be conducted by physical currency. As a consequence, retail trade requires a higher ratio of cash to sales and of cash to total assets.

The seasonality of a business may give rise to a need for cash for the purchase of inventories. For example, raw materials may be available only during a harvest season and may be perishable, as in the food-canning business. Or sales may be seasonal, as are department store sales around the Christmas and the Easter holidays, giving rise to an increase in needs for cash.

The two other traditional motives for holding "cash" are actually satisfied in large part by holdings of near-money assets—short-term government securities and the like. The precautionary motive relates primarily to the predictability of cash inflows and outflows. If the predictability is high, less cash or cash equivalent will need to be held against an emergency or any other contingency. Another factor that strongly influences the precautionary motive for holding cash is the ability to borrow additional cash on short notice when circumstances necessitate. Borrowing flexibility is primarily a matter of the strength of the firm's relations with banking institutions and other sources of potential augmentation of its cash holdings.

The speculative motive for holding cash is to be ready for profit-making opportunities that may arise. By and large, accumulations of cash for speculative purposes are not widely found. Holding cash is more a function of the behavior of individual investors. However, the cash and marketable securities account may rise to rather sizable levels on a temporary basis for accumulating the means of financing. A dramatic example of this was the rise in cash and marketable securities of Montgomery Ward in 1948 to $149 million, representing 22 percent of total assets. Ward was counting on a post-World War II depression and built up cash to take advantage of the projected price level decline.[2]

---

[2] After the fact, this turned out to be a big mistake as no depression occurred; Ward's principal competitor, Sears Roebuck, expanded rapidly and captured a large part of Ward's traditional market.

Advantages of Adequate Cash: Specific Points   In addition to these general motives, sound working capital management requires maintenance of an ample amount of cash for several specific reasons. First, it is essential that the firm have sufficient cash to take trade discounts. The payment schedule for purchases is referred to as "the term of the sale." A commonly encountered billing procedure, or term of trade, allows a 2 percent discount if the bill is paid within 10 days, with full payment required in 30 days in any event. Since the net amount is due in 30 days, failure to take the discount means paying this extra 2 percent for using the money an additional 20 days. If you were to pay 2 percent for every 20-day period over the year, there would be eighteen such periods:

$$18 = \frac{360 \text{ days}}{20 \text{ days}}$$

This represents an annual interest rate of 36 percent.[3] Most firms are able to borrow at a rate substantially lower than 36 percent a year.

Second, since the current and acid test ratios are key items in credit analysis, it is essential that the firm, in order to maintain its credit standing, meet the standards of the line of business in which it is engaged. A strong credit standing enables the firm to purchase goods from trade suppliers on favorable terms and to maintain its line of credit with banks and other sources of credit.

Third, ample cash is useful for taking advantage of favorable business opportunities that may come along from time to time. Finally, the firm should have sufficient liquidity to meet emergencies, such as strikes, fires, or marketing campaigns of competitors.

Using the knowledge about the general nature of cash flows presented in Chapter 5, the financial manager may be able to improve the inflow-outflow pattern of cash. He can do so by better synchronization of flows and by reduction of float, as will be explained in the following two sections.

Synchronization of Cash Flows   As an example of synchronization, cash flows may be improved by more frequent requisitioning of funds by divisional offices from the firm's main or central office. A concrete illustration makes the point clearly.

Some Gulf Oil Corporation divisional field offices, for instance, used to requisition funds once or twice a week; now the treasurer's office insists on daily requisitions, thus keeping some cash on tap as much as four days longer. John Shaw, assistant treasurer, told an American Management Association seminar

---

[3] The method of calculating the effective interest rate on accounts payable is described in Chapter 15.

last year that, on the basis of ten offices, each requiring $500,000 a week, these staggered requisitions free the equivalent of $10 million for one day each week. At 3 percent interest, this earns better than $42,000 a year.[4]

In addition, effective forecasting can reduce the investment in cash. The cash flow forecasting at Universal Commercial Investment Trust Credit Corporation illustrates this idea. An assistant treasurer forecasts planned purchases of automobiles by the dealers. He estimates daily the number of cars shipped to the 10,000 dealers who finance their purchases through Universal CIT. He then estimates how much money should be deposited in Detroit banks that day to pay automobile manufacturers. On one day he estimated a required deposit of $6.4 million; the actual bill for the day was $6.397 million, a difference of one-half of 1 percent. Although such close forecasting cannot be achieved by every type of firm, the system enables Universal CIT to economize on the amount of money it must borrow and thereby keeps interest expense to a minimum.

Reduction of Float

Another important method of economizing on the volume of cash required is by reduction of "float." Float refers to funds in transit between cities. Checks received from customers in distant cities are subject to two types of delays: the time required for the check to travel in the mail and the time required for clearing through the banking system.

To reduce these two types of float, a "lock-box plan" can be used. If our firm makes sales in large amounts at far distances, we can establish a lock box in a post office located in the customer's area. We can arrange to have customers send payments to the postal box in their city and then have a bank pick up the checks and deposit them in a special checking account. The bank then has the checks cleared in the local area and remits by wire to our bank of deposit. If our distant customers are scattered, we can establish the lock box in our local city and have the checks picked up by our bank. The bank begins the clearing process, notifying us that a check has been received. In this way the clearing process starts before our firm processes the check. By these methods, float may be reduced by one to five days. Examples of freeing funds in the amount of $1.5 million or more by these methods have been cited by firms.

The use of lock-box plans can be illustrated by citing an example. Northeast Airlines, a firm with headquarters in Boston, has heavy ticket sales through travel agencies in Miami. If the Miami travel agents paid for tickets by mailing checks to Boston, Northeast would deposit

[4] *Business Week,* July 12, 1958.

the checks in a Boston bank, which would then clear them through the Federal Reserve System. This would require that the checks be physically sent to the Miami bank on which they were written. After clearance, Northeast's Boston bank would be notified, and only then could Northeast use the funds. The lock-box plan avoids all the time lost in mailing checks to and from Boston and thus gives Northeast the use of funds as much as a week earlier than without the plan.

INVESTMENT OF FUNDS

A firm may have cash to invest for a number of reasons. One is seasonal or cyclical fluctuations in business. As sales expand, inventories and receivables mount. As sales fall off, inventories and receivables decrease and become cash. Thus, during a seasonal or cyclical expansion, the firm will need to finance an increase in inventories and receivables. Some firms may borrow as their seasonal or cyclical needs for financing expand. Others, particularly firms in capital goods industries where fluctuations are violent, attempt to accumulate cash or near-cash during a downturn to be ready to finance an upturn in business volume.

Firms may also accumulate resources as a protection against a number of contingencies. When they make uninsurable product warranties, firms must be ready to meet claims that may arise. Firms in highly competitive industries must have resources to carry them through substantial shifts in the market structure. A firm in an industry in which new markets are emerging—for example, foreign markets—needs to have resources to meet developments; these funds may be on hand for fairly long periods.

Thus, because of uncertain contingencies, a firm may have cash funds to invest for a few weeks, a few months, a few years, or even indefinitely. Investment alternatives are available to meet the needs of the firm. Taking both yield and risk considerations into account, these alternatives are listed in Table 14–1.

Depending on how long he anticipates holding the funds, the financial manager decides upon a suitable maturity pattern for his holdings. The numerous alternatives can be selected and balanced in such a way that he obtains the maturities and risks appropriate to the financial situation of his firm. Commerical bankers, investment bankers, and brokers provide the financial manager with detailed information on each of the forms of investments in the list. Since their characteristics change with shifts in financial market conditions, it would be misleading to attempt to give detailed descriptions of these investment outlets here. The financial manager must keep up to date on these characteristics. He should follow the principle of making investment selections that offer maturities, yields, and risks appropriate to his firm.

Because some funds are to be held for extended periods, they may be invested with the objective of a higher return than that available from government securities. Such investments may be made in the stock of other companies. "Mostly, however, these are investments pure and simple, not for the sake of control. They were purchased to put the buyer's surplus cash to work harder, producing a larger return than it could earn, say, in the government bond market."[5]

	Approximate maturities*
U.S. Treasury bills	91–182 days
U.S. Treasury certificates	9–12 months
U.S. Treasury notes	1–5 years
Prime commercial paper	Varies up to 270 days
Negotiable certificates of deposit†	Varies up to 3 years
Savings certificates at commercial banks	6 months
Savings accounts at commercial banks	
Savings accounts at savings and loan associations	
Bonds and stocks of other corporations	
Bonds and stocks of the firm in question‡	

TABLE 14–1
Alternative marketable securities for investments

* The maturities are those at issue date. For outstanding securities, maturities varying almost by day or week are available.
† See Roy L. Reierson, "A New Money Market Instrument" (New York: Bankers Trust Company, March 24, 1961).
‡ See L. A. Guthart, "More Companies Are Buying Back Their Stock," *"Harvard Business Review*, XLIII, March 1965, pp. 40–45.

Investments in other companies follow several patterns. The percentage of ownership is characteristically small; thus it cannot be said that the dominant motive is control. Often the investments are made in firms in related industries. This practice is followed partly because the nature and outlook for such industries are better understood and partly because such investments may yield additional information useful for purchasing or sales activities. For example, suppliers to larger firms may often hold shares in the larger firms for the contacts that will be provided by shareholders' information and meetings. Clearly, control cannot be exercised by the smaller firm. However, the smaller firm may in this manner obtain market information that might otherwise be more difficult to obtain.

[5] "Part-Time Portfolios," *Forbes*, vol. 95 (May 15, 1961), pp. 16–17.

MANAGEMENT OF INVESTMENT IN RECEIVABLES In the present chapter, the term "trade credit" refers to accounts *receivable,* a current *asset,* and it involves both the credit used to support and expand sales and the resulting investment required of the firm. In Chapter 15, where its potentials and limitations as a source of funds are discussed, trade credit refers to accounts *payable,* a current *liability.*

The ratio of receivables to sales generally is in the range from 8 to 12 percent for manufacturing firms, representing an average collection period of approximately one month. The ratio of receivables to total assets centers on about 16 to 20 percent. However, wide variations are experienced among firms, particularly when nonmanufacturing industries are included.

The major determinants of the level of receivables are (1) volume of credit sales, (2) seasonality of sales, (3) rules for credit limits, (4) terms of sales and credit policies of individual firms, and (5) collection policies. Variations in the ratios of receivables to sales (or the average collection periods) among firms reflect the differential impact of the factors listed above.

Variations in terms of sale reflect the customs of the line of business. A very important influence, however, is the perishability of the product. On the one hand, very short payment periods are found in the bakery products, milk products, and meat products industries. On the other hand, relatively high ratios of receivables to sales are observed in the construction, industrial machinery, agricultural machinery, office equipment, and printing and publishing industries. In addition, higher ratios of receivables to sales are found among larger firms, which obtain funds at lower cost and tend to be wholesalers of credit obtained from financial institutions and reloaned to smaller firms.

Credit Policy The basis of a firm's credit policy is its industry's characteristic credit terms; generally, a firm must meet the terms provided by other firms in the industry. However, when a customer is a poor credit risk, the company giving the trade credit must be less lenient for its own protection. A central task in formulating credit policy is an evaluation of the credit worthiness of the potential customer.

To evaluate the credit risk, the credit manager considers the five C's of credit (*character, capacity, capital, collateral, conditions*). *Character* refers to the probability that the customer will *try* to honor his obligations. This factor is of considerable importance, because every credit transaction implies a *promise* to pay. Will the creditor make an honest effort to pay his debts, or is he likely to try to get away with something? Experienced credit men frequently insist that the moral factor is the most important issue in a credit evaluation.

Capacity is a subjective judgment of the ability of the customer. This is gauged by his past record, supplemented by physical observation of the customer's plant or store and business methods. *Capital* is measured by the general financial position of the firm as indicated by a financial-ratio analysis, with special emphasis on the tangible net worth of the enterprise. *Collateral* is represented by assets that the customer may offer as a pledge for security of the credit extended to him. Finally, *conditions* refers to the impact of general economic trends on the firm or special developments in certain areas of the economy that may affect the customer's ability to meet his obligations.

The five C's of credit represent the factors by which the credit risk is judged. Information on these items is obtained from the firm's previous experience with the customer, supplemented by a well-developed system of information-gathering groups. Two major sources of external information are available. The first is the work of the credit associations. By periodic meetings of local groups and by direct communication, information on experience with creditors is exchanged. More formally, credit interchange, a system developed by the National Association of Credit Management for assembling and distributing information of debtors' past performance, is provided. The interchange reports show the paying record of the debtor, industries from which he is buying, and the trading areas in which his purchases are being made.[6]

The second is the work of the credit-reporting agencies, the best known of which is Dun & Bradstreet. Agencies that specialize in coverage of a limited number of industries also provide information. Representative of these are the National Credit Office and the Lyon Furniture Mercantile Agency. Some of the services of Dun & Bradstreet are briefly described to indicate the nature of the information obtainable.

The Dun & Bradstreet Reference Book is published six times a year and covers the entire United States and Canada. Regional and state editions are also published. The Reference Book contains listings of firms and their credit ratings by town location. The credit ratings shown in Table 14–2 indicate both estimated financial strength and a composite credit appraisal. A credit appraisal of "high" indicates that financial affairs appear healthy and meet a number of important tests with reference to the five C's of credit.

When the rating of a firm is less than high, the financial manager may wish to obtain more specific information from credit reports sold by Dun & Bradstreet. The credit reports follow the forms indicated in Table 14–3. They provide a summary of the main information about

---

[6] For additional information, see *Credit Management Handbook, Second Edition,* a publication of the National Association of Credit Management (Homewood, Ill.: Richard D. Irwin, Inc., 1965).

TABLE 14–2
Key to ratings

	Estimated financial strength			Composite credit appraisal			
				High	Good	Fair	Limited
AA	Over		$1,000,000	A1	1	1 1/2	2
A+	Over		750,000	A1	1	1 1/2	2
A	$500,000	to	750,000	A1	1	1 1/2	2
B+	300,000	to	500,000	1	1 1/2	2	2 1/2
B	200,000	to	300,000	1	1 1/2	2	2 1/2
C+	125,000	to	200,000	1	1 1/2	2	2 1/2
C	75,000	to	125,000	1 1/2	2	2 1/2	3
D+	50,000	to	75,000	1 1/2	2	2 1/2	3
D	35,000	to	50,000	1 1/2	2	2 1/2	3
E	20,000	to	35,000	2	2 1/2	3	3 1/2
F	10,000	to	20,000	2 1/2	3	3 1/2	4
G	5,000	to	10,000	3	3 1/2	4	4 1/2
H	3,000	to	5,000	3	3 1/2	4	4 1/2
J				3	3 1/2	4	4 1/2
K	Up	to	3,000	3	3 1/2	4	4 1/2
L				3 1/2	4	4 1/2	5

K and L are being phased out.

Classification for both estimated financial strength and credit appraisal

Financial Strength Bracket		Explanation
1	$125,000 and over	When only the numeral (1, 2, 3, or 4) appears, it is an indica-
2	20,000 to 125,000	tion that the estimated financial strength, while not defi-
3		nitely classified, is presumed to be within the range of the
4	Up to 20,000	($) figures in the corresponding bracket and that a condi-
		tion is believed to exist which warrants credit in keeping
4 is being phased out		with that assumption.

"*Inv.*" shown in place of a rating indicates that the report was under investigation at the time of going to press. It has no other significance.

Not classified or absence of rating

The absence of a rating, expressed by two hyphens (- -), is not to be construed as unfavorable but signifies circumstances difficult to classify within condensed rating symbols. It suggests the advisability of obtaining a report for additional information.

Absence of a listing

The absence of a listing is not to be construed as meaning a concern is non-existent or has discontinued business, nor does it have any other meaning. The letters "NQ" on any written report mean "not listed in the Reference Book."

Year business started

The numeral shown is the last digit of the year date when the business was established or came under present control or management. Thus, 8 means 1968; 9 means 1969. No dates go past ten years. Thus the absence of a numeral indicates ten years or more. This feature is not used in connection with branch listings.

Source: Courtesy of Dun & Bradstreet, Inc.

TABLE 14-3

	Dun & Bradstreet **report**		**Rating**	
SIC	**D-U-N-S**	**Date of report**	**Started**	**Rating**
34 61	803-4520	CD 13 Apr 21 19— N		
	Arnold Metal Products Co	Metal stampings	1957	D 1½

53 S Main St
Dawson Mich 66666
   Tel 215 999-0000   Summary

Samuel B. Arnold	} Partners		Payments	Disc Ppt
George T. Arnold			Sales	$177,250
			Worth	$42,961
			Employs	8
			Record	Clear
			Condition	Sound
			Trend	Up

Payments	**HC**	**Owe**	**P**	**Due**	**Terms**	**Apr 1 19—**	**Sold**
	3000	1500	1	10	30	Disc	Over 3 yrs
	2500	1000	1	10	30	Disc	Over 3 yrs
	2000	500	2	20	30	Disc	Old account
	1000				30	Ppt	Over 3 yrs
	500				30	Ppt	Over 3 yrs

Finance   **On Apr. 21 19—S. B. Arnold, Partner, submitted statement Dec 31 19—**

Cash	$ 4,870	Accts pay	$ 6,121
Accts Rec	15,472	Notes pay (Curr)	2,400
Mdse	14,619	Accruals	3,583
Current	34,961	Current	12,104
Fixed Assets	22,840	Notes pay (Def)	5,000
Other Assets	2,264	Net worth	42,961
Total assets	60,065	Total	60,065

19— sales $177,250; gross profit $47,821; net profit $4,204. Fire Insurance mdse $15,000; fixed assets $20,000. Annual rent $3,000. Signed Apr 21 19— *Arnold Metal Product Co* by Samuel B. Arnold, Partner Johnson Singer, CPA, Dawson.
   Sales and profits increased last year due to increased sub-contract work and this trend is reported continuing. New equipment was purchased last Sept for $8,000 financed by a bank loan secured by a lien on the equipment payable $200 per month. With increased capacity, the business has been able to handle a larger volume. Arnold stated that for the first two months of this year volume was $32,075 and operations continue profitable.

Banking   Medium to high four figure balances are maintained locally. An equipment loan is outstanding and being retired as agreed.

History   Style registered Feb 1 1965 by partners. *Samuel*, born 1918, married. 1939 graduate of Lehigh University with B.S. degree in Mechanical Engineering. 1939–50 employed by Industrial Machine Corporation, Detroit, and 1950–56 production manager with Aerial Motors Inc., Detroit. Started this business in 1957. *George*, born 1940, single, son of Samuel. Graduated in 1963 from Dawson Institute of Technology. Served U.S. Air Force 1963–64. Admitted to partnership interest Feb 1965.

Operation   Manufactures light metal stampings for industrial concerns and also does some work on a subcontract basis for aircraft manufacturers. Terms net 30. 12 accounts. Five production, two office employees, and one salesman. *Location:* Rents one-story cinder block building with 5,000 square feet located in industrial section in normal condition. Housekeeping is good.
   4-21   (803 77) PRA

Source: Courtesy of Dun & Bradstreet, Inc.

the customer: his credit rating and history, a discussion of the business operations and their location, financial information, and the payment experience. The payment experience indicates whether the customer takes discounts, whether he pays promptly, and by how many days he delays payment if he does not pay promptly. In the example shown in Table 14–3, the five entries in the Payments section indicate that five suppliers were queried by Dun & Bradstreet. The first column, HC, shows the highest credit that has ever been extended by each creditor. The next column shows how much is presently outstanding, while the third column gives any amounts presently past due. The terms "Disc" and "Ppt" indicate that the illustrative firm takes discounts where available and otherwise pays promptly.

The information in Tables 14–2 and 14–3 can be translated into risk classes, grouped according to the probability of loss associated with sales to a customer. The combination of rating and supplementary information might lead to the following groupings of loss experience.

Group number	Loss ratio (in percentages)
1	None
2	0–1/2
3	1/2–1
4	1–2
5	2–5
6	5–10
7	10–20
8	over 20

Conditions → If the selling firm has a 20 percent margin over the sum of direct operating costs and all delivery and selling costs, and if it is producing at less than full capacity, it may adopt the following credit policies. It may sell on customary credit terms to groups 1 to 5; sell to groups 6 and 7 under more stringent credit terms, such as cash on delivery; and require advance payments from group 8. As long as the bad debt loss ratios are less than 20 percent, the additional sales are contributing something to overhead.

Statistical techniques, especially regression analysis and discriminant analysis,[7] have been used with some success in judging credit worthi-

---

[7] Discriminant analysis is similar to multiple regression analysis, except that it partitions a sample into two components on the basis of a set of characteristics. The sample, for example, might be loan applicants at a consumer loan company. The components into which they are classified might be those likely to make prompt repayment and those likely to default. The characteristics might be such factors as whether the applicant owns his home, how long he has been with his employer, and so forth.

ness. These methods serve best when individual credits are relatively small and a large number of borrowers are involved. Thus, they have worked best in retail credit, consumer loans, mortgage lending, and the like. As the increase in credit cards and similar procedures builds up, as computers are used more frequently, and as credit records on individuals and small firms are developed, statistical techniques promise to become much more important than they are today.[8]

In reviewing credit extensions, the financial manager should not be guided by bad debt loss ratios alone. These must also be related to the potential contribution that additional sales have made to overhead costs. Accounts receivable represent an investment. The return on this investment can be calculated by taking the contribution to additional net earnings and determining the return from the investment in receivables, as in any capital budgeting problem.

Manufacturing firms generally have three kinds of inventories: (raw materials, work in process, and finished goods) The levels of raw material inventories are influenced by anticipated production, seasonality of production, reliability of sources of supply, and efficiency of scheduling purchases and production operations. **INVENTORY CONTROL**

Work-in-process inventory is strongly influenced by the length of the production period, which is the time between placing raw material in production and completing the finished product. Inventory turnover can be increased by decreasing the production period. One means of accomplishing this is perfecting engineering techniques to speed up the manufacturing process. Another means of reducing work in process is to buy items rather than make them.

The level of finished goods inventories is a matter of coordinating production and sales. The financial manager can stimulate sales by changing credit terms or by allowing credit to marginal risks. Whether the goods remain on the books as inventories or as receivables, the financial manager has to finance them. Many times, firms find it desirable to make the sale and thus take one step nearer to realizing cash. The potential profits can outweigh the additional collection risk.

Our primary focus in this section is on controlling the investment in inventories. *Inventory models* have been developed to aid in this task and have proved extremely useful in minimizing inventory requirements. As our examination of the du Pont system in Chapter 3 showed, any procedure that can reduce the investment required to generate ✕

---

[8] It has been said the biggest single deterrent to the increased automation of credit processes is George Orwell's classic book, *1984,* in which he described the social dangers of centralized files of information on individuals. Orwell's omnipresent watcher, Big Brother, is mentioned frequently in Congressional sessions discussing mass storage of information relevant to credit analysis.

a given sales volume may have a beneficial effect on the firm's rate of return and, hence, on the value of the firm.

DETERMINANTS OF SIZE OF INVENTORIES

Although wide variations occur, inventory-to-sales ratios are generally concentrated in the 12 to 20 percent range, and inventory-to-total assets ratios are concentrated in the 16 to 30 percent range.

The major determinants of investment in inventory are the following: (1) level of sales, (2) length and technical nature of the production processes, and (3) durability versus perishability or style factor in the end product. Inventories in the tobacco industry are high because of the long curing process. Likewise, in the machinery-manufacturing industries, inventories are large because of the long work-in-process period. However, inventory ratios are low in coal mining and in oil and gas production because no raw materials are used, and the goods in process are small in relation to sales. Because of the seasonality of the raw materials, inventories are large in the canning industry.

With respect to the durability and style factors, large inventories are found in the hardware and the precious-metals industries because durability is great and the style factor is small. Inventory ratios are low in baking because of the perishability of the final product. Inventories are low in printing because the items are manufactured to order and require negligible finished inventories.

Within limits set by the economics of a firm's industry, there exists a potential for improvement in inventory control from the use of computers and operations research. Although the techniques are far too diverse and complicated for a complete treatment in this text, the financial manager should be prepared to make use of the contributions of specialists who have developed effective procedures for minimizing the investment in inventory.

Illustrative of the techniques at the practical level is the following:

Raytheon's new system works like this: Tabulator cards are inserted in each package of five electronic tubes leaving Raytheon's warehouse. As the merchandise is sold, the distributor collects the cards and files his replacement order without doing paper work. He simply sends in the cards, which are identified by account number, type of merchandise, and price of the units he orders.

Western Union Telegraph Co. equipment accepts the punched cards and transmits information on them to the warehouse, where it is duplicated on other punched cards. A typical order of 5,000 tubes of varying types can be received in about 17 minutes, Raytheon says. It can be assembled in about 90 minutes and delivered to Boston's Logan Airport in an additional 45 minutes. Orders from 3,000 miles away can be delivered within 24 hours, a saving of 13 days in some cases.[9]

[9] Roger B. Rowand, "Tactics Vary as Firms Try to Cut Warehouse Costs, Speed Service," *The Wall Street Journal* (May 26, 1961), pp. 1, 11.

Managing assets of all kinds is basically an inventory-type problem—the same method of analysis applies to cash and fixed assets, as well as to inventories themselves. First, a basic stock must be on hand to balance inflows and outflows of the items, with the size of the stock depending upon the patterns of flows, whether regular or irregular. Second, because the unexpected may always occur, it is necessary to have safety stocks on hand. They represent the little extra to avoid the costs of not having enough to meet current needs. Third, additional amounts may be required to meet future growth needs. These are anticipation stocks. Related to anticipation stocks is the recognition that there are optimum purchase sizes, defined as *economical ordering quantities.* In borrowing money, or in buying raw materials for production, or in purchasing plants and equipment, it is cheaper to buy more than just enough to meet immediate needs.

With the foregoing as a basic foundation, the theoretical basis for determining the optimal investment in inventory can be developed and illustrated as in Figure 14–1. Some costs rise with larger inventories—included here would be warehousing costs, interest on funds tied up in inventories, insurance, obsolescence, and so forth. Other

GENERALITY OF INVENTORY ANALYSIS

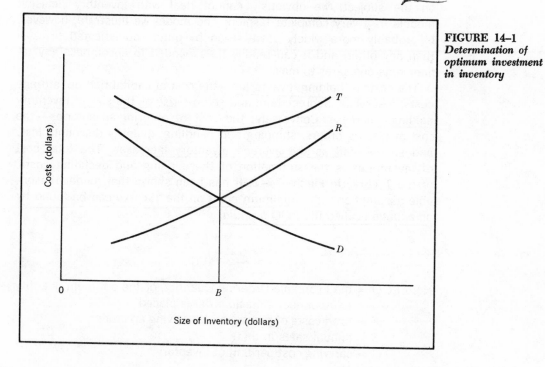

FIGURE 14–1
Determination of optimum investment in inventory

costs decline with larger inventories—included here would be the loss of profits resulting from sales lost because of running out of stock, costs of production interruptions caused by inadequate inventories, possible purchase discounts, and so on.

Those costs that decline with higher inventories are designated by curve D in Figure 14–1, while those that rise with larger inventories are designated by curve R. T is the total of the R and D curves, and it represents the total cost of ordering and holding inventories. At the point where the absolute value of the slope of the R curve is equal to the absolute value of the slope of the D curve (that is, where *marginal* rising costs are equal to *marginal* declining costs), the T curve is at a minimum. This represents the optimum size of investment in inventory.

INVENTORY DECISION MODELS The generalized statements in the preceding section can be made much more specific. In fact, it is usually possible to specify the curves shown in Figure 14–1, at least to a reasonable approximation, and to actually find the minimum point on the total cost curve. Since whole courses (in operations research programs) are devoted to inventory control techniques, and since a number of books have been written on the subject, we obviously cannot deal with inventory decision models in a very complete fashion. The model we illustrate, however, is probably more widely used—even by quite sophisticated firms—than any other, and it can readily be expanded to encompass any refinements one cares to make.[10]

The costs of holding inventories—the cost of capital tied up, storage costs, insurance, depreciation, and so on—rise as the size of inventory holdings increase. Conversely, the cost of ordering inventories—the cost of placing orders, shipping and handling, quantity discounts lost, and so on—fall as the average inventory increases. The total cost of inventories is the summation of these rising and declining costs, or the T curve in Figure 14–1. It has been shown that, under reasonable assumptions, the minimum point on the T curve can be found by an equation called the *EOQ formula:*

$$EOQ = \sqrt{\frac{2FS}{C}}.$$

Here EOQ = the Economic Ordering Quantity, or the optimum quantity
to order each time an order is placed
F = fixed costs of placing and receiving an order
S = annual sales in units
C = carrying cost per unit of inventory.

[10] In this book we simply illustrate the use of the *EOQ* inventory model; for an explanation of its development see Chapter 14, *Managerial Finance,* third edition.

For any level of sales, dividing S by EOQ indicates the number of orders that must be placed each year. The average inventory on hand—the average balance sheet inventory figure— will be

$$\text{Average inventory} = \frac{EOQ}{2}.$$

The derivation of the EOQ model assumes ① that usage is at a constant rate and ② that delivery lead times are constant. In fact, usage is likely to vary considerably for most firms—demand may be unexpectedly strong for any number of reasons, and if it is, the firm will run out of stock and suffer sales losses or production stoppages. Similarly, delivery lead times will vary depending on weather, strikes, demand in the suppliers' industries, and so on. Because of these factors, firms add *safety stocks* to their inventory holdings, and the average inventory becomes:

$$\text{Average inventory} = \frac{EOQ}{2} + \text{safety stock}.$$

The size of the safety stock will be relatively high if uncertainties about usage rates and delivery times are great, low if these factors do not vary greatly. Similarly, the safety stock will be larger if the costs of running out of stock are great. For example, if customer ill will would cause a permanent loss of business or if an elaborate production process would have to stop if an item were out of stock, then large safety stocks will be carried.[11]

Assume the following values are determined to be appropriate for a particular firm:

Illustration of the Use of the EOQ Model

S = sales = 100 units

C = carrying cost = 20 percent of inventory value = \$.20/unit

F = fixed cost of ordering = \$10.

Substituting these values into the formula, we obtain

$$EOQ = \sqrt{\frac{2FS}{C}}$$

$$= \sqrt{\frac{2 \times 10 \times 100}{.2}}$$

$$= 100 \text{ units.}$$

---

[11] Formal methods have been developed to assist in striking a balance between the costs of carrying larger safety stocks and the cost of stock-outs. A discussion of these models, which go beyond the scope of this book, can be found in most production textbooks.

If the desired safety stock is 10 units, then the average inventory (A) will be

$$A = \frac{EOQ}{2} + \text{safety stock}$$

$$= \frac{100}{2} + 10$$

$$= 60 \text{ units.}$$

If the cost of purchasing or manufacturing inventory is $100 per unit, the average inventory in dollars will be $6,000.

CASH MANAGEMENT AS AN INVENTORY PROBLEM In Chapter 6, when cash budgeting was considered, we indicated that firms generally have "minimum desired cash balances." Then, in discussing cash management, we considered the various factors that influence cash holdings. We did not, however, attempt to specify optimum cash balances. Optimum cash balances can be found by the use of inventory-type models such as those discussed in this chapter. In fact, cash management, together with inventory controls, is perhaps the area of financial management where mathematical tools have proved most useful.

Sophisticated cash management models recognize the uncertainty inherent in forecasting both cash inflows and cash outflows. Inflows are represented, in effect, by the "orders" in our inventory model; they come principally from ① receipts, ② borrowing, and ③ sale of securities. The primary "carrying cost" of cash is the opportunity cost of having funds tied up in nonearning assets (or in low yielding near-cash items), the principal "ordering costs" are brokerage costs associated with borrowing funds or converting marketable securities into cash.[12]

Cash management models have proved useful in determining the optimal amount of cash to keep on hand, but the types of models that have been used in practice are quite complex, and a discussion of them would go beyond the scope of this book.

SUMMARY The du Pont system described in Chapter 3 makes it clear that a high rate of return on investment is dependent upon controlling the size of the firm's investment. The purpose of this chapter was to examine methods of controlling the investment in current assets. Investment in current assets is important because current assets constitute

---

[12] See *Managerial Finance*, third edition, Chapter 14, for a discussion of cash management models.

more than one-half the total assets of the firm. Moreover, the relationship between sales growth and the need for funds to finance current assets is close and direct. For small, undercapitalized firms, working capital management is particularly important, because, while investment in fixed assets may be minimized by renting or leasing equipment and plant, investment in receivables and inventories cannot be reduced to the same degree.

Current assets consist primarily of cash, marketable securities, accounts receivable, and inventories. Ways of determining just how much of these assets should be kept on hand were analyzed in some detail in this chapter.

Cash and marketable securities are kept on hand for transaction purposes. There are clear advantages to having adequate cash on hand, but cash is a nonearning asset, so holdings should be kept to the minimum necessary level.

Accounts receivable are an important element of current assets. The major determinants of the level of receivables are the volume of credit sales, terms of sales, credit policies, and collection policies. The financial manager should understand how these factors interact to determine receivables and how he can alter the factors to control the level of receivables.

Inventories—raw materials, work in process, and finished goods— are necessary in most businesses. Rather elaborate systems for controlling the level of inventories have been designed. These systems frequently use computers for keeping records of all the items in stock; an inventory control model that considers anticipated sales, ordering costs, and carrying costs can be used to determine *EOQ's* for each item.

The basic inventory model recognizes that certain costs (carrying costs) rise as average inventory holdings increase, but that certain other costs (ordering costs and stock-out costs) fall as average inventory holdings rise. These two sets of costs comprise the total cost of ordering and carrying inventories, and the *EOQ* model is designed to locate an optimal order size that will minimize total inventory costs.

14–1 How can better methods of communications make it less necessary for **QUESTIONS** firms to hold large cash balances?

14–2 The highly developed financial system of the United States, with its myriad of different near-cash assets, has greatly reduced cash balance requirements. Discuss.

14–3 Assuming a firm's volume of business remained constant, would you expect it to have higher cash balances (demand deposits) during a tight-money or an easy-money period? Does this situation have any ramifications for federal monetary policy?

14–4   If a firm sells on terms of net 30 and its accounts are on the average 30 days overdue, what will its investment in receivables be if its credit sales approximate $720,000?

14–5   "It is difficult to judge the performance of many of our employees, but not that of the credit manager. If he's performing perfectly, credit losses are zero, and the higher our losses (as a percent of sales), the worse his performance." Evaluate the statement.

14–6   Explain how a firm may reduce its investment in inventory by having its supplier hold raw materials inventories and its customers hold finished goods inventories. What are the limitations of such a policy?

14–7   What factors are likely to reduce the holdings of inventory in relation to sales in the future? What factors will tend to increase the ratio? What, in your judgment, is the net effect?

14–8   What are the probable effects of the following on inventory holdings?

a) Manufacture of a part formerly purchased from an outside supplier.
b) Greater use of air freight.
c) Increase, from 7 to 17, in the number of styles produced.
d) Your firm is offered large price reductions from a manufacturer of bathing suits if they are purchased in December and January.

14–9   Inventory decision models are designed to facilitate the minimization of the cost of obtaining and carrying inventory. Describe the basic nature of the fundamental inventory control model, discussing specifically the nature of increasing costs, decreasing costs, and total costs. Illustrate your discussion with a graph.

PROBLEMS   **14–1**   The Pappas Machinery Company has sales of $50 million a year in good years and $30 million in poor years. Its fixed assets are $15 million; receivables and inventories are 40 percent of sales; total assets are constant at $40 million.

   The firm must have liquidity because of substantial risks under product warranties. In addition, the firm must be ready to meet extended terms provided by foreign competitors.

a) How much cash does the firm have available for investment in good years? in poor years?
b) Suggest three kinds of investments to be used by this firm.

14–2   The following relations for inventory purchase and storage costs have been established by analysis for the Stone Manufacturing Corporation.

1. Orders must be placed in multiples of 100 units.
2. Requirements for the year are 200,000 units. (Use 50 weeks in a year for calculations.)
3. Carrying cost is 10 cents per unit.
4. Purchasing cost per order is $16.00.
5. Desired safety stock is 3,000 units (on hand initially).
6. Two weeks are required for delivery.

a) What is the economical order size?
b) What is the optimal number of orders to be placed?
c) At what inventory level should a reorder be made?

IN Chapter 4 we traced the flow of cash through an illustrative business firm and discussed certain broad principles for managing investments in current assets. We then formalized current assets management somewhat in Chapter 14, where inventory models were considered. In the present chapter we take up the main forms of short-term credit, considering both the characteristics and the sources of this credit.

Short-term credit is defined as debt originally scheduled for repayment within one year. The three major sources of funds with short maturities are discussed in this chapter. Ranked in descending order by volume of credit supplied to business, the main sources of short-term financing are (1) trade credit between firms, (2) loans from commercial banks, and (3) commercial paper. To some degree these sources also supply funds for longer terms, but their primary importance in short-term financing justifies treatment at this point.

TRADE CREDIT[1] In the ordinary course of events, a firm buys its supplies and materials on credit from other firms, recording the debt as an *account payable*. Accounts payable, or trade credit as it is commonly called, is the largest single category of short-term credit, and it represents about 40 percent of the current liabilities of nonfinancial corporations. This percentage is somewhat larger for smaller firms; since small companies may not qualify for financing from other sources, they rely rather heavily on trade credit.

[1] In Chapter 14, we discussed trade credit from the point of view of minimizing investment in current assets. In the present chapter we look at "the other side of the coin," viewing trade credit as a *source* of financing rather than as a *use* of financing. In Chapter 14, the use of trade credit by our customers resulted in an asset investment called "accounts receivable." In the present chapter, the use of trade credit gives rise to a short-term obligation generally called "accounts payable."

Trade credit is a "spontaneous" source of financing in that it arises from ordinary business transactions. For example, suppose a firm makes average purchases of $2,000 a day on terms of net 30. On the average it will owe 30 times $2,000, or $60,000 to its suppliers. If its sales, and consequently its purchases, double, accounts payable will also double to $120,000. The firm will have spontaneously generated an additional $60,000 of financing. Similarly, if the terms of credit are extended from 30 to 40 days, accounts payable will expand from $60,000 to $80,000; thus, lengthening the credit period, as well as expanding sales and purchases, generates additional financing.

Credit Terms The terms of sales, or credit terms, describe the payment obligation of the buyer. The four main factors that influence the length of credit terms are outlined below.

1. Economic Nature of Product Commodities with high sales turnover are sold on relatively short credit terms; the buyer resells the product rapidly, generating cash that enables him to pay the supplier. Groceries have a high turnover, but perishability also plays a role. The credit extended for fresh fruits and vegetables might run from 5 to 10 days, whereas the credit extended on canned fruits and vegetables would more likely be 15 to 30 days. Terms for items that have a slow retail turnover, such as jewelry, may run six months or longer.

2. Seller Circumstances Financially weak sellers must require cash or exceptionally short credit terms. For example, farmers sell livestock to meat-packing companies on a cash basis. In some industries, variations in credit terms can be used as a sales promotion device. Although the use of credit as a selling device endangers sound credit management, the practice does occur, especially when the seller's industry has excess capacity. Also, a large seller could use his position to impose relatively short credit terms. However, the reverse appears more often in practice; that is, financially strong sellers are suppliers of funds to smaller firms.

3. Buyer Circumstances In general, financially sound retailers who sell on credit may, in turn, receive slightly longer terms. Some classes of retailers regarded as selling in particularly risky areas (such as clothing) receive extended credit terms, but they are offered large discounts to encourage early payment.

4. Cash Discounts A cash discount is a reduction in price based on payment within a specified period. The costs of not taking cash discounts often exceed the rate of interest at which the buyer can borrow, so it is important that a firm be cautious in its use of trade credit as a source of financ-ing—it could be quite expensive.[2] If the firm borrows and takes the cash discount, the period during which accounts payable remain on the books is reduced. The effective length of credit is thus influenced by the size of discounts offered.

Credit terms typically express the amount of the cash discount and the date of its expiration, as well as the final due date. Probably the most frequently encountered terms are 2/10, net 30. In other words, if payment is made within 10 days of the invoice date, a 2 percent cash discount is allowed. If the cash discount is not taken, payment is due 30 days after the date of invoice. The cost of not taking cash discounts can be substantial, as shown here. *Illustrative Credit Terms*

Credit terms	Cost of credit if cash discount not taken
1/10, net 20	36.36%
1/10, net 30	18.18%
2/10, net 20	73.44%
2/10, net 30	36.72%

Trade credit has double-edged significance for the firm. It is a source of credit for financing purchases and a way to use funds by which a firm finances credit sales to customers. For example, if a firm sells on the average $3,000 of goods a day with an average collection period of 40 days, it will have accounts receivable at any balance sheet date of approximately $120,000. *Employment of Trade Credit*

If the firm buys $2,000 worth of materials a day and the balance is outstanding for 20 days, accounts payable will average $40,000. The firm is extending net credit of $80,000, the difference between accounts receivable and accounts payable.

It is important, therefore, that the firm make the maximum use of trade credit as a source of funds, but at the same time it should

---

[2] The following equation may be used for calculating the cost, on an annual basis, of not taking discounts:

$$\text{Cost} = \frac{\text{discount percent}}{(100 - \text{discount percent})} \times \frac{360}{(\text{final due date} - \text{discount period})}.$$

The denominator in the first term, (100 — discount percent), equals the funds made available by not taking the discount. To illustrate, the cost of not taking a discount when the terms are 2/10, net 30 is computed.

$$\text{Cost} = \frac{2}{98} \times \frac{360}{20} = 0.0204 \times 18 = 36.72\%.$$

minimize the extent to which its own funds are tied up in accounts receivable.

Advantages of
Trade Credit as a
Source of
Financing

Trade credit, a customary part of doing business in most lines of activity, is convenient and informal. A firm that does not qualify for credit from a financial institution may receive trade credit because previous experience has familiarized the seller with the credit-worthiness of his customer. As the seller knows the merchandising practices of the line of business, he is usually in a good position to judge the capacity of his customer and the risk of selling to him on credit. The amount of trade credit fluctuates with the buyer's purchases, subject to any credit limits that may be operative.

Whether trade credit costs more or less than other forms of financing is a moot question. Sometimes trade credit can be surprisingly expensive to the buyer. The user often does not have other alternative forms of financing available, and the costs to the buyer may be commensurate with the risks to the seller. But in some instances trade credit is used simply because the user may not realize how expensive it is. In such circumstances, careful financial analysis may lead to the substitution of alternative forms of financing for trade credit.

At the other extreme, trade credit may represent a virtual subsidy or sales promotion device offered by the seller. The authors know, for example, of cases where manufacturers quite literally supplied *all* the financing for new firms by selling on credit terms substantially longer than those of the new company. In one instance a manufacturer, anxious to obtain a dealership in a particular area, made a loan to the new company to cover operating expenses during the initial phases and geared the payment of accounts payable to cash receipts. Even in such instances, however, the buying firm must be careful that it is not really paying a hidden financing cost in the form of higher product prices than could be obtained elsewhere.[3]

SHORT-TERM
FINANCING
BY
COMMERCIAL
BANKS

Commercial bank lending appears on the balance sheet as *notes payable* and is second in importance to trade credit as a source of short-term financing. Banks occupy a pivotal position in the short-term and intermediate-term money markets. Their influence is greater than appears from the dollar amounts they lend, because the banks provide non-spontaneous funds. As a firm's financing needs grow, the banks are called upon to provide the additional funds. If the request is denied, often the alternative is to slow down the rate of growth or to cut back operations.

[3] For numerous examples, see Robert P. Hungate, "Inter-business Financing" (unpublished Ph.D. dissertation, University of California, Los Angeles, January 1961).

The main characteristics of lending patterns of commercial banks are briefly described.

A single loan obtained from a bank by a business firm is not different in principle from a loan obtained by an individual. In fact, it is often difficult to distinguish a bank loan to a small business from a personal loan. A single loan is obtained by signing a conventional promissory note. Repayment is made in a lump sum at maturity (when the note is due) or in installments throughout the life of the loan.

A *line of credit* is a formal or an informal understanding between the bank and the borrower concerning the maximum loan balance the bank will allow the borrower. For example, a bank loan officer may indicate to a financial manager that the bank regards his firm as "good" for up to $80,000 for the forthcoming year. Subsequently, the manager signs a promissory note for $15,000 for 90 days—he is said to be "taking down" $15,000 of his total line of credit. This amount is credited to the firm's checking account at the bank. At maturity, the checking account will be charged for the amount of the loan. Interest may be deducted in advance or paid at maturity of the loan. Before repayment of the $15,000, the firm may borrow additional amounts up to a total of $80,000.

A more formal procedure may be followed if the firm is quite large. To illustrate, Chrysler Corporation arranged a line of credit for over $100 million with a group of banks. The banks were formally committed to lend Chrysler the funds if they were needed. Chrysler, in turn, paid a commitment fee of approximately $\frac{1}{4}$ of 1 percent of the unused balance of the commitment to compensate the banks for tying up their funds.

Banks make loans of all sizes. The bulk of loans from commercial banks by dollar amount is obtained by firms with total assets of $5 million and more. But, by number of loans, firms with total assets of $50,000 and less account for about 40 percent of bank loans.

Commercial banks concentrate on the short-term lending market. Short-term loans make up about two-thirds of bank loans by dollar amount, whereas "term loans" (loans with maturities longer than one year) make up only one-third.

If a potential borrower is a questionable credit risk or if his financing needs exceed the amount that the loan officer of the bank considers to be prudent on an unsecured basis, some form of security is required. More than one-half the dollar value of bank loans is secured; the forms of security are described later in this chapter. In terms of the number of bank loans, two-thirds are secured or endorsed by a third party who guarantees payment of the loan in the event the borrower defaults.

Minimum Balance   Banks typically require that a regular borrower maintain an average checking account balance equal to 15 or 20 percent of the outstanding loan. These balances, which are commonly called *compensating balances,* are a method of raising the effective interest rate. For example, if a firm needs $80,000 to pay off outstanding obligations, but must maintain a 20 percent compensating balance, it must borrow $100,000 to be able to obtain the required $80,000. If the stated interest rate is 5 percent, the effective cost is actually $6\frac{1}{4}$ percent—$5,000 divided by $80,000 equals 6.25 percent.[4]

Repayment of   Because the bulk of bank deposits is subject to withdrawal on demand,
Bank Loans   commercial banks seek to prevent firms from using bank credit for permanent financing. A bank may therefore require its borrowers to "clean up" their short-term bank loans for at least one month each year. If a firm is unable to become free of bank debt at least part of each year, it is using bank financing for permanent needs and should develop additional sources of long-term or permanent financing.

Cost of Commercial   Most loans from commercial banks have recently ranged from 7 to
Bank Loans   12 percent, with the effective rate depending upon the characteristics of the firm and the level of interest rates in the economy. If the firm can qualify as a "prime risk" because of its size and financial strength, the rate of interest will be one-half to three-quarters of 1 percent above the rediscount rate charged by federal reserve banks to commercial banks. On the other hand, a small firm with below average financial ratios may be required to provide collateral security and to pay an effective rate of interest of more than 12 percent.

Determination of the effective or true rate of interest on a loan depends upon the stated rate of interest and the method of charging interest by the lender. If the interest is paid at the maturity of the loan, the stated rate of interest is the effective rate of interest. If the bank deducts the interest in advance (*discounts* the loan), the effective rate of interest is increased. On a $10,000 loan for one year

---

[4] Note, however, that if the compensating balance is set as a minimum monthly *average,* and if the firm would maintain this average anyway, the compensating balance requirement does not entail higher effective rates.

at 5 percent, the discount is $500 and the borrower obtains the use of only $9,500. The effective rate of interest is

$$\frac{\$500}{\$9,500} = 5.3\%.$$

If the loan is repaid in twelve monthly installments, the effective rate of interest is even higher. In this event the borrower pays $500 for the use of about one-half the amount he receives. The amount received is $10,000 or $9,500, depending upon the methods of charging interest, but the *average* amount outstanding during the year is only $5,000 or $4,750. If interest is paid at maturity, the effective rate would be approximately

$$\frac{\$500}{\$5,000} = 10\%.$$

Under the discounting method, the effective cost of the installment loan would be approximately

$$\frac{\$500}{\$4,750} = 10.53\%.$$

The point to note here is that interest is paid on the *original* amount of the loan, not on the amount actually outstanding (the declining balance), and this causes the effective interest rate to be approximately double the stated rate.

Choice of Bank or Banks

Banks have close relations with their borrowers. Since there is considerable personal contact over the years, the business problems of the borrower are frequently discussed; thus the bank often provides informal management counseling services. A potential borrower seeking bank relations should recognize the important differences among banks as potential sources of funds. These differences can be summarized as follows:

1. Banks have different basic policies toward risk. Some banks are inclined to follow relatively conservative lending practices; others engage in what are properly termed "creative banking practices." The policies reflect partly the personalities of officers of the bank and partly the characteristics of the bank's deposit liabilities. Thus a bank with fluctuating deposit liabilities in a static community will tend to be a conservative lender. A bank whose deposits are growing with little interruption may follow "liberal" credit policies. A large bank with broad diversification over geographical regions or among industries served can obtain the benefit of combining and averaging risks. Thus, marginal credit risks that might be unacceptable to a small bank or to a specialized unit bank can be pooled by a branch banking system to reduce the over-all risks of a group of marginal accounts.

2. Some bank loan officers are active in providing counsel and in stimulating development loans with firms in their early and formative years. Certain banks have specialized departments to make loans to firms expected to become growth firms. The personnel of these departments can provide considerable counseling to customers.

3. Banks differ in the extent to which they will support the activities of the borrower in bad times. This characteristic is referred to as the degree of *loyalty* of the banks. Some banks may put considerable pressure on a business to liquidate its loans when the firm's outlook becomes clouded, whereas others will stand by the firm and work diligently to help it attain a more favorable condition.

4. The fourth characteristic by which banks differ is the degree of deposit stability. Instability arises not only from fluctuations in the level of deposits but also from the composition of deposits. Deposits can take the form of demand deposits (checking accounts) or time deposits (savings accounts, certificates of deposit, Christmas clubs). Total deposits tend to be more stable when time deposits are substantial. Differences in deposit stability go a long way toward explaining differences in the extent to which the banks are willing or able to help the borrower work himself out of difficulties or even crises.

5. Banks differ greatly in the degree of loan specialization. Larger banks have separate departments specializing in different kinds of loans, such as real estate, installment loans, and commercial loans, among others. Within these broad categories there may be a specialization by line of business, such as steel, machinery, or textiles. The strengths of smaller banks are likely to reflect the nature of the business and the economic environment in which the banks operate. They tend to become specialists in specific lines, such as oil, construction, and agriculture, to name a few. The borrower can obtain more creative cooperation and more active support if he goes to the bank that has the greatest experience and familiarity with his particular type of business. The financial manager should therefore choose his bank with care. A bank that is excellent for one firm may be unsatisfactory for another.

6. The size of a bank can be an important characteristic. Since the maximum loan a bank can make to any one customer is generally lim-

ited to 10 percent of capital accounts (capital stock plus surplus accounts), it will generally not be appropriate for large firms to develop borrowing relationships with small banks.

7. With the heightened competition between commercial banks and other financial institutions, the aggressiveness of banks has increased. Modern commercial banks now offer a wide range of financial and business services. Most large banks have business development departments that provide counseling to firms and serve as intermediaries on a wide variety of their requirements.

Commercial paper consists of promissory notes of *large* firms and is sold primarily to other business firms, insurance companies, pension funds, and banks. Although the amounts of commercial paper outstanding are less than 5 percent of bank loans outstanding, this form of financing is important to particular lines of business. **COMMERCIAL PAPER** *Nature*

Maturities of commercial paper vary from two to six months, with an average of about five months. The rates on prime commercial paper vary, but they are generally about ½ of 1 percent below those on prime business loans. And, since compensating balances are not required for commercial paper, the *effective* cost differential is still wider.[5] *Maturity and Cost*

The use of the open market for commercial paper is restricted to a comparatively small number of concerns that are exceptionally good credit risks. Dealers prefer to handle the paper of concerns whose net worth is $5 million or more and whose annual borrowing exceeds $500,000. *Use*

A large number of advantages are claimed for the commercial paper market. (1) It permits the broadest and most advantageous distribution of paper. (2) It provides more funds at lower rates than do other methods. (3) The borrower avoids the inconvenience and expense of financing arrangements with a number of institutions, each of which requires a compensating balance. (4) Publicity and prestige accrue to the borrower as his product and his paper become more widely known. (5) Finally, the commercial paper dealer frequently offers valuable advice to his clients. *Appraisal of Use*

[5] However, this factor is offset to some extent, as firms which issue commercial paper are generally required by commercial paper dealers to have unused bank lines of credit equal to about 10 percent of their outstanding volume of commercial paper. The usual compensating balance on regular bank loans today is 15 to 20 percent, so there is still an advantage to commercial paper.

A basic limitation of the commercial paper market is that the size of the funds available is limited to the excess liquidity that corporations, the main suppliers of funds, may have at any particular time. Another disadvantage is that a debtor who is in temporary financial difficulty receives little consideration, because commercial paper dealings are impersonal. Bank relations, on the other hand, are much more personal; a bank is much more likely to help a good customer weather a temporary storm than is a commercial paper dealer.[6]

USE OF SECURITY IN SHORT-TERM FINANCING   It is ordinarily better to borrow on an unsecured basis, as the bookkeeping costs of secured loans are often high, but frequently a potential borrower's credit rating is not sufficiently strong to justify the loan. If the loan can be secured by the borrower's putting up some form of collateral to be claimed by the lender in the event of default, then the lender may extend credit to an otherwise unacceptable firm. Similarly, a firm that could borrow on an unsecured basis may elect to use security if it finds that this will induce lenders to quote a lower interest rate.

Several different types of collateral can be employed—marketable stocks or bonds, land or buildings, equipment, inventory, and accounts receivable. Marketable securities make excellent collateral, but few firms hold portfolios of stocks and bonds. Similarly, real property (land and buildings) and equipment are good forms of collateral, but they are generally used as security for long-term loans. The bulk of secured short-term business borrowing involves the pledge of short-term assets—accounts receivable or inventories.

In the past a great deal of variation occurred in the laws of the various states with regard to the use of security in financing In the late 1960s, however, all states passed a *Uniform Commercial Code* which standardizes and simplifies the procedure for establishing loan security.

---

[6] This point was emphasized dramatically in the aftermath of the 1970 bankruptcy of Penn-Central. Penn-Central had a large amount of commercial paper which went into default and embarrassed corporate treasurers who had been holding the paper as part of their liquidity reserves. Immediately after the bankruptcy, the commercial paper market dried up to a large extent, and some companies that had relied heavily on this market found themselves under severe liquidity pressure as their commercial paper matured and could not be refunded. Chrysler, for example, had to seek bank loans of over $500 million because it could not sell commercial paper for a time. Without adequate bank lines, Chrysler might well have been forced into bankruptcy itself, even though it was basically sound, because of the "Penn-Central panic." Incidentally, the Federal Reserve Board recognized that many other firms would be in the same position as Chrysler, so the Fed expanded bank reserves in order to enable the banking system to take up the slack caused by the withdrawal of funds from the commercial paper market.

The heart of the Uniform Commercial Code is the *Security Agreement*, a standardized document, or form, on which the specific assets that are pledged are stated. The assets can be items of equipment, accounts receivable, or inventories. Procedures for financing under the Uniform Commercial Code are described in the following sections.

Accounts receivable financing involves either the *pledge* or the *sale* of receivables. The pledging of accounts receivable is characterized by the fact that the lender has a lien on the receivables but also has recourse to the borrower (seller); if the person or the firm that bought the goods does not pay, the selling firm must take the loss. In other words, the risk of default on the accounts receivable pledged remains with the borrower. Also, the buyer of the goods is not ordinarily notified about the pledging of the receivables. The financial institution that lends on the security of accounts receivable is generally either a commercial bank or one of the large industrial finance companies such as CIT, Commercial Credit, Heller, and the like.

Factoring, the second basic type of receivables financing, is the purchase of accounts receivable by the lender without recourse to the borrower (seller). The buyer of the goods is notified of the transfer and makes payment directly to the lender. Since the factoring firm assumes the risk of default on bad accounts, it must do the credit checking; so it may be fairly said that factors provide not only money but also a credit department for the borrower. Incidentally, the same financial institutions that make loans against pledged receivables also serve as factors. Thus, depending on the circumstances and the wishes of the borrower, a financial institution will provide either form of receivables financing.

FINANCING ACCOUNTS RECEIVABLE

The financing of accounts receivable is initiated by a legally binding agreement between the seller of the goods and the financing institution. The agreement sets forth in detail procedures to be followed and legal obligations of both parties. Once the working relation has been established, the seller will periodically take a batch of invoices to the financing institution. The lender reviews the invoices and makes an appraisal of the buyers. Invoices of companies that do not meet the lender's credit standards will not be accepted for pledging. The financial institution seeks to protect itself at every phase of the operation. Selection of sound invoices is the essential first step in safeguarding the financial institution. If the buyer of the goods does not pay

Procedure for Pledging Accounts Receivable

the invoice, the bank still has recourse against the seller of the goods. However, if many buyers default, the seller will doubtlessly be unable to meet his obligation to the financial institution. Additional protection is afforded the lender due to the fact that the loan will generally be for less than 100 percent of the pledged receivables; for example, the lender may advance the selling firm 75 percent of the amount of the pledged receivables.

Procedure for Factoring Accounts Receivable The procedure for factoring is somewhat different from that for pledging. Again, an agreement between the seller and the factor is made to specify legal obligations and procedural arrangements. When the seller receives an order from a buyer, a credit approval slip is written and immediately sent to the factoring company for a credit check. If the factor does not approve the sale, the seller will generally refuse to fill the order. This procedure informs the seller prior to the sale about the buyer's credit-worthiness and acceptability to the factor. If the sale is approved, shipment is made and the invoice is stamped to notify the buyer to make payment directly to the factoring company.

The factor performs three functions in carrying out the normal procedure as outlined above: (1) credit checking, (2) lending, and (3) risk bearing. The seller can select various combinations of these functions by changing provisions in the factoring agreement. For example, a small or a medium-sized firm can avoid establishing a credit department. The factor's service might well be less costly than a department that may have excess capacity for the firm's credit volume. At the same time, if the firm uses part of the time of a noncredit specialist to perform credit checking, lack of education, training, and experience may result in excessive losses.

The seller may utilize the factor to perform the credit-checking and risk-taking functions but not the lending function. The following procedure will be carried out on receipt of a $10,000 order. The factor checks and approves the invoices. The goods are shipped on terms of $n/30$. Payment is made to the factor, who remits to the seller. But assume that the factor has received only $5,000 by the end of the credit period. He must still remit $10,000 to the seller (less his fee, of course). If the remaining $5,000 is never paid, the factor sustains a $5,000 loss.

Now consider the more typical situation in which the factor performs a lending function by making payment in advance of collection. The goods are shipped and, even though payment is not due for 30 days, the factor immediately makes funds available to the seller. Suppose $10,000 of goods is shipped; the factoring commission for credit checking is 2½ percent of the invoice price, or $250; and the interest expense is computed at a 9 percent annual rate on the invoice balance, or $75.[7] The seller's accounting entry will read as follows:

Cash	$9,175	
Interest expense	75	
Factoring commission	250	
Reserve: due from factor on collection of account	500	
Accounts receivable		$10,000

The $500 "due from factor on collection of account" in the entry is a reserve established by the factor to cover disputes between sellers and buyers on damaged goods, goods returned by the buyers to the seller, and failure to make outright sale of goods. The amount is paid to the seller firm when the factor collects on the account.

Factoring is normally a continuous process instead of the single cycle described above. The seller of the goods receives orders; he transmits the purchase orders to the factor for approval; on approval, the goods are shipped; the factor advances the money to the seller; the buyers pay the factor when payment is due; and the factor periodically remits any excess reserve to the seller of the goods. Once a routine is established, a continuous circular flow of goods and funds takes place between the seller, the buyers of the goods, and the factor.

Cost of Receivables Financing

Accounts receivable pledging and factoring services are convenient and advantageous, but they can be costly. The credit-checking commission is 1 to 3 percent of the amount of invoices accepted by the factor. The cost of money is reflected in the interest rate of 8 to 12 percent charged on the unpaid balance of the funds advanced by the factor. Where the risk to the factor is excessive, he purchases the invoices (either with or without recourse) at discounts from face value.

Evaluation of Receivables Financing

It cannot be said categorically that accounts receivable financing is always either a good or a poor method of raising funds for an individual business. Among the advantages is, first the flexibility of this source of financing. As the sales of a firm expand and it needs more financing,

---

[7] Since the interest is only for one month, we take 1/12 of the stated rate, 9 percent, and multiply this by the $10,000 invoice price.

$$1/12 \times 0.09 \times \$10,000 = \$75.$$

Note that the effective rate of interest is really above 9 percent, because the borrower does not get the full $10,000. In many instances, however, the factoring contract would call for interest to be computed on the invoice price *less* the factoring commission and the reserve account.

a larger volume of invoices is generated automatically. Because the dollar amounts of invoices vary directly with sales, the amount of readily available financing increases. (Second) receivables or invoices provide security for a loan that a firm might otherwise be unable to obtain. (Third) factoring provides the services of a credit department that might otherwise be available to the firm only under much more expensive conditions.

Accounts receivable financing also has disadvantages. (First,) when invoices are numerous and relatively small in amount, the administrative costs involved may render this method of financing inconvenient and expensive. (Second,) the firm is using a highly liquid asset as security. For a long time, accounts receivable financing was frowned upon by most trade creditors. In fact, such financing was regarded as confession of a firm's unsound financial position. It is no longer regarded in this light, and many sound firms engage in receivables pledging or factoring. However, the traditional attitude causes some trade creditors to refuse to sell on credit to a firm that is pledging its receivables on grounds that to do so removes from the trade creditor a possible source of repayment.

The increased use of receivables financing has represented a substantial contribution to the financing of small businesses. It makes possible the financing of smaller firms and marginal credit risks for which other financing might not be available.

Future Use of Receivables Financing We might make a prediction at this point—in the future, accounts receivable financing will increase in relative importance. Computer technology is rapidly advancing toward the point where credit records of individuals and firms can be kept in computer memory units. Systems have been devised so that a retailer can have a unit on hand that, when an individual's magnetic credit card is inserted into a box, gives a signal that his credit is "good" and that a bank is willing to "buy" the receivable created when the store completes the sale. The cost of handling invoices will be greatly reduced over present-day costs because the new systems will be so highly automated. This will make it possible to use accounts receivable financing for very small sales, and it will reduce the cost of all receivables financing. The net result will be a marked expansion of accounts receivable financing.

INVENTORY FINANCING A relatively large volume of credit is secured by business inventories. If a firm is a relatively good credit risk, the mere existence of the inventory may be a sufficient basis for receiving an unsecured loan. If the firm is a relatively poor risk, the lending institution may insist upon security, which often takes the form of a blanket lien against the inventory. Alternatively, trust receipts or field warehouse receipts can be used to secure the loan. These methods of using inventories as security are discussed below.

The blanket inventory lien gives the lending institution a lien against all inventories of the borrower. However, the borrower is free to sell inventories, thus the value of the collateral can be reduced.   *Blanket Inventory Lien*

Because of the weaknesses of the blanket lien for inventory financing, another type of security is used, the trust receipt. A trust receipt is an instrument acknowledging that the borrower holds the goods in trust for the lender. When trust receipts are used, the borrowing firm, on receiving funds from the lender, conveys a trust receipt for the goods. The goods can be stored in a public warehouse or held on the premises of the borrower. The trust receipt provides that the goods are held in trust for the lender or are segregated in the borrower's premises on behalf of the lender, and proceeds from the sale of goods held under trust receipts are transmitted to the lender at the end of each day.   *Trust Receipts*

One defect of trust receipt financing is the requirement that a trust receipt must be issued for specific goods. For example, if the security is bags of coffee beans, the trust receipts would have to indicate the bags by number. In order to validate its trust receipts, the lending institution would have to send a man to the premises of the borrower to see that the bag numbers are correctly listed. Furthermore, complex legal requirements of trust receipts require the attention of a bank officer. Problems are compounded if borrowers are widely separated geographically from the lender. To offset these inconveniences, field warehousing is coming into wide use as a method of securing loans with inventory.

Like trust receipts, warehouse financing uses inventory as security. A public warehouse represents an independent third party engaged in the business of storing goods. Sometimes a public warehouse is not practical because of the bulkiness of goods and the expense of transporting them to and from the borrower's premises. Field warehouse financing represents an economical method of inventory financing in which the warehouse is established at the place of the borrower. To provide inventory supervision, the lending institution employs a third party in the arrangement, the field warehousing company. This company acts as the control (or supervisory) agent for the lending institution.   *Field Warehouse Financing*

A field warehouse can be illustrated very simply. Suppose that a potential borrower has stacked iron in an open yard on his premises. A field warehouse can be established if a field warehousing concern places a temporary fence around the iron and erects a sign which says "This is a field warehouse supervised and conducted by the Smith Field Warehousing Corporation." These are minimal conditions, of course.

The example illustrates the two elements in the establishment of a warehouse: (1) public notification of the field warehouse arrangement and (2) supervision of the field warehouse by a custodian of the field warehouse concern. When the field warehousing operation is relatively small, the second condition is sometimes violated by hiring an employee of the borrower to supervise the inventory. This practice is viewed as undesirable by the lending institution because there is no control over the collateral by a person independent of the borrowing concern.[8]

Example

The field warehouse financing operation is described best by a specific illustration. Assume that a tomato canner is interested in financing his operations by bank borrowing. The canner has sufficient funds to finance 15 to 20 percent of his operations during the canning season. These funds are adequate to purchase and process an initial batch of tomatoes. As the cans are put into boxes and rolled into the storerooms, the canner needs additional funds for both raw materials and labor.

Because of the credit rating of the canner, the bank decides that a field warehousing operation is necessary to secure its lending. The field warehouse is established, and the custodian notifies the lending institution of the description by number of the boxes of canned tomatoes in storage and under his control. Thereupon the lending institution establishes for the canner a deposit on which he can draw. From this point on, the bank finances the operations. The canner needs only enough cash to initiate the cycle. The farmers bring more tomatoes; the canner processes them; the cans are boxed, and the boxes are put into the field warehouse; field warehouse receipts are drawn up and sent to the bank; the bank establishes further deposits for the canner based on the receipts; the canner can draw on the deposits to continue the cycle.

Of course, the canner's ultimate objective is to sell the canned tomatoes. As the canner receives purchase orders, he transmits them

---

[8] This lack of independent control was the main cause of the breakdown that resulted in the huge losses connected with the loans to the Allied Crude Vegetable Oil Company headed by Anthony (Tino) DeAngelis. American Express Field Warehousing Company hired men from Allied's staff as custodians. Their dishonesty was not discovered because of another breakdown—the fact that the American Express touring inspector did not actually take a physical inventory of the warehouses. As a consequence, the swindle was not discovered until losses running into the hundreds of millions of dollars had been suffered. Cf. Norman C. Miller, *The Great Salad Oil Swindle* (Baltimore, Md: Penguin Books, 1965), pp. 72–77.

to the bank and the bank directs the custodian to release the inventories. It is agreed that, as remittances are received by the canner, they will be turned over to the bank. These remittances by the canner pay off the loans made by the bank.

Typically, a seasonal pattern exists. At the beginning of the tomato harvesting and canning season, the canner's cash needs and loan requirements begin to rise and reach a maximum by the end of the canning season. It is hoped that, just before the new canning season begins, the canner has sold a sufficient volume to have paid off the loan completely. If for some reason the canner has had a bad year, the bank may carry him over another year to enable him to work off his inventory.

In addition to canned foods, which account for about 17 percent of *Acceptable* all field warehouse loans, many other product inventories provide a *Products* basis for field warehouse financing. Some of these are miscellaneous groceries, which represent about 13 percent; lumber products, about 10 percent; and coal and coke, about 6 percent.

These products are relatively nonperishable and are sold in well-developed, organized markets. Nonperishability protects the lender if he should have to take over the security. For this reason a bank would not make a field warehousing loan on such perishables as fresh fish. However, frozen fish, which can be stored for a long time, can be field warehoused. An organized market aids the lender in disposing of an inventory which it takes over. Banks are not desirous of going into the canning or the fish business. They want to be able to dispose of an inventory within a matter of hours and with the expenditure of a minimum amount of time.

The fixed costs of a field warehousing arrangement are relatively high; *Cost of Financing* this type of financing is therefore not suitable for an extremely small firm. If a field warehouse company sets up the field warehouse itself, it will typically set a minimum charge of about $350 to $600 a year, plus about 1 or 2 percent of the amount of credit extended to the borrower. In addition, the financing institution will charge from 8 to 12 percent interest. The minimum size of an efficient field warehousing operation requires an inventory of about $100,000.

There are several advantages in the use of field warehouse financing *Appraisal* as a source of funds for business firms. First, the amount of funds available is flexible, because the financing is tied to the growth of inventories, which in turn is related directly to financing needs. Second, the field warehousing arrangement increases the acceptability of inventories as loan collateral. Some inventories would not be accepted by a bank as security without a field warehousing arrangement. Third, the necessity for inventory control, safekeeping, and the use of specialists in warehousing has resulted in improved warehouse practices. The services of the field warehouse companies have often saved money for the firm in spite of the costs of financing mentioned above. The field warehouse company may suggest inventory practices which reduce the labor that the firm has to employ, and reduce inventory damage and loss as well.

The major disadvantage of a field warehousing operation is the fixed cost element, which reduces the feasibility of this form of financing for small firms.

SUMMARY Short-term credit is defined as debt originally scheduled for repayment within one year. This chapter has discussed the three major sources of short-term credit—trade credit between firms, loans from commercial banks, and commercial paper—and methods of securing this credit.

Trade Credit Trade credit, represented by accounts payable, is the largest single category of short-term credit and is especially important for smaller firms. Trade credit is a *spontaneous source of financing* in that it arises from ordinary business transactions; as sales increase, so does the supply of financing from accounts payable.

Although trade credit is a most useful method of financing, it is important that the financial manager be aware of its implicit cost. If discounts are offered for prompt payment, as they very often are, then the cost of not taking the discount amounts to an interest payment. Under certain commonly encountered terms, the implicit interest cost of not taking discounts is quite high. For example, under terms of 2/10, net 30, where a 2 percent discount is allowed if payment is made within 10 days and the account is payable within 30 days, if the discount is not taken, the implicit interest cost is over 36 percent.

Bank Credit Bank credit occupies a pivotal position in the short-term money market. Banks provide the marginal credit that allows firms to expand more rapidly than is possible through retained earnings and trade credit; to be denied bank credit often means that a firm must slow its rate of growth.

Bank loans are generally represented by *notes payable*. The loan itself is frequently arranged prior to the time it is needed—this is called *establishing a line of credit*. To insure that loan customers are also deposit customers, and also to raise the effective rate of interest on loans, banks frequently require minimum deposit balances known as *compensating balances*. When used, compensating balances are generally set at about 15 to 20 percent of the outstanding amount of the loan.

Bank interest rates are quoted in three ways—regular compound interest, discount interest, and installment interest where the interest charges are computed on the original amount of the loan rather than on the outstanding balance. Regular interest needs no adjustment—it is "correct" as stated. Discount interest requires a small upward adjustment to make it comparable to regular compound interest rates. Installment interest rates require a large adjustment, and frequently the true interest rate is double the quoted rate for an installment loan.

Commercial Paper

Bank loans are personal in the sense that the financial manager meets with the banker, discusses the terms of the loan with him, and reaches an agreement that involves direct and personal negotiation. Commercial paper, however, although it is physically quite similar to a bank loan, is sold in a broad, impersonal market. A California firm might, for example, sell commercial paper notes to a manufacturer in the Midwest.

Only the very strongest firms are able to use the commercial paper markets—the nature of these markets is such that the firm selling the paper must have a reputation so good that buyers of the paper are willing to buy it without any sort of credit check. *Interest rates* in the commercial paper market are the lowest available to business borrowers.

A disadvantage of commercial paper *vis-à-vis* bank credit, however, is that if a firm gets into any kind of temporary trouble, it will be completely excluded from the commercial paper market. Commercial banks, on the other hand, are frequently willing to lend support to a long-time customer even when it is having problems. This can be a big advantage to bank credit.

Use of Security in Short-Term Financing

It is ordinarily better to borrow on an unsecured basis, but frequently a potential borrower's credit rating is not sufficiently strong to justify the loan. If the loan can be secured by the borrower's putting up some forms of collateral to be claimed by the lender in the event of default, the lender may extend credit to an otherwise unacceptable firm. The most common types of collateral used for short-term credit are inventories and accounts receivable.

Accounts receivable financing can be done either by *pledging the receivables* or by selling them outright, frequently called *factoring*. When the receivables are pledged, the borrower retains the risk that the person or firm who owes the receivable will not pay; this risk is typically passed on to the lender when factoring is involved. Because the factor takes the risk of default, he will typically investigate the purchaser's credit; therefore, the factor can perform three services—a lending function, a risk-bearing function, and a credit-checking function. When receivables are pledged, the lender typically performs only the first of these three functions. Consequently, factoring is generally quite a bit more expensive than is pledging accounts receivable.

Loans secured by inventories are not satisfactory under many circumstances. For certain types of inventory, however, the technique known as *field warehousing* is used to provide adequate security to the lender. Under a field warehousing arrangement, the inventory is under the physical control of a warehouse company, which releases the inventory only on order from the lending institution. Canned goods, lumber, steel, coal, and other standardized products are the type of goods usually covered in field warehouse arrangements.

QUESTIONS **15–1** It is inevitable that firms will obtain a certain amount of their financing in the form of trade credit, which is, to some extent, a free source of funds. What are some other factors that lead firms to use trade credit?

15–2 "Commercial paper interest rates are always lower than bank loan rates to a given borrower. Nevertheless, many firms perfectly capable of selling commercial paper employ higher cost bank credit." Discuss the statement, indicating (a) why commercial paper rates are lower than bank rates and (b) why firms might use bank credit in spite of its higher cost.

15–3 "Trade credit has an explicit interest rate cost if discounts are available but not taken. There are also some intangible costs associated with the failure to take discounts." Discuss.

15–4 What are some of the reasons that lead firms to offer high cash discounts?

15–5 A large manufacturing firm that had been selling its products on a 3/10, n/30 basis changed its credit terms to 1/20, n/90. What changes might be anticipated on the balance sheets of the manufacturer and of its customers?

15–6 The availability of bank credit is more important to small firms than to large ones. Why is this so?

15–7 What factors should a firm consider in selecting its primary bank? Would it be feasible for a firm to have a primary deposit bank (the bank where most of its funds are deposited) and a different primary loan bank (the bank where it does most of its borrowing)?

15–8 Indicate whether each of the following changes would raise or lower the cost of accounts receivable financing, and why:

a) The firm eases up on its credit standards in order to increase sales.
b) The firm institutes a policy of refusing to make credit sales if the amount

of the purchase (invoice) is below $100. Previously, about 40 percent of all invoices were below $100.

c) The firm agrees to give recourse to the finance company for all defaults.

d) The firm, which already has a recourse arrangement, is merged into a larger, stronger company.

e) A firm without a recourse arrangement changes its terms of trade from net 30 to net 90.

15–9 Would a firm that manufactures specialized machinery for a few large customers be more likely to use some form of inventory financing or some form of accounts receivable financing? Why?

15–10 "A firm that factors its accounts receivable will look better in a ratio analysis than one that discounts its receivables." Discuss.

15–11 Why would it not be practical for a typical retailer to use field warehousing?

15–12 For each of the following, list one industry, together with your reasons for including it, that might be expected to use each type of credit:

a) Field warehousing
b) Factoring
c) Accounts receivable discounting

d) Trust receipts
e) None of these

15–1 What is the equivalent annual interest rate that would be lost if a firm **PROBLEMS** failed to take the cash discount under each of the following terms?

a) 1/15, *n*/30
b) 2/10, *n*/60
c) 3/10, *n*/60

d) 2/10, *n*/40
e) 1/10, *n*/40

15–2 Given below is the balance sheet of the Consolidated Credit Corporation as of December 31, 1971.

Consolidated Credit Corporation
Balance sheet
December 31, 1971
In millions of dollars

Cash	$ 60	Bank loans	$ 220
Net receivables	2,280	Commercial paper	775
Marketable securities	120	Others	335
Repossessions	3	Total due within a year	$1,330
Total current assets	$2,463	Long-term debt	940
Other assets	137	Total shareholders' equity	330
Total assets	$2,600	Total claims	$2,600

a) Calculate commercial paper as a percent of short-term financing, as a percent of total-debt financing, as a percent of all financing.

b) Why do finance companies such as Consolidated Credit use commercial paper to such a great extent?

c) Why do they use both bank loans and commercial paper?

15–3 The Regent Corporation had sales of $2.1 million during 1971 and earned a 2 percent return after taxes on total assets.

Although its terms of purchase are 30 days, its accounts payable represent

60 days' purchases. The president of the company is seeking to increase the company's bank borrowings in order to become current in meeting trade obligations.

The company's balance sheet is shown here.

Regent Corporation
Balance sheet
December 31, 1971

Cash	$ 28,000	Accounts payable	$ 280,000
Accounts receivable	140,000	Bank loans	280,000
Inventory	672,000	Accruals	140,000
Current assets	840,000	Current debt	700,000
Land and buildings	280,000	Mortgage on real estate	280,000
Equipment	280,000	Common stock, par 10 cents	140,000
		Retained earnings	280,000
Total assets	$1,400,000	Total liabilities and net worth	$1,400,000

a) How much bank financing is needed to become immediately current on trade credit?

b) Would you as a bank loan officer make the loan? Why?

15–4 The Walden Products Company has been growing rapidly. It is suffering from insufficient working capital, however, and has therefore become slow in paying bills. Of its total accounts payable, $120,000 is overdue. This threatens its relationship with its main supplier of powders used in the manufacture of various kinds of insulation materials for aircraft and missiles. Over 80 percent of its sales are to six large defense contractors. Its balance sheet, sales, and net profit for the year ended December 31, 1971, are shown here.

Walden Products
Balance sheet
December 31, 1971

Cash	$ 36,000	Trade credit*	$ 300,000
Receivables	540,000	Bank loans	240,000
Inventories		Accruals*	60,000
Raw material	48,000		
Work in process	240,000	Total current debt	600,000
Finished goods	72,000	Mortgages on equipment	360,000
		Capital stock	120,000
Total current assets	936,000	Surplus	120,000
Equipment	264,000		
Total assets	$1,200,000	Total liabilities and net worth	$1,200,000
Sales	$2,400,000		
Profit after taxes	120,000		

* Increases spontaneously with sales increases.

a) If the same ratio of sales to total assets continues and if sales increase to $2.88 million, how much nonspontaneous financing, *including* retained earnings, will be required?

b) Could Walden obtain more funds by use of inventory financing? Explain.

c) Would receivables financing be a possibility for Walden? Explain.

d) *Assuming the facts listed below,* on the average what is the total amount of receivables outstanding at any time when sales are $2.4 million? How much cash does the firm actually receive by factoring the average amount of receivables?

What is the average duration of advances, on the basis of 360 days a year? What is the total annual dollar cost of the financing? What is the effective annual financing charge (percentage) paid on the money received?

1) Receivables turn over six times a year. (Sales/receivables = 6.)
2) All sales are made on credit.
3) The factor requires an 8 percent reserve for returns and disputed items.
4) The factor also requires a 2 percent commission to cover the costs of credit checking.
5) There is a 6 percent annual interest charge based on receivables *less* any reserve requirements and commissions. This payment is made at the beginning of the period and is deducted from the advance.

15–5 The Warren Company manufactures plastic toys. It buys raw materials, manufactures the toys in the spring and summer, and ships them to department stores and toy stores by the late summer or early fall. Warren factors its receivables. If it did not, the following would be its situation. For example, in October 1971, the balance sheet of Warren would have looked like this.

Warren Company
Pro forma balance sheet, October 31, 1971

Cash	$ 100,000	Accounts payable	$3,000,000
Receivables	3,000,000	Notes payable	2,000,000
Inventory	2,000,000	Accruals	200,000
		Total current debt	5,200,000
Total current assets	5,100,000	Common stock	500,000
		Mortgages	1,000,000
Fixed assets	2,000,000	Retained earnings	400,000
Total assets	$7,100,000	Total claims	$7,100,000

Warren provides advanced dating on its sales; thus its receivables are not due for payment until January 31, 1972. Also, Warren would have been overdue on some $2 million of its accounts payable if the above situation actually existed.

Warren has an agreement with a finance company to factor the receivables. The factoring company charges a flat commission of 2 percent, plus 6 percent per year interest on the outstanding balance; it deducts a reserve of 8 percent for returned and damaged materials. Interest and commission are paid in advance. No interest is charged on the reserved funds or on the commission.

a) Show the balance sheet of Warren on October 31, 1971, giving effect to the purchase of all the receivables by the factoring company and the use of the funds to pay accounts payable.

b) If the $3 million is the average level of outstanding receivables, and if they turn over 4 times a year (hence the commission is paid 4 times a year), what are the total dollar costs of financing and the effective annual interest rate?

Chapter 16

Intermediate-term Financing

INTERMEDIATE-TERM financing is defined as debt originally scheduled for repayment in more than one year but in less than five years. Anything shorter is a current liability and falls in the class of short-term credit, while obligations due in five or more years are thought of as long-term debt. This distinction is arbitrary, of course—we might just as well define intermediate-term credit as loans with maturities of one-to-ten years. However, the one-to-five year distinction is commonly used, so we shall follow it here.

The major forms of intermediate-term financing include (1) *term loans,* (2) *conditional sales contracts, and* (3) *lease financing.* These types of credit are described in the present chapter.

TERM LOANS A term loan is a business loan with a maturity of more than one year. There are exceptions to the rule, but ordinarily term loans are retired by systematic repayments (often called *amortization payments*) over the life of the loan. Security, generally in the form of a chattel mortgage on equipment, is often employed, but the larger, stronger companies are able to borrow on an unsecured basis.

The primary lenders on term credit are commercial banks; life insurance companies; and, to a lesser extent, pension funds. Bank loans are generally restricted to maturities of between one and five years, while insurance companies and pension funds make the bulk of their term loans for between 5 and 15 years. Therefore, insurance company term loans are generally long-term, not intermediate-term, financing. Sometimes, when relatively large loans ($10 million and up) are involved, banks and insurance companies combine to make a loan, with the bank taking the short maturities and the insurance company the long maturities. Some specific features of term loans are discussed in the following sections.

The repayment, or amortization, schedule is a particularly important *Repayment* feature of practically all term loans, so it is useful to describe how *Schedule* it is determined. The purpose of amortization, of course, is to have the loan repaid gradually over its life rather than falling due all at once. Amortization forces the borrower to retire the loan slowly, thus protecting both the lender and the borrower against the possibility that the borrower will not make adequate provisions for retirement during the life of the loan.

To illustrate how the amortization schedule is determined, let us assume that a firm borrows $1,000 on a 10-year term loan, that interest is computed at 5 percent on the declining balance, and that the principal and interest are to be paid in ten equal installments. What is the amount of each of the ten annual payments? To find this value we must use the present value concepts developed in Chapter 7.

First, notice that the lender advances $1,000 and receives in turn a 10-year annuity of R dollars each year. In the section headed Annual Receipts from an Annuity in Chapter 7 we saw that these receipts could be calculated as

$$R = \frac{A_n}{IF},$$

where R is the annual receipts, A_n is the present value of the annuity, and IF is the appropriate interest factor found either in Table 7–5 or in Appendix Table A–4. Substituting the $1,000 for A_n and the interest factor for a 10-year, 5 percent annuity, or 7.722, for IF, we find

$$R = \frac{\$1,000}{7.722} = \$130.$$

Therefore, if our firm makes ten annual installments of $130 each, it will have retired the $1,000 loan and provided the lender a 5 percent return on his investment.

Table 16–1 breaks down the annual payments into interest and repayment components and, in the process, proves that level payments of $130 will, in fact, retire the $1,000 loan and give the lender his 5 percent return. This breakdown is important for tax purposes, as the interest payments are an expense.

The typical term loan is small in terms of its dollar amount. Most *Characteristics of* commercial bank term loans are from $100,000 to $250,000. About *Term Loans* 50 percent of life insurance loans run from about $1 million to $5 *Size of Loan* million. Commercial banks typically make smaller and shorter term loans; life insurance companies make larger and longer term loans on the average, although they also make a few short-term loans.

TABLE 16–1
*Term loan
repayment schedule*

Year	Total payment	Interest*	Amortization repayment	Remaining balance
1	$ 130	$ 50	$ 80	$920
2	130	46	84	836
3	130	42	88	748
4	130	38	92	656
5	130	34	96	560
6	130	28	102	458
7	130	23	107	351
8	130	18	112	239
9	130	13	117	122
10	130	8	122	0
Totals	$1,300	$300	$1,000	

* Interest for the first year is 0.05 × $1,000 = $50; for the second year it is 0.05 × $920 = $46; and so on. The numbers are not exact because of rounding errors.

Size of Borrowers It has been estimated that 90 percent of the term loans made by commercial banks are to small firms with assets of less than $5 million. Most of the term and direct loans made by insurance companies are to larger firms.

Maturity For commercial banks, the term loan runs five years or less, typically three years. For insurance companies, the most typical maturities have been 10 to 15 years. This difference reflects the fact that liabilities of commercial banks are shorter term than are those of insurance companies. As we pointed out above, banks and insurance companies occasionally cooperate in their term lending. For example, if a firm (usually a large one) seeks a 15-year term loan, a bank may take the loan for the first five years and an insurance company for the last 10 years.

Collateral Commercial banks have required security on about 60 percent of the volume and 90 percent of the number of term loans made. They have taken as security mainly stocks, bonds, machinery, and equipment. Insurance companies also have required security on nearly a third of their loans, frequently using real estate as collateral on the longer ones.

Options In recent years institutional investors have increasingly taken compensation in addition to fixed interest payments on directly negotiated loans. The most popular form of additional compensation is an option to buy common stock, "the option being in the form of detachable warrants permitting the purchase of the shares at stated prices over a designated period."[1]

Most term loans are repayable in equal installments. Only a small percentage of the loans have any balloon segment of repayment at the end. It is possible to prepay term loans ahead of schedule, but a prepayment penalty equal to from 3 to 8 percent of the outstanding balance is usually assessed in such cases.

Repayment Provisions

A major advantage of a term loan is that it assures the borrower of the use of the funds for an extended period. On a ninety-day loan, since the commercial bank has the option to renew or not renew, the bank has frequent opportunities to re-examine the situation of the borrower. If it has deteriorated unduly, the loan officer simply does not renew the loan. On a term loan, however, the bank or insurance company has committed itself for a period of years. Because of this long-term commitment, restrictive provisions are incorporated into the loan agreement to protect the lender for the duration of the loan. The most important of the typical restrictive provisions are listed below.

Terms of Loan Agreements

The current ratio must be maintained at some specified level—2 1/2 to 1, 3 to 1, 3 1/2 to 1, depending upon the borrower's line of business. Net working capital must also be maintained at some minimum.

Current Ratio

There are restrictions on the amount of additional fixed assets that may be purchased by the borrower in the future. The lender seeks to protect himself against the borrower's sinking his funds excessively into fixed investments.

Additional Fixed Assets

Typically, there are prohibitions against incurring additional long-term indebtedness except with the permission of the lender. Furthermore, the lender does not permit the pledge of assets without the permission of the lender. The loan agreement may also prohibit the borrower from assuming any contingent liabilities, such as guaranteeing the indebtedness of a subsidiary. Finally, the loan agreement probably restricts the borrower from circumventing these provisions by signing long-term leases beyond specified amounts.

Additional Long-term Debt

The loan agreement may require that any major changes in management personnel, or in its composition, must be approved by the lender.

Management

[1] C. M. Williams and H. A. Williams, "Incentive Financing," *Harvard Business Review,* XXXVIII (March–April 1960), p. 124. See Chapter 20 of this book for more details on warrants.

The loan agreement requires life insurance on the principals of the business, especially if they are key personnel. In addition, the loan agreement may provide for the creation of a voting trust or a granting of proxies for a specified period to ensure that the management of the company will be under the control of the group on which the lender has relied in making the loan.

Financial Statements   The lender will require the borrower to submit periodic financial statements for his review.

This list does not exhaust all the kinds of terms found in loan agreements, but it is illustrative. It serves to indicate the kind of protective provisions the bank or insurance company seeks to embody in the loan agreement.

Cost of Term Loans   Another major aspect of term lending is its cost. As with other forms of lending, the interest rate on term loans varies with the size of the loan and the quality of the borrower. Surveys show that on smaller term loans the interest rate may run up to 15 percent. On loans of $1 million and above, term loan rates have been close to the prime rate. The size of the loan often reflects the quality of the borrower as well as the fixed cost involved in making small loans.

The interest rate may be related to the Federal Reserve rediscount rate. Often the loan agreement specifies that the interest rate will be based on the average of the rediscount rate in the borrower's Federal Reserve district during the previous three months, generally 1/2 percent to 1 or 2 percent above the rediscount rate. In other words, the loan rate can fluctuate during the life of the loan and is often tied to the rediscount rate. It may also be geared to the published prime rate charged by New York City banks.

CONDITIONAL SALES CONTRACTS   Conditional sales contracts are used to finance a substantial portion of the new equipment purchased by American business firms. Under the sales contract, the buyer agrees to buy a particular piece of equipment and to pay for it in installments over a one-to-five-year period. Until payment is completed, the seller of the equipment continues to hold title to the equipment. This fact gives rise to the name *conditional* sales contract—the sale is conditional upon satisfactory completion of the payments. While the contract is being paid off, the purchaser has possession of the equipment and uses it in his business. Also, it is typical for the firm that sold the equipment, a manufacturer or dealer, to sell the entire conditional sales contract to a bank or a finance company. What we have, in effect, is a long-term accounts receivable financing arrangement.

Assume that a small manufacturer needs a high-speed drill and has *Procedure*
30 percent of the purchase price. It makes the arrangements for the
purchase from the manufacturer, and it agrees to finance the remaining 70 percent of the purchase price through a finance company or
a bank. The firm signs a conditional sales contract, which schedules
payments based on the income it expects to earn. The payments are
established exactly like those examined under the term-loan
arrangement.

The conditional sales contract may be signed with the manufacturer,
who sells it to a finance company or a bank. The financing institution
usually requires a recourse agreement (guarantee) from the manufacturer for several reasons. The vendor (manufacturer) wants his money
when the equipment leaves his factory. If the equipment is returned
or repossessed, however, the manufacturer is in a better position than
the financing institution to recondition and sell it. A financing institution cannot be expected to recondition a wide variety of specialized
equipment. However, in a conditional sales contract it is usual to require that the financing institution repossess and return the equipment
to the manufacturer within 60 days after the first default.

Many kinds of equipment purchases are financed under conditional *Products, Terms,*
sales contracts. In descending order of frequency they are factory *and Appraisal*
equipment, hotel and restaurant fixtures, equipment for beauty and *Products*
barber shops, equipment for buses and trailers, medical equipment,
diners and dining equipment, and bowling alley equipment. Studies
of the credit positions of firms using installment equipment financing
reveal that a high proportion of them are small firms with low credit
ratings.

The terms of installment equipment financing are influenced mainly *Terms*
by the length of life of the equipment purchased. The down payment
runs around one third of the equipment purchase price, and the maturity generally runs from two to three years. The cost of equipment
financing is relatively high—usually 6 percent of the original amount
discounted on the face amount of the contract, an effective rate of
interest of 14 or 15 percent giving consideration to both the discount
and the installment loan features of the contract. On heavy machinery
purchased by prime credit risks, the effective rate may run as low
as 8 or 9 percent.

The main advantage of conditional sales financing is that it increases *Appraisal*
the ability of small firms to purchase equipment. Since the equipment
generally produces income, the cash flow thus generated provides for

repayment of the loan. In this sense the loan is self-liquidating. While the interest costs are high in an absolute sense, they may be low when related to the profitability of the equipment thereby acquired. The major limitation of conditional sales contract equipment financing is that it is by necessity limited to only the fixed asset portion of the assets of the firm.

LEASE FINANCING   Firms are generally interested in *using* buildings and equipment, not in owning them per se. One way of obtaining the use of facilities and equipment is to buy them, but an alternative is to lease rather than own. Prior to the 1950s, leasing was generally associated with real estate—land and buildings—but today it is possible to lease virtually any kind of fixed asset.

Leasing takes several different forms, the most important of which are sale and leaseback, service leases, and straight financial leases. These three major types of leasing are described below.

Sale and Leaseback   Under a sale and leaseback arrangement, a firm owning land, buildings, or equipment sells the property to a financial institution and simultaneously executes an agreement to lease the property back for a specified period under specific terms. If real estate—land or buildings—is involved, the financial institution is generally a life insurance company; if the property consists of equipment and machinery, the *lessor* could be an insurance company, a commercial bank, or a specialized leasing company.

Note that the seller, or *lessee*, immediately obtains the purchase price put up by the buyer, or *lessor*. At the same time, the seller-lessee retains the use of the property. This parallel is carried over to the lease payment schedule. Under a mortgage loan arrangement, the financial institution would receive a series of equal payments just sufficient to amortize the loan and provide the lender with a specified rate of return on his investment. The nature of the calculations was described above under the term loan arrangement. Under a sale and leaseback arrangement, the lease payments are set up in exactly the same manner—the payments are sufficient to return the full purchase price to the financial institution, in addition to providing it with a stated return on its investment.

Service Leases   Service or operating leases include both financing and maintenance services. International Business Machines Corporation is one of the pioneers of the service lease contract; computers, together with automobiles and trucks, are the primary types of equipment involved in service leases.

Another important characteristic of the service lease is the fact that it is frequently not fully amortized. In other words, the payments required under the lease contract are *not* sufficient to recover the full cost of the equipment. Obviously, however, the lease contract is written for considerably less than the expected life of the leased equipment, and the lessor expects to recover his cost in subsequent renewal payments or upon disposal of the leased equipment.

Service leases ordinarily call for the lessor to maintain and service the leased equipment and the costs of this maintenance are built into the lease payments.

A final feature of the service lease is the fact that such leases frequently contain a cancellation clause giving the lessee the right to cancel the lease and return the equipment before the expiration of the basic lease agreement. This is an important consideration for the lessee, for it means that he can return the equipment if technological developments render it obsolete.

Financial Leases

A strict financial lease is one that does *not* provide for maintenance services, is *not* cancelable, and *is* fully amortized (that is, the lessor receives rental payments equal to the full price of the leased equipment). The lessor is generally an insurance company, if real estate is involved, and a commercial bank or specialized leasing company, if the leased property is equipment. The typical arrangement involves the following steps:

1. The firm that will use the equipment selects the specific items it wants and negotiates the price and delivery terms with the manufacturer or the distributor.

2. Next, the user firm arranges with a bank or a leasing company to buy the equipment from the manufacturer or the distributor, and the user firm simultaneously executes an agreement to lease the equipment from the financial institution. The terms call for full amortization of the financial institution's cost, plus a return of from 6 to 10 percent a year on the unamortized balance. The lessee is generally given an option to renew the lease at a reduced rental on expiration of the basic lease, but he does not have the right to cancel the basic lease without completely paying off the financial institution.

Financial leases are almost the same as sale and leaseback arrangements, the only difference being that the leased equipment is new and the lessor buys it from a manufacturer or a distributor rather than from the user-lessee. A sale and leaseback may, then, be thought of as a special type of financial lease.

Internal Revenue Service Requirements for a Lease The full amount of the annual lease payments is deductible for income tax purposes *provided the Internal Revenue Service agrees that a particular contract is a genuine lease and not simply an installment loan called a lease.* This makes it important that a lease contract be written in a form acceptable to the Internal Revenue Service. The following are the major requirements for bona fide lease transactions from the standpoint of the IRS:

1. The term must be less than 30 years; otherwise the lease is regarded as a form of sale.

2. The rent must represent a reasonable return to the lessor, "reasonable" being in the range of 6 to 10 percent on the investment.

3. The renewal option must be bona fide, and this requirement can best be met by giving the lessee the first option to meet an equal bona fide outsider offer.

4. There shall be no repurchase option; if there is, the lessee should merely be given parity with an equal outside offer.

Cost Comparison For an understanding of the possible advantages and disadvantages of lease financing, the cost of leasing must be compared with the cost of owning the equipment. In the typical case a firm that contemplates the acquisition of new equipment must also think about how to finance the equipment. When financing is necessary, the three major alternatives are (1) a term loan secured by a chattel mortgage on the equipment, (2) a conditional sales contract, and (3) a lease arrangement. To judge the cost of leasing, we must make a comparison of leasing versus the two borrow-to-purchase alternatives.

This comparison is best carried out in the manner presented in Table 16–2. Here it is assumed that the firm is acquiring a piece of equipment costing $1,000 and that it has the choice of borrowing the $1,000 at 5 percent, to be repaid in ten annual installments of $130 each, or of leasing the machine for $150 a year. (Under the lease arrangement the firm is paying a 5 percent implicit interest rate; this is the rate the lessor is earning.) The machine will be used for ten years, at the end of which time its estimated salvage value will be $100. If the firm leases the equipment, maintenance cost is included in the lease payment, but if the machine is purchased, the company must spend $20 per year for a maintenance contract to cover servicing costs.

Note that the decision to acquire the machine is not at issue here—this decision was made previously as part of the capital budgeting process. Here we are concerned simply with whether to obtain the use of the machine by a lease or by a purchase. However, if the effective cost of the lease is substantially lower than the cost of debt—and, as will be explained later in this chapter, this could occur for a number of reasons, including the ability to obtain more debt financing if leasing is employed—then the cost of capital used in capital budgeting would have to be recalculated and, perhaps, projects formerly deemed unacceptable might become acceptable.

Columns 2 through 5 show the payment schedule for the loan—note that this section is identical with the schedule shown in Table 16–1 for a term loan and that it would apply equally well to a ten-year conditional sales contract payment schedule. Column 7 gives the annual depreciation charges, assuming the firm owns the equipment and depreciates it on a straight line basis (the depreciable cost is $900, $1,000 less $100 salvage). Column 8 gives the total tax deductible expense, interest plus depreciation plus maintenance costs. These tax deductions reduce the tax bill by one-half the amount of the deductions, assuming a 50 percent tax rate; this gives rise to the tax savings recorded in column 9.

The total cash outlay associated with the borrow-purchase arrangement is the total annual loan payment recorded in column 2 *plus* the maintenance costs shown in column 6; this is the gross cash outflow. Deducting the tax savings shown in column 9 from the total payments in columns 2 and 6 gives the net cash cost of owning shown in column 10.

Assuming that the leasing company—which might well be the same bank that is willing to make the term loan—is willing to accept a 5 percent return on its investment, the annual lease payments must be $150, the same as the loan repayment plus maintenance cost under the loan arrangement. Thus, the after-tax cost of the lease is $75 a year for 10 years; this figure is shown in column 11.

Column 10 shows the firm's net cash outlay each year if it chooses to borrow the money and purchase the machine, while column 11 shows the net cash outflow if it elects the lease alternative. Subtracting column 10 from column 11 gives the cash flow advantage—plus or minus—to owning versus leasing. This figure is recorded in column 12, which shows that owning involves smaller annual cash outlays in each of the first three years, but that leasing requires smaller cash flows during the last seven years.

We can no more add dollars payable in one year to those payable in another than we can add apples to oranges. We must, therefore, put the annual cash flow differentials between leasing and borrowing on a common basis; this requires converting them to present values.

The cash flow differentials between leasing and borrowing are known with relative certainty—if the company borrows and buys, its costs *will be* a given amount, while if it leases its costs *will be* another specified figure. Since the two cost figures are known with relative

TABLE 16–2 Comparison of cost of leasing versus buying

		Applicable to loan			Computing net cost of owning								
Year (1)	Total payment (2)	Interest (3)	Amortization payment (4)	Remaining balance (5)	Maintenance cost (6)	Depreciation (7)	(3)+(6)+(7) Tax deductible expense (8)	1/2 (8) tax saving (9)	(2)+(6)−(9) Net cost of owning (10)	Lease cost after tax (11)	(11)−(10) Advantage to owning (12)	2 1/2 percent present value factor (13)	(12)×(13) Present value of advantage to owning (14)
1	$ 130	$ 50	$ 80	$920	$ 20	$ 90	$ 160	$ 80	$ 70	$ 75	5	0.976	$ 4.88
2	130	46	84	836	20	90	156	78	72	75	3	0.952	2.86
3	130	42	88	748	20	90	152	76	74	75	1	0.929	.93
4	130	38	92	656	20	90	148	74	76	75	(1)	0.906	(.91)
5	130	34	96	560	20	90	144	72	78	75	(3)	0.884	(2.65)
6	130	28	102	458	20	90	138	69	81	75	(6)	0.862	(5.17)
7	130	23	107	351	20	90	133	67	83	75	(8)	0.841	(6.73)
8	130	18	112	239	20	90	128	64	86	75	(11)	0.821	(9.03)
9	130	13	117	122	20	90	123	61	89	75	(14)	0.801	(11.21)
10	130	8	122	—	20	90	118	59	91	75	(16)	0.781	(12.50)
									(100)		100	0.463*	46.30
Totals	$1,300	$300	$1,000	—	$200	$900	$1,400	$700	$700	$750	—		$ 7.77

Assumptions:

1. The firm can borrow $1,000 at 5% to be repaid in ten equal annual installments. The annual payments are computed as:

   a. Interest factor for 10 years, 5% annuity = 7.722

   b. Required annual payment = $1,000 ÷ 7.722 = $130

2. The firm can arrange to finance its $1,000 equipment purchase under a 10-year lease plan calling for an annual rental of $150.

3. The equipment is worth $100 at the end of 10 years. This $100 is added to column 10 as a cash inflow for the owning option.

4. The firm uses straight-line depreciation.

* 8 percent present value factor

certainty, the difference between them is also a relatively certain sum, and it should be discounted at a low interest rate to reflect its riskless nature. For this reason most interest factors shown in column 13 are for 2 1/2 percent, the after-tax cost of debt. The salvage value, on the other hand, is simply an estimate—it is not known with certainty. Accordingly, we discount it at 8 percent, the firm's average after-tax cost of capital.[2] The interest factors given in column 13, when multiplied by the cash flow differentials shown in column 12, give the present value of the differentials; these figures are shown in column 14.

When column 14 is summed, we have the net present value of the advantage to owning. This figure can be either plus or minus. A positive sum, as in the example, indicates that it is cheaper for the firm to borrow and purchase than it is to lease. A negative result would suggest that leasing has the advantage over buying.

What would happen to the relative cost of leasing versus owning if the example was modified to allow for accelerated depreciation? Accelerated depreciation would produce a higher tax deduction, hence lower taxes, in the early years. This would reduce the net cost of owning (column 10) in the early years and raise it later on. Since the lease cost after tax (column 11) is unaffected, the result would be to increase the advantage to owning (column 12) in the early years and to lower it in the later years. When the analysis is carried through to the Present Value column, the final result of accelerated depreciation would be to make owning relatively more attractive than it already is.

Raising the cost of capital factor (column 13) would have the same kind of effect as switching to accelerated depreciation. The advantage of leasing comes in the later years, which are the ones that would be penalized most heavily by a higher cost of capital factor. The net result would be to increase the advantage of owning.

However, a table similar to Table 16–2, constructed from the lessor's point of view, would show that leases provide higher returns than loans, other things the same, because under a lease the lessor can take advantage of the accelerated depreciation. In such a situation the lessor is permitted some profit flexibility in setting lease terms, and competition among leasing companies could reduce the costs of leasing.

It may be useful to summarize some of the variations and their implications for the evaluation of owning versus leasing, and this is

---

[2] We *assume* here that the salvage value is about as risky as the firm's average asset. In many instances the risk of the salvage value would be greater or less than the average riskiness, in which case some other interest factor would be used. Also, we might note that the *after-tax* cost of debt is used to maintain consistency with the cost of capital used in budgeting.

done in Table 16–3. The material in the table summarizes frequently encountered arguments about advantages and disadvantages of leasing. Each assumed condition is subject to substantial qualification, so each is considered in turn.

TABLE 16–3
*Variations in
assumed conditions
and their
implications for
costs of owning
versus leasing*

Assumed conditions	Consequences
Use of accelerated depreciation	Costs of owning lower
Implicit interest rates higher in leasing	Costs of leasing higher
Large residual values	Costs of owning lower
Rapid obsolescence	Costs of leasing lower

*Use of
Accelerated
Depreciation*

It is often argued that because of the ability to use accelerated depreciation methods, owning must be less expensive than leasing. Such an argument does not take into account the competitive aspects of the money and capital markets. Lessors benefit from accelerated depreciation, and competition will force tax advantages such as this to be shared between lessor and lessee. The payments pattern under leasing can be quite flexible. Thus, any opportunities available to equipment owners must be reflected in the competitive system of rates charged by leasing companies.

*Implicit Interest
Rates Higher in
Leasing*

The statement is frequently made that leasing always involves higher interest rates. This argument is of doubtful validity. First, when the nature of the lessee as a credit risk is considered, there may be no difference. Second, it is difficult to separate the money costs of leasing from the other services that may be embodied in a leasing contract. If, because of its specialist operations, the leasing company can perform the nonfinancial services, such as maintenance of the equipment, at a lower cost than the lessee or some other institution could perform them, the effective cost of leasing may be lower than for funds obtained from borrowing or other sources. The efficiencies of performing specialized services may thus enable the leasing company to operate by charging a lower total cost than the lessor would have to pay for the package of money plus services on any other basis.

*Large Residual
Values*

One important point that must be mentioned in connection with leasing is that the lessor owns the property at the expiration of the lease. The value of the property at the end of the lease is called the *residual value*. Superficially, it would appear that where residual values are large, owning will be less expensive than leasing. However, even this obvious advantage of owning is subject to substantial qualification. On leased equipment, the obsolescence factor may be so large that it is doubtful whether residual values will be of a great order of magnitude. If residual values appear favorable, competition between leasing companies and other financial sources, and competition among leasing companies themselves, will force leasing rates down to the point where the potentials of residual values are fully recognized in the leasing contract rates. Thus, the existence of residual values on equipment is not likely to result in materially lower costs of owning. However, in connection with decisions whether to lease or to own land, the obsolescence factor is not involved except to the extent of deterioration in areas with changing population or use patterns. In a period of optimistic expectations about land values, there may be a tendency to overestimate rates of increase in land values. As a consequence, the current purchase of land may involve a price so high that the probable rate of return on owned land may be relatively small. Under this condition, leasing may well represent a more economical way of obtaining the use of land than owning. Conversely, if the probable increase in land values is not fully reflected in current prices, it will be advantageous to own the land.

Thus it is difficult to generalize whether residual value considerations are likely to make the effective cost of leasing higher or lower than the cost of owning. Generalization is impossible—the results depend on whether the individual firm has opportunities to take advantage of overoptimistic or overpessimistic evaluations of future value changes by the market as a whole.

Another fallacy is the idea that leasing costs will be lower because of the rapid obsolescence of some kinds of equipment. If the obsolescence rate on equipment is high, leasing costs must reflect such a rate. Thus, in general terms, it might be argued that neither residual values nor obsolescence rates can basically affect the cost of owning versus leasing. *Rapid Obsolescence*

In connection with leasing, however, it is possible that certain types of leasing companies may be well equipped to handle the obsolescence problem. For example, the Clark Equipment Company is a manufacturer, reconditioner, and specialist in materials handling equipment and has its own sales organization and system of distributors. This may enable Clark to write favorable leases for equipment. If the equipment becomes obsolete to one user, it may still be satisfactory for other users with different materials handling requirements, and Clark is ably situated to locate these other users.

This illustration indicates how a leasing company, by combining lending with other specialized services, may reduce the social costs of obsolescence and increase effective residual values. By such operations the total cost of obtaining the use of such equipment is reduced.

Possibly other institutions that do not combine financing and other specialist functions, such as manufacture, reconditioning, servicing, and sales, may, in conjunction with financing institutions, perform the over-all functions as efficiently and at as low cost as do integrated leasing companies. However, this is a factual matter depending upon the relative efficiency of the competing firms in different lines of business and different kinds of equipment. To determine which combination of methods results in the lower costs, an analysis along the lines of the pattern outlined in Table 16–2 is required. Aside from the strictly quantitative considerations that would be reflected in such a table, it is useful to consider some of the possible qualitative advantages of leasing.

Possible Advantages of Leasing

If the lease is written for a period that is considerably shorter than the depreciable life of the asset, with renewals at low rentals after the lessor has recovered his costs during the basic lease period, then

Tax Deductions

deductible depreciation (column 7 in Table 16–2) is small relative to the deductible lease payment in the early years. In a sense, this amounts to a very rapid write-off, which is advantageous. However, the Internal Revenue Service correctly disallows as deductions lease payments under leases (1) that call for a rapid amortization of the lessor's costs and (2) that have a relatively low renewal or purchase option.

Increased Credit Availability

Two possible situations may exist to give leasing an advantage to firms seeking the maximum degree of financial leverage. First, it is frequently stated that firms can obtain more money for longer terms under a lease arrangement than under a secured loan agreement for the purchase of a specific piece of equipment. Second, leasing may not have as much of an impact on future borrowing capacity as borrowing and buying of equipment. This point is illustrated by examining the balance sheets of two hypothetical firms, A and B, in Table 16–4.

TABLE 16–4
Balance sheet effects of leasing

Before asset increase			After asset increase					
Firms A and B			**Firm A**			**Firm B**		
	Debt	50		Debt	150		Debt	50
Total	Equity	50	Total	Equity	50	Total	Equity	50
assets	100	100	assets	200	200	assets	100	100

Initially, the balance sheets of both firms are identical, and they both have debt ratios of 50 percent. Next, they each decide to acquire assets costing $100. Firm A borrows $100 to make the purchase, so an asset and a liability go on its balance sheet, and its debt ratio is increased to 75 percent. Firm B leases the equipment. The lease may call for as high or even higher fixed charges than the loan, and the obligations assumed under the lease can be equally or more dangerous to other creditors, but the fact that its debt ratio is lower may enable firm B to obtain additional credit from other lenders. The amount of the annual rentals is shown as a note to the financial statements, but evidence suggests that many credit analysts give less weight to firm B's lease than to firm A's loan.

This illustration indicates quite clearly a weakness of the debt ratio—if two companies are being compared and if one leases a substantial amount of equipment, then the debt ratio as we calculate it does not accurately show their relative leverage positions. It is, therefore, necessary to examine such cash flow figures as the "times fixed charges covered" ratio when making a comparative analysis of two or more firms.[3]

SUMMARY

Intermediate-term financing is defined as liabilities originally scheduled for repayment in more than one year but less than 5 years. Anything shorter is a current liability, while obligations due in 5 or more years are thought of as long-term debt. The major forms of intermediate-term financing include (1) *term loans,* (2) *conditional sales contracts,* and (3) *lease financing.*

Term Loans

A term loan is a business credit with a maturity of more than one year but less than 15 years. There are exceptions to the rule, but ordinarily term loans are retired by systematic repayments (amortization payments) over the life of the loan. Security, generally in the form of a chattel mortgage on equipment, is often employed; the larger, stronger companies are able to borrow on an unsecured basis. Commercial banks and life insurance companies are the principal suppliers of term loan credit. Commercial banks typically make smaller, shorter term loans; life insurance companies grant larger, longer term credits.

The interest cost of term loans, like rates on other credits, varies with the size of the loan and the strength of the borrower. For small loans to small companies, rates may go up as high as 15 percent; for large loans to large firms, the rate will be close to prime. Since term loans run for long periods, during which interest rates can change

---

[3] Two comments are appropriate here. First, the existence of the lease will appear in Firm B's financial statements as a footnote showing the payments made during the year on long-term lease obligations. Second, financial analysts sometimes attempt to reconstruct the balance sheets of firms such as B by "capitalizing" the lease payments, that is, estimating the value of both the lease obligation and the leased assets and transforming B's balance sheet into one comparable to A's.

radically, many loans have variable interest rates, with the rate set at a certain level above the prime rate or above the Federal Reserve rediscount rate.

Another aspect of term loans is the series of *protective covenants* contained in most loan agreements. The lender's funds are tied up for a long period, and during this time the borrower's situation can change markedly. To protect himself, the lender will include in the loan agreement stipulations that the borrower will maintain his current ratio at a specified level, limit acquisitions of additional fixed assets, keep his debt ratio below a stated amount, and so on. These provisions are necessary from the lender's point of view, but they necessarily restrict the borrower's actions.

Conditional Sales Contracts Conditional sales contracts continue to be a major method by which firms obtain the use of equipment. Under the sales contract, the buyer agrees to buy a particular piece of equipment and to pay for it in installments over a one-to-five year period. Until payment is completed, the seller of the equipment continues to hold title to the equipment; thus the completion of the sale is *conditional* upon completion of the payments.

The cost of financing under sales contracts is relatively high— usually 6 percent of the original balance discounted on the face amount of the contract, an effective rate of interest of 14 or 15 per-cent. On heavy machinery purchased by prime credit risks, the rate may run as low as 8 to 9 percent.

Lease Financing Leasing has long been used in connection with the acquisition of equip-ment by railroad companies. In recent years it has been extended to a wide variety of equipment. In the absence of major tax advantages, whether or not leasing is advantageous turns primarily on the firm's ability to acquire funds by other methods. Leasing may provide an advantage by increasing the over-all availability of nonequity financing to the firm. However, a leasing contract is very close to a straight-debt arrangement and uses some of the firm's debt-carrying ability. Also, the rental is a fixed obligation. Because of the importance of residual value, it will generally be advantageous to a firm to own its land and buildings. Because of the obsolescence factor, the residual value con-siderations may be less important in connection with the acquisition of equipment. Leasing of equipment may therefore continue to grow in importance.

QUESTIONS **16–1** "The type of equipment best suited for leasing has a long life in relation to the length of the lease; is a removable, standard product that could be used by many different firms; and is easily identifiable. In short, it is the kind of equipment that could be repossessed and sold readily. However, we would be quite happy to write a 10-year lease on paper towels for a firm such as General Motors." Discuss the statement.

16–2 On the basis of (a) the factors that make leasing a desirable means of financing and (b) your knowledge of the characteristics of different industries, name three industries that might be expected to use lease financing. Discuss.

16–3 Leasing is often called a hedge against obsolescence. Under what conditions is this actually true?

16–4 Is leasing in any sense a hedge against inflation for the lessee? for the lessor?

16–5 One of the alleged advantages of leasing is that it keeps liabilities off the balance sheet, thus making it possible for a firm to obtain more leverage than it otherwise could. This raises the question of whether or not both the lease obligation and the asset involved should be capitalized and shown on the balance sheet. Discuss the pros and cons of capitalizing leases and the related assets.

16–6 In evaluating the lease-versus-purchase decision, a low interest rate (the cost of debt) is used to discount all cash flows except the salvage value, which is discounted at the average cost of capital.
a) Why is this distinction made?
b) If the cost of debt was used throughout the analysis, would this make leasing more or less attractive vis-à-vis the present procedure?

16–7 A firm is seeking a term loan from a bank. Under what conditions would it want a fixed interest rate, and under what condition would it want the rate to fluctuate with the prime rate?

16–8 Under what conditions would a "balloon note," or loan that is not fully amortized, be advantageous to a borrower?

16–1 The Altman Department Store in considering a sale and leaseback of its **PROBLEMS** major property, consisting of land and a building, because it is 30 days late on 80 percent of its accounts payable. The recent balance sheet of Altman is shown below. Profit before taxes in 1971 is $45,000; after taxes, $25,000.

Altman Department Store
Balance sheet
December 31, 1971
In thousands of dollars

Cash		$ 360	Accounts payable	$1,800
Receivables		1,800	Bank loans, 8%	1,800
Inventories		2,340	Other current liabilities	900
Total current assets		4,500	Total current debt	4,500
Land	$1,440		Common stock	1,800
Building	900		Retained earnings	900
Fixtures and equipment	360			
Net fixed assets		2,700		
Total assets		7,200	Total claims	$7,200

Annual depreciation charges are $72,000 a year on the building and $90,000 a year on the fixtures and equipment.

The land and building could be sold for a total of $3.5 million. The annual net rental will be $300,000.

a) How much capital gains tax will Altman pay if the land and building are sold? (Assume all capital gains are taxed at the capital gains tax rate.)

b) Compare the current ratio before and after the sale and leaseback if the after-tax net proceeds are used to "clean up" the bank loans and to reduce accounts payable and other current liabilities.

c) If the lease had been in effect during 1971, what would Altman's profit for 1971 have been?

d) What are the basic financial problems facing Altman? Will the sale and lease-back operation solve them?

16-2 The Merkle Company is faced with the decision whether to purchase or to lease a new fork-lift truck. The truck can be leased on a five-year contract for $1,500 a year, or it can be purchased for $5,990. The lease includes maintenance and service. The salvage value of the truck five years hence is $1,490. The company uses the sum-of-the-years'-digits method of depreciation. If the truck is owned, service and maintenance charges (a deductible cost) would be $375 a year. The company can borrow at 8 percent for amortized term loans. It has a 50 percent marginal tax rate, and the average after-tax cost of capital is 12 percent.

a) Which method of acquiring the use of equipment should the company choose?

b) What factors could alter the results indicated by the quantitative analysis based on the above facts?

c) Explain how you chose your discount rate or rates, emphasizing risk differentials and before-tax versus after-tax costs.

Part VI

Long-term Financing

Chapter 17

The Market for
Long-term Securities

SHORT- and intermediate-term financial markets were discussed in Chapters 15 and 16. We now examine the markets in which long-term securities—stocks, bonds, warrants, and convertibles—are traded, considering efficient procedures for the financial manager to follow when raising funds by selling long-term securities. This background is necessary for an understanding of the characteristics and uses of the long-term financing instruments described in Chapters 18 through 20.

SECURITY MARKETS

There are two broad types of security markets—the *organized exchanges,* typified by the New York Stock Exchange, and the less formal *over-the-counter markets.*[1] Since the organized exchanges have actual physical market locations and are easier to describe and understand, we shall consider them first. With this foundation it will be easier to comprehend the nature of the over-the-counter market.

Organized Security Exchanges

The organized security exchanges are tangible, physical entities. Each of the larger ones occupies its own building, has specifically designated members, and has an elected governing body—its Board of Governors. Members are said to have seats on the exchange, although everybody stands up. These seats, which are bought and sold, represent the right to trade on the exchange. In 1968, seats on the New York Stock Exchange (NYSE) sold at a record high of $515,000.

Most of the larger stock brokerage firms own seats on the exchanges and designate one of the officers of the firm as a member of the exchange. The designated officer occupies the seat. The exchanges are open daily, and the members meet in a large room equipped with

---

[1] There is also a "private" market in which the borrowing firm goes directly to the lending institutions; this is the market for *private placements or direct placements,* as it is frequently called. The primary instrument used in this market is the *term* loan, described in Chapter 16.

telephones and telegraphs that enable each brokerage house member to communicate with the offices of his firm throughout the country.

Like other markets, a security exchange facilitates communication between buyers and sellers. For example, a Merrill Lynch, Pierce, Fenner, and Smith (the largest brokerage firm) office in Atlanta might receive an order from a customer to buy 100 shares of General Motors stock. Simultaneously, a brokerage house in Denver might receive an order from a customer to sell 100 shares of GM. Each broker would communicate by wire with his firm's representative of the NYSE. Other brokers throughout the country are also receiving customer orders to buy and sell GM, and they are also communicating with their own exchange members. The exchange members with *sell orders* offer the shares for sale, which are bid for by the members with *buy orders*. Thus, the exchanges operate as *auction markets*.[2]

Special procedures are available for handling large blocks of securities. For example, if a firm like General Motors, whose stock is already listed on the NYSE, plans to sell a new issue of stock, the exchange has facilities that make it easier for the market to absorb the new issue. Similarly, if a large mutual fund or pension fund wants to sell a large block of a listed stock, procedures are available that facilitate the sale without putting undue pressures on the stock price.

Two practices said to contribute to effectively functioning securities markets—margin trading and short selling—are described next. *Margin trading* involves the buying of securities on credit. For example, when margin requirements are 80 percent, 100 shares of a stock selling for $100 a share can be bought by putting up in cash only $8,000, or 80 percent of the purchase price, and borrowing the remaining $2,000. The stockbroker lends the margin purchaser the funds, retaining custody of the stock as collateral. Margin requirements are determined by the Federal Reserve Board (the Fed). When the Fed judges that stock market activity and prices are unduly stimulated by easy credit, it raises margin requirements and thus reduces the amount of credit available for the purchase of stocks. On the other hand, if the Fed desires to stimulate the market as a part of its over-all monetary policy operations, it reduces margin requirements. The last change in margin requirements prior to publication of this book was in May 1970, when the margin was lowered from 80 to 65 percent. The last change prior to that was in 1968, when margins were raised from 70 to 80 percent.

Short selling means selling a security that is not owned by the seller

---

[2] This discussion is highly simplified. The exchanges have members known as "specialists," who facilitate the trading process by keeping an inventory of shares of the stocks in which they specialize. If a buy order comes in at a time when no sell order arrives, the specialist may sell off some of his inventory. Similarly, if a sell order comes in, the specialist will buy and add to his inventory.

at the time of sale. Short selling is usually performed in anticipation of a decline in the market price. For example, a stock selling at $40 may be sold short. Suppose that in two months the market drops to $30. The short seller can buy at $30 and make delivery on stock which he sold at $40. The seller borrows the stock from his broker; often the broker has the stock because others of his customers either have purchased it on margin or have left the securities in the brokerage house's name—a so-called street name. The advantage claimed for short selling is that it increases the number of participants operating in the market and thereby reduces fluctuations in stock prices. This is, however, a controversial subject.

Insofar as margin trading and short selling provide for a more continuous market, they encourage stock ownership and have two beneficial effects. (1) They broaden the ownership of securities by increasing the ability of people to buy securities. (2) They provide for a more active market; more active trading makes for narrower price fluctuations. However, when a strong speculative psychology grips the market, margin trading can be a fuel that feeds the speculative fervor. Short selling can also aggravate pessimism on the downside. However, there are restrictions on short selling that provide that a short sale may not be made at a price lower than on the last previously recorded sale. Current rules on short selling limit speculative and manipulative practices. Similarly, flexible margin requirements have had salutary effects on the use of credit in stock market transactions.

Organized security exchanges are said to provide important benefits to businesses in at least four ways.

Benefits Provided by Security Exchanges

1. Security exchanges facilitate the investment process because they provide a marketplace in which to conduct transactions efficiently and relatively inexpensively. Investors are thus assured that they will have a place in which to sell their securities, if they decide to do so. The increased liquidity thus provided by the exchanges makes investors willing to accept a lower rate of return on securities than they would otherwise require. This means that exchanges lower the cost of capital to businesses.

2. By providing a market, exchanges create an institution in which continuous transactions test the values of securities. The purchases and sales of securities record judgments on the values and prospects of companies and their securities. Companies whose prospects are judged favorable by the investment community will have higher values, facilitating new financing and growth.

3. Security prices are relatively more stable because of the operation of the security exchanges. Organized markets improve liquidity by pro-

viding continuous markets which make for more frequent, but smaller, price changes. In the absence of organized markets, price changes would be less frequent but more violent.

4. The securities markets aid in the digestion of new security issues and facilitate their successful flotation.

Like so much else in finance, the virtues of organized exchanges vis à vis over-the-counter markets have been questioned. We personally feel that the exchanges are beneficial, and that they will become increasingly so in the future when the trading process is further automated.

OVER-THE-COUNTER SECURITY MARKETS In contrast to the formal security exchanges, the over-the-counter market is a nebulous, intangible organization. Perhaps an explanation of the name "over the counter" will help clarify exactly what this market is. The exchanges operate as auction markets—buy and sell orders come in more or less simultaneously, and the exchanges are used to match these orders. But if a stock is traded less frequently, perhaps because it is the stock of a new or a small firm, few buy and sell orders come in, and matching them within a reasonable length of time would be difficult. To avoid this problem, brokerage firms maintain an inventory of the stocks. They buy when individual investors wish to sell, and sell when investors want to buy. At one time the inventory of securities was kept in a safe, and when being bought and sold, the stocks were literally passed "over the counter."

Today, over-the-counter markets are defined as all facilities that provide for security transactions not conducted on the organized exchanges. These facilities consist primarily of (1) the relatively few brokers who hold inventories of over-the-counter securities and who are said to "make a market" in these securities and (2) the thousands of brokers who act as agents in bringing these dealers together with investors.

The majority of stocks in terms of the number of issues are traded over the counter. However, the stocks of larger companies are listed on the exchanges, and it is estimated that two-thirds of the dollar volume of stock trading takes place on the exchanges. The situation is reversed in the bond market. Although the bonds of a number of the larger companies are listed on the NYSE bond list, in excess of 95 percent of bond transactions take place in the over-the-counter market. The reason for this is that bonds typically are traded among the large financial institutions—for example, life insurance companies and pension funds—and these institutions deal in very large blocks of securities. It is relatively easy for the over-the-counter bond dealers to arrange the transfer of large blocks of bonds among the relatively few holders of the bonds. It would be impossible to conduct similar operations in the stock market among the literally millions of large and small stockholders.

The exchanges require firms to meet certain requirements before their stock can be listed. These requirements relate to size of the company, number of years in business, earnings record, number of shares outstanding and their market value, and the like. In general, requirements become higher as we move from the regional exchanges toward the NYSE. **DECISION TO LIST STOCK**

The firm itself makes the decision to seek to list or not list its securities on an exchange. Typically, the stocks of new and small companies are traded over the counter—there is simply not enough activity to justify the use of an auction market for such stocks. As the company grows, establishes an earnings record, expands the number of shares outstanding, and increases its list of stockholders, it may decide to apply for listing on one of the regional exchanges. For example, a Chicago company might list on the Midwest Stock Exchange, or a West Coast company might list its stock on the Pacific Coast Exchange. As the company grows still more, and as its stock becomes distributed throughout the country, it may seek a listing on the American Stock Exchange, the smaller of the two national exchanges. Finally, if it reaches a position as one of the nation's leading firms, it could switch to the Big Board, the New York Stock Exchange.

Assuming a company qualifies, it is generally felt that listing is beneficial both to it and to its stockholders. Listed companies receive a certain amount of free advertising and publicity, and their status as a listed company enhances their prestige and reputation. This probably has a beneficial effect on the sales of the products of the firm, and it probably is advantageous in terms of lowering the required rate of return on the common stock. Investors respond favorably to increased information, increased liquidity, and increased prestige; by providing investors with these services in the form of listing their companies' stocks, financial managers lower their firms' cost of capital.[3]

---

[3] Two industries, banking and insurance, have a tradition against listing their stocks. The historic reason given by banks was that they were afraid that a falling market price of their stocks would lead depositors to think the bank itself was in danger and, thus, cause a run on the bank. Some basis for such fears may have existed before the creation of the Federal Deposit Insurance Corporation in 1935, but the fear is no longer justified. The other reason for banks' not listing has to do with reporting financial information. The exchanges require that quarterly financial statements be sent to all stockholders; banks have been reluctant to provide financial information. Increasingly, bank regulatory agencies are requiring public disclosure of additional financial information. As this trend continues, it is expected that banks will increasingly seek listing on exchanges. A notable first is the Chase Manhattan Bank, which was listed on the New York Stock Exchange in 1965.

NATURE OF INVESTMENT BANKING In the American economy, saving is performed by one group of persons while investing is performed by another. ("Investing" is used here in the sense of actually putting money into plant, equipment, and inventory, not "investing" in the sense of buying securities.) Thus, savings are placed with financial intermediaries who, in turn, make the funds available to firms wishing to acquire plant and equipment and to hold inventories.

One of the major institutions performing this channeling role is known as *investment banking.* The term "investment banker" is somewhat misleading in that investment bankers are neither investors nor bankers. That is, they do not invest their own funds permanently, nor are they repositories for individuals' funds, as are commercial banks or savings banks. What, then, *is* the nature of investment banking?

The many activities of investment bankers may be described first in general terms and then with respect to specific functions. The historical and traditional function of the investment banker has been to act as the middleman in channeling driblets of savings and funds of individuals into the purchase of business securities, primarily bonds. The investment banker does this by purchasing and distributing the new securities of individual companies. Specifically, the investment banker performs the following functions.

Underwriting Underwriting is the insurance function of bearing the risks of adverse price fluctuations during the period in which a new issue of securities is being distributed. The nature of the underwriting function of the investment banker can best be conveyed by an example. A business firm needs $10 million. It selects an investment banker, conferences are held, and the decision is made to issue $10 million of bonds. An underwriting agreement is drawn up; on a specific day, the investment banker presents the company with a check for $10 million (less commission). In return, the investment banker receives bonds in denomination of $1,000 each, which he sells to the public.

The company receives the $10 million before the investment banker has sold the bonds. Between the time the investment banker pays the firm the $10 million and the time he has sold the bonds, the investment banker bears all the risk of market price fluctuations in the bonds. Conceivably, it can take the investment banker 10, 20, 30 days, 6 months, or longer to sell bonds. If in the interim the bond market collapses, the investment banker will be carrying the risk of loss in the sale of the bonds. There have been dramatic instances of bond market collapses within one week after an investment banker has bought $50 million or $100 million of bonds.

But the individual firm does not need to be concerned about the risk of market price fluctuations while the investment banker is selling the bonds. The firm has received its $10 million. *One fundamental economic function of the investment banker, then, is to underwrite the risk of a decline in the market price between the time the investment banker transmits the money to the firm and the time the bonds are placed in the hands of their ultimate buyers.* For this reason, the investment banker is often called an underwriter: he is an underwriter of risk during the distribution period.

The second function of the investment banker is securities marketing. **Distribution** The investment banker is a specialist who has a staff and dealer organization to distribute securities. The investment banker can, therefore, perform the physical distribution function more efficiently and more economically than could an individual corporation. Sporadically, whenever it wished to sell an issue of securities, each corporation would find it necessary to establish a marketing or selling organization. This would be a very expensive and ineffective method of selling securities. The investment banker has a permanent, trained staff and dealer organization continuously available to distribute the securities. In addition, the investment banker's reputation for selecting good companies and pricing securities fairly builds up a broad clientele over a period, further increasing the ease with which he can sell securities.

Since the investment banker is engaged in the origination and sale of **Advice and** securities, through experience he becomes an expert in advising about **Counsel** terms and characteristics of securities that will appeal to investors. The advice and guidance of the investment banker in determining the characteristics and provisions of securities so that they will be successfully marketed is valuable. Furthermore, the reputation of the investment banker, as a seller of the securities, depends upon the subsequent performance of the securities. Therefore, he will often sit on the boards of directors of firms whose securities he has sold. In this way he is able to provide continuing financial counsel and to increase the firm's probability of success.

Such, then, are the main economic functions provided by investment bankers. The investment houses engage in a wide variety of activities to provide many other services to business firms, but the other activities will best be understood after a more complete description of the investment banking operation is provided.

INVESTMENT BANKING OPERATION   To understand clearly the investment banking function it is useful to trace the history of a new issue of securities.[4]

Pre-underwriting Conferences   First, the members of the issuing firm and the investment banker hold pre-underwriting conferences. At these conferences they discuss the amount of capital to be raised, the type of security to be issued, and the terms of the agreement.

Memorandums will be written by the treasurer of the issuing company, describing alternative proposals suggested at the conferences. Meetings of the board of directors of the issuing company will be held to discuss the alternatives and to attempt to reach a decision.

At some point, the issuer enters an agreement with the investment banker that a flotation will take place. The investment banker will then begin to conduct what is called an underwriting investigation. If the company is proposing to purchase additional assets, the underwriter's engineering staff will make an engineering analysis of the proposed asset acquisition. A public accounting firm will be called upon to make an audit of the issuing firm's financial situation. In addition, the public accounting firm will aid in the preparation of the registration statements for the Securities and Exchange Commission (SEC) in connection with these issues.

A firm of lawyers will be called in to give interpretations and judgments about legal aspects of the flotation. In addition, the originating underwriter, who will be the manager of the subsequent underwriting syndicate, will make an exhaustive investigation of the prospects of the company.

When the investigations are completed, but before registration with the SEC, an underwriting agreement will be drawn up by the investment banker. Terms of the tentative underwriting agreement may be modified through discussions between the underwriter and the issuing company. Finally, agreement will be reached on all underwriting terms except the actual price of the securities.

Registration Statement   A registration statement will then be filed with the SEC. The Commission requires a 20-day waiting period, during which time its staff analyzes the registration statement to determine whether there are

[4] The process described here relates primarily to situations where the firm doing the financing picks an investment banker, then negotiates with him over the terms of the issue. An alternative procedure, used extensively only in the public utility industry, is for the selling firm to specify the terms of the new issue, then to have investment bankers bid for the entire new issue by use of *sealed bids*. The very high fixed costs that an investment banker must incur to thoroughly investigate the company and its new issue rule out sealed bids except for the very largest issues. The type of operation described in this section is called *negotiated underwriting;* competition is keen among underwriters, of course, to develop and maintain working relations with business firms.

any omissions or misrepresentations of fact. The SEC may file exceptions to the registration statement or may ask for additional information from the issuing company or the underwriters during the 20-day waiting period. During this period, the investment bankers are not permitted to offer the securities for sale, although they may print preliminary prospectuses with all the information customarily contained in a prospectus, except the offering price.

The actual price the underwriter pays the issuer is not generally determined until the close of the registration period. There is no universally followed practice, but one common arrangement for a new issue of stock calls for the investment banker to buy the securities at a prescribed number of points below the closing price on the last day of registration. For example, suppose the stock of XYZ Company has a current price of $38 and has sold in a range of $35 to $40 a share during the previous three months. The firm and the underwriter agree that the investment banker will buy 200,000 new shares at $2.50 below the closing price on the last day of registration. If the stock closes at $36 on the day the SEC releases the issue, then the firm will receive $33.50 a share. Typically, such agreements have an escape clause that provides for the contract to be voided if the price of the securities ends below some predetermined figure. In the illustrative case, this "upset" price might be set at $34 a share. Thus, if the closing price of the shares on the last day of registration is $33.50, the issuing firm will have an option of withdrawing from the agreement. *Setting the Price of the Securities*

 The preceding arrangement holds, of course, only for additional offerings of the stock of firms whose old stock was previously traded. When a company "goes public" for the first time, the investment banker and the firm will negotiate on a price in accordance with the valuation principles described in Chapter 11. But, since the value of an individual stock is very much dependent upon the state of the general market, the *final* price on a new issue is established at the close of the SEC waiting period.

 The investment banker will have an easier job if the issue is priced low and has a high yield. The issuer of the securities naturally wants as high a price and as low a yield as possible. Some conflict of interest on price therefore arises between the investment banker and the issuer. If the issuer is financially sophisticated and looks to comparisons with similar issues of securities, the investment banker is forced to price close to the market.

The investment banker with whom the issuing firm has conducted its discussions will not typically handle the purchase and distribution of the issue alone unless the issue is a very small one. If the sums *The Underwriting Syndicate* of money involved are large and the risk of price fluctuation substantial, the investment banker forms a syndicate in an effort to minimize the amount of risk he carries. A syndicate is a temporary association for the purpose of carrying out a specific objective. The nature of the arrangements for a syndicate in the underwriting and sale of a security through an investment banker may best be understood with the aid of Figure 17–1.

FIGURE 17–1
Diagram of sales of $10 million of bonds through investment bankers

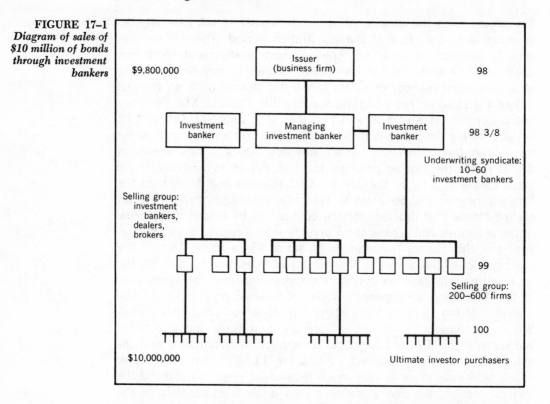

The managing underwriter invites other investment bankers to participate in the transaction on the basis of their knowledge of the particular kind of offering to be made and on the basis of their strength and dealer contacts in selling securities of the type involved in the issue.

Each investment banker has business relations with other investment bankers and dealers; thus, each investment banker has a selling group consisting of himself and other investment bankers and dealers. Some firms combine all these characteristics. For example, the firm of Merrill Lynch, Pierce, Fenner and Smith, Inc., underwrites some issues and manages the underwriting of others. On still other flotations it will be invited by the manager to join in the distribution of the issue. It also purchases securities as the dealer and carries an inventory of these securities. It publishes lists of securities it has for sale. In addition to being a dealer, Merrill Lynch, of course, carries on substantial activity as a broker. An individual investment firm may carry on all these functions, just as a department store sells many different types of merchandise.

But there are also firms with a narrower range of functions—specialty dealers, specialty brokers, and specialty investment counselors. Thus, in the financial field there is specialization of financial functions as well as department store types of operations. A *dealer* purchases securities outright, holds them in inventory as a grocery store would hold its inventory, and sells them at whatever price he can get. He may benefit from price appreciation or he may suffer a loss on declines, as any merchandiser does. A *broker,* on the other hand, takes orders for purchases and transmits them to the proper exchange; his gain is the commission he charges for the service.

Syndicates are used in the distribution of securities for three reasons. (1) A single investment banker may be financially unable to handle a large issue alone. (2) The originating house may desire to spread the risk even if it is financially able to handle the issue alone. (3) The utilization of several selling organizations, as well as other underwriters, permits an economy of selling effort and expense and encourages broader, nationwide distribution.

Participating underwriters and dealers are provided with full information on all phases of these financing transactions, and they share in the underwriting commission. To show how the underwriting commission is shared, Table 17–1 illustrates how a two-point spread is divided. An investment banker buys $10 million worth of bonds to be sold at par, or $1,000 each. If the investment banker receives a two-point spread, he will buy the bonds from the issuer at 98; thus, he must pay the issuer $9.8 million for the issue of $10 million. Typically, on a two-point spread, the manager-underwriter will receive the first 1/4 of 1 percent for originating and managing the syndicate. Next, the entire underwriting group will receive about 3/4 of 1 percent. Members of the selling group receive about 1 percent as a sales commission.

If the manager of the underwriting group makes a sale to an ultimate purchaser of the securities, he will receive the 1/4 percent as manager, 3/4 percent as underwriter, and 1 percent as the seller—the full 2 percent. If he wholesales some of the securities to members of the selling group who make the ultimate sale, the latter will receive the 1 percent selling commission, and the manager will receive the other 1 percent for managing and underwriting the issue. If the issue is managed by one firm, underwritten by a second, and sold by a third, the 2 percent commission is divided, with 1 percent going to the selling firm, 3/4 percent to the underwriter, and 1/4 percent to the manager of the underwriting group.

Ordinarily, each underwriter's liability is limited to his agreed-upon commitment. For example, if an investment banker participates in a $20 million offering and agrees to see to it that $5 million of the securities are sold, his responsibility ends when he sells his $5 million.

Selling Group The selling group is formed primarily for the purpose of distributing securities; it consists of dealers, who take relatively small participations from the members of the underwriting group. The underwriters act as wholesalers; members of the selling group act as retailers. The number of houses in a selling group depends partly upon the size of the issue. A selling group may have as many as 300 to 400 dealers; for example, the one for Communications Satellite Corporation consisted of 385 members.

The operation of the selling group is controlled by the *selling group agreement,* which usually covers the following major points.

Description of The Issue The description is set forth in a report on the issue, the *prospectus,* which fully describes the issue and the issuer.

Concession Members of the selling group subscribe to the new issue at a public offering price less the concession given to them as a commission for their selling service. In the preceding example, this was 1 percent.

Handling Purchased Securities The selling group agreement provides that no member of the selling group be permitted to sell the securities below the public offering price. The syndicate manager invariably "pegs" the quotation in the market by placing continuous orders to buy at the public offering price. A careful record is kept of bond or stock certificate numbers so that repurchased bonds may be identified with the member of the selling group who sold them. General practice is to cancel the commission on such securities and add brokerage costs incurred in the repurchase. Repurchased securities are then placed with other dealers for sale.[5]

Duration of Selling Group The most common provision in selling group agreements is that the group has an existence of 30 days, subject to earlier termination by the manager. The agreement may be extended, however, for an addi-

---

[5] Without these repurchase arrangements, a member of the selling group could sell his share of the securities on the open market instead of to new purchasers. Since the pegging operation is going on, there would be a ready market for the securities; consequently, a penalty is necessary to avoid thwarting of the syndicate operation.

tional 80 days by members representing 75 percent of the selling
group.

After the selling group has been formed, the actual offering proceeds.   *Offering and*
Publicity in advance of the offering date is developed. Advertising   *Sale*
material for release as soon as permissible is prepared. The actual
day of the offering is chosen with a view to avoiding temporary congestion in the security market and other unfavorable events or
circumstances.

The formal public offering is called "opening the books," an archaic
term reflecting ancient customs of the investment banking trade. When
the books are opened, the manager accepts subscriptions to the issue
from both selling group participants and outsiders who may wish to
buy.

If the demand for the issue is great, the books may be closed immediately. An announcement is then made that the issue is oversub-
scribed. However, when the reception is not strong, the books may
remain open for an extended period.

During the period of the offering and distribution of securities, the   *Market*
manager of the underwriting group typically stabilizes the price of   *Stabilization*
the issue. The duration of the price-pegging operation is usually 30
days. The price is pegged by placing orders to buy at a specified
price in the market. The pegging operation is designed to prevent
a cumulative downward movement in the price if it should soften.
A downward price shift would result in losses for all members of the
underwriting group. As the manager of the underwriting group has
the major responsibility, he assumes the task of pegging the price.

If the market deteriorates during the offering period, the investment
banker carries a rather substantial risk. For this reason, the pegging
operation may not be sufficient to protect the underwriters. In the
Pure Oil Company issue of $44 million convertible preferred stock
of September 3, 1937, only $1 million of shares were sold at the
$100 offering price. At the conclusion of the underwriting agreement,
initial trading took place at $74, giving the investment bankers a loss
of over $11 million ($43 × 26 percent). In the Textron issue of June
1967, the offering was reduced from $100 million to $50 million because of market congestion, and yet 5 percent of the bonds were
unsold after the initial offering. Other similar cases can be cited.

It has been charged that pegging the price during the offering period
constitutes a monopolistic price-fixing arrangement. However, investment bankers reply that not to peg the price would increase the risk
and therefore the underwriting cost to the issuer. On balance, it appears that the pegging operation is a socially useful function. The

danger of monopolistic pricing is avoided, or at least mitigated substantially, by competitive factors. If an underwriter attempts to set a monopolistic price on a particular issue of securities, the investor can turn to thousands of other securities not involved in price-pegging operations. The degree of control over the market by the underwriter in a price-pegging operation seems to be negligible.

COSTS OF FLOTATION The cost of selling new issues of securities can be put into perspective by Table 17–1. The table summarizes the data on cost of flotation in the last available report on the subject by the SEC. Although these data are somewhat old, the figures are still appropriate and two important generalizations can be drawn from them:

1. The cost of flotation for common stock is greater than for preferred stocks, and the costs of both are greater than the cost of flotation for bonds.
2. The costs of flotation as a percentage of the gross proceeds are greater for small issues than for large ones.

What are the reasons for these relationships? The explanations are found in the amount of risk involved and in the job of physical distribution. Bonds are generally bought in large blocks by a relatively few institutional investors, whereas stocks are bought by millions of individuals. For this reason the distribution job is greater for common stock, and the expenses of marketing it are greater.

The explanation for the variation in cost with the size of issue is also easily found. In the first place, certain fixed expenses are associated with any distribution of securities. Four items of expense account for 85 percent of the cost of flotation. Many of these expenses are fixed— the underwriting investigation, the preparation of the registration statement, legal fees, and so forth. Since they are relatively large and fixed, their percentage of the total cost of flotation runs high on small issues.

Second, small issues are typically those of relatively less well-known firms. The underwriting expenses may be larger than usual, because the danger of omitting vital information is greater for a small firm. Furthermore, the selling job is greater. More salesmen must exert greater effort to sell the securities of a less well-known firm. For these reasons the underwriting commission, as a percentage of the gross proceeds, is relatively high for small issues.

It has been charged that the expenses of flotation have become high since the SEC, created in 1934, began requiring that relatively elaborate registration statements be filed prior to selling securities. An analysis of the costs of flotation has been made, breaking them down into costs associated with registration and those not affected by it. Underwriting commissions account for about 65 percent of the total

TABLE 17-1 Costs of Flotation, 1961-1965 Costs expressed as percentage of gross proceeds

Size of issue (in millions of dollars)	Debt			Preferred stock			Common stock		
	Under-writing com-mission	Other expenses	Total costs	Under-writing Com-mission	Other expenses	Total costs	Under-writing Com-mission	Other expenses	Total costs
Under 0.5	7.4	8.0	15.4	7.9	8.0	16.0	11.3	7.3	18.5
0.5-0.9	7.2	3.1	10.3	8.0	3.1	11.1	9.7	4.9	14.6
1.0-1.9	7.0	3.4	10.4	8.0	3.4	11.4	8.6	3.0	11.6
2.0-4.9	4.2	1.2	5.4	4.8	1.2	6.1	7.4	1.7	9.1
5.0-9.9	1.5	0.6	2.1	1.0	0.6	1.6	6.7	1.0	7.6
10.0-19.9	1.0	0.4	1.4	1.4	0.4	1.8	6.2	0.6	6.9
20.0-49.9	1.0	0.4	1.4	2.7	0.4	3.1	4.9	0.8	5.6
50.0 and over	0.8	0.3	1.1	1.4	0.3	1.7	2.3	0.3	2.6

Sources: For common and preferred stocks: Securities and Exchange Commission, Cost of Flotation of Registered Equity Issues, 1963–1965 (Washington, D.C.: U.S. Government Printing Office, March 1970), Tables 3 and 10. For debt: Underwriting costs estimated on basis of Irwin Friend, et al., Investment Banking and the New Issues Market (Cleveland: World Publishing Company, 1967), Table 7.1, pp. 408, 409. Other expenses, based on data for preferred stock. Because of rounding errors, totals may not equal the sum of the parts. Preferred stocks were used infrequently, and because of the small sample size the figures for this group are suspect.

cost of flotation. Registration expenses account for about 30 percent, and expenses not affected by registration account for the remainder, or about 5 percent. Registration expenses as a percentage of the gross proceeds are relatively minor and do not vary greatly with the size of flotation. Costs partly affected by registration—printing, engraving, legal, accounting, and engineering costs—do increase somewhat in percentage as the size of flotation decreases. The other costs are relatively minor.

These data demonstrate convincingly that the high percentage costs of flotation on small issues are not caused by discrimination against small issues. The fixed expenses of flotation are large when expressed as a percentage of the proceeds on small issues.

In addition to the factors discussed above, flotation costs are also influenced by whether or not the issue is a rights offering, and if it is, by the extent of the underpricing.[6] If rights are used and if the underpricing is substantial, then the investment banker bears little risk of inability to sell the shares. Further, very little selling effort will be required in such a situation. These two factors combine to enable a company to float new securities to its own stockholders at a relatively low cost.

REGULATION OF SECURITY TRADING   The operations of investment bankers, the exchanges, and the over-the-counter markets described in the previous sections of this chapter are significantly influenced by a series of federal statutes enacted during and after 1933. The financial manager is affected by these laws for several reasons. (1) Corporate officers are subjected to additional liabilities. (2) The laws affect the ease and costs of financing. (3) They also affect the behavior of the money and capital markets in which the corporations' securities are sold and traded. (4) Investors' willingness to buy securities is influenced by the existence of safeguards provided by these laws.

Securities Act of 1933   The first of the securities acts, the Securities Act of 1933, followed Congressional investigations after the stock market collapse of 1929–1932. The reasons motivating the act were (1) the large losses to investors, (2) the failures of many corporations on which little information had been provided, and (3) the misrepresentations that had been made to investors.

The basic objective of the Securities Act of 1933 was to provide for both *full disclosure* of relevant information and a *record of representations.* It seeks to achieve these objectives by the following means.

---

[6] "Rights offerings" involve the sale of stock to existing stockholders. This topic is discussed extensively in Chapter 18.

1. It applies to all interstate offerings to the public (some exemptions are government bonds and bank stocks) in amounts of $300,000 or more.

2. Securities must be registered at least 20 days before they are publicly offered. The registration statement provides financial, legal, and technical information about the company. A prospectus summarizes this information for use in selling the securities. If information is inadequate or misleading, the SEC will delay or stop the public offering.

3. After the registration has become effective, the securities may be offered if accompanied by the prospectus. Preliminary or "red herring" prospectuses may be distributed to potential buyers during the waiting period.

4. Any purchaser who suffers a loss may sue for damages if the registration statement or prospectus contains misrepresentations or omissions of material facts. Liabilities and severe penalties may be imposed on the issuer, its officers, directors, accountants, engineers, appraisers, underwriters, and the others who participated in the preparation of the registration statement.

The act provides for full disclosure. It also has resulted in a procedure for obtaining a record of representations.

The Securities Exchange Act of 1934 extends the disclosure principle *Securities* as applied to new issues by the act of 1933 to trading in already *Exchange Act* issued securities (the "secondhand" securities market). It seeks to *of 1934* accomplish this by the following measures:

1. It establishes a Securities and Exchange Commission (the Federal Trade Commission had been administering the act of 1933).

2. It provides for registration and regulation of national securities exchanges. Companies whose securities are listed on an exchange must file reports similar to registration statements with both the SEC and the stock exchange and provide periodic reports as well.

3. It provides control over corporate "insiders." Officers, directors, and major stockholders of a corporation must file monthly reports of changes in holdings of the stock of the corporation. Any short-term profits from such transactions may have to be paid to the corporation, if other stockholders take the case to court.

4. The act gives the SEC the power to prohibit manipulation by such devices as pools (aggregations of funds used to effect prices artificially), wash sales (sales between members of the same group to record artificial transaction prices), and pegging the market. "Put-and-call" transactions were made subject to regulation.

5. The SEC is given control over the proxy machinery and practices.

6. Control over the flow of credit into security transactions is established by giving the Board of Governors of the Federal Reserve System the power to control margin requirements.

It will be noted that these powers extend only to listed securities. Many feel that the powers should be extended also to unlisted securities.

APPRAISAL OF REGULATION OF SECURITY TRADING Why should security transactions be regulated? If a valid answer exists, it is found in the argument that a great body of relevant knowledge is necessary for an informed judgment of the value of a security. Moreover, security values are subject to great gyrations, which influence stability and business conditions generally. Hence, social well-being requires that orderly markets be promoted.

The objectives of the regulation may be summarized into three points:

1. To protect the amateur investor from fraud and to provide him with a basis for more informed judgments

2. To control the volume of bank credit to finance security speculation

3. To provide orderly markets in securities.

Progress has been made on all three counts. There has been some cost in the increased time and expense involved in new flotations by companies. Although these burdens have not been as large as some persons have claimed, room for improvement exists. The regulations are powerless to prevent investors from investing in unsound ventures or to prevent stock prices from skyrocketing during booms and falling greatly during periods of pessimism. But requirements for increased information have been of great value.

From the standpoint of the financial manager, regulation has twofold significance. It affects the costs of issuing securities and also the effectiveness of the operation of the securities markets. With regard to the first, the data on costs of flotation reviewed above indicate that such costs have, in fact, been increased by regulation requirements. The increase, however, appears to have been only moderate except for smaller issues. The enactment of the regulatory acts of the 1930s restored public confidence in the securities markets and paved the way for renewed wide public participation in the securities markets with the post-World War II recovery in spending power. The net effect of regulation has therefore been to facilitate the raising of capital by business.

Securities are traded both on *exchanges* and in the *over-the-counter* **SUMMARY** *market*. The stocks of larger industrial and utility companies are generally listed on an exchange; stocks of financial institutions, small industrial firms, and practically all bonds are traded over the counter. From the standpoint of the financial manager, listing on an exchange seems advantageous for seasoned issues. The over-the-counter market may aid in the seasoning process until the security can meet the requirements for listing.

The investment banker provides middleman services to both the seller and the buyer of new securities. He helps plan the issue, underwrites it, and handles the job of selling the issue to the ultimate investor. The cost of the service to the issuer is related to the magnitude of the total job the banker must perform to place the issue. The investment banker must also look to the interests of his brokerage customers; if these investors are not satisfied with the banker's products, they will deal elsewhere.

The financial manager should be familiar with the federal laws regulating the issuance and trading of securities, because they influence his liabilities and affect financing methods and costs. Regulation of securities trading seeks (1) to provide information that investors can utilize as a basis for judging the merits of securities, (2) to control the volume of credit used in securities trading, and (3) to provide orderly securities markets. The laws, however, do not prevent either purchase of unsound issues or wide price fluctuations. They raise somewhat the costs of flotation but have probably decreased the cost of capital by increasing public confidence in the securities markets.

Flotation costs are lowest for bonds, higher for preferred stocks, and highest for common stock. Larger companies have lower flotation costs than smaller ones for each type of security, and most companies can cut their stock flotation costs by issuing the new securities to stockholders through rights offerings.

17–1 State several advantages to a firm that lists its stock on a major stock **QUESTIONS** exchange.

17–2 Would you expect the cost of capital of a firm to be affected if it changed its status from one traded over the counter to one traded on the New York Stock Exchange? Explain.

17–3 Evaluate the following statement: "Buying stocks is in the nature of true investment; stock is purchased in order to receive a dividend return on the invested capital. Short selling, on the other hand, is fundamentally a form of gambling; it is simply betting that a stock's price will decline. Consequently, if we do not wish to see Wall Street turned into an eastern Las Vegas, all short selling should be forbidden."

17–4   Evaluate the following statement: "The fundamental purpose of the federal security laws dealing with new issues is to prevent investors, principally small ones, from sustaining losses on the purchase of stocks."

17–5   Suppose two firms were each selling $10 million of common stock. The firms are identical—that is, they are of the same size, are in the same industry, have the same leverage, and have other similarities—except that one is publicly owned and the other is closely held. Would their costs of flotation be the same? If different, state the probable relationships. If the issue were $10 million of bonds, would your answer be the same?

17–6   Define these terms: brokerage firm, underwriting group, selling group, and investment banker.

17–7   Each month the Securities and Exchange Commission publishes a report of the transactions made by the officers and directors of listed firms in their own companies' equity securities. Why do you suppose the SEC makes this report?

17–8   The SEC forbids officers and directors to sell short the shares of their own company. Why do you suppose this rule is on the books?

17–9   Prior to 1933, investment banking and commercial banking were both carried on by the same firm. In that year, however, the Banking Act required that these functions be separated. Based on your knowledge of investment banking and commercial banking, discuss the pros and cons of this forced separation.

17–10   Before entering a formal agreement, investment bankers investigate quite carefully the companies whose securities they underwrite; this is especially true of the issues of firms going public for the first time. Since the bankers do not themselves plan to hold the securities but plan to sell them to others as soon as possible, why are they so concerned about making careful investigations? Does your answer to the question have any bearing on the fact that investment banking is a very difficult field to "break into"?

17–11   If competitive bidding was required on all security offerings, would flotation costs be higher or lower? Would the size of the issuing firm be material in determining the effects of required competitive bidding?

17–12   Since investment bankers price new issues in relation to outstanding issues, should a spread exist between the yields on the new and the outstanding issues? Discuss this matter separately for stock issues and bond issues.

17–13   What is there about the nature of insurance companies that causes them to make, on the average, (a) longer term loans, and (b) larger loans, than commercial banks?

17–14   What problems are raised by the increasing purchase of equities by institutional investors?

PROBLEMS   **17–1**   Listed below are salient facts on the terms of sale of several securities sold through investment bankers in recent years. All facts are taken from prospectuses issued in connection with the sales. Explain the differences in underwriting costs between the groups and among the firms within each group.

Company name, business, industry characteristics	Securities issued			
	Date	Size (in millions of dollars)	Unit price to public (in dollars)	Total underwriting cost (in percentages)
I. Bonds				
A. Nonconvertible				
1. General Motors Acceptance Corporation. Organized 1919. Finances distribution of new cars and dealers' installment sales of General Motors products. Industry is competitive, discount rates fluctuate depending on competitive factor. 4 1/2%, due 1985.	Nov. 1963	150.00	995.00	0.875
2. The Western Union Telegraph Company. Organized 1851. Furnishes communication services throughout the United States. Provides the only public telegraph message service. Competitive with telephone and mail. 5%, due 1982.	Mar. 1964	75.00	1,005.00	1.46
3. The Maston Company, Inc. Organized in 1923. Provides commercial and industrial loans up to three years. 5 1/2%, due 1977.	Apr. 1962	5.00	1,000.00	2.29
B. Convertible with rights				
1. Litton Industry, Inc. Organized 1953. Manufacturing and sales business, commercial and military electrical systems. Industry is highly competitive and subject to changes in defense budget. 3 1/2%, due 1987. Market price common: $138; conversion price: $160 until 1972, thereafter $170.	Apr. 1962	50.70	1,000.00	1.70*
2. Brunswick Corporation. Organized 1907. Principal product is bowling supplies. Company is one of the two leading manufacturers in its field. 4 1/2%, due 1981. Market price common: $47; conversion price: $51.	Jan. 1961	25.60	1,000.00	2.06*

Company name, business, industry characteristics	Date	Securities issued Size (in millions of dollars)	Unit price to public (in dollars)	Total under- writing cost (in per- centages)
3. Chock Full O' Nuts. Organized 1932. Oper- ates a chain of counter-service res- taurants. Restaurants principally located in the Borough of Man- hattan, New York City. 4 1/2%, due 1981. Market price com- mon: $26; conversion price: $28.50.	Aug. 1961	7.00	1,000.00	4.07*
C. Convertible: nonrights				
1. Union Oil Company of California. Organ- ized 1890. Engaged in substantially all branches of oil indus- try. The oil industry is characterized by intensive competition. 4 1/4%, due 1991. Mar- ket price common: $55; conversion price: $65.	June 1961	60.00	1,000.00	1.26
2. Baxter Laboratories, Inc. Organized 1931. One of the leading pharmaceutical com- panies in the manu- facture and sale of parental solutions. In- dustry is extremely competitive. 4%, due 1982. Market price common: $31; conver- sion price: $38.	Apr. 1962	10.00	1,020.00	2.29
3. Standard Motor Prod- ucts, Inc. Organized 1926. Engaged in the manufacture and sale of replacement parts for electrical and fuel systems, mainly for motor vehicles. Pri- mary market is the automobile industry. 4 3/4%, due 1984. Mar- ket price common: $13; conversion price: $15.	Apr. 1964	3.00	1,000.00	4.27

Securities issued

Company name, business, industry characteristics	Date	Size (in millions of dollars)	Unit price to public (in dollars)	Total under-writing cost (in per-centages)
II. Nonconvertible Preferred Stock				
1. Brockton Edison Company. Organized 1883. A Massachusetts electric utility serving an aggregate population of about 200,000. Is a member of the holding company system of Eastern Utilities Associates. No competition within its territory. 4.64%.	Oct. 1963	6.00	1,019.78	1.64
III. Common Stock				
A. With Rights				
1. Bank of America. Organized 1904. Provides banking services in California. Operates the largest system of branch banks in the nation. Market price: bid, $65.88, ask, $69.75; subscription price: $59.	Nov. 1961	94.4	59.00	1.19*
2. The Western Casualty and Surety Company. Organized 1924. Engaged in the underwriting of all major types of insurance except life. In 1960, ranked forty-seventh among 115 leading insurance company groups of all types. Market price: bid, $60.50, ask, $62; subscription price: $57.	Mar. 1962	10.7	57.00	1.96*
3. The Akron-Dime Banks. Organized in 1960 from the consolidation of the Dime Bank and the Bank of Akron. The Dime Bank was organized in 1900 and the Bank of Akron Company in 1918. Bank has 11 offices serving Summit County, Ohio. Is the second largest of 6 commercial banks in the county. Market price: bid, $34, ask, $35; subscription price: $26.	June 1965	1.7	26.00	1.92*

Company name, business, industry characteristics	Date	Securities issued		
		Size (in millions of dollars)	Unit price to public (in dollars)	Total under-writing cost (in per-centages)
B. Nonrights				
1. Communications Satellite Corporation. Organized 1963. Plans to establish and operate a global commercial communication satellite system. Authorized by the Communication Satellite Act of 1962, but not an agency of the United States government. No previous market price.	June 1964	200.0	20.00	2.3
2. Delta Air Lines, Inc. Organized 1930. Engaged in air transportation of persons, property, and mail. Industry is regulated by the government. Market price: $38.	Apr. 1962	7.6	37.25	6.38
3. Hudson Wholesale Groceries, Inc. Organized 1918. Engaged primarily in the procurement, warehousing, and sale of groceries and nonfood items to supermarkets, discount stores, and neighborhood grocery stores. No previous market price.	May 1962	0.8	8.00	19.25

*The starred figures represent the minimum cost of financing, assuming that the issue is fully subscribed. This cost will increase if the underwriter is required to buy any unsubscribed stock. In general, the subscription price is sufficiently below the market price to insure complete subscription. This point is discussed in more detail in Chapter 18.

17–2 Match each firm in list 1 with the most appropriate source of financing found in list 2, and set forth the key factors determining your choice. (There is no one right answer to this problem. Judgment is required, and where judgment is called into play, different people will reach different conclusions.)

List 1

a) Firm selling a large volume of small- and medium-sized orders to numerous medium-sized firms. Working capital position and ownership investment relatively small.

b) Medium-sized firm producing plastic toys. Profitability good, but dependent on independence of action by two owners. Growth good, requiring substantial investment in inventories of specialized packaging materials.

c) Medium-sized firm in growing industry. Needs a 15-to-20-year loan of $2 million; needs funds quickly; professional, financial, and business analysis indicates that the firm's outlook is promising.

d) Two scientists with strong technical competence have an idea for developing a product. Only technical experts could appraise the soundness of the idea. Need management guidance and encouragement as well as financing.

e) Large, highly reputable firm in the steel industry with expansion needs. Good credit rating with a 60 percent debt ratio. Fairly high price/earnings ratio.

f) Firm has large seasonal needs for funds in the autumn of each year.

g) Textile firm with declining profits because of competition of lower labor costs in other regions of the United States. Considering relocation in low-cost labor areas in cities interested in attracting new industry.

List 2

1) Commercial bank
2) Investment bankers
3) Life insurance company
4) Finance companies
5) Equity markets
6) Suppliers
7) Investment-development companies or Small Business Investment Company (SBIC).
8) Community-development companies
9) Friends and relatives

17–3 Excerpts from prospectuses, with particular focus on the underwriter agreements, are given below for three firms.

a) What differences do you find in the underwriting costs and agreements?
b) How do you explain the differences?

A summary of the financial information on the companies follows:

	Speedee Mart, Inc.	Spiegel, Inc.	Beckman Instruments, Inc.
Total assets, end of 1960	$2.3*	$291.3*	$39.0*
Net worth, end of 1960	0.7	64.2	19.5
Sales			
1958	0.097	152.7	39.8
1960	0.253	268.8	54.3
Net Income after taxes			
1958	0.018	5.0	(0.946)
1960	0.023	11.8	3.1

* Dollar amounts in millions

Speedee Mart, Inc. 90,000 shares, common stock, without par value

	Price to public	Underwriting discounts and commissions	Proceeds to company
Per share	$ 6	$ 0.60	$ 5.40
Total	540,000	54,000.00	486,000.00

Description of business

Speedee Mart, Inc. (the "company"), whose principal offices are located at 7988 Normal Avenue, La Mesa, California, was incorporated in California on April 10, 1956. It is engaged in the business of enfranchising others (franchises) to manage and operate retail food stores under the name "Speedee Mart." From October 2, 1960, 51 stores have been doing business under franchises as herein described and the company was in varying stages of establishing 33 additional stores.

Speedee Mart markets are located primarily in areas where they provide convenient neighborhood food-shopping facilities away from metropolitan shopping centers. In a sense, these convenience markets, which are open from 7 A.M. to 11 P.M., seven days a week, are in competition with several national supermarket chain store organizations, local chain stores, and large independent food stores, as well as other neighborhood markets. The Speedee Mart stores do not, however, purport to compete for the large weekly shopping trade, but rather to provide a convenient place for customers to make purchases for daily needs. The company believes that it meets supermarket prices on items comprising a majority of its sales volume.

Underwriting

The underwriter, J. A. Hogle & Company, 132 South Main Street, Salt Lake City, Utah, has made a firm commitment, subject to the terms and conditions of the underwriting agreement (a copy of which is filed as an exhibit to the registration statement), to purchase all the shares of the company offered hereby. The company has been advised by the underwriters that the common stock is proposed to be offered by the underwriter for sale initially at the public offering price set forth on the cover page of this prospectus. Concessions to selected dealers may be allowed in an amount not exceeding 35 cents a share, of which 15 cents a share may be reallowed to other dealers, provided such reallowance is retained. The public offering price and the concessions and reallowances to dealers may be changed by the underwriter after the initial public offering, by reason of changes in market conditions.

Source: Prospectus, J. A. Hogle & Company, January 31, 1961.

Spiegel, Inc., $40,000,000, 5 1/4% debentures, dated April 1, 1961; due April 1, 1983

	Price to public	Underwriting discounts and commissions	Proceeds to company
Per unit	100%	1.5%	98.5%
Total	$40,000,000	$600,000	$39,400,000

Description of business

The company is engaged, and intends to continue to engage, in the sale of merchandise by mail. Customers are offered three ways to buy: cash with order, 30-day charge, and monthly payments. The company is believed to sell a substantially larger proportion of its total volume on the monthly payment plan than any other national retailer of general merchandise does.

The company expects to continue to concentrate its efforts in the specialized techniques of catalogue credit promotion, credit acceptance, collections, and credit finance. Experience has demonstrated that monthly payment selling is more profitable than selling for cash. Monthly payment customers tend to buy more frequently and in larger amounts than do cash customers. In addition, after being charged with the company's total interest expense, the servicing of the credit accommodation now contributes materially to consolidated profit.

Underwriting

Subject to the terms and conditions set forth in the underwriting agreement, the company has agreed to sell to each of the underwriters named below, and each of the underwriters for whom Wertheim & Company is acting as representative has severally agreed to purchase, at the price set forth on the cover page of this prospectus, the principal amount of debentures set opposite its name.

The nature of the underwriting commitments is such that the several underwriters are obligated, subject to certain conditions, to purchase all the debentures offered hereby. In the event of default by any underwriter, the underwriting agreement provides that in certain circumstances other underwriters may be substituted or the agreement terminated.

The company has been advised by Wertheim & Company that in connection with the sale of the debentures by the underwriters, concessions may be allowed to other dealers not in excess of 0.25 percent.

Source: Prospectus, Wertheim & Company, April 12, 1961.

Beckman Instruments, Inc. 69,993 shares, common stock, par value $1 a share.

The company hereby offers to the holders of its common stock the right to subscribe for additional shares of its common stock at the rate of one additional share for each 20 shares held of record on the close of business on March 28, 1961, all as more fully set forth herein.

	Subscription price	Underwriting commissions		Proceeds to company	
Per share	$ 114	Min. $	2.00	Max. $	112.00
		Max.	5.40	Min.	108.60
Total	7,972,362	Min.	139,866.00	Max.	7,832,496.00
		Max.	377,638.20	Min.	7,594,723.80

Description of business

The company and its subsidiaries are engaged in the business of designing, developing, manufacturing, and selling precision instruments for scientific, industrial, medical, and laboratory use.

Underwriting

In the underwriting agreement, the several underwriters, represented by Lehman Brothers, have agreed, subject to the terms and conditions therein set forth, to purchase from the company all the shares of common stock offered hereby not purchased on exercise of rights, at the subscription price set forth on the cover page of this prospectus. For their respective commitments the underwriters are to receive compensation as set forth below and on the cover page of this prospectus. Reference is made to the underwriting agreement filed as an exhibit to the registration statement.

The company has agreed to pay the underwriters $2 a share with respect to each share of common stock offered hereby, plus $3.40 a share on all shares (herein called the "unsubscribed stock") not purchased on the exercise of rights or which are purchased by the underwriters on the exercise of rights purchased by them. The minimum underwriting commissions and maximum proceeds to the company shown on the cover page of this prospectus are based on the assumption that all shares of common stock offered hereby will be subscribed for by other than the underwriters, and the maximum underwriting commissions and minimum proceeds to the company are based on the assumption that none of such shares will be so subscribed for.

If the aggregated sales price of all unsubscribed stock sold by the several underwriters during the period of the subscription offer and within 30 days thereafter is in excess of the aggregate subscription price of the unsubscribed stock, the underwriters will pay to the company 50 percent of such excess. Such excess is to be computed after deducting all costs and expenses (including selling concessions, brokerage commissions, and transfer taxes) and any losses paid or incurred, directly or indirectly, by the underwriters in connection with the distribution of the unsubscribed stock, the purchase of rights (whether or not exercised), stabilization operations, overallotments, short sales, and related transactions.

Name	
Lehman Brothers	20.00
A. C. Allyn and Company, Inc.	6.00
Ball, Burge & Kraus	2.00
J. Barth & Company	2.00
Bear, Stearns & Company	8.00
Blyth & Company, Inc.	8.00
Burnham and Company	2.00
Eastman Dillon, Union Securities & Company	8.00
Goodbody & Company	2.00
Hayden, Stone & Company	4.50
Hornblower & Weeks	4.50
Paine, Webber, Jackson & Curtis	4.50
Paribas Corporation	8.00
Peltason, Tenebaum Company	2.00
Shearson, Hammill & Company	4.50
Stein Bros. & Boyce	2.00
Sutro & Company	2.00
Wagenseller & Durst, Inc.	2.00
Dean Witter & Company	8.00
Total	100.00

For the purpose of this paragraph, unsubscribed stock not sold or contracted to be sold by the underwriters on the date on which such 30-day period terminates will be deemed to have been sold on such date of termination at the weighted average of the sales prices of the common stock of the company on the New York Stock Exchange on such date.

Lehman Brothers has advised the company that the underwriters may offer shares of common stock as set forth on the cover page of this prospectus, that initially they may allow concessions not in excess of $2.50 a share to certain dealers, and that the underwriters and such dealers initially may reallow concessions not in excess of 50 cents a share to other dealers. Such concessions to dealers may be changed by the representative.

Source: Prospectus, Lehman Brothers, March 28, 1961.

COMMON equity or, if unincorporated firms are being considered, partnership or proprietorship interests, constitute the first source of funds to a new business and the base of support for existing firms' borrowings. Accordingly, our discussion of specific forms of long-term financing will begin with an analysis of common stock.

APPORTION- The nature of equity ownership depends upon the form of the busi-
MENT OF ness or organization. The central problem revolves around an appor-
INCOME, tionment of certain rights and responsibilities among those who have
CONTROL, AND provided the funds necessary for the operation of the business.
RISK The rights and responsibilities attaching to equity consist of positive considerations—income potential and control of the firm—and negative considerations—loss potential, legal responsibility, and personal liability.

General Rights of The rights of holders of common stock in a business corporation are
Holders of established by the laws of the state in which the corporation is
Common Stock chartered and by the terms of the charter granted by the state. The characteristics of charters are relatively uniform on many matters, including the following.

Collective Rights Certain collective rights are usually given to the holders of common stock. Some of the more important rights allow stockholders (1) to amend the charter with the approval of the appropriate officials in the state of incorporation; (2) to adopt and amend bylaws; (3) to elect the directors of the corporation; (4) to authorize the sale of fixed assets; (5) to enter into mergers; (6) to change the amount of authorized common stock; and (7) to issue preferred stock, debentures, bonds, and other securities.

Holders of common stock also have specific rights as individual own- *Specific Rights*
ers. (1) They have the right to vote in the manner prescribed by the
corporate charter. (2) They may sell their stock certificates, their evidence of ownership, and in this way transfer their ownership interest
to other persons. (3) They have the right to inspect the corporate
books.[1] (4) They have the right to share residual assets of the corporation on dissolution; however, the holders of common stock are
last among the claimants to the assets of the corporation.

There are two important positive considerations involved in equity own- *Apportionment of*
ership: income and control. The right to income carries risks of loss. *Income*
Control also involves responsibility and liability. In an individual proprietorship, using only funds supplied by the owner, the owner has
a 100 percent right to income and control and to loss and responsibility. As soon as the proprietor incurs debt, however, he has entered
into contracts that place limitations on his complete freedom to control
the firm and to apportion the firm's income.

In a partnership, these rights are apportioned among the partners
in an agreed manner. In the absence of a formal agreement, a division
is made by the laws of the locality. But the more significant issues
arise concerning the rights of the owners of a business corporation.

Through the right to vote, holders of common stock have legal control *Apportionment of*
of the corporation. As a practical matter, however, in many corpora- *Control*
tions the principal officers constitute all, or a majority, of the members
of the board of directors. In such circumstances the board of directors
may be controlled by the management, rather than vice versa. Management control, or control of a business by other than its owners, results. However, numerous examples demonstrate that stockholders can
reassert their control when dissatisfied. In recent years, proxy battles
with the aim of altering corporation policies have occurred fairly often.

As receivers of residual income, holders of common stock are frequently referred to as the ultimate entrepreneurs in the firm. They
are the ultimate owners and they have the ultimate control. Presumably
the firm is managed on behalf of its owners, the holders of common
stock, but there has been much dispute about the actual situation.
The point of view has been expressed that the corporation is an institution with an existence separate from the owners, and that the corpora-

---

[1] Obviously, a corporation cannot have its business affairs disturbed by allowing every
stockholder to go through any record that he would like to inspect. A corporation could not
wisely permit a competitor who happened to buy shares of its common stock to look at all
the corporation records. There must be, and there are, practical limitations to this right.

tion exists to fulfill certain functions for stockholders as only one among other important groups, such as workers, consumers, and the economy as a whole. This view doubtlessly has some validity, but it should also be noted that ordinarily the officers of a firm are also large stockholders. Furthermore, more and more firms are relating officers' compensation to the firm's profit performance, either by granting executives stock purchase options or by giving bonuses. These actions are, of course, designed to make management more stockholder-oriented.

Apportionment of Risk   The fact that, on liquidation, holders of common stock are last in the priority of claims signifies that the portion of capital they contribute provides a cushion for creditors if losses occur on dissolution. The equity-to-total-assets ratio indicates the percentage by which assets may shrink in value on liquidation before creditors will incur losses.

For example, compare two corporations, A and B, whose balance sheets are shown in Table 18–1. The ratio of equity to total assets in corporation A is 80 percent. Total assets would therefore have to shrink by 80 percent before creditors would lose money. By contrast, in corporation B the extent by which assets may shrink in value on liquidation before creditors lose money is only 40 percent.

TABLE 18–1
Balance sheets for
Corporations
A and B

Corporation A			Corporation B		
	Debt	$ 20		Debt	$ 60
	Equity	80		Equity	40
Total assets $100	Total claims	$100	Total assets $100	Total claims	$100

Since the average equity-to-total-assets ratio for all manufacturing is approximately two-thirds, a substantial equity cushion ordinarily exists. For some industries, such as airline transport and aircraft manufacturing, however, the equity cushion is only about one-third of total assets. Further, individual firms within industries can have abnormally high or low debt ratios.

COMMON STOCK FINANCING   Before undertaking an evaluation of common stock financing, it is desirable to describe some of its additional important characteristics. These topics include (1) the nature of voting rights, (2) the nature of the pre-emptive right, and (3) variations in the forms of common stock.

For each share of common stock owned, the holder has the right to *Nature of Voting* cast a vote at the annual meetings of stockholders of the corporation *Rights* or at such special meetings as may be called.

Provision is made for the temporary transfer of this right to vote by *Proxy* an instrument known as a proxy. A proxy is defined as a transfer of the right to vote. The transfer is limited in its duration, typically for a specific occasion such as the annual meeting of stockholders.

The SEC supervises the use of the proxy machinery and issues frequent rules and regulations seeking to improve its administration. SEC supervision is justified for several reasons. First, if the proxy machinery is left wholly in the hands of management, there is a danger that the incumbent management will be self-perpetuated. Second, if it is made easy for minority groups of stockholders and opposition stockholders to oust management, there is danger that small groups of stockholders may gain control of the corporation for temporary advantages or to place their friends in management positions.

A method of voting that has come into increased prominence is cumu- *Cumulative Voting* lative voting.[2] Cumulative voting for directors is required in 22 states, including California, Illinois, Pennsylvania, Ohio, and Michigan. It is permissible in 18, including Delaware, New York, and New Jersey. Ten states make no provision for cumulative voting.

Cumulative voting permits multiple votes for a single director. For example, suppose six directors are to be elected. The owner of 100 shares can cast 100 votes for each of the six openings. Cumulatively, then, he has 600 votes. When cumulative voting is permitted, the stockholder may accumulate his votes and cast 600 votes for *one* director, instead of 100 each for *six* directors. Cumulative voting is designed to enable a minority group of stockholders to obtain some voice in the control of the company by electing at least one director to the board.

The nature of cumulative voting is illustrated by use of a well-known formula,

$$r = \frac{d \times S}{D + 1} + 1, \tag{18-1}$$

---

[2] For an excellent discussion of all aspects of cumulative voting, see C. M. Williams, *Cumulative Voting for Directors* (Boston: Graduate School of Business Administration, Harvard University, 1951).

where

r = number of shares required to elect a desired number of directors

d = number of directors stockholder desires to elect

S = total number of shares of common stock outstanding and entitled to vote[3]

D = total number of directors to be elected.

The formula may be made more meaningful by an example. The ABC company will elect six directors. There are 15 candidates and 100,000 shares entitled to a vote. If a group desires to elect two directors, how many shares must it have?

$$r = \frac{2 \times 100,000}{6 + 1} + 1 = 28,572. \tag{18-2}$$

Observe the significance of the formula. Here, a minority group wishes to elect one-third of the board of directors. They can achieve their goal by owning less than one-third the number of shares of stock.[4]

The question may be put in another way. Assuming that a group holds 40,000 shares of stock in this company, how many directors would it be possible for the group to elect, following the rigid assumptions of the formula? The formula can be used in its present form or can be solved for d and expressed as

$$d = \frac{(r - 1)(D + 1)}{S}. \tag{18-3}$$

Inserting the figures, the calculation would be

$$d = \frac{39,999 \times 7}{100,000} = 2.8. \tag{18-4}$$

The 40,000 shares could elect 2.8 directors. Since directors cannot exist as fractions, the group can elect only two directors.

As a practical matter, suppose that in the above situation the total number of shares is 100,000. Hence 60,000 shares remain in other hands. The voting of all the 60,000 shares may not be concentrated. Suppose the 60,000 shares (cumulatively, 360,000 votes) not held by our group are distributed equally among 10 candidates, 36,000 shares held by each candidate. If our group's 240,000 votes are dis-

---

[3] An alternative that may be agreed to by the contesting parties is to define S as the number of shares *voted*, not authorized to vote. This procedure, which in effect gives each group seeking to elect directors the same percentage of directors as their percentage of the voted stock, is generally followed. When it is followed, a group that seeks to gain control with a minimum investment must estimate the percentage of shares that will be voted, then obtain control of more than 50 percent of that number.

[4] Note also that at least 14,287 shares must be controlled to elect one director. As far as electing a director goes, any number less than 14,287 constitutes a useless minority.

tributed equally for each of six candidates, we could elect all six directors even though we do not have a majority of the stock.

In actuality, it is difficult to make assumptions about how the opposition votes will be distributed. What is shown here is a good example
of game theory. One rule involved in the theory of games is to assume
that your opponents will do the worst they can do to you and to counter
with actions to minimize the maximum loss. This is the kind of assumption followed in the formula. If your opposition concentrates its votes
in the optimum manner, what is the best you can do to work in the
direction of your goal? Other plausible assumptions can be substituted
if one has sufficient facts to support alternative hypotheses about
the behavior of his opponents.

The pre-emptive right gives holders of common stock the first option *Pre-emptive Right*
to purchase additional issues of common stock. In some states the
pre-emptive right is made a part of every corporate charter. In other
states it is necessary to insert the pre-emptive right specifically in
the charter.

The purpose of the pre-emptive right is twofold. First, it protects
the power of control of present stockholders. If it were not for this
safeguard, the management of a corporation under criticism from
stockholders could prevent stockholders from removing it from office
by issuing a large number of additional shares at a very low price
and purchasing these shares itself. Management would thereby secure
control of the corporation to frustrate the will of the current
stockholders.

The second, and by far the more important, protection that the
pre-emptive right affords stockholders regards dilution of value. An
example may clarify this. Assume that 1,000 shares of common stock
with a market value of $100 are outstanding, making the total market
value of the firm $100,000. An additional 1,000 shares are sold at
$50 a share, or for $50,000, thus raising the total market value of
the firm to $150,000. When the total market value is divided by the
new total shares outstanding, a value of $75 a share is obtained.
Thus, selling common stock at below market value will dilute the price
of the stock and be detrimental to present stockholders and beneficial
to those who purchased the new shares. The pre-emptive right prevents
such occurrences. This point will be discussed at length later in this
chapter.

Classified common stock was used extensively in the late 1920s, some- *Forms of Common*
times in ways that misled investors. During that period Class A com- *Stock*
mon stock was usually nonvoting, and Class B was typically voting. *Classified*
Thus promoters could control companies by selling large amounts *Common Stock*
of Class A stock while retaining Class B stock.

In more recent years there has been a revival of Class B common for sound purposes. It is used by small, new companies seeking to acquire funds from outside sources. Common Stock A is sold to the public, and typically pays dividends of a consistent amount; it has full voting rights. Common stock B, however, is retained by the organizers of the company, but dividends are not paid on it until the company has established its earning power. By the use of the classified stock, the public can take a position in a conservatively financed growth company without sacrificing income.

Founders' Shares Founders' shares are somewhat like Class B stock except that they carry *sole* voting rights and, typically, do not have the right to dividends for a number of years. Thus the organizers of the firm are able to maintain complete control of the operations in the crucial initial development of the firm. At the same time, other investors are protected against excessive withdrawals of funds by owners.[5]

EVALUATION OF COMMON STOCK AS A SOURCE OF FUNDS Thus far, the chapter has covered the main characteristics of common stock, frequently referred to as equity shares in the company. By way of a summary of the important aspects of common stock, common stock financing will be appraised from the standpoint of the issuer.

Advantages First, common stock does not entail fixed charges. If the company generates the earnings, it can pay common stock dividends. In contrast to bond interest, however, there is no legal obligation to pay dividends. Second, common stock carries no fixed maturity date. Third, since common stock provides a cushion against losses for creditors, the sale of common stock increases the credit-worthiness of the firm.

Fourth, common stock may at times be sold more easily than debt. Common stock may appeal to certain investor groups for two reasons: (1) it typically carries a higher expected return than does preferred stock or debt, and (2) it provides the investor with a better hedge against inflation than do straight preferred stock and bonds, because it represents the ownership in the firm. Ordinarily, common stock

[5] Accountants also use the term "par value" to designate an arbitrary value assigned when stock is sold. When a firm sells newly issued stock, it must record the transaction on its balance sheet. For example, suppose a newly created firm commences operations by selling 100,000 shares at $10 per share, raising a total of $1 million. This $1 million must appear on the balance sheet, but what will it be called? One choice would be to assign the stock a "par value" of $10 and label the $1 million "common stock." Another choice would be to assign a $1 par value and show $100,000 ($1 par value times 100,000 shares) as "common stock" and $900,000 as "paid in surplus." Still another choice would be to disregard the term par value entirely—that is, use no-par stock—and record the $1 million as "common stock." Since the choice is quite arbitrary for all practical purposes, more and more firms are adopting the last procedure and abolishing the term par value. Since there are quite enough useful concepts and terms in accounting and finance, we heartily applaud the demise of useless ones such as this!

increases in value when the value of real assets rises during an inflationary period.

Disadvantages

First, the sale of common stock extends voting rights or control to the additional stockowners who are brought into the company. For this reason, among others, additional equity financing is often avoided by small and new firms. The owner-managers may be unwilling to share control of their companies with outsiders.

Second, common stock gives more owners the right to share in income. The use of debt may enable the firm to utilize funds at a fixed low cost, whereas common stock gives equal rights to new stockholders to share in the net profits of the firm.

Third, as we saw in Chapter 17, the costs of underwriting and distributing common stock are usually higher than those for underwriting and distributing preferred stock or debt. Flotation costs for selling common stock are characteristically higher because (1) the costs of investigating an equity security investment are higher than investigating the feasibility of a comparable debt security and (2) stocks are more risky, which means equity holdings must be diversified, which in turn means that a given dollar amount of new stock must be sold to a greater number of purchasers than the same amount of debt.

Fourth, as we saw in Chapter 12, the component cost of common stock is typically greater than that of debt. Therefore, if the firm has less debt than is called for in the optimum capital structure, the average cost of capital will be higher than necessary.

Fifth, common stock dividends are not deductible as an expense for calculating the corporation's income subject to the federal income tax, but bond interest is deductible. The impact of this factor is reflected in the relative cost of equity capital *vis à vis* debt capital.

Other Aspects of Equity Financing

Common stock also should be considered from a social standpoint. Common stock is a desirable form of financing because it renders business firms, hence a major segment of the economy, less vulnerable to the consequences of declines in sales and earnings. If sales and earnings decline, common stock financing involves no fixed charges, the payment of which might force the firm into reorganization or bankruptcy.

However, there is another aspect of common stock financing that may have less desirable social consequences. Common stock prices fall in recessions, and this causes a rise in the cost of equity capital.[6] The rising cost of equity raises the over-all cost of capital, which in turn reduces investment. This reduction further aggravates the recession. However, an expanding economy is accompanied by rising

[6] See Table 10–1.

stock prices, and with rising stock prices comes a drop in the cost of capital. This, in turn, stimulates investment, which may add to a developing inflationary boom. In summary, a consideration of its effects on the cost of capital suggests that stock financing may tend to amplify cyclical fluctuations.

Just how these opposing forces combine to produce a net effect is unknown, but the authors believe that the first is the stronger; that is, stock financing tends to stabilize the economy.

THE USE OF RIGHTS IN FINANCING If the pre-emptive right is contained in a particular firm's charter, then it must offer any new common stock to existing stockholders. If the charter does not prescribe a pre-emptive right, the firm has a choice of making the sale to its existing stockholders or to an entirely new set of investors. If the sale is to the existing stockholders, the stock flotation is called a *rights offering.* Each stockholder is issued an option to buy a certain number of the new shares, and the terms of the option are contained on a piece of paper called a *right.* Each stockholder receives one right for each share of stock he owns. The advantages and disadvantages of rights offerings are described in this section.[7]

THEORETICAL RELATIONSHIPS Several issues confront the financial manager who is deciding on the details of a rights offering. The various considerations can be made clear by the use of illustrative data on the Southeast Company, whose balance sheet and income statement are given in Table 18–2.

TABLE 18–2
Southeast Company. Balance sheet before rights offering

		Total debt, 5%	$ 40,000,000
		Common stock ($10 par)	10,000,000
		Retained earnings	50,000,000
Total assets	$100,000,000	Total liabilities and capital	$100,000,000

Southeast Company partial income statement

Total earnings	$10,000,000
Interest on debt	2,000,000
Income before taxes	8,000,000
Taxes (50% assumed)	4,000,000
Earnings after taxes	4,000,000
Earnings per share (1,000,000 shares)	$4
Market price of stock (price/earnings ratio of 25 assumed)	$100

Southeast earns $4 million after taxes and 1 million shares are outstanding, so earnings per share are $4. The stock sells at 25 times earnings, or for $100 a share. The company plans to raise $10 million

[7] Much of the material for this section as obtained from J. R. Nelson, *Rights* (Unpublished Ph.D. dissertation, University of California, Los Angeles, 1961).

of new equity funds through a rights offering and decides to sell the new stock to shareholders for $50 a share. The questions now facing the financial manager are:

1. How many rights will be required to purchase a share of the newly issued stock?
2. What is the value of each right?
3. What effect will the rights offering have on the price of the existing stock?

Each of these questions will now be analyzed.

Southeast plans to raise $10 million in new equity funds and to sell the new stock at a price of $50 a share. Dividing the subscription price into the total funds to be raised gives the number of shares to be issued. *Number of Rights to Purchase a New Share*

$$\text{Number of new shares} = \frac{\text{funds to be raised}}{\text{subscription price}} = \frac{\$10,000,000}{\$50}$$

$$= 200,000 \text{ shares.}$$

The next step is to divide the number of new shares into the number of previously outstanding shares to get the number of rights required to subscribe to one share of the new stock. Note that stockholders always get one right for each share of stock they own.

$$\text{Number of rights needed to buy a share of the stock} = \frac{\text{old shares}}{\text{new shares}}$$

$$= \frac{1,000,000}{200,000} = 5 \text{ rights.}$$

Therefore, a stockholder will have to surrender five rights plus $50 to receive one of the newly issued shares. Had the subscription price been set at $95 a share, 9.5 rights would have been required to subscribe to each new share, while only one right would have been needed if the price had been set at $10 a share.

It is clearly worth something to be able to buy for less than $100 a share of stock selling for $100. The right provides this privilege, so the right must have a value. To see how the theoretical value of a right is established, we will continue with the example of the Southeast Company, assuming that it will raise $10 million by selling 200,000 new shares at $50 a share. *Value of a Right*

First, notice that the *market value* of the old stock was $100 million—$100 a share times 1 million shares. (The book value is irrelevant.) When the firm sells the new stock, it brings in an additional $10 million. As a first approximation, we assume that the market value of the common stock increases by exactly this $10 million. Actually, the market value of all the common stock would go up by more than $10 million if investors think the company will be able to invest these funds at a yield substantially in excess of the cost of equity capital, but by less than $10 million if investors are doubtful of the company's ability to put the new funds to work profitably in the near future.

Under the assumption that market value exactly reflects the new funds brought in, the total market value of the common stock after the new issue will be $110 million. Dividing this new value by the new total number of shares outstanding, 1.2 million, we obtain a new market value of $91.67 a share. Therefore, we see that after the financing has been completed, the price of the common stock will have fallen from $100 to $91.67.

Since the rights give the stockholders the privilege of buying for only $50 a share of stock that will end up being worth $91.67, thus saving $41.67, is $41.67 the value of each right? The answer is "no," because five rights are required to buy one new share; we must divide $41.67 by 5 to get the value of each right. In the example each one is worth $8.33.

Ex Rights Rights are handled much like dividends in some regards. Recall that dividends go with the stock until the ex-dividend date, which is four days prior to the stock of record date. Rights are treated similarly when the old stock is traded prior to the issuance of the new stock but after the announcement of the financing. For example, on October 15, Southeast Company might announce the terms of the new financing, stating that rights will be mailed out on December 1 to stockholders of record as of the close of business on November 15. Anyone buying the old stock on or before November 11 will receive the rights; anyone buying the stock on or after November 12 will *not* receive the rights. Thus, November 12 is the *ex-rights date;* before November 12 the stock sells *rights on.* In the case of Southeast Company, the *rights on price* is $100, the *ex-rights price* is $91.67.

Formula Value of Equations have been developed for determining the value of rights
the Rights without going through all the procedures described above. (See footnote 7 at the end of this section.) While the stock is still selling rights
Rights on on, the value at which the rights will sell when they are issued can be found by use of the following formula:

Value of one right

$$= \frac{\text{market value of stock, rights on} - \text{subscription price}}{\text{number of rights required to purchase one share plus 1}}$$

$$R = \frac{M_0 - S}{N + 1}. \tag{18–5}$$

Here M_0 is the rights-on price of the stock, S is the subscription price, N is the number of rights required to purchase a new share of stock, and R is the value of one right. Substituting in the appropriate values for the Southeast Company, we obtain

$$R = \frac{\$100 - \$50}{5 + 1} = \frac{\$50}{6} = \$8.33.$$

This agrees with the value of the rights as found by the long procedure.

Suppose you are a stockholder in the Southeast Company. When you *Ex Rights* return to the United States from a trip to Europe, you read about the rights offering in the newspaper. The stock is now selling ex rights for $91.67 a share. How can you calculate the theoretical value of a right? Simply using the following formula, which follows the logic described in preceding sections, you can determine the value of each right to be $8.33:

$$\text{Value of one right} = \frac{\text{market value of stock ex rights} - \text{subscription price}}{\text{number of rights required to purchase one share}}$$

$$R = \frac{M_e - S}{N} \tag{18-6}$$

$$R = \frac{\$91.67 - \$50}{5} = \frac{\$41.67}{5} = \$8.33.$$

Here M_e is the ex-rights price of the stock.[8]

---

[8] Equation 18–6 follows directly from the verbal explanation given in the section "Value of a Right" above. Equation 18–5 can be derived from Equation 18–6 as follows:
1. Note that

$$M_e = M_0 - R. \tag{18-7}$$

2. Substitute Equation 18–7 into Equation 18–6, obtaining

$$R = \frac{M_0 - R - S}{N}. \tag{18-8}$$

3. Simplify Equation 18–8 as follows, ending with Equation 18–5. This completes the derivation.

$$R = \frac{M_0 - S}{N} - \frac{R}{N}$$

$$R + \frac{R}{N} = \frac{M_0 - S}{N}$$

$$R \left(\frac{N + 1}{N} \right) = \frac{M_0 - S}{N}$$

$$R = \frac{M_0 - S}{N} \cdot \frac{N + 1}{N}$$

$$R = \frac{M_0 - S}{N + 1} \tag{18-5}$$

EFFECTS ON POSITION OF STOCKHOLDERS A stockholder has the choice of exercising his rights or selling them. If he has sufficient funds and if he wants to buy more shares of the company's stock, the stockholder will exercise the rights. If he does not have the money or does not want to buy more stock, he will sell his rights. In either case, provided the formula values of the rights hold true, the stockholder will neither benefit nor lose by the rights offering. This statement can be made clear by considering the position of an individual stockholder in the Southeast Company.

The stockholder had 10 shares of stock before the rights offering. The 10 shares each had a market value of $100 a share, so the stockholder had a total market value of $1,000 in the company's stock. If he exercises his rights, he will be able to purchase two additional shares at $50 a share, a new investment of $100; his total investment is now $1,100. He now owns 12 shares of his company's stock, which, after the rights offering, has a value of $91.67 a share. The value of his stock is $1,100, exactly what he has invested in it.

Alternatively, if he sold his 10 rights, which have a value of $8.33 a right, he would receive $83.30. He would now have his original 10 shares of stock plus $83.30 in cash. But his original 10 shares of stock now have a market price of $91.67 a share. The $916.70 market value of his stock plus the $83.30 in cash is the same as the original $1,000 market value of stock with which he began. From a purely mechanical or arithmetical standpoint, the stockholder neither benefits nor gains from the sale of additional shares of stock through rights. Of course, if he forgets to exercise or sell his rights, or if brokerage costs of selling the rights are excessive, then a stockholder can suffer a loss. But, in general, the issuing firm makes special efforts to minimize brokerage costs, and adequate time is given to enable the stockholder to take some action, so losses are minimal.

Oversubscription Privilege Even though the rights are very valuable and *should* be exercised, some stockholders will doubtless neglect to do so. Still, all the stock *will* be sold because of the *oversubscription privilege* contained in most rights offerings. The oversubscription privilege gives subscribing stockholders the right to buy, on a pro rata basis, all shares not taken in the initial offering. To illustrate, if John Doe owned 10 percent of the stock in Southeast Company, and if 20 percent of the rights offered by the company were not exercised (or sold) by the stockholders to whom they were originally given, then John Doe could buy an additional 2.5 percent of the new stock (12.5 percent, Doe's percentage of the exercised shares, times the 20 percent unsubscribed stock, equals 2.5 percent). Since this stock is a bargain—$50 for stock worth $91.67—John Doe and other stockholders would use the oversubscription privilege, thus assuring the full sale of the new stock issue.

We can now investigate the factors influencing the use of rights and, if they are used, the level at which the subscription price will be set. The articles of incorporation of the Southeast Company permit it to use rights or not, depending on whether it judges their use to be advantageous to the company and its stockholders. The financial vice-president of the company is considering three alternative methods of raising the additional sum of $10 million. *Relation between Market Price and Subscription Price*

Southeast Company could sell additional shares through investment bankers to the public at approximately $100 a share, the company netting approximately $96 a share; thus, it would need to sell 105,000 shares in order to cover the underwriting commission. *Alternative I*

The company could sell additional shares through rights, using investment bankers and paying a commission of 1 percent on the total dollar amount of the stock sold plus an additional 3/4 percent on all shares unsubscribed and taken over by the investment bankers. Allowing for the usual market pressure when common stock is sold, the new shares would be sold at a 20 percent discount, or at $80. Thus, 125,000 additional shares would be offered through rights. With eight rights, an additional share could be purchased at $80. *Alternative II*

We noted above that stockholders are given the right to subscribe to any unexercised rights on a pro rata basis. Only shares not subscribed to on an original or secondary basis are sold to the underwriters and subjected to the 3/4 percent additional commission.

The company could sell additional shares through rights at $10 a share. Investment bankers would not be employed at all. The number of additional shares of common stock to be sold would be one million. For each right held, existing stockholders would be permitted to buy one share of the new common stock. *Alternative III*

Under Alternative I, investment bankers are used. Rights would not be utilized at all. In this circumstance the underwriting commission, or flotation cost, is approximately 4 percent. In Alternative II, where rights are used with a small discount, the underwriting commission is reduced because the discount removes much of the risk of not being able to sell the issue. The underwriting commission consists of two parts—1 percent on the original issue and an additional 3/4 of 1 percent commission on all unsubscribed shares the investment bankers are required to take over and sell. Thus, the actual commission will range somewhere between 1 percent and $1\frac{3}{4}$ percent.

Under Alternative III, the subscription price is $10 a share. With such a large concession the company does not need to use investment bankers at all, because the rights are certain to have value and to be either exercised or sold.

Which of the three alternatives is superior?

Alternative I will provide a wider distribution of the securities sold, thus lessening any possible control problems. Also, it provides assurance from the investment bankers that the company will receive the $10 million involved in the new issue. The company pays for these services in the form of underwriting charges. The stock price, after the issue, should be approximately $100.

Under Alternative II, by utilizing rights, underwriting expenses are reduced. There is also a small reduction in the unit price per share, from $100 to $98 a share. Also, since the rights do have a low value, some stockholders may neither exercise them nor sell them, thus suffering a loss.[9] Existing stockholders will buy some of the new shares, so the distribution is likely to be less wide. Because of the underwriting contract, under Alternative II the firm is also assured of receiving the funds sought. Finally, it is often argued that investors like the opportunity of purchasing additional shares through rights offerings, and that the use of rights offerings increases "stockholder loyalty."

Alternative III involves no underwriting expense, and it results in a substantial decrease in the unit price of shares. Initially, however, the shares will be less widely distributed. Note that Alternative III has a large stock-split effect, which results in a much lower final stock price per share. Many people feel that there is an optimal stock price—one that will produce a maximum total market value of the shares—and that this price is generally in the range of $30 to $60 a share. If this is the feeling of Southeast's directors, they may believe that Alternative III permits them to reach this more desirable price range, while at the same time reducing flotation costs on the new issue. Also, since the rights have a substantial value, few stockholders will fail either to exercise or to sell them, so there should be a minimum of stockholder loss from inaction.

[9] The value of each right is computed as

$$R = \frac{\$100 - \$85}{8 + 1} = \frac{\$15}{9} = \$1.67.$$

The value of the stock, after financing, is $100 − $1.67 = $98.33 a share.

The three alternatives are summarized below:

	Advantages	**Disadvantages**
Alternative I	1. Wider distribution 2. Certainty of receiving funds	1. High underwriting costs
Alternative II	1. Smaller underwriting costs 2. Lower unit price of shares 3. Certainty of receiving funds 4. Increase stockholder loyalty	1. More narrow distribution
Alternative III	1. No underwriting costs 2. Substantial decrease in unit price of shares 3. Increase stockholder loyalty	1. More narrow distribution

The alternative that is most advantageous depends upon the company's needs. If the company is strongly interested in a wider distribution of its securities, Alternative I is preferable. If it is most interested in reducing the unit price of its shares and is confident that the lower unit price will induce wider distribution of its shares, Alternative III will be chosen. If the company's needs are moderate in both directions, Alternative II may offer a satisfactory compromise. Whether rights will be used and the level of the subscription price both depend upon the needs of the company at a particular time.

Exercise of Rights

Interestingly enough, it is expected that a small percentage of stockholders may neglect to exercise their rights or to sell them. In an offering in 1955, the holders of 1 1/2 percent of the shares of General Motors common stock did not exercise their rights.[10] The loss involved to these stockholders was $1.5 million. Those who failed to exercise their rights in a number of offerings during 1955 held from 1.5 to 2.75 percent of the shares of stock outstanding. In an AT&T issue in that year, the loss to shareholders who neglected to exercise their rights was $960,000.

Market Price and Subscription Price

Measured from the registration date for the new issue of the security, the average percentage by which the subscription prices of new issues were below their market prices was 22.8 percent during the years 1946–1947, but only about 15 percent in recent years. Examples of price concessions of 40 percent or more are observed in a small percentage of issues, but the most frequently encountered discounts are from 10 to 20 percent.

[10] E. A. Grimm, "The Money You Save May Be Your Own," *Exchange,* XVI (December 1955), pp. 17–20.

Effect on Subsequent Behavior of Market Price of Stock   It is often stated that new issues of stock through rights will depress the price of the existing common stock of the company. To the extent that a subscription price in connection with the rights offering is lower than the market price, there will be a "stock split effect" on the market price of the common stock. With the prevailing market price of Southeast Company's stock at $100 and a $10 subscription price, the new market price will probably drop to about $55.

But the second question is whether, because of the rights offering, the actual new market price will be $55 or lower or higher. Again, empirical analysis of the movement in stock prices during rights offerings indicates that generalization is not practical. What happens to the market prices of the stock ex rights and after the rights trading period depends upon the prospects of the issuing company.

ADVANTAGES OF USE OF RIGHTS IN NEW FINANCING   It has been seen that the pre-emptive right gives the shareholders the protection of preserving their pro rata share in the earnings and surplus of the company. The firm also benefits. By offering new issues of securities to the existing stockholders, it increases the likelihood of a favorable reception for the stock. By their ownership of common stock in the company, these investors have already indicated a favorable evaluation of the company. They may be receptive to the purchase of additional shares, particularly when the additional reasons indicated below are taken into account.

The shares purchased with rights are subject to lower margin requirements. For example, margin requirements since May 6, 1970 have been 65 percent; in other words, a person buying listed stocks must have at least $65 of his own funds for every $100 of securities purchased. However, if shares of new issues of stocks are purchased with rights, only $25 per $100 of common stock purchased must be furnished by the investor himself; he is permitted by law to borrow up to 75 percent of the purchase price. Furthermore, the absence of a clear pattern in the price behavior of the adjusted market price of the stocks and rights before, during, and after the trading period may enhance interest in the investment possibilities of the instruments.

These factors may offset the tendency toward a downward pressure on the price of the common stock occurring at the time of a new issue.[11] With the increased interest and advantages afforded by the rights offering, the "true" or "adjusted" downward price pressure may actually be avoided.

---

[11] The downward pressure develops because of an increase in the supply of securities without a necessarily equivalent increase in the demand. Generally, it is a temporary phenomenon, and the stock tends to return to the theoretical price after a few months. Obviously, if the acquired funds are invested at a very high rate of return, the stock price benefits; if the investment does not turn out well, the stock price suffers.

A related advantage is that the flotation costs to an issuer associated with a rights offering will be lower than the costs of a public flotation. Costs referred to here are cash costs. For example, the flotation costs of industrial issues of common stock in 1955 were 9 percent on public issues compared with 3.8 percent of the proceeds to the company on rights offerings.[12] Underpricing on rights offerings increases their "costs" to 20.6 percent. However, the underpricing is not a cash outlay and, as we have seen, the underpricing accrues to stockholders by making their rights more valuable.

The financial manager may obtain positive benefits from underpricing. Since a rights offering is a stock split to a certain degree, it will cause the market price of the stock to fall to a level lower than it otherwise would have been. But stock splits will increase the number of shareholders in a company by bringing the price of a stock into a more attractive trading level. Furthermore, because a rights offering is an indirect stock split, it may result in additional dividends for the stockowners.

Finally, the total effect of the rights offering may be to stimulate an enthusiastic response from stockholders and the investment market as a whole, with the result that opportunities for financing become more attractive to the firm. Thus, the financial manager may be able to engage in common stock financing at lower costs and under more favorable terms.

SUMMARY

In this chapter, a number of characteristics of common stock financing have been presented. The advantages and disadvantages of external equity financing, compared with the use of preferred stock and debt, have been described. The purpose of the descriptive background material has been to provide a basis for making sound decisions when financing by common stock is being considered as a possible alternative.

Chapters 10, 11, and 12 have already provided a framework for analyzing the advantages and limitations to the use of debt financing versus equity financing. The more specific aspects influencing decisions will now be considered. Among the numerous factors involved, eight have particular importance:

1. Patterns of sales and profits
2. Growth rate of sales and profits
3. Existing financial position
4. Age of firm

---

[12] H. W. Stevenson, *Common Stock Financing* (Ann Arbor: University of Michigan, 1957), p. 61.

5. Control considerations
6. Cash flow requirements
7. Costs
8. Restrictions associated with the financing agreement

It is important to note that one *cannot* go through the eight factors, decide that six or even seven favor common stock, and recommend common stock over debt. The one factor that favors debt may be dominant in the particular case—it may override all those favoring common stock. In other words, here, just as in all other aspects of financial management, analytical tools provide a basis for the exercise of judgment.

The chapter also discussed the key decisions confronting the financial manager when he considers a rights offering and indicated the major features bearing on such decisions. Rights offerings may be used effectively by financial managers to increase the goodwill of shareholders. If the new financing associated with the rights represents a sound decision—one likely to result in improved earnings for the firm—a rise in stock values will probably result. The use of rights will permit shareholders to preserve their positions or to improve them. However, if investors feel that the new financing is not well advised, the rights offering may cause the price of the stock to decline by more than the value of the rights.

Because the rights offering is directed to existing shareholders, it may be possible to reduce the costs of floating the new issue.

A major decision for financial managers in a rights offering is to set the subscription price, or the amount of the concession from the existing market price of the stock. Formulas reflecting the static effects of a rights offering indicate that neither the stockholders nor the company benefits or loses from the price changes. The rights offering has the effect of a stock split. The level set for the subscription price will, to a great degree, reflect the objectives and effects of a stock split.

The subsequent price behavior of the rights and the common securities in the associated new offering will reflect the earnings and dividends prospects of the company, as well as the underlying developments in the securities markets. The new financing associated with the rights offering may be an indicator of prospective growth in the sales and earnings of the company. The stock-split effects of the rights offering may be used to alter the company's dividend payments. The effects of these developments on the market behavior of the rights and the securities before, during, and after the rights trading period will reflect the expectations of investors toward the outlook for earnings and dividends per share.

18–1   What percentage could total assets shrink in value on liquidation before creditors incurred losses in each of the following cases:

a) Equity to total asset ratio, 50 percent?
b) Debt to equity ratio, 50 percent?
c) Debt to total asset ratio, 40 percent?

18–2   What difficulties do small firms encounter in raising equity capital?

18–3   What characteristics of a new common stock issue would make its purchase more attractive to prospective investors?

18–4   How many shares must a minority group possess in order to assure election of two directors if nine new directors will be elected and 200,000 shares are outstanding? Assume cumulative voting exists.

18–5   Should the pre-emptive right entitle stockholders to purchase convertible bonds before they are offered to outsiders?

18–6   Are there advantages for a corporation to have its securities listed on more than one exchange?

18–7   What are the reasons for not letting officers and directors of a corporation make short sales in their company's stock?

18–8   It is frequently stated that the primary purpose of the pre-emptive right is to allow individuals to maintain their proportionate share of the ownership and control of a corporation. Just how important do you suppose this consideration is for the average stockholder of a firm whose shares are traded on the New York or American stock exchanges? Is the pre-emptive right likely to be of more importance to stockholders of closely held firms?

18–9   How would the success of a rights offering be affected by a declining stock market?

18–10   What are some of the advantages and disadvantages of setting the subscription price on a rights offering substantially below the current market price of the stock?

18–11   Is a firm likely to get wider distribution of shares if it sells new stock through a rights offering or directly to underwriters? Why would a company be interested in getting a wider distribution of shares?

18–1   The Florida Canning Company is principally engaged in the business of growing, processing, and marketing a variety of canned and frozen vegetables and is a major company in this field. High-quality products are produced and marketed at premium prices.

During each of the past several years the company's sales have increased and the needed inventories have been financed from short-term sources. The officers have discussed the idea of refinancing their bank loans with long-term debt or common stock. A common stock issue of 310,000 shares sold at this time (present market price is $48 a share) would yield $14 million after expenses. This same sum could be raised by selling 12-year bonds with an interest rate of 8 percent and a sinking fund to retire the bonds over their 12-year life.

Canning industry financial ratios

Current ratio (times)	2.2
Sales to total assets (times)	2.0
Sales to inventory (times)	5.6
Average collection period (days)	22.0

Current debt/total assets (percent)	25–30
Long-term debt/total assets (percent)	10–15
Preferred/total assets (percent)	0.5
Net worth/total assets (percent)	60–65
Profits to sales (percent)	2.3
Net profits to total assets (percent)	4.0
Profits to net worth (percent)	8.4
Expected growth rate of earnings and dividends (percent)	6.5

Florida Canning Company
Consolidatd balance sheet
March 31, 1971*
In millions of dollars

Current assets	$ 94	Accounts payable	$ 8	
Fixed plant and equipment	38	Notes payable	24	
Other assets	8	Accruals	10	
		Total current liabilities		42
		Long-term debt, 5%		42
		Preferred stock	6	
		Common stock	8	
		Retained earnings	42	
		Net worth		56
Total assets	$140	Total claims on assets		$140

* The majority of harvesting activities do not begin until late April or May.

Florida Canning Company
Consolidated statement of income,
year ended March 31
In millions of dollars

	1968	1969	1970	1971
Net sales	$150.0	$156.4	$195.2	$231.4
Cost of goods sold	97.4	104.4	130.2	153.6
Gross profit	52.6	52.0	65.0	77.8
Other expenses	41.2	44.0	54.0	59.0
Operating income	11.4	8.0	11.0	18.8
Other income (net)	(2.2)	(2.8)	(3.8)	6.2
Earnings before tax	9.2	5.2	7.2	12.6
Taxes	4.8	2.2	3.6	6.4
Net profit	4.4	3.0	3.6	6.2
Preferred dividend	0.2	0.2	0.2	.2
Earnings available to common stock	$ 4.2	$ 2.8	$ 3.4	$ 6.0
Earnings per share	$ 2.10	$ 1.40	$ 1.70	$ 3.00
Cash dividends per share	0.86	0.96	1.06	1.20
Price range for common stock				
High	44.00	46.00	44.00	54.00
Low	20.00	28.00	34.00	42.00

a) Should Florida refinance the short-term loans? Why?

b) If the bank loans should be refinanced, what factors should be considered in determining which form of financing to use? This question should not be answered in terms of precise cost of capital calculations. Rather, a more qualitative and subjective analysis is appropriate. The only calculations necessary are some simple ratios. Careful interpretation of these ratios is necessary, however, to understand and discuss the often complex, subjective judgment issues involved.

18–2 Pitney-Bowes has been practically the sole manufacturer of postage meters, which it leases or sells outright. Postage meters accounted for half of all the United States postage used by 1959. In addition, the company makes and sells a variety of mailing and business machines.

A few years ago the company incurred $6 million in short-term bank loans because of the expansion of its Stamford plant and offices. The officers of Pitney-Bowes discussed the desirability of refinancing the bank loans with long-term debt or common stock. Underwriters informed them that 20-year, 5½ percent sinking fund debentures or 200,000 shares of common stock could be sold to raise the desired funds. As the common stock was selling above $40 per share, the company could receive about $8,000,000 net from the sale of 200,000 shares. Financial data are shown below:

Current assets	$21	Accounts payable		$ 4	*Pitney-Bowes, Inc.,*
Fixed plant and equipment	29	Notes payable, 5%		6	*Consolidated*
		Income taxes payable		3	*balance sheet,*
		Other accruals		2	*December 31, 1959**
		Total current liabilities		$15	*In millions of dollars*
		Prepaid rental income (net)		7	
		Promissory notes, 3 3/4%, due in 1967		4	
		Cumulative preferred stock, $50			
		par, 4 1/4%		1	
		Common stock, $2 par value	8		
		Capital surplus	4		
		Retained earnings	11		
		Net worth		23	
Total assets	$50	Total claims on assets		$50	

* The balance sheet and income statement figures have been altered to simplify the calculations.

	1956	1957	1958	1959	
					Pitney-Bowes, Inc.,
					Consolidated
					statement of income,
Sales (net)	17	17	20	22	*Year ended*
Rental and service income	26	29	31	33	*December 31*
Operating income	43	46	51	55	*In millions of dollars*
Cost of products sold	7	7	9	9	
Depreciation on rental equipment	2	3	3	3	
Selling, administrative, and other					
expenses	26	27	30	33	
	35	37	42	45	
Net operating income	8	9	9	10	
Income taxes	4	5	5	5	
Net profit for the period	4	4	4	5	
Earnings per share of common	1.00	1.00	1.00	1.25	
Cash dividends per common share	0.50	0.52	0.53	0.60	
Price range for common stock					
High	24	24	33	45	
Low	15	15	18	35	

Manufacturing industry financial ratios

Current ratio (times)	2.0
Sales to total assets (times)	2.0
Sales to inventory (times)	9.0
Average collection period (days)	36
Current debt/total assets (percent)	20–25
Long-term debt/total assets (percent)	6–10
Preferred/total assets (percent)	5–10
Net worth/total assets (percent)	65–70
Profits to sales (percent)	4–6
Net profits to total assets (percent)	10–12
Profits to net worth (percent)	13–15
Expected growth in earnings and dividends (percent)	7.5

a) Should Pitney-Bowes refund the short-term bank loan? Why?

b) If you were to refinance the short-term loan, what factors would enter into your consideration of the two alternatives?

c) Indicate which means of refinancing you would suggest.

   This question should not be answered in terms of precise cost of capital calculations. Rather, a more qualitative and subjective analysis is appropriate. The only calculations neessary are some simple ratios. Careful interpretation of these ratios is necessary, however, to understand and discuss the often complex, subjective judgment issues involved.

18–3   The common stock of the Industrial Research Company is selling for $70 on the market. The stockholders are offered one new share at a subscription price of $45 for every four shares held. What is the value of each right?

18–4   Lewis has 100 shares of Nortнwood Industries. The market price per share is $80. The company now offers stockholders one new share to be purchased at $50 for every five shares held.

a) Determine the value of each right.

b) Assume that Lewis (1) uses 25 rights and sells the other 75, or (2) sells 100 rights at the market price you have calculated. Prepare a statement showing the changes in his position under the above assumptions.

18–5   National Appliance Company common stock is priced at $46 a share on the market. Notice is given that stockholders may purchase one new share at a price of $25 for every six shares held. You hold 75 shares at the time of notice.

a) At approximately what price will each right sell on the market?

b) Why will this be the approximate price?

c) What effect will the issuance of rights have on the original market price? Why?

18–6   The Wilson Company has the following balance sheet and income statement:

The Wilson Company
Balance sheet before
rights offering

		Total debt (5%)	$ 5,000,000
		Common stock ($20 par value)	2,000,000
		Retained earnings	3,000,000
Total assets	$10,000,000	Total liabilities and capital	$10,000,000

Earnings rate: 10% on total assets

Total earnings	$1,000,000
Interest on debts	250,000
Income before taxes	750,000
Taxes (40% rate assumed)	300,000
Earnings after taxes	$ 450,000

Earnings per share	$ 4.50
Dividends per share (56%)	$ 2.50
Price/earnings ratio	20 times
Market price per share	$90.00

The Wilson Company plans to raise an additional $4 million through a rights offering. The additional funds will continue to earn 10 percent. The price/earnings ratio is assumed to remain at 20 times, dividend payout will continue to be 56 percent, and the 40 percent tax rate will remain in effect. (Do not attempt to use the formulas given in the chapter for this problem. Additional information is given here which violates the "other things constant" assumption inherent in the formula.)

a) Assuming subscription prices of $20, $40, and $60 a share:

1) How many additional shares of stock will have to be sold?
2) How many rights will be required to purchase one new share?
3) What will be the new earnings per share?
4) What will be the new market price per share?
5) Selling stock through a rights offering with the subscription price set below the current market price has an effect that is somewhat similar to a stock split or stock dividend. A stock split of approximately what degree would have the same effect on earnings per share as does the rights offering under each of the three subscription prices?
6) What will be the new dividend per share if the dividend payout ratio is maintained?

b) What is the significance of your results?

Chapter 19

Fixed Income Securities: Debt and Preferred Stock

*T*HE major factors underlying the decision to use financial lever-age were set out in Part IV. It was noted that the use of leverage mag-nifies returns on common stock. Up to a point—with the particular point varying with the characteristics of the firm's line of activity—additional leverage is advantageous in terms of (1) maximizing the market value of the common stock and (2) minimizing the average cost of capital. Beyond that point, which was defined as the "optimal debt ratio," or the "optimum capital structure," additional debt raises the cost of capital and lowers the value of the firm.

In the theoretical discussion of leverage, we abstracted from reality by explaining the concepts largely in terms of one homogeneous type of fixed income security, "debt." In fact, there are a myriad of fixed income securities: long- and short-term, secured and unsecured, marketable and nonmarketable, participating and nonparticipating, senior and junior, and so on.

Different classes of investors favor different types of securities, and tastes change over time. An astute financial manager knows how to "package" his securities at a given point in time to make them most attractive to the most potential investors and thereby keep his cost of capital to a minimum. We have already analyzed the major types and forms of short-term and intermediate-term debt financing. This chapter deals with the two most important types of long-term fixed income securities, bonds and preferred stocks.

INSTRUMENTS OF LONG-TERM DEBT FINANCING For an understanding of long-term forms of financing, some familiarity with technical terminology is necessary. However, the presentation will be limited to only that descriptive material necessary to analyze important problems and to formulate financial policies. The discussion of long-term debt therefore begins with an explanation of several important instruments and terms.

Most people have had some experience with short-term promissory *Bond*
notes. A *bond* is a long-term promissory note.

A *mortgage* represents a pledge of designated property for a loan. *Mortgage*
Under a *mortgage bond* the corporation pledges certain real assets
as security for the bond. A mortgage bond is therefore secured by
real property.[1] The pledge is a condition of the loan.

A *debenture* is long-term debt unsecured in the sense that it lacks *Debenture*
a pledge of any specific property. However, like other general creditor
claims, it is secured by any property not otherwise pledged.

Funded debt is simply long-term debt. When a firm is said to be *Funded Debt*
planning to "fund" its floating debt, it will replace short-term securities by long-term securities. Funding does not imply placing money
with a trustee or other repository; it is simply part of the jargon of
finance and means "long term."

Since a bond is a long-term promissory note, a long-term relation *Indenture*
between borrower and lender is established in a document called an
indenture. When it is a matter of an ordinary 60- or 90-day promissory
note, few new developments are likely to occur in the life or affairs
of the borrower to endanger repayment. The lender looks closely at
the borrower's current position because current assets are the main
source of repayment. A bond, however, is a long-time contractual relationship between the issuer of the bond and the bondholders; over
such an extended period the bondholder has cause to worry that the
firm's position might change materially.

In the ordinary common stock or preferred stock certificate or agreement, the details of the contractual relation can be summarized in
a few paragraphs. The bond indenture, however, may be a document
of several hundred pages covering a large number of factors that
will be important to the contractual parties. It discusses the form
of the bond and the instrument. It provides a complete description
of property pledged. It specifies the authorized amount of the bond
issue. It contains protective clauses or *covenants,* which are detailed
and which usually include limits on indebtedness, restrictions on dividends, and a sinking fund provision. Generally a minimum current
ratio requirement during the bond indebtedness, as well as provisions
for redemption or call privileges, are also added.

[1] There are also *chattel mortgages,* which are secured by personal property, but these are
generally intermediate-term instruments.

Trustee Not only is a bond of long duration, but the issue is also likely to be of substantial size. Before the rise of the large aggregations of savings through insurance companies or pension funds, no single buyer was able to buy an issue of such size. Bonds were therefore issued in denominations of $1,000 each and were sold to a large number of purchasers. To facilitate communication between the issuer and the numerous bondholders, another device was instituted, the *trustee*, who is the representative of the bondholders. He is presumed to act at all times for their protection and on their behalf.

Any legal person, including a corporation, is considered competent to act as a trustee. Typically, however, the duties of the trustee are handled by a department of a commercial bank.

The trustee has three main responsibilities. (1) The trustee certifies the issue of bonds. This duty involves making certain that all the legal requirements for drawing up the bond contract and the indenture have been carried out. (2) The trustee polices the behavior of the corporation in its performance of the responsibilities set forth in the indenture provisions. (3) The trustee is responsible for taking appropriate action on behalf of the bondholders if the corporation defaults on payment of interest or principal.

It is said that in a large number of the corporate bond defaults in the early 1930s, trustees did not act in the best interests of the bondholders. The trustees did not conserve the assets of the corporation effectively. Often they did not take early action, so that corporation executives continued their salaries and disposed of assets under conditions favorable to themselves but detrimental to the bondholders. Assets pledged as security for the bonds were sold; specific security was, thus, no longer available. The result in many instances was that holders of mortgage bonds found themselves more in the position of general creditors than in that of secured bondholders.

As a consequence of such practices, the Trust Indenture Act of 1939 was passed in order to give more protection to bondholders. It provides that trustees must be given sufficient power to act on behalf of bondholders. The indenture must fully disclose rights and responsibilities and must not be deceptive. There is provision for changes in the indenture at the option of the bondholders. A specific requirement of prompt, protective action on the part of the trustees for bondholders on default is made. Provision is made for making certain that an arm's-length relation exists between the issuing corporation and the trustee. The obligor may not own more than 10 percent of the common stock of the trustee, nor the trustee more than 5 percent of the voting stock of the obligor. Finally, the corporation must make periodic reports to trustees to enable them to carry out their protective responsibilities.

A call provision gives the issuing corporation the right to call in the *Call Provision*
bond for redemption. If it is used, the call provision generally states
that the company must pay an amount greater than the par value
of the bond, with this additional sum being defined as the *call premium*.
The call premium is typically set equal to one year's interest if the
bond is called during the first year, with the premium declining at
a constant rate each year thereafter. For example, the call premium
on a $1,000 par value, 20-year, 6 percent bond would generally be
$60 if called during the first year, $57 if called during the second
year (calculated by reducing the $60, or 6 percent, premium by 1/20),
and so on.

As will be pointed out later in this chapter, the call privilege is
valuable to the firm but potentially detrimental to an investor, especially if the bond is issued in a period when interest rates are thought
to be cyclically high. Accordingly, the interest rate on a new issue
of callable bonds will exceed that on a new issue of noncallable bonds.
For example, on May 28, 1968, Monongahela Power Co. sold an issue
of AA rated bonds to yield 7.375 percent. These bonds were callable
immediately. On the same day, Union Oil of California sold an issue
of AA rated bonds to yield 6.720 percent. Union Oil's bonds were
noncallable for 10 years. Investors were apparently willing to accept
a .655 percent lower interest rate on Union Oil's bonds for the assurance that the relatively high (by historic standards) rate of interest
would be earned for at least 10 years. Monongahela Power, on the
other hand, had to incur a .655 percent higher annual interest rate
for the privilege of calling the bonds in the event of a subsequent
decline in interest rates. The analysis for determining when to call
an issue will be considered later in this chapter.

A *sinking fund* is a provision that facilitates the orderly retirement *Sinking Fund*
of a bond issue (or, in some cases, an issue of preferred stock). Typically, the sinking fund provision requires the firm to buy and retire
a portion of the bond issue each year. Sometimes the stipulated sinking fund payment is tied to sales or earnings of the current year,
but usually it is a mandatory fixed amount. If it is mandatory, a failure
to meet the sinking fund payment causes the bond issue to be thrown
into default and possibly leads the company into bankruptcy. Obviously, then, a sinking fund can constitute a dangerous cash drain
to the firm.

In most cases the firm is given the right to handle the sinking
fund in either of two ways: (1) it may call a certain percentage of
the bonds at a stipulated price each year—for example, 2 percent
of the original amount at a price of $1,050—with the actual bonds,
which are numbered serially, being determined by a lottery; or (2)

it may spend the funds provided by the sinking fund payment to buy the bonds on the open market. The firm will do whichever results in the greatest reduction of outstanding bonds for a given expenditure. Therefore, if interest rates have risen (and the price of the bonds has fallen), the firm will choose the open market alternative. If interest rates have fallen and bond prices have risen, the company will elect to use the option of calling bonds.

It must be recognized that the call provision of the sinking fund may at times work to the detriment of bondholders. If, for example, the bond carries a 7 percent interest rate, and if yields on similar securities are 4 percent, the bond will sell for well above par. A sinking fund call at par would thus greatly disadvantage some bondholders. On balance, securities that provide for a sinking fund and continuing redemption are likely to be offered initially on a lower yield basis than are securities without such a fund. Since sinking funds provide additional protection to investors, sinking fund bonds are likely to sell initially at higher prices; hence, they have a lower cost of capital to the issuer.

SECURED BONDS

Secured long-term debt may be classified according to (1) the priority of claims, (2) the right to issue additional securities, and (3) the scope of the lien.

Priority of Claims 1. A senior mortgage has prior claims on assets and earnings. Senior railroad mortgages have been called the mortgages next to the rail, implying that they have the first claim on the land and assets of the railroad corporations.

2. A junior mortgage is a subordinate lien, such as a second or a third mortgage. It is a lien or claim junior to others.

Right to Issue Additional Securities Mortgage bonds may also be classified with respect to the right to issue additional obligations pledging already encumbered property.

In the case of a *closed-end mortgage,* a company may not sell additional bonds, beyond those already issued, secured by the property specified in the mortgage. For example, assume that a corporation with plant and land worth $5 million has a $2 million mortgage on these properties. If the mortgage is closed end, no more bonds having first liens on this property may be issued. Thus a closed-end mortgage provides greater security to the bond buyer. The ratio of the amount of the senior bonds to the value of the property will not be increased by subsequent issues.

If the bond indenture is silent on this point, it is called an *open-end mortgage.* Its nature may be illustrated by the facts of the example cited. Against property worth $5 million, bonds of $2 million are sold. If an additional first mortgage bond of $1 million is subsequently sold, the property has been pledged for a total of $3 million bonds. If, on liquidation, the property sold for $2 million, the original bondholders would receive 67 cents on the dollar. If the mortgage had been closed end, they would have been fully paid.

Most characteristic is the *limited open-end mortgage.* Its nature may be indicated by continuing the example. A first mortgage bond issue of $2 million is sold secured by the property worth $5 million. The indenture provides that an additional $1 million worth of bonds—or an additional amount of bonds up to 60 percent of the original cost of the property—may be sold. Thus, the mortgage is open only up to a certain point.

These are some ways in which the limited feature of an open-end mortgage may be expressed. The limited open-end mortgage is flexible in that it provides for the issuance of additional securities. At the same time, it limits this right; thus the original bondholder is protected.

Bonds may also be classified with respect to the scope of their lien. *Scope of the Lien* When it is a matter of a *specific lien,* the security for a first mortgage or a second mortgage is a specifically designated property. A lien is granted on certain described property. On the other hand, a *blanket mortgage* pledges all real property currently owned by the company. The definition of real property is land and those things affixed thereto. Hence a blanket mortgage would not be a mortgage on cash, accounts receivables, or inventories, because these items are regarded as personal property. A blanket mortgage gives more protection to the bondholder than does a specific mortgage because it provides a claim on all real property owned by the company.

The debenture is an unsecured bond and, as such, provides no lien **UNSECURED** on specific property as security for the obligation. Debenture holders **BONDS** are therefore general creditors whose claim is protected by property *Debentures* not otherwise pledged. The advantage of debentures from the standpoint of the issuer is that he leaves his property unencumbered for subsequent financing. However, in practice the use of debentures depends on the nature of the firm's assets and its general credit strength.

If the credit positions of the borrowing companies in an industry are exceptionally strong, these firms can issue debentures—they simply do not need specific security. However, the credit position of a company may be so weak that it has no alternative to the use of debentures—all its property may already be encumbered. American Telephone & Telegraph's vast financing program since the end of World

War II has been mainly through debentures, both convertible and straight debentures. AT&T is such a strong institution that it does not have to provide security for its debt issues.

Debentures are also often issued by companies in industries where it would not be practical to provide a lien through a mortgage on fixed assets. An example of such an industry would be the large mail order houses, which characteristically do not have large fixed assets in relation to their total assets. The bulk of their assets is in the form of inventory, which is not satisfactory security for a mortgage lien.

Subordinated   The term *subordinate* means below or inferior. Thus, subordinated
Debentures   debt has claims on assets after unsubordinated debt in the event of liquidation. Debentures may be subordinated to designated notes payable—usually bank loans—or to any or all other debt. In the event of liquidation or reorganization, the debentures cannot be paid until senior debt *as named in the indenture* has been paid. Senior debt typically does not include trade accounts payable. How the subordination provision strengthens the position of senior-debt holders is shown in Table 19–1.

Where $200 is available for distribution, the subordinated debt has a claim of one half of $100, or $50. However, this claim is subordinated only to the bank debt (the only senior debt) and is added to the $100 claim of the bank. As a consequence, 75 percent of the bank's original claim is satisfied.

Where $300 is available for distribution, the $75 allocated to the subordinated debt is divided into two parts: $50 goes to the bank and the other $25 remains for the subordinated-debt holders. In this situation, the senior bank debt holders are fully paid off, 75 percent of other debt is paid, and the subordinated debt receives only 25 percent of its claim.

Subordination is frequently required. Alert credit managers of firms supplying trade credit, or commercial bank loan officers, typically will insist upon subordination, particularly where debt is owed to the principal stockholders or officers of a company.

Preferred stock, in comparison to subordinated debt, suffers from the disadvantage that preferred stock dividends are not deductible as an expense for tax purposes. The interest on subordinated debentures is an expense for tax purposes. Some people have referred to subordinated debentures as being much like a special kind of preferred stock, the dividends of which are deductible as an expense for tax purposes. Subordinated debt has therefore become an increasingly important source of corporate capital.

The reasons for the use of subordinated debentures are clear. They offer a considerable tax advantage over preferred stock, and yet they do not restrict the ability of the borrower to obtain senior debt as would be the case if all debt sources were on an equal basis.

Financial structure	Book value (1)	Percent of total debt (2)	Initial allocation (3)	Actual payment (4)	Percent of original claim satisfied (5)
I. $200 available for claims on liquidation					
Bank debt	$200	50	$100	$150	75
Other debt	100	25	50	50	50
Subordinated debt	100	25	50	0	0
Total debt	400	100	$200	$200	50
Net worth	300				0
Total	$700				29
II. $300 available for claims on liquidation					
Bank debt	$200	50	$150	$200	100
Other debt	100	25	75	75	75
Subordinated debt	100	25	75	25	25
Total debt	400	100	$300	$300	75
Net worth	300				0
Total	$700				43

TABLE 19–1
Illustration of liquidating payments to senior debt, other debt, and subordinated debt

Steps: 1. Express each type of debt as a percentage of total debt (column 2).
2. Multiply the debt percentages (column 2) by the amount available, obtaining the initial allocations shown in column 3.
3. The subordinated debt is subordinate to bank debt. Therefore, the initial allocation to subordinate debt is added to the bank debt allocation until it has been exhausted or until the bank debt is finally paid off. This is given in column 4.

Subordinated debentures are further stimulated by periods of tight money when commercial banks may require a greater equity base for short-term financing. Subordinated debentures provide a greater equity cushion for loans from commercial banks or other forms of senior debt. The use of subordinated debentures also illustrates the development of hybrid securities which emerge to meet changing situations that develop in the capital market.

The amount of subordinated debt that may be employed is limited, as is the amount of any form of debt. The rule of thumb employed by investment bankers in connection with industrial issues of subordinated debentures appears to be about $2 of net worth for each $1 of subordinated debt.

Income Bonds Income bonds typically arise from corporate reorganizations, and these bonds pay interest only if income is actually earned by the company. Because the company, having gone through reorganization, has been in difficult financial circumstances, interest is not a fixed charge; the principal, however, must be paid when due.

Income bonds are like preferred stock in that management is not required to pay interest if it is not earned. However, they differ from preferred stock in that if interest has been earned, management is usually required to pay it. In recent years, income bonds have been increasingly used as a source of ordinary financing.[2]

The main characteristic and distinct advantage of the income bond is that interest is payable only if the company achieves some earnings. Since earnings calculations are subject to differing interpretations, the indenture of the income bond carefully defines income and expenses. If it did not do so, long, drawn-out litigation might result.

Some income bonds are cumulative for a limited number of years (if interest is not paid, it "accumulates" and must be paid at some future date); others are cumulative for the first three to five years, after which time they become noncumulative. Some issues are fully cumulative.

Income bonds usually contain sinking fund provisions to provide for their retirement. The payments to the sinking funds range between 1/2 and 1 percent of the face amount of the original issue. Because the sinking fund payments are typically dependent on earnings, a fixed-cash drain on the company is avoided.

Sometimes income bonds are convertible. There are sound reasons for their being convertible if they arise out of a reorganization. Creditors who receive income bonds in exchange for defaulted obligations have a less desirable position than they had before. Since they have received something based on an adverse and problematical forecast of the future of the company, it is appropriate that if the company should prosper, income bondholders should be entitled to participate. When income bonds are issued in situations other than reorganization,

[2] See S. M. Robbins, "A Bigger Role for Income Bonds," *Harvard Business Review,* XXXII (November–December 1955), pp. 100–114.

the convertibility feature is a "sweetener" likely to make the issue more attractive to prospective bond buyers.

Typically, income bonds do not have voting rights when they are issued. Sometimes bondholders are given the right to elect one, two, or some specified number of directors if interest is not paid for a certain number of years.

Income bonds have been used instead of preferred stock in situations other than reorganization. Armour & Company has made repeated use of such bonds.[3] In 1943, Armour used subordinated income bonds to substitute for a preferred stock issue. At the close of 1954, Armour replaced convertible preferred stock with dividend arrearages by 5 percent cumulative income bonds subordinated to other debt with a warrant to buy common stock. The replacement of preferred stock by income bonds resulted in a substantial tax saving for the company.

A critical framework for analyzing the position of any security holder in a corporation includes aspects of risk, control, and income.

CHARACTER-ISTICS OF LONG-TERM DEBT

From Viewpoint of Holder

Risk

Debt is favorable to the holder because it gives him priority both in earnings and in liquidation. Debt also has a definite maturity and is protected by the covenants of the indenture.

Income

The bondholder has a fixed return; except in the case of income bonds, interest payments are not contingent on the level of earnings of the company. However, debt does not participate in any superior earnings of the company, and gains are limited in magnitude. Frequently, long-term debt is callable. If bonds are called, the investor receives funds that must be reinvested to be kept active.

Control

The bondholder usually does not have the right to vote. Yet there are periods when a substantial portion of bonds sold are convertible bonds. If bonds are convertible into common stock, under certain conditions the bondholder may obtain the position of an equity holder rather than a debt holder.

An over-all appraisal of the characteristics of long-term debt indicates that it is strong from the standpoint of risk, has limited advantages with regard to income, and is weak with respect to control.

[3] Robbins, p. 106.

From Viewpoint of Issuer

Advantages

1. The cost of debt is definitely limited. Bondholders do not participate in superior profits if earned.

2. Not only is the cost limited, but typically the expected yield is lower than the cost of common or preferred stock.

3. The owners of the corporation do not share control of the corporation when debt financing is used.

4. The interest payment on debt is deductible as a tax expense.

5. Flexibility in the financial structure of the corporation may be achieved by inserting a call provision in the indenture of the debt.

Disadvantages

1. Debt is a fixed charge; there is greater risk if the earnings of the company fluctuate, because the corporation may be unable to meet these fixed charges.

2. As was seen in Chapter 11, higher risk brings higher capitalization rates on equity earnings. Thus, even though leverage is favorable and raises earnings per share, the higher capitalization rates attributable to leverage may drive the common stock value down.

3. Debt usually has a definite maturity date. Because of the fixed maturity date, the financial officer must make provision for repayment of the debt.

4. Since long-term debt is a commitment for a long period, such debt involves risk; the expectations and plans on which the debt was issued may change. The debt may prove to be a burden, or it may prove to have been advantageous. For example, if income, employment, and the price level fall greatly, the assumption of a large amount of debt may prove to have been an unwise financial policy. The railroads are always given as an example in this regard. They were able to meet their ordinary operating expenses during the 1930s but were unable to meet the heavy financial charges they had undertaken earlier, when the prospects for the railroads looked more favorable than they turned out to be.

5. In a long-term contractual relationship, the indenture provisions are likely to be much more stringent than they are in a short-term credit agreement. Hence the firm may be subject to much more disturbing and crippling restrictions in the indenture of a long-term debt arrangement than would be the case if it had borrowed on a short-term basis or had issued common stock.

6. There is a limit on the extent to which funds can be raised through long-term debt. Some of the generally accepted standards of financial policy dictate that the debt ratio shall not exceed certain limits. These

standards of financial prudence set limits or controls on the extent to which funds may be raised through long-term debt.

The conditions favoring the use of long-term debt when a number of alternative methods of long-term financing are under consideration include the following:

DECISIONS ON USE OF LONG-TERM DEBT

1. Sales and earnings are relatively stable, or a substantial increase in future sales and earnings is expected to provide a substantial benefit from the use of leverage.

2. A substantial rise in the price level is expected in the future, making it advantageous for the firm to incur debt that will be repaid with cheaper dollars.

3. The existing debt ratio is relatively low for the line of business.

4. Management thinks the price of the common stock in relation to that of bonds is temporarily depressed.

5. Sale of common stock would involve problems of maintaining the existing control pattern in the company.

Preferred stock has claims or rights ahead of common stock, but behind all bonds. The preference may be a prior claim on earnings, it may take the form of a prior claim on assets in the event of liquidation, or it may take a preferential position with regard to both earnings and assets.

NATURE OF PREFERRED STOCK

The hybrid nature of preferred stock becomes apparent when one tries to classify it in relation to bonds and common stock. The priority feature and the (generally) fixed dividend indicate that preferred stock is similar to bonds. Payments to the preferred stockholders are limited in amount so that the common stockholders receive the advantages (or disadvantages) of leverage. However, if the preferred dividends are not earned, the company can forgo paying them without danger of bankruptcy. In this characteristic, preferred stock is similar to common stock. Moreover, failure to pay the stipulated dividend does not cause default of the obligation, as does failure to pay bond interest.

Hybrid Form

In some kinds of analysis, preferred stock is treated as debt. For example, if the analysis is being made by a potential stockholder considering the earnings fluctuations induced by fixed-charge securities, preferred stock would be treated as debt. Suppose, however, that the analysis is by a bondholder studying the firm's vulnerability to *failure* brought on by declines in sales or in income. Since the dividends on preferred stock are not a fixed charge in the sense that failure

Debt and Equity

to pay them would represent a default of an obligation, preferred stock represents a cushion; it provides an additional equity base. From the point of view of *stockholders*, it is a leverage-inducing instrument much like debt. From the point of view of *creditors*, it constitutes additional net worth. Preferred stock may therefore be treated either as debt or as equity, depending on the nature of the problem under consideration.

MAJOR PROVISIONS OF PREFERRED STOCK ISSUES   The possible characteristics, rights, and obligations of any specific security vary widely, and a point of diminishing returns is quickly reached in a descriptive discussion of different kinds of securities. As economic circumstances change, new kinds of securities are manufactured. The possibilities are numerous. The kinds and varieties of securities are limited chiefly by the imagination and ingenuity of the managers formulating the terms of the security issues. It is not surprising, then, that preferred stock can be found in a variety of forms. One need only look at the main terms and characteristics in each case and examine the possible variations in relation to the kinds of situations or circumstances in which they could occur, as is done below.[4]

Priority in Assets and Earnings   Many provisions in a preferred stock certificate are designed to reduce risk to the purchaser relative to the risk carried by the holder of common stock. Preferred stock usually has priority with regard to earnings and assets. Two provisions designed to prevent undermining these preferred stock priorities are often found. The first states that, without the consent of the holders of the preferred stock, there can be no subsequent sale of securities having a prior or equal claim on earnings. The second provision seeks to hold earnings in the firm. It requires a minimum level of retained earnings before common stock dividends are permitted. In order to assure the availability of liquid assets that may be converted into cash for the payment of dividends, the maintenance of a minimum current ratio may also be required.

Par Value   Unlike common stock, preferred stock usually has a par value, and this value is a meaningful quantity. First, it establishes the amount due to the preferred stockholders in the event of a liquidation. Second, the preferred dividend is frequently stated as a percentage of the par value. For example, J. I. Case has preferred stock outstanding that has a par value of $100, and the dividend is stated to be 7 percent of par. It would, of course, be just as appropriate for the Case pre-

---

[4] Much of the data in this section is taken from a recent study of Donald E. Fischer and Glenn A. Wilt, Jr., "Non-Convertible Preferred Stocks as a Financing Instrument," *Journal of Finance*, XXIII (September 1968), pp. 611–624.

ferred stock to state simply that the annual dividend is $7, and on many preferred stocks the dividends are stated in this manner rather than as a percentage of par value.

A high percentage of dividends on preferred stocks is cumulative—all *Cumulative* past preferred dividends must be paid before common dividends may *Dividends* be paid. The cumulative feature is therefore a protective device. If the preferred stock was not cumulative, preferred and common stock dividends could be passed by for a number of years. The company could then vote a large common stock dividend, but only the stipulated payment to preferred stock. Suppose the preferred stock with a par value of $100 carried a 7 percent dividend. Suppose the company did not pay dividends for several years, so that it accumulated an amount that would enable it to pay in total about $50 in dividends. It could pay one $7 dividend to the preferred stock and a $43 dividend to the common stock. Obviously, this device could be used to evade the preferred position that the holders of preferred stock have tried to obtain. The cumulative feature prevents such evasion. Note, however, that compounding is absent in most cumulative plans. In other words, the arrearages themselves earn no return.

Large arrearages on preferred stock would make it difficult to resume dividend payments on common stock. To avoid delays in resuming common stock dividend payments, a compromise arrangement with the holders of common stock is likely to be worked out.

A package offer is one possibility; for example, a recapitalization plan may provide for an exchange of shares. The arrearage will be wiped out by the donation of common stock with a value equal to the amount of the preferred dividend arrearage, and the holders of preferred stock are thus given an ownership share in the corporation. Whether this ownership share is worth anything depends on the future earnings prospects of the company. In addition, resumption of current dividends on the preferred may be promised.

The advantage to the company of substituting common stock for dividends in arrears is that it can start again with a clean balance sheet. If earnings recover, dividends can be paid to the holders of common stock without making up arrearages to the holders of preferred stock. The original common stockholders, of course, will have given up a portion of their ownership of the corporation.

Approximately 40 percent of the preferred stock that has been issued *Convertibility* in recent years is convertible into common stock. For example, one share of a particular preferred stock could be convertible into 2.5 shares of the firm's common stock at the option of the preferred shareholder. The nature of convertibility is discussed in Chapter 20.

Some Infrequent Provisions   Some of the other provisions occasionally encountered among preferred stocks include the following:

Voting Rights   Sometimes a preferred stock is given the right to vote for directors. When this feature is present, it generally permits the preferred to elect a *minority* of the board, say three out of nine directors. The voting privilege becomes operative only if the company has not paid the preferred dividend for a specified period, for example, 6, 8, or 10 quarters.

Participating   A rare type of preferred stock is one that participates with the common stock in sharing the firm's earnings. The following factors generally relate to participating preferred stocks: (1) the stated preferred dividend is paid first—for example, $5 a share; (2) next, income is allocated to common stock dividends *up to* an amount equal to the preferred dividend—in this case, $5; (3) any remaining income is shared equally between the common and preferred stockholders.

Sinking Fund   Some preferred issues have a sinking fund requirement. When they do, the sinking fund ordinarily calls for the purchase and retirement of a given percentage of the preferred stock each year.

Maturity   Preferred stocks almost never have maturity dates on which they must be retired. However, if the issue has a sinking fund, this effectively creates a maturity date.

Call Provision   A call provision gives the issuing corporation the right to call in the preferred stock for redemption. If it is used, the call provision generally states that the company must pay an amount greater than the par value of the preferred stock, with this additional sum being defined as the *call premium*. For example, a $100 par value preferred stock might be callable at the option of the corporation at $105 a share.

EVALUATION OF PREFERRED STOCK   An important advantage of preferred stock from the viewpoint of the issuer is that, in contrast to bonds, the obligation to make fixed interest payments is avoided. Also, a firm wishing to expand because its earning power is high may obtain higher earnings for the original owners by selling preferred stock with a limited return rather than by selling common stock.

Appraisal from Viewpoint of Issuer

Advantages   By selling preferred stock the financial manager avoids the provision of equal participation in earnings that the sale of additional common stock would require. Preferred stock also permits a company to avoid sharing control through participation in voting. In contrast to bonds, it enables the firm to conserve mortgageable assets. Since preferred stock typically has no maturity and no sinking fund, it is more flexible than bonds.

There are several disadvantages associated with preferred stock. Characteristically, it must be sold on a higher yield basis than that for bonds.[5] Preferred stock dividends are not deductible as a tax expense, a characteristic that makes their cost differential very great in comparison with that of bonds. As we have seen in Chapter 12, the after-tax cost of debt is approximately half the stated coupon rate for profitable firms. The cost of preferred, however, is the full percentage amount of the preferred dividend. This fact has greatly reduced the use of preferred stocks in recent years.[6]   *Disadvantages*

In fashioning securities, the financial manager needs to consider the investor's point of view. Frequently it is asserted that preferred stocks have so many disadvantages both to the issuer and to the investor that they should never be issued. Nevertheless, preferred stock is issued in substantial amounts. In fact, between 1930 and 1950, more preferred stock than common stock was issued and sold.   *Appraisal from Viewpoint of Investor*

From the viewpoint of the investor, preferred stock provides the following advantages. (1) Preferred stocks provide reasonably steady income. (2) Preferred stockholders have a preference over common stockholders in liquidation; numerous examples can be cited where the prior-preference position of holders of preferred stock saved them from losses incurred by holders of common stock. (3) Many corporations (for example, insurance companies) like to hold preferred stocks as investments because 85 percent of the dividends received on these shares is not taxable.   *Advantages*

[5] Historically, a given firm's preferred stock generally carried higher rates than its bonds because of the greater risk inherent in preferred stocks from the holder's viewpoint. However, as is noted below, the fact that preferred dividends are largely exempt from the corporate income tax has made them attractive to corporate investors. In recent years, high-grade preferreds, on average, have sold on a lower yield basis than high-grade bonds. In 1965, Fischer and Wilt found that bonds had a yield 0.39 percentage points *above* preferred stocks. Thus, a very strong firm could sell preferreds to yield about 0.4 percent less than bonds.

[6] By far the most important issurers of nonconvertible preferred stocks are the utility companies. For these firms, taxes are an expense for rate-making purposes—that is, higher taxes are passed on to the customers in the form of higher prices—so tax deductibility is not an important issue. This explains why utilities issue about 85 percent of all nonconvertible preferreds.

Disadvantages Some disadvantages to investors are also present. (1) Although the holders of preferred stock bear a substantial portion of ownership risk, their returns are limited. (2) Price fluctuations in preferred stock are far greater than those in bonds, yet yields on bonds are frequently higher than those on preferred stock. (3) There is no legally enforceable right to dividends. (4) Accrued dividend arrearages are seldom settled in cash comparable to the amount of the obligation that has been incurred.

Recent Trends Because of the nondeductibility of preferred stock dividends as a tax expense, many companies have retired their preferred stock. Often debentures or subordinated debentures will be offered to preferred stockholders in exchange. The interest on the debentures is deductible as a tax expense, while preferred stock dividends are not deductible.

When the preferred stock is not callable, the company must offer terms of exchange that are sufficiently attractive to induce the preferred stockholders to agree to the exchange. Characteristically, bonds or other securities in an amount somewhat above the recent value of the preferred stock will be issued in exchange. Sometimes bonds equal in market value to the preferred stock will be issued, along with additional cash or common stock to provide an extra inducement to the preferred stockholders. Sometimes the offer will be bonds equal to only a portion of the current market value of the preferred with an additional amount, represented by cash or common stock, that will bring the total amount offered to the preferred stockholders to something over its market value as of a recent date.

U.S. Steel's replacement of its 7 percent preferred stock in 1965 illustrates one of these exchange patterns. U.S. Steel proposed that its 7 percent preferred stock be changed into 4 5/8 percent 30-year bonds at a rate of $175 principal amount of bonds for each preferred share. On August 17, 1965, when the plan was announced, the preferred stock was selling at $150. U.S. Steel also announced that the conversion would increase earnings available to common stock by $10 million yearly, or 18 cents a share at 1965 federal income tax rates; this was sufficient inducement to persuade the company to give the preferred stockholders the added $25 a share.

Tax considerations have reduced the use of preferred stock. But a countertrend has been the use of convertible preferred stock in mergers.[7] The reasoning here also involves taxes. The owners of the

---

[7] Convertibles are discussed in detail in Chapter 20 and financial aspects of mergers in Chapter 21.

acquired firm frequently are willing to sell out because they are seeking to escape the worries associated with ownership and management. Consequently, they can be more easily induced to sell out if they are offered a fixed income security. But if bonds (or cash) are offered for the shares of the acquired firm, the selling stockholders must pay a capital gains tax on any proceeds received in excess of their cost basis. Frequently, this would involve a heavy capital gains tax liability. If the exchange is convertible preferred stock of the acquiring company for common stock of the acquired firm, the exchange can qualify for exemption on the capital gains liability. In this manner the stockholders of the acquired firm can receive a fixed income security, avoid an immediate capital gains liability, and receive additional benefits from the conversion feature if the price of the acquiring firm's common stock rises.

The use of convertible preferreds has been most noticeable among merger-minded conglomerate corporations. These conglomerates are frequently "growth" companies with low dividend payout policies, and they frequently buy out firms that have been paying substantial dividends. If the merger was accomplished by an exchange of stock, the stockholders of the acquired company would suffer a reduction in their dividend receipts. The use of a convertible preferred can avoid this dividend dilution and thus enhance the chances that the acquired firm's stockholders will approve the merger.

The circumstances favoring the use of preferred stock can now be distilled from the foregoing analysis. As a hybrid security type, the use of preferred stock is favored by conditions that fall between those favoring the use of common stock and those favoring the use of debt.

DECISION- MAKING ON USE OF PREFERRED STOCK

When a firm's profit margin is high enough to more than cover preferred stock dividends, it will be advantageous to employ leverage. However, if the firm's sales and profits are subject to considerable fluctuations, the use of debt with fixed interest charges may be unduly risky. Preferred stock may offer a happy compromise. The use of preferred stock will be strongly favored if the firm already has a debt ratio that is heavy relative to the reference level maximum for the line of business.

Relative costs of alternative sources of financing are always important considerations. When the market prices of common stocks are relatively low, the costs of common stock financing are relatively high; this has been shown in Chapter 10. The costs of preferred stock financing follow interest rate levels more than common stock prices; in other words, when interest rates are low, the cost of preferred stock is also likely to be low. When the costs of fixed income instruments such as preferred stock are low and the costs of variable value securities such as common stock are high, the use of preferred stock is favored.

Preferred stock may also be the desired form of financing when the use of debt would involve excessive risk, but the issuance of common stock would result in problems of control for the dominant ownership group in the company.

REFUNDING A BOND OR PREFERRED STOCK ISSUE

Suppose a company sells bonds or preferred stock at a time when interest rates are relatively high. Provided the issue is callable, as many are, the company can sell a new issue of low yielding securities and use the proceeds to retire the high rate issue. This is called a refunding operation.[8]

The decision to refund a security issue is analyzed in much the same manner as a capital budgeting expenditure. The costs of refunding—the "investment outlay"—are (1) the call premium paid for the privilege of calling the old issue and (2) the flotation costs involved in selling the new issue. The annual receipts, in the capital budgeting sense, are the interest payments that are saved each year; for example, if interest expense on the old issue is $1 million while that on the new issue is $700,000, the $300,000 saving constitutes the annual benefits.

In analyzing the advantages of refunding, the net present value method is the recommended procedure—discount the future interest savings back to the present and compare the discounted value with the cash outlays associated with the refunding. *In the discounting process, the after-tax cost of the new debt, not the average cost of capital, should be used as the discount factor.* The reason for this is that there is relatively little risk to the savings—their value is known with relative certainty, which is quite unlike most capital budgeting decisions. The following example illustrates the calculations needed in a refunding operation decision.

The Culver City Company has outstanding a $60 million, 20-year bond issue, carrying an 8 percent interest rate. The bond indenture carries a call provision making it possible for the company to retire the bonds by calling them in at a 6 percent premium. Investment bankers have assured the company that it could sell an additional $60 to $70 million worth of 20-year bonds at an interest rate of 6 percent. Predictions are that interest rates are unlikely to fall below 6 percent. Flotation costs of the new issue will amount to $2,650,000. Should the company refund the $60 million worth of bonds?

---

[8] For an excellent discussion of refunding, see O. D. Bowlin, "The Refunding Decision," *Journal of Finance*, XXI (March 1966), pp. 55–68.

What is the investment outlay required to refund the issue?   `Step 1`

a) Call premium:

Before-tax: $.06 \times \$60,000,000 = \$3,600,000.$
After-tax: $\$3,600,000 \times .5 = \$1,800,000.$

Although Culver City Company must expend $3.6 million on the call premium, this is a deductible expense in the year the call is made. Since the company is in a 50 percent tax bracket, it saves $1.80 million in taxes. Therefore, the after-tax cost of the call is only $1,800,000.

b) Flotation costs of new issue:

Total flotation costs are $2,650,000. For tax purposes, flotation costs are amortized over the life of the new bond, or twenty years. Therefore, the annual tax deduction is:

$$\frac{2,650,000}{20} = \$132,500.$$

Since Culver is in the 50 percent tax bracket, it has a tax saving of $66,250 per year for twenty years. This is an annuity of $66,250 for twenty years. The present value of this annuity, discounted at 3 percent, the after-tax cost of debt, is:

PV of tax saving $= IF \times \$66,250$
$= 14.877 \times \$66,250$
$= \$985,601.$

The net after-tax flotation cost is thus:

Cash outlay	$2,650,000
PV of tax savings	−985,601
Net after-tax flotation cost	$1,664,399

c) Total after-tax investment:

The total investment outlay required to refund the bond issue is thus:

Call premium	$1,800,000
Flotation cost	1,664,399
	$3,464,399

What are the annual savings?   `Step 2`

a) Old bond interest, after tax:

$$\$60,000,000 \times 0.08 \times 0.5 = \$2,400,000.$$

b) New bond interest, after tax:

$$\$60,000,000 \times 0.060 \times 0.5 = \$1,800,000.$$

c) Savings $\$\ 600,000.$

Step 3 What is the present value of the savings?

       a) 20-year PV of annuity factor at 3 percent:

$$14.877.$$

       b) PV of $600,000 a year for twenty years:

$$14.877 \times \$600,000 = \$8,926,200.$$

Step 4 Conclusion:

Since the present value of the receipts ($8,926,200 exceeds the required investment ($3,464,399), the issue should be refunded.

Two other points should be made. First, since the $600,000 savings is an essentially riskless investment, its present value is found by discounting at the firm's least risky rate—its after-tax cost of debt. Second, since the refunding operation is advantageous to the firm, it must be disadvantageous to bondholders—they must give up their 8 percent bond and reinvest in one yielding 6 percent. This points out the danger of the call provisions to bondholders and explains why, at any given time, bonds without a call provision command higher prices than callable bonds.[9]

SUMMARY

Bonds

A *bond* is a long-term promissory note. A *mortgage bond* is secured by real property. An *indenture* is an agreement between the firm issuing a bond and the numerous bondholders, represented by a *trustee*.

Secured long-term debt differs with respect to (1) the priority of claims, (2) the right to issue additional securities, and (3) the scope of the lien provided. These characteristics determine the amount of protection provided to the bondholder by the terms of the security. Giving the investor more security will induce him to accept a lower yield but will restrict the future freedom of action of the issuing firm.

The main forms of unsecured bonds are (1) *debentures,* (2) *subordinated debentures,* and (3) *income bonds.* Holders of debentures are unsecured general creditors. Subordinated debentures are junior in claim to bank loans. Income bonds are similar to preferred stock in that interest is paid only when earned.

The characteristics of long-term debt determine the circumstances under which it will be used when alternative forms of financing are under analysis. The cost of debt is limited, but it is a fixed obligation. Bond interest is an expense deductible for tax purposes. Debt carries a maturity date and may require sinking fund payments to prepare for extinguishing the obligation. Indenture provisions are likely to in-

---

[9] Cf. F. C. Jen and J. E. Wert, "The Effects of Call Risk on Corporate Bond Yields," *Journal of Finance,* XXII (December 1967) pp. 637–652; and G. Pye, "The Value of Call Deferment on a Bond: Some Empirical Results," *Journal of Finance,* XXII (December 1967), pp. 623–636.

clude restrictions on the freedom of action of the management of the firm.

The nature of long-term debt encourages its use under the following circumstances:

1. Sales and earnings are relatively stable.

2. Profit margins are adequate to make leverage advantageous.

3. A rise in profits or the general price level is expected.

4. The existing debt ratio is relatively low.

5. Common stock price/earnings ratios are low in relation to the levels of interest rates.

6. Control considerations are important.

7. Cash flow requirements under the bond agreement are not burdensome.

8. Restrictions of the bond indenture are not onerous.

Although seven of the eight factors may favor debt, the eighth can swing the decision to the use of equity capital. The list of factors is, thus, simply a check list of things to consider when deciding upon bonds versus stock; the actual decision is based on a judgment about the relative importance of the several factors.

The *characteristics of preferred stock* vary with the requirements of the situation under which it is issued. However, certain patterns tend to remain. Preferred stocks usually have priority over common stocks with respect to earnings and claims on assets in liquidation. Preferred stocks are usually cumulative; they have no maturity but are sometimes callable. They are typically nonparticipating and have only contingent voting rights. **Preferred Stocks**

The advantages to the issuer are limited dividends and no maturity. These advantages may outweigh the disadvantages of higher cost and the nondeductibility of the dividends as an expense for tax purposes. But their acceptance by investors is the final test of whether they can be sold on favorable terms.

Companies sell preferred stock when they seek the advantages of trading on the equity but fear the dangers of the fixed charges on debt in the face of potential fluctuations in income. If debt ratios are already high or if the costs of common stock financing are relatively high, the advantages of preferred stock will be reinforced.

The use of preferred stock has declined significantly since the advent of the corporate income tax because preferred dividends are not deductible for income tax purposes while bond interest payments are deductible. However, in recent years there has been a strong shift back to a new kind of preferred stock—convertible preferred, used primarily in connection with mergers. If cash or bonds are given to the stockholders of the acquired company, they are required to pay capital gains taxes on any gains that might have been realized. However, if convertible preferred stock is given to the selling stockholders, this constitutes a tax-free exchange of securities. The selling stockholders can obtain a fixed income security and at the same time postpone the payment of capital gains taxes.

Refunding If a bond or preferred stock issue was sold when interest rates were higher than they are at present, and if the issue is callable, it may be profitable to call the old issue and refund it with a new, lower-cost issue. The final section in the chapter examined the type of analysis required to determine whether a refunding operation should be undertaken.

QUESTIONS **19–1** There are many types of bonds—for example, mortgage, debentures, collateral trust—and varying maturities for each type. What are some factors that determine the particular type of bond a company should use?

19–2 A sinking fund is set up in one of two ways: (1) the corporation makes annual payments to the trustee, who invests the proceeds in securities (frequently government bonds) and uses the accumulated total to retire the bond issue on maturity; (2) the trustee uses the annual payments to retire a portion of the issue each year, either calling a given percentage of the issue by a lottery and paying a specified price per bond or buying bonds on the open market, whichever is cheaper. Discuss the advantages and disadvantages of each procedure from the viewpoint of both the firm and the bondholders.

19–3 Why is a financial institution such as a bank, instead of an individual, a better choice for a bond trustee?

19–4 Since a corporation often has the right to call bonds at will, do you believe individuals should be able to demand repayment at any time they so desire?

19–5 What are the relative advantages and disadvantages of issuing a long-term bond during a recession versus during a period of prosperity?

19–6 Missouri Pacific 4 3/4 percent income bonds due in 2020 are selling for $770, while the company's 4 1/4 percent first mortgage bonds due in 2005 are selling for $945. Why would the bonds with the lower coupon sell at a higher price? (Each has a $1,000 par value.)

19–7 When a firm sells bonds, it must offer a package acceptable to potential buyers. Included in this package of terms are such features as the issue price, the coupon interest rate, the term to maturity, any sinking fund provisions, and other features. The package itself is determined through a bargaining process between the firm and the investment bankers who will handle the issue. What particular features would you, as a corporate treasurer, be especially interested in, and which would you be most willing to give ground on, under each of the following conditions:

a) You believe that the economy is near the peak of a business cycle.

b) Long-run forecasts indicate that your firm will have heavy cash inflows in relation to cash needs during the next 5 to 10 years.

c) Your current liabilities are presently low, but you anticipate raising a considerable amount of funds through short-term borrowing in the near future.

19–8 Bonds are less attractive to investors during periods of inflation because a rise in the price level will reduce the purchasing power of the fixed-interest payments and also of the principal. Discuss the advantages and disadvantages to a corporation of using a bond whose interest payments and principal would increase in direct proportion to increases in the price level (an inflation-proof bond).

19–9 If preferred stock dividends are passed for several years, the preferred stockholders are frequently given the right to elect several members of the board of directors. In the case of bonds that are in default on interest payments, this procedure is not followed. Why does this difference exist?

19–10 Preferred stocks are found in almost all industries, but one industry is the really dominant issuer of preferred shares. What is this industry, and why are firms in it so disposed to use preferred stock?

19–11 From the point of view of the issuing firm, what are some of the advantages of preferred stock?

19–12 If the corporate income tax was abolished, would this raise or lower the amount of new preferred stock issued?

19–13 Investors buying securities have some expected or required rate of return in mind. Which would you expect to be higher, the required rate of return (before taxes) on preferred stocks or on common stocks (a) for individual investors and (b) for corporate investors (for example, insurance companies)?

19–14 Do you think the before-tax required rate of return is higher or lower on very high-grade preferred stocks or on bonds (a) for individual investors and (b) for corporate investors?

19–15 Discuss the pros and cons of a preferred stock sinking fund from the point of view (a) of the issuing corporation and (b) of a preferred stockholder.

19–16 For purposes of measuring a firm's leverage, should preferred stock be classified as debt or as equity? Does it matter if the classification is being made (a) by the firm itself, (b) by creditors, or (c) by equity investors?

19–1 The Clayton Company has a $200,000 long-term bond issue outstanding. **PROBLEMS** This debt has an additional 10 years to maturity and bears a coupon interest rate of 8 percent. The firm now has the opportunity to refinance the debt with 10-year bonds at a rate of 6 percent. Further declines in the interest rate are not anticipated. The bond redemption premium (call premium) on the old bond would be $10,000; issue costs on the new would be $10,500. If tax effects are ignored, should the firm refund the bonds?

19–2 In early 1970, the Micro-Meter Corporation planned to raise an additional $100 million for financing plant additions and for working capital. Micro manufactures precision instruments and tools.

Investment bankers state that the company could sell common stock at a market price of $25.75 a share to net $25, or it could sell sinking fund debentures to yield 8 percent. Costs of flotation would be slightly higher for common stock but not enough to influence the decision.

The balance sheet and the income statement of Micro-Meter prior to the financing are given as shown at top of page 438.

Micro-Meter Corporation
Balance sheet,
March 31, 1970
In millions of dollars

Current assets	$500	Accounts payable	$ 40
Investments	50	Notes payable to banks	160
Net fixed assets	250	Taxes payable	80
		Other current liabilities	70
		Total current liabilities	$350
		Long-term debt	200
		Common stock, $2 par	50
		Earned surplus	200
Total assets	$800	Total claims	$800

Micro-Meter Corporation
Income statement
for year ended
March 31, 1970
In millions of dollars

Sales	$1,400
Net income before taxes, 10%	140
Interest on debt	12
Net income subject to tax	128
Tax, 50%	64
Net income after tax	$ 64

a) Assuming that net income before interest and taxes remains at 10 percent of sales, calculate earnings per share under both the stock financing and debt financing alternatives at sales levels of $400, $800, $1,200, $1,600, and $2,000 million.

b) Make a break-even chart for the earnings under a.

c) Using a price/earnings ratio of 20 times, calculate the market value per share of common stock under both the stock financing and debt financing alternatives.

d) Make a break-even chart of the market value per share of the company for c.

e) *If the use of debt caused the price/earnings ratio to fall to 12.5,* what would the market value per share of common stock become under the debt financing alternatives in the range of sales being considered?

f) Make a break-even chart for e, keeping a price/earnings ratio of 20 for equity financing.

g) Using the data and assumptions set out, which form of financing should Micro adopt? Why? (Answer in terms of both the quantitative factors listed above and the qualitative factors discussed in the chapter.)

19–3   The Colburn Steel Company is planning a capital improvement program to provide greater efficiency and versatility in its operations. It is estimated that by mid-1972 the company will need to raise $250 million. Colburn is a leading steel producer with an excellent credit rating.

You are asked to set up a program for obtaining the necessary funds. Using the following information, indicate the best form of financing. Some of the items you should include in your analysis are profit margins, relative costs, control of the voting stock, cash flows, ratio analysis, and *pro forma* analysis.

Colburn's common stock is selling at $80 a share. The company could sell debt (25 years) at 7.5 percent or preferred stock at 8 percent.

Steel industry financial ratios

Current ratio (times)	2.1
Sales to total assets (times)	1.8
Coverage of fixed charges	7.0
Average collection period (days)	42.0
Current debt/total assets (percent)	20–25
Long-term debt/total assets (percent)	10.0
Preferred/total assets (percent)	0–5
Net worth/total assets	65–70
Profits to sales (percent)	3.3
Profits to total assets (percent)	6.0
Profits to net worth (percent)	9.5
Expected growth rate in earnings and dividends	5.3

Colburn Steel Company
Consolidated balance sheet
December 31, 1971
In millions of dollars

Assets		
Current	$ 950	
Other investments	175	
Properties (net)	1,425	
Deferred assets	50	
Total assets		$2,600
Liabilities		
Current	$ 400	
Long-term debt, 4.44%	225	
Total liabilities		$ 625
Common stock, $10 par	400	
Capital surplus	375	
Retained income	1,100	
Reserves	100	
Total net worth		1,975
Total liabilities and net worth		$2,600

Colburn Steel Company
Consolidated income statement
for years ended December 31, 1969, 1970, and 1971
In millions of dollars

	1969	1970	1971
Sales	$3,050	$2,275	$2,700
Other income	25	25	25
Total	3,075	2,300	2,725
Costs and expenses	2,650	2,000	2,400
Income before taxes	425	300	325
Federal income tax	215	150	160
Net income	210	150	165
Cash dividends	115	115	115
Interest on long-term debt	5.0	6.5	10
Depreciation	100	80	85
Shares outstanding (widely held)		40,000,000	

19–4 In late 1969 the Frontier Edison Company of Washington sought to raise $4 million to refinance present preferred stock issues at a lower rate. The company is a member of the Western Utilities Associates Holding Company system. The company could sell additional debt at 5 percent, preferred stock at 4.64 percent, or common stock at $80 a share. How should the company raise the money? Relevant financial information is provided below.

Public utilities financial ratios

Current ratio (times)	1.00
Interest earned (before taxes) (times)	4.0
Sales to total assets (times)	0.3
Average collection period (days)	28.0
Current debt/total assets (percent)	5–10
Long-term debt/total assets (percent)	45–50
Preferred/total assets (percent)	10–15
Common equity/total assets (percent)	30–35
Earnings before interest and taxes to total assets (percent)	5.9
Profits to common equity (percent)	10.1
Expected growth in earnings and dividends (percent)	4.625

Frontier Edison Company
Balance sheet
July 31, 1969
In millions of dollars

Cash	$ 0.5	Current liabilities	$ 2.0
Receivables	1.0	Long-term debt, 3.5%	18.0
Material and supplies	0.8	Preferred stock, 5.60%	4.0
Total current	2.3	Common stock, $25 par value	7.5
		Paid-in surplus	4.4
Net property	37.7	Earned surplus	4.1
Total assets	$40.0	Total claims	$40.0

Frontier Edison Company
Income statement for year
ended July 31, 1969
In millions of dollars

Operating revenues	$12.6
Operating expenses (incl. taxes)	10.5
Net operating income	2.1
Interest deductions	0.6
Net income	1.5
Earnings per share	$ 5.00
Dividends per share	$ 3.50

This question should not be answered in terms of precise cost of capital calculations. Rather, a more qualitative and subjective analysis is appropriate. The only calculations necessary are some simple ratios. Careful interpretation of these ratios is necessary, however, to understand and discuss the often complex, subjective judgment issues involved.

19–5 Addison, Inc., is a manufacturer of apparel and footwear. Although principally a manufacturer of shoes, it has in recent years acquired a number of companies that make men's and women's apparel.

The company seeks to retire its 4.5 percent unsecured notes due in 1970 and its outstanding 5 percent notes due in 1971. A substantial amount of funds ($10 million) from new financing is earmarked for additions to working capital and retirement of short-term bank notes as they mature. Addison can issue new debt at 5 1/2 percent, a preferred stock issue at 4.5 percent, or common stock at $30 a share. Total new financing is expected to be $20 million. How should the company raise the money? Relevant financial data are given below.

Footwear industry financial ratios

Current ratio (times)	2.2
Sales to total assets (times)	2.3
Sales to inventory (times)	6.1
Average collection period (days)	46.0
Current debt/total assets (percent)	30.0
Long-term debt/total assets (percent)	10.0
Preferred/total assets (percent)	0–10
Common equity/total assets (percent)	50–60
Profits to sales (percent)	2.3
Net profits to total assets (percent)	5.0
Profits to common equity (percent)	9.0
Expected growth in earnings and dividends (percent)	3.33

Addison, Inc.
Consolidated balance sheet
July 31, 1969
In millions of dollars

Current assets	$150	Current liabilities	$ 40
Plant and equipment (net)	28	Long-term debt	60
Other assets	22	Preferred stock $4.50	10
		Common stock $1 par value	3
		Paid-in capital	42
		Retained earnings	45
Total assets	$200	Total claims	$200

Addison, Inc.
Consolidated income statement
for year ended July 31, 1969
In millions of dollars

Net sales and other income	$400
Cost of sales and expenses	381
Earnings before interest and taxes	19
Taxes and interest ($3)	10
Net income	9
Earnings per share	3
Dividends	2

This question should not be answered in terms of precise cost of capital calculations. Rather, a more qualitative and subjective analysis is appropriate. The only calculations necessary are a few simple ratios. Careful interpretation of these ratios is necessary, however, to understand and discuss the often complex, subjective judgment issues involved.

Chapter 20

Warrants and Convertibles

THUS far in the discussion of long-term financing, we have examined the nature of common stock, preferred stock, and long-term debt. We also saw how offering common stock through the use of rights can facilitate low-cost stock flotations. In this chapter, we see how the financial manager, through the use of warrants and convertibles, can make his company's securities attractive to a broader range of investors, thereby lowering his cost of capital.

WARRANTS A *warrant* is an option to buy a stated number of shares of stock at a specified price. For example, Trans World Airlines has warrants outstanding that give the warrant holders the right to buy one share of TWA stock at a price of $22 for each warrant held. The warrants generally expire on a certain date—TWA's warrants expire on December 1, 1973—although some have perpetual lives. An illustrative list of warrants is shown in Table 20–1.

Theoretical Value of a Warrant Warrants have a calculated or theoretical value and an actual value or price that is determined in the marketplace. The theoretical value is found by use of the following equation:

$$\text{Theoretical value} = \left(\begin{array}{c} \text{market price} \\ \text{of} \\ \text{common stock} \end{array} - \begin{array}{c} \text{option} \\ \text{price} \end{array} \right) \times \begin{array}{c} \text{number of shares each} \\ \text{warrant entitles owner} \\ \text{to purchase.} \end{array}$$

For example, a TWA warrant entitles the holder to purchase one share of common stock at $22 a share. If the market price of the common stock is $64.50, the formula price of the warrant may be obtained as follows:

$$(\$64.50 - \$22) \times 1.0 = \$42.50.$$

TABLE 20–1   Illustrative list of warrants listed on American Stock Exchange

Name of company	Price on 7/24/67		Option to purchase common shares		Date option expires	Theoretical value	Premium†
	Common	Warrants	No.	Price			
Allegheny Airlines	20	15	1.0	$10.50	5/1/69	$ 9.50	$ 5.50
Allegheny Corporation	11 3/8	8 5/8	1.0	3.75	Perpetual	7.63	0.99
Atlas Corporation	5 5/8	3	1.0	6.25	Perpetual	0.00	3.00
Braniff Airways	65 3/4	30	1.0	73.00	12/1/86	0.00	30.00
General Acceptance Corporation	29 1/4	11 1/4	1.0	20.00	10/31/69	9.25	2.00
Hilton Hotels Corporation	38	19 3/4	1.0	46.00	10/15/70	0.00	19.75
Indian Head Corporation	29 1/2	14 1/2	1.0	20.00	5/15/70	9.50	5.00
Jefferson Lake Petrochemicals	39 1/2	30 1/2	1.04	10.00	6/1/71	30.68	(0.18)
Martin Marietta	24 1/2	29 1/8	2.73	16.50	11/1/68	21.84	7.28
McCrory	21	6 5/8	1.0	20.00	3/15/76	1.00	5.62
National General	16 1/2	7	1.0	15.00	5/15/74	1.50	5.50
Pacific Petroleum	16 1/4	5	1.1	19.00	3/13/68	0.00	5.00
Sperry Rand	34 1/4	10 1/2	1.08	28.00	9/15/67	6.75	3.75
Textron, Inc.*	73	57 3/8	1.0	15.00	5/1/84	58.00	(0.62)
Trans World Airlines	64 1/2	46 7/8	1.0	22.00	12/1/73	42.50	4.38
Tri-Continental Corporation	27 7/8	48	2.54	8.88	Perpetual	48.31	(0.31)
United Industrial Corporation	15 1/4	3 3/8	.05	17.00	11/15/69	0.00	3.38
Uris Buildings	24 3/4	15 5/8	1.06	12.50	5/1/75	12.98	2.64

* Price at which common may be purchased increases by $2.50 in 1969, 1974, and 1979.
† Price of warrant minus theoretical value.

Actual Price of a Warrant Generally, warrants sell above their theoretical values. For example, when TWA stock was selling for $64.50, the warrants had a theoretical value of $42.50 but were selling at a price of $46.87. This represented a premium of $4.37 above the theoretical value.

TABLE 20–2
Theoretical and actual values of TWA warrants at different market prices

Price of stock	Value of warrant		
	Theoretical	Actual price	Premium
$ 0.00	$ 0.00	Not available	—
22.00	0.00	$ 9.00	$9.00
23.00	1.00	9.75	8.75
24.00	2.00	10.50	8.50
33.67	11.67	17.37	5.70
52.00	30.00	32.00	2.00
75.00	53.00	54.00	1.00
100.00	78.00	79.00	1.00
150.00	128.00	Not available	—

A set of TWA stock prices, together with actual and theoretical warrant values, is given in Table 20–2 and plotted in Figure 20–1. At any stock price below $22, the theoretical value of the warrant is zero; beyond $22, each $1 increase in the price of the stock brings with it a $1 increase in the theoretical value of the warrant.[1] The actual market price of the warrants lies above the theoretical value at each price of the common stock. Notice, however, that the premium of market price over theoretical value declines as the price of the common stock increases. For example, when the common sold for $22 and the warrants had a zero theoretical value, their actual price and the premium was $9. As the price of the stock rises, the theoretical value of the warrants matches the increase dollar for dollar, but for a while the market price of the warrant climbs less rapidly and the premium declines. The premium is $9 when the stock sells for $22 a share, but it declines to $1 by the time the stock price has risen to $75 a share. Beyond this point the premium seems to be constant.

Why do you suppose this pattern exists? Why should the warrant ever sell for more than its theoretical value, and why does the premium decline as the price of the stock increases? The answer lies in the speculative appeal of warrants—they enable a person to gain a high degree of personal leverage when buying securities. To illustrate, suppose TWA warrants always sold for exactly their theoretical value.

[1] The formula gives a *negative* theoretical value when the stock is selling for less than the option price. This makes no sense, so we define the theoretical value to be zero when the stock is selling for less than the option price.

Now suppose you are thinking of investing in the company's common stock at a time when it is selling for $25 a share. If you buy a share and the price rises to $50 in a year, you have made a 100 percent capital gain. However, had you bought the warrants at their theoretical value ($3 when the stock sells for $25), your capital gain would have been $25 on a $3 investment, or 833 percent. At the same time, your total loss potential with the warrant is only $3, while the potential loss from the purchase of the stock is $25. However, a $3 decline in the stock price produces only a 12 percent loss if the stock is purchased and a 100 percent loss if you buy the warrant. The huge capital gains potential, combined with the loss limitation, is clearly worth something—the exact amount that it is worth to investors is the amount of the premium.

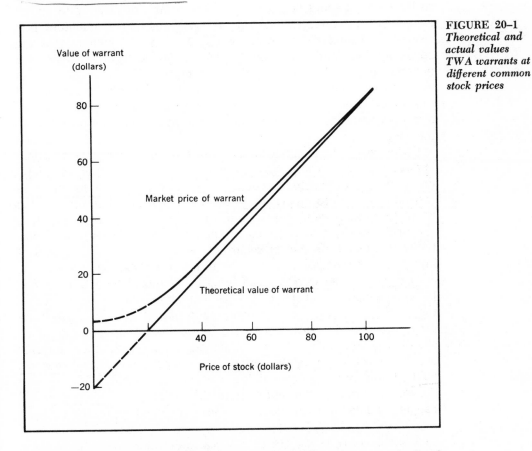

FIGURE 20–1
*Theoretical and
actual values
TWA warrants at
different common
stock prices*

Value of warrant
(dollars)

Market price of warrant

Theoretical value of warrant

Price of stock (dollars)

But why does the premium decline as the price of the stock rises? The answer here is that both the capital gains leverage effect and the loss protection feature decline at high stock prices. For example, if you are thinking of buying the stock at $75 share, the theoretical value of the warrants is $53. If the stock price doubles to $150, the theoretical value of TWA warrants goes from $53 to $128. The percentage capital gain on the stock is still 100 percent, but the percentage gain on the warrant declines from 833 percent to 142 percent. Also, notice that the loss potential on the warrant is much greater when the warrant is selling at high prices. These two factors, the declining leverage impact and the increasing danger of losses, explain why the premium diminishes as the price of the common stock rises.

Use of Warrants in Financing In the past warrants have generally been used by small, rapidly growing firms as "sweeteners" when selling either debt or preferred stocks. Such firms are frequently regarded by investors as being highly risky, so their bonds could be sold only if the firms were willing to accept extremely high rates of interest and very restrictive indenture provisions. In April 1970, however, AT&T raised $1.57 billion by selling bonds with warrants. This was the largest financing of any type ever undertaken by a business firm, and it marked the first use ever of warrants by a large, strong corporation. It may safely be anticipated that other large firms will follow AT&T's lead, so we expect to see a more widespread use of warrants in the future than has been true in the past.[2]

Giving warrants along with the bonds enables investors to share in the company's growth, if it does, in fact, grow and prosper; therefore, investors are willing to accept a lower bond interest rate and less restrictive indenture provisions. A bond with warrants has some of the characteristics of debt and some of the characteristics of equity. It is a hybrid security that provides the financial manager with an opportunity to expand his mix of securities, appeal to a broader group of investors, and thus possibly lower his firm's cost of capital.

Also, notice that warrants can bring in additional funds. The option price is generally set 15 to 20 percent above the market price of the stock at the time of the bond issue. If the firm does grow and prosper and if its stock price rises above the option price at which shares may be purchased, warrant holders will surrender their warrants and buy stock at the stated price. This happens for several reasons. First, it will surely happen if the warrants are about to expire with the market price of the stock above the option price. Second, it will happen voluntarily as the company raises the dividend on the common

[2] It is also interesting to note that the New York Stock Exchange had a policy against listing warrants prior to the AT&T issue. The NYSE's stated policy was that they could not be listed because they were "speculative" instruments rather than "investment" securities. When AT&T issued warrants, however, the Exchange changed its policy and agreed to list warrants that met certain specifications.

stock. No dividend is earned on the warrant, so it provides no current income. However, if the common stock pays an attractive dividend, it provides an attractive dividend yield. This induces warrant holders to exercise their option to buy the stock. Third, warrants sometimes have *stepped-up option prices*. For example, the Williamson Scientific Company has warrants outstanding with an option price of $25 until December 31, 1975, at which time the option price rises to $30. If the price of the common stock is above $25 just before December 1975, many warrant holders will exercise their option before the stepped-up price takes effect.

One desirable feature of warrants is that they generally bring in additional funds only if these funds are needed. If the company grows and prospers, causing the price of the stock to rise, the warrants are exercised and bring in needed funds. If the company is not successful and cannot profitably employ additional money, the price of its stock will probably not rise sufficiently to induce exercise of the options.

CONVERTIBLES

Convertible securities[3] are bonds or preferred stocks that are exchangeable, at the option of the holder, under specified terms and conditions. The *conversion ratio* gives the number of shares of common stock the holder of the convertible receives when he surrenders his security on conversion, and the *conversion price* is the effective price paid for the common stock when conversion occurs. In effect, a convertible is similar to a bond with an attached warrant.

The relationship between the conversion ratio and the conversion price is illustrated by the Adams Electric Company $1,000 par value convertible debentures. At any time prior to July 1, 1989, a debenture holder can turn in his bond and receive in its place 20 shares of common stock; therefore, the conversion ratio is 20 shares for one bond. The bond has a par value of $1,000, so the holder is giving up this amount when he converts. Dividing the $1,000 by the 20 shares received gives a conversion price of $50 a share.

$$\text{Conversion price} = \frac{\text{par value of bond}}{\text{shares received}} = \frac{\$1,000}{20} = \$50.$$

The conversion price and the conversion ratio are established at the time the convertible bond is sold. Generally, these values are fixed for the life of the bond, although sometimes a stepped-up conversion price is used. Litton Industries' convertible debentures, for example, are convertible into 12.5 shares until 1972, into 11.76 shares from 1972 until 1982, and into 11.11 shares from 1982 until they mature

[3] See Appendices A and B, *Managerial Finance*, 3rd Edition, for a more detailed discussion of convertibles.

in 1987. The conversion price thus starts at $80, rises to $85, then to $90. Litton's convertibles, like most, are callable at the option of the company.

Another factor that may cause a change in the conversion price and ratio is a standard feature of practically all convertibles—the clause protecting the convertible against dilution from stock splits, stock dividends, and the sale of common stock at low prices (as in a rights offering). The typical provision states that no common stock can be sold at a price below the conversion price, and that the conversion price must be lowered (and the conversion ratio raised) by the percentage amount of any stock dividend or split. For example, if Adams Electric had a two-for-one split, the conversion ratio would automatically be adjusted to 40 and the conversion price lowered to $25. If this protection was not contained in the contract, a company could completely thwart conversion by the use of stock splits and dividends. Warrants are similarly protected against dilution.

Like warrant option prices, the conversion price is characteristically set from 10 to 20 percent above the prevailing market price of the common stock at the time the convertible issue is sold. Exactly how the conversion price is established can best be understood after examining some of the reasons why firms use convertibles.

Relative Use of A study by C. James Pilcher[4] on the use of convertibles, during the
Convertibles period 1933 through 1952, showed that 182 convertible debentures were issued during the 20-year period. Another study, made by the late Robert R. McKenzie[5] of New York University, estimated that 419 issues were placed in the 10-year period 1956–1965. Thus, there has been a pronounced increase in the use of convertibles in more recent years.

There were clear and definite advantages to investors who bought convertibles in the post-World War II period. This was a time of great uncertainty. Many economists were forecasting a major postwar recession, while others were forecasting an unprecedented boom. The use of convertibles permitted the investor to hedge against both. In the event of a postwar collapse, he had the protection of his senior position. But if a boom and inflation caused common stock prices to soar, the convertible would rise with the price of the common stock. Thus, convertibles offered the investor both lower risk and speculative potentialities—a hedge against both deflation and inflation. Note, however, that the coupon interest rate on a convertible is *always* lower than

---

[4] C. J. Pilcher, *Raising Capital with Convertible Securities* (Ann Arbor: Bureau of Business Research, University of Michigan, 1955).

[5] Robert R. McKenzie, "Convertible Securities, 1956–1965," *Quarterly Review of Economics and Business,* VI (Winter 1966), pp. 41–48.

the interest rate of an equivalent nonconvertible bond. Accordingly, an investor who buys a convertible gives up interest income in the hope of a capital gain.

A sampling of the price behavior of convertibles issued in 1962 shows that by 1965 the market price of the common stock was approximately 150 percent of the conversion price. In other words, the market price of the stock rose approximately 50 percent above its market price at the time the convertibles were issued. Correspondingly, through 1965 there were marked profits for people who bought convertibles at the time they were originally issued. Note also, however, that profits would have been even greater had the holders of these convertibles purchased the common stock for which they were exchangeable. The reason is that the conversion price is set higher than the initial market price of the common stock.

Convertibles offer advantages to corporations as well as to individual investors. The most important of these advantages are discussed below.

Reasons for Use of Convertibles

As a sweetener when selling debt. Sometimes a company can sell debt with lower interest rates and less restrictive covenants by giving investors a chance to share in potential capital gains; convertibles, like bonds with warrants, offer this possibility.

To sell common stock at prices higher than those now prevailing. Many companies actually want to sell common stock, not debt, but feel that the price of the stock is temporarily depressed. Management may know, for example, that earnings are depressed because of a strike but that they will snap back during the next year and pull the price of the stock up with them. To sell stock now would require giving up more shares to raise a given amount of money than management thinks is necessary. However, setting the conversion price 15 to 20 percent above the present market price of the stock will require giving up 15 to 20 percent fewer shares when the bonds are converted than would be required if stock was sold directly.

Notice, however, that management is counting on the stock price rising above the conversion price to make the bonds actually attractive in conversion. If the stock price does not rise and conversion does not occur, then management is saddled with debt.

How can the company be sure that conversion will occur when the price of the stock rises above the conversion price? Characteristically, convertibles have a provision that gives the issuing firm the opportunity of calling the convertible at a specified price. Suppose the conversion price is $50, the conversion ratio is 20, the market price of the common stock has risen to $60, and the call price on the convertible bond is $1,050. If the company called the bond (by giving the usual notification of 20 days), bondholders could either convert into common stock with a market value of $1,200 or allow the company to redeem the bond for $1,050. Naturally, bondholders prefer $1,200 to $1,050, so conversion occurs. The call provision therefore gives the company a means of forcing conversion, provided that the market price of the stock is greater than the conversion price.

To have low-cost capital during a construction period. Another advantage from the standpoint of the issuer is that a convertible issue may be used as a temporary financing device. During the years 1946 through 1957, American Telephone & Telegraph Company sold $10 billion of convertible debentures. By 1959 about 80 percent of these convertible debentures had been converted into common stock. AT&T could not have sold straight debt in this amount because its financial structure would have been unbalanced. On the other hand, if AT&T had simply issued large amounts of common stock periodically, there would have been price pressure on its stock because the market is slow to digest large blocks of stock.

By using convertible debentures, which provided for a lag of some six to nine months before they were converted into common stock, AT&T received relatively cheap money to finance growth. Transmission lines and telephone exchange buildings must first be built to provide the basis for ultimately installing phones. While AT&T is installing transmission lines and telephone exchange buildings, these investments are not earning any money. Therefore it was important to AT&T to minimize the cost of money while these installations were being made. After six to nine months had elapsed and these installations were translated into telephones that were bringing in revenues, AT&T was better able to pay the regular common stock dividend.

Disadvantages of Convertibles From the standpoint of the issuer, convertibles have a possible disadvantage. Although the convertible stock gives the issuer the opportunity to sell common stock at a price 15 to 20 percent higher than it could otherwise be sold, if the common stock greatly increases in price the issuer may find that he would have been better off if he had waited and simply sold the common stock. Further, if the company truly wants to raise equity capital and if the price of the stock declines after the bond is issued, then it is stuck with debt.

But the plain fact of the matter may well be that the company has no alternative, especially if it is a small and growing company. A sufficient investment demand for the company's debt securities or preferred stock may not be present. For this reason the company may be virtually forced to use convertibles. In this kind of situation the convertibles perform a very useful function in that they enable management to raise additional debt and equity money and maintain control of the company.

The Winchester Company, an electronic circuit and component manufacturer with assets of $12 million, illustrates a typical case where
convertibles are useful.

Winchester's profits have been depressed as a result of its heavy
expenditures on research and development for a new product. This
situation has held down the growth rate of earnings and dividends;
the price/earnings ratio is only 18 times, as compared with an industry
average of 22. At the current $2 earnings per share and P/E of 18,
the stock is selling for $36 a share. The Winchester family owns 70
percent of the 300,000 shares outstanding, or 210,000 shares. It
would like to retain majority control, but cannot buy more stock.

The heavy R & D expenditures have resulted in the development
of a new type of printed circuit that management believes will be
highly profitable. Five million dollars is needed to build and equip
new production facilities, and profits will not start to flow in to the
company for some 18 months after construction on the new plant
is started. Winchester's debt amounts to $5.4 million, or 45 percent
of assets, well above the 25 percent industry average. Present debt
indenture provisions restrict the company from selling additional debt
unless the new debt is subordinate to that now outstanding.

Investment bankers inform J. H. Winchester, Jr., the financial vice-
president, that subordinated debentures cannot be sold unless they
are convertible or have warrants attached. Convertibles or bonds with
warrants can be sold with a 5 percent coupon interest rate if the
conversion price or warrant option price is set at 15 percent above
the present market price of $36, or at $41 a share. Alternatively,
the investment bankers are willing to buy convertibles or bonds with
warrants at a 5 1/2 percent interest rate and a 20 percent conversion
premium, or a conversion (or exercise) price of $43.50. If the company
wants to sell common stock directly, it can net $33 a share.

Which of the alternatives should Winchester choose? First, note that
if common stock is used, the company must sell 151,000 shares ($5
million divided by $33). Combined with the 90,000 shares held outside
the family, this amounts to 241,000 shares versus the Winchester
holdings of 210,000, so the family will lose majority control if common
stock is sold.

If the 5 percent convertibles or bonds with warrants are used and
the bonds are converted or the warrants are exercised, 122,000 new
shares will be added. Combined with the old 90,000, the outside interest will then be 212,000, so again the Winchester family will lose
majority control. However, if the 5 1/2 percent convertibles or bonds
with warrants are used, then after conversion or exercise only 115,000
new shares will be created. In this case the family will have 210,000
shares versus 205,000 for outsiders; absolute control will be
maintained.

In addition to control, using the convertibles or warrants also benefits earnings per share in the long run—the total number of shares is less because fewer new shares must be issued to get the $5 million, so earnings per share will be higher. Before conversion or exercise, however, the firm has a considerable amount of debt outstanding. Adding $5 million raises the total debt to $10.4 million against a new total assets of $17 million, so the debt ratio will be over 61 percent versus the 25 percent industry average. This could be dangerous. If delays are encountered in bringing the new plant into production, if demand does not meet expectations, if the company should experience a strike, if the economy should go into a recession—if any of these things occurs—the company will be extremely vulnerable because of the high debt ratio.

In the present case, the decision was made to sell the 5 1/2 percent convertible debentures. Two years later, earnings climbed to $3 a share, the P/E ratio to 20, and the price of the stock to $60. The bonds were called, but, of course, conversion occurred. After conversion, debt amounted to approximately $5.5 million against total assets of $17.5 million (some earnings had been retained), so the debt ratio was down to a more reasonable 31 percent.

Convertibles were chosen rather than bonds with warrants for the following reason. If a firm has a high debt ratio and its near-term prospects are favorable, it can anticipate a rise in the price of its stock and thus be able to call the bonds and force conversion. Warrants, on the other hand, have a stated life, and even though the price of the firm's stock rises, the warrants may not be exercised until near their expiration date. If, subsequent to the favorable period (during which convertibles could have been called), the firm encounters less favorable developments and the price of its stock falls, the warrants may lose their value and never be exercised. The heavy debt burden will then become aggravated. Therefore, the use of convertibles gives the firm greater control over the timing of future capital structure changes. This factor is of particular importance to the firm if its debt ratio is already high in relation to the risks of its line of business.

USE OF OPTIONS IN SMALL BUSINESS FINANCING Most of the principles of financing are equally applicable to large and small firms. However, one aspect of small business financing has received considerable attention—the fact that organizers and owners of small businesses are often reluctant to share control of the firm as it grows. This presents problems, for growth brings with it the need to obtain additional funds. Small firms characteristically do not present a record of earnings or stability that justifies long-term debt financing, and the sale of equity shares would result in dilution of ownership and control.

This basic dilemma of small business financing can be eased considerably by the use of convertibles and warrants, the subject of the present chapter. Until the necessary background on convertibles and warrants had been set forth, we could not present a rounded discussion of small business financing. We can now do so. The use of convertibles and warrants enables a small firm to raise long-term debt money from the capital markets and at the same time provide investors in such securities with a degree of participation in the potential increase in equity values. Since the convertibles and warrants provide for future purchase of the common stock at a price usually at a premium over the current common stock price, the extent of dilution of control by the present owners is diminished to some degree.

With the background of the use of options such as convertibles and warrants, it is now possible to discusss another important aspect of investment banker operations since the mid-1950s. One of the barriers to small firms' security issues has been the high cost of flotation, which until the mid-1950's according to SEC data, averaged around 20 percent of gross proceeds. Since the mid-1950s, warrants have been used to reduce direct flotation costs on both equity and debt issues for small firms. A common practice among investment bankers has been to reduce their commission from 20 percent to about 5 to 10 percent and to receive warrants to purchase up to 10 percent of the common stock of the small firm. With these kinds of inducements, investment bankers have vigorously sponsored small equity issues and have maintained a continued program of financing for small firms, especially those with good growth potential. *Investment Banker Sponsorship of Small Firms*

The original intention of the Small Business Investment Company (SBIC) Act of 1958 was able to create, with federal government financing help, institutions that would provide funds to small business firms on a debt basis with the added inducement of equity participation through the use of convertibles and warrants. Since the adoption of the act in 1958, the SBIC's have gone through alternate periods of optimistic and pessimistic evaluations of their prospects. Both government regulations providing for the nature and extent of government assistance and the investment powers of the SBIC's have undergone a series of changes. Throughout all these changes, two broad policies have characterized the operations of the small business investment corporations. First, they emphasize convertible securities and obligations with warrants, giving the SBIC a residual equity position in the companies to which funds are provided. Second, they emphasize the provision for SBIC management council, for which a fee is charged. *Small Business Investment Companies*

In order to promote small business financing, the SBIC's were granted advantageous tax provisions. Dividends received by the SBIC's from their small business investments are 100 percent deductible from the SBIC's income, compared with 85 percent for ordinary corporate dividends. Losses on the convertible debentures of small businesses that are held by SBIC's can be treated as losses chargeable against ordinary income, not against capital gains. SBIC's are exempt from penalties for improper accumulation of income if they meet certain requirements. Also, investors in SBIC's may treat their own stock losses as ordinary losses chargeable against ordinary income. In keeping with the spirit of the act, the SBIC's are under the administrative control of the Small Business Administration (SBA).

OTHER ACTIVITIES OF THE SMALL BUSINESS ADMINISTRA- TION   Since one of the activities of the Small Business Administration (SBA) was discussed in connection with the SBIC program, it may be useful to round out the discussion by describing some of the other important activities of the Small Business Administration.

Scope of Operations of the SBA   The Small Business Administration helps small business firms in a number of ways. It aids small business in obtaining a fair share of government contracts, and it also emphasizes assistance in management and production problems. These two objectives recognize that a substantial number of small business firms need management counseling and assistance. In addition, the SBA actively aids small firms with their financial problems; this aspect of SBA operations will be emphasized here.

For business loans, the SBA defines a small business as one that is independently owned and operated and is nondominant in its field. Specific standards depend upon the industry of the firm. Any manufacturing concern is defined as small if it employs 250 or fewer persons, and it is defined as large if it employs more than 1,000 persons. However, if a manufacturing concern operates in an industry that has few competitors and if it has less than 5 percent of sales, it may be called a small business; American Motors is classed as a small business under this definition. A wholesale concern is classified as small if its yearly sales are $5 million or less. Most retail businesses and service trades are defined as small if their total annual receipts do not exceed $1 million. A business operating under a franchise may obtain a loan if the SBA can be assured that the firm is not a large business through its affiliation with the franchiser. The Department of Commerce estimates that, as of the end of 1966, 95 percent of all firms were classified as small businesses. There is, therefore a wide scope for SBA operations.

By law, the SBA makes loans to small business concerns only when *Loan Policies* financing is not available to them on reasonable terms from other *and Types* sources. The SBA loans are of two types: direct and participating. In a direct loan, there is no participation by a private lender—the loan is made directly by the SBA to the borrower. In participating loans, the SBA joins with a bank or other private lending institution in making a loan to a small business firm.

A participating loan may be made under a loan guarantee or on an immediate basis. A participating loan on a *guarantee basis* provides that the SBA will purchase its guaranteed portion of the outstanding balance of the loan if the borrower defaults. When the SBA participates in a loan on an *immediate basis,* it purchases immediately a fixed percentage of the original principal amount of the loan. By law, the SBA may not enter into an immediate participation if it can arrange a guaranteed loan.

Both warrants and convertibles are forms of options used in financing **SUMMARY** business firms. The use of long-term options such as warrants and convertibles is encouraged by an economic environment combining prospects of both boom or inflation and depression or deflation. The senior position of the securities protects against recessions. The option feature offers the opportunity for participation in rising stock prices.

Both the convertibility privilege and warrants are used as "sweeteners." The option privileges they grant may make it possible for small companies to sell debt or preferred stock which otherwise could not be sold. For large companies, the "sweeteners" result in lower costs of the securities sold. In addition, the options provide for the future sale of the common stock at prices higher than could be obtained at the time. The options thereby permit the delayed sale of common stock at more favorable prices.

The conversion of bonds by their holders does not ordinarily bring additional funds to the company. The exercise of warrants will provide these funds. The conversion of securities will result in reduced debt ratios. The exercise of warrants will strengthen the equity position but will still leave the debt or preferred stock on the balance sheet. In comparing the use of convertibles with senior securities carrying warrants, a firm with a high debt ratio should choose convertibles. A firm with a moderate or low debt ratio may employ warrants.

In the past, larger and stronger firms tended to favor convertibles over bonds with warrants, so most warrants have been issued by smaller, weaker concerns. AT&T's use of warrants in its $1.57 billion 1970 financing promises to make other large firms re-examine their positions on warrants, and we anticipate that warrants will come into increasing use in the years ahead.

Options such as warrants and convertibles have been increasingly used to facilitate small business financing. One of the ways in which options have stimulated investment banker sponsorship of small firms has been in reducing the cash expenses of floating new issues of securities. SEC data showed that for a number of years flotation costs on small issues averaged as high as 20 percent of gross proceeds. The use of options has caused cash flotation costs to be reduced. The characteristic pattern has been for the investment banker to charge a commission of 5 to 10 percent of gross proceeds plus taking warrants exercisable at the issue price on up to 10 percent of the number of new shares issued.

Another institutional arrangement that encouraged the use of options in the financing of small business resulted from the establishment of Small Business Investment Corporations in 1958. The SBIC's were empowered to make debt investments in small business and to take warrants and conversion features as an inducement for making the loans.

In addition to their operations through SBIC's, the Small Business Administration has provided financing to small business firms in a number of ways. First, the SBA helps small businesses obtain government contracts. Second, the SBA has emphasized management counseling to small business. Finally, the SBA itself makes two types of loans to small business—direct loans to borrowers and participating loans through other financial institutions. Participating loans are either *immediate* loans in which a fixed percentage of the loan is made by the SBA to the small business, the remainder of the funds being supplied by a bank, or a loan *guarantee* under which the SBA will purchase its guaranteed portion if the borrower defaults.

QUESTIONS **20–1** Why do warrants typically sell at prices greater than their theoretical values?

20–2 Why do convertibles typically sell at prices greater than their theoretical values (the higher of the conversion value or straight-debt value)? Would you expect the percentage premium on a convertible bond to be more or less than that on a warrant? (The percentage premium is defined as the market price minus the theoretical value, divided by the market price.)

20–3 What effect does the trend in stock prices (subsequent to issue) have on a firm's ability to raise funds (a) through convertibles and (b) through warrants?

20–4 If a firm expects to have additional financial requirements in the future, would you recommend that it use convertibles or bonds with warrants? Why?

20–5 How does a firm's dividend policy affect each of the following?

a) The value of long-term warrants
b) The likelihood that convertible bonds will be converted
c) The likelihood that warrants will be exercised

20–6   Evaluate the following statement: "Issuing convertible securities represents a means by which a firm can sell common stock at a price above the existing market."

20–7   Why do corporations often sell convertibles on a rights basis?

20–1   The Sackett-Ziegler Company's capital consists of 8,000 shares of com-   **PROBLEMS**
mon stock and 4,000 warrants, each good to buy two shares of common at $40 a share. The warrants are protected against dilution (that is, the subscription price is adjusted downward in the event of a stock dividend or if the firm sells common stock at less than the $40 exercise price). The company issues rights to buy one new share of common at $30 for every two shares held. With the stock selling rights on at $45, compute:

a) The theoretical value of the rights before the stock sells ex rights
b) The new subscription price of the warrant after the rights issue.

20–2   The Rogers Computer Company was planning to finance an expansion in the summer of 1971. The principal executives of the company were agreed that an industrial company of this type should finance growth by means of common stock rather than by debt. However, they felt that the price of the company's common stock did not reflect its true worth, so they were desirous of selling a convertible security. They considered a convertible debenture but feared the burden of fixed interest charges if the common stock did not rise in price to make conversion attractive. They decided on an issue of convertible preferred stock.

The common stock was currently selling at $45 a share. Management projected earnings for 1971 at $3 a share and expected a future growth rate of 8 percent a year. It was agreed by the investment bankers and the management that the common stock would sell at 20 times earnings, the current price-earnings ratio.

a) What conversion price should be set by the issuer?
b) Should the preferred stock include a call-price provision? Why?

20–3   Wilson Microwave, Inc., has the following balance sheet:

Current assets	$100,000	Current debt	$ 40,000	*Balance sheet 1*
Net fixed assets	100,000	Common stock, par value $2	40,000	
		Earned surplus	120,000	
Total assets	$200,000	Total claims	$200,000	

a) The firm earns 20 percent on total assets before taxes (assume a 50 percent tax rate). What are earnings per share?
b) If the price/earnings ratio for the company's stock is 20 times, what is the market price of the company's stock?
c) What is the book value of the company's stock?

In the following few years, sales are expected to double and the financing needs of the firm will double. The firm decides to sell debentures to meet these needs. It is undecided, however, whether to sell convertible debentures or debentures with warrants. The new balance sheet would appear as follows:

Balance sheet 2

Current assets	$200,000	Current debt		$ 80,000
Net fixed assets	200,000	Debentures		120,000
		Common stock, par value $2		40,000
		Earned surplus		160,000
Total assets	$400,000	Total claims		$400,000

The convertible debentures would pay 6 percent interest and would be convertible into 25 shares of common stock for each $1,000 debenture. The debentures with warrants would carry a 7 percent coupon and entitle each holder of a $1,000 debenture to buy 20 shares of common stock at $60. Charles Wilson owns 80 percent of Microwave before the financing.

d) Assume that convertible debentures are sold and all are later converted. Show the new balance sheet, disregarding any changes in retained earnings.

Balance sheet 3

		Current debt	_____
		Debentures	_____
		Common stock, par value $2	_____
		Paid-in surplus	_____
		Earned surplus	_____
Total assets	_____	Total claims	_____

e) Complete the firm's income statement after the debentures have all been converted:

Income statement

Net income after all charges except debenture interest
   and before taxes (20% of total assets)
Debenture interest   _____
Federal income tax, 50%   _____
Net income after taxes   _____
Earnings per share after taxes   _____

f) Now, instead of convertibles, assume that debentures with warrants were issued. Assume further that the warrants were all exercised. Show the new balance sheet figures.

Balance sheet 4

		Current debt	_____
		Debentures	_____
		Common stock, par value $2	_____
		Paid-in surplus	_____
		Earned surplus	_____
Total assets	_____	Total claims	_____

g) Complete the firm's income statement after the debenture warrants have all been exercised.

Net income after all charges except debenture interest and before taxes	_____
Debenture interest	_____
Taxable income	_____
Federal income tax	_____
Net income after taxes	_____
Earnings per share after taxes	_____

20–4 The Baker Company has grown rapidly during the past five years. Recently its commercial bank has urged the company to consider increasing permanent financing. Its bank loan had risen to $200,000, carrying 6 percent interest. Baker has been 30 to 60 days late in paying trade creditors.

Discussions with an investment banker have resulted in the suggestion to raise $400,000 at this time. Investment bankers have assured Baker that the following alternatives will be feasible (flotation costs will be ignored):

Alternative 1: Sell common stock at $8.
Alternative 2: Sell convertible bonds at a 6 percent coupon, convertible into common stock at $10.
Alternative 3: Sell debentures at a 6 percent coupon, each $1,000 bond carrying 100 warrants to buy common stock at $10.

Additional information is given below.

Baker Company
Balance sheet
December 31, 1969

Current liabilities	$350,000	
Common stock, par $1.00	100,000	
Retained earnings	50,000	
Total assets $500,000	Total liabilities and capital	$500,000

Baker Company
Income statement
December 31, 1969

Sales	$1,000,000
All costs except interest	900,000
Gross profit	$ 100,000
Interest	12,000
Profit before taxes	$ 88,000
Taxes at 50%	44,000
Profits after taxes	$ 44,000
Shares	100,000
Earnings per share	$0.44
Price/earnings ratio	20×
Market price of stock	$8.80

A. B. Green, the president, owns 68 percent of the common stock of Baker Company and wishes to maintain control of the company.

a) Show the new balance sheet under each of the alternatives. For alternatives 2 and 3, show the balance sheet after conversion of the debentures or exercise of warrants. Assume that one half the funds raised will be used to pay off the bank loan and one half to increase total assets.
b) Show Green's control position under each alternative, assuming Green does not purchase additional shares.
c) What is the effect on earnings per share of each of the alternatives, if it is assumed that profits before interest and taxes will be 20 percent of total assets?
d) What will be the debt ratio under each alternative?
e) Which of the three alternatives would you recommend to Green, and why?

Part VII

Valuation in Mergers and Corporate Readjustments

Chapter 21

External Growth: Mergers and Holding Companies

GROWTH is vital to the well-being of a firm; without it, a business cannot attract able management because it cannot give them recognition in promotions and challenging creative activity. Without able executives, the firm is likely to decline and die. Much of the material in the previous chapters dealing with analysis, planning, and financing has a direct bearing on the financial manager's potential contribution to the growth of a firm. However, because of the central importance of the growth requirement, the present chapter is focused on strategies for promoting it.

Merger activity has played an important part in the growth of firms in the United States, and financial managers are required both to appraise the desirability of a prospective purchase and to participate directly in evaluating the respective companies involved in a merger.[1] Consequently, it is essential that the study of financial management provide the background necessary for effective participation in merger negotiations and decisions.

Financial managers—and intelligent laymen—also need to be aware of the broader significance of mergers. Despite the heightened merger activities in the 1920s, again after World War II, and during the mid-1960s, recent merger movements have neither approached the magnitude nor had the social consequences of the mergers that took place from 1890 to 1905. During this period, more than 200 major combinations were effected, resulting in the concentration that has characterized the steel, tobacco, and other important industries. Regardless of the business objectives and motives of merger activity, the social and economic consequences of mergers must also be taken into account.

[1] As we use the term, "merger" means any combination that forms one economic unit from two or more previous ones. For legal purposes there are distinctions between the various ways these combinations can occur, but our emphasis is on fundamental business and financial aspects of mergers or acquisitions.

REASONS FOR
SEEKING
GROWTH

One of the objectives of growth, whether by external acquisitions or by internal development, is large size for the purpose of achieving economies of large-scale operations. Economies of scale result from the following factors.

Research

Research activities are especially crucial in today's dynamic economy. The large firm can finance large-scale research which may benefit a great number of its diverse operations. But suppose a large firm is broken into 10 units. Could not the 10 units each contract to hire research from a research organization? It is true that research in the large firm is often conducted by executives hired on a salary basis, and independent research firms do sell their services on a fee basis. There are some kinds of research, however, that are the unique contribution of the large firm.

For example, suppose that a large firm which spends $50 million a year on research is divided into ten firms, each of which could allocate $5 million a year for research. If each of these ten firms hires the services of a research organization, each would attempt to buy $5 million worth of research designed to give it a competitive advantage over its nine rivals and any other firms in the industry. It seems reasonable to suppose that certain kinds of research could not be purchased by the $5 million a year but could be achieved by the $50 million budget.

Modern large-scale business organizations represent the combination of centralized and decentralized decisions. Research is an activity performed most efficiently when centralized. Although the amounts of money spent on research are relatively small, its significance is critical for the progress of the firm.

Top-Management Skills

Related to indivisibility of research expenditures is the value of the highly able executive. The very competent individual is another one of the indivisible factors that make for an advantage of large-scale operations. It cannot be denied that many decisions are decentralized; for many matters, delegation of authority to committees and subordinates takes place. However, some of the centralized decisions and the catalytic process of a great mind on policy matters are of pervasive and powerful influence on the growth pattern and performance of an organization.

Operating Economies

Often there are other economies of multiproduct operations. Lower salary ratios may be achieved by consolidating certain departments (accounting, marketing, advertising, switchboard, clerical); marketing costs may be lowered by consolidating salesmen covering the same territory for several companies, thus reducing the total number of salesmen required; production savings may come from the ability to utilize large, high-output machinery or to obtain quantity discounts on purchases.

Still another important factor is the risk reduction of multiplant operations, which is heightened by the tax structure. If a new firm attempts an innovation or a new product line and fails, the loss may force it out of business completely. However, if an established firm attempts a change or an innovation, any loss can be offset against assured income from other sources. The higher the tax rate, the higher the proportion of the innovation costs borne by taxes. This is another reason why multiproduct and multiplant firms confer economic advantages, not only on the firm itself but also on the economy as a whole, in terms of the potential rate of economic progress.

Risk Reduction

While it is not strictly an operating factor, the fact that the earnings of larger economic units are frequently capitalized at lower rates and, hence, produce higher market values has stimulated many mergers. The securities of larger firms have better marketability, these firms are more able to diversify and thus reduce risks, and they are generally better known. All these factors lead to higher price/earnings ratios. As a result, it may be possible to consolidate firms and have the resulting market value greater than the sum of their individual values, even if there is no increase in aggregate earnings. To illustrate, three companies may each be earning $100 and selling at 10 times earnings, for a total market value of ($100)(10)(3) equals $3,000. When these companies combine, the new company may obtain a Stock Exchange listing or take other actions to improve the price of its stock. If so, the price/earnings ratio may rise to 15, in which case the market value of the consolidated firm would be $4,500.[2]

Market Capitalization Rates

The five factors just discussed provide a plausible rationale for the existence and operation of large multiproduct and multiplant enterprises.

Many of the objectives of size and diversification may be achieved either through internal growth or by external growth through acquisitions and mergers. In the post-World War II period, considerable diversification was achieved by many firms through external acquisition. The reasons for utilizing external acquisition instead of internal growth to achieve diversification may be briefly indicated.

MERGERS VERSUS INTERNAL GROWTH

[2] The market capitalization rate is related to the cost of equity, as was explained in Chapter 12. A lower capitalization rate results in a lower cost of capital. Therefore, the same actions that raise the market value of the equity also lower the firm's cost of new capital.

Speed New facilities may be acquired more quickly through mergers. New products, new processes, new plants, and new productive organizations can be acquired in a fully operative condition by a merger.

Cost The desired facilities may be obtained more cheaply by purchasing the ownership stock of each existing company. For many reasons, the securities of a company may be selling below the replacement costs of the firm's assets. For example, stock market prices were relatively depressed from 1946 to 1953, and the market values of common stocks were low in relation to earnings levels. A basis was provided for developing favorable merger terms.

The mergers in the steel industry in the period immediately following 1946 are good examples of this influence. A steel company could add new capacity much more cheaply by buying another company than by building new plants to achieve the same increase in capacity. Furthermore, the speed factor mentioned above was important here. The duration of the seller's market in steel was unknown. The sooner a steel company could acquire additional facilities and get them into operation for making sales, the more likely it would be to benefit from the favorable market conditions.

Related to this is the objective of obtaining the services of desired personnel. Sometimes the inducement of higher compensation to attract an outstanding individual or management group might be either unduly expensive or useless. Simply buying the company that employs these people may prove to be the most effective means of obtaining their services. In such circumstances, a merger may be the only practicable method of obtaining the kind of superior management talent or technical skill that the acquiring firm is seeking to obtain.

Financing Sometimes it is possible to finance an acquisition when it is not possible to finance internal growth. A large steel plant, for example, involves a large investment. Steel capacity may be acquired in a merger through an exchange of stock more cheaply than it can be obtained by buying the facilities themselves. Sellers may be more willing to accept the stock of the purchaser in payment for the facilities sold than would investors in a public distribution. The use of stock reduces cash requirements for the acquisition of assets.

Risk The desired new product, new process, or new organization may be developed with less uncertainty of investment loss. The purchased facility may already have demonstrated its revenue-yielding capacity.

Stabilizing Effects A merger may represent the most effective method of achieving stability and progress at a given stage of industrial development. It may represent the most efficient method of combining facilities and disposing of obsolete and inefficient properties, as was probably true at some stages in the development of industries such as railroad transport, air transport, banking, agricultural implements, and steel.

Without question, the high level of taxation was a factor in the postwar period. A study by a Harvard group[3] indicates that taxes appear to have been a major reason for the sale of about one-third of the firms acquired by merger. Inheritance taxes precipitated these sales in some cases; in others, the advantage of buying a company with a tax loss, which was discussed in Chapter 2, provided the motivation.

Taxes

The development of new products and market areas may be accomplished through mergers. Firms in the early stages of development can in this way avoid combating difficult competition or remedy a management weakness. Market control may be obtained more rapidly with less risk through mergers than by internal expansion. The merger of two large firms may result in market dominance by the combined firms and may therefore be prevented by the antitrust authorities.

Competitive Advantages

Regardless of the motives or objectives of mergers from a business standpoint, the consequences of the market-control position of the acquiring company may lead to intervention by governmental regulatory agencies. Hence, it is not enough for the financial manager to consider only the business aspects of the merger. He must also consider the effects on market control. If the merger will have potentially adverse effects on competition, there is a strong likelihood that government action will be interposed against the merger.

For every merger actually consummated, a number of other potentially attractive combinations fail during the negotiating stage. In some of these cases, negotiations are broken off when it is revealed that the companies' operations are not compatible. In others, tangible benefits would result, but the parties are unable to agree on the merger terms. Of these terms, the most important is the price paid by the acquiring firm for the firm acquired. Factors that influence this important aspect of a merger are now considered.

TERMS OF MERGERS

A merger carries potentialities for either favorable or adverse effects on earnings, market prices of shares, or both. Previous chapters have shown that investment decisions should be guided by the effects on market values and that these effects should in turn be determined

Effects on Price and Earnings

[3] J. K. Butters, J. Lintner, and W. L. Cary, *Effects of Taxation: Corporate Mergers* (Boston, Mass.: Division of Research, Graduate School of Business Administration, Harvard University, 1951).

by the effects on future earnings and dividends. These future events are difficult to forecast, however, so stockholders as well as management give considerable weight to the immediate effects of a contemplated merger on earnings per share. Directors of companies will often state, "I do not know how the merger will affect the market price of the shares of my company because so many forces influencing market prices are at work. But the effect on earnings per share can be seen directly."

An example will illustrate the effects of a proposed merger on earnings per share and thus suggest the kinds of problems that are likely to arise. Assume the following facts for two companies:

	Company A	Company B
Total earnings	$20,000	$50,000
Number of shares of common stock	5,000	10,000
Earnings per share of stock	$ 4.00	$ 5.00
Price/earnings ratio per share	15×	12×
Market price per share	$ 60.00	$ 60.00

Suppose the firms agree to merge, with B, the surviving firm, acquiring the shares of A by a one-for-one exchange of stock. The exchange ratio is determined by the respective market prices of the two companies. Assuming no increase in earnings, the effects on earnings per share are shown in the following tabulation:

	Shares of Company B owned after merger	Earnings per share	
		Before merger	After merger
A's stockholders	5,000	$4	$4.67
B's stockholders	10,000	5	4.67
Total	15,000		

Since total earnings are $70,000 and a total of 15,000 shares will be outstanding after the merger has been completed, the new earnings per share will be $4.67. Earnings will increase by 67 cents for A's stockholders, but they will decline by 33 cents for B's.

The effects on market values are less certain. If the combined companies sell at the 15 times price/earnings ratio of company A, the new market value per share of the new company will be $70. In this

Valued
by A

case, shareholders of both companies will have benefited. This result comes about because the combined earnings are now valued at a multiplier of 15, whereas prior to the merger a portion of the earnings was valued at a multiplier of 15 and a portion valued at a multiplier of 12.

If, on the other hand, the earnings of the new company are valued at B's multiplier of 12, the indicated market value of the shares will be $56. The shareholders of each company will have suffered a $4 dilution in market value.

Valued by B

Because the effects on market value per share are less certain than those on earnings per share, the impact on earnings per share tends to be given greater weight in merger negotiations. Because of this, the following analysis also emphasizes effects on earnings per share, while recognizing that maximizing market value is the valid rule for investment decisions.

If the merger takes place on the basis of earnings, neither earnings dilution nor earnings appreciation will take place. This follows from the results shown below:

	Shares of Company B owned after merger	Earnings per old share	
		Before merger	After merger
A shareholders[4]	4,000	$4	$4
B shareholders	10,000	5	5
Total	14,000		

It is clear that the equivalent earnings per share after the merger are the same as before the merger. The effects on market values will depend upon whether the 15-times multiplier of A or the 12-times multiplier of B prevails.

Of the numerous factors affecting the valuation of the constituent companies in a merger, all must ultimately be reflected in the earnings per share or market price of the companies. Hence, all the effects

---

[4] Based on earnings, the exchange ratio is 4:5; that is, company A's shareholders receive four shares of B stock for each five shares of A stock they own. Earnings per share of the merged company is $5, but since A's shareholders now own only 80 percent of the number of their old shares, their equivalent earnings per *old* share is the same $4. For example, suppose one of A's stockholders formerly held 100 shares. He will own only 80 shares of B after the merger, and his total earnings will be $80 \times \$5 = \$400$. Dividing his $400 total earnings by the number of shares he formerly owned, 100, gives the $4 per *old* share.

on the earnings position or wealth position of stockholders are encompassed by the foregoing example. The discussion may, therefore, turn to a consideration of the factors that will influence the terms on which an acquisition or a merger is likely to take place. Both quantitative and qualitative factors receive consideration.

Quantitative Factors Affecting Terms of Mergers   Five factors have received the greatest emphasis in arriving at merger terms:

Earnings and growth rates
Dividends
Net current assets
Market values
Book values

Analysis is typically based on the per share values of the foregoing factors. The relative importance of each factor and the circumstances under which each is likely to be the most influential determinant in arriving at terms will vary. The nature of these influences is now described.

Earnings and Growth Rates   Both expected earnings and capitalization rates (P/E ratios) are important in determining the values that will be established in a merger. The analysis necessarily begins with historical data on the firms' earnings, whose past growth rates, future trends, and variability are important determinants of the earnings multiplier, or P/E ratio, that will prevail after the merger.

How future earnings growth rates affect the multiplier can be illustrated by extending the preceding example. First, we know that high P/E ratios are commonly associated with rapidly growing companies. Since company A has the higher P/E ratio, it is reasonable to assume that its earnings are expected to grow more rapidly than those of company B. Suppose A's expected growth rate is 10 percent and B's 5 percent. Looking at the proposed merger from the point of view of company B and its stockholders and assuming that the exchange ratio is based on present market prices, it can be seen that B will suffer a dilution in earnings when the merger occurs. However, B will be acquiring a firm with more favorable growth prospects; hence its earnings after the merger should increase more rapidly than before. In fact, the new growth rate may turn out to be a weighted average of the growth rates of the individual firms, weighted by their respective total earnings before the merger. In the example, the new expected growth rate is 6.43 percent.

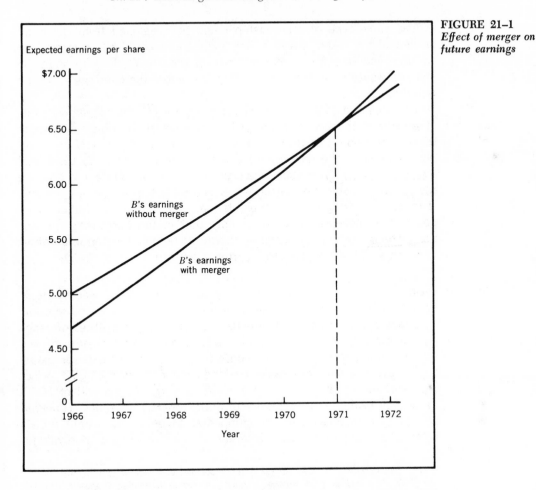

FIGURE 21–1
Effect of merger on future earnings

With the new growth rate it is possible to determine just how long it will take company B's stockholders to regain the earnings dilution. That is, how long will it take earnings per share to be back to where they would have been without the merger? This can be determined graphically from Figure 21–1.[5] Without the merger, B would have initial earnings of $5 a share, and these earnings would have grown at a rate of 5 percent a year. With the merger, earnings drop to $4.67 a share, but the rate of growth increases to 6.43 percent. Under these conditions, the earnings dilution is overcome after five years; from the fifth year on, B's earnings will be higher, assuming the merger is consummated.

[5] The calculation could also be made algebraically by solving for N in the following equation: $E_1(1 + g_1)^N = E_2(1 + g_2)^N$, where $E_1 =$ earnings before the merger, $E_2 =$ earnings after the merger, g_1 and g_2 are the growth rates before and after the merger, and N is the break-even number of years.

This same type of relationship could be developed from the point of view of the faster growing firm. Here there would be an immediate earnings increase but a reduced rate of growth. Working through the analysis would show the number of years before the earnings accretion would be eroded.

It is apparent that the critical variables are (1) the respective rates of growth of the two firms; (2) their relative sizes, which determine the actual amount of the initial earnings per share dilution or accretion, as well as the new weighted average growth rate; (3) the firms' P/E ratios; and (4) the exchange ratio. These factors interact to produce the resulting pattern of earnings per share for the surviving company. It is possible to generalize the relationships somewhat;[6] for our purposes, it is necessary simply to note that in the bargaining process the exchange ratio is the variable that must be manipulated in an effort to reach a mutually satisfactory earnings pattern.[7]

Dividends   Dividends, because they represent the actual income received by stockholders, may influence the terms of merger. However, as the material in Chapter 13 indicates, dividends are likely to have little influence on the market price of companies with a record of high growth and high profitability. For example, some companies, such as Laser Industries, have not yet paid cash dividends but command market prices representing a high multiple of current earnings. At the end of 1970, Laser was selling at a multiplier of approximately 40 times. However, for utility companies and for companies in industries where growth rates and profitability have declined, the dollar amount of dividends

---

[6] For a generalization, as well as for a more detailed examination of the interrelations, see D. F. Folz and J. Fred Weston, "Looking Ahead in Evaluating Proposed Mergers," *N.A.A. Bulletin* (April 1962).

[7] We should also mention at this point that certain companies, especially the "conglomerates," are reported to have used mergers to produce a "growth illusion" designed to increase the prices of their stocks. Whenever a high P/E company buys a low P/E ratio company, the earnings per share of the acquiring firm rise *because* of the merger. Thus, mergers can produce growth in reported earnings for the acquiring firm. This growth by merger, in turn, can cause the acquiring firm to keep its high P/E ratio. With this ratio the conglomerate can seek out new low P/E merger candidates and, thus, continue to obtain growth through mergers. The chain is broken if (1) the rate of merger activity slows, or (2) the P/E ratio of the acquiring firm falls. In 1968 and 1969 several large conglomerates reported profit declines caused by losses in certain of their divisions. This reduced the growth rate in EPS, which in turn led to a decline in the P/E ratio. A change in tax laws and antitrust suits against some conglomerate mergers also made it more difficult to consummate favorable mergers. All of these factors, along with tight money and depressed conditions in some industries, caused a further reduction in the P/E ratio and compounded these firms' problems. The net result was a drastic revaluation of conglomerate share prices, with such former favorites as LTV falling from a high of $169 to $11, and Litton Industries from $115 to $16.

paid may have a relatively important influence on the market price of the stock. Dividends may therefore influence the terms on which these companies would be likely to trade in a merger.[8]

Market Values

The price of a firm's stock reflects expectations about its future earnings and dividends, so one might expect current market values to have a strong influence on the terms of a merger. However, one could predict that the value placed on a firm in an acquisition is likely to exceed its current market price for a number of reasons. (1) If the company is in a depressed industry, its stockholders are likely to overdiscount the dismal outlook for the company; this will result in a very low current market price. (2) The prospective purchaser may be interested in acquiring the company for the contribution that it may make to the acquiring company. Thus, the acquired company is worth more to an informed purchaser than it is in the general market. (3) Stockholders are offered more than current market prices for their stock as an inducement to sell.

Book Value Per Share

Book values are now generally considered to be relatively unimportant in determining the value of a company, as they merely represent the historical investments that have been made in the company. These historical investments may have little relation to current values or prices. At times, however, especially when book values substantially exceed market values, they may well have an impact on merger terms. The book value is an index of the amount of physical facilities made available in the merger. Despite a past record of low earning power, it is always possible that, under effective management, a firm's assets may once again achieve normal earning power. If this is the case, the market value of the company will rise. Because of the potential contribution of physical properties to improved future earnings, book values may have an important influence on actual merger or acquisition terms.

Net Current Assets Per Share

Net current assets (current assets minus current liabilities) per share are likely to have an influence on merger terms because they represent the amount of liquidity that may be obtained from a company in a merger. In the postwar textile mergers, net current assets were very high, and this was one of the characteristics making them attractive

---

[8] If a company that does not pay dividends on its stock is seeking to acquire a firm whose stockholders are accustomed to receiving dividends, the exchange can be on a convertibles for common stock basis. This will enable the acquired firms' stockholders to continue receiving income.

to the acquiring firms. By buying a textile company, often with securities, an acquiring company was in a position to look for still other merger candidates, paying for the new acquisition with the just-acquired liquidity. In this same connection, if the acquired company is debt-free, the acquiring firm may be able to borrow the funds required for the purchase, using the acquired firm's assets and earning power as security for the loan.

Relative Importance of Quantitative Factors Attempts have been made to determine statistically the relative weights assigned to each of these factors in actual merger cases. However, these attempts have been singularly unsuccessful—in one case, one factor seems to dominate, in another some other determinant appears to be most important. This absence of consistent patterns among the quantitative factors suggests that qualitative forces are also at work, and we now turn our attention to these more nebulous variables.

Qualitative Influences Sometimes the most important influence on the terms of a merger is a business consideration not reflected at all in historical quantitative data. A soundly conceived merger is one in which the combination produces what may be called a *synergistic,* or "two-plus-two-equals-five" effect. By the combination, more profits are generated than could be achieved by the individual firms operating separately.

To illustrate, in the merger between Merck and Company and Sharp and Dohme, it was said that each company complemented the other in an important way. Merck had a strong reputation for its research organization. Sharp and Dohme had a most effective sales organization. The combination of these two pharmaceutical companies added strength to both. Another example is the merger in late 1954 between Carrier Corporation and Affiliated Gas Equipment, Inc. The merger enabled the combined company to provide a complete line of air-conditioning and heating equipment. The merger between Hilton Hotels and Statler Hotels led to economies in the purchase of supplies and materials. One Hilton executive estimated that the savings accruing simply from the combined management of the Statler Hotel in New York and Hilton's New York Hotel amounted to $700,000 a year. The bulk of the savings were in laundry, food, advertising, and administrative costs.

The qualitative factors may also reflect other influences. The merger or acquisition may enable one company to obtain general management ability that it lacks but which the other company possesses. Another factor may be the acquisition of a technically competent scientific or engineering staff. One of the companies may have fallen behind in the technological race and may need to combine with another company if it expects to catch up at all. In such a situation, the company lacking the technical competence possessed by the other firm may be willing to pay a substantial premium over previous levels of earnings, dividends, or market or book values.

The purpose of the merger may be to develop a production capability a firm does not possess. Some firms are strong in producing custom-made items with high-performance characteristics, yet these firms, on entering new markets, must make use of mass-production techniques. If the firm has had no experience in mass-production techniques, this skill may have to be obtained by means of a merger. The firm may perhaps need to develop an effective sales organization. For example, some of the companies previously oriented to the defense market, such as the aircraft companies, found that they had only a limited industrial sales organization; merger was the solution to the problem.

The foregoing are the kinds of qualitative considerations that may have an overriding influence on the actual terms of merger, and the values of these contributions are never easy to quantify. The all-encompassing question, of course, is how these factors will affect the contribution of each company to future earnings per share in the combined operation. The historical data and the qualitative considerations described, in addition to judgment and bargaining, combine to determine merger terms.

After merger terms have been agreed upon, the financial manager must be familiar with the principles for recording the financial results of the merger and for reflecting the initial effect on the earnings of the surviving firm. This section deals with these matters. **ACCOUNTING POLICIES IN MERGERS[9]**

The financial statements of the survivor in a merger must follow the regulations and supervision of the Securities and Exchange Commission. The SEC's requirements follow the recommendations of professional accounting societies on combinations, but interpretations of actual situations require considerable financial and economic analysis.

On August 2, 1970, the eighteen-member Accounting Principles Board (APB) of The American Institute of Certified Public Accountants issued Opinion 16, dealing with guidelines for corporate mergers, and Opinion 17, dealing with goodwill arising from mergers. The recommendations, effective October 31, 1970, modify and elaborate previous pronouncements on the "pooling of interests" and "purchase" methods of accounting for business combinations. Six broad tests are to be

---

[9] The material in this section is rather technical and is generally covered in accounting courses. The section may be omitted and the reader may skip to the section on holding companies without loss of continuity.

used to determine whether the conditions for the pooling of interests treatment are met. If all of these conditions are met, the pooling of interests method *must* be employed.

1. The acquired firm's stockholders maintain an ownership position in the surviving firm.

2. The basis for accounting for the assets of the acquired entity is unchanged.

3. Independent interests are combined; each entity had autonomy for two years prior to the initiation of the plan to combine; no more than 10 percent ownership of voting common stock is held as intercorporate investments.

4. The combination is effected in a single transaction; contingent payouts are not permitted in poolings but may be used in purchases.

5. The acquiring corporation issues only common stock with rights identical to its outstanding voting common stock in exchange for substantially all of the voting common stock of the other company; "substantially" is defined as 90 percent with much detail provided on technicalities of measurement.

6. The combined entity does not intend to dispose of a significant portion of the assets of the combining companies within two years after the merger.

In contrast, a purchase involves (1) new owners, (2) a new basis for accounting for the assets of the acquired entity, and (3) possibility of an excess or deficiency of consideration given up in the acquisition of net assets.

The latter condition refers to the creation of goodwill. In a purchase, the excess of (or deficit over) the book value of net worth purchased is set up as goodwill, and capital surplus is increased (or decreased) accordingly. In a pooling of interests, any premium over book value is charged against capital surplus. As a consequence, the combined total assets after a pooling represents a simple sum of the asset contributions of the constituent companies.

In a purchase, if the acquiring firm pays more than the acquired net worth, to the extent appropriate, the excess is associated with tangible depreciable assets. Any excess not assignable to tangible assets gives rise to a goodwill account. The goodwill is also depreciable. However, goodwill written off is not deductible for tax purposes. The new recommendations require that goodwill be written off over some reasonable period no longer than forty years in length. This requires a writeoff of at least 2.5 percent per year of the amount of goodwill arising from a purchase. Therefore, if a merger is treated as a purchase, reported profits will be lower than if it is handled as a pooling of interests. This is one of the reasons that pooling has been employed. Another stimulus to pooling was the opportunity to dispose of assets acquired at depreciated book values, selling them at their current values and recording subsequent profits on sales of assets. APB No. 16 attempted to deal with this practice by the requirement that sales of major portions of assets are not to be contemplated for at least two years after the merger has taken place.

These general statements may be made more meaningful by concrete illustrations of first a purchase and then a pooling of interests.

The financial treatment of a purchase may best be explained by use of a hypothetical example. The Mammoth Company has just purchased the Petty Company under an arrangement known as a *purchase*. The facts are as given in Table 21–1, which also shows the financial treatment. The illustration conforms to the general nature of a purchase. Measured by total assets, the Mammoth Company is 20 times as large as Petty, while its total earnings are 15 times as large. Assume that the terms of the purchase will be one share of Mammoth for two shares of Petty, based on the prevailing market value of their shares of common stock. Thus, in terms of Mammoth's stock, Mammoth is giving to Petty's stockholders $30 of market value and $7 of book value for each share of Petty stock. Petty's market value is $30 a share and its book value is $3 a share. The total market value of Mammoth paid for Petty is $60,000. The goodwill involved may be calculated as follows:

Financial Treatment of a Purchase

Value given by Mammoth	$60,000
Net worth of Petty purchased	6,000
Goodwill	$54,000

The $54,000 goodwill represents a debit in the Adjustments column and is carried to the *pro forma* balance sheet. The *pro forma* balance sheet is obtained by simply adding the balance sheets of the constituent companies.

The other adjustments to complete the entry are described below:

Common stock, Petty	$ 1,000	
Retained earnings, Petty	5,000	
Goodwill	54,000	
Common stock, Mammoth		$ 4,000
Capital surplus, Mammoth		56,000

A total value of $60,000 has been given by Mammoth. This amount represents a payment of $1,000 for the common stock of Petty, $5,000 for the retained earnings, and $54,000 goodwill. The corresponding credit is the 1,000 shares of Mammoth given in the transaction at their par value of $4 a share, resulting in a credit of $4,000. Capital surplus of Mammoth is increased by $56,000. When these adjustments are carried through to the *pro forma* balance sheet, total assets are increased from the combined total of $210,000 by the $54,000 increase in goodwill; the result is new total assets of $264,000. Total tangible assets, however, still remain $210,000.

TABLE 21–1
Financial treatment of a purchase

	Mammoth Company	Petty Company	Adjustments Debit	Adjustments Credit	Pro forma balance sheet
Assets					
Current	$ 80,000	$ 4,000			$ 84,000
Other assets	20,000	2,000			22,000
Net fixed assets	100,000	4,000			104,000
Goodwill			$54,000		54,000
Total assets	$200,000	$10,000			$264,000
Liabilities and net worth					
Current liabilities	$ 40,000	$ 4,000			$ 44,000
Long-term debt	20,000				20,000
Common stock	40,000	1,000	1,000	$ 4,000	44,000
Capital surplus	20,000			56,000	76,000
Retained earnings	80,000	5,000	5,000		80,000
Total	$200,000	$10,000			$264,000

	Mammoth	Petty
Explanation		
Par value per share common stock	$4	$0.50
Number of shares outstanding	10,000	2,000
Book value per share	$14	$3
Total earnings	$30,000	$2,000
Earnings per share	$3	$1
Price/earnings ratio	20X	30X
Market value per share	$60	$30

The effects on earnings per share for stockholders in each company are now shown:

Total earnings	$32,000
Total shares	11,000
Earnings per share	$2.91
For Petty Shareholders	
New earnings per share[10]	$1.46
Before-purchase earnings per share	$1.00
Accretion per share	$0.46
For Mammoth Shareholders	
Before-purchase earnings per share	$3.00
New earnings per share	2.91
Dilution per share	$0.09

Total earnings represent the combined earnings of Mammoth and of Petty. The total shares are 11,000, because Mammoth has given one share of stock for every two shares of Petty previously outstanding. The new earnings per share are therefore $2.91. The calculation of earnings accretion or dilution proceeds on the same principles as the calculations set forth earlier in the chapter. The results require two important comments, however.

It will be noted that although the earnings accretion per share for Petty is $0.46, the earnings dilution per share for Mammoth is relatively small, only 9 cents per share. The explanation is that the size of Mammoth is large in relation to that of Petty. This example also illustrates a general principle—when a large company acquires a small one, it can afford to pay a high multiple of earnings per share of the smaller company. In the present example, the price/earnings ratio of Petty is 30, whereas the price/earnings ratio of Mammoth is 20. If the acquiring company is large relative to the acquired firm, it can pay a substantial premium and yet suffer only small dilution in its earnings per share.

It is, however, unrealistic to assume that the same earnings on total assets will result after the merger. After all, the purpose of the merger is to achieve something that the two companies could not have achieved alone. When in late 1953, Philip Morris & Company purchased Benson & Hedges, maker of Parliament, a leading filter-tip brand, it was buying the ability and experience of Benson & Hedges. By means of this merger, Philip Morris & Company was able to make an entry into the rapidly growing filter-cigarette business more quickly than it could otherwise have done. The combined earnings per share were likely to have been higher.

---

[10] Petty shareholders, after the one for two exchange, have only one half as many shares as before the merger. Therefore their earnings per *old* share are $2.91 ÷ 2 = $1.46. The example does not reflect the write-off of goodwill.

In the previous illustration, it will be noted that the earnings rate on the tangible assets of Mammoth is 15 percent and on the total assets of Petty is 20 percent. Let us now assume that the return on total tangible assets of the combined companies rises to 20 percent. With the same total shares of 11,000 outstanding, the new earnings per share will be $3.82. Thus there will be accretion of $2.82 for the Petty shareholders, a rise of almost three dollars per share. Here, however, there will be an accretion of 82 cents for the Mammoth shareholders as well.

Another general principle is illustrated. If the purchase of a small company adds to the earnings of the consolidated enterprise, earnings per share may increase for both participants in the merger. Even if the merger results in an initial dilution in earnings per share of the larger company, the merger may still be advantageous. The initial dilution in the earnings per share may be regarded as an investment. The investment will have a payoff at some future date in terms of increased growth in earnings per share of the consolidated company.

Treatment of Goodwill In a purchase, goodwill is likely to arise; since goodwill represents an intangible asset, its treatment is subject to the exercise of judgment. It will, therefore, be useful to set out a few generalizations on good practice with respect to the treatment of goodwill.

1. When goodwill is purchased, it should not be charged to surplus immediately on acquisition. Preferably, goodwill should be written off against income and should go through the income statement. Since goodwill is to be written off against income, it would not be appropriate to write it off entirely on acquisition, because an immediate write-off would be of such magnitude that distortion of earnings for that year would result.

2. The general view is not to write off purchased goodwill by charges to capital surplus. Purchased goodwill is supposed to represent, and to be reflected in, a future rise of income. It should be written off against income rather than against capital surplus. If goodwill is set up and capital surplus is created where no actual goodwill exists, it would be appropriate to write off such goodwill; such writing off, however, is more in the nature of correcting an error.[11]

3. When goodwill is purchased, an estimate should be made of its period of life. Annual charges, based on the estimated life of the good-

---

[11] W. W. Werntz, "Intangibles in Business Combinations," *Journal of Accountancy*, CIII (May 1957), pp. 47–48.

will, should then be made against income to amortize the goodwill over the estimated period of the usefulness of the goodwill purchased.

→4. Even though the life of intangibles does not appear to be limited, they still must be written off over a maximum of forty years.

When goodwill is purchased, it should be treated as the purchase of any other valid assets. It should be written off to the extent that the value represented by any part of goodwill has a limited life, as is likely to be the situation. In a free enterprise economy, the existence of high profits represented by superior earning power attracts additional resources into that line of business. The growth of capacity and the increase in competition are likely to erode the superior earning power over time.

When a business combination is a *pooling of interests* rather than a purchase, the accounting treatment is simply to combine the balance sheets of the two companies. Goodwill will not ordinarily arise in the consolidation.

Financial Treatment of Pooling of Interests

The financial treatment may be indicated by another example, which reflects the facts as they are set forth in Table 21–2. In order to focus on the critical issues, the balance sheets are identical in every respect. However, a difference in the amount and rate of profit (after interest) of the two companies is indicated.

Book value per share is $24. The amount of profit after interest and taxes is $40,000 for company A and $20,000 for company B. Earnings per share are therefore $8 and $4, respectively. The price/earnings ratio is 15 for A and 10 for B, so that the market price of stock for A is $120 and for B $40. The working capital per share is $10 in each instance. The dividends per share are $4 for A and $2 for B.

For the example, assume that the terms of the merger would reflect either earnings or market price per share. If the terms of merger are based on earnings, 15,000 shares of stock will be outstanding. Total earnings are $60,000. The number of shares of stock in the new company AB is 15,000; hence, earnings per share in the company will be $4. As the owners of company A receive two shares, they are receiving the equivalent of $8 per share of stock that they originally held. Stockholders of both A and B have experienced neither earnings dilution nor earnings accretion.

When the terms of exchange are based on market price per share, the terms of exchange are 3 to 1. The number of shares of stock outstanding increases to 20,000, so that earnings per share become $3. The stockholders in company A now each receive three shares of stock

TABLE 21-2 Financial treatment of pooling of interest

	A	B	Adjustments or ratios	New firm AB if exchange basis is 2/1	3/1
Current assets	$100,000	$100,000		$200,000	$200,000
Fixed assets	100,000	100,000		200,000	200,000
Total assets	$200,000	$200,000		$400,000	$400,000
Current liabilities	$ 50,000	$ 50,000		$100,000	$100,000
Long-term debt	30,000	30,000		60,000	60,000
Total debt	80,000	80,000		160,000	160,000
Common stock, par value $10	50,000	50,000	$ 50,000* 100,000†	150,000	200,000
Capital surplus	60,000	60,000	$ 50,000* 100,000†	70,000	20,000
Earned surplus	10,000	10,000		20,000	20,000
Total claims on assets	$200,000	$200,000		$400,000	$400,000
Number of shares of stock	5,000	5,000	1.0	15,000	20,000
Book value	$ 24	$ 24			
Amount of profit after interest and taxes	$ 40,000	$ 20,000	2.0	$ 60,000	$ 60,000
Earnings per share	$8	$4		4.0	3.0
Price/earnings ratio	15	10			
Market price of stock	$120	$40	3.0		
Working capital per share	$10	$10	1.0		
Dividends per share	$4	$2	2.0		
Exchange ratio No. 1—earnings basis	2/1	1/1	2/1		
Equivalent earnings per share	$8	$4			
Exchange ratio No. 2—price basis	3/1	1/1			
Equivalent earnings per share	$9	$3			

* = 2/1 ratio basis.   † = 3/1 ratio basis.

with earnings per share of $3. Nine dollars of earnings per original share represents an accretion of $1 for the stockholders of company A. The earnings per share of $3 for the stockholders of company B represents dilution of $1 a share.

The adjustment to common stock reflects the fact that, since more shares of $10 par value stock will be outstanding after the merger, the common stock account must rise to either $150,000 ($10 × 15,000 shares) or $200,000 ($10 × 20,000 shares). The capital surplus adjustment offsets the increase in the common stock account.

The general principle is that when terms of merger are based on the market price per share and the price/earnings ratios of the two companies are different, earnings accretion and dilution will occur. The company with a higher price/earnings ratio will attain earnings accretion; the company with the lower price/earnings ratio will suffer earnings dilution. If the sizes of the companies are greatly different, the effect on the larger company will be relatively small, whether in earnings dilution or in earnings accretion. The effect on the smaller company will be large.

HOLDING COMPANIES

In 1889, New Jersey became the first state to pass a general incorporation law permitting corporations to be formed for the sole purpose of owning the stocks of other companies. This law was the origin of the holding company. The Sherman Act of 1890, which prohibits combinations or collusion in restraint of trade, gave an impetus to holding company operations as well as to outright mergers and complete amalgamations, because companies could do as one company what they were forbidden to do, by the terms of the act, as separate companies.

Many of the advantages and disadvantages of holding companies are no more than the advantages and disadvantages of large-scale operations already discussed in connection with mergers and consolidations. Whether a company is organized on a divisional basis or with the divisions kept as separate companies does not affect the basic reasons for conducting a large-scale, multiproduct, multiplant operation. However, the holding company form of large-scale operations has different advantages and disadvantages from those of completely integrated divisionalized operations.

Advantages

Control with Fractional Ownership

Through a holding company operation a firm may buy 5, 10, or 50 percent of the stock of another corporation. Such fractional ownership may be sufficient to give the acquiring company effective working control or substantial influence over the operations of the company in which stock ownership has taken place. An article in the *New York Times* makes this point clearly.

Working control is often considered to entail more than 25 percent of the common stock, but it can be as low as 10 percent if the stock is widely distributed. One financier says that the attitude of management is more important than the number of shares owned, adding that "if they think you can control the company, then you do." In addition, control on a very slim margin can be held through friendship with large stockholders outside the holding company group.

Sometimes holding company operations represent the initial stages of the transformation of an operating company into an investment company, particularly when the operating company is in a declining industry. When the sales of an industry begin to fall off permanently and the firm begins to liquidate its operating assets, it may use these liquid funds to invest in industries having a more favorable growth potential. An illustration of this is provided by the same *New York Times* article.

Former investment banker Gordon W. Wattles, who holds many corporate directorships, is the architect of the pyramid built on Century Investors and Webster Investors. The former was once an aviation investment concern, while the latter began as a cigar maker.

Isolation of Risks Because the various operating companies in a holding company system are separate legal entities, the obligations of any one unit are separate from the obligations of the other units. Catastrophic losses incurred by one unit of the holding company system are therefore not transmitted as claims on the assets of the other units.

Although this is the customary generalization of the nature of a holding company system, it is not completely valid. In extending credit to one of the units of a holding company system, an astute financial manager or loan officer will look through the holding company veil and require a guarantee or a claim on the assets of all the elements in a complete holding company system. Therefore, to some degree, the assets in the various elements of a holding company are joined. The advantage remains to the extent that unanticipated catastrophies that may occur to one unit in a holding company system will not be transmitted to the other units.

Approval Not Required If a holding company group is seeking to obtain effective working control of a number of companies, it may quietly purchase a portion of the stock of the companies in which it is interested. This is a completely informal operation, and the permission or approval of the stockholders of the acquired company or companies is not required. Thus the guiding personalities in a holding company operation are not dependent upon negotiations and approval of the other interest groups in order to obtain their objectives.

Provided the holding company owns at least 80 percent of a sub-   *Disadvantages*
sidiary's voting stock, the Internal Revenue regulations permit the filing   *Partial*
of consolidated returns, in which case dividends received by the parent   *Multiple*
are not taxed. However, if less than 80 percent of the stock is owned,   *Taxation*
returns may not be consolidated, but 85 percent of the dividends
received by the holding company may be deducted. With a tax rate
of 48 percent, this means that the effective tax on intercorporate dividends is 7.2 percent. This partial double taxation somewhat offsets
the benefits of holding company control with limited ownership, but
whether the penalty of 7.2 percent of dividends received is sufficient
to offset other possible advantages is a matter that must be decided
in individual situations.[12]

While pyramiding magnifies profits if the operations are successful,   *Risks of*
as was seen in the financial leverage analysis, it also magnifies   *Excessive*
losses. The greater the degree of pyramiding, the greater the degree   *Pyramiding*
of risk involved for any degree of fluctuations in sales or earnings
of the company. This is one of the potential disadvantages of pyramiding operations through holding companies.

In the case of a holding company operation that falls into disfavor   *Ease of*
with the U.S. Department of Justice, it is relatively easy to require   *Enforced*
dissolution of the relationship by disposal of stock ownership. A clear   *Dissolution*
case in point is the recent requirement that du Pont dispose of its
23 percent stock interest in General Motors Corporation. The acquisition took place in the early 1920s. Because there was no fusion between the corporations, there were no difficulties, from an operating
standpoint, in requiring the separation of the two companies. However,
if complete amalgamation had taken place, it would have been much
more difficult to break up the company after a lapse of so many years.

The problem of excessive leverage is worthy of further note, for the   *Leverage in*
degree of leverage in certain past instances has been truly stagger-   *Holding*
ing. For example, in the 1920s, Samuel Insull and his group controlled   *Companies*
electric utility operating companies at the bottom of a holding company
pyramid by a 1/20 of 1 percent investment. As a ratio, this represents
1/2000. In other words, $1 of capital at the top holding company
level controlled $2,000 of assets at the operating level. A similar situa-

---

[12] The 1969 Tax Reform Law also empowers the Internal Revenue Service to prohibit the
deductibility of debt issued to acquire another firm where the following conditions hold:
(1) the debt is subordinated to a "significant portion" of the firm's other creditors, (2)
the debt is convertible or has warrants attached, (3) the debt/assets ratio exceeds 67
percent, and (4) on a *pro forma* basis the times interest-earned ratio is less than 3.
The IRS can use discretion in invoking this power.

tion existed in the railroad field. It has been stated that Robert R. Young, with an investment of $254,000, obtained control of the Allegheny system consisting of total operating assets of $3 billion.

The nature of leverage in a holding company system and its advantages and disadvantages are illustrated by the hypothetical example developed in Table 21–3. As in the previous examples, although this is a hypothetical case, it illustrates actual situations. One thousand dollars of class B common stock of holding company 2 controls $2 million of assets at the operating company level. Further leverage could, of course, have been postulated in this situation by setting up a third company to own the common stock B of holding company 2.

TABLE 21–3
Leverage in a holding company system

Holding company 2			
Common stock B of holding company 1	5,000	Debt	2,000
		Preferred stock	1,000
		Common stock: class A*	1,000
		Common stock: class B	1,000
Holding company 1			
Common stock B of operating company	100,000	Debt	50,000
		Preferred stock	10,000
		Common stock: class A*	30,000
		Common stock: class B	10,000
Operating company			
Total assets	2,000,000	Debt	1,000,000
		Preferred stock	150,000
		Common stock: class A*	650,000
		Common stock: class B	200,000

*Common stock A is nonvoting.

Table 21–4 shows the results of holding company leverage on gains and losses at the top level. In the first column it is assumed that the operating company earns 12 percent before taxes on its $2 million of assets, while in the second column it is assumed that the return on assets is 8 percent. The operating and holding companies are the same ones described in Table 21–3.

A return of 12 percent on the operating assets of $2 million represents a total profit of $240,000. The debt interest of $40,000 is deducted from this amount, and the 50 percent tax rate applies to the remainder. The amount available to common stock after payment of debt interest, preferred stock dividends, and an 8 percent return to the nonvoting common stock A is $40,500. Assuming a $40,000 divi-

TABLE 21–4
*Results of holding
company leverage on
gains and losses*

Assume that each company pays: 4% on debt
5% on preferred stock
8% on common stock A

	Earnings before taxes	
Operating Company	12%	8%
Amount earned	$240,000	$160,000
Less tax*	100,000	60,000
Available to meet fixed charges	140,000	100,000
Debt interest	40,000	40,000
Preferred stock	7,500	7,500
Common stock A	52,000	52,000
Total charges	99,500	99,500
Available to common B	40,500	500
Dividends to common B	40,000	500
Holding Company 1		
Amount earned	20,000	250
Less tax (0.5 × 0.15 × $18,000)*	1,350	0
Available to meet fixed charges	18,650	250
Debt interest	2,000	2,000
Preferred stock	500	500
Common stock A	2,400	2,400
Total charges	4,900	4,900
Available to common B	13,750	loss
Dividends to common B	10,000	
Holding Company 2		
Amount earned	5,000	
Less taxes (0.5 × 0.15 × $4,920)*	369	
Available to meet fixed charges	4,631	
Debt interest	80	
Preferred stock	50	
Common stock A	80	
Total	210	
Available to common B	4,421	
Percent return on common B	442%	

* Tax computed on earnings less interest charges at a 50 percent tax
rate. Since earnings are entirely in the form of inter-corporate dividends,
only 15 percent of the holding company's earnings are taxable.

dend payout, the amount earned on the assets of holding company 1 is $20,000. If the same kind of analysis was followed through, the amount available to the common stock B in holding company 2 would be $4,421. This return is on an investment of $1,000, representing a return on the investment in common stock B of holding company 2 of about 440 percent. The power of leverage in a holding company system can indeed be great.

On the other hand, if a decline in revenues caused the pretax earnings to drop to 8 percent of the total assets of the operating company, the results would be disastrous. The amount earned under these circumstances is $160,000. After deducting the bond interest, the amount subject to tax is $120,000, resulting in a tax of $60,000. The after-tax-but-before-interest earnings are $100,000. The total prior charges are $99,500, leaving $500 available to common stock B. If all earnings are paid out in dividends to common stock B, the earnings of holding company 1 are $250. This is not enough to meet the debt interest. The holding company system would be forced to default on the debt interest of holding company 1 and, of course, holding company 2.

This example illustrates the potentiality for tremendous gains in a holding company system. It also illustrates that a small decline in earnings on the assets of the operating companies would be disastrous.

Tender Offers In a tender offer, one party, generally a corporation seeking a controlling interest in another corporation, asks the stockholders of the firm it is seeking to control to submit, or "tender," their shares in exchange for a specified price. The price is generally stated as so many dollars per share of acquired stock, although it can be stated in terms of shares of stock in the acquiring firm. The tender offer is a direct appeal to stockholders, so the tender need not be cleared with the management of the target firm. Tender offers have been used for a number of years, but the pace greatly accelerated after 1965.

If one firm wishes to gain control over another, the acquiring firm typically approaches the to-be-acquired firm's management and seeks its approval of the merger. If approval cannot be obtained, the company wishing to gain control can appeal directly to stockholders by means of the tender offer, unless the management of the to-be-acquired firm holds enough stock to retain control. If the potential acquiring firm has reason to believe that the to-be-acquired firm's management will not approve the merger, it may use a tender offer without ever informing the to-be-acquired firm's management of its intentions. In this situation, the potential acquirer will frequently buy the stock of the acquired firm in the name of a stockbroker ("street name") to conceal its intentions. Because of the frequency of tender offers and because of the views of some that (1) the recent merger trend is leading to "too much concentration" in the economy and (2) the feeling that tender offers are somehow "unfair" to the managements of firms acquired through this vehicle, Congressional investigations were conducted during 1967 with the idea of obtaining information that could be used to legislate controls over the use of tender offers. A new law became effective on July 29, 1968, placing tender offers under full SEC jurisdiction. Disclosure requirements written into the statute include the following: (1) The acquiring firm must give thirty days' notice of its intentions to make the acquisition both to the management of the acquired firm and to the SEC. (2) When substantial blocks are purchased through tender offers (or through open market purchases—that is, on the stock exchange), the beneficial owner of the stock must be disclosed together with the name of the party putting up the money for the transaction.

The example of Tenneco's acquisition of Kern County Land Company illustrates many of these points. First, Kern was a relatively old, conservatively managed company whose assets consisted largely of oil properties and agricultural land together with some manufacturing subsidiaries. Many informed investors believed that Kern's assets had a potential long-run value in excess of its current market price. Occidental Petroleum, a relatively aggressive company, made an investigation of Kern's assets and decided to make a tender offer for the company. At that time, Kern's market price was about $60 a share, while the price Occidental decided to offer Kern's stockholders was $83.50 a share. According to Kern's management, Occidental's management got in touch with the former over a weekend and informed Kern that the tender offer would be made the following Monday.

Kern's management resisted the offer. Because the published statements of Occidental indicated that it felt Kern's undervalued position was partly the result of an unaggressive management, Kern's management could anticipate being replaced in the event that Occidental effected the takeover. One could anticipate that Kern's management would resist the takeover, and it did indeed. Kern's president wrote a letter to stockholders condemning the merger and published the letter as an advertisement in the *Wall Street Journal*. His position was that Kern's stock was indeed valuable, but it was worth more than had been offered by Occidental Petroleum.

How would Kern County's stockholders react to this exchange? In the first place, the stock had been selling at about $60 a share, and now they were offered $83.50 a share. One might anticipate that stockholders would accept the tender unless Kern's management could do something to keep the price above $83.50. What Kern did was to obtain "marriage proposals" from a number of other companies.

Kern's management reported to the newspapers—while Occidental's tender offer was still outstanding—that it had received a substantial number of proposals calling for the purchase of Kern's stock at a price substantially in excess of $83.50.

The offer Kern's management finally accepted—and presumably the one giving Kern's stockholders the highest price—was from Tenneco Corporation. Tenneco offered one share of a new $5.50 convertible preferred stock for each share of Kern's stock. The market value of this convertible preferred was estimated at the time of Tenneco's offer to be worth about $105 a share. Further, Kern's stockholders would not have to pay capital gains tax on this stock at the time of the exchange. (Had they accepted Occidental's offer, the difference between $83.50 and the cost of their stock would be taxable income to Kern's stockholders.) According to newspaper reports, Tenneco planned to keep Kern's existing management after the merger was completed.

The Kern-Tenneco merger was completed in the fall of 1967. Tenneco owns the Kern stock and is thus a holding company, with Kern being one of its operating subsidiaries.

SUMMARY Growth is vital to the well-being of a firm, for without it a business cannot attract able management because it cannot give men recognition in promotions and challenging creative activity. Mergers have played an important part in the growth of firms, and since financial managers are required both to appraise the desirability of a prospective merger and to participate in evaluating the respective companies involved in the merger, the present chapter has been devoted to background materials on merger decisions.

Terms of Mergers The most important term that must be negotiated in a merger arrangement is the price the acquiring firm will pay for the acquired business. Some of the factors that influence this decision are given below.

Earnings Present earnings, expected future earnings, and the effects of the merger on the rate of earnings growth of the surviving firm, are perhaps the most important determinants of the price that will be paid for a firm that is being acquired.

Market Prices Current market prices are the second most important determinant of prices in mergers.

Book Value Depending on whether or not asset values are at all indicative of the earning power of the merged firm, book values may exert an important influence on the terms of the merger.

Net current assets are an indication of the amount of liquidity being *Net Current* purchased in a merger, and this can be an important factor. *Assets*

The factors listed above are all *quantitative;* qualitative, or nonmeasurable, factors are sometimes the overriding determinant of merger terms. Qualitative considerations may suggest that *synergistic,* or "two-plus-two-equals-five," effects may be present to a sufficient extent to warrant paying more for the acquired firm than the quantitative factors would suggest.

A merger may be treated as either a *purchase* or a *pooling of interests.* *Accounting* In a purchase, a larger firm generally takes over a smaller one and *Policies and* assumes all management control. The amount actually paid for the *Mergers* smaller firm is reflected in the acquiring firm's balance sheet; if more was paid for the acquired firm than the book value of its assets, goodwill is reflected on the acquiring firm's financial statements. In a pooling of interests, the merged firms should be about the same size and both managements should carry on important functions after the merger, and common stock rather than cash or bonds should be used in payment. The total assets of the surviving firm in a pooling are equal to the sum of the assets of the two independent companies, so no goodwill is required to be written off as a charge against earnings.

In mergers, one firm disappears. However, an alternative is for one *Holding* firm to buy all or a majority of the common stock of another and *Companies* to run the acquired firm as an operating subsidiary. When this occurs, the acquiring firm is said to be a *holding company.* A number of advantages arise when a holding company is used:

1. It may be possible to control the acquired firm with a smaller investment than would be necessary if a merger were to occur.

2. Each firm in a holding company is a separate legal entity, and the obligations of any one unit are separate from the obligations of the other units.

3. Stockholder approval is required before a merger can take place. This is not necessary in a holding company situation.

There are also some disadvantages to holding companies, some of which are:

1. If the holding company does not own 80 percent of the subsidiary's stock and does not file consolidated tax returns, it is subject to taxes on 15 percent of the dividends received from the subsidiary.

2. The leverage effects possible in holding companies can subject the holding company to a great deal of risk.

3. The Antitrust Division of the U.S. Department of Justice can much more easily force the breakup of a holding company situation than it can the dissolution of two completely merged firms.

QUESTIONS   **21–1**   The number of mergers tends to fluctuate with business activity, rising when GNP rises and falling when GNP falls. Why does this relationship exist?

21–2   A large firm has certain advantages over a smaller one. What are some of the *financial* advantages of large size?

21–3   What are some of the potential benefits that can be expected by a firm that merges with a company in a different industry?

21–4   Mergers can often be important to rapidly growing firms. How?

21–5   Distinguish between a holding company and an operating company. Give an example of each.

21–6   Which appears to be more risky, the use of debt in the holding company's capital structure or the use of debt in the operating company? Why?

21–7   Is the public interest served by an increase in merger activity? Give arguments both pro and con.

21–8   Would the book value of a company's assets be considered the absolute minimum price to be paid for a firm? Why? Is there any value that would qualify as an absolute minimum?

21–9   Discuss the situation where one firm, Midwest Motors, for example, calls off merger negotiations with another, American Space Labs, because the latter's stock price is overvalued. What assumption concerning dilution is implicit in the above situation?

21–10   Thus far, many methods by which a company can raise additional capital have been discussed. Can a merger be considered a means of raising additional equity capital? Explain.

21–11   A particularly difficult problem regarding business combinations has been whether to treat the new company as a purchase or as a pooling of interests.

a) What criteria can be set down to differentiate between these two forms of business combinations?
b) Would you as a stockholder in one of the firms prefer a purchase or a pooling arrangement? Why?
c) Which combination would you prefer if you were a high-ranking manager in one of the firms?

21–12   Question 21–11 discusses purchases and pooling arrangements. Why is it important to make a distinction between these two combination forms?

21–13   Are the negotiations for merger agreements more difficult if the firms are in different industries or in the same industry? If they are about the same size or quite different in size? Why?

21–14   How would the existence of long-term debt in a company's financial structure affect its valuation for merger purposes? Could the same be said for any debt account regardless of its maturity?

21–15   During 1964–1965, the Pure Oil Company was involved in merger negotiations with at least three other firms. The terms of these arrangements varied from a transfer of stock to a direct cash purchase of Pure Oil. Discuss the relative advantages to a corporation of paying for an acquisition in cash or in stock.

21–16 In late 1968 the SEC and the New York Stock Exchange each issued sets of rulings on disclosure of information which, in effect, required that firms disclose the fact that they have entered into merger discussions as soon as they start such discussions. Since the previous procedure had been to delay disclosure until it was evident that there was a reasonably good expectation the merger under discussion would actually go through (and not to bring the matter up at all if the merger died in the early stages), it can safely be predicted that, in a statistical sense, a larger percentage of prospective mergers will be "abandoned" in the future than in the past.

a) Why do you suppose the new rulings were put into effect?
b) Will the new rulings have any adverse effects? Why?

21–1   Given the following balance sheets: **PROBLEMS**

Maxi Company
Consolidated balance sheet

Cash	$1,200	Borrowings	$ 900
Other current assets	900	Common stock	1,500
Net property	1,500	Surplus	1,200
Total assets	$3,600	Total claims on assets	$3,600

				Mini Company
Current assets	$300	Net worth	$600	*Balance sheet*
Net property	300			
Total assets	$600	Total net worth	$600	

a) The holding company, Maxi, buys the operating company, Mini, with "free" cash of $600. Show the new consolidated balance sheet for Maxi after the acquisition.
b) Instead of buying Mini, Maxi buys Midi Company with free cash of $900. The balance sheet of Midi follows:

				Midi Company
Current assets	$ 600	Borrowings	$ 600	*Balance sheet*
Net property	900	Net worth	900	
Total assets	$1,500	Total claims on assets	$1,500	

Show the new consolidated balance sheet for Maxi after acquisition of Midi.
c) What are the implications of your consolidated balance sheets for measuring the growth of firms resulting from acquisitions?

21–2   H Company is a holding company owning the entire common stock of Trite Company and Trivial Company. The balance sheet as of December 31, 1972, for each subsidiary is identical with the following one.

Current assets	$ 6,000,000	Current liabilities	$ 1,000,000	*Balance sheet*
Fixed assets, net	4,000,000	First mortgage bonds (8%)	2,000,000	*December 31, 1972*
		Preferred stock (6%)	2,000,000	
		Common stock	4,000,000	
		Surplus	1,000,000	
Total assets	$10,000,000		$10,000,000	

Each operating company earns $1,100,000 annually before taxes and before interest and preferred dividends. A 50 percent tax rate is assumed.

a) What is the annual rate of return on each company's net worth (common stock plus surplus)?

b) Construct a balance sheet for H Company based on the following assumptions: (1) The only asset of the holding company is the common stock of the two subsidiaries; this stock is carried at par (not book) value. (2) The holding company has $1,400,000 of 8 percent coupon debt and $2,600,000 of 6 percent preferred stock.

c) What is the rate of return on the book value of the holding company's common stock?

d) How could the rate of return in c be increased?

e) What investment is necessary to control the three companies under the assumptions of the conditions specified in b?

f) If ownership of 25 percent of the holding company's common stock ($4 million of common) could control all three firms, what percentage would this be of the total assets?

21–3 You are given the following data on two companies:

	Company A	Company B	Adjustments	Consolidated statement
Current assets	$ 60,000	$ 60,000		1. _____
Fixed assets	40,000	40,000		2. _____
Total assets	$100,000	$100,000		3. _____
Current liabilities	$ 30,000	$ 30,000		4. _____
Long-term debt	20,000	20,000		5. _____
Total debt, 5%*	$ 50,000	$ 50,000		6. _____
Common stock, par value $5	$ 25,000	$ 25,000	1. _____	7. _____
Capital surplus	20,000	20,000	2. _____	8. _____
Earned surplus	5,000	5,000	3. _____	9. _____
Total claims on assets	$100,000	$100,000		10. _____

			Ratios	
(1) Number of shares of stock	5,000	5,000		1. _____
(2) Book value per share	_____	_____	1. _____	2. _____
(3) Amount of profit before interest and taxes†	$ 32,500	$ 12,500		3. _____
(4) Earnings per share	_____	_____	2. _____	4. _____
(5) Price/earnings ratio	20	15		
(6) Market price of stock	_____	_____	3. _____	
(7) Working capital per share	_____	_____	4. _____	
(8) Dividends per share, 50% payout	_____	_____	5. _____	
(9) Exchange ratio	_____	_____	6. _____ (A/B)	
(10) Equivalent earnings per old share	_____	_____		

* Average rate on interest-bearing and noninterest-bearing debt combined.
† Assume a 50 percent tax rate.

a) What in your judgment would be a reasonable basis for determining the terms at which shares in company A and in company B would be exchanged for shares in the new AB company? What exchange ratio would you recommend and why?

b) Use the market price of stock relation as the basis for the terms of exchange of stock in the old company for stock in the new company (2 shares of AB for 1 share of A, or 1/2 share of AB for 1 share of B). Then complete all calculations for filling in all the blank spaces, including the adjustments for making the consolidated statement. Treat this problem as a situation that the SEC and accountants would refer to as a pooling of interests.

21–4 The Alpha Company has just purchased the Beta Company under an arrangement known as a purchase. The purchase was made by stock in a settlement based exactly on the indicated market prices of the two firms. The data on the two companies are given below.

a) Fill in the blank spaces and complete the Adjustments and *Pro Forma* Balance Sheet columns, and show the journal entries for the stock purchase. Give an explanation for your entries.

b) Calculate earnings dilution or accretion for both companies on the assumption that total earnings are unchanged.

c) Calculate the earnings dilution or accretion on the assumption that the return on combined tangible assets rises to 20 percent after interest and taxes.

d) Comment on your findings.

	Alpha	Beta	Adjustments	Pro forma balance sheet
Current assets	$ 900,000	$14,000		
Other assets	300,000	10,000		
Fixed assets	800,000	16,000		
Intangibles				
Total assets	$2,000,000	$40,000		
Current liabilities	$ 400,000	$16,000		
Long-term debt	300,000			
Common stock	400,000	4,000		
Capital surplus	300,000			
Retained earnings	600,000	20,000		
Total claims	$2,000,000	$40,000		
Par value	$ 8.00	$ 1.00		
Number of shares	————	————		
Total earnings available to common	$ 250,000	$16,000		
Book value	————	————		
Earnings per share	————	————		
Price/earnings ratio	10 times	25 times		
Market value per share	————	————		

21–5 Every merger agreement is subject to negotiation between the companies involved. One significant indicator of the compensation received by the acquired company is the respective market prices of the companies' stocks relative to the merger items. Some actual merger data are given below.

Calculate the percent premium or discount received by the acquired company, using market prices as the criteria. Compare the results of your calculations based on the stock prices of the two previous quarters with that of your results based on the prices immediately preceding the merger. Which is the proper measure of the actual discount or premium received: the one indicated by the earlier stock prices or the one indicated by the stock prices immediately preceding the merger? Explain.

	Company	Date	Terms	Market price two quarters before merger		Market price preceding merger	
				A	B	A	B
1 { A	Celanese Corporation	9/21/64	2 shares of Celanese for every 3 shares of Champlain				
B	Champlain Oil			62	34	67	42
2 { A	Cities Service Company	6/14/63	0.9 shares (2.25 pref.) for each Tenn. Corp. share (common)				
B	Tennessee Corporation			65	48	61	55
3 { A	Ford Motor Company	12/11/61	1 share of Ford for every 4 1/2 shares of Philco				
B	Philco Corporation			81	22	113	25
4 { A	General Telephone	3/5/59	Share for share basis				
B	Sylvania Electric			52	46	69	69

*T*HUS far the text has dealt with issues associated mainly with the growing, successful enterprise. Not all businesses are so fortunate, however, so we must examine financial difficulties, their causes, and their possible remedies. This material is significant for the financial manager of successful, as well as potentially unsuccessful, firms. The successful firm's financial manager must know his firm's rights and remedies as a creditor and must participate effectively in efforts to collect from financially distressed debtors. Conversely, the financial manager must know how to handle his own firm's affairs if financial difficulties arise. Often such understanding may mean the difference between loss of ownership of the firm and rehabilitation of the operation as a going enterprise.

The life cycle of an industry or firm is often depicted as an S-shaped curve, as shown in Figure 22–1. The figure represents a hypothetical life cycle of a representative firm. Although it is an oversimplification, it provides a useful framework for analysis. The hypothesis represented by the four-stage life-cycle concept is based on a number of assumptions. It assumes competent management in the growth periods and insufficient management foresight prior to the decline phase. Obviously, one of management's primary goals is to prolong phase *B* and completely forestall phase *D*, and a great many firms are apparently successful in these endeavors. **THE FIRM'S LIFE CYCLE**

If an industry experiences the period of decline, financial readjustment problems will arise, affecting most firms in the industry. In addition, specific events may result in business failure—for example, a prolonged strike, a fire not adequately covered by insurance, or a bad decision on a new product.

FIGURE 22–1
*Hypothetical life
cycle of a firm*

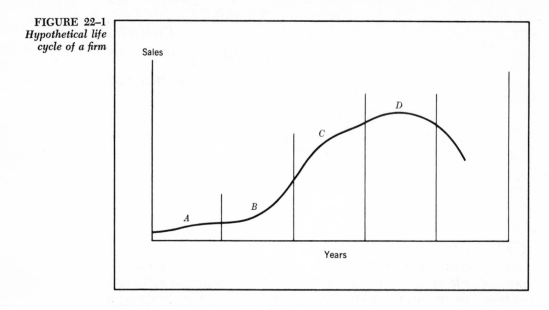

FAILURE   Although failure can be defined in several ways, according to various applications of the term, it does not necessarily result in the collapse and dissolution of a firm.

Economic Failure   Failure in an economic sense usually signifies that a firm's revenues do not cover costs. Another formulation states that a firm has failed if the rate of earnings on the historical cost of investment is less than the firm's cost of capital. According to still another possible definition, a firm can be considered a failure if its actual returns have fallen below expected returns. There is no consensus on the definition of failure in an economic sense.[1]

Financial Failure   Failure from a financial standpoint is a less ambiguous term than the concept of economic failure. Financial failure signifies insolvency; even here, however, two aspects are generally recognized.

1. A firm can be considered a failure if it is insolvent in the sense that it cannot meet its current obligations as they come due, even though its total assets may exceed its total liabilities.

---

[1] In still another economic sense, a firm that goes bankrupt may not be a failure at all. To illustrate, suppose someone starts a business to *attempt* to develop a product that, if successful, will produce very large returns and, if unsuccessful, will result in a total loss of invested funds. The entrepreneur *knows* that he is taking a risk but thinks the potential gains are worth the chance of loss. If the loss in fact results, then it was expected (in a probability sense).

② A firm is a failure or is bankrupt if its total liabilities exceed a fair valuation of its total assets. The "real" net worth of the firm is negative.

When we use the word "failure" hereafter, we include both of these aspects.

According to data compiled regularly by Dun & Bradstreet, Inc., the yearly rate of failure per 10,000 firms was about 50 immediately prior to World War II.[2] In the years immediately following World War II, the failure rate was low, about 20 to 30 per 10,000 firms, because of the vigorous rate of business activity in making up the war postponements of production. In recent years the failure rate has risen to 60 per 10,000 firms, reflecting the resumption of stronger competition between firms.

CAUSES OF FAILURE

The liability per failure averaged about $20,000 prewar but has risen to nearly $100,000 in recent years. The Dun & Bradstreet compilations also indicate that about 60 percent of these firms fail during the first five years of their lives, and another 25 percent fail during the second five years.[3]

Different studies assign the causes of failure to different factors. The Dun & Bradstreet compilations assign these causes as follows:

Cause of failure	Percentage of total
Neglect	4
Fraud	2
Disaster	1
Management incompetence	91
Unknown	2

A number of other studies of failures may be generalized into the following groupings:[4]

Cause of failure	Percentage of total
Unfavorable industry trends (secular)	20
Management incompetence	60
Catastrophes	10
Miscellaneous	10

[2] *The Failure Record through 1965* (New York: Dun & Bradstreet, Inc. 1966), p. 3.

[3] *The Failure Record,* p. 12.

[4] See studies referred to in A. S. Dewing, *The Financial Policy of Corporations* (New York: Ronald, 1953), vol. II, Chap. 28.

Both classifications presumably include the effects of recessions and place the resulting failures in the category of managerial incompetence. This method is logical—managements should be prepared to operate in environments in which recessions take place and should frame their policies to cope with downturns as well as to benefit from business upswings. Also, managements must anticipate unfavorable industry trends.

A number of financial remedies are available to management when it becomes aware of the imminence or occurrence of insolvency. These remedies are described in the remainder of this chapter.

EXTENSION AND COMPOSITION Extension and composition are discussed together because they both represent voluntary concessions by creditors. *Extension postpones* the date of required payment of past-due obligations. *Composition* voluntarily *reduces* the creditors' claims on the debtor. Both have the purpose of keeping the debtor in business and avoiding court costs. Although creditors absorb a temporary loss, the recovery is often greater than if one of the formal procedures had been followed, and the hope is that a stable customer will emerge.

Procedure A meeting of the debtor and his creditors is held. The creditors appoint a committee consisting of four or five of the largest creditors and one or two of the smaller ones. These meetings are typically arranged and conducted by *adjustment bureaus* associated with local credit managers' associations or by trade associations. The facts are presented in a general statement to the adjustment bureaus.

After a meeting is held at the adjustment bureau and it is judged that the case can be worked out, the bureau assigns investigators to make an exhaustive report. The bureau and the creditors' committee use the facts of the report to formulate a plan for adjustment of claims. Another meeting between the debtor and the creditors is then held in an attempt to work out an extension or a composition or a combination of the two. Subsequent meetings may be required to reach final agreements.

Necessary Conditions At least three conditions are usually necessary to make an extension or composition feasible:

1. The debtor is a good moral risk.
2. The debtor shows ability to make a recovery.
3. General business conditions are favorable to recovery.

An extension is preferred by creditors in that it provides for payment *Extension*
in full. The debtor buys current purchases on a cash basis and pays
off his past balance over an extended time. In some cases, creditors
may agree not only to extend time of payment but also to subordinate
existing claims to new debts incurred in favor of vendors extending
credit during the period of the extension. The creditors must have faith
that the debtor will solve his problems. Because of the uncertainties involved, however, creditors will want to exercise controls over the debtor
while waiting for their claims to be paid.

As examples of controls, the committee may insist that an assignment (turnover of assets to the creditors' committee) be executed, to be
held in escrow in case of default. Or if the debtor is a corporation,
the committee may require that stockholders transfer their stock certificates into an escrow until repayment as called for under the extension has been completed. The committee may also designate a representative to countersign all checks. Furthermore, the committee may
obtain security in the form of notes, mortgages, or assignment of accounts receivable.

In a composition a pro rata cash settlement is made. Creditors receive *Composition*
from the debtor in cash a uniform percentage of the obligations. The
cash received is taken as full settlement of the debt. The ratio may
be 10 percent or higher. Bargaining will take place between the debtor
and the creditors over the savings that result in avoiding certain costs
associated with the bankruptcy: costs of administration, legal fees,
investigators, and so on. In addition to financial considerations, the
debtor gains in that the stigma of bankruptcy is avoided, and thus
he may be induced to part with most of the savings that result from
avoiding bankruptcy.

Often the bargaining process will result in a compromise involving *Combination*
both an extension and a composition. For example, the settlement may *Settlement*
provide for a cash payment of 25 percent of the debt and six future
installments of 10 percent each. Total payment would thereby aggregate 85 percent. Installment payments are usually evidenced by notes.
Creditors will also seek protective controls.

The advantages of voluntary settlements are informality and simplicity. *Appraisal of*
Investigating, legal, and administrative expenses are held to a minimum. *Voluntary*
The procedure is the most economical and results in the largest return *Settlements*
to creditors.

One possible disadvantage is that the debtor is left in control of
his business. This situation may involve legal complications or erosion
of assets still operated by the debtor. However, numerous controls
are available to give the creditors protection.

A second disadvantage is that small creditors may take a nuisance role in that they may insist on payment in full. As a consequence, settlements typically provide for payment in full for claims under $50 or $100. If a composition is involved and all claims under $50 are paid, all creditors will receive a base of $50 plus the agreed-on percentage of the balance of their claims.

REORGA- Reorganization is a form of extension or composition of the firm's obli-
NIZATION gations. However, the legal formalities are much more involved than the procedures thus far described. Regardless of the legal procedure followed, the reorganization processes have several features in common.

1. The firm is insolvent either because it is unable to meet cash obligations as they come due or because claims on the firm exceed its assets. Hence, some modifications in the nature or amount of the firm's obligations must be made. A scaling down of terms or amounts must be formulated. This procedure may represent scaling down fixed charges or converting short-term debt into long-term debt.

2. New funds must be raised for working capital and for property rehabilitation.

3. The operating and managerial causes of difficulty must be discovered and eliminated.

The procedures involved in effecting a reorganization are highly legalistic and are, in fact, thoroughly understood only by attorneys who specialize in bankruptcy and reorganization. We shall therefore confine our remarks to the general principles involved.

A reorganization is, in essence, a composition, a scaling down of claims. In any composition, two conditions must be met: (1) the scaling down must be fair to all parties and (2) in return for the sacrifices, the likelihood of successful rehabilitation and profitable future operation of the firm must be feasible. These are the standards of *fairness* and *feasibility*, which are analyzed further in the next section.

FINANCIAL When a business becomes insolvent, a decision must be made whether
DECISIONS to dissolve the firm through liquidation or to keep it alive through
IN REORGA- reorganization.[5] Fundamentally, this decision depends upon a deter-
NIZATION mination of the value of the firm if it is rehabilitated versus the value of the sum of the parts if the firm is dismembered.

Liquidation values depend upon the degree of specialization of the

---

[5] This discussion is based on the excellent treatment by N. S. Buchanan, *The Economics of Corporate Enterprise* (New York: Holt, Rinehart and Winston, Inc., 1964), pp. 363–388.

capital assets used in the firm and, hence, their resale value. In addition, liquidation itself involves costs of dismantling, including legal costs. Successful reorganization also involves costs. Typically, better equipment must be installed, obsolete inventories must be disposed of, and improvements in management must be made.

Net liquidation values are compared with the value of the firm after reorganization, net of the costs of rehabilitation. The procedure that promises the higher returns to the creditors and owners will be the course of action favored. Often the greater indicated value of the firm in reorganization, compared with its value in liquidation, is used to force a compromise agreement among the claimants in a reorganization, even when they feel that their relative position has not been treated fairly in the reorganization plan.

In reorganizations both the SEC and the courts are called upon to determine the *fairness* and the *feasibility* of proposed plans of reorganization.[6] In developing standards of fairness in connection with such reorganizations, both the courts and the SEC have adhered to two court decisions which established precedent on these matters.[7]

The basic doctrine of fairness states that claims must be recognized in the order of their legal and contractual priority. Junior claimants may participate only to the extent that they have made an additional cash contribution to the reorganization of the firm. *Standards of Fairness*

The carrying out of this concept of fairness involves the following steps:

1. An estimate of future sales must be made.

2. An analysis of operating conditions must be made so that the future earnings on sales can be estimated.

3. A determination of the capitalization rate to be applied to these future earnings must be made.

4. The capitalization rate must be applied to the estimated future earnings to obtain an indicated value of the properties of the company.

5. Provision for distribution to the claimants must then be made.

The meaning and content of these procedures may best be set out by the use of an actual example of reorganization involving the Northeastern Steel Corporation. *Illustrative Case*

---

[6] The federal bankruptcy laws specify that reorganization plans be worked out by court-appointed officials and be reviewed by the Securities and Exchange Commission.

[7] *Case v. Los Angeles Lumber Products Co.*, 308 U.S. 106 (1939) and *Consolidated Rock Products Co. v. duBoise*, 213 U.S. 510 (1940). Securities and Exchange Commission, Seventeenth Annual Report, 1951 (Washington, D.C.: U.S. Government Printing Office), p. 130.

Table 22–1 gives the balance sheet of the Northeastern Steel Corporation as of March 31, 1957. The company had been suffering losses running to $2.5 million a year, and on February 1, 1957, it filed a petition for reorganization with a federal court. The court, in accordance with the law, appointed a disinterested trustee. On June 13, 1957, the trustee filed with the court a plan of reorganization, which was subsequently analyzed by the SEC.

TABLE 22–1
Northeastern Steel Corporation
Balance sheet
March 31, 1957
Amounts in millions

Current assets	$ 3.50
Net property	12.50
Miscellaneous assets	0.70
Total assets	$16.70
Accounts payable	$ 1.00
Taxes	0.25
Notes payable	0.25
Other current liabilities	1.75
4 ½% First-mortgage bonds, due 1970	6.00
6% Subordinated debentures, due 1975	7.00
Common stock ($1)	1.00
Paid-in capital	3.45
Earned surplus	(4.00)
Total liabilities and capital	$16.70

The trustee found that the company could not be internally reorganized, and he concluded that the only feasible program would be to combine Northeastern with an established producer of stainless and alloyed steel. Accordingly, the trustee solicited the interest of a number of steel companies. Late in March 1957, Carpenter Steel Company showed an interest in Northeastern. On June 3, 1957, Carpenter made a formal proposal to take over the $6 million of 4½ percent first-mortgage bonds of Northeastern, to pay $250,000 taxes owed by Northeastern, and to pay 40,000 shares of Carpenter Steel common stock to the company. Since the stock had a market price of $75 a share, the value of the stock was equivalent to $3 million. Thus, Carpenter was offering this sum, plus the $6 million takeover and the $250,000 taxes, a total of $9.2 million on assets that had a net book value of $16.7 million.

Trustee's Plan The trustee's plan, based on 40,000 shares at $75 equaling $3 million, is shown in Table 22–2. The total claims of the unsecured creditors equal $10 million. However, the amounts available total only $3 million. Thus, each claimant would be entitled to receive 30 percent before the adjustment for subordination. Before this adjustment, holders of notes payable would receive 30 percent of their claim of $250,000, or $75,000. However, the debentures are subordinated to *the notes payable,* so an additional $175,000 would be transferred to notes payable from the subordinated debentures. In the last column of Table 22–2, the dollar claims of each class of debt are restated in terms of the number of shares of Carpenter common stock received by each class of unsecured creditors.

TABLE 22–2
Northeastern Steel Corporation
Trustee's plan

Prior claims	Amount	Receives
Taxes	$ 250,000	Cash paid by Carpenter
First mortgage, 4 ½%, 1970	6,000,000	Same assumed by Carpenter

Trustees' plan for remainder of claims

Valuation based on 40,000 shares at $75 equals $3 million, or 30% of $10 million liabilities.

Claims	Amount	30 percent × amount of claim	Claim after subordination	Number of shares of common stock
Notes payable	$ 250,000	$ 75,000	$ 250,000	3,333
General unsecured creditors	2,750,000	825,000	825,000	11,000
Subordinated debentures	7,000,000	2,100,000	1,925,000	25,667
	$10,000,000	$3,000,000	$3,000,000	40,000

The Securities and Exchange Commission, in evaluating the proposal *SEC Evaluation* from the standpoint of fairness, made the following analysis. The SEC began with an evaluation of the prospective value of Northeastern Steel (Table 22–3). After a survey and discussion with various experts, they arrived at estimated sales of Northeastern Steel Corporation of $25 million a year. It was further estimated that the profit margin on sales would equal 6 percent, thus giving an indicated future earnings of $1.5 million a year.

The SEC analyzed price/earnings ratios for comparable steel companies and arrived at 8 times future earnings for a capitalization factor. Multiplying 8 by $1.5 million gave an indicated total value of the company of $12 million. Since the mortgage assumed by Carpenter Steel was $6 million, a net value of $6 million is left for the other claims. This value is exactly double that of the 40,000 shares of Carpenter Steel stock paid for the remainder of the company. Because the SEC felt that the value of these claims was $6 million rather than $3 million, the SEC concluded that the trustee's plan for reorganization did not meet the test of fairness. It will be noted that under both the trustee's plan and the SEC plan, the holders of common stock would receive nothing, while the holders of the first-mortgage bond were paid in full.

TABLE 22–3
Northeastern Steel Corporation
SEC evaluation of fairness

Valuation	
Estimated sales of Northeastern Steel Corp.	$25,000,000 per year
Earnings at 6% of sales	1,500,000
Price/earnings ratio of 8 times earnings	12,000,000
Mortgage assumed, $6,000,000	6,000,000
Net value	$ 6,000,000

Claims	Amount	Claim	Claim after sub-ordination
Notes payable	$ 250,000	$ 150,000	$ 250,000*
General unsecured creditors	2,750,000	1,650,000	1,650,000
Subordinated debentures (subordinate to notes payable)	7,000,000	4,200,000	4,100,000*
Totals	$10,000,000	$6,000,000	$6,000,000
Total available	6,000,000		
Percentage of claims	60%		

* Notes payable must be satisfied before subordinated debentures receive anything.

Because no better alternative offer could be obtained, the proposal of Carpenter Steel was accepted despite the SEC disagreement with the valuation. This example illustrates how the standard of fairness is actually applied in a reorganization plan.

Standard of Feasibility The primary test of feasibility is that the fixed charges on the income of the corporation after reorganization are amply covered by earnings or, if a value for a firm that is to be sold is established, that a buyer at that price can be found. Adequate coverage of fixed charges for a company that is to continue in operation generally requires an improvement in earnings or a reduction of fixed charges, or both.

Policies Required Among the actions that will have to be taken to improve the earning power of the company are the following:

1. Where the quality of management has been inefficient and inadequate for the task, new talents and abilities must be brought

into the company if it is to operate successfully subsequent to the reorganization.

2. If inventories have become obsolete to a considerable degree, the useless inventory should be disposed of and the operations of the company streamlined.

3. Sometimes the plant and the equipment of the firm need to be modernized before it can operate and compete successfully on a cost basis.

4. Reorganization may also require an improvement in production, marketing, advertising, and other functions, to enable the firm to compete successfully and earn satisfactory profits.

5. Sometimes it is necessary to develop new product activity of the firm so that it can move from areas where economic trends have become undesirable into areas where the growth and stability potential is greater.

Referring again to the Northeastern Steel Corporation example, the SEC observed that the reorganization involved taking over the properties of the Northeastern Steel Corporation by the Carpenter Steel Company. It judged that the direction and aid of the Carpenter Steel Company would remedy the production and operation deficiencies that had troubled Northeastern Steel. Whereas the debt-to-assets ratio of Northeastern Steel had become unbalanced, the Carpenter Steel Company went into the purchase with only a moderate amount of debt. After the consolidation had taken place, the total debt of Carpenter Steel was approximately $17.5 million compared with total assets of more than $63 million. Thus the debt ratio of 27 percent after the reorganization was not unreasonable. *Application of Feasibility Tests*

The net income after taxes of Carpenter Steel had been running at a level of approximately $6 million. The interest on the debt of Carpenter Steel would be $270,000 on the long-term debt and, taking other borrowings into account, would total a maximum of $600,000 a year. The $6 million profit after taxes would therefore provide a 10-times coverage of fixed charges; this exceeds the standard of 8 times set forth in Chapter 10.

Notice that the question of feasibility would have been irrelevant (from the standpoint of the SEC) had Carpenter Steel offered $3 million in cash rather than in stock. It is the SEC's function to protect the interests of Northeast Steel's creditors. Since they are being forced to take common stock in another firm, the SEC must look into the feasibility of the transaction. However, if Carpenter had made a cash offer, the feasibility of Carpenter's own operation after the transaction was completed would have been none of the SEC's concern. [Notice that the SEC feasibility study is much more important if a small, weak firm buys the assets of a reorganized firm for stock than if the purchase is made by a stronger firm.] Thus, the SEC would be more concerned with the feasibility of a takeover of Northeast by Wesbrig Corporation than it would be if General Motors made the takeover.

LIQUIDATION PROCEDURES Liquidation of a business takes place when the estimated value of the firm is greater "dead than alive."

Assignment is a liquidation procedure that does not go through the courts, although it can be used to achieve full settlement of claims on the debtor. *Bankruptcy* is a legal procedure carried out under the jurisdiction of special courts in which a business firm is formally liquidated and claims of creditors are completely discharged.

Assignment Assignment (as well as bankruptcy) takes place when the debtor is insolvent and the possibilities of restoring profitability so remote that the enterprise should be dissolved—that is, when the firm is "'worth more dead than alive." Assignment is a technique for liquidating a debt and yielding a larger amount to the creditors than is likely to be achieved in formal bankruptcy.

Technically, there are three types of assignments:

1. Common law assignment
2. Statutory assignment
3. Assignment plus settlement

Common Law Assignment The common law provides for an assignment whereby a debtor transfers his title to assets to a third person, known as an assignee or a trustee. The trustee is instructed to liquidate the assets and to distribute the proceeds among the creditors on a pro rata basis.

Typically, an assignment is conducted through the adjustment bureau of the local credit managers' association. The assignee may liquidate the assets through what is known as a bulk sale, which is a public sale through an auctioneer. The auction is preceded by sufficient advertising so that there will be a number of bids at the auction. Liquidation may also be by a piecemeal auction sale conducted on the premises of the assignor by a competent licensed auctioneer, rather than by a bulk sale. On-premises sales are particularly advantageous in the liquidation of large machine shops or manufacturing plants.

The common law assignment, as such, does not discharge the debtor from his obligations. If a corporation goes out of business and does not satisfy all its claims, there will still be claims against the corporation, but in effect the corporation has ceased to exist. The people who have been associated with the corporation can then proceed to organize another corporation free of the debts and obligations of the previous corporation. There is always the danger, however, that the court may look through the corporate veil and hold the individuals responsible. It is therefore usually important to obtain a statement from creditors that claims have been completely settled. Such a statement is, of course, even more important for a nonincorporated business.

Although a common law assignment has taken place, the assignee in drawing up checks paying the creditors, may write on the check the requisite legal language to make the payment a complete discharge of the obligation. There are technical legal requirements for this process, which are best carried out with the aid of a lawyer, but essential is a statement that endorsement of this check represents acknowledgment of full payment for the obligation.

Statutory assignment is similar in concept to common law assignment. Legally, it is carried out under state statutes regulating assignment; technically, it requires more formality. The debtor executes an instrument of assignment, which is recorded. This recordation provides notice to all third parties. A court is utilized: the court appoints an assignee and supervises the proceedings, including the sale of the assets and distribution of the proceeds. As in the common law assignment, the debtor is not automatically discharged from the balance of his obligations. He can discharge himself, however, by printing the requisite statement on the settlement checks.

Statutory Assignment

Both the common law assignment and the statutory assignment may take place with recognition and agreement beforehand with the creditors that the assignment will represent a complete discharge of obligation. Normally, the debtor will communicate with the local credit managers' association. The adjustment bureau of the association will arrange a meeting of all the creditors. A trust instrument of assignment is drawn up. The adjustment bureau is designated to dispose of the assets, which are sold through regular trade channels, by bulk sales, by auction, or by private sales. The creditors will, typically, leave all responsibility for the liquidation procedure with the assignee, the adjustment bureau of the local credit managers' association.

Assignment Plus Settlement

Having disposed of the assets and obtained funds, the adjustment bureau will then distribute the dividends pro rata among the creditors, with the designation on the check that this is in full settlement of the claims on the debtor. Ordinarily, a release is not agreed upon prior to the execution of the assignment. After full examination of the facts, the creditors' committee will usually make a recommendation for the granting of a release following the execution of the assignment. If releases are not forthcoming, the assignor may, within four months of the date of the assignment, file a voluntary petition in bankruptcy. In this event the assignment is terminated and the assignee must account and report to the trustee and the referee in bankruptcy, and deliver to the trustee all assets in the estate (usually by that time assets have been reduced to cash).

Advantages   Assignment has substantial advantages over bankruptcy. Bankruptcy through the courts involves much time, legal formalities, and accounting and legal expenses. An assignment saves the substantial costs of bankruptcy proceedings, and it may save time as well.

Furthermore, an assignee usually has much more flexibility in disposing of property than does a bankruptcy trustee. He may be more familiar with the normal channels of trade. Since he takes action much sooner, before the inventories become more obsolete, he may achieve better results.

BANKRUPTCY   Although the bankruptcy procedures leave room for improvement, the Federal Bankruptcy Acts themselves represent two main achievements. (1) They provide safeguards against fraud by the debtor during liquidation and, simultaneously, they provide for an equitable distribution of the debtor's assets among his creditors. (2) Insolvent debtors may discharge all their obligations and start new businesses unhampered by a burden of prior debt.

Prerequisites for   A voluntary petition of bankruptcy may be filed by the debtor. But
Bankruptcy   if an involuntary petition of bankruptcy is to be filed, three conditions must be met.

1. The total debts of the insolvent must be $1,000 or more.

2. If the debtor has less than 12 creditors, any one of the creditors may file the petition if the amount owed him is $500 or more. If there are 12 or more creditors, the petition must be signed by three or more creditors with provable total claims of $500 or more.

3. Within the four preceding months, the debtor must have committed one or more of the six acts of bankruptcy.

Acts of   The six acts of bankruptcy can be summarized briefly.
Bankruptcy

1. Conceal-   Concealment constitutes hiding assets with intent to defraud creditors.
ment or
Fraudulent   Fraudulent conveyance is transfer of property to a third party without
Conveyance   adequate consideration and with intent to defraud creditors.

A preferential transfer is the transfer of money or assets by an in- ② *Prefer-*
solvent debtor to a creditor, giving the creditor a greater portion of *ential*
his claim than other creditors would receive on liquidation.   *Transfer*

If an insolvent debtor permits any creditor to obtain a lien on his ③ *Legal Lien*
property and fails to discharge the lien within 30 days, or if the debtor *or Distraint*
permits a landlord to distrain (to seize property that has been pledged
as security for a loan) for nonpayment of rent, he has committed
an act of bankruptcy. In this way creditors, by obtaining a lien, may
force an insolvent but obdurate debtor into bankruptcy.

If a debtor makes a general assignment for the benefit of his creditors, ④ *Assignment*
an act of bankruptcy likewise exists. Again, this enables creditors who
have become distrustful of the debtor in the process of assignment
to transfer the proceedings to a bankruptcy court. As a matter of
practice, typically in common law assignments, creditors will require
that a debtor execute a formal assignment document to be held in
escrow, to become effective if informal and voluntary settlement negotiations fail. If they do fail, the assignment becomes effective and
the creditors have their choice of throwing the case into the bankruptcy
court.

If an insolvent debtor permits the appointment of a receiver or a ⑤ *Appointment*
trustee to take charge of his property, he has committed an act of *of Receiver*
bankruptcy. In this event, the creditors may remove a receivership *or Trustee*
or an adjustment proceeding to a bankruptcy court.

If the debtor admits in writing his inability to pay his debts and his ⑥ *Admission*
willingness to be judged bankrupt, he has committed an act of bank- *in Writing*
ruptcy. The reason for this sixth act of bankruptcy is that debtors are
often unwilling to engage in voluntary bankruptcy because it carries
some stigma of avoidance of obligations. Sometimes therefore, negotiations with a debtor reach an impasse. Admission in writing is one
of the methods of forcing the debtor to commit an act of bankruptcy
and of moving the proceedings into a bankruptcy court, where the
debtor will no longer be able to reject all plans for settlement.

On the filing of the petition of involuntary bankruptcy, a subpoena *Adjudication and*
is served on the debtor. There is usually no contest by the debtor, *the Referee*
and the court adjudges him bankrupt. On adjudication, the case is
transferred by the court to a referee in bankruptcy. A referee in bankruptcy is generally a lawyer appointed for a specified term by the
judge of the bankruptcy court to act in his place after adjudication.
    In addition, on petition of the creditors, the referee in voluntary

proceedings, or the judge in involuntary proceedings, may appoint a receiver, who serves as the custodian of the property of the debtor until the appointment of a trustee. This arrangement was developed because a long period elapses between the date of the filing of a petition in bankruptcy and the election of a trustee at the first creditors' meeting. To safeguard the creditors' interest during this period, the court, through either the referee or the judge, may appoint a receiver in bankruptcy. The receiver in bankruptcy has full control until the trustee is appointed.

First Creditors' Meeting: Election of Trustee   At the first meeting of the creditors, a trustee is elected. If different blocks of creditors have a different candidate for trustee, the election may become drawn out. Frequently, the trustee will be the adjustment bureau of the local credit managers' association. At this first meeting the debtor may also be examined for the purpose of obtaining necessary information.

Subsequent Procedure   The trustee and the creditors' committee act to convert all assets into cash. The trustee sends a letter to people owing the debtor money, warning that all past-due accounts will result in instant suit if immediate payment is not made, and if necessary he will institute such suit. Appraisers are appointed by the courts to set a value on the property. With the advice of the creditors' committee and by authorization of the referee, the merchandise is sold by approved methods. As in an assignment, auctions may be held.

Property may not be sold without consent of the court at less than 75 percent of the appraised value that has been set by the appraisers appointed by the court. Cash received from the disposition of the property is used first to pay all expenses associated with the proceedings of the bankruptcy. The trustee will then pay any remaining funds to the claimants.

Final Meeting and Discharge   When the trustee has completed his liquidation and has sent out all the claimants' checks, he makes an accounting, which is reviewed by the creditors and the referee. After all the payments have been made by the trustee, the bankruptcy is discharged and the debtor is released from all debts.

If the hearings before the referee indicate the probability of fraud, the FBI is required to undertake an investigation. If fraud was not committed and the bankruptcy is discharged, the debtor is again free to engage in business. Since business is highly competitive in many fields, he will probably not have great difficulty in obtaining credit again. Under the National Bankruptcy Act, however, a debtor may not be granted a discharge more often than at six-year intervals.

The order of priority of claims in bankruptcy is as follows:

1. Costs of administrating and operating the bankrupt estate.

2. Wages due workers if earned within three months prior to the filing of the petition in bankruptcy. The amount of wages is not to exceed $600 a person.

3. Taxes due the United States, state, county, or any other governmental agency.

4. Secured creditors with the proceeds of the sale of specific property pledged for a mortgage.

5. General or unsecured creditors. This claim consists of the remaining balances after payment to secured creditors from the sale of specific property, and includes trade credit, bank loans, and debenture bonds. Holders of subordinated debt fall into this category, but they must turn over required amounts to the holders of senior debt.

6. Preferred stock.

7. Common stock.

Priority of Claims on Distribution of Proceeds of a Bankruptcy

To illustrate how this priority of claims works out, let us take a specific example. The balance sheet of the bankrupt firm is shown in Table 22–4. Assets total $90 million. The claims are those indicated on the right-hand side of the balance sheet. It will be noted that the subordinated debentures are subordinated to the notes payable to commercial banks.

TABLE 22–4
Bankrupt firm balance sheet

Current assets	$80,000,000	Accounts payable	$20,000,000
Net property	$10,000,000	Notes payable (due bank)	10,000,000
		Accrued wages, 1,400 @ $500	700,000
		U.S. taxes	1,000,000
		State and local taxes	300,000
		Current debt	$32,000,000
		First mortgage	$ 6,000,000
		Second mortgage	1,000,000
		Subordinated debentures*	8,000,000
		Long-term debt	$15,000,000
		Preferred stock	2,000,000
		Common stock	26,000,000
		Capital surplus	4,000,000
		Earned surplus	11,000,000
		Net worth	$43,000,000
	$90,000,000	Total	$90,000,000

* Subordinated to $10 million notes payable to the First National Bank.

TABLE 22–5
*Bankrupt firm
order of
priority of claims*

Distribution of proceeds on liquidation

1. Proceeds of sale of assets	$33,000,000
2. Fees and expenses of administration of bankruptcy	$ 6,000,000
3. Wages due workers earned three months prior to filing of bankruptcy petition	700,000
4. Taxes	1,300,000
	$25,000,000
5. First mortgage, paid from net property	5,000,000
6. Available to general creditors	$20,000,000

Claims of general creditors	Claim (1)	Application of 50 percent (2)	After subordination adjustment (3)	Percentage of original claims received (4)
Unsatisfied portion of first mortgage	$ 1,000,000	$ 500,000	$ 500,000	92
Unsatisfied portion of second mortgage	1,000,000	500,000	500,000	50
Notes payable	10,000,000	5,000,000	9,000,000	90
Accounts payable	20,000,000	10,000,000	10,000,000	50
Subordinated debentures	8,000,000	4,000,000	0	0
	$40,000,000	$20,000,000	$20,000,000	56

Notes: 1. Column (1) is the claim of each class of creditor. Total claims equal $40 million.
2. From line 6 in the top part of the table we see that $20 million is available. This sum, divided by the $40 million of claims, indicates that general creditors will receive 50 percent of their claims. This is shown in column (2).
3. The debentures are subordinated to the notes payable. Four million dollars is transferred from debentures to notes payable in column (3).
4. Column (4) shows the results of dividing the column (3) figure by the original amount given in Table 22–4, except for first mortgage, where $5 million paid on sale of property is included. The 56 percent total figure includes the first mortgage transactions, that is, ($20,000,000 + $5,000,000) ÷ ($40,000,000 + $5,000,000) = 56%.

Now assume that the assets of the firm are sold. The following amounts are realized on liquidation:

Current assets	$28,000,000
Net property	5,000,000
Total	$33,000,000

The order of priority of payment of claims is shown by Table 22–5. Fees and expenses of administration typically are about 20 percent of gross proceeds. In this example they are assumed to be $6 million.

Next 'in priority are wages due workers, which total $700,000. The total amount of taxes to be paid is $1.3 million. Thus far the total paid from the $33 million is $8 million. The first mortgage is then paid from the net proceeds of $5 million from the sale of fixed property, leaving $20 million available to the general creditors.

The claims of the general creditors total $40 million. Since $20 million is available, each claimant would receive 50 percent of his claim before the subordination adjustment. The subordination adjustment requires that the subordinated debentures turn over to the notes to which they are subordinated all amounts received until the notes are satisfied. In this situation, the claim of the notes payable is $10 million, but only $5 million is available. The deficiency is $5 million. After transfer by the subordinated debentures of $4 million, there remains a deficiency of $1 million, which will be unsatisfied. It will be noted that 90 percent of the bank claim is satisfied, whereas only 50 percent of other unsecured claims will be satisfied. These figures illustrate the usefulness of the subordination provision to the security to which the subordination is made. Since no other funds remain, the claims of the holders of preferred and common stock are completely wiped out.

Studies of the proceeds in bankruptcy liquidations reveal that unsecured creditors receive, on the average, about 15 cents on the dollar. Consequently, where assignment to creditors is likely to yield more, assignment is to be preferred to bankruptcy.

SUMMARY

Problems associated with the decline and failure of a firm, as well as methods of rehabilitating or liquidating one that has failed, were the subjects treated in this chapter. The major cause of failure is incompetent management. Bad managers should, of course, be removed as promptly as possible; if failure has occurred, a number of remedies are open to the interested parties.

The first question to be answered is whether the firm is better off dead or alive—whether it should be liquidated and sold off piecemeal or rehabilitated. Assuming the decision is made that the firm should survive, it must be put through what is called a *reorganization*. Legal procedures are always costly, especially in the case of a business failure. Therefore, if it is at all possible, both the debtor and the creditors are better off if matters can be handled on an informal basis rather than through the courts. The informal procedures used in reorganization are (1) *extension*, which postpones the date of settlement, and (2) *composition*, which reduces the amount owed.

If voluntary settlement through extension or composition is not possible, the matter is thrown into the courts. If the court decides on reorganization rather than liquidation, it will appoint a trustee (1) to control the firm going through reorganization and (2) to prepare a formal plan of reorganization. The plan, which must be reviewed by the SEC, must meet the standards of *fairness* to all parties and *feasibility* in the sense that the reorganized enterprise will stand a good chance of surviving rather than being thrown back into the bankruptcy courts.

The application of standards of fairness and feasibility developed in this chapter are tools to determine the probable success of a particular plan for reorganization. The concept of *fairness* involves the estimation of sales and earnings and the application of a capitalization rate to the latter to determine the appropriate distribution to each claimant.

The *feasibility test* examines the ability of the new enterprise to carry the fixed charges resulting from the reorganization plan. The quality of management and the company's assets must be assured. Production and marketing may also require improvement.

Finally, where liquidation is treated as the only solution to the debtor's insolvency, the creditors should attempt procedures that will net them the largest recovery. *Assignment* of the debtor's property is the cheaper and the faster procedure. In addition, there is more flexibility in disposing of the debtor's property and thus providing larger returns. *Bankruptcy* provides formal procedures in liquidation to safeguard the debtor's property from fraud and provides equitable distribution to the creditors. The procedure is long and cumbersome. In addition, the debtor's property is generally poorly managed during bankruptcy proceedings unless the trustee is closely supervised by the creditors.

QUESTIONS **22–1** "A certain number of business failures is a healthy sign. If there are no failures, this is an indication (1) that entrepreneurs are overly cautious, hence not as inventive and as willing to take risks as a healthy, growing economy requires, (2) that competition is not functioning to weed out inefficient producers, or (3) that both situations exist." Discuss, giving pros and cons.

22–2 How can financial analysis be used to forecast the probability of a given firm's failure? Assuming that such analysis is properly applied, can it always predict failure?

22–3 Why do creditors usually accept a plan for financial rehabilitation rather than demand liquidation of the business?

22–4 Would it be possible to form a profitable company by merging two companies both of which are business failures? Explain.

22–5 Distinguish between a reorganization and a bankruptcy.

22–6 Would it be a sound rule to liquidate whenever the liquidation value is above the value of the corporation as a going concern? Discuss.

22–7 Why do liquidations of all types usually result in losses for the creditors or the owners, or both? Would partial liquidation or liquidation over a period limit their losses? Explain.

22–8 Are liquidations likely to be more common for public utility, railroad, or industrial corporations? Why?

22-1   The financial statements of the Sandy Publishing Company for 1972 are **PROBLEMS**
shown below.

A recapitalization plan is proposed in which each share of the $4 preferred will
be exchanged for one share of $1.60 preferred (stated value, $25) plus one
8 percent subordinated income debenture (stated principal, $50). The $7 preferred would be retired from cash.

a) Show the *pro forma* balance sheet (in millions of dollars) giving effect to the
recapitalization and showing the new preferred at its stated value and the common stock at its par value.
b) Present the *pro forma* income statement (in millions of dollars carried to
two decimal places).
c) How much does the firm increase income available to common stock by the
recapitalization?
d) How much less is the required pretax earnings after the recapitalization compared to those before the change? Required earnings is that amount that is just
enough to meet fixed charges, debenture interest, and/or preferred dividends in
this case.

Sandy Publishing Company
Balance sheet
December 31, 1972
In millions of dollars

Current assets	$ 80	Current liabilities	$ 28
Investments	32	Advance payments for subscriptions	52
Net fixed assets	102	Reserves	4
Good will	10	$4 preferred stock, $75 par	
		(1,200,000 shares)	90
		$7 preferred stock, no par	
		(60,000 shares, callable at $100)	6
		Common stock, par value	
		of $1 (6,000,000 shares outstanding)	6
		Retained earnings	38
Total assets	$224	Total claims	$224

Sandy Publishing Company
Consolidated statement of
income and expense for year ended
December 31, 1972
In millions of dollars

Operating income		$360.0
Operating expense		344.0
Net operating income		$ 16.0
Other income		2.0
Other expense		0.0
Earnings before income tax		$ 18.0
Income tax at 50 percent		9.0
Income after taxes		$ 9.0
Dividends on $4 prior preferred stock	4.8	
Dividends on $7 preferred stock	0.4	5.2
Income available for common stock		$ 3.8

e) How is the debt-to-net-worth position of the company affected by the recapitalization?

f) Would you vote for the recapitalization if you were a holder of the $4 prior preferred stock?

22–2 The Unitex Instrument Company produces precision instruments. The company's products are designed and manufactured according to specifications set out by its customers and are highly specialized.

Declines in sales and increases in development expenses in recent years resulted in a large deficit by the end of 1972.

Unitex Instrument Company
Balance sheet
December 31, 1972
In thousands of dollars

Current assets	$ 750	Current liabilities	$ 900
Fixed assets	750	Long-term debt (unsecured)	450
		Capital stock	300
		Earned surplus or (deficit)	(150)
Total assets	$1,500	Total claims	$1,500

Independent assessment led to the conclusion that the company would have a liquidation value of about $1,200,000. As an alternative to liquidation, the management concluded that a reorganization was possible with additional investment of $600,000. The management was confident of eventual success of the company and stated that the additional investment would restore earnings to $250,000 a year after taxes and before fixed charges. The appropriate multiplier to apply is 8 times. The management is negotiating with a local investment group to obtain

Unitex Instrument Company
Sales and profits, 1969–1972
In thousands of dollars

Year	Sales	Net profit after tax before fixed charges
1969	$5,250	$ 525
1970	$4,800	$ 450
1971	$2,850	$(150)
1972	$2,700	$(225)

the additional investment of $600,000. If the funds are obtained, the holders of the long-term debt would be given one half the common stock in the reorganized firm in place of their present claims.

Should the creditors agree to the reorganization or should they force liquidation of the firm?

22–3* On September 13, 1956, a voluntary petition for reorganization under Chapter X of the Bankruptcy Act was filed by Green River Steel Corporation in

---

* Based on SEC Reorganization Release No. 1940. *In the matter of Green River Steel Corporation, Debtor, in proceedings for the reorganization of a corporation pursuant to Chapter X of the Bankruptcy Act* (Washington, D.C.: January 24, 1957), pp. 1–25. Facts altered and rounded to facilitate calculations.

the U.S. District Court for the Western District of Kentucky, Owensboro Division. The petition was approved and a trustee was named. On November 12, 1956, the trustee filed a plan for reorganization with the court.

Green River Steel Company
Balance sheet, July 31, 1956
In thousands of dollars

Assets		Current liabilities	
Current assets	$ 4,000	4 1/2% mortgage due RFC	
Net property account	9,000	($2,100 past due)	$ 4,000
		Notes payable to banks	1,000
		Accounts payable	1,500
		Interest due to RFC	1,000
		Accruals	200
		Total current liab.	$ 7,700
		Long-term debt	
		4 1/2% mortgage due RFC	$ 4,500
		Deferred interest	300
		3 1/2% debentures, due 1961	4,000
		Interest accrued on	
		3 1/2% debentures	18
		Total long-term debt	$ 8,818
		Capital stock	
		Common (10 cents par)	7
		Paid-in surplus	80
		Earned surplus (deficit)	(3,605)
Total assets	$13,000	Total claims	$13,000

On November 22, 1950, Green River Steel was incorporated under the laws of Kentucky for the purpose of engaging in the production and sale of semifinished steel products. In July 1953, Green River started operations. In early 1954, when the plant was ready to produce at its rated capacity, the entire industry was hit by a recession. In addition, the company lacked working capital as shown by the balance sheet below.

All attempts to secure additional funds failed. In spite of the difficulties, there has been a steadily improving trend in both sales and net profits.

However, with the entire $4 million principal amount of one of the mortgage notes held by RFC falling due on January 1, 1957, it was obvious to the management that the company could not meet its obligations.

Green River Steel Company
Sales and profits, 1954–1956
In thousands of dollars

Year ended	Net sales	Net operating profit before interest charges	Net profits
July 31, 1954	$ 5,413	(1,603)	(2,185)
July 31, 1955	10,790	947	575
July 31, 1956	17,270	826	204

The trustee's plan of reorganization was based on an offer by Jessop Steel Company. The trustee's plan follows:

1) The United States, as the holder of RFC notes, will receive a new first-mortgage note in the principal amount of $9.8 million at the date of consummation, maturing 18 years thereafter and bearing interest at 3 percent a year for the first 3 years and 4½ percent a year thereafter.

2) The holders of outstanding debentures will receive, in exchange for each $1,000 principal amount and the interest accumulated thereon to the date of consummation, a new $1,000 income subordinated debenture note, maturing 25 years thereafter and bearing interest if earned, but noncumulative, of 2 percent for the third through the sixth years, 2 1/2 for the seventh and eighth years, and 3 1/2 percent thereafter. The new debentures will be subordinate (a) to a $9.8 million first-mortgage note, (b) to new 10-year notes payable to Jessop in the principal amount of not less than $1.5 million, and (c) to bank loans of $3 million.

3) The holders of the common stock of the debtor will receive in exchange for each 10 shares of such stock one share of common stock of Jessop. New common stock will be issued by Green River to Jessop, which will become the sole stockholder of the reorganized enterprise.

4) The trustee's plan provides for the issuance of 10-year notes to Jessop in exchange for cash advanced to the debtor in the principal amount of $1.5 million at the consummation date, maturing in 10 years and bearing interest of 4 percent a year.

5) The plan also provides for sinking funds for the retirement of the first-mortgage note, the 10-year note, and the new debentures.

The *pro forma* liabilities and net worth, giving effect to the trustee's plan, are:

Notes payable to banks	$3,000	
Accounts payable	1,500	
Accruals	200	
Current liabilities		$ 4,700
First mortgage due RFC	$9,800	
10-year note to Jessop	1,500	
Subordinated income debentures	4,000	
Long-term debt		15,300
Common stock, par value $10	$3,000	
Capital surplus	1,000	
Net worth		4,000
Total claims		$24,000

The *pro forma* statement is based on continuing the accounts payable at $1.5 million, on increasing the bank loans to $3 million, and on additional investment of $1.5 million by Jessop Steel.

a) What is the value of the assets of Green River less the new capital invested in the business?

b) Using the capitalization of income method, if the sales of Green River rise to $30 million, the profit rate on sales (before interest) is 7 percent and the price/earnings ratio is 8, what is the amount of the total assets of Green River after reorganization?

c) What is the amount of total assets of Green River if sales are $25 million but all other conditions are as in b?

d) Assume that sales of Green River are $25 million but that the profit rate rises to 8 percent. What is the amount of total assets of Green River now?

e) Because Jessop Steel would become the sole owner of Green River, does it make any difference whether Jessop's $1.5 million is treated as debt or as ownership investment?

f) What is your appraisal of the fairness of the proposed reorganization plan?

g) What is your opinion of the feasibility of the reorganization plan?

22–4   On May 10, 1972, the Alberta Company filed an involuntary petition in bankruptcy, having defaulted interest on its outstanding debt. At this date, it issued the following balance sheet.

				Alberta Company
Cash	$ 10,000	Accounts payable	$ 500,000	*Balance sheet*
Receivables	190,000	Notes payable, 8%	500,000	*May 10, 1972*
Inventory	800,000	First mortgage, 5%	1,000,000	
Machinery	2,000,000	Second mortgage, 6%	1,000,000	
Plant	5,000,000	Debentures, 6%	2,000,000	
Surplus	1,000,000	Preferred stock, 7%	1,000,000	
		Common stock	3,000,000	
Total	$9,000,000	Total	$9,000,000	

The Alberta Company, after the necessary reorganization, can earn $320,000. You have determined that 8 percent is an appropriate capitalization rate.

a) State your plan of reorganization, using (1) absolute priority doctrine and (2) relative priority doctrine.

b) Defend both your plans for (1) "fairness" in legal connotation and (2) "feasibility" in legal connotation.

22–5   The Carver Company has suffered several years of operating losses. Because of the unfavorable outlook for the firm, it goes into bankruptcy and is dissolved.

				Carver Company
Cash	$ 20,000	Accounts payable	$ 1,000,000	*Balance sheet*
Accounts receivable	100,000	Loans from banks	2,000,000	*September 30, 1971*
Inventories	2,000,000	Property taxes	5,000	*Last balance sheet*
Building	10,000,000	Accrued wages*	60,000	*before dissolution*
Equipment	5,000,000	Federal income taxes	5,000	
		First mortgage on building	4,000,000	
		Second mortgage on building	2,000,000	
		Subordinated convertible		
		debentures†	1,000,000	
		Preferred stock	3,000,000	
		Common stock	3,000,000	
		Retained earnings	1,050,000	
Total	$17,120,000	Total	$17,120,000	

* Incurred during the last two months, no claim exceeds $600.
† Subordinated to bank loan only.

On liquidation, the following amounts are received from respective items:

Cash	$ 20,000
Receivables	50,000
Inventories	1,000,000
Building	5,000,000
Equipment	2,000,000

What would be the priority of payment, and how much would each class of creditor receive?

Part VIII

An Integrated View of Financial Management

*T*HIS chapter deals with the timing of financial policy. Variations in the relative cost and availability of funds require comparisons of the changes in the cost and availability of equity money, long-term money, and short-term money over time. Fluctuations in the level of business activity produce a number of impacts on the firm. For satisfactory financial timing, the financial manager must take into account prospective changes in asset requirements that will have to be financed over time. He must also consider prospective prices and returns from capital assets. Finally, he must plan his needs to meet future maturing obligations.

The significance of financial timing is suggested by two quotations from *Business Week:*

SIGNIFICANCE TO FINANCIAL MANAGEMENT

> Even a modest increase in monetary restraint will be hard for most companies to handle. Ever since the end of last year's credit drought, companies have worked hard to rebuild liquidity.
>
> However, there's a "difference between actual and desired liquidity," says an economist for a major New York City bank, "and companies haven't succeeded in loosening up balance sheets."
>
> In contrasting money market conditions that lie ahead with 1966, economists stress the expected impact of inflation itself. During late 1966, the wholesale price index remained relatively stable. But if price increases get larger in coming months, interest rates are almost sure to climb.
>
> "People who borrow under conditions of sharp inflation are willing to pay any amount for money," says Milton Friedman of the University of Chicago, "and people who lend ask high rates to protect themselves from loss of purchasing power." If the Fed doesn't tighten, Friedman expects prices to rise by at least 5% and possibly 7% during 1968 and predicts that interest rates will be in the 9% to 10% range."[1]

[1] "Is a Money Crunch on Its Way?" *Business Week* (September 29, 1967), p. 36.

Professor Friedman's position was subsequently borne out, and the second *Business Week* quotation suggests that financial executives may have to adjust to a long period of high interest rates:

> "There will be times in the next 10 years," says a Wall Street bond dealer, "when we will look back on today's interest rates as being very reasonable."
>
> Since money has never cost more than it does today, that is a very dour forecast indeed. Yet most financial executives—bankers and corporate treasurers alike—expect the 1970s to produce a tremendous demand for credit and do not have much hope that interest rates will slip very far from today's extremely high levels.[2]

Financial managers are divided on the question of whether significant fluctuations in money costs will occur in the future or whether interest rates will trend upward with only occasional dips. Recent experience suggests that both possibilities are worth consideration. Accordingly, in this chapter we first consider cyclical patterns in the costs of financing, then review the nature of monetary and fiscal policies with particular emphasis on the implications of these policies for future interest rate patterns. The chapter concludes with an analysis of the changing financial practices that have resulted from recent shifts in the money and capital markets.

HISTORICAL PATTERNS IN THE COSTS OF FINANCING Figure 23–1 gives an indication of patterns of interest rate changes in the U.S. economy during the period of 1929–1969. One outstanding characteristic of interest rate behavior is the wide magnitude of the changes in the price of money over the years. For example, the borrowing rate on 4 to 6 months commercial paper, which is the best indication of the cost of short-term money to large corporations, reached a low of 0.53 percent in 1941. By 1953, this rate stood at 2.52 percent, but it declined to 1.58 percent during the business recession of the following year. In the early 1960s prime commercial paper rates rose to over 3 percent, and during the credit stringency of the late 1960s they rose to the 8 percent level.

Yields on high grade long-term corporate bonds have fluctuated similarly, but not to the same degree. For example, the corporate Aaa bond rate reached a low of 2.53 percent in 1946. It rose to over 3 percent in 1953 and, after declining to 2.90 percent during the business downturn of 1954, climbed to 4.41 percent by 1960. During August 1966, yields on Aaa corporates rose above 5 1/2 percent, and the rise continued to over 9 percent in 1969.

This brief review of fluctuations in short-term and long-term interest rates is sufficient to demonstrate that fluctuations in the cost of capital

---

[2] "Not Enough Money to Go Around," *Business Week*, December 6, 1969, p. 167.

FIGURE 23–1 *Long-term and short-term interest rates*

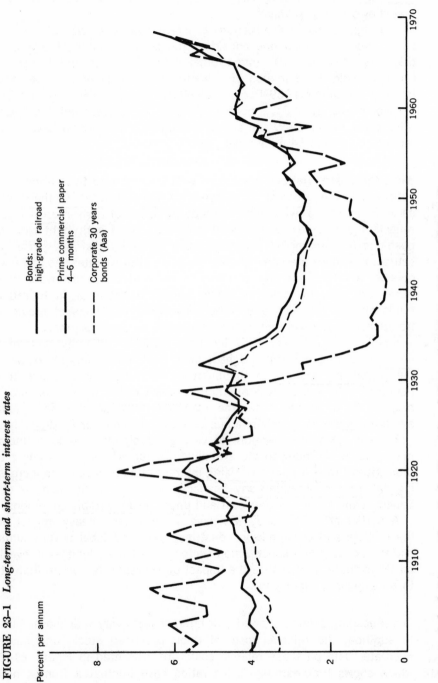

Source: *Federal Reserve Chart Book, Financial and Business Statistics,* February 1970, p. 23.

to business represent one of the most volatile of the inputs purchased by firms. Within relatively short time periods, money costs have fluctuated by over 100 percent.

The significance of fluctuations in interest rates is seen to be especially important when one considers the large amounts of financing that may be involved. In mid-1968, Pacific Telephone and Telegraph Company sold $165 million of debentures at a cost of 6.53 percent. In early December 1969 Pacific Telephone sold another $150 million of debentures at a 9.10 percent yield to investors. Had the 1968 rates prevailed in 1969 the company's interest cost would have been reduced by almost $4 million per year.

INTEREST RATES AS AN INDEX OF AVAILABILITY OF FUNDS While the cost variations associated with interest rate fluctuations are substantial, the greatest significance of interest rates is their role as an index of the availability of funds. A period of high interest rates reflects tight money, which is in turn associated with tight reserve positions at commercial banks. At such times interest rates rise, of course, but there are conventional limits on interest rates. As a consequence, a larger quantity of funds is demanded by borrowers than banks are able to make available. Banks therefore begin to ration funds among prospective borrowers by continuing lines of credit to traditional customers but restricting loans to new borrowers.

Small firms characteristically have greater difficulty obtaining financing during periods of tight money. Even among large borrowers, the bargaining position of the financial institutions is stronger in a period of tight money. It is a lender's market rather than a borrower's market. As a consequence, the restrictive conditions in term loan agreements are especially onerous when the demand for funds is high.

Interest rates are therefore of very great significance to financial managers as an index to the availability of funds. For small- and medium-sized firms, a period of rising interest rates may indicate increasing difficulty in obtaining any financing at all. Or, if financing is obtained, it will be at a higher cost and under less favorable conditions.

A period of tight money will have a particularly heavy impact on the utilities and other heavy industries, state and local governments, and the housing and construction sectors. The heavy, long-term investments in these areas cause the impact of interest rates on profitability to be especially significant.

COSTS OF DIFFERENT TYPES OF FINANCING OVER TIME The preceding section showed that interest rates vary widely over time. In addition, the relative costs of debt, preferred stock, and equity fluctuate. Data on these relative costs are presented in Figure 23–2, which shows that earnings/price ratios have fluctuated from a high

FIGURE 23-2 *Long-term security yields*

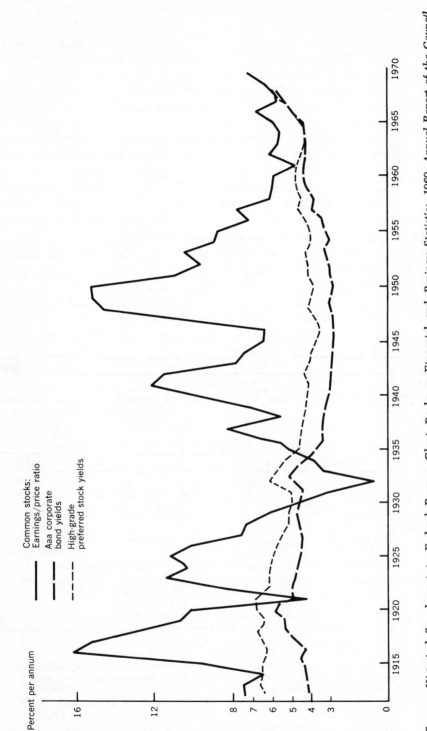

Percent per annum

Common stocks:
Earnings/price ratio

Aaa corporate
bond yields

High-grade
preferred stock yields

16

12

8
7
6
5

4

3

0

1915   1920   1925   1930   1935   1940   1945   1950   1955   1960   1965   1970

Source: Historical Supplement to Federal Reserve Chart Book on Financial and Business Statistics, 1969; Annual Report of the Council of Economic Advisors, 1970.

of 16 percent to a low of 1 percent.[3] During the 1960s, earnings/price ratios averaged about 6 percent, ranging from 4.7 to 6.7 percent. Yields on bonds and preferred stocks have fluctuated to a much lesser extent. Also, since bonds and preferred stocks both provide a stable, fixed income to investors, they are close substitutes for one another, and their yields parallel one another closely.[4]

The pronounced decline in earnings/price ratios that began in the early 1950s resulted largely from investors' increasing awareness of the growth potential in common stock earnings, dividends, and stock prices. The economy was strong during this period, and security analysts and investors became aware of the importance of the "*g*" component in the realized rate of return equation $k = D/P + g$. A recognition of the dangers of inflation and the effect it has on fixed income securities was driving bond and preferred stock yields up, further closing the gap between interest rates and earnings/price ratios.

RELATION BETWEEN LONG-TERM AND SHORT-TERM INTEREST RATES[5]

One of the important elements in the financial manager's timing decisions is an understanding of the relationship between long- and short-term interest rates. Long-term interest rates are rates on securities with maturities in excess of five years. Short-term interest rates are those on securities with maturities of under one year.

Figure 23–3 graphs the relationship between long- and short-term interest rates. In some periods short-term interest rates were higher than long-term interest rates; this was true in 1966 and again in 1969, when the money market was extremely tight. Under certain conditions there is greater risk to holding long-term than short-term securities. For one thing, the longer the maturity of the security, the greater the danger that the issuer may not make an effective adaptation to its environment and, therefore, may not be able to meet its obligations

Causes high short term rates

---

[3] An earnings/price ratio, the reciprocal of a P/E ratio, does not measure exactly the cost of equity capital but does indicate *trends* in this cost. In other words, when earnings/price ratios are high, the cost of equity capital is high, and vice-versa.

[4] Note also that bond yields tended to lie below those on preferred stocks during most of the period covered; this relationship resulted from the fact that bonds have priority over preferred stocks and, hence, are less risky. However, preferred stock dividends are largely tax exempt to corporate owners, so after-tax yields (to corporations) are considerably higher than those on bonds. Recall that 85 percent of the dividends received by a corporate stockholder are tax exempt to the receiver, whereas interest income is fully taxable to the recipient. During the 1960s, certain corporations which had previously paid very low taxes became subject to higher taxes (insurance companies, savings and loans, mutual savings banks); these firms bought preferred stocks and closed the gap between bond and preferred stock yields.

[5] The relationship between long- and short-term interest rates—generally referred to as the term structure of interest rates—is developed in summary fashion here and in some detail in the Appendix to Chapter 23 of *Managerial Finance*, third edition.

FIGURE 23-3 *Long- and short-term interest rates*

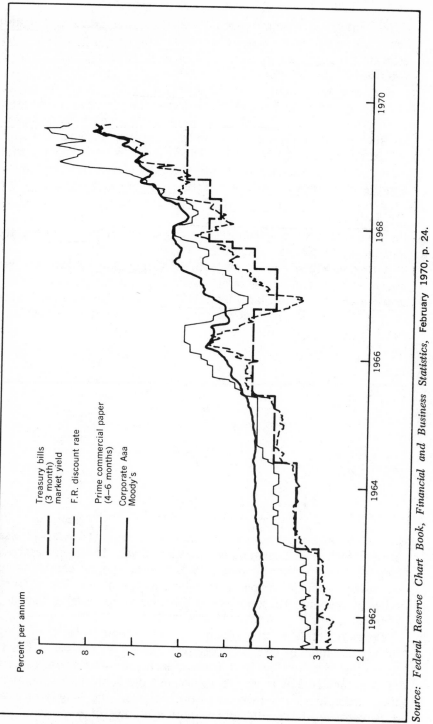

Percent per annum

Treasury bills
(3 month)
market yield

F.R. discount rate

Prime commercial paper
(4–6 months)

Corporate Aaa
Moody's

Source: Federal Reserve Chart Book, Financial and Business Statistics, February 1970, p. 24.

in ten, fifteen, or twenty years. In addition, the *prices* of long-term bonds are much more volatile than short-term bond prices when interest rates change; the reason for this is largely arithmetic and was described in Chapter 11.

However, many other kinds of uncertainties are faced by the firm and the investor, and these other considerations may dominate at some point in time. One of these uncertainties concerns changes in the supply and demand of loanable funds over time. When the supply of funds is tight, relative to the demand for them at prevailing prices, there will be strong pressure for short-term interest rates to rise. Short-term interest rates reflect current supply-and-demand situations. Long-term interest rates reflect an average of supply-and-demand conditions over the life of the security. This characteristic accounts for the fact that short-term interest rates are much more volatile than long-term interest rates (Figure 23–3).

A theory, which economists call the *expectations theory*, has been advanced that long-term interest rates may appropriately be regarded as an average of short-term interest rates. Thus the relation between long rates and short rates will depend upon what is happening to the future of short-term interest rates, as illustrated in Table 23–1.

TABLE 23–1
Relation between short-term and long-term interest rates

Year	A		B	
	5-year note	Short-term rates	5-year note	Short-term rates
1	4	2	4	6
2		3		5
3		4		4
4		5		3
5		6		2

In section A it is assumed that short-term interest rates will rise 1 percent each year, beginning at 2 percent in year 1. The corresponding long-term interest rate in year 1 for a five-year period can be approximated by taking a simple arithmetic average of the five short-term rates, 4 percent. Thus, in year 1, the long-term rate is double the short-term rate.

Consider, however, the situation under section B. Here, in a tight-money situation in year 1, short-term rates are 6 percent, but they are expected to decline by 1 percent each year. The average of these rates is the same as in section A, because the numbers are identical— their order is simply reversed. Now, however, the long-term rate of 4 percent lies below the initial short-term rate of 6 percent.

These examples do not prove the relation between short-term rates and long-term rates. They do, however, illustrate the pattern that would exist if the only factor operating was expected changes in interest rate movements, which themselves reflect a broad group of supply-and-demand factors. However, many other factors do operate in the market. Some of these include differences in the risks of loss and failure among individual business firms, in the economic outlook for different industries, in the degree to which price-level changes affect different products and industries, and in the impact that changes in government legislation will have on different firms in an industry.

CHARACTERISTIC PATTERNS IN COST OF MONEY

The general nature of the relationships between long- and short-term interest rates, and between interest rates and Gross National Product (GNP), are shown in Figure 23–4. Short-term interest rates show the widest amplitude of swings. Since long-term interest rates are *averages* of short-term rates, they are not as volatile as short-term rates—short-term rates move more quickly and fluctuate more than long-term rates. The cost of debt money tends generally to lag behind movements in general business conditions, both at the peak and at the trough. But the movements of long-term rates lag more than short-term rates.

The cost of equity funds may best be approximated by equity yields, dividends plus capital gains. To understand the behavior of equity yields, one must analyze the behavior of earnings, dividends, and stock prices. Corporate earnings are highly volatile. They lead the business cycle both on the upturn and on the downturn, and dividends follow earnings. Prices of common stocks anticipate changes in corporate earnings. Prices of equities are also influenced by money market conditions. Owing to the gradual tightening in money market conditions as expansion continues, bond yields rise and attract money out of stocks and into bonds, causing the prices of equities to turn down before corporate profits reach their peak. Hence, the cost of equity financing turns up because firms receive lower prices for the stocks they sell.[6] In other words, the cost of equity capital begins to rise in the later stages of the business cycle.

Relationships

The relationships between the costs of financing over time set forth in Figure 23–4 represent generalizations that provide a frame of reference for the financial manager; the patterns are not intended as pre-

---

[6] Recall that in Chapter 12 we showed that, at least conceptually, stock prices may be determined by the equation

$$P = \frac{D}{k - g}$$

where P = the price of a share of stock, D = the dividend on the stock, k = the required rate of return on the stock (or the cost of equity capital), and g = the expected growth rate. Since stocks and bonds compete with one another for investors' funds, if monetary policy drives interest rates up, k will likewise rise and P must decline.

cise guidelines. A basic requirement for sound financial management is the ability to make judgments about future economic and financial conditions that will affect financial timing and the forms and sources of financing that are used. The next section seeks to provide a foundation for evaluating trends in financial markets.

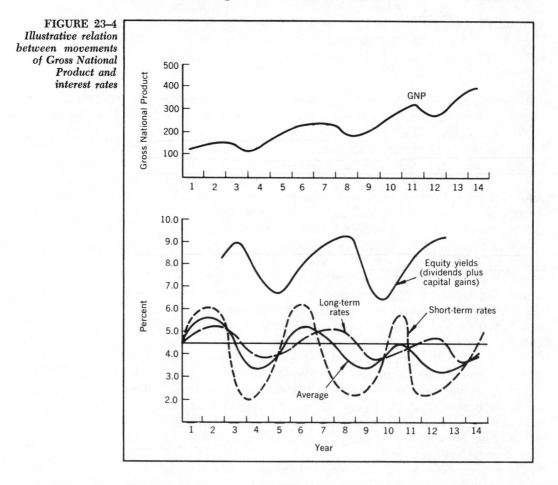

FIGURE 23–4
Illustrative relation between movements of Gross National Product and interest rates

MONEY AND CAPITAL MARKET BEHAVIOR

Federal Reserve Policy

Fundamental to an understanding of the behavior of the money and capital markets is an analysis of the role of the central bank, which in the United States is the Federal Reserve System. The "Fed," as it is called, has a set of instruments with which to influence the operations of commercial banks, whose loan and investment activities in turn have an important influence on the cost and availability of money. The most powerful of the Fed's instruments, hence the one used most sparingly, is changing *reserve requirements*. The one most often used is changing the pattern of *open-market operations*.

Changes in the *discount rate* (the interest rate charged to commercial banks when they borrow from Federal Reserve Banks) shown in Figure 23–3 above are likely to have more of a psychological influence than direct quantitative effects. These changes represent an implicit announcement by Federal Reserve authorities that a change in economic conditions has taken place, and that these new conditions call for a tightening or easing of monetary conditions. The data in the figure demonstrate that increases in the Federal Reserve bank discount rate have been followed by rising interest rate levels, and conversely.

Fed a way of affecting rates

When the Federal Reserve System purchases or sells securities in the open market, makes changes in the discount rate, or varies the reserve requirement, this produces changes in interest rates on most securities.

The fiscal policy of the federal government has considerable impact on movements in interest rates. A cash budget deficit represents a stimulating influence by the federal government, and a cash surplus exerts a restraining influence from the government-spending sector of the economy. However, this generalization must be modified to reflect the way a deficit is financed and the way a surplus is used. To have the most stimulating effect, the deficit should be financed by sale of securities through the banking system, particularly the central bank—this provides a maximum amount of bank reserves and permits a multiple expansion in the money supply. To have the most restrictive effect, the surplus should be used to retire bonds held by the banking system, particularly the central bank, thus reducing bank reserves and causing a multiple contraction in the supply of money.

FISCAL POLICY

The impact of Treasury financing programs will be different at different times. Ordinarily, when the Treasury needs to draw funds from the money market, it competes with other potential users of funds; the result may be a rise in interest rate levels. However, the desire to hold down interest rates also influences Treasury and Federal Reserve policy. To ensure the success of a large new offering, Federal Reserve authorities may temporarily ease money conditions, a procedure that will tend to soften interest rates. If the Treasury encounters resistance in selling securities in the nonbanking sector, securities may be sold in large volume to the commercial banking system, which expands its reserves and thereby increases the monetary base. This change in turn tends to lower the level of interest rates.

Procedure

Price-level trends affect interest rates in two important ways. First, the "nominal" interest rate—the contract, or stated, interest rate—reflects expectations about future price level behavior. If prices are rising, and are expected to rise further, the expected rate of inflation is added to the interest rate that would have prevailed in the absence of inflation to adjust for the decline in purchasing power represented

EFFECTS OF PRICE-LEVEL CHANGES ON INTEREST RATES

by price increases. This is illustrated in Figure 23–5. Nominal interest rates on high-grade corporate bonds were relatively stable at 4.5 percent from 1962 through mid-1965. However, as the rate of inflation increased, starting in 1966, nominal interest rates began to rise sharply, interrupted only by declines of short duration and of less than one percentage point in early 1967 and again in late 1968. But after adjustment for price-level changes, the "real" rate of return on high-grade corporate bonds fluctuated in a relatively narrow range around 3.5 percent.

FIGURE 23–5
Yields on highest-grade corporate bonds

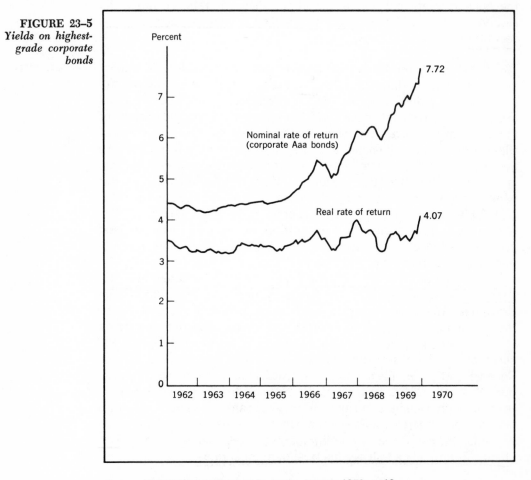

Source: Federal Reserve Bank of St. Louis, January 1970, p. 19.

The second way that price inflation influences interest rates is through federal actions. If prices are rising at a rate of more than about 2 percent a year, restrictive monetary policy can be expected in an effort to reduce inflationary forces. As a consequence, relative tightness will prevail in monetary and credit markets, and nominal interest rate levels will be high.

Within this framework of general economic and financial patterns, short-term interest rate patterns and forecasts may be analyzed through the use of flow of funds accounts. The flow of funds accounts are summarized in Table 23–2 to depict the behavior of the major categories of suppliers and demanders of funds. By projecting the sources and uses of funds in different categories, the direction of the pressure on interest rates can be estimated.[7]

INTEREST RATE FORECASTS

The table can be used in the following way: Historical patterns can be established to show uses and sources of funds in relation to the growth of the economy as a whole as measured by GNP. When in any particular year the demand for funds grows faster than the supply in relation to historical patterns, interest rates are likely to rise. These extra funds are supplied by drawing on the commercial banking system, which is the pivot in the financial mechanism. Whenever the demand for funds must be met by drawing on the commercial banking system to a greater-than-normal degree, interest rates rise.

Another significant statistic in the table is the rise in the supply of funds from "Individuals and Miscellaneous"; funds from this source doubled during 1966, and a further increase of almost $30 billion occurred during 1968. Because of restrictive Federal Reserve policies, the ability of the commercial banks and other financial institutions to supply funds was held back relative to demand. This produced high interest rates, and these high rates induced individuals, businesses, and others to make their surplus funds available to borrowers. Thus, the supply of funds was augmented from nonbanking sources, but only at substantially higher interest rates.

Most longer-term predictions for the financial market call for continued high interest rates with only moderate declines of short duration from time to time. The causes are diverse, but a major factor reflects efforts of governments throughout the world to achieve full employment and high growth rates.[8] A worldwide capital shortage has resulted.

The outlook for continued price-level increases and high interest rates has already had a number of effects on corporate financial policy. Table 23–3 presents the sources and uses of corporate funds for the

---

[7] Compilations of studies of this kind are facilitated by the flow of funds data developed by the Federal Reserve System, published monthly in the *Federal Reserve Bulletin.*

[8] The reasons for this forecast are set forth in the papers by R. Solomon, O. Eckstein, R. E. Moor, J. W. Knowles, R. A. Kavesh, W. C. Freund, and J. J. O'Leary in *Business Economics*, V (January 1970) pp. 12–49.

TABLE 23-2 *Summary of supply and demand for credit   Annual net increases, $ billions*

	1963	1964	1965	1966	1967	1968	1969e	1970e
Net investment demand								
Mortgages, publicly held	26.6	25.6	24.6	18.2	20.2	23.8	21.8	19.7
Corporate bonds	5.6	6.6	8.1	11.1	16.0	14.0	14.6	17.0
State and local securities	6.1	5.8	7.4	5.7	9.8	10.0	8.6	9.5
Foreign bonds	1.1	0.9	1.2	0.9	1.2	1.4	1.1	1.5
Subtotal—long term	39.4	38.9	41.3	35.9	47.2	49.2	46.1	47.7
Net other demand								
Business loans (banks and financial companies)	6.6	7.2	15.4	9.8	5.7	14.1	15.1	9.3
Consumer loans (banks and financial companies)	6.6	8.8	9.0	3.8	2.8	10.8	9.4	4.8
All other bank loans*	1.3	0.4	0.8	0.7	2.2	1.3	-1.1	-0.8
Open market paper	0.9	2.1	0.7	4.4	3.9	4.1	12.1	6.0
Publicly held treasury debt	0.9	2.6	-2.4	-1.9	3.4	6.1	-6.3	0.0
Publicly held federal agency debt	1.6	0.6	2.9	4.8	3.7	5.4	8.1	9.1
Total net demand for credit	57.3	60.6	67.7	57.5	68.9	91.0	83.4	76.1
Net supply†								
Mutual savings banks	3.6	4.1	3.6	2.5	5.0	4.1	2.3	3.2
Savings and loan associations	13.0	10.9	9.4	4.7	9.0	10.0	9.3	9.2
Life insurance companies	5.9	6.4	6.7	6.3	6.4	6.0	4.9	5.4
Fire and casualty insurance companies	0.9	0.8	1.0	1.5	1.3	1.9	2.1	2.0
Private noninsured pension funds	1.9	2.1	2.1	1.9	0.8	1.2	0.7	0.4
State and local retirement funds	2.5	2.7	2.8	2.8	3.0	3.6	4.0	4.5
Open-end mutual funds	0.2	0.3	0.7	1.5	-0.5	0.9	1.4	0.2
Total nonbank investing institutions	28.0	27.3	26.3	21.2	25.0	27.7	24.7	24.9
Commercial banks	18.8	21.5	27.9	17.2	36.6	38.9	9.5	22.0
Finance companies	4.3	3.9	5.0	2.3	0.6	5.3	7.9	5.3
Business corporations	1.6	0.3	-0.6	1.8	-1.4	6.7	9.6	4.6
State and local governments	0.6	-0.3	2.0	1.4	1.8	4.1	2.8	2.2
Foreigners	1.0	1.8	0.3	-0.9	1.6	-0.9	-0.9	-1.0
Subtotal	54.3	54.5	60.9	43.0	64.2	81.8	53.6	58.0
Residual: Individuals and miscellaneous	3.0	6.1	6.8	14.5	4.7	9.2	29.8	18.1
Total net supply of credit	57.3	60.6	67.7	57.5	68.9	91.0	83.4	76.1

* Exclusively agricultural and security loans.
† Excludes funds for equities, cash and miscellaneous demands not tabulated above.
Source: Sidney Homer, Henry Kaufman, and James McKeon, *Supply and Demand for Credit in 1970* (Salomon Brothers & Hutzler, March 1970), Table I.

period 1963–1970, expressed as a percentage of the total. A dramatic change has taken place in the role of internal financing. Total internal financing declined from 79 percent of total sources in 1963 to under 64 percent in 1970. Most of the decline has taken place in retained earnings, reflecting larger capital outlays in relation to profits.

	Percentages of total sources or uses								
	1963	1964	1965	1966	1967	1968	1969e	1970e
Uses								
Plant and equipment	66	68	66	71	74	69	73	79
Total physical investment (includes inventory)	81	84	83	92	87	81	88	88
Accounts receivable	6	9	9	6	8	11	10	6
Other	13	7	8	2	5	8	2	6
Total uses	100	100	100	100	100	100	100	100
Sources								
Retained profits	22	28	27	26	23	19	16	15
Depreciation	53	50	44	44	48	45	46	51
Total internal sources	79	79	74	71	66	68	63	64
Bank loans	6	6	13	10	7	10	8	5
Net new stock issues	m	2	m	1	3	m	4	6
Net new bond issues	7	6	7	12	17	13	12	15
Total external sources	21	21	26	29	34	32	37	36
Total sources or uses	100	100	100	100	100	100	100	100

e—estimated
m—less than 1 percent

Source: Sidney Homer, Henry Kaufman, and James McKeon, *Supply and Demand for Credit in 1970* (Salomon Brothers & Hutzler, March 1970), Table I.

TABLE 23–3
Selected elements of corporate sources and uses of corporate funds expressed as percentages of total sources or uses, 1963–1970

Another significant change has been a reduction in dependence on commercial bank financing as compared with external long-term financing from stocks and bonds. New common stock financing rose from negligible amounts in 1963 to 6 percent of total sources of funds in 1970, and this percentage was of course much higher in certain industries and for some individual firms. Long-term bond financing likewise grew from 7 percent to 15 percent by 1970.

These relations are further emphasized in Table 23–4. Part A of the table presents data on gross proceeds (total funds raised before using part of the cash proceeds to retire obligations previously outstanding). Part B presents data on net proceeds after refundings and other adjustments. Part C analyzes some patterns in convertible debt financing. These data indicate, as one would expect, a changing pattern of financing as interest rates rose during the 1960s.

TABLE 23–4 *Bond and stock financing by type, 1963–1970*

Part A—Gross proceeds of bond and stock financing (percentages)

	1963	1964	1965	1966	1967	1968	1969e	1970e
Straight debt, public offerings	42	30	43	40	50	42	48	53
Straight debt, privately placed	53	64	46	44	28	29	22	23
Convertible debt for cash	3	4	9	12	21	17	20	21
Convertible debt in mergers	2	2	2	4	1	12	10	3
Total bond	100	100	100	100	100	100	100	100
Total bond	91	79	86	87	88	82	72	72
Total stocks	9	21	14	13	12	18	28	28
Total bond and stocks	100	100	100	100	100	100	100	100

Part B—Net proceeds of bond and stock financing (percentages)

	1963	1964	1965	1966	1967	1968	1969e	1970e
Straight debt, public offerings	41	29	51	46	59	49	55	60
Straight debt, privately placed	55	65	38	35	19	19	10	12
Convertible debt	4	6	11	19	22	32	35	28
Total bond	100	100	100	100	100	100	100	100
Total bond	104	82	100	90	87	107	80	73
Total stocks	(4)	18	0	10	13	(7)	20	27
Total bond and stocks	100	100	100	100	100	100	100	100

Part C—Analysis of convertible bond offerings ($ billions)

	1963	1964	1965	1966	1967	1968	1969e	1970e
Total convertibles, gross	0.5	0.6	1.4	2.6	4.6	5.6	6.0	5.4
Convertibles, called or retired	0.3	0.2	0.5	0.5	1.1	1.0	0.9	0.6
Percent of total called or retired	60.0	33.3	35.7	19.2	23.9	17.8	15.0	11.1
Yearly net convertible debt	0.2	0.4	0.9	1.9	3.5	4.6	5.1	4.8
Cumulative net convertible debt outstanding	0.2	0.6	1.5	3.4	6.9	11.5	16.6	21.4

e—estimated

Source: Sidney Homer, Henry Kaufman, and James McKeon, *Supply and Demand for Credit in 1970* (Salomon Brothers & Hutzler, March 1970), Table I.

1. The total amount of financing by stocks and bonds—external long-term financing—almost tripled on a gross basis and more than quadrupled on a net basis.

2. Bond financing dropped from 90 to 72 percent of the total.

3. Private placement of debt dropped from over one-half of total long-term debt financing to 23 percent on a gross basis and only 12 percent on a net basis. This dramatic change reflects the impact of tight money on the financing demands of insurance companies, a major source of direct placement financing.

4. With rising price levels, buyers of debt increasingly sought potential equity participation through the convertibility feature, and convertible debt rose from less than 5 percent to approximately one-fourth of total bond financing.

5. Convertible debt issued in mergers rose from less than 2 percent through 1967 to over 10 percent in 1968 and 1969.

6. The reduction of convertible debt by conversion into stock was large in percentage terms in 1963–1965, but with the acceleration of inflation and the increased use of convertible debt, conversions and other retirements had declined to only 11 percent by 1970.

7. The cumulative total of net convertible debt outstanding rose from $6.9 billions in 1967 to an estimated $21.4 billions for 1970. It is clear that the increased uncertainties about the rate of inflation and the increased difficulties of forecasting interest rate patterns have led to the greater use of hybrid forms of financing—debt with equity participation such as convertibles or warrants. The percentage of direct loans with such equity sweeteners, or interest adjustment provisions, is reported to be even higher than was true in the public flotations on which data is available.

A continuing period of high interest rates and tight money markets has produced major changes in financing patterns. The further significance of these developments is discussed in the following section.

Variations in the cost of money and its availability are likely to be of great significance to financial managers. The importance of sound financial timing is further underscored by the mistakes observed in the past and the uncertainties of the future.

IMPLICATIONS OF INTEREST RATE PATTERNS FOR FINANCIAL TIMING

A question that has challenged financial managers since 1966 is whether interest rates, which have trended upward, are near a peak or are going to increase even further? Long-term rates are at the highest level of the Twentieth Century; should firms finance now with long-term debt in anticipation of even higher rates in the future? Or would it be a mistake to lock the company into high-cost, long-term capital?

Easy answers to these questions are not available, and the uncertainties have given rise to new forms and patterns of financing as documented throughout this book. No one can give definitive answers to the questions raised above, but financial executives must make decisions and they must, therefore, make judgments about these issues.

SUMMARY   Financial managers have at least some flexibility in their operations. Even though a firm may have a target debt/assets ratio, it can deviate from this target to some extent in a given year to take advantage of favorable conditions in either the bond market or the stock market. Similarly, although it may have a target relationship between its long- and short-term debt, it can vary from this target if market conditions suggest that such action is appropriate.

As a basis for making sound decisions with respect to financial timing, we have analyzed data covering both cyclical and long-term trends. Uncertainties about the future have increased in recent years, and this has increased the importance of sound financial timing. Also, attempts to deal with an increasing level of uncertainty in the economy have given rise to new innovations in financing techniques and patterns. Some important changes in financing that have developed in response to changes in the economy, especially in the money and capital markets, include:

1. Long-term financing has increased in comparison to the use of short-term commercial bank financing. Bond flotations in the capital markets have risen to record levels.

2. Public flotations of equity issues have increased substantially.

3. A large increase in debt ratios has occurred in response to the inflationary environment. From 1966 to 1969 the ratio of debt to assets for all manufacturing companies rose from 33 to 41 percent.

4. An increase has occurred in the use of equity participations in the form of convertibility or warrants.

5. Insurance companies and other institutional lenders have virtually ceased to provide credit to small and medium-sized borrowers on a straight-debt basis. For business loans, warrants are usually required, while on mortgages supplementary payments based on a percentage of gross or net income are stipulated in loan contracts.

6. New equity securities have been issued in spite of the decline in equity prices beginning in early 1969. As the debt ratios of large corporations rose, and as their liquidity positions declined, larger corporations began selling equity issues in substantial amounts.

7. Since larger firms have greater access to the financial markets, an increase in the volume of trade credit has occurred, with larger firms increasing their extension of credit to smaller ones.

These developments indicate that trends in the money and capital markets are increasing in importance to financial managers. The changes have been so massive that not only has financial timing been involved but also innovations in forms of financing used have been stimulated. Thus, financial policies have been broadened and have taken on greater importance in the over-all management of business firms.

23–1 "It makes good sense for a firm to fund its floating debt, because this **QUESTIONS** relieves the possibility that it will be called upon to pay off debt at an awkward time. However, from the standpoint of cost, it is always cheaper to use short-term debt than long-term debt." Discuss the statement.

23–2 Historical data indicate that more than twice as much capital is raised yearly by selling bonds as by selling common stocks. Does this indicate that corporate capital structures are becoming overburdened with debt?

23–3 Distinguish between the money market and the capital market. How are they related?

23–4 Is the Federal Reserve's tight money policy restraining the country's economic growth? Discuss the pros and cons from the corporation's viewpoint.

23–5 Why do interest rates on different types of securities vary widely?

23–6 What does GNP represent? Why are its levels and growth significant to the financial manager?

23–7 Figure 23–5 indicates that short-term interest rates were higher than long-term interest rates for most of the period 1900–1930. Is there any reason to believe that this relationship may again prevail during the period 1970–1980?

23–8 Are short-term rates of any value in forecasting future rates in the long-term market?

23–1 In mid-1958 the Central Company made a reappraisal of its sales fore- **PROBLEMS** casts for the next one, two, and five years. It was clear that the product development program which had been under way for the previous five years was now coming to fruition. The officers of Central were confident that a sales growth of 12 to 15 percent a year (on a compound basis) for the next five years was strongly indicated unless general business declined.

The Central Company has total assets of $10 million. It has a debt-to-total assets ratio of 29 percent. Since it has been spending heavily on research and development during the past five years, its profits have been depressed and the stock has not been favorably regarded by investors.

The Central Company learned that it could borrow on a short-term basis at 2.5 percent (the rate for prime commercial paper at mid-1958 was 1.6 percent) and sell some common stock or float some nonconvertible long-term bonds at 4 percent. Central financed by selling $2 million of common stock (the maximum to avoid control problems) and by short-term loans at the lower rates until early 1960, when it found that its growing financial requirements could not be met by short-term borrowing. Its need for financing was so great that Central sold $10 million convertible debentures at 5.5 percent (the rate on prime commercial paper at this time was almost 5 percent) and with terms requiring a strong current ratio and limitations on fixed assets purchases. The price of its common

stock had quadrupled by mid-1959 but had dropped by 10 percent in early 1960.
Evaluate the timing of the selection of forms of financing by the Central Company.

23–2 In July 1958, as the economy in general was emerging from the 1957–1958 downturn and the Flexible Container Corporation's business was resuming its strong growth in sales, Fred Bolden, the treasurer, concluded that the firm would require more working capital financing during the year ending June 30, 1959. Below are the historical and *pro forma* income statements and balance sheets of the Flexible Container Corporation.

Flexible Container Corporation
Balance sheets, 1958 and 1959
Pro Forma
In thousand dollars

Assets	1958	1959
Cash	$ 200	$ 600
Receivables	800	1,200
Inventories	1,000	1,600
Total current assets	$2,000	$3,400
Fixed assets, net	1,000	2,000
Total assets	$3,000	$5,400

Liabilities and capital	1958	1959
Accounts payable	300	500
Accruals	100	200
Reserves for taxes	600	800
Total current liabilities	$1,000	$1,500
Additional financing needed	0	800
Common stock, $10 par	1,000	1,000
Surplus	1,000	2,100
Total liabilities and capital	$3,000	$5,400

Flexible Container Corporation
Income statements
for years ended
June 30, 1958 and 1959

	1958	1959
Sales, net	$10,000	$14,000
Cost of sales	8,000	10,000
Gross profit	2,000	4,000
Operating expenses	1,000	1,500
Operating profit	1,000	2,500
Other income, net	200	100
Profits before taxes	1,200	2,600
Taxes	600	1,300
Net profit after taxes	600	1,300
Dividends	100	200
Retained earnings	$ 500	$ 1,100

How should the financing needs be met? Why? (Although the $800,000 *pro forma* financial requirements are shown in the long-term section of the balance sheet, they can be met with either long- or short-term funds.)

23-3 On January 21, 1970, the American Telephone and Telegraph Company announced plans for new corporate financing. The details of the financing provided for the issuance to shareholders of record on April 10, 1970, of rights to subscribe for $100 principal amount of debentures with detachable warrants to purchase two common shares of the company. Thirty-five shares of common stock (that is, 35 rights) would be required to purchase one debenture. It was provided that the rights would expire on May 18, 1970. The financing was a success, as all the debentures were sold.

The balance sheet of the American Telephone and Telegraph Company as of the end of 1968 is summarized below:

American Telephone
and Telegraph Company
Balance sheet
December 31, 1968
Amounts in billions of dollars

Current assets	$ 3	Current debt	$ 3
Investments	2	Long-term debt	16
Net fixed assets	38	Net worth	24
Total assets	$43	Total liabilities plus capital	$43

The number of common shares of stock, for purposes of this analysis, may be considered to be 549,500,000. The bonds were $100 principal amount with a thirty-year maturity, carrying an interest rate of 8 3/4 percent, maturing May 15, 2000. Two warrants, entitling the holder to purchase for cash one common share of the company at any time from November 15, 1970, through May 15, 1975, at $52 per share, accompany each bond.

Data on the number of telephones in service, average conversations per day, net income to AT&T common stock, construction expenditures, total capital, debt to total capital, earnings per share, dividends per share, price range, return on total capital, and return on equity are shown in the table on page 546.

a) The financing provided for the sale of how many debentures?

b) At a price of $100 each, how much financing would be obtained initially by the sale of the debentures?

c) What was the total number of warrants issued?

d) If all the warrants were exercised at the exercise price of $52, how much additional financing would be raised by AT&T by May 15, 1975?

e) What total amount is AT&T raising for the five-year period from this financing?

f) What was the increase in plant during the years 1965–1969? What was the total of construction expenditures less the total of depreciation charges ($9.8 billions) during the same period? What was the increase in capital during the same period of time?

g) On the basis of the answer to the previous question, we may take as an approximate measure of AT&T's future financing needs the sum of construction expenditures less the total of depreciation charges for the same period. On this basis, estimate AT&T's total financing needs for the period 1970–1975, if

Some basic data on the American Telephone & Telegraph Company, 1959–1969

Year	Number of telephones in service, year end (in millions)	Average number of conversations per day (in millions)	Operating revenues (in billions)	Net income to AT & T shares (in millions)	Total number of shares (in millions)	Total plant (year end) (in billions)	Construction expenditures (in millions)	Total capital (in billions)	Debt to total capital (in percents)	Earnings per share (in dollars)	Dividends per share (in dollars)	Price range (rounded)	Return on total capital (in percents)	Return on equity (in percents)
1959	57.9	208	$ 7.4	$1,113	427	$22.2	$2,249	$18.9	36	2.61	1.58	44–37	7.55	9.77
1960	60.7	219	7.9	1,213	438	24.1	2,658	20.5	36	2.79	1.65	54–40	7.69	10.00
1961	63.2	226	8.4	1,285	465	26.0	2,696	22.3	35	2.76	1.72	70–52	7.41	9.46
1962	66.0	242	9.0	1,388	479	28.0	2,976	24.3	35	2.90	1.80	68–49	7.45	9.47
1963	68.6	251	9.6	1,480	488	30.1	3,136	25.6	35	3.03	1.80	71–57	7.45	9.49
1964	72.0	262	10.3	1,659	512	33.5	3,519	28.0	33	3.24	1.95	75–65	7.56	9.51
1965	75.9	280	11.1	1,796	527	35.3	3,918	29.8	33	3.41	2.00	70–60	7.65	9.53
1966	79.0	295	12.1	1,979	536	38.4	4,193	32.0	33	3.69	2.20	64–50	7.91	9.86
1967	83.8	307	13.0	2,049	540	41.5	4,310	34.5	35	3.79	2.20	63–50	7.77	9.73
1968	88.0	323	14.1	2,052	547	45.0	4,742	36.9	36	3.75	2.40	58–48	7.50	9.26
1969	92.7	350	15.7	2,199	549	49.2	5,731	40.2	39	4.00	2.45	58–48	7.73	9.04
5-year growth rate { 1959–1964	4.5	4.7	6.8	8.3	3.7	8.4	9.4	8.2	—	4.4	4.3	11.5[a]	7.52[b]	9.62[b]
{ 1964–1969	5.2	6.0	8.8	5.8	1.4	8.0	10.2	7.5	—	4.3	4.7	5.5[a]	7.69[c]	9.49[c]

[a] Based on average of high and low values.
[b] Average for years 1959-64.
[c] Average for years 1964-69.
Source: American Telephone & Telegraph Annual Reports and Prospectus, April 13, 1970.

construction expenditures grow at a 10 percent rate and depreciation expenses, which were $2,316 millions in 1969, grow at an 8 percent rate.

h) What would retained earnings be for this period, if net income grew at a 7 percent rate and a 60 percent dividend payout policy were followed?

i) What portion of total financing requirements estimated under (g) would not be covered by retained earnings plus the financing under consideration?

j) If AT&T established a 45 percent debt to capital ratio, how much additional debt and outside equity financing would be required for the 1970–1975 period?

k) In financing immediately after World War II, AT&T utilized convertible debentures in connection with its financing. In this present instance it utilized warrants rather than convertibles. Can you suggest some reasons for the shift from convertibles to debentures with warrants?

l) Discuss how the amount, timing, and form of financing employed by AT&T in this financing episode was influenced by the economic and financial developments of the late 1960s.

Chapter 24

An Integrated View of Managerial Finance: A Summary

NOW that we have examined all the component parts of managerial finance, it is appropriate to conclude by drawing the pieces together. If one sees clearly how they interrelate, he will better understand the logic of the parts themselves and, of course, the over-all nature of managerial finance.

THE ROLE OF MANAGERIAL FINANCE WITHIN THE ECONOMY Because business firms produce the vast majority of the economy's goods and services, if the economy is to function efficiently so must the firms within it. By efficient operations we mean that firms must accurately determine what goods and services consumers want, then produce and distribute these products at the lowest possible cost.[1]

The financial manager plays a key role in the operations of his firm. Through his exercise of internal controls he helps insure that the resources available to the firm are used as efficiently as possible. Included here are both cost control and analysis designed to achieve the most efficient use of assets. The financial manager also plays a key role with regard to the use of external resources, or the decision to acquire resources not presently under the control of the firm. In the first place the capital budgeting decision is designed to insure that the firm makes desirable investments but forgoes undesirable

---

[1] Cost must include all social costs such as air and water pollution. One procedure for forcing the inclusion of such costs in firms' operating decisions is for a governmental agency to assess charges to polluters, with the charges being an increasing function of the level of pollution and the estimated social cost of the particular pollution. This is a thorny problem, but it is perfectly obvious that business firms can and will reduce pollution, just as they reduce labor usage or raw materials wastage, if their pollution costs are assessed against them. Charges based on the extent to which a firm creates pollution would provide this incentive. We might also note that it is unrealistic to expect voluntary controls to work in a competitive industry, as even one noncooperative firm can gain an advantage over other firms and literally force them to abandon voluntary controls. Thus, mandatory industry-wide controls are necessary.

ones. If all costs, social as well as private, are taken into account, and if the cost of capital is estimated appropriately, then the capital budgeting process will insure that the firm's capital expenditures are optimal from the points of view of both stockholders and society as a whole. The cost of capital, if it is determined in the correct manner, will reflect the opportunity cost of employing resources in the particular firm versus using them elsewhere in the economy. Further, if the firm is to procure funds in the least-cost manner, it must provide the package of investment securities that investors (that is, savers) consider to be the most desirable.

Finance, then, plays an important role both in increasing operating efficiency within individual business units and in allocating productive resources among firms.

Following the introduction, we reviewed some aspects of the federal tax system. Since corporations pay about half of their profits to the federal government as income taxes, and since personal incomes are taxed at a rate of up to 70 percent, taxes are clearly important in many financial decisions. Next, we considered the areas of financial analysis, planning, and control, which are summarized below. **FINANCIAL ANALYSIS, PLANNING, AND CONTROL**

We examined a number of financial ratios and saw how ratio analysis could be used to appraise key aspects of a firm's operating position. *Liquidity ratios*, especially the current and the quick ratios, were seen to provide information on the firm's ability to meet its short-run obligations. *Leverage ratios*—particularly the debt ratio, the times interest earned, and the times burden covered—were used to make judgments about the firm's risk of financial leverage. *Activity ratios*—relating to the turnover of such asset categories as inventories, accounts receivable, and fixed assets, as well as total assets—were studied to see how intensively the firm is employing its assets. Finally, the *profitability ratios*—the profit margin on sales, and the rate of return on net worth and total assets—were examined. The firm's primary operating objective is to earn a good return on its invested capital, and the rate-of-return ratios show how successfully it is meeting this objective. *Ratio Analysis*

The ratios are interrelated, and the set of relationships can be studied through the so-called du Pont system. Basically, the du Pont system makes use of the fact that the profit margin on sales times the turnover of total assets equals the rate of return on investment:

$$\frac{profit}{sales} \times \frac{sales}{assets} = \frac{profit}{assets}.$$

This equation can be expanded to include financial leverage, in which case the final product is the rate of return on net worth.

The significant advantage of the du Pont approach is that it helps the financial manager focus on problem areas. If the rate of return on net worth is lower than that of other firms in the same industry, one can trace back through the du Pont system to see where the trouble lies—for example, is some category of assets (such as inventories) too high, or are labor costs excessive? Note that in addition to comparing a firm with others in its industry, the financial manager can use the du Pont system of ratio analysis to study the trend in his firm's performance over time, thus helping to forestall developing problems.

By categorizing the ratios into four groups we stressed the uses of the ratios rather than their definitions. Our emphasis was on the generality of ratio analysis, and we sought to show that the purpose of a ratio determines how it is defined. The financial manager faces a myriad of situations calling for analysis—for example, appraising the credit-worthiness of his firm's customers, and analyzing the performance of his own firm's various operating divisions. Ratios facilitate this analysis, and because of their simplicity and flexibility they are one of the most widely used tools in the financial manager's kit.

Profit Planning Ratio analysis is used to examine the firm's current operating posture. Such constant surveillance is a critical part of the control process, but even if no current weaknesses are detected, the firm must still plan for future growth. One important element of such planning relates to decisions about expansion of existing operations, as well as movements into new product lines. Also, whatever type of expansion occurs, the firm must choose between using more or less highly automated productive processes. If a greater degree of automation is to be employed, then relatively heavy investments in fixed assets must be made, and this will increase fixed costs. Variable costs will, however, be relatively low in such cases. The extent to which fixed costs are incurred in the production process is defined as *operating leverage,* while the relationship between changing levels of sales and profits was considered at length under the topic of *break-even analysis.*

Financial Forecasting Although each specific asset expansion decision must be evaluated in detail in reaching the capital budgeting decision, the financial manager should also make broad-brush, aggregate forecasts of future asset requirements to assure that funds will be available to finance new investment programs. The first step in the aggregate forecast is to obtain an estimate of sales during each year of the planning period. This estimate is worked out jointly by the marketing, production, and finance departments—the marketing manager estimates demand, the production manager estimates capacity, and the financial manager estimates the availability of funds to finance new accounts receivable, inventories, and fixed assets.

Given the approximate level of sales, the financial manager must determine, as accurately as possible, the amount and timing of financial requirements over the planning horizon. On the basis of past relationships between sales and individual balance sheet items, the funds requirements can be forecast by using either (1) the *percent of sales method*, or (2) *regression analysis* (simple or multivariate, linear or curvilinear). Asset requirements by balance sheet category are forecast, spontaneously generated funds (increases in accounts payable plus retained earnings) are estimated, and the difference is determined. If the growth rate is quite rapid, asset requirements will exceed internal sources of funds, so plans must be made to obtain new debt or external equity money. If growth is slow, then more funds will be generated than are required to support the estimated growth in sales. In this case the financial manager will consider a number of alternatives including increasing the dividend payout ratio, retiring debt, using excess funds to acquire other firms or, perhaps, going back to the operating departments to encourage more R & D expenditures and a further search for profitable investment opportunities.

Control through Budgeting

Once the firm's broad goals for the planning period have been established, the next step is to set up a detailed plan of operation—the *budget*. A complete budget system encompasses all aspects of the firm's operations over the planning horizon; modifications in plans as required by variations in factors outside the firm's control, especially the level of economic activity, are accounted for by use of *flexible budgets*.

One aspect of the budget system—the cash budget—is especially important to the financial manager. In fact, the cash budget is the principal tool for making short-run forecasts of financial requirements. While forecasting procedures, such as the percent of sales method, are used to make rough estimates of the level of financial requirements over the next several years, the cash budget is used to estimate precisely how much money will be required and exactly when it will be needed during the coming year.

Interrelationships between Ratio Analysis, Profit Planning, Forecasting, and Budgeting

Ratio analysis is used to highlight certain key features of a firm's operations. Such an analysis can be conducted relatively quickly, and it can be updated frequently to permit early detection of developing problems. Further, ratio analysis is useful in that it facilitates a comparison between the firm in question and other firms in the industry. Once ratio analysis has been used to take stock of the firm's present condition, actions must be taken to exploit its strong points and to strengthen weak ones. Here, the planning techniques come into play. Break-even analysis can be used both to appraise the prospects of new product decisions and to analyze the effects of expansion or plant modernization decisions on earnings variability.

Sales forecasts are made and used to determine asset requirements and the funds needed to finance these assets. Specific, detailed plans for the current year are drawn up to implement the firm's long-run goals and objectives—this is the annual budget. A key part of the total budget—the cash budget—pinpoints when and how much money will be required during the budget period.

Finally, the financial manager continually compares actual operating results with budgeted figures: Are sales running at the forecasted level? Are costs being kept within the estimated limits? Are cash flows running on schedule? Are all divisions meeting their own individual budgeted objectives? This process, called budgetary control, is an important key to successful operations.

LONG-TERM In addition to his role in the analysis-planning-control process de-
INVESTMENT scribed above, the financial manager must make decisions on specific
DECISIONS individual investments. These capital budgeting decisions involve the whole process of evaluating projects whose returns are expected to extend beyond one year.

Compound Since long-term returns are involved, the effects of compound interest
Interest must be considered. Chapter 7 was devoted to a discussion of compound interest and the ways of taking it into account in financial analysis. Perhaps the most fundamental idea developed in Chapter 7 was that of *present value:* The present value of any asset is equal to the sum of future cash flows from the asset, discounted at an "appropriate" interest rate later defined as the firm's cost of capital.

Capital Capital budgeting, as it is practiced by sophisticated firms, involves
Budgeting (1) estimating the cost of each prospective project, (2) estimating annual net cash flows from each project, (3) determining the appropriate risk-adjusting discount rate (cost of capital) for the project, and (4) using the present value equation to see if the project's net present value (*NPV*) is positive. If the *NPV* is positive or, alternatively, if the internal rate of return (the *IRR*) exceeds the cost of capital, the project should be accepted.

This sketch of capital budgeting is, of course, highly simplified. At times it is difficult to estimate either the cost of a project or the cash flows that will come from it. Ordinarily, the *NPV* and the *IRR* give identical answers to these questions: Which of two mutually exclusive projects should be selected? How large should the total capital budget be? However, under certain circumstances conflicts may arise. In general, the *NPV* is preferred in the absence of capital rationing, but the *IRR* may be the better method if capital rationing is imposed. Under capital rationing, or if the cost of capital is not constant, only mathematical programming techniques can provide truly optimum solutions to the capital budgeting decision.

Both logic and empirical evidence suggest that investors prefer investments with relatively certain returns. This being the case, investment decisions should encompass more than just the *expected return* from a project—the decision-maker should also take into account any *risk differentials* that may exist among projects.

> *Uncertainty, or Risk Analysis*

The first task in risk analysis is to measure the riskiness of various projects. The measure of risk that we employ, and the one used most frequently in practice, is the *standard deviation* of the probability distribution of expected returns from a project. The larger the standard deviation, the greater the probability that the actual return will deviate significantly from the expected return, and the greater the riskiness of the project.

The risk to the firm embodied in a single project is dependent upon the correlation between returns on the project at hand and the remainder of the firm's assets. If this correlation is positive, returns on the project are high when other assets are also providing high returns, and vice-versa. However, if the correlation is negative, returns on the project will be high when those on other assets are low, so taking on the project in question will reduce earnings fluctuations for the firm as a whole. In this case, favorable *portfolio effects* are said to be present because the over-all risk to the firm is less than the apparent risk of the project considered alone. Portfolio effects are taken into account when the firm considers diversification measures in its capital budget.

The typical method for dealing with risk in capital budgeting is to employ a lower cost of capital for less risky projects and a higher cost for more risky ones—this is called the *risk-adjusted discount rate method.* For example, a firm may determine that its average cost of capital is 10 percent and use this discount rate to find the NPV of "average risk" projects. It will use rates less than 10 percent for low-risk projects and more than 10 for high-risk investments.

In Chapter 9 we saw that risk aversion leads investors to seek higher returns on more risky investments—the riskier the investment, the greater the *risk premium* (the amount by which the expected return on a risky investment exceeds the riskless rate of return). These concepts were extended in Chapters 10, 11, and 12, where we showed

> **FINANCIAL STRUCTURE AND THE COST OF CAPITAL**

the effect of capital structure on risk and, thus, on the firm's cost of capital.

Financial Leverage Whenever a firm uses debt capital, it is employing *financial leverage*. Since debt typically involves a fixed interest charge, any fluctuation in operating income will produce a magnified fluctuation in earnings available to common stock. The greater the extent of financial leverage, the greater the potential earnings variability of the common stock.

The impact of financial leverage can be examined graphically, but it can also be studied more rigorously and measured in terms of the *degree of financial leverage*. In addition, the effects of financial and operating leverage may be combined, with the *combined leverage factor* showing the percentage change in earnings per share that results from a given percentage change in sales.

Valuation and When the present value concepts developed in Chapter 7 were used
Rates of Return in Chapter 8 to determine the desirability of investing in specific assets, we determined the value of the asset *to the firm* by discounting the expected cash flows by the appropriate cost of capital. This same valuation technique may be applied to the firm as a whole by investors—common and preferred stockholders, and bondholders. In this latter case the cash flows are the expected returns on the firm's securities—interest plus maturity value on bonds, dividends on preferred stocks, and dividends plus capital gains on common stocks. The appropriate discount rate is dependent primarily on the riskiness of the particular security and supply and demand conditions in the capital market—the riskier the security, the higher the appropriate discount rate, and the greater the demand for funds, vis-à-vis the supply of funds, the higher the rate.

Notice particularly that the firm can influence its cost of capital. If it uses a high degree of operating leverage and invests in assets which produce highly uncertain returns, then it will be subject to a high degree of *basic business risk*, which will cause its cost of capital to be relatively high. If it superimposes financial leverage on top of its basic business risk, it further increases the risk borne by investors.

The Cost Each component of the capital structure has what we have called a
of Capital *component cost*, and each individual component cost is a function of (1) the riskiness of the income stream expected by owners of the particular component securities (for example, bondholders or stockholders), and (2) the opportunity cost of the security holders (for example, the interest rate on other bonds or the expected rate of return on comparable stocks of other companies). The firm can do little to influence opportunity costs, but its decisions with regard to both asset

purchases and the use of financial leverage affect the riskiness of its securities.

Both theory and empirical evidence suggest that for each firm there is an *optimum capital structure*, that is, a mix of debt and equity securities that minimizes the cost of raising any given amount of capital.[2] Shifts in this optimum structure as capital market conditions vary is the issue discussed in Chapter 23. However, at any point in time there is an optimum structure.[3]

Recall that we have two primary reasons for wanting to know the cost of capital: (1) we need it for capital budgeting purposes, and (2) we want to minimize it. The cost of capital needed for capital budgeting is the *marginal cost*, while the cost we want to minimize is the *average cost* of new capital raised during the planning period (generally a year). The procedure for determining these two cost figures is as follows:

1. Decide upon a tentative optimum capital structure.

2. Determine the cost of the various capital components under this capital structure:

  a. Debt cost = (interest rate)(1 — tax rate).

  b. Preferred cost = (preferred dividend)/(price of preferred net of flotation costs).

  c. Retained earnings   cost = k = expected   dividend   yield + expected capital gains = $\dfrac{D}{P} + g$.

  d. New outside equity (newly issued common stock) cost

$$= \frac{k}{1 - \text{flotation cost}}.$$

3. Use the capital structure percentages and the estimated component costs to calculate a weighted average cost.

4. The marginal and average costs are constant and equal to one another until retained earnings have been used up. At this point, newly issued common stock must be sold, raising the component cost of equity. Here, the marginal cost rises above the average cost, and this now higher marginal cost causes the average cost to begin increasing.

[2] Theories have been advanced by Modigliani and Miller, among others, that no optimum capital structure would exist if there were no corporate taxes and if capital markets were perfect. Since neither condition holds, even advocates of these theories agree that in the real world there is an optimum capital structure.

[3] Empirical evidence suggests that the average cost of capital curve is U-shaped, not V-shaped, so there is generally a *range* of capital structures within which the average cost of capital is *approximately* minimized. This greatly facilitates the financial manager's task, as it is much easier to locate a range than a unique point.

Dividend Policy   Our study of the cost of capital makes it clear that because of flotation costs, if for no other reason, retained earnings have a lower cost than new outside equity. However, dividends, which constitute an important part of the return to common stockholders, must be lowered if a firm increases its retained earnings. Thus, dividend policy—determining how net income will be split between dividends and reinvestment—is an important component of over-all financial policy.

We found in Chapter 13 that because of capital budgeting and cost of capital considerations a firm with many good investment opportunities will tend to have a low dividend payout ratio, while a firm with few good investments will have a high payout. We also found that the firm's own individual situation—its cash or liquidity position, its access to capital markets, the tax position of its stockholders, and so on—have an important bearing on its dividend policy.

REVIEW OF FINANCIAL THEORY   It is useful to recap developments to this point. First, the operating goal of the firm is to maximize the market value of stockholders' equity.

To achieve this maximization the firm must satisfy a number of conditions:

1. Operating efficiency.   The firm must operate efficiently in the sense of recognizing customer demands, both actual and potential, and producing to meet this demand at a minimum cost.[4] The planning and control techniques introduced earlier are designed to enhance operating efficiency.

2. Rate of expansion.   Expansion decisions (capital budgeting) should be made if, and only if, the expected present value of a specific project exceeds the cost of undertaking the project. In this connection note that since more efficient firms have higher expected cash flows than inefficient ones, resources shift over time to efficient businesses.

3. Risk characteristics.   The degree of business risk inherent in a firm's assets combines with any additional risk resulting from financial leverage to determine its over-all risk characteristics. These, in turn, affect the firm's cost of capital.

4. Average cost of capital.   To maximize its value the firm must minimize the cost of capital for financing its chosen set of assets. This means selecting the set of securities—long and short-term debt, preferred and common stock, retained earnings and new outside equity, convertibles or bonds with warrants, and the specific provisions attached to each of these instruments—that minimizes capital costs.

---

[4] We emphasized that for the firm to be efficient in a *social* sense cost must include social costs as well as private costs. Governmental agencies must assess the level of these costs and force firms either to eliminate them or be taxed to cover them.

5. Marginal cost of capital. The marginal cost of capital is dependent upon basic business risk and financial leverage. It is also a function of the amount of capital the firm raises during a given time period. If the rate of expansion is quite rapid, the firm must bring in new outside equity capital, which causes the marginal cost of capital to rise.

6. Simultaneous determination. The cost of capital is a necessary ingredient in asset expansion decisions because we must know the marginal cost of capital to determine whether or not each particular project should be accepted or rejected. We must also know the size of the capital budget before we can determine the marginal cost of capital. Therefore, the cost of capital and the capital budget must be determined simultaneously. If we knew the cost of capital schedule and the investment opportunity schedule *precisely*, then we could use mathematical techniques to obtain the simultaneous solution to a system of equations and, thus, arrive at a precise value-maximizing set of investments. As a practical matter, we do not have sufficient information to warrant using this approach.

Although we cannot obtain the simultaneous solution, the pragmatic usefulness of the theoretical concepts that have been developed should not be ruled out. The financial manager can obtain an estimate of his cost of capital which, if not exact, is sufficiently accurate to use in the capital-budgeting process. Further, under normal conditions the rate of expansion, or even changes in the firm's mix of assets that would cause significant changes in its basic business risk, is not large enough to alter its cost of capital seriously. If the cost of capital is relatively constant, the simultaneity conditions are not important, and straight-forward capital-budgeting techniques, such as the risk-adjusted *NPV* method, are appropriate. Further, even if the firm is contemplating a significant change in operations—such as a shift in product lines, entry into a new industry, or an important change in dividend or capital structure policy—the wisdom of such a move can certainly be better ascertained if it is considered within the framework of our theory of financial policy.

From Chapter 7 to Chapter 13 we covered most of the important theoretical issues in managerial finance. In the remaining chapters of the book—Chapters 14 through 23—we completed the picture of managerial finance, filling in such important details as the nature and use of various types of long-term financial instruments, merger policy, financial timing, and working capital management. **WORKING CAPITAL MANAGEMENT**

In theory, investments in current assets should be analyzed in the same way as investments in capital assets. In practice, however, important differences in the two types of assets lead to variations in the way the financial manager controls current and fixed asset investments. The most important difference is the fact that investments in capital assets commit the firm to a certain course of action over an extended period, while current asset investments can be modified relatively quickly. This means that capital budgeting must emphasize long-run projections, discounting procedures, and the like. Current asset management, in contrast, is more short-run oriented; the primary objective is to use current assets efficiently. There is an opportunity cost of tying funds up in inventories, cash, and accounts receivable. If the investment in these assets can be reduced without increasing costs or reducing sales, then such a reduction increases the firm's profitability. Thus, current asset management deals largely with the use of techniques such as EOQ models, lock box systems, and so forth, which are designed to control the investment in working capital.

A knowledge of certain institutional arrangements is essential to an understanding of managerial finance. Chapters 15 and 16 describe the types of institutions that provide short- and intermediate-term funds to businesses, as well as such important financial arrangements as factoring, term loans, and leasing. A variety of different sources of funds and different types of appropriate security arrangements exist for use under different conditions, and a financial manager must be knowledgeable about these institutional factors if he is to minimize his firm's cost of obtaining funds.

LONG-TERM FINANCING　In our discussion of capital structure and the cost of capital we emphasized the risk differences between debt and equity. We did not consider other differences, nor did we attempt to show the alternative ways "debt" and "equity" securities can be packaged. These points, which are essential to a thorough understanding of managerial finance, were covered in Chapters 17, 18, 19, and 20.

One critical distinction between debt and equity is the fact that equity—the common stock—has control of a firm's operations. In theory, management should operate in strict accordance with "what is best for stockholders"—subject to external constraints imposed by labor, government, and so on. In practice, however, if a firm's managers are not also its major stockholders, management will also be concerned about maintaining its control position. This factor can influence the stock-versus-bonds decision and, thus, perhaps affect the firm's capital structure.

Long-term debt can be issued in many forms: secured and unsecured, marketable and nonmarketable, senior and junior, callable and noncallable, convertible and nonconvertible, with and without a sinking fund, and so on. Preferred stock can also be issued with a number of alternative features. Depending on the firm's own position and investors' preferences, it will be advantageous for the financial manager to use different ones of these features at different times. For example, if the financial manager feels that interest rates are high presently and likely to decline in the near future, he will probably insist on making new long-term debt callable. Similarly, if investors think that a sinking fund will reduce the riskiness of the firm's bonds, they will accept a lower interest rate if the bonds have a sinking fund. However, a sinking fund will increase the cash flow requirements for servicing the debt, and this may be unattractive from the firm's standpoint. The financial manager must balance all these alternatives and decide upon the specific set of features that will be in the best interests of his firm.

Convertible debt and preferred stock, or bonds with warrants, can be issued to raise new money. When either convertibles or bonds with warrants are used, the purchaser receives a package consisting of both a fixed income component and the possibility of a capital gain. Thus, the investor is able to hedge his position somewhat—he is more protected against losses than if he owned only common stock, yet he can still share the benefits if the firm is highly successful or if inflation dilutes the value of fixed return securities. Because of this protection, investors may be willing to accept lower over-all expected rates of return on convertibles or bonds with warrants than on straight debt plus common stock.

The usefulness of convertibles and warrants varies over time. They are most attractive in times of uncertainty such as the early 1970s, and at such times the financial manager can use them to lower his firm's cost of capital.

Because of his strategic position, the financial manager has a key **MERGER** role in corporate mergers and acquisitions. In a sense, a merger is **POLICY** like any other long-term investment decision—one firm acquires another in much the same way that it would acquire a new plant or office building. From this point of view, the merger decision should be analyzed in the capital budgeting framework, and the acquisition should be made if it increases the acquiring firm's net present value as reflected in the price of its stock. However, mergers are frequently quite significant both in terms of their impact on the acquiring firm and on the economy. Not only can a bad merger decision literally wreck a firm, but mergers among competing firms can turn a competitive market into an oligopolistic one. Accordingly, both managements and the federal government are generally more concerned over merger decisions than over most other decisions made by corporations.

THE TIMING OF FINANCIAL POLICY

Financial managers have at least some flexibility in their operations. Even though a firm may have a target debt/total assets ratio, it can deviate from this target to some extent in a given year to take advantage of favorable conditions in either the bond market or the stock market. Similarly, although it may have a target relationship between its long- and short-term debt, it can vary from this target if market conditions suggest that such action is appropriate.

As a basis for making sound decisions with respect to financial timing, we analyzed data covering both cyclical and long-term trends. Uncertainties about the future have increased in recent years, and this has increased the importance of sound financial timing. Also, attempts to deal with the greater uncertainties have given rise to innovations in financing techniques and patterns. Some important changes in financing that have developed in response to changes in the economy and in the money and capital markets include:

1. Long-term financing has increased in comparison to the use of short-term commercial bank financing. Bond flotations in the capital markets have risen to record levels.

2. Public flotations of equity issues have increased substantially.

3. A large increase in debt ratios has occurred in response to the inflationary environment. From 1966 to 1969 the ratio of debt to assets for all manufacturing companies rose from 33 percent to 41 percent.

4. An increase has occurred in the use of convertibles and warrants.

5. Insurance companies and other institutional lenders have virtually ceased providing credit to small and medium-sized borrowers on a straight-debt basis. For business loans warrants are usually required, while on mortgages supplementary payments based on a percentage of gross or net income are stipulated in loan contracts.

6. New equity securities have been issued in spite of the decline in equity prices beginning in early 1969. As the debt ratios of large corporations rose, and as their liquidity positions declined, larger corporations began (in 1970) to sell equity issues in substantial amounts.

7. Since larger firms have greater access to the financial markets, an increase in the volume of trade credit has occurred, with larger firms increasing their extension of credit to smaller ones.

The developments outlined above indicate that trends in the money and capital markets have become of increased importance to financial managers. The changes have been so massive that not only has financial timing been involved but also innovations in the forms of financing used have been stimulated.

Finance is a complex subject, blending together abstract theory, practical decision models and techniques, and a description of the institutional setting in which financial decisions are made. Further, it is a dynamic area, ever-changing in response to new technology and developments within the economy. These characteristics make finance a difficult subject, but one which is exciting and challenging. Finance is also important to the economy, for we must have efficient firms if the economy is to cope with the problems it faces. We can only hope that this book has, by helping the reader to understand the theory and methodology of finance, assisted in preparing him to meet the challenges of the future.

CONCLUSION

QUESTIONS

24–1 Discuss the relationship between size of firm and the life-cycle concept.

24–2 Discuss the relationship between diversification and the life-cycle concept.

24–3 Should a firm always attempt to forestall the declining phase of the life cycle? What about a firm created for the purpose of exploiting a given mineral deposit, say an iron ore mine?

24–4 Explain how each of the following factors could be expected to influence the extent to which actual firms conform to the life-cycle hypothesis:

a) Development of the corporate form of organization
b) Corporate diversification
c) Research and development expenditures
d) Trend toward larger firms

24–5 If the average cost of capital is actually minimized when the firm has a certain amount of debt in its capital structure, is it logical for older, slower growing firms to retire all their debt by retaining earnings? If such a tendency is observed, what is the implication for the economists' notion that firms seek to maximize stockholder wealth?

24–6 A fast-growing firm usually has a higher profit rate than a firm growing more slowly. Yet the former will be less able to finance its growth from retained earnings. Explain.

24–7 A large, well-established firm typically retains a lower percentage of its earnings than does a smaller, faster growing firm. Yet the larger firm finances a higher percentage of its financing needs from retained earnings than does the smaller firm. Explain.

24–8 Two firms each earn 6 percent on sales and have an asset turnover of 2 times. Firm A has a debt-to-total-assets ratio of one third. Firm B has a ratio of two thirds. What is the respective profit rate on net worth for each firm?

24–9 A firm has a 5 percent return on sales. It has a debt-to-net-worth ratio of 100 percent. What turnover of total assets is required for a 20 percent return on net worth?

24–10 Which firms are likely to have the higher asset turnover—new, small, rapidly growing firms or the largest firms in American industry?

24–11 What are the major sources of initial financing of new, small firms? Why?

24–12 Are large firms likely to have a higher or a lower ratio of trade receivables to trade payables than have smaller firms in the same line of business?

24–13 At what stage in its development is an industrial firm likely to make the greatest use of long-term debt? Explain.

24–14 Explain the characteristics of the economy and the stage of development of a firm and of its financial structure that will favor the use of convertible debt to raise funds equal to 20 percent of its present total assets.

PROBLEMS **24–1*** To obtain a position in the underwriting department of a major investment banking house is difficult, but it is especially hard to land a job that calls for contact with the top partners so that one may really learn the inside of the business. Through family connections, however, Gordon Hammrick was fortunate enough to get the job of assistant to William Murray, Senior Partner and Managing Officer of Murray, Finch, Price, Farmer & Smith. Hammrick received his bachelor's degree in history only two weeks ago, and this is his first day on the job. After a rather pleasant morning spent meeting various people around the office, including some attractive secretaries, Hammrick was given his first task.

Murray had not only been forced to miss his regular Thursday afternoon golf match, but he also had to stay up until 3 A.M. Thursday night finishing some recommendations on the types of financing that a group of clients should use. The next morning, having completed the analyses and made his recommendations, Murray turned over to Hammrick the folder on each client and, attached to each of the folders, the recommendations as to the types of financing that each should use. He then told Hammrick, first, to have the analyses and financing recommendations typed up and sent immediately to each of the client companies and, second, that he was taking his secretary away for a weekend of uninterrupted dictation. Murray particularly stressed that he should be contacted during the weekend only in the event of an emergency.

The first thing Hammrick did was to detach the analyses and recommendations from the folders and give them to one of the secretaries to type up. When the secretary returned the typed reports, Hammrick discovered that he did not know which recommendation belonged to which company! He had folders on nine different companies and financing recommendations for nine companies, but he could not match them up. Hammrick's major was history, so he could not be expected to be able to match the financing recommendations with the appropriate companies. However, as a finance student, you should be able to help Hammrick by telling him which companies in Section B should use the financing methods shown in Section A.

Section A

1. Common stock: nonrights.

2. Debt with warrants.

3. Factoring.

* This case study is taken from Eugene F. Brigham, Timothy J. Nantell, Robert T. Aubey, and Stephen L. Hawk, *Cases in Managerial Finance* (New York: Holt, Rinehart and Winston, Inc., 1970).

4. Friends or relatives.

5. Preferred stock (nonconvertible).

6. Common stock: rights offering.

7. Long-term bonds.

8. Leasing arrangement.

9. Convertible debentures.

Section B

(a) Arizona Mining Company

Arizona Mining needs $10 million to finance the acquisition of mineral rights to some land in south-central Arizona, as well as to pay for some extensive surveys, core-borings, magnetic aerial surveys, and other types of analyses designed to determine whether the mineral deposits on this land warrant development. If the tests are favorable, the company will need an additional $10 million. Arizona Mining's common stock is currently selling at $12, while the company is earning approximately $1 a share. Other firms in the industry sell at from 10 to 15 times earnings. Arizona Mining's debt ratio is 25 percent, which compares with an industry average of 30 percent. Total assets at the last balance sheet date were $105 million.

(b) New York Power Company

Since New York Power, a major electric utility, is organized as a holding company, the Security and Exchange Commission must approve all security issues; such approval is automatic if the company stays within conventional norms for the electric utility industry. Reasonable norms call for long-term debt in the range of 55–65 percent, preferred stock in the range of 0–15 percent, and common equity in the range of 25–35 percent. New York Power Company currently has total assets of $1 billion financed as follows: $600 million debt, $50 million preferred stock, and $350 million common equity. The company plans to raise an additional $25 million at this time.

(c) Wilson Brothers, Inc.

A wholesale grocery business in Cincinnati, Ohio, this company is incorporated, with each of the three Wilson brothers owning one-third of the outstanding stock. The company is profitable, but rapid growth has put it under a severe financial strain. The real estate is all under mortgage to an insurance company, the inventory is being used under a blanket chattel mortgage to secure a bank line of credit, and the accounts receivable are being factored. With total assets of $5 million, the company now needs an additional $100,000 to purchase 20 forklift trucks and related equipment to facilitate handling in the shipping and receiving department.

(d) Alabama Milling Company

Alabama Milling manufactures unbleached cotton cloth, then bleaches the cloth and dyes it in various colors and patterns. The finished cloth is packaged in bulk and sold on 60-day credit terms, largely to relatively small clothing companies operating in the New York City area. The company's plant and equipment have been financed in part by a mortgage loan, and this is the only long-term debt. Raw materials—cotton and dyes—are purchased on terms calling for payment within 30 days of receipt of goods, but no discounts are offered.

Because the national economy is currently so prosperous, apparel sales have experienced a sharp increase. This, in turn, has produced a marked increase in the demand for Alabama Milling's products. To finance a higher level of output, Alabama Milling needs approximately $500,000.

(e) Florida-Pacific Corporation

Florida-Pacific is a major producer of plywood, paper, and other forest products. The company's stock is widely held, actively traded, and listed on the New York Stock Exchange; recently it has been trading in the range of $30–$35 a share. The latest 12 months' earnings were $2.12; the current dividend rate is 80 cents a year, and earnings, dividends, and the price of the company's stock have been growing at a rate of about 7 percent over the last few years. Florida-Pacific's debt ratio is currently 42 percent versus 25 percent for other large forest product firms. Other firms in the industry, on the average, have been growing at a rate of about 5 percent a year, and their stocks have been selling at a price earnings ratio of about 13. Florida-Pacific has an opportunity to acquire a substantial stand of forest in Northern California. The current owners of the property are asking $20 million in cash for the land and timber.

(f) Toy World

Joseph Marino is an employee of the state of Pennsylvania and an avid model airplane and model automobile builder, and he has just learned that some of the stores in a new neighborhood shopping center are still available to be leased. Marino knows that no good toy and hobby store exists in the southwest section of the city of Harrisburg, and he believes that if he can obtain approximately $20,000 for fixtures and stock, he can open a successful store in the new shopping center. His liquid savings total $5,000, so Marino needs an additional $15,000 to open the proposed store.

(g) Knight Electronics Corporation

Knight Electronics is a medium-sized electronics company whose sales distribution is approximately 30 percent for defense contracts and 70 percent for nonmilitary uses. The company has been growing rapidly in recent years, and projections based on current research and development prospects call for continued growth at a rate of 10–12 percent a year. Although recent reports of several brokerage firms suggest that the firm's rate of growth might be slowing down, Knight's management believes, on the basis of internal information, that no decline is in sight. The company's stock, which is traded on the Pacific Stock Exchange, is selling at 20 times earnings; this is slightly below the 23 times ratio of Standard & Poor's electronics industry average. The firm's debt ratio is 40 percent, just above the 38 percent average for the industry. The company has assets of $28 million and needs an additional $4 million, over and above retained earnings, to support the projected level of growth during the next 12 months.

(h) Utah Chemical Company

Utah Chemical is a closely held company that was founded in 1952 to extract from the Great Salt Lake minerals used in agricultural fertilizers. The company's debt ratio is 48 percent versus an average ratio of 36 percent for agricultural fertilizer producers in general. The stock is owned in equal parts by 10 individuals, none of whom is in a position to put additional funds into the business. Sales for the most recent year were $10 million, and earnings after taxes amounted to $600,000. Total assets, as of the latest balance sheet, were $8 million. Utah Chemical needs an additional $3 million to finance expansion during the current fiscal year, and, given the worldwide growth in demand for agricultural chemicals, the firm can anticipate additional outside capital needs in the years ahead.

(i) Universal Container Corporation

Universal Container is engaged in the manufacture of cans, glass bottles, paper boxes of various sorts, a variety of plastic tubes, and other packaging materials. Since the firm sells to a great many producers of nondurable consumer goods, sales are relatively stable. The current price of the company's stock, which is listed on the New York Stock Exchange, is $42, and the most recent earnings and dividends per share are $4 and $2, respectively. The rate of growth in sales, earnings, and dividends in the last few years has averaged 5 percent. Universal Container has total assets of $360 million. Current liabilities, which consist primarily of accounts payable and accruals, are $25 million; long-term debt is $75 million; and common equity totals $260 million. An additional $30 million of external funds is required to build and equip a new can-manufacturing complex in Central California and to supply the new facility with working capital.

24–2 Allied Chemists, Inc., has experienced the following sales, profit, and balance sheet patterns. Identify the financial problem that has developed, and recommend a solution for it.

Allied Chemists, Inc.
Financial data, 1963–1972
In millions of dollars

Income statements	1963	1964	1965	1966	1967	1968	1969	1970	1971	1972
Sales	$100	$140	$180	$200	$240	$400	$360	$440	$480	$680
Profits after tax	10	14	18	20	24	40	36	44	48	68
Dividends	8	10	12	12	14	20	20	28	36	48
Retained earnings	2	4	6	8	10	20	16	16	12	20
Cumulative retained earnings	2	6	12	20	30	50	66	82	94	114
Balance sheets										
Current assets	20	30	40	50	60	100	80	110	120	160
Net fixed assets	30	40	50	50	60	100	100	110	120	180
Total assets	$ 50	$ 70	$ 90	$100	$120	$200	$180	$220	$240	$340
Trade credit	8	12	16	18	20	36	30	40	40	120
Bank credit	8	12	20	20	26	58	28	40	40	40
Other	2	10	12	12	14	16	16	18	16	16
Total current liabilities	18	34	48	50	60	110	74	98	96	176
Long-term debt	0	0	0	0	0	10	10	10	20	20
Total debt	18	34	48	50	60	120	84	108	116	196
Common stock	30	30	30	30	30	30	30	30	30	30
Retained earnings	2	6	12	20	30	50	66	82	94	114
Net worth	32	36	42	50	60	80	96	112	124	144
Total claims on assets	$ 50	$ 70	$ 90	$100	$120	$200	$180	$220	$240	$340

24–3 a) A firm with $60 million of assets judges that it is at the beginning of a three-year growth cycle. It is a manufacturing firm with a total-debt-to-assets ratio of 16 percent. It expects sales and net earnings to grow at a rate of 10 percent a year.

Stock prices are expected to rise 30 percent a year over the three-year period. The firm will need $6 million at the beginning of the three-year period and another $3 million by the middle of the third year. It is at the beginning of a general business upswing, when money and capital costs are what they generally are after about a year of recession and at the beginning of an upswing. By the middle of the third year, money and capital costs will have their characteristic pattern near the peak of an upswing.

How should the firm raise the $6 million and the $3 million?

b) An aerospace company with sales of $25 million a year needs $5 million to finance expansion. It has a debt-to-total-assets ratio of 65 percent. Its common stock, which is widely held, is selling at a price/earnings ratio of 25 times. It is comparing the sale of common stock and convertible debentures.

Which do you recommend? Why?

c) A chemical company has been growing steadily. To finance a growth of sales from $40 million a year to $50 million over a two-year period, it needs $2 million in additional equipment. When additional working capital needs are taken into account, the total additional financing required during the first year is $5 million. Profits will rise by 50 percent after the first 10 months. The stock is currently selling at 20 times earnings. It can borrow on straight debt at 7 1/2 percent. It could borrow with a convertibility or warrant "sweetner" for 3/4 percent less. The present debt-to-total-asset ratio is 25 percent.

Which form of financing should it employ?

Glossary

Accelerated Depreciation Depreciation methods that write off the cost of an asset at a faster rate than the write-off under the straight-line method. The three principal methods of accelerated depreciation are: (1) sum-of-years-digits, (2) double declining balance, and (3) units of production.

Accruals Continually recurring short-term liabilities. Examples are accrued wages, accrued taxes, and accrued interest.

Aging Schedule A report showing how long accounts receivable have been outstanding. It gives the percent of receivables not past due and the percent past due by, for example, one month, two months, or other periods.

Amortize To liquidate on an installment basis; an amortized loan is one in which the principal amount of the loan is repaid in installments during the life of the loan.

Annuity A series of payments of a fixed amount for a specified number of years.

Arrearage Overdue payment; frequently, omitted dividends on preferred stocks.

Assignment A relatively inexpensive way of liquidating a failing firm that does not involve going through the courts.

Balloon Payment When a debt is not fully amortized, the final payment is larger than the preceding payments and is called a "balloon" payment.

Benefit/Cost Ratio (See Profitability Index)

Bankruptcy A legal procedure for formally liquidating a business carried out under the jurisdiction of courts of law.

Bond A long-term debt instrument.

Book Value The accounting value of an asset. The book value of a share of common stock is equal to the net worth (common stock plus surplus) of the corporation divided by the number of shares of stock outstanding.

Break-even Analysis An analytical technique for studying the relation between fixed cost, variable cost, and profits. A break-even *chart* graphically depicts the nature of break-even analysis. The break-even *point* represents that volume of sales at which total costs equal total revenues (that is, profits equal zero).

Call (1) An option to buy (or "call") a share of stock at a specified price within a specified period. (2) The process of redeeming a bond or preferred stock issue before its normal maturity.

Call Premium The amount in excess of par value that a company must pay when it calls a security.

Call Price The price that must be paid when a security is called. The call price is equal to the par value plus the call premium.

Call Privilege A provision incorporated into a bond or a share of preferred stock that gives the issuer the right to redeem (call) the security at a specified price.

Calling The action of exercising the call privilege and redeeming securities prior to their maturity date.

Capital Asset An asset with a life of more than one year that is not bought and sold in the ordinary course of business.

Capital Budgeting The process of planning expenditures on assets whose returns are expected to extend beyond one year.

Capital Gains Profits on the sale of capital assets held for six months or more.

Capital Losses Losses on the sale of capital assets.

Capital Rationing A situation where a constraint is placed on the total size of the capital investment during a particular period.

Capital Structure   The permanent long-term financing of the firm represented by long-term debt, preferred stock, and net worth (net worth consists of capital, capital surplus, and earned surplus). Capital structure is distinguished from *financial structure*, which includes short-term debt plus all reserve accounts.

Capitalization Rate   A discount rate used to find the present value of a series of future cash receipts; sometimes called *discount rate*.

Carry-back; Carry-forward   For income tax purposes, losses that can be carried backward or forward to reduce federal income taxes.

Cash Budget   A schedule showing cash flows (receipts, disbursements, and net cash) for a firm over a specified period.

Cash Cycle   The length of time between the purchase of raw materials and the collection of accounts receivable generated in the sale of the final product.

Certainty Equivalents   The amount of cash (or rate of return) that someone would require *with certainty* to make him indifferent between this certain sum (or rate of return) and a particular uncertain, risky sum (or rate of return).

Chattel Mortgage   A mortgage on personal property (not real estate). A mortgage on equipment would be a chattel mortgage.

Coefficient of Variation   Standard deviation divided by the mean.

Collateral   Assets that are used to secure a loan.

Commercial Paper   Unsecured, short-term promissory notes of large firms, usually issued in denominations of $1 million or more. The rate of interest on commercial paper is typically somewhat below the prime rate of interest.

Commitment Fee   The fee paid to a lender for a formal line of credit.

Compensating Balance   A required minimum checking account balance that a firm must maintain with a commercial bank. The required balance is generally equal to 15 to 20 percent of the amount of loans outstanding. Compensating balances can raise the effective rate of interest on bank loans.

Composition   An informal method of reorganization that voluntarily reduces creditors' claims on the debtor firm.

Compound Interest   An interest rate that is applicable when interest in succeeding periods is earned not only on the initial principal but also on the accumulated interest of prior periods. Compound interest is contrasted to *simple interest*, in which returns are not earned on interest received.

Compounding   The arithmetic process of determining the final value of a payment or series of payments when compound interest is applied.

Conditional Sales Contract   A method of financing new equipment by paying it off in installments over a one- to five-year period. The seller retains title to the equipment until payment has been completed.

Consolidated Tax Return   An income tax return that combines the income statement of several affiliated firms.

Continuous Compounding (Discounting)   As opposed to discrete compounding, interest is added continuously rather than at discrete points in time.

Conversion Price   The effective price paid for common stock when the stock is obtained by converting either convertible preferred stocks or convertible bonds. For example, if a $1,000 bond is convertible into 20 shares of stock, the conversion price is $50 ($1,000/20).

Conversion Ratio or Conversion Rate   The number of shares of common stock that may be obtained by converting a convertible bond or share of convertible preferred stock.

Convertibles   Securities (generally bonds or preferred stocks) that are exchangeable at the option of the holder for common stock of the issuing firm.

Cost of Capital The discount rate that should be used in the capital budgeting process.

Coupon Rate The stated rate of interest on a bond.

Covenant Detailed clauses contained in loan agreements. Covenants are designed to protect the lender and include such items as limits on total indebtedness, restrictions on dividends, minimum current ratio, and similar provisions.

Cut-off Point In the capital budgeting process, the minimum rate of return on acceptable investment opportunities.

Decision Tree A device for setting forth graphically the pattern of relationship between decisions and chance events.

Debt Ratio Total debt divided by total assets.

Debenture A long-term debt instrument that is not secured by a mortgage on specific property.

Default The failure to fulfill a contract. Generally, default refers to the failure to pay interest or principal on debt obligations.

Degree of Leverage The percentage increase in profits resulting from a given percentage increase in sales. The degree of leverage may be calculated for financial leverage, operating leverage, or both combined.

Discount Rate The interest rate used in the discounting process; sometimes called *capitalization rate*.

Discounted Cash Flow Techniques Methods of ranking investment proposals. Included are (1) internal rate of return method, (2) net present value method, and (3) profitability index or benefit/cost ratio.

Discounting The process of finding the present value of a series of future cash flows. Discounting is the reverse of compounding.

Discounting of Accounts Receivable Short-term financing where accounts receivable are used to secure the loan. The lender *does not* buy the accounts receivable but simply uses them as collateral for the loan. Also called "pledging of accounts receivable."

Dividend Yield The ratio of the current dividend to the current price of a share of stock.

Earnings Multiplier The price/earnings ratio (the P/E ratio).

EBIT Abbreviation for "earnings before interest and taxes."

EPS Abbreviation for "earnings per share."

Economical Ordering Quantity (EOQ) The optimum (least cost) quantity of merchandise which should be purchased.

Equity The net worth of a business, consisting of capital stock, capital (or paid-in) surplus, earned surplus (or retained earnings), and, occasionally, certain net worth reserves. *Common equity* is that part of the total net worth belonging to the common stockholders. *Total equity* would include preferred stockholders. The terms "common stock," "net worth," and "equity" are frequently used interchangeably.

Excise Tax A tax on the manufacture, sale, or consumption of specified commodities.

Ex-dividend Date The date on which the right to the current dividend no longer accompanies a stock. (For listed stock, the ex-dividend date is four working days prior to the date of record.)

Exercise Price The price that must be paid for a share of common stock when it is bought by exercising a warrant.

Expected Return The rate of return a firm expects to realize from an investment. The expected return is the mean value of the probability distribution of possible returns.

Extension An informal method of reorganization in which the creditors voluntarily postpone the date of required payment on past-due obligations.

Factoring A method of financing accounts receivable under which a firm sells its accounts receivable (generally without recourse) to a financial institution (the "factor").

Field Warehousing A method of financing inventories in which a "warehouse" is established at the place of business of the borrowing firm.

Financial Leverage The ratio of total debt to total assets. There are other measures of financial leverage, especially ones that relate cash inflows to required cash outflows. In this book, the debt/total asset ratio is generally used to measure leverage.

Financial Structure The entire right-hand side of the balance sheet—the way in which a firm is financed.

Fixed Charges Costs that do not vary with the level of output.

Float· The amount of funds tied up in checks that have been written but are still in process and have not yet been collected.

Flotation Cost The cost of issuing new stocks or bonds.

Funded Debt Long-term debt.

Funding The process of replacing short-term debt with long-term securities (stocks or bonds).

Goodwill Intangible assets of a firm established by the excess of the price paid for the going concern over its book value.

Holding Company A corporation operated for the purpose of owning the common stocks of other corporations.

Improper Accumulation Earnings retained by a business for the purpose of enabling stockholders to avoid personal income taxes.

Income Bond A bond that pays interest only if the current interest is earned.

Incremental Cost of Capital The average cost of the increment of capital raised during a given year.

Indenture A formal agreement between the issuer of a bond and the bondholders.

Insolvency The inability to meet maturing debt obligations.

Interest Factor (IF) Numbers found in compound interest and annuity tables.

Internal Rate of Return (IRR) The rate of return on an asset investment. The internal rate of return is calculated by finding the discount rate that equates the present value of future cash flows to the cost of the investment.

Intrinsic Value That value that, in the mind of the analyst, is justified by the facts. It is often used to distinguish between the "true value" of an asset (the intrinsic value) and the asset's current market price.

Investment Banker One who underwrites and distributes new investment securities; more broadly, one who helps business firms to obtain financing.

Investment Tax Credit Business firms can deduct as a credit against their income taxes a specified percentage of the dollar amount of new investments in each of certain catgeories of assets.

Leverage Factor The ratio of debt to total assets.

Line of Credit An arrangement whereby a financial institution (bank or insurance company) commits itself to lend up to a specified maximum amount of funds during a specified period. Sometimes the interest rate on the loan is specified; at other times, it is not. Sometimes a commitment fee is imposed for obtaining the line of credit.

Liquidity Refers to a firm's cash position and its ability to meet maturing obligations.

Listed Securities Securities traded on an organized security exchange—for example, the New York Stock Exchange.

Lock-box Plan A procedure used to speed up collections and to reduce float.

Margin—Profit on Sales The *profit margin* is the percentage of profit after tax to sales.

Margin—Securities Business The buying of stocks or bonds on credit, known as *buying on margin.*

Margin Trading Buying securities on credit (margin).

Marginal Cost The cost of an additional unit. The *marginal* cost of *capital* is the cost of an additional dollar of new funds.

Marginal Efficiency of Capital A schedule showing the internal rate of return on investment opportunities.

Marginal Revenue The additional gross revenue produced by selling one additional unit of output.

Merger Any combination that forms one company from two or more previously existing companies.

Money Market Financial markets in which funds are borrowed or loaned for short periods. (The money market is distinguished from the capital market, which is the market for long-term funds).

Mortgage A pledge of designated property as security for a loan.

Net Present Value (NPV) Method A method of ranking investment proposals. The NPV is equal to the present value of future returns, discounted at the appropriate cost of capital, minus the present value of the cost of the investment.

Net Worth The capital and surplus of a firm—capital stock; capital surplus (paid-in capital); earned surplus (retained earnings); and, occasionally, certain reserves. For some purposes, preferred stock is included; generally, net worth refers only to the common stockholders' position.

Objective Probability Distributions Probability distributions determined by statistical procedures.

Operating Leverage The extent to which fixed costs are used in a firm's operation. Break-even analysis is used to measure the extent to which operating leverage is employed.

Opportunity Cost The rate of return on the best *alternative* investment that is available. It is the highest return that will *not* be earned if the funds are invested in a particular project. For example, the opportunity cost of *not* investing in common stocks yielding 8 percent might be 6 percent, which could be earned on bonds.

Ordinary Income Income from the normal operations of a firm. Operating income specifically excludes income from the sale of capital assets.

Organized Security Exchanges Formal organizations having tangible, physical locations. Organized exchanges conduct an auction market in designated ("listed") investment securities. For example, the New York Stock Exchange is an organized exchange.

Over-the-counter Market   All facilities that provide for security transactions not conducted on organized exchanges. The over-the-counter market is typically a "telephone market," as most business is conducted over the telephone.

Over-the-counter Securities   Securities that are not traded on an organized security exchange.

Par Value   The nominal or face value of a stock or bond.

Payback Period   The length of time required for the net revenues of an investment to return the cost of the investment.

Payout Ratio   The percentage of earnings paid out in the form of dividends.

Perpetuity   A stream of equal future payments expected to continue forever.

Pledging of Accounts Receivable   Short-term borrowing from financial institutions where the loan is secured by accounts receivable. The lender may physically take the accounts receivable but typically has recourse to the borrower; also called *discounting of accounts receivable.*

Pooling of Interest   An accounting method for combining the financial statements of two firms that merge. Under the pooling of interest procedure, the assets of the merged firms are simply added together to form the balance sheet of the surviving corporation. This method is different from the "purchase" method, where goodwill is put on the balance sheet to reflect a premium (or discount) paid in excess of book value.

Portfolio Effect   The extent to which the variation in returns on a combination of assets (a "portfolio") is less than the sum of the variations of the individual assets.

Pre-emptive Right   A provision contained in the corporate charter and bylaws that gives holders of common stock the right to purchase on a pro rata basis new issues of common stock (or securities convertible into common stock).

Present Value (PV)   The value today of a future payment, or stream of payments, discounted at the appropriate discount rate.

Price/earnings Ratio (P/E)   The ratio of price to earnings. Faster growing or less risky firms typically have higher P/E ratios than either slower growing or riskier firms.

Prime Rate   The rate of interest commercial banks charge very large, strong corporations.

Pro Forma   A projection. A *pro forma* financial statement is one that shows how the actual statement will look if certain specified assumptions are realized. *Pro forma* statements may be either future or past projections. An example of a backward *pro forma* statement occurs when two firms are planning to merge and show what their consolidated financial statements would have looked like had they been merged in preceding years.

Profit Margin   The ratio of profits after taxes to sales.

Profitability Index (PI)   The present value of future returns divided by the present value of the investment outlay.

Progressive Tax   A tax that requires a higher percentage payment on higher incomes. The personal income tax in the United States, which is at a rate of 14 percent on the lowest increments of income to 70 percent on the highest increments, is progressive.

Prospectus   A document issued for the purpose of describing a new security issue. The Securities and Exchange Commission (SEC) examines prospectuses to insure that statements contained therein are not "false and misleading."

Proxy   A document giving one the authority or power to act for another. Typically, the authority in question is the power to vote shares of common stock.

Put   An option to sell a specific security at a specified price within a designated period.

Rate of Return   The internal rate of return on an investment.

Recourse Arrangement   A term used in connection with accounts receivable financing. If a firm sells its accounts receivable to a financial institution under a recourse agreement, then, if the account receivable cannot be collected, the selling firm must repurchase the account from the financial institution.

Refunding   The process of retiring an old bond issue and replacing it with a new debt or equity issue.

Regression Analysis   A statistical procedure for predicting the value of one variable (dependent variable) on the basis of knowledge about one or more other variables (independent variables).

Reinvestment Rate   The rate of return at which cash flows from an investment are reinvested. The reinvestment rate may or may not be constant from year to year.

Reorganization   When a financially troubled firm goes through reorganization, its assets are restated to reflect their current market value, and its financial structure is restated to reflect any changes on the asset side of the statement. Under a reorganization the firm continues in existence; this is contrasted to bankruptcy, where the firm is liquidated and ceases to exist.

Required Rate of Return   The rate of return that stockholders expect to receive on common stock investments.

Residual Value   The value of leased property at the end of the lease term.

Retained Earnings   Profits after taxes that are retained in the business rather than being paid out in dividends.

Right   A short-term option to buy a specified number of shares of a new issue of securities at a designated "subscription" price.

Rights Offering   A securities flotation offered to existing stockholders.

Risk-adjusted Discount Rates   The discount rate applicable for a particular risky (uncertain) stream of income: the riskless rate of interest plus a risk premium appropriate to the level of risk attached to the particular income stream.

Risk Index (RI)   Calculated as a function of the present value interest factor for a riskless cash flow divided by the present value interest factor for the risky asset.

Risk Premium   The difference between the expected rate of return on a particular risky asset and the rate of return on a riskless asset with the same expected life.

Salvage Value   The value of a capital asset at the end of a specified period. It is the current market price of an asset being considered for replacement in a capital budgeting problem.

Selling Group   A group of stock brokerage firms formed for the purpose of distributing a new issue of securities; part of the investment banking process.

Short-selling   Selling a security that is not owned by the seller at the time of the sale. The seller borrows the security from a brokerage firm and must at some point repay the brokerage firm by buying the security on the open market.

Securities, Junior   Securities that have lower priority in claims on assets and income than other securities (*senior securities*). For example, preferred stock is junior to debentures, but debentures are junior to mortgage bonds. Common stock is the most junior of all corporate securities.

Securities, Senior   Securities having claims on income and assets that rank higher than certain other securities (*junior securities*). For example, mortgage bonds are senior to debentures, but debentures are senior to common stock.

Simulation   A technique whereby probable future events are simulated on a computer. Estimated rates of return and risk indices can be generated.

Sinking Fund   A required annual payment designed to amortize a bond or a preferred stock issue. The sinking fund may be held in the form of cash or marketable securities, but more generally the money put into the sinking fund is used to retire each year some of the securities in question.

Stock Dividend   A dividend paid in additional shares of stock rather than in cash. It involves a transfer from earned surplus to the capital stock account; therefore, stock dividends are limited by the amount of earned surplus.

Stock Split   An accounting action to increase the number of shares outstanding; for example, 3-for-1 split, shares outstanding would be tripled and each stockholder would receive three new shares for each one formerly held. Stock splits involve no transfer from surplus to the capital account.

Subjective Probability Distributions   Probability distributions determined through subjective procedures without the use of statistics.

Subordinated Debenture   A bond having a claim on assets only after the senior debt has been paid off in the event of liquidation.

Subscription Price   The price at which a security may be purchased in a rights offering.

Surtax   A tax levied in addition to the normal tax. For example, the normal corporate tax rate is 22 percent, but a surtax of 26 percent is added to the normal tax on all corporate income exceeding $25,000.

Tangible Assets   Physical assets as opposed to such tangible assets as goodwill and the stated value of patents.

Tender Offers   A situation wherein one firm offers to buy the stock of another, going directly to the stockholders, frequently over the opposition of the management of the firm whose stock is being sought.

Term Loan   A loan generally obtained from a bank or insurance company with a maturity greater than one year. Term loans are generally amortized.

Trade Credit   Interfirm debt arising through credit sales and recorded as an account receivable by the seller and as an account payable by the buyer.

Trust Receipt   An instrument acknowledging that the borrower holds certain goods in trust for the lender. Trust receipt financing is used in connection with the financing of inventories for automobile dealers, construction equipment dealers, appliance dealers, and other dealers in expensive durable goods.

Underwriting   (1) The entire process of issuing new corporate securities. (2) The insurance function of bearing the risk of adverse price fluctuations during the period in which a new issue of stock or bonds is being distributed.

Underwriting Syndicate   A syndicate of investment firms formed to spread the risk associated with the purchase and distribution of a new issue of securities. The larger the issue, the more firms will typically be involved in the syndicate.

Utility Theory   A body of theory dealing with the relationships among money income, utility (or "happiness"), and the willingness to accept risks.

Warrant   A long-term option to buy a stated number of shares of common stock at a specified price. The specified price is generally called the "exercise price."

Working Capital   Refers to a firm's investment in short-term assets—cash, short-term securities, accounts receivable, and inventories. *Gross working capital* is defined as a firm's total current assets. *Net working capital* is defined as current assets minus current liabilities. If the term "working capital" is used without further qualification, it generally refers to gross working capital.

Yield   The rate of return on an investment—the internal rate of return.

TABLE A–1   COMPOUND SUM OF $1

Year	1%	2%	3%	4%	5%	6%	7%
1	1.010	1.020	1.030	1.040	1.050	1.060	1.070
2	1.020	1.040	1.061	1.082	1.102	1.124	1.145
3	1.030	1.061	1.093	1.125	1.158	1.191	1.225
4	1.041	1.082	1.126	1.170	1.216	1.262	1.311
5	1.051	1.104	1.159	1.217	1.276	1.338	1.403
6	1.062	1.126	1.194	1.265	1.340	1.419	1.501
7	1.072	1.149	1.230	1.316	1.407	1.504	1.606
8	1.083	1.172	1.267	1.369	1.477	1.594	1.718
9	1.094	1.195	1.305	1.423	1.551	1.689	1.838
10	1.105	1.219	1.344	1.480	1.629	1.791	1.967
11	1.116	1.243	1.384	1.539	1.710	1.898	2.105
12	1.127	1.268	1.426	1.601	1.796	2.012	2.252
13	1.138	1.294	1.469	1.665	1.886	2.133	2.410
14	1.149	1.319	1.513	1.732	1.980	2.261	2.579
15	1.161	1.346	1.558	1.801	2.079	2.397	2.759
16	1.173	1.373	1.605	1.873	2.183	2.540	2.952
17	1.184	1.400	1.653	1.948	2.292	2.693	3.159
18	1.196	1.428	1.702	2.026	2.407	2.854	3.380
19	1.208	1.457	1.754	2.107	2.527	3.026	3.617
20	1.220	1.486	1.806	2.191	2.653	3.207	3.870
25	1.282	1.641	2.094	2.666	3.386	4.292	5.427
30	1.348	1.811	2.427	3.243	4.322	5.743	7.612

Year	8%	9%	10%	12%	14%	15%	16%
1	1.080	1.090	1.100	1.120	1.140	1.150	1.160
2	1.166	1.188	1.210	1.254	1.300	1.322	1.346
3	1.260	1.295	1.331	1.405	1.482	1.521	1.561
4	1.360	1.412	1.464	1.574	1.689	1.749	1.811
5	1.469	1.539	1.611	1.762	1.925	2.011	2.100
6	1.587	1.677	1.772	1.974	2.195	2.313	2.436
7	1.714	1.828	1.949	2.211	2.502	2.660	2.826
8	1.851	1.993	2.144	2.476	2.853	3.059	3.278
9	1.999	2.172	2.358	2.773	3.252	3.518	3.803
10	2.159	2.367	2.594	3.106	3.707	4.046	4.411
11	2.332	2.580	2.853	3.479	4.226	4.652	5.117
12	2.518	2.813	3.138	3.896	4.818	5.350	5.936
13	2.720	3.066	3.452	4.363	5.492	6.153	6.886
14	2.937	3.342	3.797	4.887	6.261	7.076	7.988
15	3.172	3.642	4.177	5.474	7.138	8.137	9.266
16	3.426	3.970	4.595	6.130	8.137	9.358	10.748
17	3.700	4.328	5.054	6.866	9.276	10.761	12.468
18	3.996	4.717	5.560	7.690	10.575	12.375	14.463
19	4.316	5.142	6.116	8.613	12.056	14.232	16.777
20	4.661	5.604	6.728	9.646	13.743	16.367	19.461
25	6.848	8.623	10.835	17.000	26.462	32.919	40.874
30	10.063	13.268	17.449	29.960	50.950	66.212	85.850

TABLE A–1 (*Continued*)

Year	18%	20%	24%	28%	32%	36%
1	1.180	1.200	1.240	1.280	1.320	1.360
2	1.392	1.440	1.538	1.638	1.742	1.850
3	1.643	1.728	1.907	2.067	2.300	2.515
4	1.939	2.074	2.364	2.684	3.036	3.421
5	2.288	2.488	2.932	3.436	4.007	4.653
6	2.700	2.986	3.635	4.398	5.290	6.328
7	3.185	3,583	4.508	5.629	6.983	8.605
8	3.759	4.300	5.590	7.206	9.217	11.703
9	4.435	5.160	6.931	9.223	12.166	15.917
10	5.234	6.192	8.594	11.806	16.060	21.647
11	6.176	7.430	10.657	15.112	21.199	29.439
12	7.288	8.916	13.215	19.343	27.983	40.037
13	8.599	10.699	16.386	24.759	36.937	54.451
14	10.147	12.839	20.319	31.691	48.757	74.053
15	11.974	15.407	25.196	40.565	64.359	100.712
16	14.129	18.488	31.243	51.923	84.954	136.97
17	16.672	22.186	38.741	66.461	112.14	186.28
18	19.673	26.623	48.039	85.071	148.02	253.34
19	23.214	31.948	59.568	108.89	195.39	344.54
20	27.393	38.338	73.864	139.38	257.92	468.57
25	62.669	95.396	216.542	478.90	1033.6	2180.1
30	143.371	237.376	634.820	1645.5	4142.1	10143.

Year	40%	50%	60%	70%	80%	90%
1	1.400	1.500	1.600	1.700	1.800	1.900
2	1.960	2.250	2.560	2.890	3.240	3.610
3	2.744	3.375	4.096	4.913	5.832	6.859
4	3.842	5.062	6.544	8.352	10.498	13.032
5	5.378	7.594	10.486	14.199	18.896	24.761
6	7.530	11.391	16.777	24.138	34.012	47.046
7	10.541	17.086	26.844	41.034	61.222	89.387
8	14.758	25.629	42.950	69.758	110.200	169.836
9	20.661	38.443	68.720	118.588	198.359	322.688
10	28.925	57.665	109.951	201.599	357.047	613.107
11	40.496	86.498	175.922	342.719	642.684	1164.902
12	56.694	129.746	281.475	582.622	1156.831	2213.314
13	79.372	194.619	450.360	990.457	2082.295	4205.297
14	111.120	291.929	720.576	1683.777	3748.131	7990.065
15	155.568	437.894	1152.921	2862.421	6746.636	15181.122
16	217.795	656.84	1844.7	4866.1	12144.	28844.0
17	304.914	985.26	2951.5	8272.4	21859.	54804.0
18	426.879	1477.9	4722.4	14063.0	39346.	104130.0
19	597.630	2216.8	7555.8	23907.0	70824.	197840.0
20	836.683	3325.3	12089.0	40642.0	127480.	375900.0
25	4499.880	25251.	126760.0	577060.0	2408900.	9307600.0
30	24201.432	191750.	1329200.	8193500.0	45517000.	230470000.0

TABLE A–2

Present Value of $1

Year	1%	2%	3%	4%	5%	6%	7%	8%	9%	10%	12%	14%	15%
1	.990	.980	.971	.962	.952	.943	.935	.926	.917	.909	.893	.877	.870
2	.980	.961	.943	.925	.907	.890	.873	.857	.842	.826	.797	.769	.756
3	.971	.942	.915	.889	.864	.840	.816	.794	.772	.751	.712	.675	.658
4	.961	.924	.889	.855	.823	.792	.763	.735	.708	.683	.636	.592	.572
5	.951	.906	.863	.822	.784	.747	.713	.681	.650	.621	.567	.519	.497
6	.942	.888	.838	.790	.746	.705	.666	.630	.596	.564	.507	.456	.432
7	.933	.871	.813	.760	.711	.665	.623	.583	.547	.513	.452	.400	.376
8	.923	.853	.789	.731	.677	.627	.582	.540	.502	.467	.404	.351	.327
9	.914	.837	.766	.703	.645	.592	.544	.500	.460	.424	.361	.308	.284
10	.905	.820	.744	.676	.614	.558	.508	.463	.422	.386	.322	.270	.247
11	.896	.804	.722	.650	.585	.527	.475	.429	.388	.350	.287	.237	.215
12	.887	.788	.701	.625	.557	.497	.444	.397	.356	.319	.257	.208	.187
13	.879	.773	.681	.601	.530	.469	.415	.368	.326	.290	.229	.182	.163
14	.870	.758	.661	.577	.505	.442	.388	.340	.299	.263	.205	.160	.141
15	.861	.743	.642	.555	.481	.417	.362	.315	.275	.239	.183	.140	.123
16	.853	.728	.623	.534	.458	.394	.339	.292	.252	.218	.163	.123	.107
17	.844	.714	.605	.513	.436	.371	.317	.270	.231	.198	.146	.108	.093
18	.836	.700	.587	.494	.416	.350	.296	.250	.212	.180	.130	.095	.081
19	.828	.686	.570	.475	.396	.331	.276	.232	.194	.164	.116	.083	.070
20	.820	.673	.554	.456	.377	.312	.258	.215	.178	.149	.104	.073	.061
25	.780	.610	.478	.375	.295	.233	.184	.146	.116	.092	.059	.038	.030
30	.742	.552	.412	.308	.231	.174	.131	.099	.075	.057	.033	.020	.015

Year	16%	18%	20%	24%	28%	32%	36%	40%	50%	60%	70%	80%	90%
1	.862	.847	.833	.806	.781	.758	.735	.714	.667	.625	.588	.556	.526
2	.743	.718	.694	.650	.610	.574	.541	.510	.444	.391	.346	.309	.277
3	.641	.609	.579	.524	.477	.435	.398	.364	.296	.244	.204	.171	.146
4	.552	.516	.482	.423	.373	.329	.292	.260	.198	.153	.120	.095	.077
5	.476	.437	.402	.341	.291	.250	.215	.186	.132	.095	.070	.053	.040
6	.410	.370	.335	.275	.227	.189	.158	.133	.088	.060	.041	.029	.021
7	.354	.314	.279	.222	.178	.143	.116	.095	.059	.037	.024	.016	.011
8	.305	.266	.233	.179	.139	.108	.085	.068	.039	.023	.014	.009	.006
9	.263	.226	.194	.144	.108	.082	.063	.048	.026	.015	.008	.005	.003
10	.227	.191	.162	.116	.085	.062	.046	.035	.017	.009	.005	.003	.002
11	.195	.162	.135	.094	.066	.047	.034	.025	.012	.006	.003	.002	.001
12	.168	.137	.112	.076	.052	.036	.025	.018	.008	.004	.002	.001	.001
13	.145	.116	.093	.061	.040	.027	.018	.013	.005	.002	.001	.001	.000
14	.125	.099	.078	.049	.032	.021	.014	.009	.003	.001	.001	.000	.000
15	.108	.084	.065	.040	.025	.016	.010	.006	.002	.001	.000	.000	.000
16	.093	.071	.054	.032	.019	.012	.007	.005	.002	.001	.000	.000	
17	.080	.030	.045	.026	.015	.009	.005	.003	.001	.000	.000		
18	.089	.051	.038	.021	.012	.007	.004	.002	.001	.000	.000		
19	.030	.043	.031	.017	.009	.005	.003	.002	.000	.000			
20	.051	.037	.026	.014	.007	.004	.002	.001	.000	.000			
25	.024	.016	.010	.005	.002	.001	.000	.000					
30	.012	.007	.004	.002	.001	.000	.000						

TABLE A—3 SUM OF AN ANNUITY OF $1 FOR N YEARS

Year	1%	2%	3%	4%	5%	6%
1	1.000	1.000	1.000	1.000	1.000	1.000
2	2.010	2.020	2.030	2.040	2.050	2.060
3	3.030	3.060	3.091	3.122	3.152	3.184
4	4.060	4.122	4.184	4.246	4.310	4.375
5	5.101	5.204	5.309	5.416	5.526	5.637
6	6.152	6.308	6.468	6.633	6.802	6.975
7	7.214	7.434	7.662	7.898	8.142	8.394
8	8.286	8.583	8.892	9.214	9.549	9.897
9	9.369	9.755	10.159	10.583	11.027	11.491
10	10.462	10.950	11.464	12.006	12.578	13.181
11	11.567	12.169	12.808	13.486	14.207	14.972
12	12.683	13.412	14.192	15.026	15.917	16.870
13	13.809	14.680	15.618	16.627	17.713	18.882
14	14.947	15.974	17.086	18.292	19.599	21.051
15	16.097	17.293	18.599	20.024	21.579	23.276
16	17.258	18.639	20.157	21.825	23.657	25.673
17	18.430	20.012	21.762	23.698	25.840	28.213
18	19.615	21.412	23.414	25.645	28.132	30.906
19	20.811	22.841	25.117	27.671	30.539	33.760
20	22.019	24.297	26.870	29.778	33.066	36.786
25	28.243	32.030	36.459	41.646	47.727	54.865
30	34.785	40.568	47.575	56.085	66.439	79.058

Year	7%	8%	9%	10%	12%	14%
1	1.000	1.000	1.000	1.000	1.000	1.000
2	2.070	2.080	2.090	2.100	2.120	2.140
3	3.215	3.246	3.278	3.310	3.374	3.440
4	4.440	4.506	4.573	4.641	4.770	4.921
5	5.751	5.867	5.985	6.105	6.353	6.610
6	7.153	7.336	7.523	7.716	8.115	8.536
7	8.654	8.923	9.200	9.487	10.089	10.730
8	10.260	10.637	11.028	11.436	12.300	13.233
9	11.978	12.488	13.021	13.579	14.776	16.085
10	13.816	14.487	15.193	15.937	17.549	19.337
11	15.784	16.645	17.560	18.531	20.655	23.044
12	17.888	18.977	20.141	21.384	24.133	27.271
13	20.141	21.495	22.953	24.523	28.029	32.089
14	22.550	24.215	26.019	27.975	32.393	37.581
15	25.129	27.152	29.361	31.772	37.280	43.842
16	27.888	30.324	33.003	35.950	42.753	50.980
17	30.840	33.750	36.974	40.545	48.884	59.118
18	33.999	37.450	41.301	45.599	55.750	68.394
19	37.379	41.446	46.018	51.159	63.440	78.969
20	40.995	45.762	51.160	57.275	72.052	91.025
25	63.249	73.106	84.701	98.347	133.334	181.871
30	94.461	113.283	136.308	164.494	241.333	356.787

TABLE A-3 (*Continued*)

Year	16%	18%	20%	24%	28%	32%
1	1.000	1.000	1.000	1.000	1.000	1.000
2	2.160	2.180	2.200	2.240	2.280	2.320
3	3.506	3.572	3.640	3.778	3.918	4.062
4	5.066	5.215	5.368	5.684	6.016	6.362
5	6.877	7.154	7.442	8.048	8.700	9.398
6	8.977	9.442	9.930	10.980	12.136	13.406
7	11.414	12.142	12.916	14.615	16.534	18.696
8	14.240	15.327	16.499	19.123	22.163	25.678
9	17.518	19.086	20.799	24.712	29.369	34.895
10	21.321	23.521	25.959	31.643	38.592	47.062
11	25.733	28.755	32.150	40.238	50.399	63.122
12	30.850	34.931	39.580	50.985	65.510	84.320
13	36.786	42.219	48.497	64.110	84.853	112.303
14	43.672	50.818	59.196	80.496	109.612	149.240
15	51.660	60.965	72.035	100.815	141.303	197.997
16	60.925	72.939	87.442	126.011	181.87	262.36
17	71.673	87.068	105.931	157.253	233.79	347.31
18	84.141	103.740	128.117	195.994	300.25	459.45
19	98.603	123.414	154.740	244.033	385.32	607.47
20	115.380	146.628	186.688	303.601	494.21	802.86
25	249.214	342.603	471.981	898.092	1706.8	3226.8
30	530.312	790.948	1181.882	2640.916	5873.2	12941.0

Year	36%	40%	50%	60%	70%	80%
1	1.000	1.000	1.000	1.000	1.000	1.000
2	2.360	2.400	2.500	2.600	2.700	2.800
3	4.210	4.360	4.750	5.160	5.590	6.040
4	6.725	7.104	8.125	9.256	10.503	11.872
5	10.146	10.846	13.188	15.810	18.855	22.370
6	14.799	16.324	20.781	26.295	33.054	41.265
7	21.126	23.853	32.172	43.073	57.191	75.278
8	29.732	34.395	49.258	69.916	98.225	136.500
9	41.435	49.153	74.887	112.866	167.983	246.699
10	57.352	69.814	113.330	181.585	286.570	445.058
11	78.998	98.739	170.995	291.536	488.170	802.105
12	108.437	139.235	257.493	467.458	830.888	1444.788
13	148.475	195.929	387.239	748.933	1413.510	2601.619
14	202.926	275.300	581.859	1199.293	2403.968	4683.914
15	276.979	386.420	873.788	1919.869	4087.745	8432.045
16	377.69	541.99	1311.7	3072.8	6950.2	15179.0
17	514.66	759.78	1968.5	4917.5	11816.0	27323.0
18	700.94	1064.7	2953.8	7868.9	20089.0	49182.0
19	954.28	1491.6	4431.7	12591.0	34152.0	88528.0
20	1298.8	2089.2	6648.5	20147.0	58059.0	159350.0
25	6053.0	11247.0	50500.0	211270.0	824370.0	3011100.0
30	28172.0	60501.0	383500.0	2215400.0	11705000.0	56896000.0

TABLE A—4   PRESENT VALUE OF AN ANNUITY OF $1

Year	1%	2%	3%	4%	5%	6%	7%	8%	9%	10%
1	0.990	0.980	0.971	0.962	0.952	0.943	0.935	0.926	0.917	0.909
2	1.970	1.942	1.913	1.886	1.859	1.833	1.808	1.783	1.759	1.736
3	2.941	2.884	2.829	2.775	2.723	2.673	2.624	2.577	2.531	2.487
4	3.902	3.808	3.717	3.630	3.546	3.465	3.387	3.312	3.240	3.170
5	4.853	4.713	4.580	4.452	4.329	4.212	4.100	3.993	3.890	3.791
6	5.795	5.601	5.417	5.242	5.076	4.917	4.766	4.623	4.486	4.355
7	6.728	6.472	6.230	6.002	5.786	5.582	5.389	5.206	5.033	4.868
8	7.652	7.325	7.020	6.733	6.463	6.210	5.971	5.747	5.535	5.335
9	8.566	8.162	7.786	7.435	7.108	6.802	6.515	6.247	5.985	5.759
10	9.471	8.983	8.530	8.111	7.722	7.360	7.024	6.710	6.418	6.145
11	10.368	9.787	9.253	8.760	8.306	7.887	7.499	7.139	6.805	6.495
12	11.255	10.575	9.954	9.385	8.863	8.384	7.943	7.536	7.161	6.814
13	12.134	11.348	10.635	9.986	9.394	8.853	8.358	7.904	7.487	7.103
14	13.004	12.106	11.296	10.563	9.899	9.295	8.745	8.244	7.786	7.367
15	13.865	12.849	11.938	11.118	10.380	9.712	9.108	8.559	8.060	7.606
16	14.718	13.578	12.561	11.652	10.838	10.106	9.447	8.851	8.312	7.824
17	15.562	14.292	13.166	12.166	11.274	10.477	9.763	9.122	8.544	8.022
18	16.398	14.992	13.754	12.659	11.690	10.828	10.059	9.372	8.756	8.201
19	17.226	15.678	14.324	13.134	12.085	11.158	10.336	9.604	8.950	8.365
20	18.046	16.351	14.877	13.590	12.462	11.470	10.594	9.818	9.128	8.514
25	22.023	19.523	17.413	15.622	14.094	12.783	11.654	10.675	9.823	9.077
30	25.808	22.397	19.600	17.292	15.373	13.765	12.409	11.258	10.274	9.427

Year	12%	14%	16%	18%	20%	24%	28%	32%	36%
1	0.893	0.877	0.862	0.847	0.833	0.806	0.781	0.758	0.735
2	1.690	1.647	1.605	1.566	1.528	1.457	1.392	1.332	1.276
3	2.402	2.322	2.246	2.174	2.106	1.981	1.868	1.766	1.674
4	3.037	2.914	2.798	2.690	2.589	2.404	2.241	2.096	1.966
5	3.605	3.433	3.274	3.127	2.991	2.745	2.532	2.345	2.181
6	4.111	3.889	3.685	3.498	3.326	3.020	2.759	2.534	2.339
7	4.564	4.288	4.039	3.812	3.605	3.242	2.937	2.678	2.455
8	4.968	4.639	4.344	4.078	3.837	3.421	3.076	2.786	2.540
9	5.328	4.946	4.607	4.303	4.031	3.566	3.184	2.868	2.603
10	5.650	5.216	4.833	4.494	4.193	3.682	3.269	2.930	2.650
11	5.988	5.453	5.029	4.656	4.327	3.776	3.335	2.978	2.683
12	6.194	5.660	5.197	4.793	4.439	3.851	3.387	3.013	2.708
13	6.424	5.842	5.342	4.910	4.533	3.912	3.427	3.040	2.727
14	6.628	6.002	5.468	5.008	4.611	3.962	3.459	3.061	2.740
15	6.811	6.142	5.575	5.092	4.675	4.001	3.483	3.076	2.750
16	6.974	6.265	5.669	5.162	4.730	4.033	3.503	3.088	2.758
17	7.120	5.373	5.749	4.222	4.775	4.059	3.518	3.097	2.763
18	7.250	6.467	5.818	5.273	4.812	4.080	3.529	3.104	2.767
19	7.366	6.550	5.877	5.316	4.844	4.097	3.539	3.109	2.770
20	7.469	6.623	5.929	5.353	4.870	4.110	3.546	3.113	2.772
25	7.843	6.873	6.097	5.467	4.948	4.147	3.564	3.122	2.776
30	8.055	7.003	6.177	5.517	4.979	4.160	3.569	3.124	2.778

Subject Index